MW01140597

Beginning Java Networking

Chád Darby
John Griffin
Pascal de Haan
Peter den Haan
Alexander V. Konstantinou
Sing Li
Sean MacLean
Glenn E. Mitchell
Joel Peach
Peter Wansch
William Wright

Wrox Press Ltd. ®

Beginning Java Networking

Published by Wrox Press Ltd,
Arden House, 1102 Warwick Road, Acocks Green,
Birmingham, B27 6BH, UK
Printed in the United States
ISBN 1861005601

Trademark Acknowledgements

Wrox has endeavored to provide trademark information about all the companies and products mentioned in this book by the appropriate use of capitals. However, Wrox cannot guarantee the accuracy of this information.

Credits

Authors
Chád Darby
John Griffin
Pascal de Haan
Peter den Haan
Alexander V. Konstantinou
Sing Li
Sean MacLean
Glenn E. Mitchell
Joel Peach
Peter Wansch
William Wright

Technical Architect
Louay Fatoohi

Technical Editors
Helen Callaghan
John R. Chapman
Benjamin Hickman

Category Manager
Louay Fatoohi

Author Agent
Velimir Ilic

Project Administrator
Laura Hall

Cover Design
Dawn Chellingworth

Technical Reviewers
Kapil Apshankar
Steve Baker
Raj Betapudi
Richard Bonneau
Carl Burnham
Brian Campbell
Jeremy Michael Crosbie
Sam Dalton
John Davies
Will Henton
Brian Higdon
Sachin Khanna
Manzoor Hussain
Tony Loton
Stéphane Osmont
Michael Oyach
Phil Powers-DeGeorge
Gavin Smyth
Paul Wilt

Production Manager
Simon Hardware

Production Coordinator
Pip Wonson

Production Assistants
Paul Grove
Natalie O'Donnell

Indexer
Adrian Axinte

Proofreader
Agnes Wiggers

About the Authors

Chád Darby

Chád Darby is the founder of J9 Consulting, a Java consulting firm. He has experience developing n-tier web applications for Fortune 500 companies and the Department of Defense. Chád is a contributing author for the book, *Professional Java E-Commerce, Wrox Press; ISBN 1861004818*, he has also published articles in Java Report, Java Developer's Journal, and Web Techniques.

Chád has been an invited speaker at conferences including SD West 99, XML DevCon 2000 and JavaCon 2000. He recently gave a presentation on JSP Custom Tags in Mumbai, India. In between consulting and writing projects, he teaches Java courses for Learning Tree International.

Chád is a Sun Certified J2EE Architect and BEA Certified WebLogic Developer. He holds a B.S. in Computer Science from Carnegie Mellon University.

Chád can be reached at darby@j-nine.com or http://www.j-nine.com/.

Chád would like to thank his wife Janine and daughter Chadé for understanding his absence during the writing process.

John Griffin

John Griffin is a software consultant specializing in large-scale distributed application architecture and development. In 1997, John founded Aries Software Technologies, Inc., an IT consulting company providing software solutions and testing services to the financial and healthcare industries.

John has designed, built and deployed n-tier applications using CORBA and/or Java for many Fortune 500 companies, spanning platforms from handhelds to mainframes.

For my parents Theresa and John and my brother Daniel. Thank you so much for your love, support and guidance.

Pascal de Haan

Pascal de Haan works for Cap Gemini Ernst & Young in a high technology unit, called Warp11. His tasks vary from architecting or consulting on large application architectures, the creation of frameworks, the setting up of software factories, the development of Java awareness and the coaching of Java talents.

Upon completing a Bachelor's degree in Informatics, Pascal started working on Java web applications before there was an Enterprise Edition of the platform. These applications were mainly intended for clients in the insurance sector. Pascal has since completed several projects that featured message-oriented middleware and his main focus at the moment lies with web services, marketplaces and related technologies.

My special thanks go out to Eric Hol from Warp11 of Cap Gemini Ernst &Young, for arranging that I could work on this book during office hours. Also many thanks go to Claudia, who was very supportive of my efforts, even if it resulted in working during our holiday.

Peter den Haan

Peter den Haan is a senior systems engineer at Objectivity Ltd, a UK-based systems integration company. He started out programming at 13 on a Radio Shack TRS-80 model I with 16KB of memory, but has progressed since to J2EE systems architect and lead developer in projects for customers ranging from dotcoms (UMBRO.COM) to blue chips (Shell Finance).

Peter is a Sun-certified Java 2 developer, a JavaRanch bartender, self-confessed geek, and holds a doctorate in theoretical physics.

He loves his job, his books, his music, but most of all, his wife Inger.

Alexander V. Konstantinou

Alexander V. Konstantinou is currently completing his doctoral degree in Computer Science at Columbia University in the city of New York. His general research interests include programming languages, computer networks, network management, and distributed systems. His thesis work is focused on a novel architecture for automating network configuration management, called NESTOR. As part of his thesis work, Alexander has implemented a large Java/Jini-based prototype including a distributed object repository, IDL compiler, a constraint interpreter, graphical configuration and network topology visualization tool, and several adapters to instrumentation repositories such as SNMP, Cisco IOS, Linux, and so on. The prototype is currently being used by researchers in industry and academia and will soon be deployed on a DARPA-funded experimental active networks backbone.

Alexander was awarded the M.S. degree in Computer Science from Renselaer Polytechnic Institute (RPI) in Troy, NY (1996), and a B.A. magna cum laude in History and Computer Science from Macalester College in St. Paul, MN (1994). In his RPI master's thesis project he designed and implemented a port of the C++ Standard Template Library into Ada 95. Consulting projects have included a Jini home network prototype, and inevitably a few SQL applications.

Alexander first caught the computer bug after receiving a Sinclair ZX81 and has not stopped learning and applying since. He may be contacted at akonstan@acm.org.

Alexander would like to thank his family for all their support and encouragement, Scott Epter and Mary Krembs for the gracious hospitality in Martha's Vineyard which made writing all the more fun, and the staff at Wrox for the opportunity to write about Java.

Sing Li

First bitten by the computer bug in 1978, Sing has grown up with the microprocessor revolution. His first PC was a $99 do-it-yourself COSMIC ELF computer with 256 bytes of memory and a 1-bit LED display.

For two decades, Sing has been an active author, consultant, speaker, instructor, and entrepreneur. His wide-ranging experience spans distributed architectures, multi-tiered Internet/Intranet systems, computer telephony, call center technology, and embedded systems.

Sing has participated in several Wrox projects in the past, and has been working with (and writing about) Java and Jini since their very first alpha releases.

Sean MacLean

Sean is a Sun-Certified Java programmer and holds a Bachelor's degree in Computer Science as well as a Bachelor's degree in Music.

After pursuing a career as a classical musician, Sean could not resist the lure of technology that has plagued him since first seeing a Sinclair ZX81. He currently focuses on the design and development of multi-tiered distributed Internet applications, particularly distributed content management systems.

Though primarily a Java developer since its earliest release, Sean's interest in the world of computers also includes cryptography, signal processing and digital audio editing.

For Sean, an ideal day begins by brewing an espresso and practicing flamenco guitar and ends in the kitchen preparing a great meal – with a little computing thrown in the middle for good measure, of course.

Glenn E. Mitchell

Glenn E. Mitchell II wears several different hats. To the undergraduate students at the University of South Florida, he's Dr. Mitchell. He prefers "Mitch" and that's what his colleagues and graduate students call him. In addition to being the faculty administrator at USF who directs the State Data Center on Aging, Mitch is also an active consultant, writer, and speaker. His consulting firm is called .Com Consulting Group.

Mitch co-authored two other titles for Wrox this past year, "*Professional Oracle 8i Application Programming*" and "*Professional Java Data.*" He also writes lots of articles and speaks at professional conferences. Mitch is a technical evangelist on object-oriented analysis/design, C++, Java, .NET, Visual Basic, and Microsoft SQL Server.

You might also recognize Mitch as the author of the weekly developer newsletter for BrainBuzz.com.

His other passions include music, movies, and nature photography. Mitch earns lots of frequent flyer miles flying every week between his university office in Tampa, FL, and his home in Tallahassee, FL. His wife is Lillian. She's a terrific small animal veterinarian in Tallahassee. He's also dad to Jessica, who is just starting high school as a freshman International Baccalaureate student. Mitch earned his Ph.D. at the University of Iowa. You can reach Mitch at mitchell@dot-com-group.com.

Joel Peach

Joel Peach is Vice President of Professional Services and co-founder of Tracer Information Systems, Ltd. in Columbus, OH. He has several years of experience building distributed applications for both private and public sector firms.

You can e-mail him at jpeach@traceris.com.

Joel would like to acknowledge Brian Campbell of L^3Com, for his insightful review comments, many of which helped make his writing a better text to read. Thanks also to Laura Hall at Wrox for being such a pleasure to work with when writing as well as reviewing.

Peter Wansch

Peter is a software developer at IBM's Toronto Lab working on the DB2Universal Database administration tools, which are largely written in Java. He is a certified Java programmer and holds a master degree in computer science from the Vienna University of Technology in Austria.

His interests include web-based learning, large-scale Java application development, time-based media processing in Java, relational databases and theoretical computer science subjects such as software analysis and verification.

Thanks to Carole, Wolfgang and Susi for their support and encouragement.

William Wright

William Wright is a division engineer with BBN Technologies in Arlington, Virginia. His current work is in the areas of real-time signal processing systems and distributed agent applications.

William holds a Bachelor of Music Education degree from Indiana University and a Master of Computer Science degree from George Mason University.

Table of Contents

Table of Contents

Table of Contents

Table of Contents

Table of Contents

Table of Contents

xvi

Introduction

Unlike many other programming languages, Java has had support for network programming built in from its early days. Java provides the programmer with an extensive set of core classes and interfaces to handle a wide range of network protocols. As network programming continued to develop, Java kept on expanding its versatile Application Programming Interfaces (APIs), providing the programmer with powerful tools for developing applications that tackle emerging, more complicated networking tasks.

In this book, we will look at various network protocols and explore Java toolkits that can be used to develop a variety of network applications. Starting from the basics of networking, through core Java network classes, and moving on to more advanced Java networking APIs, this book provides comprehensive coverage of networking with Java. In addition to JDK 1.3, the book covers new networking features in JDK 1.4.

This book does not assume any knowledge of networking, so basic and more advanced networking concepts are appropriately covered. While requiring a working knowledge of Java, the book does cover core Java classes that are relevant to networking. Thus, this book caters for both the beginner and the more advanced programmer. By the end of the book, you should have acquired a deep understanding of various network concepts and protocols and developed extensive knowledge of a large number of Java APIs that you can use to develop sophisticated network applications.

Throughout, this book has used numerous examples to show the practical contexts of theoretical issues and abstract concepts.

Structure and Content of This Book

This book is divided into five sections that follow a logical sequence. Network basics and core Java networking classes are first covered before more advanced topics are tackled. What follows is a brief description of the contents of each of the twenty-one chapters and two appendices of the book.

Section I: Network Fundamentals

While this section is intended mainly for readers with no background in networking, the clear and structured introduction to many network protocols and concepts can be useful for more advanced readers also. The four chapters in this section provide the reader with an overview of many of the topics that are explored in detail later in the book.

Chapter 1: Introduction To Java Network Networking

This chapter starts with a general introduction to the main categories of network applications. It then mentions, briefly, the main packages that Java provides for developing network applications.

Chapter 2: Network Basics

Whether using Java or any other language, there are some basic concepts that you need to understand before you can start developing network applications. Here we learn about the various network layers, in both the OSI seven-layer reference model and the simpler TCP/IP four-layer model. The chapter then covers the Internet Protocol (IP), and the Transmission Control Protocol (TCP) and User Datagram Protocol (UDP) both of which work over IP. The chapter also covers the most important Internet protocols and concludes with an introduction to the Internet standards.

Chapter 3: Network Application Models

In this chapter we read about the main models of network applications: the classical client-server model and the more recent peer-to-peer model. Clients, servers, and the two-tier, three-tier and multi-tier architectures of the client-server model are covered. Similarly, the anatomy of the peer-to-peer model is explained in this chapter.

Chapter 4: Web Basics

There are many standards used on the web, and this chapter covers the most important amongst them. The Uniform Resource Identifier (URI), Locator (URL) and Name (URN) are all explained. Hypertext Transfer Protocol (HTTP), which is the standard protocol used to communicate between web browsers and web servers, is introduced. Hypertext Markup Language (HTML), eXtensible Markup Language (XML) and eXtensible Hypertext Markup Language (XHTML), which are the most common web languages, are also covered in this chapter. The chapter then concludes with an introduction to client- and server-side technologies.

Section II: Java Preliminaries

Having introduced network basics in the previous section, we now explore Java classes and packages that are related to network programming.

Chapter 5: Java I/O

Java's network programming model is built upon a broad foundation of classes that provide input and output facilities to Java programmers. This chapter covers first basic Java I/O concepts, such as streams, filters and pipes. Next, it covers various classes in the `java.io` package including `java.io.InputStream`, `java.io.OutputStream`, `java.io.Reader` and `java.io.Writer`. By the end of the chapter, you should have developed a solid understanding of Java I/O fundamentals that will help you when programming network I/O.

Chapter 6: Threads

Since network applications usually have to deal with many streams of data, assigning a thread to each of these data streams is a convenient and robust way to make sure each I/O channel is serviced. This chapter shows how to implement a class that runs as a separate thread by extending `java.lang.Thread` and implementing `java.lang.Runnable`. There are a number of examples on the various methods that can be used to manipulate threads, leading to more efficient code.

Chapter 7: Java Security Model

Security is a major concern in all network applications. This chapter explains why Java, with its unique security model, is exceptionally well suited to writing network-enabled code. The chapter starts with an introduction to the approach of the two main Java programs – applets and applications – to security. The sandbox and Java 2 security models are both covered. The chapter shows you how to sign your code to authenticate it to others and make it tamper-proof, how to give Java classes specific permissions to access parts of the system using a security policy, and how to create your own permissions and securely grant access to services you provide.

Section III: Java Networking

After covering network basics and Java networking preliminaries in the previous two sections, this section introduces Java classes that can be used to write a variety of Java network applications, including transport layer protocol applications.

Chapter 8: Internet Addressing and Naming

This chapter covers the basic functions of the Internet, which are addressing, naming and routing. After introducing the structure and use of Internet addresses, the chapter explains how names are translated into IP addresses and how the latter can be manipulated. The basics of Internet routing are also covered.

Chapter 9: TCP Programming

Nearly all current Internet services make use of the Transport Control Protocol (TCP), which is a transport layer protocol that builds a reliable end-to-end channel over the unreliable and connectionless Internet Protocol (IP). After introducing TCP operations and explaining the concept of "socket", which is a programming abstraction through which Java networking applications communicate, the chapter focuses on developing TCP client and server sockets.

Chapter 10: UDP Programming

The topic of this chapter is the second major Internet transport layer protocol, after TCP, User Datagram Protocol (UDP). The chapter compares TCP and UDP operations and explains the kind of applications that each of these two protocols is better suited for. The chapter includes an example implementation of the Echo protocol, which demonstrates use of the `java.net.DatagramPacket` and `java.net.DatagramSocket` classes.

Chapter 11: Multicasting

While both TCP and UDP provide a one-to-one transport service, the Internet multicast protocol, which is the subject of this chapter, is used for one-to-many transmission on the Internet. This chapter outlines how the multicast protocol works, explains how to control the scope of multicast transmissions, and introduces the support of Java for UDP/IP multicast programming. The second half of the chapter is an in-depth example of a group chat application.

Chapter 12: Java URL Handler Architecture

The first two sections of this chapter provide a solid introduction to URIs and the Java URL handling architecture. The remaining sections will cover the Java classes involved, starting with the `java.net.URL` entry-point class and navigating from there to the remaining classes. Small complete examples are presented to demonstrate use of the APIs presented, with two realistic, in-depth examples of Java handlers (plugins) for the WHOIS protocol and the Comma Separated Value (CSV) file format.

Chapter 13: Implementing an HTTP Server

This chapter discusses the basics of HTTP operations and how CGI programs can be used to create dynamic HTTP responses. Next, the chapter implements a well-designed HTTP server in Java and shows how to tackle all the networking issues involved. The design and implementation of the application are explained in detail. The HTTP server is further developed in the next chapter.

Chapter 14: Making Network Applications More Secure

Security and cryptography play an important role in today's networked world. This chapter explores the Java Cryptography Architecture (JCA) and its three extensions: Java Authentication and Authorization Services (JAAS), Java Cryptography Extension (JCE), and Java Secure Sockets Extension (JSSE). One of the many examples in this chapter uses JSSE to add HTTPS support to the HTTP server from the previous chapter.

Section IV: Java Distributed Networking

The focus of this section is distributed programming over a network and the various options that Java makes available to developers of distributed applications.

Chapter 15: Object Serialization

Serialization is the process of converting the state of objects into byte streams and restoring objects from those byte streams. After introducing how serialization works, the chapter proceeds to explain working with object streams, creating serializable classes, and customizing the serialization process. Next, the chapter explores versioning.

Chapter 16: RMI

When combined with object serialization as a way of distributing objects over a network, Remote Method Invocation (RMI) provides a unique yet powerful distributed computing model that non-Java platforms simply cannot match. The chapter contrasts RMI with Remote Procedure Call (RPC) and compares it to TCP/UDP socket-based programming, before embarking on a detailed investigation of how RMI works. A detailed example is provided to show RMI in action.

Chapter 17: CORBA

Unlike RMI, which is a purely Java-based mechanism, CORBA is a language-independent specification for a distributed application framework. The chapter first provides an overview of CORBA and explains its fundamental concepts. Next, RMI-IIOP is investigated. The introduction of RMI-IIOP makes it possible to integrate RMI clients with CORBA objects and vice versa because RMI clients, CORBA clients, RMI objects and CORBA objects all transfer their requests using the same protocol, IIOP.

Chapter 18: Servlets

A servlet is a small Java application that extends the functionality of the server that it runs on. After comparing servlets to other similar technologies, the chapter looks at how to build, deploy, and debug servlets. Topics covered in the chapter include the servlet life cycle, multithreaded servlets, managing sessions and exception handling.

Chapter 19: E-Mail with JavaMail

This chapter examines e-mail messaging systems before moving to cover JavaMail. The latter is a powerful Java API that provides support for sending and receiving e-mail. Sending e-mail (with and without attachments) and receiving e-mail with JavaMail are covered. The chapter develops a sophisticated, web-based mail application similar to Yahoo! Mail and Hotmail. The web application makes use of servlets and JavaServer Pages (JSP).

Chapter 20: Messaging with JMS

This chapter explains the basics of using enterprise messaging with Java applications. It covers the different techniques for enterprise messaging and makes clear what the respective advantages and drawbacks are. The chapter covers message oriented middleware, hub and spoke architecture, and Java Messaging Service (JMS). Both the point-to-point and publish/subscribe messaging domains are covered.

Section V: JDK 1.4 Networking

The JDK 1.4 API includes many new features that enhance and extend the Java networking model. The last chapter of the book investigates some of these new capabilities and features.

Chapter 21: Networking in JDK 1.4

The chapter covers first the new I/O API, introducing the new buffer and channel classes. Selectable channels, selectors and selection keys are explored. Using the new non-blocking I/O facilities, a scalable server application is built. The chapter explains the new JDK 1.4 support for IPv6 addresses and how they co-exist with the IPv4 addressing. The `java.net.URI` class is also introduced. The chapter concludes with brief coverage of a number of other new networking features in JDK 1.4.

Appendices

The book contains two appendices as back-up material.

Appendix A: Java Network Connectivity Exceptions

After a quick introduction to how exceptions are handled in Java, this appendix focuses on the `java.net` exceptions, which are subclasses of `IOException`.

Appendix B: Installing and Configuring Tomcat 4.0

This appendix explains how to install and configure Tomcat 4.0. This servlet and JSP engine is used in Chapters 18 and 19.

Tools Needed for Using This Book

The code in the book was tested with JDK 1.3. Examples on new features in JDK 1.4 were tested using release Beta 2 of the SDK, which was the latest release at the time when the book went to the press. Some chapters are based on APIs that are part of the Java 2 Enterprise Edition rather than the Standard Edition. Running the examples in these chapters requires downloading and installing the respective APIs.

Conventions

We have used a number of different styles of text and layout in this book to help differentiate between the different kinds of information. Here are some examples of the styles we use and an explanation of what they mean.

Code has several styles. If it's a word that we're talking about in the text, then we use the font shown in this example: "The `accept()` method blocks until an incoming TCP connection successfully negotiates the handshake phase, and then returns a `java.net.Socket` object encapsulating the streaming connection". If it's a block of code that you can type as a program and run, then it's in a gray box:

```
String host = args[0];
String user = args[1];
String password = args[2];
```

Sometimes you'll see code in a mixture of styles, like this:

```
String host = args[0];
String user = args[1];
String password = args[2];
int msgNum = Integer.parseInt(args[3]);
```

In cases like this, the code with a white background is code we are already familiar with; the line highlighted in gray is a new addition to the code since we last looked at it.

Advice, hints, and background information come in this type of font:

> **Important pieces of information come in boxes like this.**

Bullets appear indented, with each new bullet marked as follows:

❑ **Important Words** are in a bold type font

❑ Words that appear on the screen, in menus like File or Window, are in a similar font to that you would see on a Windows desktop

❑ Keys that you press on the keyboard like *Ctrl* and *Enter*, are in italics

Command lines are written as below, their output is written as the line that follows:

```
C:\Beg_Java_Networking\Ch01>java DaytimeClient
It is Tue Aug 28 12:09:39 2001 at tock.usno.navy.mil.
```

Customer Support

We always value hearing from our readers, and we want to know what you think about this book: what you liked, what you didn't like, and what you think we can do better next time. You can send us your comments, either by returning the reply card in the back of the book, or by e-mail to feedback@wrox.com. Please be sure to mention the book title in your message.

How To Download the Sample Code for the Book

When you log on to the Wrox site, http://www.wrox.com/, simply locate the title through our Search facility or by using one of the title lists. Click on Download in the Code column, or on Download Code on the book's detail page.

The files that are available for download from our site have been archived using WinZip. When you have saved the attachments to a folder on your hard-drive, you need to extract the files using a de-compression program such as WinZip or PKUnzip. When you extract the files, the code is usually extracted into chapter folders. When you start the extraction process, ensure your software (WinZip, PKUnzip, etc.) is set to extract to Use Folder Names.

Errata

We've made every effort to make sure that there are no errors in the text or in the code. However, no one is perfect and mistakes do occur. If you find an error in one of our books, like a spelling mistake or a faulty piece of code, we would be very grateful for feedback. By sending in errata you may save another reader hours of frustration, and of course, you will be helping us provide even higher quality information. Simply e-mail the information to support@wrox.com, your information will be checked and if correct, posted to the errata page for that title, or used in subsequent editions of the book.

To find errata on the web site, log on to http://www.wrox.com/, and simply locate the title through our Advanced Search or title list. Click on the Book Errata link, which is below the cover graphic on the book's detail page.

E-mail Support

If you wish to directly query a problem in the book page with an expert who knows the book in detail, then e-mail support@wrox.com, with the title of the book and the last four numbers of the ISBN in the subject field of the e-mail. A typical e-mail should include the following things:

- ❑ The **name**, **last four digits of the ISBN**, and **page number** of the problem in the Subject field

- ❑ Your **name**, **contact information**, and the **problem** in the body of the message

We **won't** send you junk mail. We need the details to save your time and ours. When you send an e-mail message, it will go through the following chain of support:

- ❑ Customer Support – Your message is delivered to our customer support staff, who are the first people to read it. They have files on most frequently asked questions and will answer anything general about the book or the web site immediately.

❑ Editorial – Deeper queries are forwarded to the technical editor responsible for that book. They have experience with the programming language or particular product, and are able to answer detailed technical questions on the subject. Once an issue has been resolved, the editor can post the errata to the web site.

❑ The Authors – Finally, in the unlikely event that the editor cannot answer your problem, he or she will forward the request to the author. We do try to protect the author from any distractions to their writing; however, we are quite happy to forward specific requests to them. All Wrox authors help with the support on their books. They will e-mail the customer and the editor with their response, and again all readers should benefit.

The Wrox Support process can only offer support on issues that are directly pertinent to the content of our published title. Support for questions that fall outside the scope of normal book support, is provided via the community lists of our http://p2p.wrox.com/ forum.

p2p.wrox.com

For author and peer discussion join the P2P mailing lists. Our unique system provides **programmer to programmer**™ contact on mailing lists, forums, and newsgroups, all **in addition** to our one-to-one e-mail support system. Be confident that your query is being examined by the many Wrox authors and other industry experts who are present on our mailing lists. At p2p.wrox.com you will find a number of different lists that will help you, not only while you read this book, but also as you develop your own applications.

To subscribe to a mailing list just follow these steps:

1. Go to http://p2p.wrox.com/.

2. Choose the appropriate category from the left menu bar.

3. Click on the mailing list you wish to join.

4. Follow the instructions to subscribe and fill in your e-mail address and password.

5. Reply to the confirmation e-mail you receive.

6. Use the subscription manager to join more lists and set your e-mail preferences.

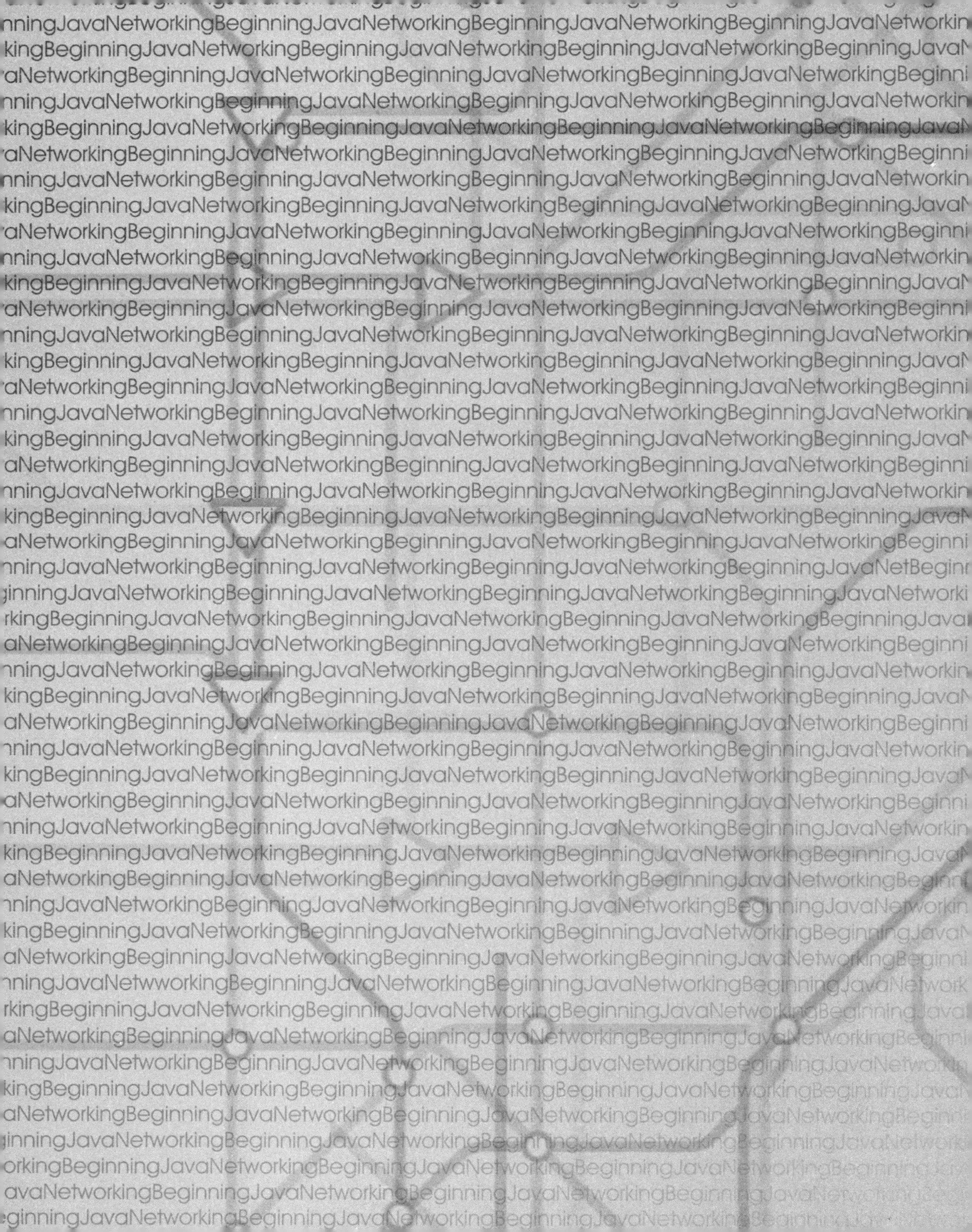

Introduction to Java Network Programming

It is easier to write network applications in Java than it is in most programming languages as support for network programming was built right into Java from the start. The core API for Java includes classes and interfaces that provide uniform access to a diverse set of network protocols. As the Internet and network programming have evolved, Java has maintained its cadence. New APIs and toolkits have expanded the available options for the Java network programmer.

This chapter will give you a good understanding of what Java network programming is all about. It starts with "a definition" of network programming. The emphasis on "a definition" is important. Network programming is one of those concepts that has many different meanings.

We're going to take a look at the broadest interpretation of Java network programming in this chapter. We'll start with low-level programming and work our way to interactive Internet applications. Here's a quick list of the topics we'll cover:

❑ What is network programming?

❑ What can network programs do?

❑ Network programming with Java

What Is Network Programming?

Network Programming is a bit of jargon that means different things to different people. To some programmers, network programming means low-level programming: reading and writing network sockets, translating network protocols, encrypting/decrypting data, and so on. To others, the meaning of network programming is broader and includes the design and programming of distributed applications.

Distributed computing is another piece of jargon that has lots of interpretations. Client-server applications that use a network server for important services, such as security and database access, are one popular interpretation. We can broaden distributed computing further to include agents and peer-to-peer services. We'll get to these terms a little later in this chapter. The important feature of distributed computing is that it involves two or more computers communicating with each other.

Some programmers interpret network programming as Internet/Intranet programming. The highly interactive web application that uses the web browser as its user interface is a good, generic example.

There is some truth in each of the above interpretations, but since there is no consensus on what a network program is, we have a chance to offer our own definition. The defining characteristic of network programs is that they use a network *in some way* to do their work. Network programs do any, all or some of the following:

- ❏ Send data across a network

- ❏ Provide services over a network

- ❏ Receive data over a network

- ❏ Invoke services across a network

Client and server are two overloaded terms in network programming. We'll soon see that they are not just overused by Java network programmers; they are widely used terms in programming *generally*.

One common meaning for **server** is a computer or some other device on a network that manages a network resource. A **file server**, for example, manages some sort of storage device to share files over a network. A **print server** manages access to a network printer. A **database server** is used to store, query, and retrieve large amounts of data efficiently.

Another meaning for the term *server* is a computer program that provides data and/or services to another computer program. One of the reasons we call these programs *servers* is because they typically run on another computer and are accessed over a network.

A web site is an excellent example of both meanings of the word *server* – there's a remote computer involved and a computer application running on that machine. While it is possible to create a web site on a workstation that is not even connected to a network, it is more common to think of another computer serving up web pages. The remote computer alone doesn't serve up web pages – there's a network program running on that remote machine waiting for web browsers to request pages, and the web server application handles the incoming requests for web pages.

A **client** is a computer application that relies on another computer program for some of its data or services. Typically, the client will run on a local computer and access a server application across a network. A web browser is a network client – you can use your web browser exclusively to read text files and view graphic images on your local PC, but most people use their web browsers as a network client in order to access web sites over the Internet.

Clients and servers don't just talk randomly to each other – they communicate. That means they share information in a predictable way.

Protocol is another bit of network programming jargon. A protocol is an agreed-upon way of exchanging information and service requests between clients and servers. FTP (File Transfer Protocol), for example, is a frequently used protocol for transferring files on the Internet. FTP file transfers use two network programs. We can use an FTP client program to connect to an FTP server over a network and transfer files. We can upload files from our machine to the remote FTP server. We can also download files from the FTP server to our local machine. Other operations are also possible with FTP, such as creating directories, deleting files, and so on.

Gnutella is a relatively new protocol for transferring files on the Internet. Gnutella relies on just one program (called a **servant** in Gnutella-speak) to transfer files. That one network program can switch back and forth, acting as a client one moment, searching for files and retrieving them from other computers, and acting as a server in the next moment, sending files and responding to queries from other computers. **Peer-to-peer** network protocols, like Gnutella, allow individual computers to interact as equals. Peer-to-peer protocols are symmetrical for example, each computer running a Gnutella servant has the potential to be a client, a server, or both. It can simultaneously interact with many different computers: querying some, downloading files from others, fulfilling upload requests from still others. You can see a screenshot of Gnotella, a popular Gnutella servant, in the figure below. (Gnotella is available from http://www.gnotella.com/).

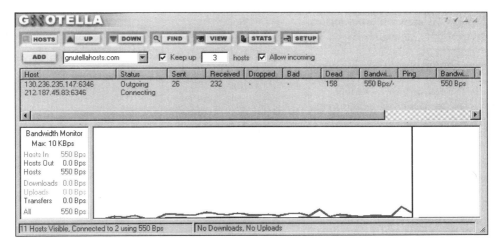

What Can Network Programs Do?

Networking extends the power of a single computer. Networks let one computer communicate with thousands, even millions, of other computers.

Let's consider Gnutella for a moment. Gnutella is a protocol where one computer can retrieve information from thousands of other computers. Suppose you want to find information on the price of widgets. There is no single Gnutella server indexing all of the available information on the Internet. There is no Gnutella equivalent of Yahoo! or AltaVista; no giant Gnutella file server mirroring data from across the Internet.

With Gnutella, when you want to find information on the price of widgets, your computer asks neighboring computers if they know anything about the price of widgets. At the same time, it also asks those computers to ask their neighbors. Those neighbors pass the query along and ask their neighbors. Depending on how many computers are running Gnutella at the time you submit your query, thousands of computers might be involved in the search for your data. When matches are found, the computers with matches send the information directly back to your computer.

Share Information

At their simplest, network programs either send data or they receive data.

The Daytime protocol is a basic Internet protocol for exchanging a simple piece of data – the current time of day and date. A Daytime server application ignores any data that a client might send. It checks its local clock and returns the current time and date as a string – the client can then do whatever it wants with the string. Not very elaborate, perhaps, but the Daytime protocol does have its uses. You can use it, for example, to keep your enterprise servers synchronized to a time standard, like the U.S. Naval Observatory's atomic clocks, rather than a network engineer's wristwatch.

Data displays for network programs can range from simple, character-based interfaces to highly interactive user interfaces. Simple network utilities tend to favor character-based interfaces. While these sorts of interfaces feel foreign to many Windows developers, UNIX and mainframe developers prefer them for basic network utilities, tasks like fetching the current date and time. Windows users have gotten used to highly interactive user interfaces. Even the time of day sports a flashy user interface on the Web. The example below comes from the U.S. National Institute of Standards and Technology (NIST) at http://www.time.gov/.

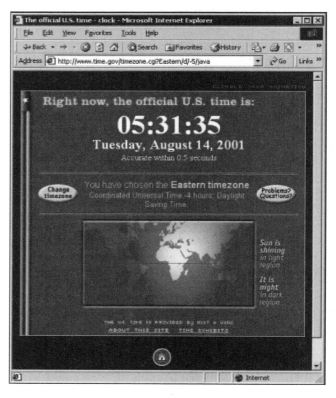

It is common these days to equate network programming with Internet programming generally and web browser programming in particular. While web browsers are certainly pervasive and they have become increasingly sophisticated, they are not a universal network programming solution. The typical web browser cannot connect to Daytime protocol server and just display the current date and time. You don't see the whole stream of data that an HTTP request generates, but a Daytime protocol server would just ignore it all if you tried to use your web browser and your web browser wouldn't know what to do with string that comes back from the Daytime protocol server. Web browsers and Daytime protocol servers don't use the same protocol. They don't know how to communicate with each other. Instead, if you want to get the current time and date from a Daytime protocol server, your web browser needs to connect with a web server that knows how to talk to a Daytime protocol server.

Web browsers and web servers communicate with a protocol called HTTP (Hypertext Transfer Protocol). When you type the name of a web site in your web browser, the browser sends an HTTP command to the web server that asks it to transmit its home page to your browser. If the home page contains some links to graphic images, the web browser can send HTTP requests for the graphic images and display them along with the text of the home page. Web browsers typically work with text files and a few supported binary files (mostly multimedia files, although the list continues to grow). Browsers can incorporate lots of functionality beyond the HTTP protocol, but these involve extensions that are far from universal in their acceptance.

Java network programs offer greater power and flexibility than browser-based technologies alone. Browser-based technologies are a just a subset of the possibilities open to the Java network programmer. Browsers make excellent user interfaces, but obtaining a consistent look and feel to browser-based applications can be a challenge as different browsers support different feature sets.

Automated processes are usually better suited to Java applications, because browser applications assume a human being is sitting at the browser. Returning to our Daytime protocol client again, what if we want to automate the synchronizing of day/time for our enterprise servers with the U.S. Naval Observatory? We can write a small Java application to fetch the current date and time and then update all of the servers in our enterprise without any user intervention at all.

Web browsers retrieve information on demand. They are ideal for retrieving information that changes infrequently. It is certainly possible to use a web browser to go out and fetch stock prices, but each time you want an update, you will need to refresh the page. Browser applications are also not well-suited when constant updates are required. A Java stock analysis program, however, can easily pull stock prices at frequent intervals from a remote server, store that information in a file, and then analyze it. Even a Java applet can periodically fetch stock prices and display the results in a small browser window, as in the figure above.

This is not to say that browser applications have little or no utility – quite the opposite. They can be a very valuable means of sharing information and other resources on the Internet or on a corporate intranet. Browser applications can employ applets, servlets, and other Java technologies to prove a richer, more interactive user experience. The NASDAQ stock ticker applet in the previous figure enhances NASDAQ's web site at http://www.nasdaq.com/.

Web browsers are better at retrieving data than they are at collecting information and submitting it. When a web browser is involved in submitting data, it is usually through an HTML form. Validating data on an HTML form involves important design trade-offs – client-side solutions risk browser incompatibilities and server solutions can involve network roundtrips. Web browsers are optimized for displaying data, but Java network programs do not have that same narrow specialization – they can send data just as easily as retrieving it and can easily validate the data as it is entered, giving the user immediate corrective feedback.

Parallel Computing

Java includes the basic infrastructure to integrate computers into a parallel computational resource – many different computers can participate in helping to solve a single problem. They each work on a part of it, and when they finish their task, they pass their results back.

Parallel computing extends the ideas of multitasking and multithreading. **Multitasking** is the ability of a single processor to give the appearance of performing more than one task simultaneously. What really happens is the processor switches from one task to another so quickly that it gives the appearance of executing all of the tasks at the same time. **Multithreading** divides a program's work into separate threads of execution. The threads can then be run by separate processors, improving application performance. Ordinarily, the processors are all part of the same physical server, but there are servers today that contain 16, 32, even 64 separate processors.

Parallel computing does not confine its work to a single physical server. Network communications make it possible for the threads of execution to run on computers distributed across a network. The SETI@Home Project (http://setiathome.ssl.berkeley.edu/) developed at U.C. Berkeley, uses thousands of home computers to analyze radio telescope data, searching for evidence of extraterrestrial life.

If you visit the SETI@Home site and read their web pages, you'll be told that the SETI@Home software "borrows" unused clock cycles on machines running the software. What's really going on is the software uses the ability of your computer to multitask. The SETI@Home software downloads a chunk of data to analyze when you install the software. Then, a task runs in the background, analyzing the data. When the chunk is analyzed, the results are returned and another chunk is fetched. On a PC, the SETI@Home task typically runs when the screen saver is active. An active screen saver is the signal that the processor has "spare" cycles available to "borrow".

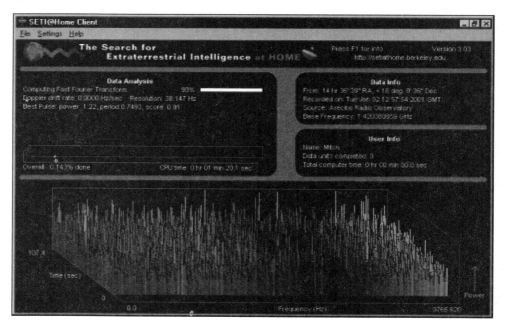

Application Services

Java has included the ability to listen for network connections and respond to those connections since its first release. Java has been used to create clients and servers for many popular Internet services, including e-mail, chat, and file transfer.

Java is an excellent tool for implementing custom clients and servers because it supports multiple technologies for sending and receiving data over a network. Java network applications can use technologies that are 100% Java and can also use non-Java technologies.

Java applications can use network connections to pass data and request services. Chapter 5, which covers Java I/O, will give you a solid introduction to using network connections in this way. If you're an object-oriented programmer, network connections are a less than elegant solution. OOP programmers prefer to work with objects and invoke methods. We'll be discussing RMI (Remote Method Invocation) in Chapter 16. RMI lets a Java client work with objects on a remote server just as if those objects were running locally. If you need to work with objects written in another OOP language, C++ perhaps, Java network applications can work with CORBA (Common Object Request Broker Architecture) to access those objects. Chapter 17 covers working with CORBA.

Java is widely used to implement electronic commerce applications. Applets can provide an enhanced user interface right inside a web browser window. Java network APIs make it relatively easy to authenticate people and encrypt information, making it easier to handle sensitive transactions securely, like credit card sales.

Chat applications are very popular network applications that allow users to send messages to each other in real-time. Yahoo!, for example, uses a Java applet to connect your web browser with thousands of concurrent users engaged in hundreds of simultaneous conversations. You can even use a microphone and stream audio to other chat room visitors, thanks to another Java technology, the Java Multimedia Framework (JMF – http://java.sun.com/products/java-media/jmf/).

While Java applets can handle many chat implementations, like Yahoo! chat rooms, some implementations require a Java application instead. For example, a complete implementation of Internet Relay Chat (IRC) includes the ability to share files between IRC clients. Sharing files between one IRC client and another would violate an important security restriction imposed on applets. Applets are not allowed to access a client machine's file system, whereas Java applications can access files on a local machine.

Multiplayer games are another popular example of network applications that can be written in Java. Yahoo! uses Java applets for their multiplayer games, like the chess applet in the following figure. The chess applet uses a network connection to pass moves between the players and then multicasts the moves to anyone else who cares to watch the game.

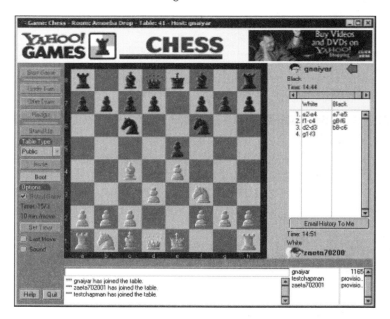

Collaborative Computing

Collaborative computing is another term that means different things to different people. Popular definitions include:

- ❑ Interactive desktop conferencing

- ❑ Distributed network presentations

- ❑ Shared simulations and experiments

- ❑ Group workflow

It is possible to write collaborative applications, such as whiteboards and desktop conferencing with Java's network APIs. Until recently, that was your only alternative. The Java Shared Data Toolkit (JSDT) is a recent addition that makes it much easier to write collaborative applications in Java. JSDT is a 100% pure Java toolkit that allows developers to easily add collaborative features to applets and network applications. For more information, please visit http://java.sun.com/products/java-media/jsdt/.

Network Programming

The available network programming features in the earliest release of Java included only low-level network programming. It was possible to create sophisticated Internet applications with Java 1.0 but you had to know how to do it with basic network programming techniques, like socket programming (which we will discuss in more detail in Chapter 2).

As Java has matured, so has its set of network programming features. New APIs and new tools were added to shield programmers from low-level network programming. These new APIs and tools use low-level network programming "under the hood". They provide developers with some important benefits:

❑   Productivity: The new APIs and tools make developers more productive so network applications can be written quicker and with less code.

❑   Maintainability: The new APIs provide high-level object models and function libraries. A single method call can replace dozens of lines of low-level network programming, making source code more readable.

❑   Robustness: Low-level network programming is error-prone. It can be complicated, with many possibilities for subtle errors; therefore, thorough testing and considerable debugging are usually required. The new APIs and tools undergo thorough testing and debugging, allowing the developer to leverage that effort. Network applications become less fragile.

The foundation for Java networking is located in the `java.net` and `java.io` packages. The `java.net` package provides the classes for implementing network applications. We will spend a lot of time in this book exploring the fundamental features of this package, since its classes are used to build applications that rely upon TCP/IP and UDP. We will introduce TCP/IP and UDP (the network protocols used by the Internet) in Chapter 2. The `java.io` package provides classes for system input and output through data streams, serialization, and the file system. Our interest in `java.io` will focus primarily on data streams and serialization.

Here is just a little background on the evolution of Java network programming features:

❑   **Java 1.0** included the basics for network programming, such as:

    ❑   The ability to make connections to other computers and listen for new connections

    ❑   A customizable handler for Uniform Resource Locators (URLs). More about URLs later

    ❑   Primitive network programming; handling basic considerations, like connection timeouts, required lots of effort

❑   **Java 1.1** gave developers more control over networking features:

    ❑   `Socket` and `SocketHandler` were no longer declared final

    ❑   The ability to create low-level content and protocol handlers was enhanced

- ❏ Multicast networking was added
- ❏ Remote Method Invocation (RMI) gave applications the ability to use objects on another machine just like they were part of the local application

- ❏ **Java 2.0** developers were given very little in the area of low-level network programming features. Instead, the big changes occurred in distributed computing:
  - ❏ Servlets and JavaServer Pages (JSPs) allowed Java developers to build sophisticated web applications
  - ❏ Enterprise JavaBeans (EJBs) took the basic ideas of RMI to a whole new level
  - ❏ Remote objects became components with the EJB server providing important services like transactions and security

- ❏ **JDK 1.4 Beta** adds and improves low-level network features:
  - ❏ Developers get a new I/O library (called NIO), which supplements the I/O features in the `java.io` package
  - ❏ Character-set handling is improved
  - ❏ Pattern-matching, based on Perl regular expressions, is added
  - ❏ There is a new primitive I/O abstraction, called `Channels`, which allows multiplexed, non-blocking I/O, making it easier to build scalable server applications

The various `java.rmi` packages were added to Java with JDK 1.1. We will spend considerable time with the `java.rmi` packages, because they support Java's Remote Method Invocation (RMI), a mechanism that enables an object on one Java virtual machine to invoke methods on an object in another Java virtual machine. The RMI mechanism is fundamental to creating distributed network applications with Java.

Java network programming also uses other classes, depending upon the application:

- ❏ The `java.security` package provides the interfaces and classes for Java's security framework (see Chapter 7)
- ❏ The various `org.omg.CORBA` packages add CORBA support to Java (covered in Chapter 17)
- ❏ The `javax.rmi` packages provide the APIs for RMI-IIOP (described in Chapter 16)

Daytime Protocol Example

Since this is a book that is intended to be a programmer-to-programmer experience, complete with practical examples, it is time to give you your first brief example. We won't explain the code at this point – we'll save that for a later chapter, but we do want you to see how easy it is to write Java network programs.

Earlier in this chapter, we showed you a Daytime protocol client. The Daytime protocol is a standard Internet protocol, which means there is an agreed-upon standard (RFC 867 – http://www.ietf.org/rfc/rfc0867.txt). We'll discuss the standards process in detail later. For now, it's enough to know that our Daytime protocol client complies with the Internet Daytime standard. The code below will return the date and the time of day from a remote server that implements the Daytime protocol. If you do not enter a server name, the client will default to the U.S. Naval Observatory's server, `tock.usno.navy.mil`. This code is available as a download from http://www.wrox.com/.

```
// DaytimeClient

import java.net.*;
import java.io.*;

public class DaytimeClient {
  public static void main(String[] args) {
    String sHostName;

    /* Get the name of the server from the command line.
       No entry, use tock.usno.navy.mil */
    if (args.length > 0) {
      sHostName = args[0];
    } else {
      sHostName = "tock.usno.navy.mil";
    }

    try {

      /* Open a socket to Port 13.
         Prepare to receive the Daytime information. */
      Socket oSocket = new Socket(sHostName, 13);
      InputStream oTimeStream = oSocket.getInputStream();
      StringBuffer oTime = new StringBuffer();

      int iCharacter;

      // Fetch the Daytime information.
      while ((iCharacter = oTimeStream.read()) != -1) {
        oTime.append((char) iCharacter);
      }

      // Convert Daytime to a string and output.
      String sTime = oTime.toString().trim();
      System.out.println("It is " + sTime + " at " + sHostName + ".");

      // Close the stream and the socket.
      oTimeStream.close();
      oSocket.close();
    } catch (UnknownHostException e) {
      System.err.println(e);
    } catch (IOException e) {
      System.err.println(e);
    }
  }
}
```

If you compile and run the code from a command prompt you should get the current date and time displayed.

C:\Beg_Java_Networking\Ch01>**javac DaytimeClient.java**

C:\Beg_Java_Networking>\Ch01**java DaytimeClient**
It is Tue Aug 14 12:09:39 2001 at tock.usno.navy.mil.

Summary

This chapter is just a brief introduction to Java network programming. We have discussed the definition of Java network programs, summarized some of the important uses of network programs, and had a brief overview of Java network programming features.

Here is a quick list of the important points in this chapter:

- ❑ The defining characteristic of network programs is that they use a network *in some way* to do their work.

- ❑ Network programs do any, all or some combination of the following: send data, provide services, receive data, invoke services.

- ❑ A **server** is a network program that provides data and services to another network program.

- ❑ A **client** is a network program that consumes data and services provided by another network program, such as a server.

- ❑ **Peer-to-peer** network programs are symmetrical. Each computer has the potential to be both a client and a server simultaneously.

- ❑ Java network programs offer greater power and flexibility than browser-based technologies alone. Browser-based technologies are a subset of the possibilities open to the Java network programmer.

- ❑ The available network programming features in the earliest release of Java included only low-level network programming. As Java has matured, so has its set of network programming features.

Network Basics

Before we discuss Java network programming in great detail, we need to cover some basics. This chapter covers network basics, fundamental network concepts you need to understand before you try to write network programs with Java or any other programming language. None of this information is Java-specific, so there is no Java code – there will be plenty of Java code in subsequent chapters, after we get a good grounding in fundamental concepts.

Here's a list of the topics we will cover in this chapter:

❑   What is a Network?

❑   The Layers of a Network

❑   IP, TCP, UDP, and Multicasting

❑   The Internet

❑   Important Internet Protocols

❑   Internet Standards

What is a Network?

A **network** is a collection of computers and other devices that can move information around from one device to another. Traditionally, network devices were connected together with wires with shared information converted into electrical signals that were passed across the wires. Later, fiber optic cables were used to convert the information into light signals instead of electrical signals and today, some networks use radio transmitters and receivers and do not use cabling at all.

Each device on a network is called a **node**. These include computers as well as routers, bridges, and gateways (these are used to route network data). When printers are connected directly to the network they also become nodes.

Another word you will hear is **host**. A host is a node that provides one or more services to other nodes over a network. A host usually refers to a network device that is a fully functional computer, although there are some special purpose devices that provide network services to other network nodes. Common examples include database servers, network proxy servers (which offer a shared Internet connection to other network nodes), web servers, and so on.

Each node on a network is uniquely identified by a **network address**. The nodes use it to identify each other, a first step in communicating. A node needs more than a network address to communicate with other nodes, they also need a shared set of rules for passing information back and forth. They might be using different operating systems, for example, therefore in order to share data, the nodes need a **network protocol**. Network protocols define precise sets of rules for communication among the nodes on a network. There are many different network protocols; after all, nodes can communicate about many different things, from exchanging the time of day to displaying highly-interactive web pages.

Networks communicate by sharing packets of information. Each packet contains the network address of the node that sent it and the network address of its destination. They also include a checksum, to make sure the packet wasn't damaged in some way during transmission. **Packet-switching** gives networks the ability to use a single wire (sometimes called the backbone) to handle simultaneous communications between many different nodes.

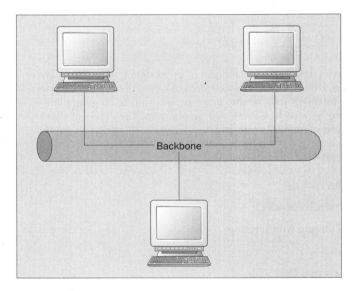

There are lots of different kinds of networks. The most common are **LANs** (**Local Area Networks**) and **WANs** (**Wide Area Networks**). LANs are used to connect computers in a local area, such as an office or a home. WANs connect computers over a wider area, such as an entire campus, across a city, and so on.

Networks are laid out with some common geometric relations. The most common are bus, ring, and star topologies.

- ❏ **Ring topologies**: Connect all of the nodes together in one closed circuit
- ❏ **Bus topologies**: Connect all of the nodes to one circuit that runs through the network like a backbone
- ❏ **Star topologies**: Connect nodes together in smaller circuits, which are then connected to a circuit that runs through the network

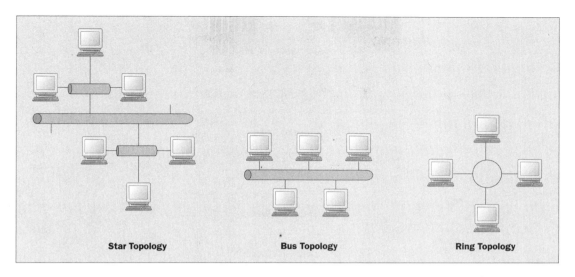

Star Topology **Bus Topology** **Ring Topology**

Networks can be connected together, that's how the LAN in your office, for example, can connect to the Internet. When networks are connected, we need a way of routing packets from one node on one network to a node on another network. Different network protocols use different addressing schemes. There are several types of devices that are used for routing messages between networks. A **gateway** (or **switch**) is a computer that has two network interface cards (NICs). The gateway accepts network packets from one network on one network interface card and then routes those packets to a different network with the second network interface card. **Routers** and **bridges** are dedicated hardware devices that route packets from one network to a different network. Routers are more complicated and more expensive than bridges. Routers can communicate and share information that helps them pick the best route for transmitting data to another network.

Most networks today use the Ethernet network protocol, but some networks may use IBM's Token Ring protocol or some other network protocol. Ethernet networks use a hub to connect the network interface card in your PC to the network. Typically, a cable will connect your NIC to the hub. You'll hear people talking about **fast Ethernet** and throwing around terms like **10-baseT** and **100-baseT**. 10-baseT Ethernet networks use twisted pair cable (that's the "T") and transmit data at speeds up to 10 million bits per second (10 Mbps). 100-baseT Ethernet has a maximum speed of 100 Mbps.

The Layers of a Network

Moving information from one computer to another is a complex set of operations. It involves many different standards and protocols. Network engineers solved the complex web of protocols and standards by breaking them down into an abstract set of layers, with each layer building on the services provided by the layers beneath it. The layers of a network only speak to the layers immediately above and below them. The convention, when diagramming network services, is to organize the layers vertically. Together, this set of layers is referred to as a **stack**.

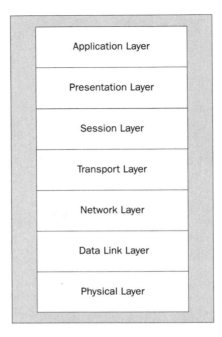

The OSI (Open System Interconnect) Reference Model, shown above, defines seven layers that every network stack *should* provide. This model is defined by the ISO, the International Standards Organization (http://www.iso.org/).

Here are some quick definitions for those seven layers:

- **Physical Layer**: The physical layer is at the bottom of the OSI stack, it defines the cable or physical medium used to tie network nodes together. Common examples include Type I, twisted pair, fiber optic and wireless. From the perspective of network theory, all media are functionally equivalent. Modern network operating systems can work with a heterogeneous physical media (for example, some nodes tied together with unshielded twisted pair, some tied together with fiber optic cable). Different physical media require different network adapter cards and different device drivers for those cards, they also involve different cabling standards. The physical layer also determines how data is transmitted over the network, for example, what voltages represent 1 and 0 bits and what control signals are used.

- **Data Link Layer**: Connecting two computers together with the right cables and connectors is not sufficient to move information across the cable. The data link layer defines the format of data on the network. We've already mentioned that modern networks are packet-switched. Network packets (also called **data frames**) are defined in the data link layer and include a checksum, the source and destination addresses, and the data. The data layer converts data bits into packets and defines parameters, like the largest packet that can be sent (the **Maximum Transmission Unit** or **MTU**). The data link layer handles the physical and logical connections to the packet's destination, using a network interface card. Common network interface cards include Ethernet, Token-Ring, ARCNET, StarLAN, LocalTalk, FDDI, and ATM. The data link layer also provides low-level error detection and correction. If a packet is corrupted during transit, the data link layer is responsible for retransmitting the packet.

- **Network Layer**: Now that we have packets of data, the network layer is responsible for routing those packets of data across the network. The network layer is also responsible for routing packets across multiple networks. When a packet crosses from one network to another, it may encounter a smaller MTU. The network layer is responsible for breaking packets larger than MTU into smaller packets. It is also the layer responsible for reassembling those fragmented data packets when they arrive at the destination node.

- **Transport Layer**: The transport layer is an intermediate layer used by the higher levels to communicate with the network layer. It offers a level of abstraction for the higher layers, shielding them from the low-level details of the network, data link, and physical layers. The transport layer gets its name from its primary responsibility, packet handling. It divides streams of data into packets and ensures that packets are delivered in sequence. It also performs error-checking, to guarantee error-free delivery with no data loss.

- **Session Layer**: The session layer establishes, maintains and ends sessions across the network. A **session** establishes communication between nodes. The session layer provides synchronization, security authentication, and network naming. Synchronization establishes check points in the data stream, improving network performance. If a session fails, only data after the most recent checkpoint needs to be retransmitted.

- **Presentation Layer**: The presentation layer is another intermediate layer. It handles the mapping of data to the layers immediately above and below itself, translating data between the computer and the network format. Presentation layer services include character set conversion, protocol conversion, data encryption, and data compression.

- **Application Layer**: The application layer is all about application services. These are services needed to support user applications, such as messaging, network access and file transfers.

The *OSI Reference Model* is useful for network vendors, it helps them ensure that their products interoperate. In theory, you should be able to mix-and-match network layers from different vendors, since each layer has well-defined APIs and protocols. In practice, the *OSI Reference Model* has never won the enthusiastic support of network vendors. Each offers their network operating system as a complete stack, with the separate layers designed to interoperate and be used as a single stack architecture.

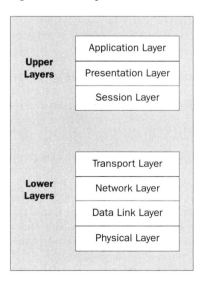

Before we move on to the TCP/IP stack, it is helpful to note that the *OSI Reference Model* refers to the application, presentation, and session layers as **upper layers**. These layers perform application-specific functions like data formatting, encryption, and connection management. The **lower layers** provide more primitive functions, such as routing, addressing, and flow control.

The TCP/IP Stack

The *OSI Reference Model* is more detail than you will need for Java network programming. Java network programming is limited to TCP/IP. **TCP/IP** (**Transmission Control Protocol/Internet Protocol**) was originally developed by the US Defense Advance Research Projects Agency (DARPA) to interconnect the computer networks managed by the US Department of Defense. It is now the network protocol preferred by most UNIX vendors and by Microsoft for networking computers running Microsoft Windows 9x/NT/2000.

The TCP/IP protocols operate over nearly any underlying local or wide area network technology. Ethernet is the most common network transport protocol. **Serial Line Internet Protocol** (**SLIP**) and **Point-to-Point Protocol** (**PPP**) provide data link layer protocol services where no other underlying data link protocol is in use, such as in leased line or dial-up environments. If you connect to the Internet from your home over a telephone line, you almost certainly use SLIP or PPP. PPP also provides support for using multiple protocols simultaneously over a single connection.

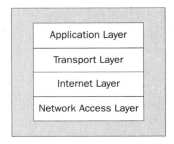

TCP/IP uses a simpler four-layer model that omits some of the features of the *OSI Reference Model*. The services of some adjacent OSI layers are merged, others are separated. Here's a brief description of the four TCP/IP layers:

❑ **Network Access Layer**: This is the bottom layer in the TCP/IP stack. The network access layer merges the functions of the physical layer and the data link layer in the *OSI Reference Model*. It includes the network hardware and device drivers. The network access layer also includes the protocols that a node uses to deliver data to the other devices attached to the network.

❑ **Internet Layer**: This layer is used for basic communication, addressing and routing. TCP/IP uses IP and ICMP (Internet Control Message Protocol) protocols at the network layer. The Internet layer protocols also provide a **Datagram** (or data packet) network service. The IP datagram service does not support any concept of a session or connection, it makes no guarantee that packets will be received at all, let alone, that they will arrive in the order they were sent. There is no ability to retransmit data, so if the receiving node detects a transmission error using the datagram's checksum, it simply ignores the datagram.

❑ **Transport Layer**: This layer handles communication among programs on a network. The transport layer uses the idea of a connection to provide an extended two-way communication between nodes. This layer ensures end-to-end data integrity, in that packets are guaranteed to arrive at their destination in the order they were transmitted and if an error is detected, the packet can be retransmitted. TCP/IP uses TCP and UDP as its transport layer protocols. We will have a lot more to say about TCP and UDP – the User Datagram Protocol – in subsequent sections of this chapter.

❑ **Application Layer**: Services that process application data, such as character set conversion, protocol conversion, data encryption, and data compression reside on this layer. The application layer also manages sessions (that is, connections). TCP/IP uses the terms **sockets** and **ports** to describe the connection over which applications communicate. Socket is synonymous with connection and session. Because a host can have more than one application, the port number is a way of addressing which application you want to connect to on that host.

IP, TCP, and UDP

The Java networking APIs deal only with IP-based networks. **IP** (**Internet Protocol**) is a network layer protocol. It is the network protocol underlying the Internet. Every device attached to the Internet must use the IP protocol. **TCP** (**Transmission Control Protocol**) is a connection-oriented transport layer protocol. It provides data streams that are guaranteed to arrive at the destination network node in the order they were transmitted by the source node. **UDP** (**User Datagram Protocol**) is another transport layer protocol for TCP/IP networks. UDP is fast but unreliable as it makes no guarantee that packets will arrive, let alone, that they will arrive in the same order they were transmitted, so it is best suited to small, independent data packets.

IP (Internet Protocol)

IP is the foundation on which TCP/IP is built. The primary responsibilities for IP are the addressing of hosts and the routing of datagrams between hosts. In addition to routing between hosts, IP also provides error relaying and services for fragmenting and reassembling datagrams so they can be transmitted over networks with different MTUs.

Version 4 of IP, also known as IPv4 has been in use since the early 1980s. However, due to the growth of the Internet and new emerging applications, a new version of IP – IP version 6 (IPv6) – has entered the Internet Standards Track. The primary description of IPv6 is contained in RFC 1883 (http://www.ietf.org/rfc/rfc1883.txt) and described in Chapter 21.

IP Addresses

Each host on a TCP/IP network is assigned a unique 32-bit logical address. The address is divided into two main parts: the network number and the host number. The network number identifies a particular network. If the network will be connected to the Internet, then the network number must be assigned by the Internet Network Information Center (InterNIC), this ensures a globally unique network number. The host number identifies a host on a network and is assigned by the local network administrator. Together, the network number and the host number provide a globally unique address for every host on every network connected to the Internet.

IP addresses are usually represented as four decimal numbers separated by dots. The dots are for our convenience. The real address is just a 32-bit number. Here's an example:

```
199.174.242.68
```

In this case, `199.174.242` is the network address and `68` is the host address.

IP addressing supports five different classes of addresses. The first byte in the network address determines the class of the address. Commercial addresses are limited to classes A, B, and C.

❑ **Class A**: Network addresses `001-126`. 16 million available hosts for each network. The first 8 bits are the network address; the remaining 24 bits are the host address.

❑ **Class B**: Network addresses `128-191`. 65,536 available hosts for each network. The first 16 bits are the network address; the remaining 16 bits are the host address.

❑ **Class C**: Network addresses `192-223`. 256 available hosts for each network. The first 24 bits are the network address; the remaining 8 bits are the host address.

❑ **Class D**: Network addresses `224-239`. Multicast mode only (more on multicasting later on).

❑ **Class E**: Network addresses `240-255`. Reserved for future use.

> **Several IP addresses are deliberately unassigned. They can be used on internal networks and nodes employing these addresses are not allowed on the Internet. Home networks and small LANs often use them and they are also used to test networks. The non-routable addresses are all IP addresses beginning with 10, IP addresses between 172.16 and 172.31, and IP address 192.168.**

IP networks can be divided into smaller networks called subnets. **Subnets** provide more efficient use of network addresses and simplify network administration. They also restrict broadcast traffic. (Every IP network and subnet has a broadcast address. Packets addressed to this address are received by every node on the network or subnet. Broadcasts do not cross a router.)

Subnets are under local administration, the rest of the Internet sees a network with subnets as a single network. Each subnet contains a range of addresses from their IP network, they borrow bits from the host address and designate them as the subnet address. **Subnet masks** identify the portion of an IP address that identifies the network and subnetwork for routing purposes. Subnet masks for networks without subnets are easy:

Class A	`255.0.0.0`	8 bits
Class B	`255.255.0.0`	16 bits
Class C	`255.255.255.0`	24 bits

When a network is divided into subnets, the subnet mask divides the address space. A network with a B class address, such as `176.16.0.0`, might use four bits from the host address to identify the subnet. All NICs on that particular subnet would share the subnet mask, `255.255.240.0`. This would divide the IP address into a 16-bit network address, a 4-bit subnet address, and a 12-bit host address.

IP addresses are computer-friendly, but are not human-friendly as people have a hard time remembering four digit addresses. The **Domain Name Service** (**DNS**) maps globally unique names to IP addresses. IP addresses are used at the network level, domain names are used at the application level, for example wrox.com. We will have more to say about IP addresses and domain names when we discuss the `java.net.InetAddress` class in Chapter 8.

IP Datagrams

An IP datagram includes a header and data. The header is 20 to 60 bytes long and contains items like the source IP address, destination IP address, and type of service. The data portion of an IP datagram can contain up to 65,516 bytes of data. Typically, the packets are much smaller.

Routing

The routing of datagrams is central to IP. Sending information from one network host to another can be very complicated. There can be multiple routes between the source of a datagram and its destination. The quickest route between two nodes can change because of network congestion (and other factors). A number of different protocols are used to keep distributed networks operating efficiently.

Here's a short list of important datagram routing protocols:

❑ **Internet Control Message Protocol (ICMP)**: IP uses ICPM to exchange information about routing difficulties with IP datagrams, echo transactions, and so on

❑ **Routing Information Protocol (RIP)**: Routers use RIP to exchange information, helping them calculate the most efficient path for passing datagrams along to their destination

❑ **Border Gateway Protocol (BGP)** and **Exterior Gateway Protocol (EGP)**: Used to convey network reachability information between routers and gateways

TCP (Transmission Control Protocol)

TCP provides two important services. First, it provides reliable packet delivery, giving the appearance of passing a continuous stream of information. Second, TCP provides a virtual connection service, based on sockets and ports.

TCP comes first in TCP/IP because TCP does the heavy lifting. TCP is responsible for breaking a stream of information into a set of datagrams, reassembling those datagrams at the destination host, and resending any datagrams that are lost or corrupted during transit.

We have mentioned that TCP is a connection-oriented transport protocol. That means a connection must be established before sending any information. The connection remains available until the requestor closes the connection or the connection "times out" because of inactivity. TCP connections are bi-directional, which means a client can listen to the same connection for error messages and other information from the server.

TCP uses three different kinds of sockets and a client creates a **sending socket** to request a service. Servers make their services available through **listening sockets**. Servers listen for connection attempts on these sockets and when a client attempts to connect, the server application responds by creating a **receiving socket**. The receiving socket is used to process service requests from the client and to pass information back to the client. Using separate processes to listen for connection attempts and to respond to client service requests improves server performance, as it prevents the listening socket from blocking while the application responds to client requests.

The sending socket includes the port number for the server – sending the address alone is not enough to specify a particular service as hosts can offer many different services simultaneously. Each TCP/IP host can specify up to 65,535 ports so port numbers help TCP multiplex and demultiplex many different connection streams.

Network engineers love standards. There are standard ports assigned to "well-known" services. For example, web browsers typically use port 80 to connect with HTTP servers. The first 1,024 ports are reserved for system use, here are a few of them:

Port	Service	Description
21	ftp	Used to send command strings to an FTP server
23	telnet	Used by Telnet for terminal emulation
25	smtp	Simple Mail Transfer Protocol, used to send e-mail between hosts
80	http	Hypertext Transfer Protocol, used by web servers
110	pop3	Post Office Protocol, used to receive e-mail sent between hosts

> **The official list of "well-known" ports is available online. You can access it at http://www.iana.org/assignments/port-numbers.**

UDP (User Datagram Protocol)

UDP is a one-shot network service. Like TCP, it sits in the transport layer and builds on the services in IP.

Since UDP is connectionless, all UDP communication involves single datagrams. UDP also uses sockets, but once a UDP datagram is sent, the socket is destroyed, so if you need to send more data, you need to create another socket. The same process occurs at the destination node – once a datagram is received, the socket is discarded and a new socket is required to listen for another datagram.

UDP is not well-suited to large datagrams as UDP provides no error correction or retransmission. Therefore, if any portion of a fragmented datagram becomes lost or corrupted during transmission, the entire data packet is discarded. This means that UDP works best with small, independent packets of information.

UDP datagrams are under-appreciated by novice network programmers. UDP is a lightweight network protocol with important uses. Here are a few scenarios to consider:

❑ **Multimedia Streaming**: Speed is critical and information flow is unidirectional. If an occasional packet gets lost, error correction protocols can compensate, so an occasional drop-out can be tolerated. All good reasons to use UDP datagrams instead of TCP segments.

❑ **Network Discovery Services**: You broadcast queries to hosts on a network and each host responds with information about the services they provide using a UDP datagram.

❑ **Control Services**: The classic case here is a periodic "I'm still alive" message to a server. Why go to the overhead of maintaining a collection of open sockets when a periodic message will do?

❑ **Basic Information Services**: Many services do not require a session, instead, they invoke a service in order to obtain a single piece of information, like the time of day. No need for the overhead of TCP in this case.

Multicasting

Multicasting and broadcasting are closely related. Multicasting allows hosts to communicate in a peer-to-peer fashion. With **multicasting**, an application can send a packet to the network and have that packet delivered to multiple destinations. Those destinations can be on the same network or distributed across multiple networks (for example, across the Internet). **Broadcasting** also sends the same packet to multiple recipients, but all the recipients have to be on the same network as the sender.

Multicasting works much like UDP. Instead of sending the packet to a particular node, multicasting transmits the packet to a host group. The host group has its own IP address. D Class IP addresses (224.0.0.0 through 239.255.255.255) are set aside specifically for multicast host addresses. Clients that are interested in a multicast group listen on the same multicast IP address. To send a message, hosts just send a packet to the IP address for a multicast group. Some multicast host groups are permanent, with administratively-assigned IP addresses. Others are transient, using dynamic assignment of IP addresses that expire when the group has no members.

Membership of a host group is dynamic – hosts may join and leave the group at any time. A host that sends a multicast datagram might be speaking to no one.

Multicasting is built on the IP datagram service. It is a "send and pray" service, just like UDP, as there is no guarantee that packets will arrive. Java 1.0 did not include IP Multicast support, but subsequent versions have included it.

Multicasting is the subject of Chapter 11, where we include a multicast chat program, as a practical example of multicast network programming.

The Internet

The Internet is more than the World Wide Web, it is a world-wide network of networks. The uppercase version – the Internet – got its name from its less expansive cousin – internet. An **internet** is any collection of networks that are interconnected with IP.

The World Wide Web (or WWW) is a relatively recent addition to the Internet, being only a decade old, and graphical browsers are even more recent. The World Wide Web uses a protocol called HTTP (Hypertext Transfer Protocol) to share information on the Internet, but this is not the only protocol for sharing information – we can use FTP, for example, to share files.

The networks that make up the Internet are varied. They include small Local Area Networks (LANs), Metropolitan Area Networks (MANs), Wide Area Networks (WANs), and even PCs and laptops dialing into ISPs over SLIP/PPP accounts. Some of the networks do not even run TCP/IP, they could use a different network protocol, such as AppleTalk. Networks on the Internet must use IP to communicate with each other. If a network uses some other network protocol, such as AppleTalk, a gateway can handle the translation between TCP/IP on the connection to the Internet and the unrelated network protocol used on the LAN.

Another related term that you will encounter frequently is Intranet. An **Intranet** uses Internet technologies within a single organization or company. For the most part, Intranets refer to in-house web servers, providing web pages and other web-based services to members of the organization. They are intended to be private Internet services.

Internet Security

Unless you're brand new to the Internet, you will know that there are unscrupulous people intent on vandalism and data theft. **Firewalls** are one means of preventing this, they partition networks from the rest of the Internet, serving as a single access point, inspecting every data packet that comes in or goes out.

Firewalls can be configured in different ways to restrict Internet traffic:

❑ **Dual-homed host for Internet access**: A dual-homed host has two network cards, one is connected to the local network, the other is connected to the Internet. Access to the Internet requires an account on the dual-homed host.

❑ **Packet filtering**: A packet filter inspects every packet coming into or out of a local network. It uses rules to determine whether to allow the packet to proceed. Usually, the rules are based on IP addresses and ports. It is possible, for example, to block all incoming packets from another network entirely, based on the network address portion of the IP address. For example, an Intranet might block incoming requests on port 80, keeping its corporate web server private from the rest of the Internet.

Proxy servers are related to firewalls. Firewalls operate at the transport or internet layer, whereas proxy servers operate at the application layer, sitting between clients and services on the local network and clients and services on the Internet. Local hosts do not communicate directly with Internet hosts, instead, they communicate with the proxy. All communication with hosts on the Internet is indirect.

Firewalls and proxy servers can log attempts to reach hosts. Proxy servers not only examine packets, they also understand important features of protocols like HTTP and FTP. They can examine the data payloads and determine if their contents are appropriate. They can log not only attempts to reach hosts but also specific activities, such as the URLs for downloaded resources. Many organizations and businesses use proxy servers to restrict Internet activities and monitor what members of the organization do while they are on the Internet.

Proxy servers are also sometimes used to cache resources. Caching lowers bandwidth and speeds access to the same data for the next user. When a web page is requested, the proxy server can check to see if a copy of the file exists in its cache; if it finds the page, it can supply the page from the cache instead of forwarding the request to the web server. If not, it can store the requested resource in its cache and then forward it to the requesting node.

The major problem with proxy servers is their tunnel vision, they understand a limited set of Internet protocols. Often, proxy servers are configured to block requests for newer and less-established protocols. This can keep employees from frittering time on downloading full-length movie AVI files with Gnutella, but it can also limit the possibilities for Java network programmers. Java client-server applications often use their own protocols, but a proxy server set to allow only HTTP, outgoing FTP, POP3, and SMTP will block any custom protocol for your Java network applications.

> **Applets that run inside a web browser are automatically configured to use the proxy server settings of the web browser. Standalone Java applications need to set the `http.proxyHost` and `http.proxyPort` system properties when the application is run:**

```
java -Dhttp.proxyHost=proxy.someOrg.com -Dhttp.proxyPort=8080 someApp
```

**An application can instead set these same system properties through the
System.getProperties() and System.setProperties() methods.**

Important Internet Protocols

TCP/IP network stacks usually come bundled with some common network services. Some of the services are important to network administrators and are used to test network communications and synchronize servers in an enterprise setting.

There are also some important TCP/IP services that have become widespread on the Internet. It's common to think of these network protocols as Internet protocols because the Internet is their typical context. Each can be used on an isolated TCP/IP network, although it is more common to see them on the Internet.

Each of these TCP/IP services uses a particular port. With the exception of Simple Network Management Protocol (SNMP), each of the protocols in this section uses client TCP rather than UDP.

Ping (Packet InterNetwork Grouping)

Ping is a familiar network utility. Network administrators use ping to determine if a host is active/inactive and whether there are significant delays between the sender and the receiver.

Ping uses a series of ICMP (Internet Control Message Protocol) messages. ICMP is a routing protocol that is used to announce problems on a network, such as network congestion. Ping uses ICMP echo request packets to test remote hosts. **Echo** is another familiar network protocol, where a remote host just returns whatever it receives. Once ping sends an ICMP echo request packet, it waits for a response from the remote host.

It should be noted that Java does not support ICMP to send raw IP data, so ping cannot be implemented in Java. However, Java network developers should become familiar with the ping utility on their network as a useful development tool. You can use Ping to test that an active connection exists between a client and a remote server. This is an important troubleshooting step when your client application fails to connect to a server. When ping fails, you know there is a problem preventing the client from reaching the server. The problem could be as simple as a disconnected network cable at the client (or the server). The problem could also be more complicated, but at least you know where to start – the connection between client and server.

You can create your own ping client, or you can use the utility that comes with your network. The ping utilities that ship with network operating systems provide some useful functionality:

❑   Ping utilities typically place a unique sequence number on each packet they transmit. This sequence number will be echoed back and can be used to determine if packets were dropped, duplicated, or reordered.

❑   Ping utilities can add checksums to each packet. These can be used to detect some forms of packet damage.

❑   Ping typically places a timestamp in each packet. This is echoed back. You can use it to compute the Round Trip Time (RTT) for each packet.

FTP (File Transfer Protocol)

FTP is one of the oldest TCP/IP protocols, it is used to transfer text and binary files between hosts. FTP can use password controlled access or anonymous access. Anonymous access lets you set up an FTP server to make information available to the public, no account or password is required. Allowing anonymous access requires careful planning and administration, since it does expose your server to hackers on the Internet.

FTP uses two ports. TCP port 21 is used to initiate and control FTP connections, for example, requests to download/upload a file or change directory. TCP port 20 is used for the actual transfer of data.

HTTP (Hypertext Transfer Protocol)

HTTP is the protocol of the World Wide Web. It is used for communication between web browsers and web servers and uses TCP port 80.

HTTP is a stateless protocol and connections are one-shot. The browser opens a connection and makes a request, the server returns the requested information – typically a web page – and then immediately closes the connection.

HTTP is also a file transfer protocol – it defines how an HTTP client and server establish a connection, how the client submits a request, how the server responds to the request, and how a connection is closed. Every request in HTTP generates a response, this could be a web page or the result of running a CGI script, but often, the response is no more elaborate than a simple response code for example 404 File Not Found.

We will be covering HTTP in greater detail in Chapter 4, and in Chapter 13 we use Java to build an HTTP Server.

NNTP (Network News Transfer Protocol)

NNTP is used by the USENET Internet news system. USENET is a distributed conference system where conferences are called USENET newsgroups and messages are called articles.

If you have ever logged onto a computerized bulletin board system (BBS), then USENET will be a familiar concept. USENET functions as a large BBS that has thousands of newsgroups. Comparable names from other systems include forums and discussion groups.

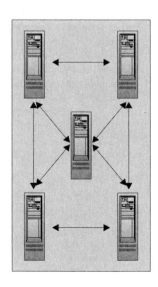

NNTP uses a **flooding protocol** to transfer messages between servers, this is illustrated in the figure previous page. An NNTP server tells all of the adjacent servers about the articles it holds and those servers can then request any articles it hasn't yet received by a different route.

Flooding protocols are very fast and reliable, but they are also inefficient in the use of network bandwidth. A single NNTP server will receive article notifications from every adjacent NNTP server, but NNTP servers avoid article duplication by maintaining two lists – a trace list and a list of Message-IDs stored on the server.

Clients are responsible for maintaining their own list of viewed articles, which is just a list of Message-IDs. NNTP servers do not need to maintain client state or even know which clients are currently accessing them.

NNTP uses TCP port 119.

SMTP (Simple Mail Transfer Protocol)

Most e-mail systems that send mail over the Internet use SMTP to send messages from one server to another. It is also widely used to send e-mail messages from a client to a mail server.

SMTP uses TCP port 25. The client establishes a connection with an SMTP server via a simple request/response dialogue. The client transmits the mail addresses of the originator and the recipient(s) for a message; if the server process accepts the mail addresses, the client then transmits the message.

POP3 (Post Office Protocol 3)

E-mail servers typically use SMTP for both sending and receiving e-mail between servers.

SMTP servers can and do fail upon occasion and when that happens, the sender will be unable to connect to the destination server and it will attempt to retry delivery of the message. Eventually, the sending server will give up and return the message, marked as undeliverable.

Hosts that are not permanently connected to the Internet continuously need a different protocol. The host may be offline for days, weeks, even months – people go on vacation, take sabbaticals, turn off their PCs, and so on. The POP3 protocol works like a post office: mail is held in a mailbox until a POP3 client connects and removes the e-mail from the mailbox.

The server host listens on TCP port 110. When a client wants to access a mailbox, it establishes a TCP connection with the server host. Once the connection is established, the POP3 server sends a greeting – in network jargon, they **handshake** – the client and POP3 server then exchange commands and responses until the connection is closed or aborted.

SNMP (Simple Network Management Protocol)

SNMP is used to control and monitor devices connected to a network and is based on a manager-agent paradigm. Bridges, hubs, routers, and network servers are examples of devices that are typically monitored via SNMP. Vendors of hardware and software can easily add SNMP-compliant services to their products.

SNMP assumes a connectionless communication network. SNMP makes no guarantees about the reliable delivery of the data, typically relying on UDP as its transport protocol. SNMP is actually transport protocol independent, so it can use TCP, but in its typical configuration, SNMP uses UDP ports 161 and 162.

Each network resource that SNMP monitors and manages is called a **managed object**. A managed object can be a network device, a host, a software application, or even a performance monitor. SNMP-compliant devices and software incorporate SNMP **agents**. Agents store data about their managed objects in **Management Information Bases** (**MIBs**). SNMP is used to inspect and alter MIB variables.

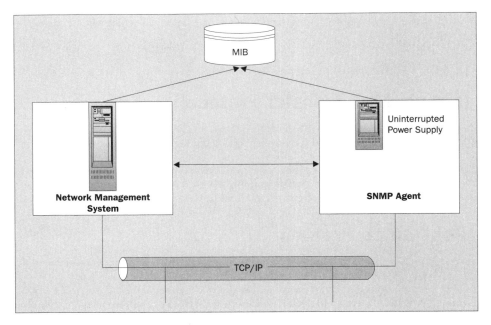

A simple example of SNMP is the monitoring software that comes with an enterprise-strength uninterrupted power supply (UPS). In an enterprise setting, each server will have its own UPS. It is common for UPS to be SNMP-compliant. That way, performance information about the UPS can be tracked from a central management console. If the status of the UPS changes, perhaps as the result of a power failure, the management console can be notified through an SMTP **trap**. Traps are asynchronous notifications from an SNMP agent to an SNMP manager.

SNMP is a relatively simple protocol, suitable for relatively simple management of network components. While SNMP has the ability to alter the values of managed objects, in practice this usually goes unimplemented. SNMP is not secure; it just includes a trivial form of authentication, therefore SNMP is used almost exclusively for monitoring managed objects.

Telnet (Telecommunications Network)

Telnet is a protocol used to emulate terminals providing an interactive, character-based session. The typical use for Telnet is to allow users to communicate with a server using a remote login. Users can interact with the remote server via Telnet, using a keyboard to submit commands and printing the results on the screen. Telnet uses TCP port 23.

Telnet client software needs to emulate one or more terminals that are compatible with the remote server. To keep Telnet compatible with heterogeneous networks, Telnet clients and servers use the concept of a **Network Virtual Terminal** (**NVT**) to communicate. The NVT is implemented as a generic device with a printer and a keyboard. The printer responds to incoming data and the keyboard sends outgoing data.

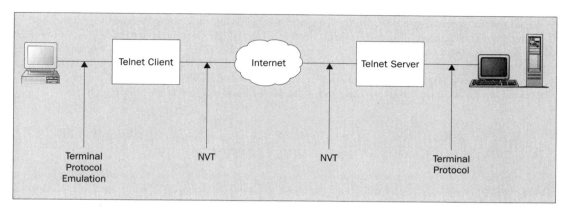

The NVT is implemented as a half-duplex device. That means data can be sent or received but cannot do both simultaneously. When you send a command to a server through a Telnet session, the NVT keyboard on the client sends the command to the NVT printer on the server. The response from the server is sent through its NVT keyboard to the NVT printer on the client. The typical result is some sort of character string printed to a client terminal emulation window.

Internet Standards

Each of the protocols that we have discussed in this chapter has associated standards. Standards are important, because the Internet is a loosely organized collaboration among interconnected TCP/IP networks around the world. In order for host-to-host communication to work, there need to be open protocols supported by published standards. RFC 2026 (http://www.ietf.org/rfc/rfc2026.txt) defines an Internet Standard as a specification that:

❏ Is stable and well-understood

❏ Is technically competent

❏ Has multiple, independent, and interoperable implementations

❏ Has substantial operational experience

❏ Has significant public support

❏ Is recognizably useful in some or all parts of the Internet

There are many standards organizations around the world. The two largest and most visible are the IETF (Internet Engineering Task Force – http://www.ietf.org/) and the W3C (World Wide Web Consortium – http://www.w3.org/). IETF standards govern most of the Internet protocols and W3C standards focus on web protocols, particularly HTTP, HTML, and XML.

Internet Drafts, RFCs, and STDs

The IETF is open to any interested individual. It is a relatively informal, democratic body. The actual technical work of the IETF is done in its working groups, and a lot of that work is done via e-mail distribution lists.

The standards process involves Internet Drafts and RFCs. RFC stands for Request for Comments. During the development of a specification, draft versions of the document are made available for informal review and comment – these are **Internet Drafts**. IETF standards and specifications actively under consideration as standards are published as **RFCs** and each RFC has a unique number. All of the protocols we have discussed in this chapter have one or more RFCs. Once an RFC is adopted as a standard, a new unique number is assigned – this is the standard's **STD** number.

> **You can obtain a list of RFCs from the IETF web site – http://www.ietf.org/rfc.html**

The concept of the RFC process should be familiar to Java developers as it is similar to the Java Community Process (JCP) and the Java Specification Requests (JSRs). JCP is an open organization of international Java developers and licensees who develop and revise Java technology specifications and reference implementations. JSRs are the actual descriptions of proposed and final specifications for the Java platform.

RFCs are a very important source of information for network programmers and it is very common to refer to Internet protocols by their RFC numbers. The RFC points to a particular protocol, but as standards evolve, new RFCs and STDs replace obsolete numbers. For example, here's a brief history of the POP3 and its predecessors:

❑   The original POP protocol is defined in RFC 918

❑   RFC 918 was superseded by RFC 937 (which is where POP2 is described)

❑   POP3 is described in RFC 1081, which was published in 1988

RFCs are extremely technical and provide us with a complete specification of a standard, but unfortunately they are not very reader friendly. Here's an example, the Internet Time Protocol. The interaction between the server and the client is specified in detail for both TCP and UDP transports.

```
Network Working Group                              J. Postel - ISI
Request for Comments: 868                    K. Harrenstien - SRI
                                                       May 1983


                            Time Protocol


This RFC specifies a standard for the ARPA Internet community.  Hosts on the ARPA
Internet that choose to implement a Time Protocol are expected to adopt and
implement this standard.

This protocol provides a site-independent, machine readable date and time.  The
Time service sends back to the originating source the time in seconds since
midnight on January first 1900.
```

One motivation arises from the fact that not all systems have a date/time clock, and all are subject to occasional human or machine error. The use of time-servers makes it possible to quickly confirm or correct a system's idea of the time, by making a brief poll of several independent sites on the network.

This protocol may be used either above the Transmission Control Protocol (TCP) or above the User Datagram Protocol (UDP).

When used via TCP the time service works as follows:

    S: Listen on port 37 (45 octal).

    U: Connect to port 37.

    S: Send the time as a 32 bit binary number.

    U: Receive the time.

    U: Close the connection.

    S: Close the connection.

The server listens for a connection on port 37. When the connection is established, the server returns a 32-bit time value and closes the connection. If the server is unable to determine the time at its site, it should either refuse the connection or close it without sending anything.

When used via UDP the time service works as follows:

    S: Listen on port 37 (45 octal).

    U: Send an empty datagram to port 37.

    S: Receive the empty datagram.

    S: Send a datagram containing the time as a 32 bit binary number.

    U: Receive the time datagram.

The server listens for a datagram on port 37. When a datagram arrives, the server returns a datagram containing the 32-bit time value. If the server is unable to determine the time at its site, it should discard the arriving datagram and make no reply.

The Time

The time is the number of seconds since 00:00 (midnight) 1 January 1900 GMT, such that the time 1 is 12:00:01 am on 1 January 1900 GMT; this base will serve until the year 2036.

For example:

    the time   2,208,988,800 corresponds to 00:00   1 Jan 1970 GMT,

               2,398,291,200 corresponds to 00:00   1 Jan 1976 GMT,

               2,524,521,600 corresponds to 00:00   1 Jan 1980 GMT,

               2,629,584,000 corresponds to 00:00   1 May 1983 GMT,

       and   -1,297,728,000 corresponds to 00:00 17 Nov 1858 GMT.

Some RFCs are not intended to serve as standards. Instead they clarify other RFCs or provide useful information. The IETF Internet standards process, for example, is described in painful detail in RFC 2026.

RFCs undergo change as they mature toward becoming a standard. Within the IETF Internet standards process, these stages are formally labeled **maturity levels:**

❑   **Proposed Standard**: This is the entry level. A Proposed Standard specification must be generally stable, resolve known design choices, be well-understood, receive significant community review, and enjoy enough community interest to be considered valuable. Implementers should treat Proposed Standards as immature specifications.

❑   **Draft Standard**: The Draft Standard has at least two independent and interoperable implementations from different code bases, and there is sufficient successful operational experience. The requirement for at least two independent and interoperable implementations applies to all of the options and features. Draft Standards are normally considered to be final specifications and changes are likely to be made only to solve specific problems.

❑   **Internet Standard**: Significant implementation and successful operational experience. The specification has achieved a high degree of technical maturity and acceptance and the specified protocol provides significant benefit to the Internet community.

W3C Recommendations

W3C is a very different organization. Where the IETF is democratic and imposes no barriers to membership and participation, W3C is a vendor organization so membership is open only to official representatives of dues-paying organizations. The fees are high, with corporations paying $50k a year in order to participate.

The W3C standards process works essentially the same as the IETF's process. Working drafts are discussed in working groups, usually by an e-mail loop. Recommendations usually progress in the following stages:

❑   **Working Draft**: A work in progress and a commitment by W3C to pursue work

❑   **Candidate Recommendation**: Work that has received significant review from its immediate technical community

❑   **Proposed Recommendation**: Work that represents consensus within the group that produced it and has been proposed to the Advisory Committee for review

❑   **Recommendation**: W3C believes the ideas or technology are appropriate for widespread deployment

Summary

We have certainly covered a lot of territory in this chapter. We have discussed the basic features of a network, took a brief look at network stacks (the TCP/IP stack, in particular), summarized some important Internet protocols, and closed with a quick look at the Internet standards.

Here is a quick list of the important points in this chapter:

❑ Each device on a network is called a node. Another word we came across is host. A host usually refers to a network device that is a fully functional computer providing some sort of network service.

❑ Network engineers solved the complex web of protocols and standards by breaking them down into an abstract set of layers. Each layer builds on the services provided by the layers beneath it. The convention, when diagramming network services, is to organize the layers vertically. Together, this set of layers is referred to as a stack.

❑ Java network programming is limited to TCP/IP. TCP/IP is the network protocol used by the Internet and intranets and consists of four layers: Network Access Layer, Internet Layer, Transport Layer, and Application Layer.

❑ IP (Internet Protocol) is a network layer protocol that underlies the Internet. Every device attached to the Internet must use the IP protocol.

❑ TCP (Transmission Control Protocol) is a connection-oriented transport layer protocol. It provides data streams that are guaranteed to arrive at the destination network node in the order they were transmitted by the source node.

❑ UDP (User Datagram Protocol) is another transport layer protocol for TCP/IP networks. UDP is fast but unreliable. It makes no guarantee that packets will arrive, or that they will arrive in the same order they were transmitted, so it is best suited to small, independent data packets.

❑ IP networks can be divided into smaller networks called subnets. Subnets provide more efficient use of network addresses and simplify network administration. Subnets also restrict broadcast traffic.

❑ Multicasting allows hosts to communicate in a peer-to-peer fashion.

❑ There are many standards organizations around the world. The two largest and most visible are the IETF (Internet Engineering Task Force) and the W3C (World Wide Web Consortium). IETF standards govern most of the Internet protocols. W3C standards focus on web protocols, particularly HTTP, HTML, and XML.

❑ IETF standards and specifications that are actively under consideration are published as RFCs (Request for Comments). RFCs are a very important source of information for network programmers, they provide a complete specification of a network protocol.

Network Application Models

Modern network programming is based on two models: the client-server model and the peer-to-peer model. The client-server model has been undergoing profound change in recent years. Attention has shifted away from the basic client-server model with two tiers to multi-tier architecture. Peer-to-peer networking has also attracted a lot of attention during the last few years.

Here's a brief list of the topics we will cover in this chapter:

- ❑ The basic client-server model
- ❑ The anatomy of servers and clients
- ❑ Two-tier, three-tier, and multi-tier architecture
- ❑ The peer-to-peer model

The Basic Client-Server Model

Many trees have been sacrificed in recent years on discussions of client-server computing. Client-server programming is a popular paradigm for building applications that use resources dispersed over a network. It is also a popular topic for Java technical writers.

One reason why client-server programming generates so many articles and books is the breadth of the topic. Successful client-server programming requires experience with many different technical skills: database design, network protocols, transaction processing, user interface design, component architecture, remote procedure calls, asynchronous messaging, etc.

Most of the interest in client-server programming centers on two broad categories of applications:

- ❑ **Custom business applications**: These are created by corporate IT departments or outsourced to contract programmers and consultants. These are typically designed to run on PC workstations connected over a LAN.

- ❑ **Internet applications**: The World Wide Web is certainly redefining client-server computing. E-Commerce and Business-to-Business (B2B) solutions are also driven largely by client-server computing.

Definition of Client-Server

The term client-server although widely understood is poorly defined: software vendors use it (and, sometimes, abuse it) to refer to all sorts of things. Many people use it loosely, to describe nearly every interaction on network between computers and computer applications. We will give you our definition of client-server programming. Like our definition of network programming, our definition of client-server programming is *a* definition, not necessarily *the* definition of client-server programming.

For our purposes, client-server programs have the following characteristics:

- ❑ **Services**: Servers respond to service requests from clients.

- ❑ **Separate processes**: Servers and clients run in their own distinct processes. Those processes do not need to run on separate machines to qualify as client-server. Client and server could instead operate in their own address spaces on the same machine.

- ❑ **Asymmetrical relationship**: Clients and servers are not peers they cannot and do not swap roles. Clients initiate communication by requesting a service. Servers fulfill those requests. Between service requests, servers passively wait for clients to request a service.

- ❑ **Loose coupling**: Servers encapsulate their functionality. A client can initiate a service in several ways such as making a remote procedure call or passing a message to the server. Implementation details for the service are unknown by the client.

- ❑ **Location transparency**: The server process can run on the client machine or it can run on a remote machine.

- ❑ **Scalability**: This is done in two ways distributing the processing load across more processors or through techniques like multithreading. The whole of Chapter 6 is devoted to threads so we'll just discuss multi-processors here. A client-server system can be scaled by distributing the processing across multiple machines – "distributed computing". Clustering is a form of distributed processing that uses multiple machines to work together as a single system, sharing the same namespace. This improves both scaling and reliability. If one machine in a cluster crashes, other servers can redistribute the load. The load is balanced across the machines in the cluster to provide maximum performance.

The figure below shows the typical exchange of information in a client-server program. A client initiates a request of some sort and the server provides an appropriate response.

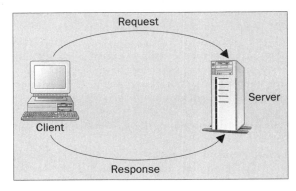

Sometimes, servers make remote procedure calls or pass messages back to clients. A common example is a client that exposes a method for server callbacks. This makes it possible for the server to communicate asynchronously with the client. Once the server finishes the request, the server can invoke the callback method on the client. It is important to realize that the original relationship between client and server is still preserved. The client initiated a request, the server responded. In this case, the response is a callback from the server.

> It is important to remember here when we talk about client and server this does not necessarily refer to a particular computer. The server (or client) can just be a process running on a computer, in fact a single computer could run numerous client and server processes if needed.

The same process can be a client or a server, it can even be both at the same time. For example, Client A can invoke a method on Server B. Server B can then invoke a method on another server, Server C. Which role a process plays, client or server, depends upon the relationship between the two processes for a particular context. Change the context and their respective roles can change.

Applications of the Client-Server Model

Client-server is a useful model for sharing and managing resources on a network. Here are some common examples of network applications for client-server architecture:

- ❑ **File Servers**: LANs gained their early popularity due to file servers. The network server often performed dual duty – managing the network and acting as a shared repository for documents, images, and other information.

- ❑ **Database Servers**: Database servers also became quickly popular on LANs. The client merely passes SQL requests as messages to the database server. The database server then performs the queries and returns the results.

- ❑ **Print Servers**: Providing every workstation with its own printer is rarely an option in an enterprise. Printer servers allow multiple workstations to access a shared printer. Printer servers also allow for remote administration of servers, such as the cancellation of print jobs.

- ❑ **E-mail Servers**: Unless individual workstations are online 24-7, using a protocol like SMTP for receiving e-mail is impractical. E-mail servers provide 24-7 reliability. Client workstations can fetch their e-mail by making calls to the e-mail server with the POP3 and other e-mail protocols.

- ❑ **Proxy Servers**: We have already discussed proxy servers in Chapter 2. They are used to manage Internet connections for an organization. There original role was to reduce external bandwidth by caching frequently requested content. They are often implemented as part of a security firewall denying those behind it direct access to the internet and more importantly access from the internet to an internal network.

- ❑ **Application Servers**: Application servers are one of the more recent additions to many networks. Application servers make it easier to encapsulate and reuse business logic. They do this by providing business logic services, often through components, such as Enterprise JavaBeans (EJB). Application servers frequently offer additional features, such as transaction management and load balancing.

- ❑ **Web Servers**: Lest we forget, the ubiquitous web server also operates on the client-server model!

Client-server programming makes extensive use of sockets. The idea of sockets originated in Berkeley Unix. Sockets treat a network connection as a simple data stream for reading or writing data. Sockets shield network programmers from low-level network details. While socket programming is the most common technology for client-server programming, Java offers us other options.

One option, if we are building a web application, is to use Java servlets (see Chapter 18) to extend and enhance the web server. These behave like server-side applets without a user interface. They are Java's (superior) alternative to CGI programming. Servlets have an important advantage over CGI programs; they scale better because they do not have to spawn a separate process on the web server for each instance. All this means they are an excellent choice for middle-tier services in three-tier and multi-tier web applications.

Another option is to use distributed objects. Distributed object technologies let a local machine run programs on a remote host. That's what client-server programs do, too. The twist with distributed objects is the ability to access methods of objects running on a remote machine. Invoking remote object methods simplifies communication for the programmer compared with handling input/output streams and parsing/composing those streams. Java gives us options when it comes to distributed objects. We can use RMI, which is native to Java; also there is CORBA, which has broader cross-platform support. RMI stands for Remote Method Invocation. RMI allows a host to expose object methods to clients running in a different process (usually on another host). CORBA is another technology for distributed access to objects. Unlike RMI, which is specific to Java, CORBA is language- and platform-independent.

We will cover servlets and distributed objects in considerable detail in subsequent chapters. Our discussion of distributed objects will include both RMI and CORBA. Before we get to distributed objects, we will devote a lot of attention to socket programming.

Anatomy of a Server Program

When a server program is deployed on a TCP/IP network, the program will typically use sockets and ports. Both TCP and UDP have 65,535 logical ports available. Port numbers from 1 to 1023 are reserved for "well-known" services. That leaves a wide range of available port numbers for custom applications.

Creating a server socket is quite simple in Java, it takes just a few lines of code. Here's a code snippet that creates a server socket on port 10,000:

```
ServerSocket oServerSocket = new ServerSocket(10000);
```

This example is just to illustrate how simple socket programming can be. When we actually get to the Java details behind socket programming in Chapter 9, we will see that our code here is not very robust and totally ignores exception handling.

Most TCP/IP servers follow a similar lifecycle. The basic lifecycle for a server socket written in Java is:

❑ A new ServerSocket instance is created on a selected port using one of the constructors for the ServerSocket class.

❑ The ServerSocket instance listens for incoming connection attempts on its designated port. It uses its accept() method for listening, blocking on that method until a client attempts to connect.

❑ Once a client connects, the `accept()` method returns an instance of the `Socket` class, which it uses as a receiving socket. Client "sending" sockets and server "receiving" sockets use the same Java class, the `Socket` class.

❑ The client and server interact according to the agreed-upon protocol. Java servers typically use `getInputStream()` and `getOutputStream()` to handle socket communication.

❑ The server, the client, or both close the socket.

❑ The server returns to listening for connections on its designated port.

Incoming connection requests are stored by the operating system in a FIFO (first in, first out) queue. Those requests will block while the server is handling client interactions. The Java network developer faces an important design choice. If servicing the client will take a long or indefinite amount of time, it is best to spawn a new thread to handle the client interaction. If not, it may be more efficient and result in more easily maintained code to forego spawning a thread.

Anatomy of a Client Program

Client programs also typically use sockets on TCP/IP networks. They have a Java lifecycle that resembles server sockets:

❑ A new `Socket` instance is created, using a constructor of the `Socket` class.

❑ The socket attempts to connect to a remote host, passing an IP address (or URL) and a port number.

❑ Once the client connects, the client and server interact according to the agreed-upon protocol.

❑ Finally the server, the client, or both close the socket.

Some protocols allow a single connection to be used for multiple requests between the client and the server, FTP is a good example of this. Other protocols require that the connection be closed after each request receives a response. HTTP is an example of a one-shot protocol, requiring a new socket and new connection for each request.

Below is the basic code for establishing a client socket:

```
Socket oClientSocket = new Socket("www.someWebSite.com", 10000);
```

Again this just illustrates the point that creating a client socket is a task that even beginning network programmers should not find intimidating. Real production code would have to include exception handling for instance.

Client-Server: From Two Tiers to Many

With all of the flexibility Java offers us, there are many ways to do everything. One of the most difficult things about developing client-server applications is deciding how to split the work between client processes and server processes.

Two-Tier Architecture

Back in the days before PCs, applications used a "thin" client and a "fat" server. The functionality of the client-server system was predominantly on the server-side.

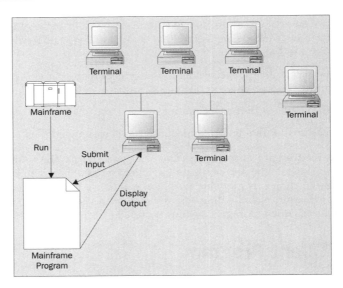

The figure above is typical of client-server processing in the past. Here is a list of the most important features of a traditional mainframe-based client-server environment:

❑ Dumb terminals connected over communication links to mainframe computers.

❑ Application logic resides in the mainframe application.

❑ The terminal provided a character-based user interface.

❑ The mainframe application could use various character sequences to position output. A "screen scraper" program could read data from the terminal and return it to the mainframe. Simpler programs could just use simple character streams for input and output.

PC-Based Two-Tier Applications

Traditionally, PC client-server applications separated data services from the rest of the application's logic. A separate database server stored shared data and executed queries, returning the results back to the client. The data server was optimized to store and retrieve information as efficiently as possible. The rest of the application logic was the responsibility of the client. This was the so-called "fat" client. Separating out the data services in this manner offered important advantages. Data persistence became a shared resource that was more secure and scaled better as the enterprise grew.

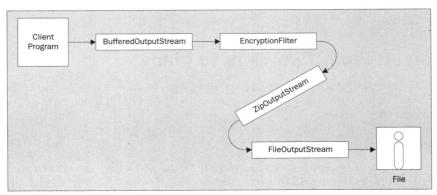

Another twist to the two-tier application was to partition the business rules logic. Business rules that were data-oriented could move from the client to the database server. Using stored procedures (precompiled database operations used to improve performance) and triggers (procedures in the database triggered by some event) slimmed the client somehow, but it did it at the expense of the database server. Moving data-oriented business logic in this way has benefits and drawbacks. When the data-oriented business logic changes, theses changes can migrate to the database server. The alternative is to make the changes to the application, recompile, and then redeploy the application on dozens or hundreds of workstations. This also spreads the business logic across the application and the database server. This makes the code less readable and more resistant to change.

Two-tier applications became victims of their own success. Enterprises began to convert their applications from the desktop to the client-server model. Demands on their database servers increased. The database server often became a performance bottleneck as the enterprise converted to two-tier architecture. Each concurrent client consumed database server resources. It soon became apparent that two-tier client server applications were not flexible enough to scale well beyond a few dozen concurrent users. Hence, three-tier applications soon emerged.

Three-Tier Architecture

Three-tier architecture partitions the application into three sets of services

❑ **User Interface Services Tier**: This tier handles the UI logic; this is normally on the client.

❑ **Business Rule Services Tier**: This handles all of the business rules logic and validates user input from the user interface tier. The roles performed at this level include combining heterogeneous data and performing data manipulation.

❑ **Data Persistence Services Tier**: Here the focus is solely the storage and retrieval of data from databases, files, and other data sources.

In a typical three-tier application, the client application becomes a thin client. The client provides the user interface for the system. It no longer has responsibility for enforcing business rules. The user interface services tier becomes especially thin when a web browser hosts the user interface.

Application servers handle business rule processing and ensure that all input is validated against these rules. The application servers interact directly with the database server. Once they are separated from the user interface and data persistence, the business rule services can easily be encapsulated in business rule components. The resulting business rule components can then be installed on one or more application servers. This greatly improves the scalability of the client server applications.

Three-tier applications can conserve database server resources by reducing the number of concurrent database connections. We can see this in the figure overleaf. Once we encapsulate business rule services into components and move the components to an application server, the database server no longer needs separate connections for each client. Instead, it needs a separate connection for each running instance of the business rule component. Users no longer require separate logins. They don't even need database drivers. This not only saves database resources, it also eases database account maintenance and improves data security.

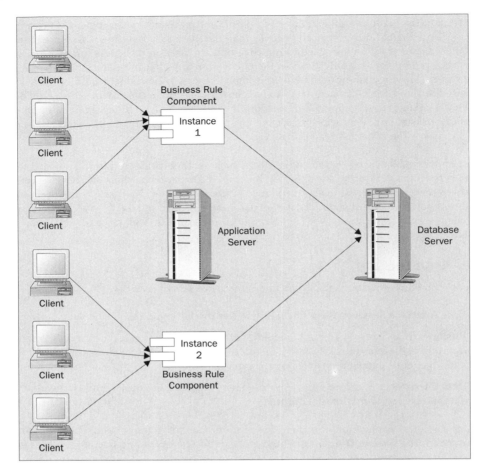

Separating business rule services from the rest of the application offers other important advantages:

❑ Moving business rule components to an application server can boost performance.

❑ Multiple application servers can take advantage of load balancing and improve system fault tolerance.

❑ Changes to business rules can migrate to a small number of application servers instead of a large number of workstations.

❑ This also provides better code encapsulation allowing different people or even companies to implement each tier.

Three-tier applications became victims of their own success even faster than two-tier applications. Three-tier applications can generate a lot of network activity. Consider for a moment what happens when you validate fields on a form. Because users expect highly interactive forms, validating all of the fields at one time quickly becomes impractical. Therefore, each validation can require a separate call to the application server. Validating the data on one form might involve dozens of cross-network calls to an application server.

Multi-Tier Architecture

Multi-tier architecture (sometimes called n-tier architecture) takes the partitioning of application services even further. They divide the business rule services tier into two collaborating tiers – one for business rule processing that supports the user interface and the other for business rule processing that integrates and manipulates data.

❑ **User Interface Services Tier**: This handles the UI logic, which includes the actual presentation of screens, the types of widgets that will collect information, and so on.

❑ **UI-Oriented Business Rule Services Tier**: A layer that handles business rule logic that supports the user interface. This layer mainly performs validation of input from the user interface services tier.

❑ **Data-Oriented Business Rule Services Tier**: This is responsible for data manipulation and integration. It can combine data from SQL databases with legacy mainframe data, flat files, or even Internet resources.

❑ **Data Persistence Services Tier**: Just like in three-tier models this layer handles the storage and retrieval of data from databases, files, and other data sources.

The central idea in multi-tier architecture is to keep the services physically close to the data they work with and so cut down on cross-network calls.

Three-tier architecture assumes we can easily decide where to separate business rule services from user interface functionality and data services. Multi-tier architecture recognizes that it is sometimes very difficult to partition business rules neatly from the remaining application logic.

The classic example is validating text in a textbox. Here's the scenario in a three-tier application, with a business rule component:

❑ We have a textbox on a form.

❑ We decide the textbox cannot be empty.

❑ We also decide to display all the text in uppercase.

The decisions that the textbox cannot be empty and the text should be all uppercase are both business rules. Where do we place the validation code? Do we put it in a business rules component? If we do, our application will pay a severe performance penalty. If a network call crosses to an application server every time our application validates the textbox, we will generate a lot of network activity.

What will happen if our form has twenty textboxes to validate? Do we make twenty cross-network calls just to validate each textbox? Unnecessary network calls degrade network bandwidth and impede application performance. Enter design tradeoffs. Many developers decide not to be slavish to principle and keep their validation code in their user interface code. Other developers decide to validate at the form level, offering a user interface that many users find objectionable.

The difference between three-tier and multi-tier appears trivial. We simply partition the business rule services tier. However, what appears to be a trivial change provides considerably more flexibility.

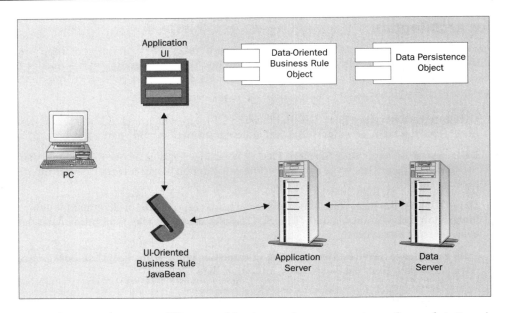

Multi-tier architecture lets us put UI-oriented business rule components on the workstation. As we see in the figure above, UI-oriented business rule components are excellent candidates for JavaBeans. The JavaBeans API lets developers create reusable, platform-independent components that can be combined into applets, applications, or composite components. Keeping UI-oriented business rule components on the workstation keeps them close to the client, improving the performance of the user interface.

Data-oriented business rule components are best deployed on the database server or a separate application server. This makes them excellent candidates for Enterprise JavaBeans (EJBs). The EJB API extends the idea of JavaBeans to the realm of distributed programming. With the EJB technology, components can be deployed on a remote server and then accessed as if they were installed locally.

Multi-tier applications scale well because multi-tier architecture is a component-based architecture. The performance of core business logic and data persistence can be tuned with extreme precision. Business logic services that support the UI can remain physically close to the client. Remaining application services can scale as additional resources become available. We can add more processors to the application server, add another server, or whatever is needed to maintain performance.

The multi-tier architecture is flexible about the placement *and* the presence of application servers. A small enterprise might elect to use their database server as an application server. As the enterprise grows, the system can scale by adding a separate server to take over as the application server task. More growth and the system can scale again. The single application server can become a small server farm.

Data persistence services tend to be very efficient compared to data manipulation services. Data manipulation services spawn data persistence services in a multi-tier application. Therefore, whatever speed the data persistence services run at, they will always finish before the data manipulation services that spawn them.

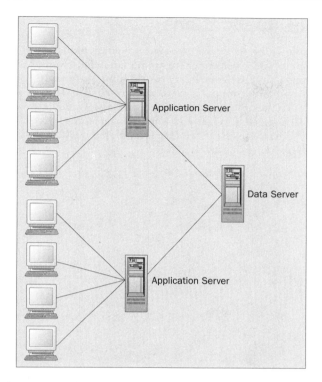

The longer lifecycle that is typical of the business rule objects means they consume server resources differently compared to data persistence services. As the number of concurrent users grows, tuning the application servers can result in more performance improvement than additional tuning of the database server. Better performance can sometimes result when multiple application servers are present. We can see an example of this in the figure above, where a second application server is used to increase the number of clients concurrently using the application.

The Peer-to-Peer Model

Peer-to-peer networking is another networking term that is often abused or misunderstood. Most of the current, so-called, peer-to-peer network programs do not meet the strict definition of peer-to-peer networking. A true peer-to-peer network program brings two or more computers into direct communication so they interact with each other without involving other computers in their workflow. The computers can shift roles; acting as client, server, or both, therefore they can't be adequately described in the client-server model. Programs commonly thought of as peer-to-peer, such as Napster and ICQ do not meet this strict definition. They are hybrids, combining features of peer-to-peer and client-server programming.

The classic example of true peer-to-peer networking is the telephone system. One party initiates a telephone conversation. After answering the call, there is no asymmetry: the parties can both speak, listen, or do both at the same time. Either party can end the telephone conversation at any time, by just hanging up the telephone. If the telephone system followed the client-server model, you would need two telephones; one for incoming calls and one for outgoing calls.

True Peer-to-Peer Applications

The Gnutella protocol follows the strict peer-to-peer interaction model. That is one of the fundamental differences between Gnutella and Napster. There are no Gnutella servers. When a Gnutella servant initializes, it knows nothing about the Gnutella network. It points to an IP address or a URL, such as gnutellahosts.com. Your servant is not pointing to a server as such. It's just a Gnutella servant that runs continuously as a point of contact to the Gnutella network. The Gnutella network itself is nothing more than a collection of interacting peers. When you want to locate a file, your Gnutella servant asks all of the adjacent Gnutella servants if they have the file. They respond with a message if they have the file and they also pass the query along to other peers.

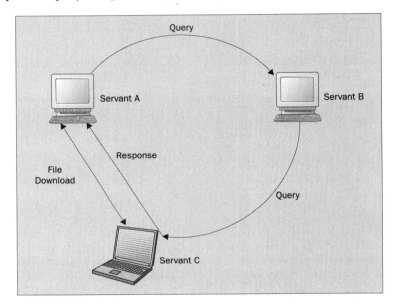

We can see a typical peer-to-peer interaction in the figure above. Servant A queries Servant B, searching for a particular file. Servant B does not have the file. However, it does know about Servant C. It forwards the query to Servant C who has the file, so it sends a message to Servant A. Servant A then sends a download request to Servant C, which then sends the file to Servant A.

Anatomy of a Peer-to-Peer Program

When we use socket programming for peer-to-peer networking, our peers will need to implement both Socket and ServerSocket. They need to be able to connect to other peers and they need to listen for incoming connections. Here's a typical scenario:

❑ The peer-to-peer host application starts by creating a listening socket. A new ServerSocket instance is created on a selected port using one of the constructors for the ServerSocket class.

❑ The ServerSocket instance listens for incoming connection attempts on its designated port. It uses the accept() method for listening, blocking on that method until a remote peer-to-peer host attempts to connect.

❑ Once a remote host connects, the `accept()` method returns an instance of the `Socket` class, which the local host uses to pass responses and requests to the remote host. Communication across the socket is fully duplex. Both hosts are able to make requests and send responses.

❑ The local host process can also connect to remote hosts. A new `Socket` instance is created for each connection, using a constructor of the `Socket` class.

❑ The socket attempts to connect to a remote host, passing an IP address (or URL) and port number.

❑ Once the peer-to-peer hosts connect, they interact according to the agreed-upon protocol.

❑ Finally one of the hosts closes the socket ending the interaction.

It is normal for peer-to-peer programs to communicate with multiple peers simultaneously. For example, a Gnutella servant might service simultaneous connections from many other Gnutella servants. It is typical for a Gnutella servant to respond to requests from other servants while it is submitting queries, tabulating responses, and downloading files. Multithreading is usually required in order to keep performance at an acceptable level.

Performance can also be improved by actively managing connections. For example, assume a remote host already has an open connection to your local host, perhaps to download a file from your machine. You submit a query to your application. You're trying to locate a file that interests you. Your local host begins to search remote hosts to find the file. Rather than open a new connection to a host that is already connected, your application could instead use the existing connection to post its query, saving the overhead of a second connection to the same host.

The Hybrid Model

The hybrid model is popular for programs like Napster and ICQ. And is a natural extension to the strict peer-to-peer model. The typical case uses a server to locate available peers. Once the peers are connected, the server is removed from their communication loop. The peers communicate directly. The role of the server, in this case, is to provide a directory service.

When compared to the pure peer-to-peer model the hybrid model includes an extra step. The connection to the directory server would occur before the local peer-to-peer host creates a socket to connect with a remote host. Here is that scenario:

❑ The local host creates a new `Socket` instance, using a constructor of the `Socket` class.

❑ The socket attempts to connect to a directory server, passing an IP address (or URL) and port number.

❑ Once the local host connects as a client, it passes a query to the server.

❑ The server responds with a list of peer-to-peer hosts matching the query criteria.

❑ The hosts undertake whatever interactions are necessary without further reference to the directory server.

This process is illustrated in the diagram overleaf:

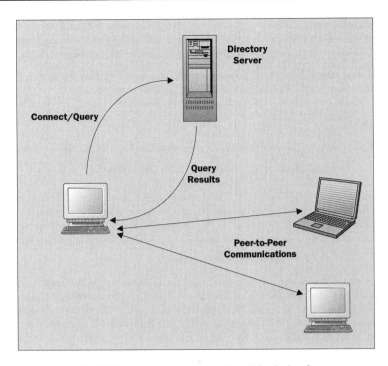

Instant messaging services, like ICQ, are a good example of the hybrid peer-to-peer model. The client software can initiate searches of the remote server's database to find users to swap messages with. Once you find a user to share messages with, communication becomes peer-to-peer. An instant messaging system (such as ICQ) would lose a lot of its appeal if the directory server was removed from the communication model. You could still identify other ICQ users by using a directory posted to a web site or periodically downloading a carefully selected subset of profiles matching some query. Adding a limited client-server interaction for directory services increases the flexibility of the peer-to-peer model.

Summary

Modern network programming has main several important models:

- ❏ Client-server applications are the most widely deployed paradigm in network programming. Here the server responds to request from the client and most of the application logic resides on the server-side.

- ❏ Peer-to-peer network programs bring two or more computers into direct communication so they interact with each other without bringing other computers into their workflow.

- ❏ The hybrid model is a natural extension to the strict peer-to-peer model. The role of the server is to provide a directory service.

While socket programming is the most common technology for client-server programming, Java offers us several options. One option, if we are building a Web application, is to use Java servlets. Another option is to use distributed objects.

In client-server programming the server can consist of one or more tiers:

- ❏ Two-tier applications use two models: a "thin" client and a "thick" client.
  - ❏ Thin clients, the client is responsible for the user interface and the server handling everything else.
  - ❏ Thick clients typically use the server for access to shared resources, such as a database.
- ❏ Three-tier architecture partitions the application into three sets of services:
  - ❏ User interface services (usual on the client-side)
  - ❏ Business rule services
  - ❏ Data persistence services
- ❏ Multi-tier architecture takes the partitioning of application services even further. They divide the business rules tier into two collaborating tiers:
  - ❏ Business rule processing that supports the user interface.
  - ❏ Business rule processing that integrates and manipulates data.

Web Basics

Many Java network programs need to interact with web servers to post data or retrieve files. Even, if you consider building flashy web sites to be more graphic art than programming, the typical network programmer works with web servers a lot. Some Java network programs are applets that run in a web browser, so to be a proficient Java network programmer, you need to understand how web servers and web browsers interact.

This chapter will give you a good foundation in Web and Internet basics. Here's a short list of the topics we will cover:

- ❏ Uniform resource identifiers
- ❏ Hypertext and web client-server programming
  - ❏ HTTP
  - ❏ HTML and XML
- ❏ Interactivity and web client-server programming
  - ❏ Server-side technologies
  - ❏ Client-side technologies

Uniform Resource Identifiers

The World Wide Web is an information space. That's a fancy mathematical way of saying that the Web is a set (or, if you prefer, a collection) of information resources. **Uniform Resource Identifiers** (**URIs**) are short strings that identify resources on the Web. We use them to identify documents, downloadable files, images, services, mailboxes, and other shared information resources.

In order to reach a worldwide audience, the Web relies on three elements:

- ❏ A uniform naming scheme to locate resources on the Web
- ❏ Standard protocols to access resources over the Web
- ❏ A standard markup language to easily navigate within resources and display the results to the user

Every resource available on the Web has an address that may be represented by a URI. Here's a simple example: http://www.ietf.org/rfc/rfc2396.txt . This is the URI that points to the RFC 2396 document on the IETF's web site. RFC 2396 specifies the general syntax for URIs. The example that we have used is a typical one containing three parts:

❑ The naming scheme of the protocol used to access the resource. The URI specifies that the resource is accessible with the HTTP protocol. So, if we want to get the resource, we will be interacting with a web server.

❑ The domain name of the machine hosting the resource. The resource is located on a machine registered with the domain name www.ietf.org. The machine will have an IP address, but the domain name is much more human-readable and maps to the IP address by a lookup on a domain name server.

❑ The name of the resource itself (given as a path). The resource is a file named rfc2396.txt that is located at the path /rfc/. The web server at http://www.ietf.org is responsible for mapping the path we provide to an actual resource. The resource, in this case, is probably a plain text file, although the file extension is not guaranteed to be an accurate indicator of a resource's contents.

Here's a screenshot of http://www.ietf.org/rfc/rfc2396.txt, displayed in Microsoft Internet Explorer (version 5):

URIs provide a flexible *and* extensible means for identifying resources on the Internet. URIs can point to files, like our example above, but a "resource" is not necessarily a "file". Take for instance the following URI.

mailto:someone@someaddress.com

This specifies an electronic mailbox. A web browser, when properly configured, will launch your e-mail program and start an e-mail message to someone@someaddress.com. Web pages use URIs extensively to identify documents, graphics images, and multimedia streams.

New protocols can easily be accommodated with the URI mechanism. Here is a brief list of Internet protocols that are used to access resources through URIs:

❑ **file**: This specifies a file accessible by the local machine. The file does not need to reside on the local machine itself. It might be on some sort of network file system such as a mapped network drive in the Windows OS.

❑ **ftp**: This is used to access resources on an FTP server.

❑ **http**: This is used to access web pages and other resources on a web server using the HTTP protocol.

❑ **mailto**: This is an electronic mailbox address. The web browser is responsible for invoking an electronic mail service (typically, SMTP) to send the message.

❑ **nntp**: Usenet news servers are accessed using this URI.

❑ **telnet**: This can be used to start a Telnet terminal session.

Not all URIs are intended for use in web documents. Java, for example, also specifies its own schema names to use with URIs. Here is another short list of commonly used Java-based URIs:

❑ **jar**: This is used to access Java classes inside a Java `.jar` file

❑ **jndi**: This is used to access network resources with the Java JNDI mechanism

❑ **rmi**: This is used to access remote objects through the Java RMI mechanism

Uniform Resource Locators

If you are familiar with the Web, you are probably familiar with **Uniform Resource Locators (URLs).** A URL is a specific kind of URI, although most people assume that URI and URL refer to the same thing.

URLs identify a resource by specifying its exact location on the Internet. Our first example was a URL. It identifies the exact location of the `rfc2396.txt` file. Our second example is a more generic URI. It specifies an electronic mailbox, but it does not specify the e-mail protocol to use to send the message or the e-mail server to use to deliver it. We could use SMTP, IMAP, or any other suitable protocol.

The URI path for URLs has multiple parts. Here is an example of a completely specified URL:

http://SomeUser:my_password@www.some_server.com:8080/path/file.html

This URL specifies a web resource that requires user authentication. The user ID and the password are passed to the web server named `www.some_server.com`. The web server is not located at the "well-known" port number for HTTP servers, which is 80, so we need to specify the port (8080 in this case). The path on the web server and the name of the web page are appended to the rightmost end of the URL string.

URLs can contain information in addition to resource locations. A web URL, for example, can include two additional elements: a query and parameters. When you fill out information on an HTML form, the information is often passed back to the web server in a URL. A web page, for example, might contain links to various discussion groups or "boards". When the user selects one of these links, the selected board is passed back as a key/value pair, with `board` being equal to `320`.

http://www.MyServer.com/boards.asp?board=320

URLs do not have to be completely specified. If a protocol uses a "well-known" port, the port number can be excluded. If a user ID and password do not need to be passed to the host, they can also be excluded.

If a URL appears inside an object with a well-defined URL, the URL can use an abbreviated form, called a relative URL. A **relative URL** can refer to its parent object without specifying the parent URL. This makes it a lot easier to move documents on a web site. It also cuts down on network bandwidth, since full paths do not have to be transmitted with every request for a resource. For example, the file.html document in the example above could refer to another document in the same path this way:

```
<a href="file2.txt">
```

In this case, the URL for file2.txt would inherit its protocol, host name, and path from the URL for file.txt. If file2.txt was located on the same server but in a different directory, we could specify a different path, like this:

```
<a href="/path2/file2.txt">
```

URLs can also optionally specify the subsection of a resource to access. In a file, this can be a specific section to jump to. For example:

```
<a href="/book/chapter.txt#section2">
```

This URL would cause a web browser to jump straight to section2 of a document called chapter.txt.

Some characters have special meanings inside a URL. The basic encoding rules are simple.

- ❑ A space is replaced with a plus (+) sign
- ❑ A forward slash (/) is used to separate directories and subdirectories
- ❑ A question mark (?) separates the URL from the query
- ❑ A percent sign (%) is used to specify special characters
- ❑ A pound sign (#) is used to specify a bookmark
- ❑ The ampersand (&) is used to separate parameters

While these characters have special meanings in a URL, we human beings sometimes use them for other purposes, for example, sometimes we want to include a plus sign in our resource names. When that's the case, we replace them with their hexadecimal values as shown in the table below:

Special Character	Hexadecimal Value
+	%20
/	%2F
?	%3F

Special Character	Hexadecimal Value
%	%25
#	%23
&	%26

Uniform Resource Name

Another important subset of URIs are **Uniform Resource Names** (**URNs**). These are used to identify persistent information on the Internet by a logical name (that is, by an alias). URNs are becoming increasingly important as more information moves from one location to another on the Web. URNs are handy for identifying resources that migrate around the Internet or are mirrored on multiple servers and have the following syntax:

```
urn:namespace:resource_name
```

The URN namespace refers to a collection of resources that is maintained by some authority. Many people use namespaces based on URLs as they are one of the few sets of characters that you can guarantee are unique and you can buy. RFC 1737 (http://www.ietf.org/rfc/rfc1737.txt), which describes the functional requirements for URNs, delegates the authority for assigning namespaces to the same naming authorities who assign URLs. The resource name refers to a particular resource within that collection. The syntax for resource names is entirely up to the namespace authority.

The current use of URNs is limited, but in the future, as indexing improves and naming services become more widespread, URNs will play an increasingly important role in accessing Internet resources. A current implementation of URNs is **Persistent Uniform Resource Locators** (**PURL**). A PURL works in the same way as a URL but points to an intermediate naming service rather than directly to a resource. The PURL resolution service then returns the URL associated with that PURL to the client. This has the advantage that you can change the URL of a resource then simply update the PURL service to point to the new location. For more information on PURLs see http://purl.oclc.org/.

RFC 2276 (http://www.ietf.org/rfc/rfc2276.txt) provides the details on how a URN is resolved into a URL. The process is quite simple. Let's assume that we want to download a file from the Internet and we see a link to the file on a web page somewhere. Instead of a link to an ftp:// URL, the page contains a link to a URN. Translating the URN into a URL is called **resolving**. A **resolver** does the translation *and* it may also provide direct access to the resource as well, although this is not required. The resolver might return the same URL to every requestor, or it might return different instances of a resource under different conditions – perhaps owing to some policy relating to the nature of the requestor or to balance the load demands for the resource.

Hypertext and Web Client-Server Programming

The World Wide Web goes back just one decade. Tim Berners-Lee, working at CERN in Switzerland, posted the first computer code of the World Wide Web on the news://alt.hypertext Usenet newsgroup in 1991. In its earliest incarnation, the Web was just a global hypertext system. **Hypertext** refers to software protocols that link references in one document to other documents. Those documents can be located on the same machine or distributed across a network.

The web experience as we now know it – with a graphical web browser – emerged in 1993 and has been constantly evolving ever since. People who had not previously heard of the Web and the Internet now wanted to get online to access its content. In essence, though, the Web worked like a global file server. Three-tier client-server web applications had to wait until 1995 when the **Common Gateway Interface (CGI)** protocol let web servers process information from HTML in background processes on the web server.

Recent changes to web clients and web servers have transformed the everyday web experience from static pages that provide limited information back to the web server into dynamic web pages, personalized by the user, with highly interactive content. The remainder of this chapter will look at some of the technologies responsible for this transformation.

HTTP

Hypertext Transfer Protocol (HTTP) is the standard protocol used to communicate between web browsers and web servers. It's a detailed protocol, and we cannot cover it in its entirety in just a few pages. We will give you an overview of how HTTP works.

HTTP is an RPC-like protocol. There's another bit of jargon. **RPC** stands for **Remote Procedure Call**, which is a mechanism for requesting services on a remote machine and processing responses. RPCs work just like a procedure call in a programming language. In the case of HTTP, a web browser makes a request of a web server, using a URL to submit that request. The web browser then waits for a reply from the web server.

HTTP was originally designed to use UDP datagrams, therefore, it is stateless (see Chapter 10). HTTP uses connections, but until recently, those connections were one-shot. A connection lasted just long enough to service one request from a client and its response from the server. HTTP 1.1 includes limited support for multiple transactions between an HTTP client and server over the same connection.

The interaction between the HTTP client and server involves just a few steps:

❑ **HTTP server listens for requests**: An HTTP server opens a listening socket, usually on TCP port 80. This is usually done in a thread, which then blocks, waiting for an incoming HTTP request.

❑ **HTTP client composes an HTTP URL**: The HTTP client needs to establish an initial connection with the HTTP server. This is done with a URL, typically in the form of: http://www.some_server.com. In this form, the HTTP client is specifying the default resource on the HTTP server, usually a page called index.htm or default.htm. The default web page is usually the home page for the site. In some cases, the URL is more intricate. We discussed some of the URL basics in the previous section of this chapter. If a port other than 80 is used, perhaps to access a corporate intranet, then the URL might take the form http://www.some_server.com:8080 (8080 is a popular alternative HTTP port).

❑ **HTTP client establishes a connection**: HTTP client creates a sending socket to connect with the web server. The sending socket will be used by the client to submit HTTP requests to the server.

❑ **HTTP server accepts the connection**: HTTP server creates a receiving socket to receive a request from the HTTP client. Typically, receiving sockets run in their own threads in order to improve web server performance.

❑ **HTTP client composes an HTTP request to send to the HTTP server**: Once the connection with the HTTP server is established, the client composes an HTTP request and passes it through the socket to the HTTP server. We will be looking at HTTP requests in more detail further on in this chapter.

❏ **HTTP server processes the request**: The HTTP server continues to listen on its receiving socket for incoming requests. When a request is received, the server parses the incoming request and takes whatever action is required by the request.

❏ **HTTP server sends an HTTP response to the HTTP client**: The HTTP server composes an HTTP response. We will also take a more detailed look at HTTP responses in this chapter. The server passes the response back through the connection to the HTTP client.

❏ **HTTP client processes the response**: When the HTTP client receives a response from a server, the client parses and then handles the response.

❏ **Socket connection is closed**: The HTTP client and/or server close the connection.

HTTP 1.1

HTTP 1.1 is the proposed standard, and it includes three mechanisms to improve performance when downloading web pages.

HTTP 1.1 addresses a very common situation: an HTTP client downloads an HTML file from an HTTP server, and the HTML page contains links to, perhaps, a dozen graphic images. With HTTP 1.0, downloading the page will require thirteen connections, one to download the HTML page, and one each to download the twelve graphic images. Remember, in HTTP 1.0, the connections are all one-shot.

HTTP 1.1 addresses this problem with these three mechanisms:

❏ **Persistent connections**: With these, multiple transactions can pass between the HTTP client and server over the same connection. Either client or server can close the connection at any point. Persistent connections are the default.

❏ **Pipelining**: This is used by HTTP clients that do not need to block between each request. HTTP clients can instead send multiple requests without waiting for a response. The HTTP server sends its responses in the same order that HTTP requests were received from the client.

❏ **Cache validation commands**: These are used by HTTP clients to maintain a consistent cache of documents from an HTTP server by determining the expiration date for a document.

Therefore, HTTP 1.1 handles our previous scenario more efficiently as only one connection is needed to download the HTML page and the twelve graphic images.

MIME

A lot of the information that passes between HTTP clients and HTTP servers is binary data (for example a `.gif` image). HTTP clients and servers need a standard way to describe the data they are passing and where the binary data starts and ends inside each message.

HTTP borrows its standard for describing message contents from Internet Mail (RFC 822 – http://www.ietf.org/rfc/rfc822.txt) and the **Multipurpose Internet Mail Extensions** (RFC 1521 – http://www.ietf.org/rfc/rfc1521.txt). MIME is used by both HTTP clients and HTTP servers – HTTP clients use it to tell HTTP servers what kinds of data they can handle and HTTP servers use it to tell HTTP clients what kind of data they are sending.

A MIME header includes both a type and a subtype. A type specifies the general class of information such as a text file, bitmap graphic image, streaming video file. The subtype identifies the specific type of information, an HTML file, GIF file, AVI file and so on. The general form for a MIME header is type/subtype. Here's an example:

```
image/gif
```

Non-standard MIME types are prefixed with `x-`. These are MIME types supported by a subset of HTTP clients/servers. For example, the `x-bitmap` subtype identifies binary files for Microsoft bitmap images (`.bmp` files).

MIME supports nearly one hundred predefined subtypes. The average HTTP client-server, however, supports just a small subset. At a minimum, it is reasonable to expect an HTTP client or server to support the following MIME subtypes: `text/html`, `text/plain`, `image/gif`, and `image/jpeg`. Here is a brief list of common predefined MIME type/subtypes:

MIME Type	MIME Subtype	Description
text	html	HTML files (`*.htm`, `*.html`)
	plain	ASCII text files (`*.txt`)
image	gif	.GIF image files (`*.gif`)
	jpeg	.JPG image files (`*.jpg`)
	tiff	Adobes tagged image files (`*.tif`, `*.tiff`)
audio	basic	.AU audio files (`*.au`)
video	mpeg	Movie Pictures Experts Group video files (`*.mpg`)
	quicktime	Apple QuickTime video files (`*.mov`)
application	java	Java class files (`*.class`)
	pdf	Adobe Acrobat files (`*.pdf`)

How ever long the list of predefined subtypes is, it does not necessarily cover all the types of data you might want to send – this is where x-types come in; these allow you to define a MIME type for whatever you want. The problem is that unlike the predefined subtypes you cannot guarantee that they will be supported by client applications. Despite this, many of these x-types are now so widely accepted that this is not a major problem. Here are a few examples of common x-types:

MIME Type	MIME Subtype	Description
image	x-bitmap	Microsoft bitmap image files (`*.bmp`)
audio	x-wav	Microsoft audio files (`*.wav`)
video	x-msvideo	Microsoft audio video interleave files (`*.avi`)

HTTP Requests

HTTP requests have a simple structure to them. There are five parts to an HTTP request, two of which are optional:

❑ **Request Method**: This specifies the command to be applied. The two most common request methods are GET and POST. GET asks the server to send a resource to the client and POST is used to send data to the server.

❑ **Resource ID**: This specifies the name of the target resource. Typically, it is a URL without the protocol and server domain name.

❑ **HTTP Version**: As the name suggests, this specifies the version of the HTTP protocol supported by the client

❑ **Request Header Fields** (Optional): These are used to pass additional information about the request and the client to the server. Each request header field consists of a name, a colon (`:`), and a value. One of the most common HTTP Request fields is `Accept`. The `Accept` field is used to inform the HTTP server about the kinds of MIME types the client can handle. Here is a simple example:

```
Accept: text/html, text/plain, image/gif, image/jpeg
```

❑ **Request Body** (Optional): Here you can include bulk data as part of a request. A blank line separates the response body from the remainder of the HTTP request.

The most basic HTTP request is a single line containing a request method, a resource ID, and an HTTP version. The line ends with a carriage return and linefeed pair (`\r\n`):

```
GET /index.htm HTTP/1.0
```

If the request is just a simple one-line request, a second carriage return and linefeed pair signals the HTTP server to begin processing the request.

Here is a quick list of the basic HTTP request methods:

❑ **GET**: Without question, this is the most common HTTP request method. It is used to fetch resources, such as web pages and graphic images, from an HTTP server. No data is included in the request body using this method.

❑ **POST**: The next most widely used request, `POST` is used to send data to the server. The typical use is to pass information from an HTML form back to the server. Request header fields are often used to pass this information.

❑ **HEAD**: The simplest of the HTTP request methods, it returns only the MIME header for a resource. It is typically used to check whether a resource has changed since it was last cached.

❑ **PUT** (HTTP 1.1): This method allows clients to upload a resource to the HTTP server and place it in the server's file system. Many servers ignore this request method, since it is a clear security risk.

❑ **DELETE** (HTTP 1.1): This can delete a resource from the HTTP server; again many servers ignore this request for security reasons

❑ **TRACE** (HTTP 1.1): This is used to send back the MIME header that the server received from the client. It is often useful to see what a proxy server might be changing in an HTTP request.

❑ **OPTIONS** (HTTP 1.1): This method is used to get the list of options supported by a particular URL. If an asterisk (*) is substituted for the URL, the request applies to the HTTP server as a whole.

Even a simple `GET` request can generate several request headers. A more complete `GET` request is shown below:

```
GET /index.htm   HTTP/1.1
Connection: Keep-Alive
User-Agent: Java1.3
Host: www.SomeSite.com
Accept: text/html, text/plain, image/gif, image/jpeg
Accept-Language: en
Accept-Encoding: gzip, compress, no-identity
Accept-Charset: iso-8859-1, utf-8
Content-Length: 2750
```

Here's a list of the most common request headers:

❑   **Connection**: This is used in HTTP 1.1 to request a persistent connection. An example appears in the code above – Connection: Keep-Alive

❑   **User-Agent**: This passes browser information to the server

❑   **Host**: This specifies the host name and port number

❑   **Accept**: This is the most common request header, it is used to specify the kinds of MIME types the client can handle

❑   **Accept-<Behavior>**: This specifies other types of data or behaviors supported by the HTTP client. In the example above:

  ❑   Accept-Language indicates the English language

  ❑   Accept-Charset indicates the supported character sets

  ❑   Accept-Encoding specifies acceptable encoding types for data, such as compressed files, .zip files

❑   **Content-Length**: This specifies the length of the data in the request body

HTTP Responses

An HTTP response looks a lot like an HTTP request. It has six parts as well, but only the first two are required.

❑   **HTTP Version**: This specifies the version of the HTTP protocol supported by the server

❑   **HTTP Status Code**: This numeric code identifies the status of the response

❑   **HTTP Status Description** (Optional): This is a short description of the HTTP status code

❑   **Response Header Fields** (Optional): These are used to pass additional information about the response from the server, this is then used by the client to control response handling

❑   **Response Body** (Optional): This method allows you to include bulk data as part of a request. A blank line separates the response body from the remainder of the HTTP response.

❑   **Content-Length** (Optional): As before, this specifies the length of the data in the request body

Here's an example of an HTTP response (without the response body):

```
HTTP/1.1    200    OK
Date: Sun, 02 Jun 2001 16:27:54 GMT
Server: Apache/1.2.5
Connection: close
Content-Type: text/html
```

As we can see in the code example, the first three parts of an HTTP response are usually concatenated on a single physical line.

There are many status codes in HTTP 1.0 and there are even more in HTTP 1.1. The codes fall into several general:

❑   100 – 199: Informational responses

❑   200 – 299: Successful responses

❑   300 – 399: Redirected responses

❑   400 – 499: Indicate a client error

❑   500 – 599: Indicate a server error

The bulk of HTTP responses involves a small set of response headers:

❑   **Connection** (HTTP 1.1): The default behavior is to keep a persistent connection open for a default timeout period. If the server closes the connection after the request for some reason, it can issue a `close` response header

❑   **Content-Encoding**: This identifies the MIME encoding scheme

❑   **Content-Length**: This specifies the length of the data in the response body

❑   **Content-Type**: This identifies the MIME type of the response body

❑   **Date**: This identifies the date and time of the response

❑   **Server**: This identifies the HTTP server

> The standards for HTTP 1.0 are available in RFC 1945
> (http://www.ietf.org/rfc/rfc1945.txt). The proposed standards for HTTP 1.1 are
> contained in RFC 2616 (http://www.ietf.org/rfc/rfc2616.txt). The standards include the
> complete lists for request methods, request headers, response codes, and response headers.

Displaying and Describing Data

Information is useless to any application unless it knows what to do with it. There are many ways to approach this, but one of the most powerful is to use a language which describes your data, usually called a markup language. Most markup languages in use are based on **SGML** (**Standard Generalized Markup Language**) that has its roots in the early 1970s. This was an early attempt to provide a universal markup language. This is rather a heavyweight standard, though, so a number of more familiar languages have developed for more specific purposes, principally HTML and XML.

HTML

HTML (**Hypertext Markup Language**) is the lingua franca of the World Wide Web. HTML is a basic standard for describing the context of information intended for display in a web browser.

Here is a brief introduction to HTML:

❑ The HTTP client requests a web page with an HTTP GET request

❑ The requested HTML page is sent in the response body of the HTTP response from the HTTP server

❑ The HTML code tells the web browser what information to provide to the user and how to display it. HTML can be used to display text, hyperlinks, lists, submit buttons and so on

❑ As users interact with various HTML elements, like textboxes and submit buttons, the web browser sends information back to the HTTP server as an HTTP POST request

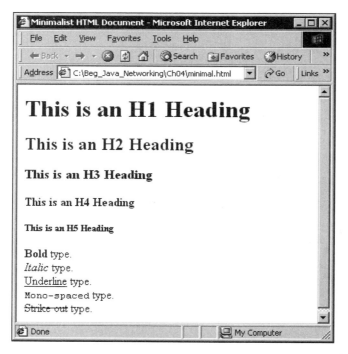

HTML is plain, unadorned ASCII text. The magic that web browsers perform when they convert an HTML document into a flashy web page is done by translating tags embedded in the text. Let's take a quick look at the code for the minimalist HTML page in the figure above:

```
<! minimal.html>
<html>
  <head>
    <title>Minimalist HTML Document</title>
  </head>
```

```
    <body>
        <h1>This is an H1 Heading</h1>
        <h2>This is an H2 Heading</h2>
        <h3>This is an H3 Heading</h3>
        <h4>This is an H4 Heading</h4>
        <h5>This is an H5 Heading</h5>
        <b>Bold</b> type.<br>
        <i>Italic</i> type.<br>
        <u>Underline</u> type.<br>
        <tt>Mono-spaced</tt> type.<br>
        <strike>Strike out</strike> type.
    </body>
</html>
```

Most of the document is just a text stream. The tags stand out and most are paired. To make a portion of text bold, for example, we enclose the text inside a pair of bold tags: <b></b>. Because the text in an HTML document is just a stream of text, we use the <br> tag to delimit paragraphs (br being an abbreviation for BREAK). We can instead use the <p> tag at the beginning of a paragraph to indicate a new paragraph.

HTML has gone through several changes. The current recommendation is HTML 4.01, while the major web browsers support most of HTML 4.0 standard. Browser wars among companies like Microsoft and Netscape meant that vendors added their own incompatible extensions to HTML.

XML

Enter **XML**, short for **eXtensible Markup Language**. XML isn't about displaying data, but it is about describing it. It can be used to convey information to people, between software applications, and even to other machines. The extensible part of XML's name is important. XML lets web page authors create new tags.

XML and HTML share the same ancestor: SGML, so they look alike, but they are not the same. Remember the <b></b> tags from HTML in our previous example? We used them to denote bold text. With XML, those same tags could mean anything. Bold, blue, backward what ever you want. The meaning can change, depending on the context where <b></b> is used. XML lets you make up your own markup language.

HTML became rather eclectic over time. For example, Cascading Style Sheets (CSS) were added to give web page authors more precise control over the display of page elements. HTML 4.0 is a family of technologies, and so is XML. XML even relies on cascading style sheets to display XML data in a browser. Here are some of the evolving family members (some are very much works in progress, some have reached maturity):

❑ **DOM and SAX**: These are APIs for accessing XML documents from programming languages

❑ **XLINK**: This defines a standard for adding hypertext links to an XML document

❑ **XPOINTER**: This adds navigation links to XML documents

❑ **XML Schemas**: These are used to define valid document properties and attributes for an XML document

❑ **XSL**: This defines CSS-like style sheets for XML

❑ **XSLT**: This is part of XSL. It is a language for describing structural transformations of XML. This allows you to transform data from one document format to another and has important applications for Java network programmers as a tool for integrating different systems and applications.

XML's strength is the ability to manage and exchange complex data structures. If you want to sum up XML, it's a language for describing structured data and storing it in plain, unadorned Unicode text files. It was created so that structured data could be used over the Web. You can even take data, load it into an XML document, and then put this in an HTML file. Microsoft calls this an XML **data island**.

Embedding XML in an HTML page as a data island is simple enough. You need to use a browser that supports XML and the XML element in the HTML Document Object Model (DOM). XML can be embedded inline or with an SRC attribute.

Here's a very brief example of XML embedded inline:

```
<XML ID="XMLID">
<XMLDATA>
    <DATA>TEXT</DATA>
  </XMLDATA>
</XML>
```

If you want to use the SRC attribute instead you do it like this:

```
<XML SRC="http://localhost/XMLDATA.xml"></XML>
```

Why Unicode text instead of binary representations? Text files are more portable. We can take a data file from an IBM mainframe, create an XML document to hold the data, and pass it to a PC, a Macintosh, or a Prime minicomputer. We don't have to worry about converting packed decimals, zoned decimals, and other IBM binary formats into something the PC can understand. Converting everything to text strings means we can use XML to pass legacy data from an IBM mainframe to a PC.

XML is important to Java network programmers for several reasons:

❑ XML is all the rage so it looks good on your résumé. While this may seem trivial it's not, by its very nature the more applications that use XML the more useful it will become.

❑ XML is a powerful tool for integrating systems. In a heterogeneous enterprise application, all of our components might not be written in Java. JDBC can be used to pass recordsets between Java components, but it won't work for passing data between a Java component and a C++ component. The same information, converted into an XML document, can easily pass between Java and C++ components, using the XML API of the respective language. XML is thoroughly agnostic; it is platform, protocol, and language independent. That's why it's becoming so popular in the IT industry.

❑ XML can be used to store and describe data. Application configuration files are an excellent example: object data can be temporarily persisted to text files with XML.

Java and XML complement each other as both are simple, portable, and flexible. XML is the ideal companion for Java when creating enterprise applications that leverage web technologies. The Java APIs for XML Processing (JAXP) supports processing XML documents with DOM, SAX, and XSLT.

Before we move along, let's look at a small piece of XML:

```xml
<?xml version="1.0"?>
<contacts>
  <person>
    <name>
      <first_name>John</first_name>
      <last_name>Smith</last_name>
    </name>
    <profession>professor</profession>
    <profession>consultant</profession>
    <profession>author</profession>
  </person>
</contacts>
```

This is, admittedly, a very simple example. It's just a simple person object; one that captures first name, last name, and multiple professions for someone. We have the start here for information that a Personal Information Manager (PIM) might track; the sort of information a data component might send to a client user interface. If we had two records to pass along, instead of one, there's no problem. We just fill out the information for two people in our XML file.

```xml
<?xml version="1.0"?>
<contacts>
  <person>
    <name>
      <first_name>John</first_name>
      <last_name>Smith</last_name>
    </name>
    <profession>professor</profession>
    <profession>consultant</profession>
    <profession>author</profession>
  </person>
  <person>
    <name>
      <first_name>Jane</first_name>
      <last_name>Doe</last_name>
    </name>
    <profession>veterinarian</profession>
  </person>
</contacts>
```

Our sample XML documents are **well-formed**. That means they don't break any XML syntax rules. Being well-formed is one requirement for a valid XML document, but it's not the only requirement. **Valid** means an XML document is well-formed *and* it meets the rules of some sort of standard. We can define the standard for an XML document in a **DTD** (**Document Type Definition**) or a **Schema**. When XML data is shared, the document can be compared with the agreed rules in a DTD or Schema.

DTDs and schemas are alternative ways for businesses and groups of people to agree on a common format for sharing data. Since XML lets developers create their own markup languages, DTDs and schemas are the mechanisms for self-imposed standards on our ad hoc markup languages.

> The W3C is the standards body responsible for defining the syntax of XML. You can get further information from **http://www.w3.org/xml**.

77

XHTML

HTML does a reasonably good job of displaying information and it has become more powerful since cascading style sheets and internationalization were made part of the HTML standard. However, HTML still has one big problem, incompatibility. We see it in the different extensions to HTML from companies like Microsoft and Netscape. Also, it is quite possible that HTML code that does not conform to the standard will work in some browsers, but not others, a far from ideal situation.

The solution to this is **eXtensible Hypertext Markup Language** (XHTML) which is the reformulation of HTML 4.0 as an XML application. It can be seen as a stricter form of HTML, which must conform to the XML rules for well-formedness and validate against one of the available XHTML DTDs. The application of these stricter rules should ensure that an XHTML document would work with most current browsers and all future ones. In addition, any XML-enabled device from mobile phones to supercomputers can read XHTML and then decide what to do, taking into account its own capabilities.

Some of the major differences between XHTML and HTML include:

❑ All tags in XHTML must be lowercase

❑ All tags must be closed, even empty ones

❑ All attributes must have arguments

❑ All XHTML files must contain a document type declaration

Further information can be found in the XHTML specification, which is located at http://www.w3.org/TR/xhtml1/.

Interactivity and Web Client-Server Programming

After all of this discussion of HTTP, HTML, and XML, it should be obvious that web-enabled enterprise applications involve two sets of technologies: client-side technologies that operate in the browser environment and server-side technologies that operate in the server environment.

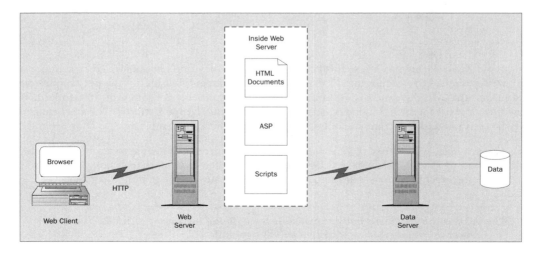

Server-Side Technologies

The Web is constantly evolving in the direction of greater interactivity, richer multimedia, and personalized content. The challenge for developers is to deliver dynamic content, not just static web pages. Web pages need to be constructed "on the fly" as users interact with the site. Popular choices for generating personalized web content include Common Gateway Interface (CGI) programs, PHP, Active Server Pages (ASP), Servlets, and JavaServer Pages (JSP).

CGI is used to generate dynamic web page content. The HTTP server delegates the responsibility for responding to an HTTP request to a CGI application. One common scenario is the CGI application adopts a three-tier architecture and makes calls to the data server. The CGI program acts like a business rules service component, adding value to the data from the data server and preparing a web page to return to the HTTP client. CGI programs can be written in almost any language, Perl and C are the favored languages, although Java can be used too.

The CGI interface is supported on a wide variety of web servers, but CGI programs are not necessarily portable across different platforms. Cross-platform compatibility requires careful design and testing.

When an HTTP request includes a URL for a CGI application, the web server runs the CGI application in a separate process. This has some important consequences:

❑   The CGI program has little access to the web server process. It receives its inputs from environment variables and standard input, output from the CGI program is returned via standard output.

❑   Because they run in an independent process, CGI programs that crash are not likely to crash the HTTP server or other applications running on the host machine.

❑   CGI programs can cause a web server to crash under high load conditions. This happens because each new request creates a separate process and if numerous concurrent requests must be dealt with, the server quickly runs out of resources.

❑   CGI programs impose a performance penalty compared to returning a static web page. Initiating a separate process requires substantial clock cycles and host machine resources.

The need to spawn a new process for each HTTP request means CGI programs do not scale well. As the number of concurrent connections increase, so does the demand for server-side processes. The use of standard input and standard output can also be a performance bottleneck.

Scripting languages – like **JavaScript**, **PHP**, and **Active Server Pages** (**ASP**) – are a popular alternative to CGI programming. Server-side scripting relies on a script engine to process pages containing special HTML tags. These tags are extensions to HTML that are meaningful only to the scripting engine and result in the dynamic generation of HTML code. When an HTTP client requests a page containing server-side script, the web server passes the page to the script engine, and the script engine processes the page, generating any dynamic HTML required. The output from the script engine is then passed to the client as an HTTP response. Developers can use scripting languages to write sophisticated application code.

Scripting languages like PHP and ASP scale better than CGI because they run in the process space of the scripting engine. The web server does not have to spawn a new process every time a page with script commands is processed. You do pay a small performance penalty, however, as scripting languages tend to be interpreted, rather than compiled.

Active Server Pages rely on technology with an architecture that is closely tied to Microsoft's IIS web server. There are scripting solutions that are more platform agnostic than ASP; these include PHP, PerlScript, and JavaScript.

Java technology allows web developers to rapidly develop and easily maintain highly interactive web pages that contain lots of dynamic content. Java-based web programming relies heavily on servlets and JavaServer Pages (JSP).

Servlets are Java's answer to CGI programming. Java servlets are essentially server-side applets that run on a web server. They differ from applets in one important respect – servlets contain no user interface. They provide Java with a component-based method for building web applications that is platform-independent and more easily scaled than CGI applications. Servlets make the entire Java language available to developers for extending web server functionality.

Servlet requests are handled by a separate thread inside the JVM. That means that Java servlets can easily share data and maintain information from request to request, simplifying session tracking – tasks difficult to do with CGI programs. Unlike scripting languages, which offer limited programming features, Java servlets have access to the entire family of Java APIs, including JDBC. That makes Java servlets an ideal candidate for three-tier and multi-tier web-based applications.

JavaServer Pages (JSP) is a Java-based technology for creating dynamic web content – JSP adds Java to HTML pages. Like Active Server Pages and PHP, JavaServer Pages embed commands inside HTML pages with XML-like tags, but rather than using a script engine to process the HTML, JSP pages are converted into Java servlets.

Client-Side Technologies

Scripting is also an option on the client-side for making web applications more responsive. On the client-side, scripting languages like JavaScript are useful for performing data and input validation. Web developers also use client-side script to display basic messages to users in windows rather than HTML pages. JavaScript is a popular scripting language for client-side interactions as well as server-side programming.

Applets are Java programs that only run inside the framework of a web browser and can be embedded into a web page. Applets were the feature that made Java famous as they could do things that HTML just couldn't do.

Adding an applet to a web page is just as easy as adding an image, it is achieved in HTML 4.0 by using the <OBJECT> tag. The tag attributes denote the class name for the applet and its location. Earlier versions of HTML use the <APPLET> tag. Here's an example:

```
<OBJECT
    CLASSID="HelloWorld.class"
    CODEBASE="applets"
    ARCHIVE="Archive.jar"
    WIDTH=300 HEIGHT=200 ALIGN=LEFT
</OBJECT>
```

Java applets can be stored inside compressed .jar files. The ARCHIVE attribute in our example tells the web server that the applet is stored in a .jar file named Archive.jar. We can also pass parameters to a Java applet:

```
<OBJECT
   CLASSID="HelloWorld.class"
   CODEBASE="applets"
   ARCHIVE="Archive.jar"
   WIDTH=300 HEIGHT=200 ALIGN=LEFT
   <PARAM NAME=Phrase VALUE="Ain't life grand!">
</OBJECT>
```

Java applets can define as many parameters as they need, we just include a separate PARAM attribute for each.

> If you want your HTML code to be compatible with newer and older browsers, use both the <OBJECT> and the <APPLET> tag on your pages. One of the virtues of web browsers is they ignore tags they do not understand.

Summary

This chapter was a quick introduction to the most important concepts behind WWW and Internet programming. This should give you a good overall picture of the important technologies and how they fit together. Many of these subjects will be revisited in later chapters where they touch on Java network programming. Here's a quick summary of the topics we have discussed:

- ❏ The Web is a collection of information resources. URLs (Uniform Resource Locators) are used to identify resources by specifying their exact location on the Internet. URNs (Uniform Resource Names) identify resources on the Internet, instead, by a logical name.

- ❏ Hypertext Transfer Protocol (HTTP) is the standard protocol used to communicate between web browsers and web servers. Web browsers send HTTP requests to web servers, web servers respond with HTTP responses.

- ❏ A lot of the information that passes between HTTP clients and HTTP servers is binary data. MIME is a standard way to describe the data being passed and where the binary data starts and ends inside each message.

- ❏ XML is a language for describing structured data and storing it in plain, unadorned text files. It was created so that structured data could be passed between applications in a totally platform-independent manner.

- ❏ Web-enabled enterprise applications involve two sets of technologies: client-side technologies that operate in the browser environment and server-side technologies that operate in the server environment.

- ❏ Popular choices for generating personalized web content include common gateway interface (CGI) programs, PHP, Active Server Pages, Servlets, and JSP.

- ❏ Java-based solutions to web programming rely heavily on servlets and JavaServer Pages (JSP).

Java I/O

Before we get busy learning how to utilize Java's rich network programming libraries, we must first gain an understanding of the APIs upon which that functionality is based. Java's network programming model is built upon a broader foundation of classes that provide input and output (**I/O**) facilities to Java programmers. Like many Java APIs, the I/O library is composed fundamentally of a few classes that provide basic input and output functions. It is from these general purpose classes that more sophisticated classes are built which allow you to read from and write to memory, the console, the file system, and even network sockets.

In this chapter, we will begin by covering the conceptual origin of the Java I/O classes. The "plumbing" metaphor for Java I/O, utilizing sources, streams, pipes, filters, and sinks for data will provide us with an intuitive way to connect the classes of the `java.io` package.

Next, we will look at the two base classes, `java.io.InputStream` and `java.io.OutputStream`, from which the more sophisticated I/O functionality is provided. These classes give us the ability to move data into, around, and out of our programs a byte at a time.

Once we have our foundation established, we will move on to the abstract `java.io.Reader` and `java.io.Writer` classes that allow us to move data around in two-byte (or character) sized chunks. We'll look at some examples along the way that use the file system to mimic the way we'll be reading from and writing to network sockets later in the book.

We'll also see some examples of Java I/O facilities that can be used to filter, encode, and decode data, as it's being read or written. The chapter will wrap up with a demonstration of how you can link input to output as you create more sophisticated network programs throughout the rest of the book. Realizing that intricacies of network programming are presented later in this text, we will focus on the broader picture of I/O, using more familiar means, like files and the console, for demonstration. We will always discuss how the particular concept or technique will be of use to you later on.

> **Serialization is another important topic in network I/O that usually falls into the domain of a chapter like this. However, rather than rush through an overview of serialization in this chapter, we will cover it in depth in Chapter 15.**

By the time the chapter is finished, you should have a solid understanding of Java I/O fundamentals that will give you confidence when programming network I/O. Let us begin with the basics.

Streams, Filters, and Pipes

Many of the core Java APIs make use of rich metaphors to explain how they work, and the I/O classes are no exception. The concept upon which Java I/O is founded is that input and output data are represented as **Streams**. Conceptually, a stream is nothing more than a sequence of data moving from one place to another. This data can be bits, characters, bytes, and so on.

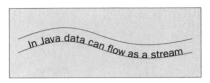

You might ask, "If streams represent bits and bytes, how are they different from say, a String?" That's a good question, and the answer is that a String is an in-memory object that can only contain an array of characters. A Stream on the other hand can represent all kind of data. Primitive types, strings, and entire objects can flow in a stream. A stream is also connected to an **endpoint**. An endpoint acts as either a provider of data, or a receiver of data. The stream is the way you either get the data from, or send the data to, an endpoint. Endpoints are also called sources and sinks depending on whether they provide or receive data.

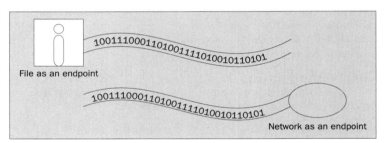

The word itself, "Stream", is particularly descriptive since the important point is that the data is intended to be moved. Data can flow from a source to be consumed by the program. In this case what you have is an input stream. If your program is the source of the data that is written to, or consumed by, an external entity, you are making use of an output stream. As you can see, depending on where the stream is coming from, and where it is going, it's possible for a stream of data to be both an input and an output stream. We can also construct new streams on top of old streams to manipulate the data as it's passing through the new stream. The new stream is usually a "filter" stream. This makes it possible to do things like create encryption and compression stream filters.

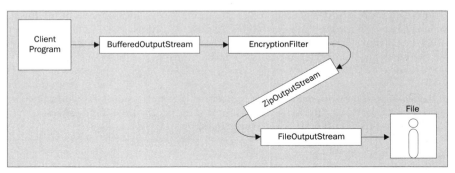

In many cases, creating even the most complex arrangements and processing of input and output is as simple as "hooking up" the right pieces. For example, to send an encrypted file from your file system to a network socket, you might open an input stream using the file as a source. Then you could get an output stream from the network connection, wrap it with an encrypting filter and then you could read the data from the file input stream and pass it to the filter that would send it out over the network in encrypted form.

Streams pipes and filters are provided for data that is accessed a byte at a time and data that is accessed a character at time. This division is necessary because there is much data (primitive types, binary data), which is adequately represented by bytes. But text data is also important and the native representation for text in Java occurs as 2-byte chars. We begin by discussing the classes that support the byte-based approach and see how this develops into a need (and JDK implementation) for the character-based classes.

The java.io Foundation Classes

Basic input and output starts in two very simple places: the InputStream class and the OutputStream class. Earlier we defined "streams" as ordered sequences of data. In an InputStream and an OutputStream, this data is provided and output as a stream of bytes. If you've done I/O in other languages, particularly 8-bit file I/O, the byte should seem like a natural unit to move data back and forth in.

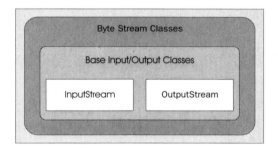

If you look at the Javadocs for the InputStream and OutputStream class, something should strike you immediately: both classes are declared abstract. This means that we can't instantiate them directly. In order to make use of them, we would either have to create custom concrete extensions of the classes, or get them as predefined implementations in the JDK. As luck would have it, there are several such implementations provided throughout the JDK and we will discuss them later in this chapter. InputStream and OutputStream objects are also available from the sources we discussed earlier, like network sockets and files. In fact, let's look at a brief code example and then go into the details of the base java.io classes.

> **Java network programming relies on many I/O concepts and techniques. Many of the examples in this chapter will obtain input from and generate output to sources other than network sockets. This is so that we may focus on the I/O aspects without distraction from the network programming information that is forthcoming in the text. Most techniques are identical with the exception of the technique used to obtain an original input or output stream from the network socket. Any serious deviations will be noted in the text.**

```java
// SimpleTest.java

import java.io.InputStream;
import java.io.OutputStream;
import java.io.IOException;

public class SimpleTest {

  public static void main(String args[]) {

    try {
      InputStream input = null;
      OutputStream output = null;

/* Here you would assign the input and output to actual streams.
      If you had a variable s that was of type java.net.Socket, you might
      write:

      input = s.getInputStream();
      output = s.getOutputStream();*/

      byte[] b = new byte[255];
      int bytesRead = 0;

      while ((bytesRead = input.read(b)) != -1) {
        output.write(b, 0, bytesRead);
      }

      input.close();
      output.close();
    } catch (IOException io) {
      io.printStackTrace();
    }

  }
}
```

Of course, running this example would generate a NullPointerException at the input.read() call since we never assigned a real InputStream to input, but it is sufficient for our purposes of exploring some of the functionality of both the InputStream and OutputStream classes. Let's look at what's going on in the SimpleTest class.

The first thing we need to do is import the relevant Java I/O classes.

```java
import java.io.InputStream;
import java.io.OutputStream;
import java.io.IOException;
```

We create references for InputStream and OutputStream objects. As indicated in the comment, these streams would likely be provided by a native system implementation such as from a java.io.File object or a java.net.Socket object.

```
public class SimpleTest {

    public static void main(String args[]) {

    try {
        InputStream input = null;
        OutputStream output = null;

        /* Here you would assign the input and output to actual streams.
           If you had a variable s that was of type java.net.Socket, you might
           write:

           input = s.getInputStream();
           output = s.getOutputStream();*/
```

Next, we create a byte array to hold bytes that are returned from the input stream, and to provide bytes to the output stream. We also create a variable to hold an indicator for the number of bytes returned from a read operation:

```
        byte[] b = new byte[255];
        int bytesRead = 0;
```

We then invoke the `public int read(byte[] b) throws IOException` method on our `InputStream` object:

```
        while ((bytesRead = input.read(b)) != -1) {
```

This method attempts to read bytes from the underlying stream implementation and stores them in array b. If the stream is available and there are no bytes ready to be read, such as is the case with an open network socket that has received no input, this method will block the executing thread until either data is ready, or the underlying stream is closed due to an exception or reaching end of available data (End of file, for files). The `read` method returns an `int` indicating the number of bytes that were actually read. If no bytes were read due to reaching the end of the stream, a value of −1 would be returned. If for some reason you had passed in a byte array with length `zero`, this method would return a `zero` value. In the condition for the `while` statement, we're calling the `read()` method, setting the result of that call to `bytesRead` and checking to make sure the value of that assignment (and hence the result value of the `read()` method) is not −1. Sometimes network I/O will terminate when the end of the stream is reached and a value of −1 returns. In the case of a file, this will happen when there is no more data available to be read from the file.

> **You should be aware though that many network applications define a messaging protocol where an open socket connection is maintained and a certain number of bytes are sent at the beginning of the message which give the length of the remainder of the message. In this "length encoded" protocol, many messages can be sent back and forth this way with the message termination not being the same as terminating the stream.**

If the amount of data available to be read exceeds the capacity of the byte array parameter, 255 bytes in our case, the `read()` method will return with a value of 255 and store the first 255 available bytes in array b. Since we are in a `while` loop, this will continue to occur until the stream is exhausted, closed, or an exception is generated.

The underlying stream also has the option of returning from the read() method before the array is full, even if the stream hasn't been closed. A hypothetical network socket InputStream implementation might buffer 128 bytes and then return, in which case bytesRead would be 128, and there would be 128 bytes stored in array b. Once we have retrieved some bytes from the input stream, we make the following call to the output stream:

```
output.write(b, 0, bytesRead);
```

This method pushes the data in array b, from index position 0 for bytesRead number of bytes to the underlying output stream. Note, this does not necessarily mean the data will get written to the underlying output stream. OutputStream implementations are allowed to conserve resources and buffer data to be written. As we will see in the upcoming detailed section on OutputStream, there is a method available that allows us to flush any buffers programmatically.

Our example finishes up with a few short steps. First the input and output stream are closed. Since input and output streams obtained from network sockets and files use system level resources, this allows us to explicitly free these resources. The system resources would eventually be freed when garbage collection occurs had we not made a call to the public void close() throws IOException methods.

```
    input.close();
    output.close();
} catch (IOException io) {
    io.printStackTrace();
}
```

Finally, virtually all I/O methods in Java are capable of throwing an IOException. The IOException itself is quite simple providing no additional functionality beyond that which is declared in the java.lang.Exception class it extends. There are, however, several specific IOException subclasses located throughout the JDK that provide additional information related to the type of I/O being performed.

Now that we've seen the InputStream, OutputStream in action, let's take a more detailed look at the functionality we can access with these base classes.

java.io.InputStream

The most basic class for getting a data stream into a Java program is implemented as the InputStream class. The smallest increment the data is provided in is an 8-bit chunk. The most basic of algorithms for reading data from an input stream would look something like this:

```
Obtain an input stream.
While there is more data available {
    Read data.
}
Close input stream.
```

In the example above we saw one method signature for reading bytes from an InputStream object. The class provides two additional read methods that are quite similar in function. They are:

```
public int read(byte[] b, int offset, int length) throws IOException

public abstract int read() throws IOException
```

The first additional `read()` method looks quite similar in its signature to the method we used to write data to an output stream. We specify the same byte array to hold any return bytes. Additionally, we specify an offset, the index position from which the input stream will return bytes to us. Our last parameter is the desired number of bytes to read.

| stream data | H | e | l | l | o | . | | W | o | r | l | d | ! |
| position | 0 | 1 | 2 | 3 | 4 | 5 | 6 | 7 | 8 | 9 | 10 | 11 | 12 |

In the hypothetical stream pictured above, if we made a call to the `read` operation using an offset parameter of 7 and a length parameter of 5, one of the following will happen:

- ❏ The method will return a value of 5 and the first five bytes of the byte array will be W, o, r, l, d
- ❏ The method will return a value less than 5 and that same number of bytes will be stored in the array
- ❏ The method will throw an `IOException`

If all of these outcomes are possible, how can we program I/O operations with any degree of certainty? While it is true that many outputs could occur, if we understand the reasons for variation we will find this makes a good deal of sense.

First, remember that the `InputStream` class is abstract and any number of implementations can be provided to support network, file, and in-memory I/O. Some implementations will buffer the data internally and make it available in quantities smaller than the length specified. Even though you ask for 25 bytes, a particular `InputStream` implementation might only give you 5 at a time. Many stream types rely on system-level resources, and if those should become unavailable for any reason an exception could potentially be thrown.

This brings us to final parameterless version of the read method. There is no default implementation of this method; hence it must be implemented by a subclass of `InputStream`. The method specification itself is quite simple; the method simply returns the next byte available in the stream as an `int` between 0 and 255, or –1 if the end of the stream is reached. This method will block the executing thread if no bytes are available and the end of the stream hasn't yet been reached.

It might seem strange that this method reads a `byte`, but returns an `int`. This is necessary since a `byte` can have a value from –127 to 128 and in that range there is no room for a return value to indicate the end of a stream has been reached. An `int`, with its 32-bit capacity, has more than enough space to accommodate the range of a `byte` (256 values), and provide an end-of-stream result. This `int` may be converted to a `byte` by the following algorithm:

```
int b;
byte result;
if (b <= 0) {
      result = (byte)b;
} else {
      result = (byte)(b-256);
}
```

There are two other methods provided with the InputStream class that you may have occasion to use when you're using Java's I/O facilities for network programming. These methods are:

```
public int available() throws IOException

public long skip(long l) throws IOException
```

The available() method tells us how many bytes we can successfully read or skip from the stream in a single operation. If we were to request to read or skip more than the available value of bytes, we would run the risk of hitting the end of the stream, or having the InputStream block our thread until all of the requested bytes were available.

The skip() method causes the stream to discard ("skip over") the specified number of bytes in the stream. This method has the potential to return before skipping over the specified number of bytes for a variety of reasons, the most common being if the end of the stream is reached before the requested quantity of bytes can be skipped. When this occurs, the actual number of bytes skipped, or −1 if no bytes are skipped, will be returned.

InputStream provides a few more methods that can be used to interact with a byte stream, but are more relevant to file I/O since they aren't supported by network stream implementations. For completeness, they are:

❏ public void mark(int readlimit): Allows you to mark a position in the input stream that you can jump back to at any time before readlimit bytes have been read, by calling the reset() method.

❏ public void reset() throws IOException: Allows you to return to the point in the stream at which you last called the mark() method.

❏ public boolean markSupported(): Exposes whether the mark() and reset() methods are supported in a particular input stream implementation. If this method returns false, calls to the reset method will generate IOExceptions.

Now that we've discussed how the InputStream class functions, let's look at the workings of the OutputStream class.

java.io.OutputStream

OutputStream is the logical complement to the InputStream. It exposes methods that allow byte data to be written to an underlying output stream implementation. Like the InputStream class, OutputStream is also abstract and relies on subclass implementations to provide a good portion of its output-type specific functionality.

Writing

In our earlier sample, we saw how to write bytes to the output stream by specifying a byte array, offset and length of bytes to be written. The general algorithm for writing data to an output stream is straightforward:

```
Obtain an output stream.
While there is more data to be written {
    Write data.
}
Close the output stream.
```

The OutputStream provides two additional method signatures for the write method that can be used to write a byte of data to the output stream:

```
public void write(byte[] b) throws IOException

public abstract void write(int b) throws IOException
```

The first method has an identical effect to the call write(b, 0, b.length); it writes all of the data contained in the byte array to the output stream. The second method is abstract and is implemented by a stream-specific subclass of OutputStream. It writes a single byte (or the eight low-order bits of an int) to the stream.

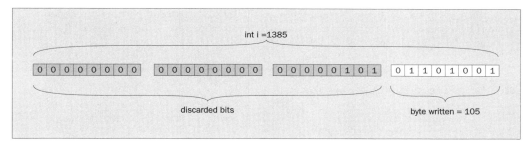

This is similar to the truncation that occurs when an integer is downcast to a byte. We find this behavior quite natural considering an output stream is meant to operate at the byte level, but it quickly becomes inconvenient when we want to output data which is greater than 8 bits, such as a 16-bit character, or 64-bit long. Later in this chapter we will look at the mechanisms Java provides to handle the output (and input) of wider data types.

Flushing

Another method of the OutputStream that wasn't covered in our example, but warrants attention, is flush():

```
public void flush() throws IOException
```

For efficiency reasons subclass implementations of OutputStream may buffer bytes written via one of the write methods before sending them to their actual destination (such as a client socket, file, or console). Therefore, a call to a write() method does not mean the byte(s) will be immediately transferred. Calling the flush() method of an OutputStream tells it to go ahead and deliver any bytes it may have buffered to their intended destination.

Cleaning up

When we've finished using an output stream, we can explicitly trigger the release of any underlying system resources by making a call to the close() method. Once close() has been called the stream cannot be reopened, and subsequent calls to methods on the same instance will generate an IOException.

> Note: if the close() method is not called, the system resources will eventually be freed when the OutputStream object is garbage collected. Generally speaking it is still considered good form to call the close() method so the system resources in use can be made available as soon as possible.

java.io.IOException

So far the actual functionality specified in the base I/O classes has been pretty bland, and the IOException is no exception. Taking a look at the Javadoc for this exception, will show that it has two constructors, one that takes a message, and one with no parameters. It doesn't define any additional methods beyond those provided in its parent class, java.lang.Exception. This is standard fare for just about any base classes in a JDK package. Providers of subclasses to streams (and as we'll see soon, filters, readers and writers) can create specific exceptions that are subclasses of IOException to be thrown in response to error conditions. Many of these specialized children of IOException will provide methods to gain additional information about the error.

The IOException subclasses are spread amongst the JDK, and several pertinent to network programming appear in the java.net package. Refer to Appendix A for discussion of the following networking-related subclasses of IOException:

- ❑   java.net.BindException
- ❑   java.net.ConnectException
- ❑   java.net.MalformedURLException
- ❑   java.net.NoRouteToHostException
- ❑   java.net.ProtocolException
- ❑   java.net.SocketException
- ❑   java.net.UnknownHostException
- ❑   java.net.UnknownServiceException

Making I/O More Convenient

So far, we've had a basic introduction to Java I/O and have seen how it allows us to move data into and out of a program a byte at a time. This is fantastic if all you ever want to move across the wire or from a file is bytes. However, as you've probably already noticed, a byte is the smallest of the Java data types. With only 8-bits, it doesn't provide nearly enough capacity for larger primitive types like int, long, or double, let alone more complex object types.

You might also remember that characters in Java (and therefore Java Strings) utilize the 16-bit Unicode character set. This means that we can't read and write text as streams from the network or files unless we perform a little conversion magic – relying on specialized I/O helper classes in the JDK to do this work for us.

It just so happens that the JDK builds many classes on top of the ones we have just covered to enable us to move complex data structures in and out of our applications. From stream implementations that allow us to treat access to an in-memory array of bytes as a stream, to character-converting readers and writers, and even to compression and encryption streams, there are a multitude of classes at your disposal to create fully-featured I/O applications such as network clients and servers.

For the duration of this chapter, we will discuss several of these classes with detailed examples you can use. Because it's early in the book and you haven't had time to master network programming, we'll use text files as I/O sources and sinks. As we'll see many of these convenience classes are actually constructed by passing in instances of `InputStream` or `OutputStream` objects. Obtaining input and output streams from a socket is nearly as simple as doing the same thing with a file. In fact, let's look at the code needed to create an input stream from a file:

```
FileInputStream in = new FileInputStream("MyTextFile.txt");
```

and to create an input stream from a network socket:

```
Socket s = new Socket("www.wrox.com");
InputStream in = s.getInputStream();
```

About the only difference between these two techniques is the exceptions they can throw related to their construction. Once we have this input stream (or output stream, which is just as easy to get) we're off and running into the plentiful offerings of the Java I/O package.

Filtered Streams

One of the simplest ways the basic functionality of streams can be extended to provide ease of use is via filtering. A filter essentially does what its name implies: it filters a stream of bytes on the way in, or on the way out to give them more meaning in either direction. A filter is typically constructed around an available stream and then we make calls against this filter.

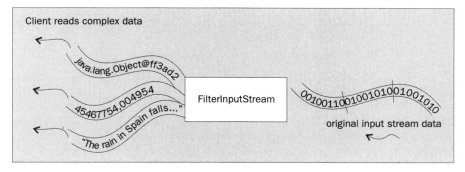

When we make a call against an input stream filter to read a piece of data that's bigger than a `byte`, the filter is responsible for making repeated calls to the underlying stream, and then massaging the data into the format we requested. The inverse works for output stream – we can construct an output filter around an output stream, and then pass in more meaningful pieces of data. The filter is responsible for breaking the data down into bytes and then making repeated calls to the write method of the underlying output stream.

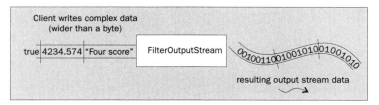

The JDK provides base implementations of filter streams in the `java.io.FilterInputStream` and `java.io.FilterOutputStream` classes. `FilterInputStream` is a subclass of `InputStream` and `FilterOutputStream` is a subclass of `OutputStream`. Both classes can be instantiated, but are only implemented to pass all method calls on to the underlying stream without any modification. To see where filter streams are useful we'll now look at some specialized subclasses of `FilterInputStream` and `FilterOutputStream` and see what kind of convenience functionality they provide.

DataOutputStream & DataInputStream

`java.io.DataOutputStream` and `java.io.DataInputStream` are subclasses of `FilterOutputStream` and `FilterInputStream` respectively and provide some assistance when reading and writing data that comes in chunks larger than bytes. You can see the relationship of these classes to the filter and byte stream classes in the diagram below.

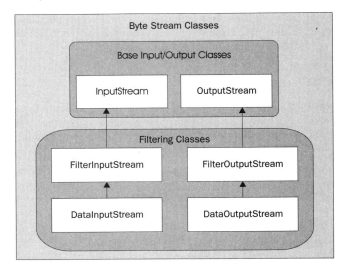

Let's look at a code example where we'll use a `DataOutputStream` to write primitive data to a file. We'll look at the file, and then write a program that uses a `DataInputStream` to take the file and turn the data back into its original primitive form.

```java
// DataOutputTest.java

import java.io.DataOutputStream;
import java.io.FileOutputStream;
import java.io.IOException;

public class DataOutputTest {

  public DataOutputTest() {}

  public static void main(String args[]) {
    FileOutputStream fileOut = null;
    DataOutputStream dataOut = null;

    try {
```

```
            fileOut = new FileOutputStream("datatest.txt");
            dataOut = new DataOutputStream(fileOut);

            dataOut.writeBoolean(true);
            dataOut.writeInt(98765);
            dataOut.writeFloat(1.5f);
            dataOut.writeLong(3210L);
            dataOut.writeDouble(25.65d);
            dataOut.flush();

            dataOut.close();
        } catch (IOException ioe) {
            ioe.printStackTrace();
        }
    }
}
```

Much of this file is straightforward, but we'll look at a few of the statements in detail. The first is the creation of the stream and the stream filter.

```
            fileOut = new FileOutputStream("datatest.txt");
            dataOut = new DataOutputStream(fileOut);
```

We use a constructor to the `FileOutputStream` class that accepts the name of the file we are going to create and write to. Next, we construct a `DataOutputStream` object passing in an `InputStream` (our newly created `FileOutputStream`) as an argument. Keep in mind that both `DataOutputStream` and `FileOutputStream` are both subclasses of `OutputStream`. We could call any `OutputStream` method on either of these references, but the real value lies in being able to call special methods on `dataOut` to have primitive data written to the underlying output stream.

```
            dataOut.writeBoolean(true);
            dataOut.writeInt(98765);
            dataOut.writeFloat(1.5f);
            dataOut.writeLong(3210L);
            dataOut.writeDouble(25.65d);
```

The next five statements all write a different primitive data value out to the `DataOutputStream`. There is a method available in `DataOutputStream` to write out every primitive Java type, as well as to write out `String` data. Writing out `String` data often involves conversion from 16-bit Unicode char values to 8-bit byte representations, and while it is possible to do this using `DataOutputStream`, we will discuss some more common methods, as well as character conversion, shortly.

```
            dataOut.flush();
            dataOut.close();
```

Finally we flush the `DataOutputStream` to make sure it has written the data we requested to the intended destination: a file in this case, but it could just as easily be a remote host. In most cases, calling the `close()` method will cause `OutputStream` subclasses to purge their data immediately, but it is good form to flush the stream when you are ready for the data to be passed on. Also note that we didn't explicitly close the original `FileInputStream`. Consulting the documentation for `FilterOutputStream` (the parent class of `DataOutputStream`) reveals that we're in luck. When we close `dataOut`, it automatically closes the underlying output stream.

To run the example, type the following from a command prompt in the directory where you have saved and compiled `DataOutputTest.java`:

C:\Beg_Java_Networking\Ch05>**java DataOutputTest**

When execution completes, you should see a file in the directory called `datatest.txt`. If we look at that file in a hex or regular text editor it looks like the following (hex is on the left, the text values are on the right):

```
 0: 01 00 01 81 CD 3F CO 00   00 00 00 00 00 00 00 0C   ...|I?A........
10: 8A 40 39 A6 66 66 66  66 66                         |@9:fffff
```

The data looks very different because we are using a text editor to read data that is raw binary data. When a text editor encounters this, it attempts to group the raw data into 8 or 16-bit segments (depending on your platform) and translate this into a character.

This look quite a bit different than the data we put in as primitives, but have faith, our data is in there. If you look at the size of the file, it should be 25 bytes. Given the types of data we output and their sizes, this seems more reasonable.

Data type	Size
boolean	8 bits
int	32 bits
float	32 bits
long	64 bits
double	64 bits
Total	**200 bits (25 bytes)**

Looking at this, perhaps we've built a little more assurance that the `DataOutputStream` has faithfully written out our data. To be sure, let's look at another program that reads in the data using the complementary class `DataInputStream`.

```java
// DataInputTest.java

import java.io.DataInputStream;
import java.io.FileInputStream;
import java.io.IOException;

public class DataInputTest {

  public DataInputTest() {}

  public static void main(String args[]) {
    FileInputStream fileIn = null;
    DataInputStream dataIn = null;

    try {
      fileIn = new FileInputStream("datatest.txt");
```

```
        dataIn = new DataInputStream(fileIn);

        System.out.println("boolean:" + dataIn.readBoolean());
        System.out.println("int:    " + dataIn.readInt());
        System.out.println("float:  " + dataIn.readFloat());
        System.out.println("long:   " + dataIn.readLong());
        System.out.println("double: " + dataIn.readDouble());

        dataIn.close();
    } catch (IOException ioe) {
        ioe.printStackTrace();
    }
  }
}
```

This program looks strikingly similar to our last. As we gain more exposure to I/O in this chapter and throughout the rest of the book, we'll see that many I/O operations are symmetric. Writing and reading differ by very few steps, and this helps make working with Java I/O a breeze. We begin by constructing our base stream and filter stream in a familiar fashion.

```
        fileIn = new FileInputStream("datatest.txt");
        dataIn = new DataInputStream(fileIn);
```

First, we specify the name of the file we just wrote out and then we pass the InputStream subclass to the DataInputStream Constructor. Again, the original stream could (and later in this book, will) be an input stream returned from a network socket. Next we read in the data record with the same types and order in which it was originally output.

```
        System.out.println("boolean:" + dataIn.readBoolean());
        System.out.println("int:    " + dataIn.readInt());
        System.out.println("float:  " + dataIn.readFloat());
        System.out.println("long:   " + dataIn.readLong());
        System.out.println("double: " + dataIn.readDouble());
```

Similar to how the DataOutputStream had methods available to write all primitive types, the DataInputStream provides the ability to read those same primitive types. When we invoke a read method, DataInputStream retrieves the appropriate number of bytes from the underlying input stream and converts them to the primitive type in a manner specified by the java.io.DataInput interface. The interface documentation is worded somewhat trickily, but suffice it to say, the behavior should be what you expect. The data being read in should be in the correct format, which it will if you wrote it using a DataOutputStream, and are reading it back in the same order. Other conditions make sense as well. If you only have two bytes left before you reach the end of the stream and you attempt to read an int (a 4-byte type), you will get an "end of file (or stream)" EOFException.

To see this example in action, type the following:

```
C:\Beg_Java_Networking\Ch05>java DataInputTest
boolean:true
int:     98765
float:   1.5
long:    3210
double: 25.65
```

By these two examples, we have seen that the DataOuputStream and DataInputStream may be used to read and write primitive data using lower-level streams. For a simple client-server application, a protocol could be defined that listed which primitive types would be sent back and forth and when. DataOutputStream and DataInputStream could then be employed to eliminate the hassle of converting primitive data to bytes and vice versa when reading and writing streams.

This could work well for simple scenarios, but Java provides much more powerful functionality such as the ability to decompose, send, and reconstruct entire objects at a time using its serialization facilities. Serialization takes a similar path of decomposing objects all the way down to bytes and then reconstructing them the same way using the actual class file itself as a template for breaking down and building up objects. Detailed coverage of serialization can be found in Chapter 15.

Buffered Filter Streams

An important set of streams that can help improve your efficiency of resource when doing I/O programming are the buffered filter streams. We discussed earlier how the low-level reading and writing of streams makes use of precious system resources. We also talked about how buffering, if provided by the underlying stream implementation, can help us queue up stream operations and make more efficient use of the streams. However, some implementations may not provide this buffering, and that's where a set of filter stream subclasses comes in handy. The java.io.BufferedInputStream and java.io.BufferedOutputStream allow us to wrap any InputStream or OutputStream with buffering support, including the ability to mark and reset an input stream, and to queue up writes to an output stream. An example of the BufferedOutputStream follows:

```java
// OutputBufferTest.java

import java.io.IOException;
import java.io.ByteArrayOutputStream;
import java.io.BufferedOutputStream;

public class OutputBufferTest {

  public OutputBufferTest() {
  }

  public static void main(String args[]) {
    try {
      ByteArrayOutputStream byteOut = new ByteArrayOutputStream();
      BufferedOutputStream bos = new BufferedOutputStream(byteOut);

      bos.write(new byte[255]);

      System.out.println("We've written 255 bytes and the byte stream shows:" +
                         byteOut.size() +" bytes");
      bos.flush();

      System.out.println("After flushing the buffer, the byte stream shows:" +
                         byteOut.size() +" bytes");

    } catch (IOException ioe) {
      ioe.printStackTrace();
    }
  }
}
```

Starting from the top with this example, we introduce something new, but simple:

```
ByteArrayOutputStream byteOut = new ByteArrayOutputStream();
BufferedOutputStream bos = new BufferedOutputStream(byteOut);
```

The first object we create is a `ByteArrayOutputStream`. We haven't discussed it previously, but its operation is straightforward. A `ByteArrayOutputStream` functions as an in-memory data sink. As we write bytes to it, the `ByteArrayOutputStream` grows dynamically, its growth being limited only by memory. Think of its functionality as being similar to an `ArrayList`, but for byte primitives. The stream is traditionally used as a mechanism to collect data as a stream to eventually be converted to a string. We use it here to illustrate the buffering effect of the `BufferedOutputStream`, which is the next object created. Next we add some data to the buffered stream.

```
bos.write(new byte[255]);
```

This statement constructs an array of 255 0-value bytes that are written to the buffer. In our next statement we determine if the bytes were written to the underlying `ByteArrayOutputStream`.

```
System.out.println("We've written 255 bytes and the byte stream shows:" +
                   byteOut.size() +" bytes");
```

The `size()` method of a `ByteArrayOutputStream` returns an `int` indicating the number of bytes that have been written to the stream.

```
bos.flush();

System.out.println("After flushing the buffer, the byte stream shows:" +
                   byteOut.size() +" bytes");

} catch (IOException ioe) {
ioe.printStackTrace();
}
```

Next we make a call to the `flush()` method of the buffer stream that tells it to release any bytes it has queued up and write them to the underlying stream. Our next statement uses the byte array stream size method again to show us how many bytes the stream contains after we flush the containing buffer. Finally, we catch any `IOExceptions`.

Type the following to run the program:

C:\Beg_Java_Networking\Ch05>**java OutputBufferTest**
We've written 255 bytes and the byte stream shows:0 bytes
After flushing the buffer, the byte stream shows:255 bytes

From the output we can see that even though we wrote 255 bytes to the buffered stream sitting on top of the byte array, the bytes didn't show up in the underlying array until we called the flush method on the buffer. In most situations we'll encounter, it is unlikely that we'll want to write single bytes at a time. We'll usually have more complex data that can take advantage of the efficiency provided by output buffering.

> It's worth noting that there's an additional constructor for the
> **BufferOutputStream** that lets you specify a buffer size other than the default of
> 512. You might make this size smaller if system memory is at a premium. Going to a
> native system resource for data repeatedly is more expensive than grabbing large
> chunks of data at a time, so you might use a larger buffer to minimize this type of
> access. The contract of the **BufferOutputStream** says that the data will be flushed
> to the underlying stream automatically when this buffer size is exceeded, or if the
> buffer stream is closed.

There may be other cases where it is advantageous for us to buffer incoming data, particularly when we need to mark a position in the stream and return to it for further processing. This doesn't happen so much in network I/O but it is used in applications like text parsing where you need to return to previously read bytes. In a normal, unbuffered situation, once you read bytes from a stream, unless you have saved them off somehow, you are unable to reread them. Let's look at input stream buffering in action.

```java
// InputBufferTest.java

import java.io.IOException;
import java.io.ByteArrayInputStream;
import java.io.BufferedInputStream;

public class InputBufferTest {

  public InputBufferTest() {}

  public static void main(String args[]) {
    try {
      byte[] b = new byte[] {
        (byte) -8, (byte) -4, (byte) -2, (byte) 0, (byte) 2, (byte) 4
      };
      ByteArrayInputStream byteIn = new ByteArrayInputStream(b);
      BufferedInputStream bis = new BufferedInputStream(byteIn);

      int readByte = bis.read();
      System.out.println("Reading the first byte: "
                  + ((readByte <= 0) ? readByte : (readByte - 256)));

      bis.mark(16);

      readByte = bis.read();
      System.out.println("Reading the second byte: "
                  + ((readByte <= 0) ? readByte : (readByte - 256)));

      readByte = bis.read();
      System.out.println("Reading the third byte: "
                  + ((readByte <= 0) ? readByte : (readByte - 256)));

      readByte = bis.read();
      System.out.println("Reading the fourth byte: "
                  + ((readByte <= 0) ? readByte : (readByte - 256)));

      bis.reset();

      readByte = bis.read();
      System.out.println("Reading the second byte again: "
                  + ((readByte <= 0) ? readByte : (readByte - 256)));
```

```
    } catch (IOException ioe) {
      ioe.printStackTrace();
    }
  }
}
```

In this example, we start by creating a `java.io.ByteArrayInputStream` that is populated from an array containing 6 bytes. We then wrap the array in a `BufferedInputStream`.

```
byte[] b = new byte[] {
   (byte) -8, (byte) -4, (byte) -2, (byte) 0, (byte) 2, (byte) 4
};
ByteArrayInputStream byteIn = new ByteArrayInputStream(b);
BufferedInputStream bis = new BufferedInputStream(byteIn);
```

`ByteArrayInputStream` is the counterpart to the `ByteArrayOutputStream` we worked with in the last example and acts as a data source. Once a byte input stream is initialized with a byte array, that data may be read from like any other stream. Next we read the first byte in via our buffered stream.

```
int readByte = bis.read();
System.out.println("Reading the first byte: "
               + ((readByte <= 0) ? readByte : (readByte - 256)));
```

Earlier in the chapter we discussed that since the parameterless `read()` method of `InputStream` returned an `int`, we had to do some maneuvering to convert the `int` into the proper `byte`. The third operator expands as follows:

```
If (readByte <= 0) {
    Concatenate readByte;
} else {
    Concatenate (readByte -256);
}
```

After we have read the first byte, the underlying byte array stream is positioned at the second byte, so we place a marker here and then continue to read the next three bytes. The parameter we pass to the `mark` method is an integer "read limit". If we read bytes in excess of the read limit, the buffer treats us as though we had never marked the stream. This allows the buffer to periodically purge buffered input bytes that have not been re-requested.

```
bis.mark(16);

readByte = bis.read();
System.out.println("Reading the second byte: "
               + ((readByte <= 0) ? readByte : (readByte - 256)));

readByte = bis.read();
System.out.println("Reading the third byte: "
               + ((readByte <= 0) ? readByte : (readByte - 256)));

readByte = bis.read();
System.out.println("Reading the fourth byte: "
               + ((readByte <= 0) ? readByte : (readByte - 256)));
```

After those bytes have been read, to demonstrate the power of the input buffer, we make a call to `reset()`, which tells the buffer, (not the underlying byte array stream), to jump back to the last location we marked.

```
        bis.reset();
```

This method will generate an IOException if the specified readlimit has been exceeded since the mark method was invoked, or if a mark was never set. Finally, we make a call to read() again to demonstrate that the mark() and reset() methods indeed worked, as well as catch any IOExceptions that may have been thrown.

```
        readByte = bis.read();
        System.out.println("Reading the second byte again: "
                        + ((readByte <= 0) ? readByte : (readByte - 256)));
    } catch (IOException ioe) {
        ioe.printStackTrace();
```

To see this example in action, type the following:

C:\Beg_Java_Networking\Ch05>**java InputBufferTest**
Reading the first byte: -8
Reading the second byte: -4
Reading the third byte: -2
Reading the fourth byte: 0
Reading the second byte again: -4

There is one other input stream class that provides buffer-like functionality.

PushbackInputStream

Another buffer-like wrapper class, the java.io.PushbackInputStream buffers data so we can effectively "push" the stream back and reread a series of previously read bytes, thus "pushing back" the stream. PushbackInput doesn't support the ability to mark and reset the stream. Its pushback features are often employed by parsers that search for tokens in a stream, such as a parser attempting to match regular expressions. This class is used quite a bit in conjunction with text file parsing. There might be interesting advanced applications for the parsing of data coming in via the network, such as an incoming XML request for data in the SOAP protocol.

As you can see the buffered streams provide elegant ways to filter and move around within stream data and make stream access more efficient. We will wrap up our discussion of the filter streams by giving a brief overview of some additional filter stream classes you may encounter when programming Java I/O.

Miscellaneous Filter Stream Classes

The following is a list of the remaining I/O filter stream classes along with a listing of their uses:

java.io.PrintStream

The PrintStream class is almost identical in operation to a DataOutputStream, with a few notable exceptions. Both classes provide the ability to write primitive data types and strings to underlying output streams, but the PrintStream does so without side effects. This means that if the PrintStream traps an IOException, it will not forward it to the caller, but will instead set an error flag, which can be checked programmatically. This is meant to support things like logging programs where you wouldn't want an attempt to log data (particularly error data) to generate additional exceptions. The other difference worth mentioning which is also console- and log-oriented is that PrintStream provides the ability to append newline characters after a write operation is performed. The System.out object is a PrintStream object which delivers output to the system console.

java.security.DigestInputStream and java.security.DigestOutputStream

You are probably most likely to encounter the digest filter streams when you are coding network programming that uses digesting to validate the integrity of a transmitted message. A message digest is basically a fingerprint that you can send along with your data to allow the recipient to verify that it wasn't altered in transit. The message digest is updated automatically as data is written to or read from the stream.

java.util.zip.DeflaterOutputStream and java.util.zip.InflaterInputStream

The deflater and inflater filter streams are used to compress and decompress data coming by in a stream. There are implementations available in the JDK for GZIP, ZIP, and JAR compression as:

- ❑   `java.util.zip.ZipInputStream`
- ❑   `java.util.zip.ZipOutputStream`
- ❑   `java.util.zip.GZIPInputStream`
- ❑   `java.util.zip.GZIPOutputStream`
- ❑   `java.util.jar.JARInputStream`
- ❑   `java.util.jar.JAROutputStream`

java.util.zip.CheckedInputStream and java.util.zip.CheckedOutputStream

The checked filter streams can be used in concert with the compression and decompression streams to allow you to calculate a checksum of the data as it's to be written to or read from a stream. This is a simple means of checking for errors in the stream. The JDK provides implementations to calculate both a `CRC32` and `Adler-32` checksum.

javax.swing.ProgressMonitorInputStream

This filter class is provided in the Swing windowing toolkit and is used to glean data about the progress of a stream being used. The progress information can then be relayed to a visual component such as a progress bar.

Now that we have seen the other filter streams available in the JDK, our last topic for streams will be covering the remaining stream classes.

Other Useful Streams

The JDK contains a couple more stream classes in the same vein as those we have already seen demonstrated in this chapter. They are divided among the object streams and the pipe streams. Object streams will be dealt with in greater depth in the chapters on serialization, RMI, and CORBA, and piped streams will be covered at the end of this chapter, but a quick note is in order.

Object streams

Object streams provide a convenient way to move an in-memory object as stream data. An object output stream can decompose an object into a series of bytes that can then be utilized like any other stream. An object input stream can take a decomposed series of bytes and reconstitute it back into a normal Java object. This decomposition and reconstruction is not unlike what occurs with a `DataOutputStream` and a `DataInputStream`. In the case of an `Object`, the object's class file is used as a template for tearing down and rebuilding the object.

Piped streams

Pipes provide a way to share data between threads by hooking an input stream being accessed in one thread, to an output stream being accessed in another. More coverage on pipe usage comes at the end of this chapter.

Character Streams: I/O Support for Text Data

Now that we've had a chance to see the types of I/O processing arrangements that are possible with the basic stream-based facilities of Java, it's time to turn our attention to a serious limitation of the stream processing classes. As agreed upon earlier, most programs need input or output to be useful. We also alluded in the section on streams, that quite often the data that needs to be shuttled in or out of the program is text in nature. Java uses the Unicode character set natively to hold text data as `Strings`. The Unicode character set is quite large and includes the symbols used for text in dozens upon dozens of languages worldwide. Everything seems fine until we realize that the Unicode defines an individual text character to be 16-bits (2-bytes) wide. Fortunately, Sun have designed the JDK to support just this kind of I/O.

Through the rest of the chapter, we will discuss the classes provided in the JDK to handle text-based input and output. We will begin with a brief discussion of characterset encodings and how they are used in Java to interact with the native operating system. The characterset encoding is nothing more than this mapping between the Java world and the native operating system world. Then we will discuss the text-oriented counterparts to the abstract `InputStream` and `OutputStream`: Reader and Writer. From there we will move on to some code examples that utilize concrete implementations of the `Reader` and `Writer` classes. We will finish up with a look at piped readers, writers and their stream counterparts.

> The same rules from the beginning of the chapter apply: because chances are you aren't a network programming expert yet, we'll use means other than network sockets to obtain base input and output. The only thing that's different for many of these examples is the underlying stream implementation. It can be a network socket just as easily as it can be a file!

Character Encoding in Java

Character encoding allows us to provide a map between a visual representation of a symbol and a number. Whenever we store data we take the intended symbol, perhaps an *M* keystroke, and convert it to an numeric encoding such as the ASCII code 77, or Unicode value 0x004D. Whenever we want to display that data, we simply perform the reverse mapping and provide the appropriate numeric output, perhaps displaying the symbol M on screen.

There are a number of encoding schemes in use in the world today and Java understands a large number of them. Java has to because the majority of the world's character encoding schemes are 8-bits or smaller per character, leaving only enough room for 256 characters. Internally, Java works on the 16-bit Unicode encoding, an international standard which, with its 65,536 character capacity, can hold most of the world's alphabets, symbols, and pictograms: everything from the Latin alphabet, to the Arabic alphabet, to Japanese Kanji.

Let's look at some of the more common encoding mechanisms in place today and their relationships.

ASCII

The American Standard Code For Information Interchange was ratified by the United States government in 1968. Available in a 7-bit encoding, the 127-character capacity of ASCII was enough to hold the English alphabet, some punctuation, and miscellaneous computer control characters, such as the 'Bell' (*Ctrl-G*). Eventually, ASCII was extended with another bit that enabled the addition of some extra Latin alphabet characters that provided coverage of many European languages.

ISO Latin-1

The International Standards Organization specified this character set in an effort to provide a character encoding that encompassed a wider cultural and linguistic radius. ISO Latin-1 supplied the diacriticals and punctuation that were used by a large percentage of the world population. To maintain compatibility with the widespread usage of ASCII encoding, the lower 127 character positions are the same in ISO Latin-1 as they are in ASCII.

Unicode

To further extend the uniformity of character encoding by specifying a character encoding for just about every character set in use around the world. Unicode was the result of collaboration by the members of the Unicode consortium. The very beginning of the Unicode character set (the first 256) characters contains the ISO Latin-1 character set.

UTF-8

UTF-8 is another encoding in use in Java primarily to store literal strings in class files. It is an extremely efficient way to store ASCII characters and can handle the entire Unicode set.

Encoding Choices

With all of these encoding choices (and many more in existence that we didn't cover) it's a wonder Java is able to handle them all. Since JDK 1.1, indicating the default character encoding is as simple as setting the −encoding flag and providing the correct encoding argument to the Java command line. You can find out what your default character encoding is by using the statement:

```
System.getProperty("file.encoding");
```

Once that has been done, Java knows how to take care of the encoding conversion, providing you access to read and write character data free of charge via its Reader and Writer I/O classes. This makes inter-platform, and cross-platform I/O a piece of cake when it comes to character encoding conversion.

Character Stream Foundation: Reader and Writer

If we think back to the structure and operation of the InputStream and OutputStream classes, we will have a very easy time understanding the basic java.io.Reader and java.io.Writer classes (also called the **character stream classes**). Basically, they provide a character-based view to stream data.

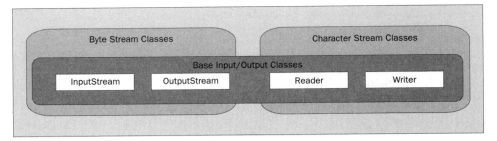

The InputStream and OutputStream interact with data in a stream one byte at a time and the Reader and Writer class see two bytes in a single read or write operation. It sounds relatively simple, and for the most part, it is. Although the mechanics are similar, there are some important feature enhancements in the character stream classes, namely:

❑ **More efficient reading and writing**: The byte stream classes are set up for reading a byte of data at a time unless external buffering is employed. However, the character stream classes are geared toward reading or writing a buffered amount of data each time without such a need for explicit buffering in our code.

❑ **More efficient synchronization**: The byte stream classes allow for very little internal control over the synchronization of streams, meaning there is a greater chance that multiple threads will contend for resources. The character stream classes are set up to allow for smaller critical sections of code, thereby reducing the possibility of contention for stream resources.

❑ **Support for the Unicode character set**: As has just been mentioned, the Unicode set is very rich and the character stream classes allow us to leverage this by performing any necessary conversions under the hood.

Let's look at the difference between Reader and InputStream method signatures that are available:

Reader

The java.io.Reader class provides read methods with the following signatures:

```
public int read() throws IOException
public int read(char[] cbuf) throws IOException
public abstract int read(char[] cbuf, int offset, int length) throws IOException
```

As you notice, these are similar to the read methods of InputStream, but utilize a character array instead of a byte array. Something else that may strike you is that the read(char[], int, int) method is abstract in a writer. This means any concrete subclass must provide an implementation for this method that attempts to get data in chunks. The default implementation of the other read methods is to utilize the subclass definition of this method as shown in the following:

```
public int read() throws IOException {
    char buf[] = new char[1];
    if (read(buf, 0, 1) == -1) {
        return -1;
    }
    return buf[1];
}
public int read(char[] buf) throws IOException {
    return read(buf, 0, buf.length);
}
```

Another substitution made in the `Reader` class is the method:

```
public boolean ready() throws IOException;
```

Similar to the `available()` method of `InputStream`, this method returns `true` if the next read call is guaranteed not to block the calling thread.

The last feature the `Reader` has that the `InputStream` does not is the ability to specify an object to use for synchronization. A complete discussion of threading is outside the scope of this text, but this essentially means you can require a person to have access to a particular object before they're able to execute certain parts of certain reader methods. This is of great importance in increasing the performance when doing I/O in a multithreaded environment such as a web or file server.

Writer

There are just a few changes from the `OutputStream` to the `writer` class as well. The main change occurs in the available write methods.

```
public abstract void write(char[] buf, int off, int len) throws IOException
public void write(char[] buf) throws IOException
public void write(int c) throws IOException
public void write(String s) throws IOException
public void write(String s, int off, int len) throws IOException
```

Like the `Reader` class, the `Writer` declares its multi-character `write()` method to be abstract, requiring subclasses to provide an implementation. The rest of the methods have default implementations which forward the method call to the `write(char[], int, int)` method. This includes the `write()` methods that take string arguments. A string is nothing more than an immutable array of character primitives so making this method call is quite easy to implement.

Special note should be given to the `write(int c)` method. This method takes an `int`, but will perform a conversion resulting in a `char` containing the lowest 16 bits of the original `int`.

The `Writer` also provides thread synchronization facilities similar to the `Reader` class. The `Writer` class provides a constructor that subclasses can use to set an object against which write operations should be synchronized.

Character Stream Subclasses

Since many of the character stream classes align themselves with the functionality provided by byte stream classes, we'll look at an overview of the `Reader` and `Writer` subclasses, highlighting the additional features the character stream subclasses provide. We'll start with three classes that don't have direct equivalents among the byte stream classes.

InputStreamReader

The `java.io.InputStreamReader` class allows you to take an existing `InputStream` of bytes and read it as a stream of characters. You can specify the character encoding used to translate the bytes to characters, or use the system default encoding. The `InputStreamReader` is constructed by specifying the `InputStream` to use and optionally the name of a character encoding. Consult the Javadocs for a complete list of accepted character encodings.

This class is a great way to provide character-reading functionality when you're only able to get an InputStream, such as with a network socket.

OutputStreamWriter

The java.io.OutputStreamWriter provides the inverse functionality of the InputStreamReader. It is also constructed passing an OutputStream instance and an optional character encoding. This is another great class to use when you're only able to get your hands on an OutputStream but would like to output text data. We'll use this class in our upcoming example.

StringReader

Much like we were able to use a ByteArrayInputStream to provide a sequence of bytes to another stream that required an InputStream, we can use a java.io.StringReader to allow us to access a piece of String data as a stream. This can be useful in a variety of applications from text parsing, to access of large data strings in an efficient stream-like fashion.

StringWriter

Comparable to a ByteArrayOutputStream, a StringWriter allows us to collect output character data that is made available in a string representation.

Now we'll cover the remaining classes that mirror functionality provided in byte stream classes.

- ❑ FilterReader: This class is similar in function to a FilterInputStream. It allows you to change the data while reading from its character form into something that may be more appropriate in your particular application.

- ❑ PushbackReader: This is a subclass of the FilterReader, the java.io.PushbackReader provides similar functionality to the PushbackInputStream. Instead of providing a back buffer of bytes, this class provides access to a back buffer of characters.

- ❑ FilterWriter: This complements FilterReader, and is counterpart to FilterOutputStream. FilterWriter allows data to be altered before it is sent to the underlying writer in character form.

- ❑ BufferedReader: This is similar in function to a BufferedInputStream. By constructing it around a reader, you can enable buffering, marking, and resetting in a Reader implementation that might otherwise not support those functions.

- ❑ LineNumberReader: This is a specialized buffered reader that allows a stream of data to be read a single line at a time. When using this class, every time you make a call to retrieve and entire line as a string, you can also make a call to retrieve the current line number. This is useful when reading text files where the line number is important, such as a source code file.

- ❑ BufferedWriter: This class runs parallel to the BufferedOutputStream. It provides the ability to define a custom buffer size for stream data being output to a Writer.

- ❑ FileReader: This is a specialized reader that is constructed to provide Reader access to a file as a stream source. This is similar in use to the FileInputStream.

- ❑ FileWriter: This is a specialized writer that is constructed to provide Writer access to a file as a sink. This is similar in use to the FileOutputStream.

- ❑ PrintWriter: This method provides the ability to output several different data types much like the PrintStream. Like PrintStream, the PrintWriter is meant to support logging, so it doesn't generate any IOExceptions that might disrupt our ability to generate output.

❏ CharArrayReader: This is similar to the ByteArrayInputStream and allows a sequence of characters to be used as a data source. This is like a StringReader, but the data originates as a mutable char array instead of a fixed string.

❏ CharArrayWriter: This method is similar to the ByteArrayOutputStream and allows a sequence of characters to be used as a data sink.

For quick reference, here is a table showing each character stream class and its corresponding byte stream class.

Character stream class	Byte stream class
java.io.Reader	java.io.InputStream
java.io.Writer	java.io.OutputStream
java.io.BufferedReader	java.io.BufferedInputStream
java.io.BufferedWriter	java.io.BufferedOutputStream
java.io.LineNumberReader	*none*
java.io.CharArrayReader	java.io.ByteArrayInputStream
java.io.CharArrayWriter	java.io.ByteArrayOutputStream
java.io.InputStreamReader	*none*
java.io.OutputStreamWriter	*none*
java.io.FileReader	java.io.FileInputStream
java.io.FileWriter	java.io.FileOutputStream
java.io.FilterReader	java.io.FilterInputStream
java.io.FilterWriter	java.io.FilterOutputStream
java.io.PushbackReader	java.io.PushbackInputStream
java.io.PrintWriter	java.io.PrintStream
java.io.StringReader	*none*
java.io.StringWriter	*none*

Now that we understand how similarly character streams and byte streams behave, let's try a character stream example.

Character Stream Example

This example will set up a very simple network server which listens to a port for an incoming connection and upon connecting, reads a text file and writes it to the network socket. We will ignore the relatively simple details of the network programming and instead focus on the I/O concepts being applied.

This example uses a simple text file (serverfile.txt) which is included with the code download for this chapter:

```
Hello World!

I read this document with a FileReader
and sent it to you with an OutputStreamWriter!

Aren't I/O and network programming great?
```

This is the file our network server will serve up whenever anyone connects. Now let's look at the actual program:

```java
// SimpleServerTest.java

import java.io.IOException;
import java.io.FileReader;
import java.io.OutputStreamWriter;
import java.net.ServerSocket;
import java.net.Socket;

public class SimpleServerTest {

  public SimpleServerTest() {}

  public static void main(String args[]) {
    try {
      ServerSocket server = new ServerSocket(5000);
      System.out.println("Listening for incoming connection...");
      Socket s = server.accept();

      char[] buf = new char[64];
      int charsRead = 0;
      FileReader fr = new FileReader("serverfile.txt");
      OutputStreamWriter ow = new OutputStreamWriter(s.getOutputStream());

      while ((charsRead = fr.read(buf)) > -1) {
        ow.write(buf, 0, charsRead);
      }

      ow.close();
      fr.close();

    } catch (IOException ioe) {
      ioe.printStackTrace();
    }
  }
}
```

As we begin to traverse the code, the first thing we encounter are some network-related import statements. We are importing the ServerSocket class which will allow us to register and listen for incoming network connections. We also import the Socket class to hold our socket connection once the server accepts an incoming connection. The IOException is a standard import since we don't intend to do anything fancy with exception handling. We'll use the FileReader to bring in the file we just created, and we'll use the OutputStreamWriter to send the file data to our socket output.

```
ServerSocket server = new ServerSocket(5000);
System.out.println("Listening for incoming connection...");
Socket s = server.accept();
```

The next thing we do is open up the `ServerSocket` to listen for incoming requests on port 5000. The port number is not significant, but should be higher than 1023 so it is not reserved for system use. In the following statement we tell the server to begin listening for connection. This method will stall (or block) until an incoming connection request is received. Once the request is received, the active network `Socket` object is returned.

```
char[] buf = new char[64];
int charsRead = 0;
```

Once a connection has come through and the method returns a socket, we begin preparing to read our file. First we allocate a read buffer, as well as an `int` variable to hold the number of characters actually returned from a read operation.

```
FileReader fr = new FileReader("serverfile.txt");
OutputStreamWriter ow = new OutputStreamWriter(s.getOutputStream());
```

Next we create a new `FileReader` object by passing the constructor the name of the file we want to read. If we passed the name of a file that didn't exist, this constructor would throw a `FileNotFoundException`. We then instantiate an `OutputStreamWriter` passing it the `OutputStream` we retrieved from the network socket.

```
while ((charsRead = fr.read(buf)) > -1) {
  ow.write(buf, 0, charsRead);
}
```

Like our byte stream example, our next task is to begin filling our buffer with characters we're reading from the file, and then turning around and writing those via our `OutputStreamWriter`.

```
ow.close();
fr.close();

} catch (IOException ioe) {
  ioe.printStackTrace();
```

When we're all done, we close our `Reader` and `Writer` to free up any system resources that we were using and are now finished with.

To get this example running, you must ensure that `SimpleServerTest.java` is in the same directory as your `serverfile.txt` file.

C:\Beg_Java_Networking\Ch05>**java SimpleServerTest**
Listening for incoming connection...

This output indicates that your example is ready to receive an incoming connection. To complete the test of this program, use your favorite Telnet utility and telnet to `localhost` port 5000. A Telnet utility can be accessed in Windows 9x/NT/2000 by typing:

C:\Beg_Java_Networking\Ch05>**telnet localhost 5000**

Upon executing this command, you should see the following output:

Hello World!

I read this document with a FileReader and sent it to you with an
OutputStreamWriter!

Aren't I/O and network programming great?

Connection to host lost.

This indicates your example has worked.

Hooking Things Up with Pipes

The only subject left to cover to end this review of Java I/O programming is the use of pipes. Conceptually, piping is a way to join an input to an output so that data, be it bytes or characters, flows from one source all the way through perhaps multiple pipes to the destination sink. The pipe classes are essentially FIFO buffers that allow a sequence of data to be pushed into one end and then retrieved from the other.

In other words, a piped output connected with a piped input allows one thread to write bytes to an output and have those bytes transferred and available to another thread as an input via the piped input.

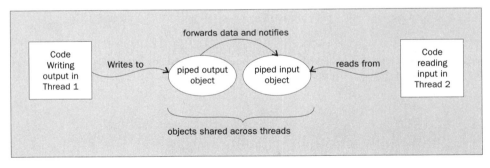

It is recommended that piped streams be used only where separate threads will access them to add input and read output. Ignoring this guideline and accessing both from a single thread can lead to deadlock situations.

Let's look at the piped stream implementations in the java.io package.

java.io.PipedOutputStream

PipedOutputStream is the OutputStream component of a pipe that acts as a byte sink to a thread. When this object is constructed we have the option to attach a sink, which will receive notification whenever we have written bytes to this stream. When a PipedInputStream is connected to this PipedOutputStream, writing bytes, calling the flush() method will alert the PipedInputStream that there are new bytes that can be read.

If we choose not to attached a `PipedInputStream` during object construction, we have the option to do so later by invoking the following method:

```
public void connect(PipedInputStream sink) throws IOException
```

Once a `PipedOutputStream` is in place, it is written to just as you would with a normal `OutputStream`. The `PipedInputStream` takes care of communicating with the attached `PipedInputStream` to make it aware of any new data you have output.

java.io.PipedInputStream

`PipedInputStream` is the `InputStream` component of a pipe that acts as a byte source to a thread. When we construct this object, we can connect it immediately to a `PipedOutputStream`, or we can wait and call the following method to attach a `PipedInputStream`:

```
public void connect(PipedOutputStream source) throws IOException
```

You may also notice another method in the `PipedInputStream` called `receive(int i)`. This method is used by the attached `PipedOutputStream` to transmit bytes into the `PipedInputStream` buffer. It is not intended to be called explicitly by any code other than the `PipedOutputStream`.

Once you have a `PipedInputStream` constructed and connected to a `PipedOutputStream`, you interact with it in the same way you would with a normal `InputStream`. The availability of bytes for reading is based on the bytes being written by another thread to the attached `PipedOutputStream`.

Finally there are two more methods for dealing with characters:

❑   `java.io.PipedReader`: As you probably guessed, the `PipedReader` class provides identical functionality to the `PipedInputStream` class, but acts as a connect source for characters instead of bytes

❑   `java.io.PipedWriter`: The `PipedWriter` class operates parallel to the `PipedOutputStream`, acting as a connected sink for characters instead of bytes

Summary

In this chapter we have taken a comprehensive look at the I/O facilities Java provides that will assist you in developing network programming. We began by exploring the basic metaphors that Java I/O is based upon:

- ❑ Data flows from a source
- ❑ Data flows to a sink
- ❑ Data flows via a stream

After this conceptual overview we learned that input and output in Java can be accomplished at two basic levels of granularity:

- ❑ Byte-based streams
- ❑ Character-based (or text-based) streams

Both of these stream views are implemented by classes in the `java.io` package with parallel methods; some taking bytes, some taking characters.

We learned that the Java I/O classes make use of a rich inheritance hierarchy to provide building block functionality for more complicated I/O classes that can be used to get complex data structures into and out of streams.

Finally, threads can share stream data via piping classes.

Hopefully by now you feel comfortable around the Java I/O classes and will be able to leverage your new skills as you apply them to the world of network I/O programming.

Threads

To take advantage of the powerful networking features of the Java programming language, it's important to have a good understanding of threads and multithreaded programming. When we use threads, our program can actually be executing at more than one point at the same time. For example, it might be reading from an I/O stream, as we saw previously, while simultaneously responding to user input and updating a display. While it's possible to do these things without multiple threads, the code to do it tends to be very convoluted with event handling for the various activities scattered throughout the program.

Java is one of the few common programming languages to include facilities for multithreading as language primitives. Classes and interfaces for creating threads are part of the core `java.lang` package and the class `java.lang.Object`, from which all Java objects descend, has methods to support multithreaded programming.

With many threads of execution going at once, building correct multithreaded programs can be enormously complex and poorly written multithreaded programs are common. Buggy multithreaded programs tend to fail unpredictably or when under heavy load, or slow down a program.

Debugging a multithreaded program is difficult because traditional debugging tools can't show how threads interact, so it's important to keep the fundamental principles of multithreaded programming in mind when writing the program.

In this chapter, we'll look at the great capabilities and potential complexity of multithreaded programming in Java.

Overview

Before we get into the details of writing multithreaded programs in Java, let's look at the implications of using threads in our program. Most modern operating systems can run multiple **processes** at the same time. That means we might be running our e-mail client, editor, and compiler all at once. Modern desktop operating systems enforce a separation between the memory areas used by these programs, so a bug in the compiler can't crash the editor and the e-mail client can't break the compiler. Each of these separate memory areas is called an **address space**.

In the old days, before operating systems divided programs into separate address spaces, it was common for a bug-ridden application to bring down the whole system by destroying some critical shared data. Separating the programs from each other and the operating system increases the reliability of the system tremendously.

The operating system is responsible for scheduling the processes and managing the address space for each one. Switching between processes is called **context-switching** and requires the operating system to save the whole state of the running process and load the state of another process before resuming the original process. If we are talking about a computer with more than one processor, the operating system could even schedule them to run simultaneously. Because the processes are completely independent, the system as a whole is reliable even if the individual programs are not.

A process contains one or more independent units of execution called **threads**. Threads are similar to processes in that they are independent flows of control, but they are also different in important ways:

❑ The threads within a process run within a single address space (the address space of the process), so the threads operate using the same body of code and the same body of data.

❑ Because the threads are operating within a single process, the Java Virtual Machine rather than the operating system can do the thread scheduling. This can make context-switching much more efficient.

The figure below shows the relationships between the operating system, processes, and threads. To reiterate: the operating system can run any number of processes and each process can contain any number of threads.

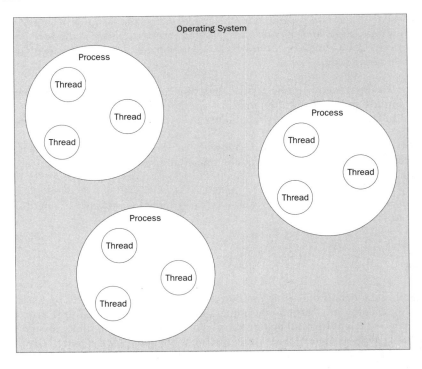

Because they inhabit separate address spaces, processes can only communicate with one another by using operating system services like files or network connections. Threads, because they inhabit the same address space, share the same data and can communicate with one another much more conveniently. There is no need to write an object to a file or transmit data on the network to get data from one thread to another; they can see the same object.

This is a blessing and a curse. While threads can easily communicate through shared objects, they also need to be aware that other threads may change those objects while they are using them. For example, take this simple operation:

```
if (o != null) {
  x = o.someField;
}
```

This will never throw a `NullPointerException` in a single-threaded program. However, what happens if there is another thread with this line of code?

```
o = null;
```

We might think that we're still safe because we checked for `null` before referencing `o.someField`. The problem comes when the other thread sets `o` to `null` after the check and before the reference. Even if the check is right before the call, it's still possible for the other thread to sneak in and set the variable to `null`. The program might run for days and then throw a `NullPointerException`. We look at the code and think "I checked it for `null`. It *can't* be `null`." But it is – the other thread just happened to catch it at the wrong time.

How often will this happen? Not very often, but if it's possible, it *will* happen and probably at the worst time. These timing-dependent bugs are the hardest part of writing multithreaded programs. Fortunately, Java provides some robust mechanisms for dealing with these types of problems. We'll examine these mechanisms later in this chapter.

Using Threads for Networking

Why are threads important for networking? Network applications usually have to deal with many streams of data. A server may have to service several clients at once or a client might need to pull data from several servers. Assigning a thread to each of these data streams is a convenient and robust way to make sure each I/O channel is serviced.

At the highest level, a network server has this function:

```
start:
wait for a request
create a thread to service the request
goto start
```

The server can treat each request as an independent event that is not affected by other requests. This allows the server to make the most efficient use of the CPU because at any one time, most of the threads will be waiting for I/O activity. The others don't need to wait; they can proceed when they are ready.

Thread Mechanics

Now we will look at how to create and use threads in Java programs. As I mentioned before, the Java programming language includes many features that make creating multithreaded programs possible. We will look at the classes and interfaces used to control threads and discuss the issues associated with sharing state amongst threads.

Writing Thread Classes

There are two ways to implement a class that is to run as a separate thread.

❑   Extend the `java.lang.Thread` class

❑   Create a class that implements the `java.lang.Runnable` interface and associate an instance of it with an instance of `java.lang.Thread`

Subclassing `java.lang.Thread` is slightly more convenient, but because Java does not support multiple inheritance, sometimes implementing `java.lang.Runnable` is the only option available. We'll look at both of these techniques below.

The java.lang.Thread Class

The most important method of the `Thread` class is the `run()` method. The `run()` method is the method that the new thread will execute, so when we subclass `java.lang.Thread`, we must override `run()` with the code that the new thread should execute, as the default implementation of this method does nothing in the `Thread` class.

The example below shows a simple class that inherits `java.lang.Thread` and overrides the `run()` method. When the Java Virtual Machine starts a program, it creates one thread and uses it to call the `main()` method of the program's main class. This example's `main()` method creates a new thread which continuously prints T (for "thread"). After starting the other thread, the main thread continues and continuously prints M (for "main"). These two threads continue printing T or M until the program stops.

```
//PrintThread.java

public class PrintThread extends Thread {

  public static void main(String[] args) {
    PrintThread p = new PrintThread();
    p.start();
    for (; ; ) {
      System.out.print("M");
    }
  }
  public void run() {
    for (; ; ) {
      System.out.print("T");
    }
  }
}
```

To escape from this program, hit *Ctrl-C*. The output should resemble something like the following:

C:\Beg_Java_Networking\Ch06>**javac PrintThread.java**

C:\Beg_Java_Networking\Ch06>**java PrintThread**
MMMMMMMMMMMTTTTTTTTTTTTTTTTTTTMMMMMMMMMMMMMMMMMTTTTTTTTTTTTTTTTTTTTTT
TTTTTTTTTTTTTTTTTTMMMMMMMMMMMMMMMMMMMMMMMMMMMTTTTTTTTTTTTTTTTTTTTTTT
TTTTTTTTTTTTTTTTTTTTMMMMMMMMMMMMMMMMMMMMMM

The figure below shows how the two threads relate over time with the start of execution at the top. The thread running `main()` initializes the new thread and starts it. From then on, there are two independent flows of control in the program, each one trying to print its character as fast as it can.

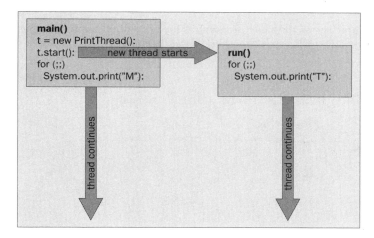

The outputs of these two threads are interleaved depending on which thread is scheduled. Both of these threads are always **schedulable**. That is, either thread, if given the chance to run, would have some work to do. Threads are not schedulable if they are waiting for something like an I/O stream, user input, or another thread. Threads that are not schedulable are called **blocked** threads.

If we run the example a few times, the output is likely to be different each time. Here's the output from a few sample runs:

C:\Beg_Java_Networking\Ch06> **java PrintThread**
MMMMMMMMMMTTTTTTTTTTTTTTTTTTTTTMMMMMMMMMMMMMMMMMTTTTTTTTTTTTTTTTTTTTTT
TTTTTTTTTTTTTTTTTTMMMMMMMMMMMMMMMMMMMMMMMMMMMMMTTTTTTTTTTTTTTTTTTTTTT
TTTTTTTTTTTTTTTTTTTTMMMMMMMMMMMMMMMMMMMM
C:\Beg_Java_Networking\Ch06> **java PrintThread**
MMMMMMTTTTTTTTTTTTTTTTTTTTTTTTTTTTTTTTTTMMMMMMTTTTTTTTTTTTTTTTTMMMMMMTTT
TTTTTTTTTTTTTTTTTTTTTTTTTTTMMMMMMMMMMMMMM
C:\Beg_Java_Networking\Ch06> **java PrintThread**
TTTTTTTTTTTTTTTTTTTTMMMMMMMMMMMMMMMMMMMMMMMMMTTTTTTTTTTTTTTTTTTTTTTTTTTTTT
TTTTTTTMMMMMMMMMMMMMMMMMMMMMMMMMMMMMMMMMMMMMMMMMMMMMTTTTTTTTT
TTTTTTTTTTTTTTTTTTTTT
C:\Beg_Java_Networking\Ch06> **java PrintThread**
TTTTMMMMMMMMMMMMMMMMMMMMMMTTTTTTTTTTTTTTTTTTTTTTTTTTTTTTTTTTTTTTTTTT
TTTTTTTTTTTTTTTTTTTTTTTTMMMMMMMMMMMMMMMMMMMMTTTTTTTTT

This example shows that we can't predict how the threads will be scheduled. We must assume that any schedulable thread can be executing at any time. This is critical to keep in mind when writing multithreaded code. Every place where one thread interacts with another is a potential problem, and the exact interleaving of the threads' operations can't be guaranteed.

The java.lang.Runnable Interface

Often the class we want to run as a thread class will already extend another class so the method described above will not work. When this happens, we can implement the java.lang.Runnable interface rather than extending the java.lang.Thread class. Then we simply need to create a thread to run the class. The Thread class has several constructors, some of which take a java.lang.Runnable as argument. When a thread that is bound to a Runnable is started, it calls the Runnable object's run() method.

The following example shows the same program as the preceding example, implementing the Runnable interface rather than extending the Thread class.

```java
//PrintRunnableThread.java

public class PrintRunnableThread implements Runnable {

  public static void main(String[] args) {
    Thread t = new Thread(new PrintRunnableThread());
    t.start();
    for (; ; ) {
      System.out.print("M");
    }
  }
  public void run() {
    for (; ; ) {
      System.out.print("T");
    }
  }
}
```

The output of this example is just as unpredictable as the previous example.

Daemon Threads

When a Java program has more than one thread and one of those threads finishes, the JVM needs a way to know whether the whole program is finished or whether it should continue with the other threads. Often the other threads are simply servicing the main thread and when main() finishes the program is done. Other times, the program should continue until all of the threads exit. Daemon threads let the programmer express this distinction.

The JVM exits when either:

1. The exit() method of the java.lang.Runtime class is called *or*

2. All of the remaining threads are daemon threads

The JVM starts with one non-daemon thread that executes the `main()` function of the program's main class. New threads are not by default daemon threads unless the creating thread is a daemon, so the JVM will continue until they terminate. The `java.lang.Thread` class has a method called `setDaemon(boolean)` that controls whether a thread is a daemon thread or not. `setDaemon()` must be called before the thread is started, so a thread cannot be turned into a daemon thread after it starts.

This example is like the example above, except that the main thread prints 30 Ms and then finishes.

```
//PrintDaemon.java

public class PrintDaemon extends Thread {

  public static void main(String[] args) {
    PrintDaemon p = new PrintDaemon();

    p.start();
    // Just print M 30 times, then stop
    for (int i=0; i<30; i++)
      System.out.print("M");

    // After the 30 Ms are printed, main returns
  }

  public void run() {
    // The thread will print Ts as long as it exists
    for (;;)
      System.out.print("T");
  }
}
```

However, just because `main()` finished, this doesn't mean the JVM will exit. There is still a non-daemon thread running, so the output looks like this:

C:\Beg_Java_Networking\Ch06>**java PrintDaemon.java**

C:\Beg_Java_Networking\Ch06>**java PrintDaemon**
MMMMMMMMMMMMMMMTTTTTTTTTTTTTTTTTTTTTTTTTTTTTTTTTTTTTTTTTTTTTTTTTTTTTTMMMM
MMMMMMMMMMMMTTTTTTTTTTTTTTTTTTTTTTTTTTTTTTTTTTTTTTTTTTTTTTTTTTTTTTTTTTTTTT
TTTTTTTTTTTTTTTTTTTTTTTTTTTTTTTTTTTTTTTTTTTTTTTTTTTTTTTTTTTTTTTTTTTTTTTTTT
TTTTTTTTTTTTTTTTTTTTTTTTTTTTTTTTTTTTTTTTTTTTTTTTTTTTTTTTTTTTTTTTTTTTTTTTTT
TTTTTTTTTTTTTTTTTTTTTTTTTTTTTTTTTTTTTTTTTTTT

This will continue to run until we stop it with *Ctrl-C*. If we change the example to make the new thread a daemon thread, the presence of the new thread will not prevent the JVM from exiting.

```
//PrintDaemon2.java

public class PrintDaemon2 extends Thread {

  public static void main(String[] args) {
    PrintDaemon2 p = new PrintDaemon2();
    p.setDaemon(true);
    p.start();
```

```
      // Just print M 30 times, then stop
      for (int i=0; i<30; i++)
        System.out.print("M");

      // After the 30 Ms are printed, main returns
    }

  public void run() {
    // The thread will print Ts as long as it exists
    for (;;)
      System.out.print("T");
  }
}
```

Now when `main()` finishes, the presence of the daemon thread will not keep the JVM from exiting. After running the program four times the output looked like this:

C:\Beg_Java_Networking\Ch06>**java PrintDaemon2.java**

C:\Beg_Java_Networking\Ch06>**java PrintDaemon2**
MMMMMMMMMMMMMMMMMMMMMMMMMMMMMMTTTTTTTTTTTTTTTTTTTTTTTTTTTTTTTTTTT
TTTTTTTTTTTTTTTTTTTTTTTTTTTTTTTTTTTTTTTTTTTTTTTTTTTTTTTTTT
C:\Beg_Java_Networking\Ch06>**java PrintDaemon2**
MMMMMMMMMMTTTTTTTTTTTTTTTTTTTTTTTTTTTTTTTTTTTTMMMMMMMMMMMMMMMMMMMMMMMTTT
TTTTTTTTTTTTTTTTTTTTTTTTTTTTTTTTTTTTTTTTTTTTTTTTTTTTTTTTTTTTTTTTTTT
C:\Beg_Java_Networking\Ch06>**java PrintDaemon2**
TTTTTTTTMMMMMMMMMMMMMMMMMMMMMMMMMMMMMMMMMTTTTTTTTTTTTTTTTTTTTTTTTT
TTTTTTTTTTTTTTTT
C:\Beg_Java_Networking\Ch06>**java PrintDaemon2**
MMMMMMMMMMMMMMMTTTTTTTTTTTTTTTTTTTTTTMMMMMMMMMMMMMMMMTTTTTTTTTTTTTTT
TTTTTTTTTTTTTT

As we can see, once the Ms are printed, the JVM exits, and the thread printing T is stopped. Again, we see that the interactions between the threads are slightly different each time. In each case, the thread printing the Ts continues for a few more iterations after the Ms stop and before the JVM exits.

It's important to be aware that when daemon threads are killed by the exiting JVM, they have no opportunity to clean up after themselves. Any thread that will be carrying out operations like writing important files should probably not be a daemon thread.

Handling Threads

Now that we've seen how to create and start threads, let's look at how to control running threads. We'll see that the `java.lang.Thread` class has capabilities for pausing, naming, and interrogating running threads.

The Thread.sleep() Methods

The `java.lang.Thread` class includes several static methods that are useful when dealing with threads. One of these is the `sleep()` method, which causes the current thread to pause its execution. The `sleep()` method comes in two forms:

❑   `sleep(long millisecs)` – This version of the method causes the current thread to pause for the specified number of milliseconds

❑   sleep(long millisecs, int nanosecs) – This version of the method causes the
current thread to pause for the specified number of milliseconds plus the specified number of
nanoseconds. The number of nanoseconds must be in the range 0 to 999999 or an
IllegalArgumentException is thrown.

The duration of time that these methods actually suspend execution of the thread is not as exact as the
method signatures might suggest. They suspend the thread for the specified time (subject to the
resolution of the system clock) and then make it schedulable. It may not be scheduled right away, so the
actual time the thread is suspended will be a little greater than the specified sleep time.

A thread can be interrupted while it is sleeping, so code that calls sleep() must be ready to catch a
java.lang.InterruptedException. The following example shows how the Thread.sleep()
method can be used to suspend the execution of a thread:

```
//PrintSleep.java

public class PrintSleep {

  public static void main(String[] args) {
    long startSleepTime = System.currentTimeMillis();
    try {
      Thread.sleep(5000);    // sleep for 5 seconds (5000 milliseconds)
    } catch (InterruptedException ie) {
      System.out.println("Oh no! I was interrupted!");
    }
    long endSleepTime = System.currentTimeMillis();
    System.out.println("Finished sleeping. Slept for "
                       + (endSleepTime - startSleepTime) + " milliseconds");
  }
}
```

When I run this program a few times on my own machine, it takes about five seconds and then prints
that it slept for 5007 or 5008 milliseconds.

C:\Beg_Java_Networking\Ch06>**javac PrintSleep.java**

C:\Beg_Java_Networking\Ch06>**javac PrintSleep**
Finished sleeping. Slept for 5007 milliseconds.

This will vary on different machines, obviously. As we can see, the Thread.sleep() functions
are handy if we need a thread to wait a while before proceeding, but they can't be used for high-
precision timing.

The Thread.yield() method can be used to allow other threads the opportunity to execute. Usually
the Java thread scheduler does fine without threads explicitly yielding, but occasionally an unusually
intensive operation can monopolize the CPU. In these cases, Thread.yield() can be added to the
intense operation to encourage the scheduler to run other threads.

Naming Threads

When we create a thread, we can give it a name. A meaningful name can be very helpful for debugging a multithreaded application. The Thread class can take various arguments in its constructor and one of the arguments can be a String that will be the name of the new thread. If we don't supply a name, a new unique name will be assigned. The previous example didn't give the thread a name, so a name was generated for it automatically. The example could be changed to assign a name to the thread by creating the thread using this code:

```
Thread t = new Thread(new PrintRunnableThread(), "T-Printer");
```

This code will give the name T-Printer to the new thread.

Manipulating Running Threads

The java.lang.Thread class also has static methods for listing the set of current threads and getting information about the thread that is currently executing. The method Thread.activeCount() returns the number of active threads; the Thread.enumerate() method fills an array with the currently active threads. We'll see how these are used in the next example.

Sometimes it's important to know something about the thread that is currently executing. The Thread class has static methods for this, too. The Thread.currentThread() method returns the current thread, which could be used to get the name of the current thread, for example. Thread.dumpStack() is useful for debugging. It prints the current method and all of the calling methods to the console stream.

The next example shows how to use the static methods of the Thread class to manipulate threads. It creates two threads, named First Thread and Second Thread, starts them, and then uses the Thread static methods to look at them.

```java
//PrintStatic.java

public class PrintStatic implements Runnable {

  public static void main(String[] args) {

    // Create two threads
    Thread t1 = new Thread(new PrintStatic(), "First Thread");
    t1.start();
    Thread t2 = new Thread(new PrintStatic(), "Second Thread");
    t2.start();

    // Now, use the Thread static methods to look at these threads.
    int numThreads = Thread.activeCount();
    System.out.println("The number of threads is: " + numThreads);
    Thread[] threads = new Thread[numThreads];
    Thread.enumerate(threads);
    for (int i = 0; i < threads.length; i++) {
      System.out.println("  Thread named: " + threads[i].getName());
    }
  }

  public void run() {
```

```
    try {
      Thread.sleep(1000);    // wait a second...
    } catch (InterruptedException ie) {
      System.out.println("Oh no! I was interrupted!");
    }

    // Call a method that will print the chain of method calls.
    aMethod();
  }

  private void aMethod() {
    Thread.dumpStack();
  }
}
```

This class implements the `Runnable` interface rather than extending the `Thread` class. The `main()` method creates two new instances of the `Runnable`, and assigns them each to a thread. These threads each `sleep()` for a second and then print the list of method calls that led to them being invoked.

This is what the output looks like:

C:\Beg_Java_Networking\Ch06>**javac PrintStatic.java**

C:\Beg_Java_Networking\Ch06>**java PrintStatic**
The number of threads is: 3
 Thread named: main
 Thread named: First Thread
 Thread named: Second Thread
java.lang.Exception: Stack trace
    at java.lang.Thread.dumpStack(Thread.java:993)
    at PrintStatic.aMethod(PrintStatic.java:38)
    at PrintStatic.run(PrintStatic.java:31)
    at java.lang.Thread.run(Thread.java:484)
java.lang.Exception: Stack trace
    at java.lang.Thread.dumpStack(Thread.java:993)
    at PrintStatic.aMethod(PrintStatic.java:38)
    at PrintStatic.run(PrintStatic.java:31)
    at java.lang.Thread.run(Thread.java:484)

Notice that we see a total of three threads. In addition to the two we created, there is another one called main. This is the thread that calls `public static void main()` to start the program. Next, after a short pause, each thread prints the sequence of method calls that led up to its invocation. The trace includes the file name and line number of each call, so it's very useful for debugging.

Thread Priorities

We saw before how threads can be scheduled in an unpredictable order. By assigning priorities to threads, the programmer can exercise some control over the scheduling of the threads.

Thread priorities are integers in the range `Thread.MIN_PRIORITY` to `Thread.MAX_PRIORITY`. Schedulable threads with higher priority tend to be scheduled before those with lower priority, but the exact behavior varies between JVMs. Some will always run a higher priority thread before a lower one; some will just tend to run the higher priority thread first. The default priority for a new thread is the same as the thread in which it was created.

The following example shows how to set the priority of the thread created in the previous example. Here we set it to the maximum possible priority.

```
//PrintPriority.java

public class PrintPriority extends Thread {

  public static void main(String[] args) {
    PrintPriority t = new PrintPriority();
    t.setPriority(Thread.MAX_PRIORITY);
    t.start();
    for (; ; ) {
      System.out.print("M");
    }
  }
  public void run() {
    for (; ; ) {
      System.out.print("T");
    }
  }
}
```

This is an example of the output. As before, it is different with each run. Note that the higher priority thread is run more than the lower priority thread, but the lower priority thread still does get some time to execute. In this case, run on a Windows JVM, the thread priorities are used by the JVM to proportion the execution time, but the higher priority thread does not always get preference.

C:\Beg_Java_Networking\Ch06>**javac PrintPriority.java**

C:\Beg_Java_Networking\Ch06>**java PrintPriority**
TTTTTTTTTTTTTTTTTTTTTTTTTMTTTTTTTTTTTTTTTTTTTTTTTTTTMTTTTTTTTTTTTTTTTTTTTTTTTMTTT
...

However, when we run the same code on a Linux JVM, no Ms are printed at all. The thread printing T is the only thread scheduled. Using thread priorities to control the scheduling of threads can make code less portable and is best avoided. We'll look at some better ways to control threads later in this chapter.

The ThreadGroup Class

The java.lang.ThreadGroup class represents a set of threads. It can also contain other ThreadGroups resulting in a tree of ThreadGroups. Every ThreadGroup has a parent except the first ThreadGroup, which is created by the Java Virtual Machine when it starts. Every thread belongs to a ThreadGroup and the thread's getThreadGroup() method can be used to find that group. When a thread is created, it can be assigned to a ThreadGroup by passing the ThreadGroup to the Thread constructor. If no ThreadGroup is passed to the Thread constructor, the new thread is placed in the same group as the thread that created it.

Several of the characteristics of a thread can also be applied to a ThreadGroup. A ThreadGroup has a maximum priority which can be set and retrieved with setMaxPriority() and getMaxPriority(), respectively. No thread in the thread group can be given a priority higher than the maximum priority of the ThreadGroup. A ThreadGroup can be a daemon ThreadGroup. A daemon ThreadGroup is automatically destroyed when its last thread finishes or its last subgroup is destroyed.

This example shows how thread groups are used. It creates a new `ThreadGroup` and sets its maximum priority to `Thread.NORM_PRIORITY`. So, no threads in that group can have a higher priority. Then the example creates two threads in the new thread group. Finally, it calls the `ThreadGroup`'s `list()` method which prints debugging information.

```java
//PrintGroup.java

public class PrintGroup implements Runnable {

  public void run() {}

  public static void main(String[] args) {

    // Create a new thread group and put a couple of threads in it.
    ThreadGroup tg = new ThreadGroup("New Group");
    tg.setMaxPriority(Thread.NORM_PRIORITY);
    Thread t1 = new Thread(tg, new PrintGroup(), "Thread 1");
    Thread t2 = new Thread(tg, new PrintGroup(), "Thread 2");

    // Find the top-level parent group
    // (the one with a null parent)
    ThreadGroup parent = Thread.currentThread().getThreadGroup();
    while (parent.getParent() != null) {
      parent = parent.getParent();
    }

    // This method prints the contents of the group and
    // all sub-groups.
    parent.list();

  }
}
```

The output of this program looks like this:

```
C:\Beg_Java_Networking\Ch06>javac PrintGroup.java

C:\Beg_Java_Networking\Ch06>java PrintGroup
java.lang.ThreadGroup[name=system,maxpri=10]
    Thread[Reference Handler,10,system]
    Thread[Finalizer,8,system]
    Thread[Signal Dispatcher,10,system]
    java.lang.ThreadGroup[name=main,maxpri=10]
        Thread[main,5,main]
        java.lang.ThreadGroup[name=New Group,maxpri=5]
            Thread[Thread 1,5,New Group]
            Thread[Thread 2,5,New Group]
```

The `list()` method shows the structure and content of the `ThreadGroup` tree. The top-level group is named `system` and has a maximum priority of 10 (`Thread.MAX_PRIORITY`). There are three threads in this group – `Reference Handler` and `Signal Dispatcher` which run at the highest priority – and `Finalizer` which runs at priority 8 – slightly lower than the other two threads.

Within the system thread group, there is a sub-group called main which contains the thread that called the main() method of the program. Within the main group is also the ThreadGroup that we created called New Group. As we can see, its maximum priority is 5 (Thread.NORM_PRIORITY) as we set it, and the group contains the two threads that we created.

Variable Visibility

As mentioned before, because threads share variables they can communicate very easily. This flexibility comes at a price, however. They can also interfere with each other in unexpected ways. In this section, we will look at how variables can be shared among threads.

Shared Variables

The Java scoping rules and the structure of the program determine which variables can be shared among threads. If two different threads can legally reference the object, those threads can use it.

The following example shows two threads sharing a variable. The variable is initialized to zero. The main thread calls the modify() method to increment it 100 times and then it prints the value. The other thread calls the modify() method to decrement it 100 times and prints the value.

```java
//SharedVariable.java

public class SharedVariable extends Thread {
  private int shared = 0;

  public int modify(int amount) {
    for (int i = 0; i < 100; i++) {
      shared = shared + amount;
      System.out.println("shared = " + shared);
    }
    return shared;
  }

  public static void main(String[] args) {
    SharedVariable t = new SharedVariable();
    t.start();
    System.out.println("FINISHED main: shared = " + t.modify(+1));
  }
  public void run() {
    System.out.println("FINISHED thread: shared = " + modify(-1));
  }
}
```

We might expect main to see 100 and the other thread to see -100 but they interact so the results are unpredictable. On my machine the last thread to finish usually saw the value 0 but the other thread's value varied widely. When threads share an object, the results can be unpredictable unless their access to that object is carefully controlled. We'll see how to control threads' access to objects later in this chapter.

Stack-local Variables

Each thread is assigned a scratch space in memory by the JVM called a **stack**. This is where the virtual machine can store things like method arguments and local variables. Variables that are declared within a method are stored on the thread's stack and are not visible to other threads. If we change the previous example to use a variable on the stack, the behavior is very different.

```java
//StackVariable.java

public class StackVariable extends Thread {

  public int modify(int amount) {
    int stack = 0;    // each call gets another copy of this variable
    for (int i = 0; i < 100; i++) {
      stack = stack + amount;
      System.out.println("stack = " + stack);
    }
    return stack;    // after return, "stack" is destroyed
  }

  public static void main(String[] args) {
    StackVariable t = new StackVariable();
    t.start();
    System.out.println("FINISHED main: stack = " + t.modify(+1));
  }
  public void run() {
    System.out.println("FINISHED thread: stack = " + modify(-1));
  }
}
```

The first part of the output looks like this:

C:\Beg_Java_Networking\Ch06>**javac StackVariable.java**

C:\Beg_Java_Networking\Ch06>**java StackVariable**
stack = 1
stack = 2
stack = 3
stack = 4
stack = 5
stack = -1
stack = -2
stack = -3
stack = -4
stack = -5
stack = -6
stack = -7
stack = -8
stack = -9
stack = -10
stack = -11
stack = -12
stack = -13
stack = -14
stack = -15
stack = -16
stack = -17
stack = -18
stack = -19
stack = -20
...

In this example, the integer called `stack` is local to the `modify()` method so each thread gets its own copy of it. When this finishes, the main thread sees the value `100` and the other thread sees `-100`. The threads don't affect each other.

Thread-local Variables

Java also has a mechanism for explicitly associating data with threads. This allows the programmer to be sure that different threads have independent data. This example shows the same example using thread-local data.

```java
//ThreadVariable.java

public class ThreadVariable extends Thread {

  // This piece of data will be maintained by the VM
  // so that each thread gets its own copy
  private static ThreadLocal threadLocal = new ThreadLocal();

  public int modify(int amount) {
    for (int i = 0; i < 100; i++) {
      Integer local = (Integer) threadLocal.get();
      local = new Integer(local.intValue() + amount);
      threadLocal.set(local);
      System.out.println("local = " + local);
    }
    return ((Integer) threadLocal.get()).intValue();
  }

  public static void main(String[] args) {
    ThreadVariable t = new ThreadVariable();
    t.start();

    // initialize this thread's local data to zero
    threadLocal.set(new Integer(0));
    System.out.println("FINISHED main: local = " + t.modify(+1));
  }
  public void run() {

    // initialize this thread's local data to zero
    threadLocal.set(new Integer(0));
    System.out.println("FINISHED thread: local = " + modify(-1));
  }
}
```

This example behaves just like the previous example. The main thread sees a final value of `100` and the other thread sees a final value of `-100`. The code is more difficult to follow, though.

First, a `java.lang.ThreadLocal` object is initialized. These are often private static variables so several threads with access to the same class can reference them. Then each thread initializes its thread-local data to `Integer 0`. Note that the data stored as thread-local data must be an instance of `java.lang.Object`, so we use an `Integer` rather than an `int`.

Within the `modify()` method, the thread-local variable is retrieved using `ThreadLocal`'s `get()` method. It is incremented or decremented, then updated using the `ThreadLocal`'s `set()` method.

The JVM has to maintain all of the `ThreadLocal` variables when it context, so using a lot of `ThreadLocal` variables can have an impact on the efficiency of our programs. All in all, it's a fairly complicated syntax and only needed on rare occasions. `ThreadLocal` data isn't used very often.

Synchronization

As we have seen, unpredictable interactions between threads can affect the results of a Java program. Fortunately, the Java Programming Language provides several tools for controlling thread interactions. One of the most important concepts to understand to make effective use of Java threads is the concept of the **monitor**.

A monitor is not a Java object, but each object has a monitor that can be owned by no more than one thread at a time. Because each monitor can only be owned by zero or one thread, an object's monitor can be used to control how many threads have simultaneous access to a particular section of code. If we require each thread to acquire ownership of a single monitor before executing the code, only one thread will execute the code at the same time. This access is controlled by the synchronized keyword.

The synchronized Keyword

The synchronized keyword can be used like this:

```
synchronized (anyObject) {
  // This code will be executed by only one thread at a time
}
```

In the example above, a thread must successfully acquire anyObject's monitor before it will enter the synchronized body of code.

Very often, whole methods need to be synchronized with respect to the this object. For example, the java.util.Vector method addElement() is synchronized on the vector's monitor so it can search through and update the vector's internal data structures without some other thread modifying it at the same time. For these instances, the synchronized keyword can be added to the method declaration. This method:

```
public synchronized void addElement(Object obj) {
  // Some code here
}
```

is exactly the same as:

```
public void addElement(Object obj) {
  synchronized (this) {
    // Some code here
  }
}
```

In both cases, the thread executing addElement() must acquire the monitor of the vector before executing the body of the method.

wait() and notify()

Sometimes we need one thread to wait for some event in another thread before continuing. For example, a thread may need to wait for a buffer to be filled before processing the data in the buffer. The java.lang.Object class contains several methods that provide this functionality.

133

The wait() method causes the current thread to stop (that is, become not schedulable) until some other thread signals it using the notify() or notifyAll() methods explained below. A thread must own the monitor of the object it is waiting on. It can acquire the monitor by synchronizing on the object as we saw above. If the thread does not own the monitor when it calls wait(), an IllegalMonitorStateException is thrown. Once the thread is blocked and waiting, it releases the monitor. We'll see why this is important below.

This example shows the use of the wait() method:

```
synchronized (obj) { // acquire the monitor
  // ...
  obj.wait();          // wait indefinitely
  // When we get here, we have been notified
}
```

The wait() method can also take arguments that control the amount of time the thread is willing to be suspended.

❑ wait(long millisecs) causes the thread to stop until notified or millisecs milliseconds have elapsed, whichever comes first

❑ wait(long millisecs, int nanosecs) causes the thread to stop until notified or millisecs milliseconds plus nanosecs nanoseconds have elapsed whichever comes first

As with the sleep() methods described above, despite the fact that we can specify individual nanoseconds to wait, these timeouts are approximate and can't be used for high-precision timing.

A thread can also exit a wait() by being interrupted. Another thread can call the interrupt() method of the waiting thread, which causes it to receive an InterruptedException.

The example above with the required exception handling looks like this:

```
synchronized (obj) { // acquire the monitor
  // ...
  try {
    obj.wait();          // wait indefinitely
  } catch (InterruptedException ie) {
    // When we get here, we have been interrupted
  }
  // When we get here, we have been notified
}
```

However a thread exits the wait, it can't continue until it can re-acquire the monitor. When the notify() method of an object is called, one of the threads waiting on the object is awakened. If more than one thread is waiting, then one is picked in a manner that is implementation-dependent. That is, each JVM vendor is free to implement a different scheme for waking up waiting threads. This means that we can't count on threads being notified in a first-in-first-out basis or any other scheme.

In contrast, notifyAll() wakes up all waiting threads. As with wait(), the thread calling notify() or notifyAll() must own the monitor for the object being notified. Because the threads blocked on the wait() owned the monitor when they started waiting, after they are notified, they must re-acquire the monitor before continuing. This example shows how notifyAll() is used:

```
synchronized (obj) { // acquire the monitor released by wait()ers
   obj.notifyAll();    // wake up all wait()ers --
   // wait()ers must still acquire the monitor, so this thread
   // continues at least until the end of the synchronized block
}
```

In summary, a thread must always acquire the object's monitor to successfully enter a wait(). To exit the wait, one of three things must happen:

❑   Another thread calls notify() or notifyAll()

❑   The timeout period for the wait elapses

❑   The thread is interrupted

In all of these cases, the waiting thread must re-acquire the monitor before continuing.

The following example shows how synchronized, wait(), and notify() can be used to coordinate multiple threads. It shows a single thread filling a queue and two other threads waiting for objects to become available and removing them from the queue. This is called a producer/consumer or reader/writer scenario. It comes up often when there is a stream of tasks to be completed and some number of resources (threads) to complete them. It's important that no tasks are lost and that no tasks are done twice, so coordination between the threads is crucial.

The figure below illustrates how this works:

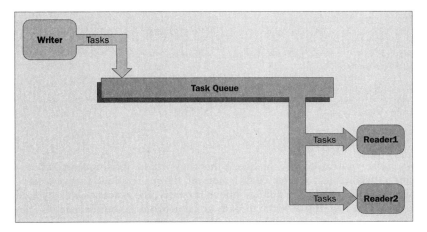

The figure above depicts the flow of tasks from the writer on the left, through a queue, to the set of readers on the right. Notice how the task producer is separated from the task consumer(s) by the queue. There could be any number of readers on the receiving end of the task queue.

For example, take the case of a network server mentioned earlier. The task producer would receive the network service requests and queue them for a worker thread. When a thread finishes its previous task and becomes available, it can take a service request from the queue and work on it independently of any other thread or request. By controlling the number of worker threads available, the network server can increase the efficiency of the server. Of course, this depends on the ability of the worker threads and the producer thread to properly synchronize their manipulation of the queue.

The next code example will illustrate how this works. In the example below, the `Writer` class contains the `main()` method which creates and starts two reader threads. Then it fills the queue with some integers for the readers. The three threads are synchronized using the `queue` vector. Notice that the `fill()` method must have a `synchronized (queue)` section so it can call `notifyAll()` without triggering an `IllegalMonitorStateException`.

```java
//Writer.java

package com.wrox.syncserver;

import java.util.Vector;

public class Writer {

  public void fill(Vector queue) {
    for (int i = 0; i < 20; i++) {
      queue.add(new Integer(i));
      synchronized (queue) {
        queue.notifyAll();
      }
    }
  }
  public static void main(String[] args) {

    // This vector will be the communication channel
    // between the writer and the readers.
    Vector queue = new Vector();
    Writer writer1 = new Writer();

    // Start two readers.
    Reader reader1 = new Reader(queue, "Reader1");
    reader1.start();
    Reader reader2 = new Reader(queue, "Reader2");
    reader2.start();

    // Fill up the queue. The waiting readers will wake up
    // and start emptying the queue.
    writer1.fill(queue);
  }
}
```

The readers start with their name and the queue that they will be reading from, which are passed into their constructor as arguments. In their `run()` method, the readers loop forever, reading from the queue when an object is available. When the queue is empty, the readers block by calling the `wait()` method of the vector `queue`. Because the threads are synchronized on the `queue` object, they can't remove the same object or lose track of one.

```java
//Reader.java

package com.wrox.syncserver;

import java.util.Vector;

public class Reader extends Thread {

  // The queue is the communication channel between
  // this reader and the writer.
```

```
    private Vector queue;

    // A name so we can tell the readers apart.
    private String name;

    public Reader(Vector queue, String name) {
      this.queue = queue;
      this.name = name;
    }

    public void run() {
      for (; ; ) {
        synchronized (queue) {    // acquire the monitor
          while (queue.isEmpty()) {
            try {
              queue.wait();         // releases the monitor
            } catch (InterruptedException ex) {

              // Nothing to do here. If the queue is empty,
              // might as well go back to waiting.
            }
          }

          // At this point the monitor has been re-acquired
          Object o = queue.remove(0);
          System.out.println(name + " got job number: " + o);
        }                // release the monitor at the end of the synchronized block
      }
    }
  }
```

join()

Threads complete by exiting from the `run()` method either by reaching the end of the method or executing a `return` statement. Sometimes it is necessary for a thread to wait until another thread completes.

The `join()` method is used to cause the calling thread to wait until the other thread completes. Like `wait()`, it can also accept timeout arguments that will limit the number of milliseconds and nanoseconds that the current thread will wait for the other thread to complete.

It looks like this in use:

```
try {
  reader1.join(); // wait indefinitely for the reader1 thread to finish
} catch (InterruptedException ie) {
  // interrupted
}
```

The output for this application is as follows:

C:\Beg_Java_Networkin\Ch06g>**javac com\wrox\syncserver\Writer.java**

C:\Beg_Java_Networking\Ch06>**java com.wrox.syncserver.Writer**
Reader1 got job number: 0
Reader1 got job number: 1

```
Reader1 got job number: 2
Reader1 got job number: 3
Reader1 got job number: 4
Reader1 got job number: 5
Reader1 got job number: 6
Reader1 got job number: 7
Reader2 got job number: 8
Reader2 got job number: 9
Reader2 got job number: 10
Reader2 got job number: 11
Reader2 got job number: 12
Reader2 got job number: 13
Reader2 got job number: 14
Reader2 got job number: 15
Reader2 got job number: 16
Reader2 got job number: 17
Reader2 got job number: 18
Reader2 got job number: 19
```

Common Issues with Threaded Applications

As we have seen, writing multithreaded applications can be complicated. Here are some common problems associated with multithreaded code to keep in mind when designing and developing our programs.

Deadlock

When two or more threads are each waiting on one another, the whole program can appear to stop. This situation is called **deadlock**. Just looking at the code for each thread may not show a problem – the problem is with the interaction of the threads.

The example that follows shows a classic deadlock scenario. Here two threads are each trying to acquire two monitors. No problem yet. The problem is that they try to acquire them in different orders. One acquires o1 then o2; the other acquires o2 then o1. Deadlock happens when one of them holds the monitor for o1 and is waiting for o2 while the other one holds the monitor for o2 and is waiting for o1. They both block forever.

```
//Deadlock.java

public class Deadlock extends Thread {

  // These are the two objects used for synchronization
  static Object o1 = new Object();
  static Object o2 = new Object();

  // if doO1First is true, the thread will synchronize on o1 then o2.
  // if doO1First is false, the thread will synchronize on o2 then o1.
  boolean doO1First;
  public Deadlock(boolean doO1First) {
    this.doO1First = doO1First;
  }

  public static void main(String[] args) {
```

```
      // This thread will synchronize on o1 then o2
      Deadlock d1 = new Deadlock(true);
      d1.start();

      // This thread will synchronize on o2 then o1
      Deadlock d2 = new Deadlock(false);
      d2.start();
    }
    public void run() {
      for (; ; ) {
        if (doO1First) {
          synchronized (o1) {        // acquire o1's monitor
            synchronized (o2) {      // acquire o2's monitor
              System.out.println(Thread.currentThread().getName()
                                  + "Got both monitors");
            }                        // release o2's monitor
          }                          // release o1's monitor
        } else {
          synchronized (o2) {        // acquire o2's monitor
            synchronized (o1) {      // acquire o1's monitor
              System.out.println(Thread.currentThread().getName()
                                  + "Got both monitors");
            }                        // release o1's monitor
          }                          // release o2's monitor
        }
      }                              // end for(;;) loop
    }
  }
```

When we run this example, it usually prints only a few lines before deadlocking. This is a very simple example and the deadlock is fairly easy to see, but a large server with hundreds of threads might run for days before deadlocking. Try this for yourself. Be sure you understand the way your threads are using synchronization.

C:\Beg_Java_Networking\Ch06>**javac Deadlock.java**

C:\Beg_Java_Networking\Ch06>**java Deadlock**
Thread-0Got both monitors
Thread-0Got both monitors
Thread-0Got both monitors
Thread-0Got both monitors
Thread-0Got both monitors
Thread-0Got both monitors
Thread-0Got both monitors
Thread-1Got both monitors
Thread-1Got both monitors
Thread-1Got both monitors
Thread-1Got both monitors
Thread-1Got both monitors
Thread-1Got both monitors
Thread-1Got both monitors
Thread-1Got both monitors
Thread-1Got both monitors
...

There are some commercial tools that can be used to detect deadlock, but one useful tool that is included with the JVM is the stack backtrace. By typing *CTRL-* under UNIX or *Ctrl-BREAK* under Windows, we can make the JVM dump a trace of all currently active threads. Sometimes we can see which threads are deadlocked.

Here is a trace of the deadlock example:

```
Thread-0Got both monitors
Thread-0Got both monitors
Thread-0Got both monitors
Thread-0Got both monitors
Thread-0Got both monitors
Thread-1Got both monitors
Full thread dump:

"Thread-2" prio=5 tid=0x234360 nid=0x808 waiting on monitor [0..0x6fb38]

"Thread-1" prio=5 tid=0x7fa720 nid=0x790 runnable [0x8eaf000..0x8eafdc4]
        at Deadlock.run(Deadlock.java:38)

"Thread-0" prio=5 tid=0x7fa808 nid=0x758 runnable [0x8e6f000..0x8e6fdc4]
        at Deadlock.run(Deadlock.java:31)

"Signal Dispatcher" daemon prio=10 tid=0x889d80 nid=0x7b4 waiting on monitor [0.
.0]

"Finalizer" daemon prio=9 tid=0x7e9c60 nid=0x814 waiting on monitor [0x8c4f000..
0x8c4fdc4]
        at java.lang.Object.wait(Native Method)
        at java.lang.ref.ReferenceQueue.remove(ReferenceQueue.java:108)
        at java.lang.ref.ReferenceQueue.remove(ReferenceQueue.java:123)
        at java.lang.ref.Finalizer$FinalizerThread.run(Finalizer.java:162)

"Reference Handler" daemon prio=10 tid=0x7e8428 nid=0x4c4 waiting on monitor [0x
8c0f000..0x8c0fdc4]
        at java.lang.Object.wait(Native Method)
        at java.lang.Object.wait(Object.java:420)
        at java.lang.ref.Reference$ReferenceHandler.run(Reference.java:110)

"VM Thread" prio=5 tid=0x23f5b8 nid=0x7fc runnable

"VM Periodic Task Thread" prio=10 tid=0x889c48 nid=0x74c waiting on monitor
```

It's interesting to note that even this simple example has eight threads. The two of interest are `Thread-0` and `Thread-1` that are both referenced in `Deadlock.java`. One thread is trying to synchronize on `o1`; the other is trying to synchronize on `o2`. The way to avoid deadlock is to avoid cases where a thread needs to acquire two monitors and make sure that for any object that is used for `wait()`, there is a different thread that calls `notify()` or `notifyAll()`.

Race Conditions

A **race condition** exists any time the behavior of a program is dependent on the uncontrolled timing of threads. We saw race conditions in earlier examples where one thread was incrementing a variable while another was decrementing it. The results of a program with race conditions can be very erratic. It might work as expected 99% of the time and only fail on rare occasions. These are among the most difficult problems to debug and are best avoided by careful use of synchronized blocks to ensure safe access to shared variables.

The Thread.stop(), Thread.suspend(), and Thread.resume() Methods

The first version of the Java Development Kit (JDK) included the stop(), suspend(), and resume() methods in java.lang.Thread. The intent was to allow a programmer to do things like kill an arbitrary thread using the stop() method. A thread that was stopped could not be restarted and was effectively dead. When the thread was killed, all of its monitors were immediately released by the JVM to avoid the deadlock that was likely. The problem was if the thread was killed while in the process of updating a shared object, even though the monitor was released, the object might be left in an inconsistent state. That is, it might be left half-updated and be unusable by other threads.

So the stop(), suspend(), and resume() methods are deprecated because they are inherently unsafe. If a thread is suspended while it holds a monitor, no other threads can acquire that monitor and deadlock usually results. If a thread is stopped, the JVM can release all of the monitors held by that thread, but it might leave some objects in inconsistent states.

The next example shows how the stop() method was used. In it, main() creates a thread, waits 5 seconds, then kills the thread with stop() Note that the other thread could be doing anything and may not be in a state where it can be safely stopped.

```
//PrintStop.java

public class PrintStop extends Thread {

  public void run() {
    for (; ; ) {
      try {
        sleep(1000);
      } catch (InterruptedException ie) {}
      System.out.print(".");
    }
  }

  public static void main(String[] args) {
    Thread t = new PrintStop();
    t.start();
    try {
      sleep(5000);
    } catch (InterruptedException ie) {}

    // Kill the thread. Possibly leaving some object in an
    // inconsistent state.  THIS IS BAD!
```

```
      t.stop();

      // Make sure the thread has finished.
      try {
        t.join();
      } catch (InterruptedException ie) {}
      System.out.println("The thread has finished");
    }

  }
```

The output is as follows:

C:\Beg_Java_Networking\Ch06>**javac PrintStop.java**

C:\Beg_Java_Networking\Ch06>**java PrintStop**
....The thread has finished

There are some simple practices that make the stop() method unnecessary and don't lead to inconsistent objects. One possibility is, rather than using stop() to terminate a thread, simply set a variable that the thread checks before each iteration of its task. So the updated example above looks like this:

```
//PrintStop2.java

public class PrintStop2 extends Thread {

  private boolean should_stop = false;

  public void run() {
    for (; ; ) {

      // This is a safe place to quit.
      // Check to see if I should stop.
      if (should_stop) {
        break;
      }
      try {
        sleep(1000);
      } catch (InterruptedException ie) {}
      System.out.print(".");
    }
  }

  public static void main(String[] args) {
    PrintStop2 t = new PrintStop2();
    t.start();
    try {
      sleep(5000);
    } catch (InterruptedException ie) {}

    // Signal the thread to stop by setting the boolean flag.
    t.should_stop = true;
```

```
                // Wait for the thread to finish.
                try {
                    t.join();
                } catch (InterruptedException ie) {}
                System.out.println("The thread has finished");
            }

        }
```

Now the next time the thread reaches the top of its loop, it will exit. The thread itself can make sure that it exits in a safe state. This thread only waits one second between iterations of its loop, but if the thread is in wait() mode for a long time, use the interrupt() method to get the thread's attention. Then the thread can handle the cleanup in the InterruptedException exception handler.

The output will be the same as before.

Here's the example again using the interrupt() technique.

```
//PrintStop3.java

public class PrintStop3 extends Thread {

    private boolean should_stop = false;

    public void run() {
        for (; ; ) {

            // This is a safe place to quit.
            // Check to see if I should stop.

            if (should_stop) {
                break;
            }
            try {
                sleep(1000 * 60 * 60 * 24);    // sleep for one day
            } catch (InterruptedException ie) {


                if (should_stop) {
                    break;
                }
            }
            System.out.print(".");
        }
    }

    public static void main(String[] args) {
        PrintStop3 t = new PrintStop3();
        t.start();
        try {
            sleep(5000);
        } catch (InterruptedException ie) {}
```

```
      // Signal the thread to stop by setting the boolean flag.
      t.should_stop = true;

      // Wake it up by interrupting it.
      t.interrupt();

      // Wait for the thread to finish.
      try {
        t.join();
      } catch (InterruptedException ie) {}
      System.out.println("The thread has finished");
    }
  }
```

Now, we see that the output is slightly different, though the result is the same:

C:\Beg_Java_Networking\Ch06>**javac PrintStop3.java**

C:\Beg_Java_Networking\Ch06>**java PrintStop3**
The thread has finished

Writing Efficient Multithreaded Applications

One of the prime reasons for writing multithreaded applications is to maximize the efficiency of the code. When multiple threads are available, some threads can be productive while others are waiting for I/O or other slow events. The careful use of `synchronized` blocks and the use of thread pools can make multithreaded code much more efficient.

Thread Pools

Threads are relatively expensive objects to create. The JVM has to keep records of the state of all threads so it can schedule them and switch between them. When an application calls for many transient threads, keeping a resource pool of threads can be much more efficient than creating new threads for each use. Network servers, for example, often make extensive use of thread pools for servicing network requests. If these requests are frequent and quick to fulfill, creating a new thread for each one can noticeably hurt the server's responsiveness. Each one must be created and scheduled, and then quickly given up to the garbage collector. If we're just going to need a new thread again in a few milliseconds, it's much better to save the thread and reuse it.

Below is an example of a simple thread pool. It creates a number of threads when it starts and assigns those threads to tasks as the tasks arrive. When a task is finished, the thread is not destroyed, but goes back into the pool to be reused. This avoids the expensive operations of creating and destroying a thread for each request. The example package `com.wrox.threadpool` contains two classes:

❑   `ThreadPool` – This is the thread pool class used by clients of the pool.

❑   `PoolableThread` – This is a class used by the pool to manage each thread.

❑   `PoolTest.java` – This is the class we will use to test our thread pool.

But first, let's look at `ThreadPool.java`.

```
//ThreadPool.java

package com.wrox.threadpool;

import java.util.*;

public class ThreadPool {

  private Vector freeThreads = new Vector();
  private Vector inUseThreads = new Vector();

  private static int INITIAL_SIZE = 10;

  public ThreadPool() {
    fillPool(INITIAL_SIZE);
  }

  private void fillPool(int poolSize) {
    for (int i = 0; i < poolSize; i++) {
      PoolableThread pt = new PoolableThread(this);
      pt.start();
      freeThreads.add(pt);
    }
    try {
      Thread.sleep(2000);
    } catch (InterruptedException ie) {}
  }

  public synchronized void runTask(Runnable task) {
    if (freeThreads.isEmpty()) {
      throw new RuntimeException("All threads are in use");
    }
    PoolableThread t = (PoolableThread) freeThreads.remove(0);
    inUseThreads.add(t);
    t.setTask(task);
  }

  synchronized void free(PoolableThread t) {
    inUseThreads.remove(t);
    freeThreads.add(t);
  }
}
```

The second class in the package is used by the pool to manage each thread:

```
//PoolableThread.java

package com.wrox.threadpool;

class PoolableThread extends Thread {

  Runnable task = null;
  ThreadPool pool;

  PoolableThread(ThreadPool pool) {
    this.pool = pool;
  }
```

```
synchronized void setTask(Runnable task) {
  this.task = task;
  notify();
}

synchronized void executeTasks() {
  for (; ; ) {
    try {
      if (task == null) {
        wait();
      }
    } catch (InterruptedException ex) {

      // Interrupted
    }
    task.run();
    task = null;
    pool.free(this);
  }
}
public void run() {
  executeTasks();
}
}
```

The pool is used by clients through the `runTask()` method of `ThreadPool`. They can create a thread pool and assign it tasks as in this example:

```
ThreadPool tp = new ThreadPool();
tp.runTask(new SomeTask());       // SomeTask implements Runnable
tp.runTask(new SomeOtherTask());// SomeOtherTask implements Runnable
```

Let's look at how the pool works. When the pool is created, its `fill()` method makes and starts ten `PoolableThread` objects and stores them in a vector called `freeThreads`. These threads don't have anything to do, so they just wait. At the beginning of `PoolableThread`'s `executeTasks()` method, this code makes the thread block if there is no task for it to do:

```
try {
  if (task == null)
    wait();
} catch (InterruptedException ex) {
  // Interrupted
}
```

By just calling `wait()`, the thread is blocking on the `this` object, so it will stop until another thread calls `notify()` or `notifyAll()` on it.

Back in the `ThreadPool` class, when a client has a task to run, it calls the pool's `runTask()` method with the `Runnable` task as its argument. First, the pool checks to make sure there is an available thread; it throws an exception if no threads are available. If there is a thread available, the pool moves it from the `freeThreads` vector to the `inUseThreads` vector and assigns the task to the thread by calling the `PoolableThread`'s `setTask()` method.

These lines assign the task to the thread:

```
PoolableThread t = (PoolableThread)freeThreads.remove(0);
inUseThreads.add(t);
t.setTask(task);
```

In the `setTask()` method, the `PoolableThread` keeps a reference to the task and then notifies the waiting thread. As soon as it can re-acquire the monitor, the waiting thread wakes up and executes the task by calling its `run()` method.

```
task.run();
task = null;
pool.free(this);
```

The last two lines above get the `PoolableThread` ready to re-enter the pool as a free thread. For purposes of clarity, this pool is very simple. It doesn't have any mechanism for changing the number of threads in the pool or trapping a thread's completion with `join()`. Its error handling is also not very robust. It's intended as an illustration of the concept rather than a finished component.

This small file basically returns the results of the threads to the screen:

```java
//PoolTest.java

package com.wrox.threadpool;

public class PoolTest implements Runnable {

  public PoolTest() {
    ThreadPool tp = new ThreadPool();
    for (int i=0; i<10; i++)
      tp.runTask(this);

    try {Thread.sleep(400000);} catch (Exception e) {}
  }

  public static void main(String[] args) {
    PoolTest poolTest1 = new PoolTest();
  }
  public void run() {
    System.out.println("Start on "+Thread.currentThread().getName());
    try {Thread.sleep(2000);} catch (InterruptedException ie) {}
    System.out.println("Done on "+Thread.currentThread().getName());
  }
}
```

To see the output, run the following:

C:\Beg_Java_Networking\Ch06>**javac com\wrox\threadpool\PoolTest.java**

C:\Beg_Java_Networking\Ch06>**java com.wrox.threadpool.PoolTest**
Start on Thread-0
Start on Thread-1
Start on Thread-2
Start on Thread-3

Start on Thread-4
Start on Thread-5
Start on Thread-6
Start on Thread-7
Start on Thread-8
Start on Thread-9
Done on Thread-0
Done on Thread-1
Done on Thread-2
Done on Thread-3
Done on Thread-4
Done on Thread-5
Done on Thread-6
Done on Thread-7
Done on Thread-8
Done on Thread-9

Using Synchronized Appropriately

As we have seen, the use of the synchronized keyword is critical for robust multithreaded applications. Some newcomers to Java assume that the more synchronized blocks and methods, the better. This is not the case. We have already seen how misuse of synchronized can lead to deadlock when multiple monitors are acquired in different threads.

Using unnecessary synchronized blocks can also greatly affect a program's performance. Every time a program synchronizes on an object, the JVM must make sure that no other thread already owns the monitor and updates the monitor status accordingly. If the monitor is already owned by another thread, the current thread blocks and the JVM must schedule another thread for execution. synchronized is a time-consuming operation and should only be used where necessary.

Here's an example that shows the performance impact of synchronized blocks. This little program counts up to one million and times how long it takes.

```
//PrintSync.java

public class PrintSync {

  // public static String syncObject = "sync";

  public static void main(String[] args) {
    long count = 0;
    long start = System.currentTimeMillis();
    for (int i = 0; i < 1000000; i++) {

      // Gratuitous synchronization
      // synchronized (syncObject) {
      // Do something useful
      count = count + 1;

      // }
    }
    long stop = System.currentTimeMillis();
    System.out.println("Time = " + (stop - start) + " milliseconds");
  }
}
```

This program is not too useful, but it's informative as a benchmark. When we run it, the program prints the following output (obviously this will vary greatly from machine to machine):

C:\Beg_Java_Networking\Ch06>**java PrintSync.java**

C:\Beg_Java_Networking\Ch06>**java PrintSync**
Time = 10 milliseconds

It took ten milliseconds to run to completion. Now if we add an unnecessary synchronized block like this:

```java
//PrintSync2.java

public class PrintSync2 {

  public static String syncObject = "sync";

  public static void main(String[] args) {
    long count = 0;
    long start = System.currentTimeMillis();
    for (int i = 0; i < 1000000; i++) {

      // Gratuitous synchronization
      synchronized (syncObject) {
      // Do something useful
      count = count + 1;

      }
    }
    long stop = System.currentTimeMillis();
    System.out.println("Time = " + (stop - start) + " milliseconds");
  }
}
```

the program now prints:

C:\Beg_Java_Networking\Ch06>**java PrintSync2.java**

C:\Beg_Java_Networking\Ch06>**java PrintSync2**
Time = 40 milliseconds

This program took four times as long to run with an extra synchronized block. Granted, this program wasn't doing much else, but the effects of the synchronized block on the performance of the program were significant nonetheless. The rule is, use synchronized when two threads must not execute the same code simultaneously. Don't use it if the code can safely be executed in multiple threads at once.

Summary

Using multiple threads in network programs can enable them to service many requests at once, leading to greater efficiency and responsiveness. This capability is supported by the Java programming language's built-in support for thread creation and synchronization. This support comes in the form of these features:

❑ The `java.lang.Thread` class and `java.lang.Runnable` interface are subclassed to create classes that can be executed by independent threads. `java.lang.Thread` can be extended to make a class that can execute in its own thread. If the class already extends another class, we can implement the `java.lang.Runnable` interface to create a class that can be run in a thread.

❑ The `synchronized` keyword is used to control threads' access to shared data. Each Java object has a monitor associated with it, which can only be owned by one thread at a time. In order to enter a synchronized block, a thread must acquire the monitor for the object on which the block is synchronized. If another thread already owns the monitor, the current thread will block until the monitor is released.

❑ The `wait()`, `notify()`, and `join()` methods, are used by threads to communicate and coordinate with other threads. A thread that calls `wait()` on an object will block until another thread calls `notify()` or `notifyAll()` on that same object. This mechanism allows threads to wait for events that are signaled by other threads as we saw in the reader/writer example, above. The `join()` method enables one thread to wait for the completion of another thread before continuing or terminating.

As we saw, there are some hazards associated with writing multithreaded applications. Deadlock results when two or more threads are all waiting for the others to do something like release a monitor or call `notify()`. Deadlocked threads are blocked forever. Race conditions are difficult to debug because the failure can be infrequent and unpredictable. They occur when two threads interfere with each other in the manipulation of a shared object. The careful use of `synchronized` blocks helps avoid race conditions.

The use and abuse of Java's multithreading features can affect the efficiency of our programs. Using thread pools can increase the efficiency of programs by eliminating the expensive creation and destruction of `Thread` objects, while the careless overuse of `synchronized` blocks can cause a program to run much more slowly.

Java Security Model

If you are studying Java Networking with an eye on writing networked client software, you should be acutely aware of the security implications of downloading executable content over the network. A basic knowledge of the Java security framework can help you to decide when you can trust code, and how to limit the trust you extend to downloaded code. Should you be planning to write network services, such as web servers, security is absolutely vital. You should assume that the server *will* be attacked sooner or later. Most of the Java preliminaries on network programming have been covered now, but the final ingredient needed before we can safely embark on it is security.

In this chapter, you will see why Java is exceptionally well suited to writing network-enabled code, and be shown how the Java security model can help you make it even more secure. You will:

- ❏ See why security is important in a heavily networked environment
- ❏ Understand the fundamentals of access control as introduced in Java 1.0 and extended in Java 1.1, notably the "sandbox model"
- ❏ Sign your code to authenticate it to others and make it tamper-proof
- ❏ Understand the Java 2 platform security model which introduces permissions and policies
- ❏ Give Java classes specific permissions to access parts of the system using a security policy
- ❏ Create your own permissions, and securely grant access to services you provide
- ❏ Use the Java 2 security tools

Although some cryptography terms cannot be avoided, this chapter covers only those that are absolutely necessary. An in-depth treatment of the topic follows later in Chapter 14.

Why Security?

Don't just trust any executable code – not even when it's coming from an apparently trustworthy source. This lesson was first learned the hard way with the famous Internet worm of November 3, 1988, which effectively shut down the net. A 23-year-old student, Robert Morris, had created a program that would propagate over the network, installing a copy of itself on every computer it met along the way. But the bit of code that was supposed to ensure that each machine only got a single copy of the worm didn't work, and thousands of Internet hosts ground to a halt as they became infested with hundreds of worms each. Administrators of clean machines axed their net connections to avoid infection, and for a few days the Internet ceased to exist.

Amazingly enough, this lesson is still being learned at great cost every day. Some of the most popular e-mail applications and word processors are perfectly happy to execute macros, scripts, and active controls without any user intervention. Such executable content can gain access to the most sensitive system services, such as the hard drive or the operating system. This is possible because what little security is in place appears to be an afterthought. More than a decade after the worm, its descendants thrive. The worm was, in fact, a fairly benign creature, which had run amok due to a programming error. Most of the current crop is spread by design, and some of them have been created to cause as much damage as possible.

The Internet worm actually spread through a vulnerability in the commonly-used **sendmail** mail transport program. Sendmail featured a handy facility allowing programmers to debug it over the net. For the worm, this turned out to be a handy facility allowing it to run just about anything on any mail host. Clearly, it pays to be very careful about the services provided by an Internet server. Sensitive services need to be carefully protected so that only authorized users can access them. Services must also be able to handle unexpected input so they cannot be subverted.

For example, one of the most common security holes in server software is insufficient protection of memory buffers. An unprotected buffer will overflow when the input is unexpectedly long, and overwrite other memory locations. Hackers have used such carelessness to break into the most tightly secured machines. This, too, is a lesson still being learnt daily.

New vulnerabilities are being discovered every week in some of the world's most popular server software. For up to date information and security bulletins, see the website of the Computer Emergency Response Team (CERT, http://www.cert.org).

Java Security

In Java, Sun has addressed security issues from the very start:

❑ The Java language ensures that array access never goes out of bounds. Any attempt to access memory beyond the array boundaries results in an `ArrayIndexOutOfBoundsException`. This prevents buffer overflows and underflows.

❑ The pointers and unions that lie at the root of so many bugs in C and C++ are not supported. Together with garbage collection, this prevents uncontrolled memory access.

❑ Casts are always checked and throw a `ClassCastException` if illegal. That way, code can never get around security features by casting an object to an incompatible type.

❑ Before Java bytecode (that is, a `.class` file) is loaded as a class, the virtual machine runs a bytecode verifier to ensure that the code is valid. This makes it impossible to construct invalid bytecode that could cause the JVM to behave in unexpected ways.

❑ The language does not contain any low-level constructs that would allow direct hardware access. All access has to go through the Java libraries, with the sole exception of **Java Native Interface (JNI)** calls.

❑ The libraries enforce security by blocking Java programs from accessing the system unless they are allowed to do so. Any attempt to perform a prohibited operation will cause a `SecurityException` to be thrown.

❑ Finally, there is extensive support for cryptography. Cryptography is essential to data protection and authentication. We will return to it in Chapter 14.

These features make Java arguably the best language to implement Internet-secure applications, although it is important to remember that there may still be security bugs in the JVM implementation itself. If we want to safely use Java networking to connect to services on the net, or to implement services made available over the net, we need to be familiar with its security support.

Broadly speaking, there are two types of Java programs. **Applications** need to be installed by the user before they can be used. An application is typically purchased or downloaded from a trusted source. It takes an explicit action to install and run it. Traditionally, the user implicitly trusts an application with full access to the machine; later in this chapter, we will see how Java 2 refines this by allowing the user to confer specific levels of trust using **certificates**.

Applets, on the other hand, are primarily Java programs embedded within web pages. They can be used to make a page more interactive, or to access a server resource such as a database without the delay associated with server-side processing. They execute automatically when you view the web page that contains the applet, unless Java is disabled on the user's browser. The user does not know whether a web page contains an applet and if the applet can be trusted. Like executable content within an e-mail, an applet should be treated as if it contained malicious code.

The basic Java security model directly reflects this fundamental difference between applications and applets. Applications get full access to all system resources, while applets run in a protected environment known as a **sandbox**.

The Sandbox Model

We have seen that a Java applet in a web page is downloaded from the web and executed without explicit permission from the user, provided that the user had enabled Java on their browser. In fact, the user may not even realize that the web page uses an applet. There is no reason why it could not contain malicious code, such as a virus, a function to delete all the files on the hard drive, or a program which tracks all the passwords typed in and sends the results to some e-mail address. The only safe thing to do is to treat the applet as **untrusted code** and deny it access to all system resources that could potentially be abused. This is known as the **sandbox model**. Basically, the applet is put in a virtual container, separate from the rest of the system, where it can cause no harm.

The Basic Sandbox

The sandbox model has been with Java from the first production release, version 1.0:

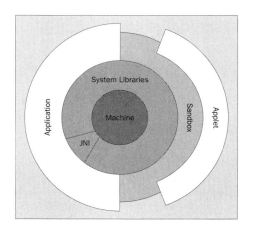

While applications get full access to the libraries and the machine, the Java 1.0 sandbox subjects an applet to a large number of restrictions. Every facility that could allow the applet to damage data, access confidential information, or otherwise compromise system security, is blocked from access.

Before we discuss these restrictions in more detail, let's examine how it works with an example. The following code implements a simple applet performing some simple privileged operations. The class has a main() method, so you can run it as an application and compare results.

```java
//SecurityApp.java

package com.wrox.security;

import java.awt.*;
import java.awt.event.*;

public class SecurityApp extends java.applet.Applet {

  private SecurityTestWindow window;

  public void init() {
    window = new SecurityTestWindow("Applet Security Test");
    window.addWindowListener(new WindowAdapter() {
      public void windowClosing(WindowEvent e) {
        window.hide();
      }
    });
    window.showTestResults();
  }

  public void destroy() {
    window.dispose();
  }
```

This is a small applet. Its only purpose is to create the SecurityTestWindow, which runs a number of security tests and displays their results. In addition, there is a static main() method to allow the tests to be run from an application:

```java
  public static void main(String[] args) {
    SecurityTestWindow window =
      new SecurityTestWindow("Application Security Test");
    window.addWindowListener(new WindowAdapter() {
      public void windowClosing(WindowEvent e) {
        System.exit(0);
      }
    });
    window.showTestResults();
  }
}
```

The SecurityTestWindow class itself attempts to perform a selection of three security-sensitive operations: it lists a file from the root directory, opens a network connection to the Wrox site and retrieves the length of its homepage, and finally displays the location of your home directory. All three operations are security-sensitive and generally forbidden to untrusted code.

156

```java
//SecurityTestWindow.java

package com.wrox.security;

import java.awt.*;
import java.io.File;
import java.net.URLConnection;

class SecurityTestWindow extends Frame {

  private TextArea textArea;

  public SecurityTestWindow(String title) {
    super(title);

    textArea = new TextArea();
    textArea.setEditable(false);
    add(textArea);

    pack();
    show();
  }

  public void showTestResults() {
    println("Running tests...");
    try {
      fileTest("/");
    } catch (Exception e) {
      println(e);
    }
    try {
      socketTest("http://www.wrox.com");
    } catch (Exception e) {
      println(e);
    }
    try {
      systemTest("user.home");
    } catch (Exception e) {
      println(e);
    }
    println("Done.");
  }

  private void fileTest(String path) {
    String[] files = new java.io.File(path).list();
    if (files.length > 0) {
      println("First file in " + path + " is " + files[0]);
    }
  }

  private void socketTest(String url) throws java.io.IOException {
    URLConnection connection = new java.net.URL(url).openConnection();
    connection.connect();
    println(url + " is " + connection.getContentLength() + " bytes");
    connection.getInputStream().close();
  }

  private void systemTest(String property) {
    println(property + " has value " + System.getProperty(property));
  }
```

```
    private void println(Object toPrint) {
        textArea.append(toPrint + "\n");
    }
}
```

It is not necessary to have anything in particular in your classpath. After compilation, the code can be run as an application:

C:\Beg_Java_Networking\Ch07>**set CLASSPATH=.;**

C:\Beg_Java_Networking\Ch07>**javac com.wrox.security.SecurityApp.java**

C:\Beg_Java_Networking\Ch07>**java com.wrox.security.SecurityApp**

As an application has full access to the system, you should be seeing something like the following window:

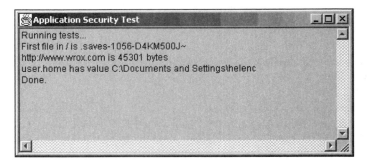

If you are running the application from behind a firewall, you may find that instead of returning the number of bytes from the connection, an UnknownHostException is thrown. In such an instance, the information being returned is effectively hidden by the firewall.

It is possible to run a workaround on a proxy server or another machine that is not behind this firewall, providing you know the IP address for the proxy you will use. If you yourself do not have this information, contact your system administrator who can advise you further.

For the purposes of this example, we shall say that the proxy IP address is 123.456.7.89. The port will be 99. The workaround explicitly names the IP address and port that the application will run against on the command line, and it looks like this:

C:\Beg_Java_Networking\Ch07>**java -Dhttp.proxyHost=123.456.7.89 -Dhttp.proxyPort=99 SecurityApp**

Obviously, your address and port will be different, but when included on the command line as in the example above, this command should run successfully.

To view the program as a browser applet, we need a small HTML file:

```
<HTML>
    <HEAD><TITLE>Applet Security Example</TITLE></HEAD>
    <BODY>
```

```
        <HR WIDTH="100%">
        <H3>Applet Security Example</H3>
        <HR WIDTH="100%">
        <APPLET
            code="com.wrox.security.SecurityApp.class"
            archive="com.wrox.security.SecurityDemo.jar" width=0 height=0></APPLET>
    </BODY>
</HTML>
```

After saving this file as `SecurityApp.html` in the same directory as the Java source, open it in a browser or the `appletviewer` tool:

C:\Beg_Java_Networking\Ch07>**appletviewer SecurityApp.html**

If you are operating behind a firewall, the syntax for this command is as follows:

C:\Beg_Java_Networking\Ch07>**appletviewer -J"-Dhttp.proxyHost=123.456.7.89" -J"-Dhttp .proxyPort=99" SecurityApp.html**

A window like the one below should appear.

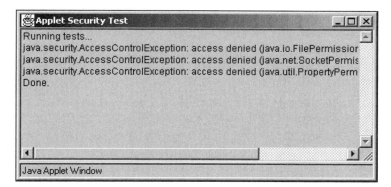

All three tests failed with a security `AccessControlException` or a subclass of it, depending on the browser. Had this demo been loaded from the Wrox web site, the download from **www.wrox.com** would have succeeded, as an applet can always access the host it was loaded from.

In the `fileTest()`, `socketTest()` and `systemTest()` methods of `SecurityTestWindow`, the program attempts to do things which could potentially be abused by malicious code. For that reason, they are forbidden to applets and throw a `java.lang.SecurityException` (or, as in this case, a subclass). The forbidden operations that `SecurityApp` tries to accomplish are as follows:

❑   **Read a directory**: Untrusted code cannot read from or write to the file system in any way. This applies to both files and directories, as even checking for the existence of a file can reveal sensitive information such as the presence of software with known security holes.

❑   **Access the Internet**: The networking operations that can be performed are strictly limited. These restrictions ensure that network communications are only possible within the machine the code was loaded from.

Untrusted code can only create network connections to the computer it was loaded from, and server sockets created by it cannot accept connections from anywhere else. It cannot create server sockets on the privileged ports (port 1023 or lower); on UNIX, this would even apply to the root use. It cannot create multicast sockets, and none of the network object factories – `SocketImplFactory`, `URLStreamHandlerFactory` or `ContentHandlerFactory` – may be created or registered. This prevents an applet from creating or accessing unauthorized services.

❑ **Read a system property**: Only a few selected properties, typically `java.version`, `java.vendor`, `java.vendor.url`, `java.class.version`, `os.name`, `os.arch`, `os.version`, `file.separator`, `path.separator` and `line.separator`, can be retrieved using `System.getProperty()`. `System.setProperties()` would allow the modification of system properties and cannot be used at all.

Many other methods of the `Runtime` and `System` classes are also security-sensitive. Untrusted code may not access the `exit()` methods, as these would stop the JVM. The `Runtime.exec()` methods which run external commands are likewise inaccessible. The ability to run commands would allow untrusted code to perform just about any operation.

The `load()` and `loadLibrary()` methods cannot be accessed either. Allowing these would enable malicious code to gain direct access to the machine using JNI.

These are only some of the sandbox restrictions. They partly depend on the applet container (for example, a web browser or the Sun `AppletViewer`), but in addition to what has been mentioned above you can typically expect the following:

❑ The system clipboard and event queue cannot be accessed. Printing is not possible.

❑ Threads can be accessed or created only within the thread group in which the code is running.

❑ From the libraries installed on the client machine, only `java.*` classes can be directly used. No `ClassLoader` can be instantiated or used.

❑ Access to the `java.security` package is limited. In particular, security properties are inaccessible and untrusted code cannot create or register its own `SecurityManager`, as this would enable it to circumvent the security restrictions. `SecurityManager` will be discussed later in this chapter.

❑ The applet gets its own **namespace**, so it cannot gain access to classes loaded by other Java applications running in the same JVM.

Together, these restrictions ensure that untrusted applet code can safely be run. The flip side is that a lot of useful things have become impossible. For example, if you would want to create a word processing applet capable of saving its files to the user's hard drive, that would be impossible. This problem was addressed in version 1.1 of the JDK.

Escaping the Sandbox

Confining all applets to the sandbox means that many types of applications are impossible to realize for applet writers. Some applets simply need to be able to escape in order to perform their task. To support this, JDK 1.1 introduced **signed applets**.

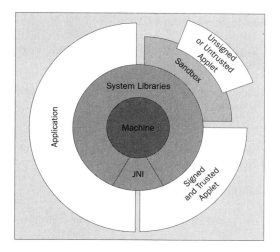

Signed applets are ordinary applets in a JAR archive with a cryptographically secure **signature**. The signature both identifies the code's author or publisher, and indicates that they vouch for the integrity of the code. It is almost impossible for a third party to forge the publisher's signature or to change existing code without invalidating the signature. This makes it safe for a user to indicate that applets from a specific publisher should be **trusted**. The JVM can then give the applet full access rights. An applet that is both signed by its author and trusted by the user is allowed to do everything an application can do.

It is also possible to obtain a **trusted certificate** from a **certificate authority** such as VeriSign (http://www.verisign.com/) or Thawte (http://www.thawte.com/). A certificate contains your signature's **public key** and information about your identity, signed by the authority. Browsers are generally pre-configured to trust certificates issued by such authorities. Users can set up their trust by simply acknowledging a dialog box, provided you sign with a certificate signed by a recognized authority. The level of security granted to the applet will also depend on the security settings of the browser, such as the "zones" that can be set within Internet Explorer.

Unfortunately, Microsoft Internet Explorer does not recognize signed JAR archives as such, but needs to have its code packaged and signed in **Windows Cabinet (CAB)** files. On the other hand, Netscape uses its own JAR signing tools and a proprietary security API. This fragmentation of Java applet support is one of the things that make applets less viable in an Internet environment. Signed applets can still be useful in the more controlled and uniform world of intranet applications, but for the Internet world server-side technologies or Java Web Start are more viable.

Certificates and cryptography in general will be discussed in more detail in Chapter 14.

Code Signing

To allow the applet described in the previous section to escape the sandbox, we need to sign it. This procedure is best illustrated by a simple example. Assuming you are using JDK 1.2 or better, the steps are the following. First, in order to sign code it needs to be packaged in a JAR archive. Save the following text as C:\Beg_Java_Networking\Ch07\SecurityApp.manifest, or alternatively this file is in the code download for this chapter:

```
Manifest-Version: 1.0
Main-Class: com.wrox.security.SecurityApp
```

This is the manifest to be used in creating the JAR:

C:\Beg_Java_Networking\Ch07>jar cfm SecurityApp.jar SecurityApp.manifest com\wrox\security\Security*.class

This creates a file called `SecurityApp.jar` containing the security demo classes. Before we can sign it, we first need to generate a keystore database with our signature key, which we will give the alias signkey.

If you are using Windows, you need to ensure that the JDK's `bin` directory is in your path. The tool will prompt you for the information it needs, such as passwords for both the `SecurityApp.keystore` file and the generated signature key, and information about your identity. The contents of the square brackets are the current or default settings.

C:\Beg_Java_Networking\Ch07>keytool -genkey -keystore SecurityApp.keystore -alias signkey -keyalg rsa

Enter keystore password: **bronte**
What is your first and last name?
  [Unknown]: **Ellen Callaghan**
What is the name of your organizational unit?
  [Unknown]: **Mathe Group**
What is the name of your organization?
  [Unknown]: **Breuil Holdings**
What is the name of your City or Locality?
  [Unknown]: **Angouleme**
What is the name of your State or Province?
  [Unknown]: **France**
What is the two-letter country code for this unit?
  [Unknown]: **FR**
Is <CN=Ellen Callaghan, OU=Mathe Group, O=Breuil Holdings, L=Angouleme, ST=France, C=FR> correct?
  [no]: **yes**

Enter key password for <signkey>
    (RETURN if same as keystore password): **bronte**

C:\Beg_Java_Networking\Ch07>

Answer the prompts and the tool will generate a **key pair** (signature) for your named signkey. The keytool will be described more fully later in this chapter.

At this point, we could let the tool generate a certificate request, send that off to an authority, and import the certificate they will return. Everyone would then be able to trust our signed applet. Unfortunately, that would probably cost rather more time and money than you'd be willing to spend on an example like this, so we will continue without an "official" certificate.

At this stage we are ready to sign the code with our signature.

C:\Beg_Java_Networking\Ch07>jarsigner -keystore SecurityApp.keystore SecurityApp.jar signkey

When asked for a **passphrase**, merely re-enter your password. Browsers do not yet trust the signed applet – after all, anyone can sign an applet. To achieve this, we would either have to get a certificate signed by a **certificate authority (CA)** that the browser has been set up to trust, or import our own certificate into the browser as a trusted root certificate, so we effectively become our own CA – at least, that is how it would work in an ideal world. (We will discuss CAs in more detail below.) As mentioned above, Internet Explorer and Netscape are incompatible in their approach to code signing.

Rather than deal with all this, we can for the moment use the JDK applet viewer tool and create a security policy file for the signed code. Save the following as `SecurityApp.policy1` (it is also included in the code download for this chapter):

```
keystore "file:SecurityApp.keystore";

grant SignedBy "signkey" {

    permission java.security.AllPermission;
};
```

The applet viewer can now be run with the following prompt:

C:\Beg_Java_Networking\Ch07>**appletviewer -J"-Djava.security.policy=SecurityApp.policy1"
SecurityApp.html**

Or if you are behind a firewall:

C:\Beg_Java_Networking\Ch07>**appletviewer -J"-Dhttp.proxyHost=123.456.7.89" -J"-
Dhttp.proxyPort=99" -J"-Djava.security.policy=SecurityApp.policy1" SecurityApp.html**

where `proxyHost` and `proxyPort` are equal to the proxy server and port that your system is configured to.

The policy allows applets signed by signkey to execute outside the sandbox, and the applet should run as if it were an application installed on the machine.

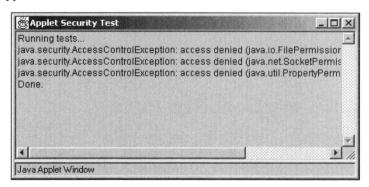

By signing the `SecurityApp.jar` file we have achieved two things:

❑ We have established the authorship of the archive. The archive is signed with the **private key** of the key pair generated by keytool. This signature can be verified with the other, **public key**. We can then freely give the public key away so others can verify that we really signed the archive. As long as the private key is kept secret, it is impossible for anyone else to create an archive that will verify against our public key.

163

❏ We have protected the archive against tampering. The signature includes a checksum (digest) of all the archive contents. Any modification of the classes or other files will change the checksum and invalidate the signature.

Security is based on trust, so don't just believe it – try it! Change one of the classes, recompile and update the archive, then run the applet viewer again. Rename your keystore file and generate a new key pair with the same name. Convince yourself that it really works.

The applet viewer uses the Java **security policy file** to check whether applets signed with our specific signature should be trusted. Few people use Sun's applet viewer, of course. And you will generally not want to force all of your users to set up a policy file or reconfigure their browser just so they can use your applet anyway. So, how are they to know that you are indeed who you say you are, and that you can be trusted?

With this issue in mind, browsers generally trust applets signed with certificates issued by one of a list of common **certificate authorities (CA)**. These authorities will check your identity before they issue you with a certificate signed by them. Because the certificate is signed, it is unforgeable and tamper-proof. Should your code be found to be doing something unsavory, you can be easily tracked down using the information from the certificate you used to sign the code with.

When we come to explore secure web sites (HTTPS, SSL), we will see that virtually the same considerations apply there. Browsers will only accept an SSL connection from the server without complaint if it uses a certificate signed by a reputable certificate authority.

Java Web Start

Slow downloads and incompatible implementations have all but killed off Java applets. Our discussion would therefore not be complete without at least mentioning the **Java Web Start** plugin. This is a comparatively new technology to deploy Java applications from a web server. With a minimum of user interaction, it features good security, incremental downloads and updates.

Although Java Web Start uses a sandbox model similar to the applet sandbox, applications can gain limited, controlled access to the local disk. Upon acceptance of the certificate by the user, signed applications can get unrestricted access without the cross-browser compatibility problems that affect applets. The price to pay is that browsers do not support it by default; the user will have to install a plugin first. The plugin is also included in version 1.4 of the JDK.

The Command Line Security Tools

We have already been using two of the security-related tools shipped with JDK 1.2 and higher: `keytool` and `jarsigner`. It is worth taking a slightly closer look at each. We will not discuss every command line option in minute detail, but you can find more information in the JDK documentation itself or from http://java.sun.com/j2se/1.3/docs/index.html.

Keytool

The **keytool** will manage a small database with keys and trusted certificates. These are used to sign code and to verify signatures:

❑ **Private key**: this half of a key pair can be used to sign a JAR file. The private key needs to be kept secret, so that we will be the only one able to sign code and other files.

❑ **Public key**: the public key of a key pair is necessary to verify the signature. If we only know someone's public key, it is currently impossible to discover the corresponding private key. For this reason it is safe to spread the public key far and wide so that others can authenticate our code.

❑ **Trusted certificate:** This contains your identity, your public key, and some other information, signed by a trusted certificate authority. Such certificates remove the need of disseminating your public key before your code can be trusted. If you sign using the certificate, the other party will know that the authority vouches for the authenticity of your public key.

Using the keytool, it is possible to generate a **key pair** of public and private keys using the -genkey option. We've already seen this in operation in the previous example. The key's alias defaults to mykey, but you can specify an alias with the -alias option:

```
keytool -genkey -alias signkey -keyalg rsa
```

The -keyalg option tells the tool to use generate a key pair for the given encryption algorithm. The default is DSA, but most browsers support only RSA key pairs. Other options include setting a limited validity period (-validity), the key size (-keysize), and a password for the key in addition to the keystore password (-keypass). The password will protect any usage of the private key.

It is also possible to generate the **certificate request** an authority needs before they can give you a certificate, using -certreq -file certificate_file:

```
keytool -certreq -alias signkey -file codeCertReq.cer
```

Please refer to the individual certificate authorities' guidelines on submitting a certificate request.

The following command will display the contents of a certificate file:

```
keytool -printcert -file fred.cer
```

If you wish to import certificates from people you trust, once you have firmly convinced yourself that the certificate is genuinely theirs, this is possible using the -import option:

```
keytool -import -alias fredsCertificate -file fred.cer
```

You can also import the certificate signed and returned to you by a certificate authority:

```
keytool -import -trustcacerts -alias fredsCertificate -file codeCertReq.cer
```

The -trustcacerts option tells the keytool to trust certificates from the ${java.home}/lib/security/cacerts keystore file, which contains the keys of certificate authorities. If you use an authority other than VeriSign, you will probably need to import their certificate in this keystore first. Without the -trustcacerts option, the cacerts keystore is ignored.

Should you wish to export your certificate or public key so that someone else can import it in his or her key database, the command is as follows:

```
keytool -export -alias signkey -file peter.cer
```

If you want to change any details in your certificate without generating a new key pair, this is possible though self-signing certificates with -selfcert. The keytool documentation contains a step-by-step description of the procedure.

It is also possible to perform common maintenance tasks with the tool, such as displaying all keystore entries or a particular alias using the -list option, deleting a keystore entry using -delete -keystore *keystorename*.keystore and then deleting entries using -delete -alias *alias*, cloning one with -keyclone -alias *alias* -dest *destination_alias*, or changing the keystore and entry passwords using -storepasswd and -keypasswd.

There are a number of options common to virtually all keytool commands. The most important are the -keystore option to specify a keystore file other than the default ${user.home}/.keystore; -alias to specify a key or certificate alias different from mykey; and -file to read the input from, or write output to, a file.

> *The keystore file is by default stored in the Java Key Store (JKS) format, a Sun proprietary file format. You can provide your own keystore implementation to change this, or use the alternative keystores provided by some Java extensions. The keytool will work with any file-based keystore, but not with implementations that load their information from a database or the network. The other security tools in the JDK, jarsigner and policytool, have no such restriction.*

Jarsigner

Signing JAR archives is done using the jarsigner tool. Once an archive has been signed, its integrity and authenticity can be verified by the Java classloader. A signed archive cannot be modified without invalidating the signature. The most important usage options are the following:

```
jarsigner -keystore mystore -storepass mystorePassword -keypass signkeyPassword -
signedjar MySignedJarFile.jar MyJarFile.jar signkey
```

This command would sign MyJarFile.jar using the alias myCodeSigningKey from the keystore located in the mystore file. The signed archive will be written to MyJarFile.jar. You can omit the passwords if you wish; the tool will prompt for them. The keystore can be omitted too if you are using the default keystore file.

The tool can also be used to check the validity of signatures:

```
jarsigner -verify -keystore mystore MySignedJarFile.jar
```

The public key of the signature or certificate authority needs to be in your keystore file for verification to work. Multiple people can sign an archive simply by running the jarsigner tool multiple times.

Browser Compatibility

It has been mentioned before that Microsoft Internet Explorer does, unfortunately, not recognize signed JAR archives. To create an applet for use with IE, you will need to download the Microsoft SDK for Java from http://www.microsoft.com/java/sdk/ and use their archiving and signing tools. For a truly cross-browser applet, you will need to package it in both JAR and the CAB archives and use Internet Explorer's CABBASE applet parameter:

```
<HTML>
    <HEAD><TITLE>Applet Security Example</TITLE></HEAD>
    <BODY>
        <HR WIDTH="100%">
        <H3>Applet Security Example</H3>
        <HR WIDTH="100%">
        <APPLET
            CODE="/com/wrox/security/SecurityApp.class"
            ARCHIVE="/come/wrox/security/SecurityApp.jar" WIDTH=0 HEIGHT=0>
            <PARAM NAME="CABBASE" VALUE="SecurityApp.cab">
        </APPLET>
    </BODY>
</HTML>
```

This HTML will load and verify `SecurityApp.cab` in IE and `SecurityApp.jar` in most other browsers.

Although Netscape supports JAR archives, it introduces its own incompatibilities by requiring the use of the Netscape signing tools available from http://developer.netscape.com/software/signedobj/jarpack.html, and a proprietary **Capabilities API** to perform privileged operations.

This turns writing cross-browser code to escape the sandbox into a developer's nightmare. You could require your users to download and install the Sun Java 2 plugin, but if they have to install a plugin anyway, Java Web Start (discussed above) is likely to be the best option.

The Java 2 Model

The sandbox model has two important limitations. First, it is very coarse-grained: either you are inside the sandbox and you cannot access the system in a meaningful way at all, or you are outside of it and free to do completely as you please. There is no middle way. If, for example, you are an Application Service Provider hosting a number of your customers' web applications on a single application server, you cannot set up security so that each application can only access the directories assigned to that customer. The **principle of least privilege** means that, if you are concerned about security, you give a program exactly those privileges it needs to perform its function. The sandbox does not support this model.

The second limitation of the sandbox is that it is only concerned with applet security. In practice, there are many other situations where you may need security. The example above clearly illustrates this. To give another example, an Enterprise JavaBean (EJB) may not create threads. Yet without a better security model, an EJB container will actually not be able to enforce this.

In the Java 2 platform (JDK 1.2 and higher), the security model was completely overhauled to address these problems. The new model offers fine-grained, highly configurable access control to applications as well as applets. Separate permissions can be set up for each major API, such as file access, networking, and AWT/Swing.

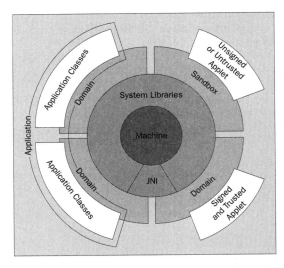

In the Java 2 security model, every Java class (including both applets and applications) runs inside a **protection domain**. Each domain has a set of **permissions** associated with it. For example, classes in a specific domain might be able to access the hard disk but not be allowed any network connections. Yet another domain might allow read-only access to the disk and limited networking.

A Java class is assigned to exactly one protection domain based both on where it was loaded from, and who signed it. There is little that sets applets apart from applications anymore; the only difference is that applets default to strict security settings, while applications don't. Such defaults can easily be changed. Finally, it is worth noting that an application may consist of classes from more than one protection domain; this is quite common in secure applications where access to sensitive resources is granted only through libraries.

At the lowest level are the Java libraries, running inside the **system domain**. The system domain always enjoys full privileges. For each privileged operation that the libraries implement, they check with the **security manager** to see if the protection domains of the calling code have permission to perform that operation, and throw a `SecurityException` if they don't. It follows that the security system is critically dependent on the fact that all machine access goes through the libraries – in other words, if you grant code access to native code libraries (JNI) you no longer have any serious security in place.

Looking back at the two examples of protection domains given above – one with full hard disk access but no networking privileges, one with disk read access and networking – a potential problem comes up. There is no reason why a Java object from one domain cannot call an object in another domain. In fact, this happens all the time when Java code makes use of the system libraries. It is important that restricted code cannot get more permissions simply by calling more privileged code, or by arranging to receive a callback from such code. The security manager has to examine the call chain and work out the *combined* permissions of all protection domains involved in the call. If any of the domains do not have enough permissions to perform the operation, a `SecurityException` will be thrown.

As we have seen, every class gets assigned to one, and only one, protection domain. This is done by the classloader as the class is loaded. To construct protection domains and decide which domain a class belongs to, the Java `SecureClassLoader` normally uses a configuration file called the **security policy file**. Before going into details about the Java classes that implement the Java 2 security model, we will first take a look at the policy file to get a better high-level feel for what the model actually can do.

The Security Policy File

The security policy file controls the permissions granted to code coming from one or more code sources. In fact, we already constructed a simple policy for the applet-signing example that simply granted all possible permissions to the applet, which is the Java 2 way of emulating the JDK 1.1 sandbox model.

A policy file consists of a `keystore` entry, which tells the policy manager where to find the public keys for signers or certificate authorities, and one or more `grant` entries. Each `grant` entry specifies permissions for code based on who signed the code, where the code is located, or a combination of both. With the latest JDK, version 1.4, you can even specify permissions based on who executes the code.

In everyday life, you will probably prefer working with the JDK's `policytool` application. The policy tool gives you a simple graphical front-end to the policy file settings, so you don't have to remember all the system permission names, targets and actions. However, in the examples below, we will edit policy files directly because this offers valuable insights into the way the Java 2 security model operates.

Anatomy of a Policy File

The example below illustrates a policy file assigning three different levels of trust. This file demonstrates most of the features you may find in security property files. We will go through the entries line by line:

```
// The keystore file is "myapp.keystore" in the "keystores" directory

keystore "keystores/myapp.keystore"

// give everyone access to the temporary directory
grant {
    permission java.io.FilePermission "C:\\tmp\\*", "read,write,delete";
};

// code from the company applets directory get limited permissions
grant CodeBase "http://www.mycompany.com/applets/*" {
    permission java.io.FilePermission "<<ALL_FILES>>", "read";
    permission java.io.FilePermission "${user.home}${/}-",
               "write,delete,execute";
    permission java.io.SocketPermission "*.mycompany.com", "connect";
    permission com.mycompany.application.CustomPermission, SignedBy "signkey";
};

/* code from anywhere on the company website, which is also signed by *
 * both my key and the authorization key, gets full permissions       */
grant CodeBase "http://www.mycompany.com/-",
SignedBy "signkey,authorizationkey" {
    permission java.security.AllPermission;
};
```

The keywords appearing in this file, such as keystore, grant, codeBase, signedBy, and permission, are all case-insensitive. The permission names represent case-sensitive class names.

```
keystore "keystores/myapp.keystore"
```

This is the location of the keystore file that stores the public keys of signers, necessary to authenticate signed code. It is given relative to the location of the policy file itself; in this case, it is a file called java in the keystores subdirectory of wherever the policy is located. If the policy file was retrieved from a web server, the keystore file will be retrieved from the same server. If you want, it is also possible to specify an absolute keystore location, for instance http://www.mycompany.com/keystores/myapp.keystore.

These three lines form a simple grant entry that allows all code to read, write and delete files in the temporary directory.

```
grant {
    permission java.io.FilePermission "C:\\tmp\\*", "read,write,delete";
};
```

Running executable code from this directory is not permitted because permission to execute has not been granted. Because neither a signer nor a codebase is given for this grant (which would be specified between the grant keyword and the open curly brace), it applies to all code irrespective of where it came from or who signed it, or indeed of whether it is signed at all.

Note how the temporary directory c:\tmp\ is specified – the first argument to the FilePermission, its **target**, is not a URL but a filesystem path. Because of this, it needs to use system-specific notation (Windows, in this case). Backslashes need to be escaped as in ordinary Java strings. The second argument, its **action**, tells what the permissible actions on the target are; in this case reading, writing, and deleting files.

The next grant specifies a code base:

```
grant CodeBase "http://www.mycompany.com/applets/*" {
```

This grant is only valid for code loaded from the http://www.mycompany.com/applets/ web site directory. Code loaded from any subdirectories is *not* included. You can denote a directory and all its subdirectories by replacing the star by a dash, "-". The code base can be any URL, including file:URLs for locations on the local hard disk.

```
permission java.io.FilePermission "<<ALL_FILES>>", "read";
```

This permission entry grants full read access. The string <<ALL_FILES>> is a special constant denoting all files on the system. The next line is also a file permission entry:

```
permission java.io.FilePermission "${user.home}${/}-",
                "write,delete,execute";
```

Full access is granted to files in the user's home directory and all its subdirectories. This entry uses **property expansion**: ${user.home} is replaced by the value of the user.home Java system property. If you are familiar with UNIX shell variables you will no doubt recognize the syntax. The ${/} is a special property which will be expanded to the system-specific path separator, that is, the backslash in Windows and the forward slash in UNIX. This helps to make property files a bit more portable.

The action omits read permission, because read permission has already been granted to all files on the system in the previous line. When a single permission occurs multiple times like this, the privileges granted are those of the permissions combined. Put differently, permissions are combined using an OR operation.

```
permission java.io.SocketPermission "*.mycompany.com", "connect";
```

In the next line, connections are possible to any host within the mycompany.com domain, and all ports on those hosts, but the code is not allowed to operate as a server (this would require the listen and accept actions).

```
permission com.mycompany.application.CustomPermission SignedBy "signkey";
};
```

The Java 2 security framework is extensible – we can create our own permissions and grant them in the policy file. Every permission name is actually the name of the Java class that implements it. In this case, a custom permission implemented by com.mycompany.application.CustomPermission is granted to code loaded from the company web site *and* signed with the signkey private key. We will take a closer look at implementing our own permissions later on in this chapter.

The next grant shows that it is possible to require multiple signatures and combine them with a code base:

```
grant CodeBase "http://www.mycompany.com/-",
SignedBy "signkey,authorizationkey" {
    permission java.security.AllPermission;
};
```

This code states that code loaded from anywhere on the company web site that is signed by both keys signkey *and* authorizationkey, gets all permissions. java.security.AllPermission is a special permission which implies all other permissions.

When the Java classloader loads a new Java class, it compares the signers of the class and the location it was loaded from with the grant entries in the policy file. The permissions granted by all matching entries are combined into the class's protection domain. Every combination of code base and signers (and, as of JDK 1.4, principals) corresponds to a domain. Whenever the class attempts to perform a privileged operation such as network access, the security manager examines the call chain to trace the path taken through the code. For each protection domain involved, it verifies that the domain actually has permission to perform this operation. If not, a SecurityException is thrown.

In JDK 1.4 policy files, you can specify not only CodeBase and SignedBy in your grant statements, but also Principal classname "principalname", enabling you to assign permissions to code based on who executed it (the principal).

```
grant principal javax.security.auth.x500.X500Principal "cn=Joe" {
    permission java.net.SocketPermission "www.wrox.com:80", "connect";
}
```

This grant gives code run by Joe access to the www.wrox.com web site, provided he has been properly authenticated and the application was written to support principal-based permissions. If the principal has an entry in your keystore, there is a useful shorthand whereby you omit the class and simply specify the user's keystore alias:

```
grant principal "Joe" {
    permission java.net.SocketPermission "www.wrox.com:80", "connect";
}
```

Authentication and principals will be fully discussed in Chapter 14.

A Policy for the Security Application

Having seen a number of different ways to determine exactly what code gets granted permissions, and quite a few of those permissions themselves, it is useful to see how this can be applied to the policy file from the security demo applet.

```
keystore "file:SecurityApp.keystore";

grant SignedBy "signkey" {
    permission java.io.FilePermission "/", "read";
    permission java.net.SocketPermission "www.wrox.com", "connect";
    permission java.util.PropertyPermission "user.home", "read";
    permission java.awt.AWTPermission "showWindowWithoutWarningBanner";
};
```

This policy file grants the applet precisely those permissions it needs to operate the way a normal application would – no more, no less – in the spirit of the principle of least privilege. Assuming the policy is saved as `SecurityApp.policy2`, running

C:\Beg_Java_Networking\Ch07>**appletviewer -J"-Djava.security.policy=SecurityApp.policy2"**
SecurityApp.html

should remove any difference between applet and application mode.

If you are operating behind a firewall, then the command prompt is as follows:

C:\Beg_Java_Networking\Ch07>**appletviewer -J"-Dhttp.proxyHost=123.456.7.89" -J"-**
Dhttp.proxyPort=99" -J"-DtrustProxy=true" --J"-Djava.security.policy=SecurityApp.policy2"
SecurityApp.html

where, once again, the `proxyHost` and `proxyPort` values are equal to the proxy IP address and its port that is not behind your firewall. In addition, there is a new instruction here: – DtrustProxy=true. Without this, an `AccessControlException` is thrown as the `SocketPermission` needs to use DNS lookup to reconcile proxy-returned data with the hostname-based permission it has. The `trustProxy` property tells it to trust the proxy for DNS lookup.

You might want to try removing a few permissions, or changing the permissions' actions, to verify that an exception gets thrown. Or add a `CodeBase` to the `grant` entry, for example:

```
grant SignedBy "signkey", CodeBase "file:C:/Program Files/-" {
```

This will cause the code to be granted permissions only if it was loaded from the `Program Files` directory, or (thanks to the dash) a subdirectory underneath it. You can find a description of the most important permissions, their targets and actions in the table a few pages onwards.

The Java 2 security model does not only work for applets, but for any Java code including applications. To enable application-mode security for the above `SecurityApp`, we need to do two things:

❑ Because applications do not normally run with security restrictions, we have to set the `java.security.manager` system property to indicate that the application needs to be run with a security manager. Alternatively, the application can install its own security manager using

```
System.setSecurityManager(new SecurityManager());
```

❑ The security manager needs to be told that, rather than the system policy file, we want to use our own security policy. Setting the `java.security.policy` system property will cause an application to be run under the specified policy file.

To execute the demo as an application with a security policy, run:

C:\Beg_Java_Networking\Ch07>**java -Djava.security.manager -Djava.security.policy=SecurityApp.policy2 -jar SecurityDemo.jar**

Again, if you are behind a firewall, the prompt is:

C:\Beg_Java_Networking\Ch07>**java -Dhttp.proxyHost=123.456.7.89 -Dhttp.proxyPort=99 - DtrustProxy=true -Djava.security.manager -Djava.security.policy=SecurityApp.policy2 -jar SecurityApp.jar**

It is worthwhile to experiment with the various settings and become comfortable with them. Setting up a well thought out security policy file can make networked applications more secure and help reduce the impact if your server is compromised.

Policytool

The `policytool` is a simple graphical front-end to create and maintain policy files. The greatest advantage is that it knows about all the standard permissions, their targets, and their actions, which saves quite a bit of browsing through the documentation. Take, for example, the policy constructed in the security policies example.

```
keystore "file:SecurityApp.keystore";

grant SignedBy "signkey" {
    permission java.io.FilePermission "/", "read";
    permission java.net.SocketPermission "www.wrox.com", "connect";
    permission java.util.PropertyPermission "user.home", "read";
    permission java.awt.AWTPermission "showWindowWithoutWarningBanner";
};
```

The following picture shows its contents when edited by the policytool:

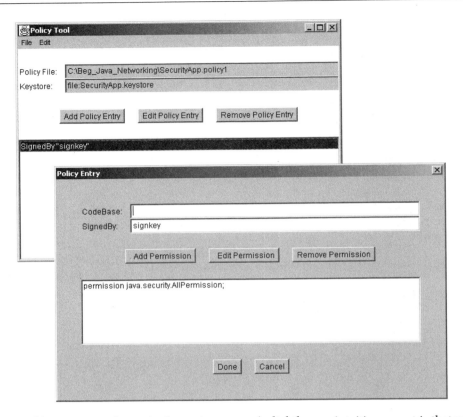

Filename and keystore are shown in the main screen. A slightly non-intuitive aspect is that you can't just overtype the location of the keystore file on the main screen, but have to set it using Change KeyStore in the Edit menu. Every grant policy entry is shown in the list underneath. Pressing Add or Edit brings up the policy entry window.

In the policy entry window, you can set the code base and signers the grant applies to, and add, edit, or remove the individual permissions inside it. If you have worked through the discussion of policy files, the tool should be straightforward to use.

Types of Permissions

The table below lists some of the most important permissions and targets. You can find an exhaustive listing in your JDK directory at docs/guide/security/permissions.html, or consult the Javadoc documentation for the various java.security.Permission classes. We will talk more about actions and targets in the section on *Defining a Custom Permission*:

Permission	Target	Action	Description
java.security. AllPermission	None *	None	Grants every other permission, including user-defined permissions.

Permission	Target	Action	Description
java.awt.AWT Permission	AccessClipboard	None	Posts to and retrieves from the AWT clipboard.
	AccessEvent Queue	None	Grants access to the AWT event queue.
	ListenToAll AWTEvents	None	Installs an arbitrary event listener. This could allow malicious code to read keyboard input.
	ShowWindow WithoutWarning Banner	None	Removes the applet warning from windows.
java.io.File Permission	File pattern, or <<ALL FILES>>	read write execute delete	Grants permission for the writing, execution and deletion of files. The file pattern may contain the star (*) denoting all files in the directory, or the dash (–) for all files and subdirectories.
			Other than on UNIX systems, execute permission is meaningless for directories, and the delete option is not applicable to UNIX.
			<<ALL FILES>> gives access to all files.
			Code *always* has read access to files and subdirectories in the directory it was loaded from.
java.net.Net Permission	SetDefault Authentication	None	Sets the authentication method when a proxy or HTTP server asks for authentication.
	RequestPassword Authentication	None	Asks the registered authenticator for a password.
	SpecifyStream Handler	None	Grants ability to specify a stream handler when constructing an URL.
java.util. Property Permission	Property pattern	read write	Grants permission to read and write system properties. The last character of the property pattern may be a star (*), for example, java.*.

Table continued on following page

Permission	Target	Action	Description
`java.lang.Runtime Permission`	`ExitVM`	None	Exits the Java virtual machine.
	`SetFactory`	None	Sets socket factories and URL stream handlers.
	`SetIO`	None	Modifies `System.in`, `System.out` and `System.err`.
	`GetProtection Domain`	None	Gives access to policy information for a code domain.
	`LoadLibrary`	None	Allows access to native libraries (JNI).
	`AccessDeclared Members`	None	Accesses reflection information for a class.
	`QueuePrintJob`	None	Initiates a print job.
`java.net.Socket Permission`	`Host:port pattern`	`accept` `connect` `listen` `resolve`	Accepts connections from a host, connects to a host, listens on a port (as in `ServerSocket`; this only makes sense for `localhost`), and provides DNS and service lookups. `resolve` is implied if any of the other three is present.
			In the target pattern, the host may be either a hostname or an IP address. If it is a hostname, a single wildcard may be included in the leftmost position, for instance `*.wrox.com`. The port may be a single port or a port range, for example, `hostname:1024-2048`.

System and User Policy Files

In the examples discussed so far, a -Djava.security.policy argument was passed to the Java runtime telling it which policy file to use. Two more policies are always loaded: the **system security policy** located in the JDK directory under /lib/security/java.policy, and the **user security policy**, .java.policy, located in the user's home directory. (In Windows, the default home directory is the parent directory of My Documents.)

These default locations are, in turn, determined by the values of some system properties:

```
policy.url.1=file:${java.home}/lib/security/java.policy
policy.url.2=file:${user.home}/.java.policy
```

If you want, you can redefine these properties, or load additional policy files by defining new properties along the same lines: `policy.url.3`, and so forth. The file `${java.home}/lib/security/java.security`, where `${java.home}` is the location of the Java runtime environment, specifies the default values for these system properties.

Defining a Custom Permission

We have seen that the permissions in the security policy file are actually class names; unsurprisingly, the Java security framework uses these classes to represent the permissions at runtime. All of them directly or indirectly extend `java.security.Permission`. To create a new permission, all you have to do is subclass it.

Permission and BasicPermission

Let's first examine how the `Permission` class works. It is an abstract class with the following attributes:

❏ A name, returned by `getName()`; in the policy file, this was referred to as the *target* of the permission. For example, the name of a `java.io.FilePermission` is a filename pattern.

❏ Zero or more **actions** returned by `getActions()`, for example `read` or `execute` to indicate permission to read or execute the files matching the pattern.

You will recognize these properties from the policy file settings discussed in the previous sections. In addition, there are two more abstract methods that help the access controller to query permissions:

❏ An `implies(Permission)` method returns a Boolean indicating whether the argument is implied by the permission object. Taking `java.net.SocketPermission` as an example: `resolve` permission for www.wrox.com:80 is implied by a `connect` permission for `*.wrox.com:1-1023`. The security code uses this method to check permissions and simplify permission collections.

❏ The `newPermissionCollection()` factory method is used by the security code to create collections holding multiple permissions of the same class. That way, a number of permissions such as `SocketPermissions` can be conveniently bundled and checked as a whole.

To create your own permission class, you need to subclass `Permission` and provide implementations for at least the `equals()`, `hashCode()`, `implies()` and `getActions()` methods.

There are a few things to watch out for when creating your own permissions:

❏ The `equals(Object)` and `hashCode()` contracts, as set out in the documentation of `java.lang.Object`, should be satisfied so that `Permissions` can be put in a hashtable.

❏ It should correctly implement `implies(Permission)` or the security manager will get all confused about whether a required permission is covered by the granted permissions or not.

❑ The action list returned by getActions() should be in *canonical form*, meaning that the same string should be returned regardless of the order in which the actions where listed in the security properties file.

❑ If a set of permissions can *between them* imply a permission – even if no single permission in the set explicitly implies it completely by itself – you will need to provide your own implementation of PermissionCollection. We will go into this in more detail when we discuss permission collections. If you don't need to implement your own PermissionCollection, the newPermissionCollection() method should simply return null.

If you are creating a permission that recognizes wildcard patterns in the name (target), you can probably save yourself implementing the implies() method. The BasicPermission class provides an implementation of implies() that recognizes wildcards in the target name, so that the name my.permission.* implies my.permission.special.

Checking the Permission

Defining a permission is only one side of the coin. Presumably, some privileged operation is being implemented where we should check that the calling code has that permission. This is done using the security manager, implemented by the java.lang.SecurityManager class. This class can seem daunting at first because of its bewildering array of methods, all checking for specific privileges. They actually date back to the old sandbox model. In Java 2, all of them delegate the checking to a single method, checkPermission(Permission).

```
SecurityManager security = System.getSecurityManager();
if (security != null) {
    Permission toCheck = new CheckPasswordPermission(arguments);
    security.checkPermission(toCheck);
}
```

First, the currently installed security manager is retrieved. If the code is not running under a security manager, this returns null, so we should remember to check for this. A Permission object representing the privileges we need is constructed, and checkPermission() is called. This method does not return a value, but simply throws a SecurityException if any of the calling code does not have enough privileges.

In fact, the default SecurityManager does in turn delegate the checkPermission() call to java.security.AccessController.checkPermission(Permission). The AccessController has a number of static methods that actually implement the permission checks and a couple of other facilities, which we will examine below.

Performing the Privileged Operation

When we build code to perform a privileged function, it is vital that the client code does not have any access to the resources we need. After all, anyone can run a Java decompiler against our classes, figure out what they do, implement the functionality themselves and circumvent any security we want to impose. We could try to keep our classes secret, of course, but that still doesn't prevent a determined attacker from reverse engineering the logic. **Security through obscurity is very bad security**. In fact, openness tends to encourage security because it exposes your algorithms to peer review, and prevents you from lazily relying upon your algorithm being "secret".

This immediately runs us into problems. Suppose for a moment that we need to access a database over a network. If the client code calling our function does not have network access to the database machine, then neither have we. Remember, the security model requires that *all* the code in the call chain has the required privileges. Clearly we need a way to perform a **privileged operation** subject to the protection domain of our class only, disregarding any code further up the chain.

The `java.security.AccessController` class provides a number of static methods:

❑ `checkPermission(Permission)` checks whether all code in the call chain has sufficient privileges to perform the operation specified by the permission, as described previously.

❑ A number of `doPrivileged(PrivilegedAction, ...)` methods give the ability to execute a section of code without being restricted by the protection domains of the calling code.

❑ `getContext()` returns an `AccessControlContext`, which essentially is a snapshot of the current permissions, looking at all the code in the call chain. This can be useful if the actual permission checking needs to happen in another thread, where the current call chain is not available.

Clearly, the `doPrivileged(PrivilegedAction)` method provides exactly the facility we need. The privileged code is encapsulated in an object implementing the `PrivilegedAction` interface. This interface is virtually identical to `Runnable`, except for the fact that the `run()` method is not defined as `void` but returns an `Object`. In the simplest cases, you can instantiate an inner class:

```
AccessController.doPrivileged(new PrivilegedAction() {
    public Object run() {
        // start of privileged code
        doDatabaseAccess();
        return null; // no return value
        // end of privileged code
    }
});
```

For actions that need to throw exceptions we can use `PrivilegedExceptionAction`. We will take a closer look at this class after an example.

Putting It All Together

To see the entire process in action, we will use a password-checking library example. It will read its passwords from a simple, unencrypted password file. This file should be unreadable to normal code so that a client program will only have access to it through the library. The library will never directly return a user's password, but simply `true` or `false` to indicate whether the password is correct. The password verification process itself will be regarded as a privileged operation, subject to a `CheckPasswordPermission`. Finally, a simple command line application is written to allow some basic testing of the library.

The first ingredient is the password-checking permission. The password library will need to be signed, so its classes need to live in a separate `password` package.

```
//CheckPasswordPermission.java

package com.wrox.password;

import java.security.*;
```

```
public class CheckPasswordPermission extends Permission {

  public CheckPasswordPermission() {
    super("<CheckPasswordPermission>");
  }

  public CheckPasswordPermission(String name, String actions) {
    this();
  }

  public boolean equals(Object obj) {
    return obj instanceof CheckPasswordPermission;
  }

  public String getActions() {
    return "";
  }

  public boolean implies(Permission p) {
    return equals(p);
  }

  public int hashCode() {
    return CheckPasswordPermission.class.hashCode();
  }
}
```

There is little to this class except very basic implementations for the abstract methods in `Permission`. The actual password-checking code is a bit more involved. The `CheckPassword` class living in the password package is responsible for performing the actual check:

```
//CheckPassword.java

package com.wrox.password;

import java.io.*;
import java.net.*;
import java.security.*;

public class CheckPassword {
```

The following is little more than a `doPrivileged()` wrapper around the second method. Ensuring that the caller has `CheckPasswordPermission` takes just a few lines of code. Note that the Boolean value returned by `privilegedCheck()` needs to be "boxed" inside a Boolean object because `PrivilegedAction.run()` cannot return a primitive type.

```
public boolean check(final String username, final String password,
                      final String passwordLocation) {

  // First verify that the callers have permission to check passwords
  SecurityManager security = System.getSecurityManager();
```

```
      if (security != null) {
        security.checkPermission(new CheckPasswordPermission());
      }

      // Then check the password in a privileged code block
      Boolean passwordOk =
        (Boolean) AccessController.doPrivileged(new PrivilegedAction() {
        public Object run() {

          // start of privileged code
          try {
            boolean ok = privilegedCheck(username, password,
                                    passwordLocation);
            return new Boolean(ok);
          } catch (IOException e) {
            return Boolean.FALSE;
          }
          // end of privileged code
        }
      });

      return passwordOk.booleanValue();
  }
```

The meat of the password checker is the `privilegedCheck()` method. It opens the password file from any URL, and attempts to find the given username in it. Once it has found the user, it compares the password to the one passed into the function. We would normally make this method private, but it is declared public here so that the test program can call it for demonstration purposes.

```
    public boolean privilegedCheck(String username, String password,
                              String passwordLocation) throws IOException {
      String toSearch = username + ":";
      String passwordFound = null;
      URL passwordUrl = new URL(passwordLocation);
      BufferedReader passwords =
        new BufferedReader(new InputStreamReader(passwordUrl.openStream()));

      try {
        while (true) {
          String line = passwords.readLine();
          if (line == null) {
            break;

          }
          if (line.startsWith(toSearch)) {
            passwordFound = line.substring(toSearch.length());
            break;
          }
        }
      }
      finally {
        passwords.close();
      }
      return passwordFound != null && password.equals(passwordFound);
    }
  }
```

The CheckPassword and CheckPasswordPermission classes make up the password-checking library. After compilation, they need to be packaged in a JAR and signed so they can be given exclusive permission to read the password file:

C:\Beg_Java_Networking\Ch07>**javac com\wrox\password*.java**

C:\Beg_Java_Networking\Ch07>**jar cf CheckPassword.jar com\wrox\password*.class**

C:\Beg_Java_Networking\Ch07>**jarsigner -keystore SecurityApp.keystore CheckPassword.jar signkey**

We will assume the archive is signed with the signkey signature generated for the security application above. The CheckPassword class needs to access a password file, consisting of a list of *username*:*password* combinations, one per line. For example:

```
bill:clinton
joe:secret
```

In this example, the name of the file should be password.txt. The use of the library can be demonstrated with a simple command line client called CheckPasswordApp:

```
import com.wrox.password.*;

public class CheckPasswordApp {

  public static void main(String args[]) {
    if (args.length == 2) {
      try {

        // install a security manager if none has been installed yet
        if (System.getSecurityManager() == null) {
          System.setSecurityManager(new SecurityManager());
        }

        // check the password
        CheckPassword checker = new CheckPassword();
        System.out.println(checker.check(args[0], args[1],
                                   "file:password.txt"));
      } catch (Exception e) {
        System.out.println(e);
      }
    } else {
      System.out.println("Arguments: username password");
    }
  }
}
```

After compilation, the application needs to be packaged in a JAR with the following manifest file, saved as CheckPasswordApp.manifest:

```
Manifest-Version: 1.0
Main-Class: CheckPasswordApp
Class-Path: CheckPassword.jar
```

This tells the Java interpreter that the password application needs to use classes from `CheckPassword.jar`.

Next, we compile the class and create `CheckPasswordApp.jar`:

C:\Beg_Java_Networking\Ch07>**javac CheckPasswordApp.java**

C:\Beg_Java_Networking\Ch07>**jar cfm CheckPasswordApp.jar CheckPasswordApp.manifest CheckPasswordApp.class**

`CheckPasswordApp` has a `CheckPasswordPermission` but is otherwise unprivileged code, so there is no need to sign this JAR. To set up the permission, and allow the password library free access to the password file, a security policy needs to be set up:

```
//CheckPassword.policy

keystore "file:SecurityApp.keystore";

// give the password library permission to read the password file
grant CodeBase "file:CheckPassword.jar", SignedBy "signkey" {
  permission java.io.FilePermission "password.txt", "read";
};

/* give password-checking permission only to locally installed code, but *
 * not to anything loaded over the internet                              */
grant CodeBase "file:/-" {
   permission com.wrox.password.CheckPasswordPermission;
};
```

Assuming this policy file is saved as `CheckPassword.policy`, the demonstration application can be run by typing:

C:\Beg_Java_Networking\Ch07>**java -Djava.security.policy=CheckPassword.policy –jar CheckPasswordApp.jar joe secret**

The application should respond with

true

to indicate that joe does indeed have the password secret. It is worth experimenting with a couple of user names and passwords to convince yourself that it really works.

The fact that normal, unprivileged code really does not have the ability to directly read the password file can be verified by changing `CheckPasswordApp` and replacing the call to check() by a call to privilegedCheck():

```
    CheckPassword checker = new CheckPassword();
    System.out.println(checker.privilegedCheck(
       args[0], args[1], "password.txt"));
}
```

Upon recompiling and running the example, an `AccessControlException` is now thrown because the `CheckPasswordApp` class is not allowed to access the password file. The same exception is thrown when the `CheckPasswordPermission` is commented out of the policy file so that the application is no longer allowed to access the password-checking library.

You may want to experiment some more with the policy file settings. For example, to retrieve the password file from the **password.mycompany.com** web server, the first `grant` in the policy file would need to be modified to:

```
// give the password library permission to read the password file
grant CodeBase "file:CheckPassword.jar", SignedBy "signkey" {
   permission java.net.SocketPermission "password.mycompany.com:80",
                                         "connect";
};
```

SecurityManager, AccessController and All That

To understand the roles of protection domains, the security manager, and the `AccessController` class, we can stick with the example and track its progress through the internals of the Java security system. When the classloader loads the classes from `CheckPassword.jar` and `CheckPasswordApp.jar`, it assigns them to two different protection domains, both characterized by their code base and signers.

Predictably, these protection domains are represented by `ProtectionDomain` objects. The protection domain of `CheckPassword.jar` has the `FilePermisson` necessary to access the password file, while both domains are granted a `CheckPasswordPermission`.

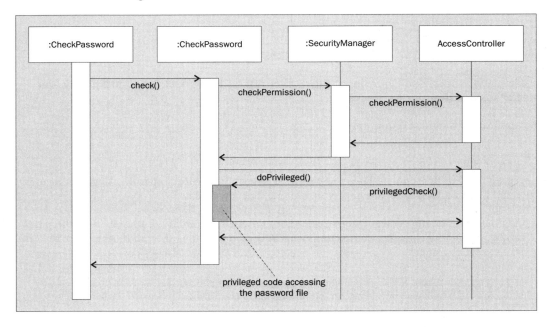

privileged code accessing
the password file

The sequence diagram above illustrates what is happening in the example. The vertical "swimlanes" represent the objects; time flows from top to bottom. The arrows represent the method calls taking place. The gray area is where the program is executing the `privilegedAction()` (itself not drawn, because it is little more than a call to `privilegedCheck()`). In this area, it is subject only to the privileges of `CheckPassword`'s protection domain and therefore able to read the password file.

The first thing `CheckPassword.check()` does is call the security manager to verify that the calling code does have password-checking permission. If you want this check to happen regardless whether there is a security manager installed or not, you can also call `AccessController.checkPermission()` directly.

When the main class calls `CheckPermission.check()`, the code would not normally be allowed to open and read the password file. The security manager would find `CheckPermissionApp()` in the call chain, which does not have the necessary `FilePermisson`. This is why replacing the call to `check()` by one to `privilegedCheck()` led to an `AccessControlException`.

For this reason, the `AccessController.doPrivileged()` method is used to execute the `privilegedCheck()` in the protection domain of `CheckPassword.jar`, disregarding all domains further up in the call chain. However, if the code inside a `PrivilegedAction` would make further calls to classes in other protection domains, the permissions of those domains *would* be imposed.

Finally, it is worth noting at this point that `CheckPassword` cannot reside in the same package as `CheckPasswordApp`. When a class is loaded from a signed archive, the classloader demands that *all* of the classes in that package are signed with the same key. This prevents malicious code from compromising security by redefining classes in the package.

Throwing Exceptions in Privileged Operations

The password-checking implementation given above has one problem: it does not handle exceptions very well. If there is a problem reading the password file, for example because it doesn't exist or because there are errors on the disk or network, the `check()` method simply returns `false`. It would be much better to propagate the exception to the calling code, and fortunately the security framework provides a way of doing this.

The `PrivilegedExceptionAction` interface is just like `PrivilegedException`, except that the `run()` method is defined to throw `Exception`. The `doPrivileged()` method will wrap the exception inside a `PrivilegedActionException` and throw that. In your code, you can catch the exception in `CheckPassword.java`, recover the original exception, and re-throw it:

```java
public boolean check(final String username, final String password,
                     final String passwordLocation)
throws IOException {
    // First verify that the callers have permission to check passwords
    SecurityManager security = System.getSecurityManager();
    if (security != null) {
        security.checkPermission(new CheckPasswordPermission());
    }

    // Then check the password in a privileged code block
    try {
        Boolean passwordOk = (Boolean)
            AccessController.doPrivileged(new PrivilegedExceptionAction() {
```

```
                public Object run() throws IOException {
                    // start of privileged code
                    boolean ok = privilegedCheck(username, password,
                                                passwordLocation);
                    return new Boolean(ok);
                    // end of privileged code
                }
            });

        return passwordOk.booleanValue();
    }
    catch(PrivilegedActionException e) {
        throw (IOException) e.getException();
    }
}
```

This technique does require you to keep careful track of the exceptions that can be thrown by your `PrivilegedExceptionAction`. If you modify your code to throw a new type of exception and forget to cater for it in the final catch clause, the compiler will not warn you; a `ClassCastException` will be thrown at runtime. Because this is in exception-handling code that can be difficult to test, it is easy for this bug to slip through unnoticed.

Guarding Access from Other Threads

Sometimes, checking if the calling code has the right permissions isn't quite as easy as calling the security manager. Take another look at the relevant code from `CheckPassword`:

```
// First verify that the callers have permission to check passwords
SecurityManager security = System.getSecurityManager();
if (security != null) {
    security.checkPermission(new CheckPasswordPermission());
}
```

To determine if the caller has `CheckPasswordPermission`, it examines all the protection domains involved in the call chain. But what if `CheckPassword` was a system service running in a different thread? The relevant call chain would not be available in this thread and it would be impossible to determine its domains. The security check would have to be delayed until *after* the privileged operation has completed and returned its result, when we are back in the calling thread and its protection domain information is at our disposal.

To give another example, the library could be made available to other applications as a remote service with an RMI interface. The password checking service would have no information about the permissions available to the client code, yet it needs this information to determine whether the client is allowed to check passwords.

To achieve this, we return the result in a **guarded object**. The `java.security.GuardedObject` class acts as a "safe" in which the result of the call is locked away. When the client code attempts to retrieve the result by calling `getObject()`, the guarded object calls the **guard**, which then performs the necessary security checks first. `Guard` is a simple interface with a single `checkGuard(Object)` method. Your security check has to implement this interface.

Sticking with the password-checking library as an example, this is how you implement a simple guard:

```
import java.security.*;

public class CheckPasswordGuard implements Guard {

    public void checkGuard(Object toGuard) throws SecurityException {
        SecurityManager security = System.getSecurityManager();
        if (security != null) {
            security.checkPermission(new CheckPasswordPermission());
        }
    }
}
```

With this guard, returning a guarded object with the Boolean result of the password check takes just a single line of code:

```
return new GuardedObject(passwordOk, new CheckPasswordGuard());
```

The permissions are now checked only when the calling code attempts to retrieve the result from the GuardedObject.

In fact, if you only have a single permission to check you do not even need to create your own Guard as the Permission class already implements it! The implementation is basically identical to that of CheckPasswordGuard above. This class can therefore be scrapped and the code simplified even further to:

```
return new GuardedObject(passwordOk, new CheckPasswordPermission());
```

Of course, the password-checking library does not actually need guarded objects as everything is handled in a single thread, but in network services that typically make heavy use of multi-threading or remote method calls you may well encounter this technique.

Permission Hierarchies

If you need to implement multiple permission classes in your application, you could of course make all of them subclasses of java.security.Permission. It is recommended, however, that in those cases you insert your own base class in the hierarchy:

```
package com.wrox.password;

public abstract class PasswordLibraryPermission
extends java.security.Permission {
    // insert whatever part of the implementation can be shared by your subclasses
}
```

It is then possible to subclass your permission classes off that. You could also extend BasicPermission or any other permission class if that is more convenient.

Permission Collections

In most of the code we write, we aren't interested in the individual permissions granted to code. Instead, we have something we want to do, create a `Permission` that encapsulates the privileges we need to do it, and are only interested in the question whether the permissions associated with a protection domain imply the `Permission` we need. In other words, in most cases we are only interested in the permissions as a group. An important part of the security API comes down to grouping and querying `Permission` collections.

PermissionCollection

The `Permission` class declares a factory method `newPermissionCollection()` which produces a collection object for its own permission type. What is so special about this collection? Why not a simple `Vector` or `ArrayList`?

The abstract class `PermissionCollection` is what the name suggests: a collection of `Permission` objects. Unlike a `Vector` or `ArrayList`, it has an `implies()` method that determines whether a given permission is granted by the `Permissions` in the collection. Permission collections are, in general, permission-specific, exactly because of this `implies()` method. Consider for example the following fragment of a security policy file:

```
permission java.io.FilePermission "<<ALL_FILES>>", "read";
permission java.io.FilePermission "${user.home}${/}-",
           "write,delete,execute";
```

What if we need to determine whether we can read from and write to files in the directory `/home/jack/`?

```
permissonCollection.implies(
    new java.io.FilePermission("/home/jack/*", "read,write"));
```

If Jack is indeed the current user, this should return `true`. Although neither permission in the policy file actually implies it by itself, between them they *do* imply the permission.

It is the job of `PermissionCollection.implies(Permission)` to figure this out. There is no simple generic algorithm to do this; the implementation depends on the way the targets and actions of a particular type of permission are organized. That is why these collections are necessarily permission-specific and **homogeneous**, containing only a single class of permission. When you are creating a `Permission` with non-trivial implication rules, you need to implement a `PermissionCollection` to be returned by the `newPermissionCollection()` method of your permission class.

Permissions

Homogeneous collections alone are not enough, though. Looking at a protection domain, the set of permissions it encapsulates is **heterogeneous**, consisting of many different types of permissions. How to reconcile this with the argument that a collection is permission-specific?

The answer is that a heterogeneous `PermissionCollection` must not contain any `Permission` objects directly – it would be extremely difficult to write a generic `implies()` method – but only further, homogeneous `PermissionCollections`. You would no longer need any logic to figure out if permissions interact to grant a given `Permission`, because that can be left completely to the individual homogeneous sub-collections.

The `java.security.Permissions` class implements such a heterogeneous permission collection. When you add a permission to it, it will put it in the appropriate homogeneous subcollection, instantiating this collection if necessary.

Summary

In this chapter, we thoroughly explored the Java security model. We discussed:

❑   Why security is important, especially when running executable content from over the network, or when offering services to a network

❑   The "sandbox" security model and the difference between applets and applications, both in terms of trustworthiness and in terms of the privileges granted to them by the JDK

❑   Packaging and signing code using secure cryptographic signatures

❑   How the code base and signers of Java code are mapped to protection domains and permissions using the Java security policy file in the Java 2 security model

❑   Constructing a policy file, and the meaning of the most important permissions supported by the Java library

❑   Securely implementing your own privileged operations by defining your own `Permission`, checking that the calling code has this permission, and accessing the protected resource using `AccessController.doPrivileged()`

❑   How exceptions thrown in privileged code can be propagated to the calling code

❑   How security can be enforced using guarded objects if a privileged service does not execute in the caller's thread

❑   Coding a permission collection when your `Permissons` imply each other in nontrivial ways

❑   What the JDK security tools do

Armed with this knowledge, we are better able to implement networked services in a secure way.

Internet Addressing and Naming

In the previous chapters, we explored network concepts at a high-level and developed some essential Java programming skills. This chapter will move us to more concrete ground by focusing on the protocols and technologies used on the Internet.

This chapter will cover the basic functions of the Internet, which are addressing, naming and routing:

- ❑ Internet addresses are used to identify the unique location of an Internet node
- ❑ Names provide a second layer of direction by providing a location-independent and human-friendly identification of Internet nodes
- ❑ Routing is the core function of the Internet whose role is to move data from source to destination

The chapter also covers the Java library support for Internet addressing and naming, illustrated by two complete examples. Unlike older programming languages that were developed before the time of ubiquitous networking, Java was designed from the start with standard library support for network communications. Therefore, Java is one of the few languages supporting standardized cross-platform network programming. Moreover, the Java language was developed at a time when the protocols used on the Internet had already become the de-facto standard for wide-area communications. As a result, the Java libraries provide core support for the Internet Protocol suite discussed in Chapter 2.

At the end of this chapter you will know:

- ❑ The structure and use of Internet addresses
- ❑ How names are translated (resolved) into IP addresses
- ❑ How to write Java programs that manipulate IP addresses and resolve names to addresses
- ❑ The basics of Internet routing

The Internet

The Internet is a network of networks, all of which agree to communicate using a standard set of protocols. Several inter-networking technologies were developed in the 1970s and 1980s. One of these was the collection of protocols standardized by the Internet Engineering Task Force (IETF – http://www.ietf.org/). The **Internet Protocol** (IP) is the core of this protocol suite. The basic communications model of the Internet Protocol is that of a connectionless, best-effort packet service. Internet nodes wishing to send data across the network to a destination node must first break down that data into smaller data-segments called **packets**. Each packet is then transmitted individually on a hop-by-hop basis towards the destination node. Internet nodes performing forwarding functions are called routers. IP Packets are forwarded with best effort so they may not be lost, get corrupted or arrive out of order at the destination.

The Internet Protocol suite evolved from the experience of developing a research network for the United States Department of Defense, known as ARPANET. The ARPANET was the first network to demonstrate reliable, highly scalable wide area communications using a simple set of protocols. As the technologies used in the ARPANET matured, and the network became used for real communications, as opposed to research, it was split into a public network, known as "the Internet" and a private network used by the US military and known as MILNET. The value of a network increases with the number of services available. The Internet had the advantage of size, simplicity, and demonstrated scalability. Therefore, with the exception of high-security organizations, such as the US military, most organizations preferred to join their networks to the growing global Internet in order to obtain access to the largest array of services possible. This created a snowball effect under which all other competing inter-networking technologies were relegated to obscurity. As a result, network programming today is almost synonymous with Internet programming.

> **The global Internet has become synonymous with the IETF Internet Protocol (IP) suite, therefore, the terms "Internet" and "Internet Protocol" may be used interchangeably. Because other internets (networks-of-networks) may exist, by convention we capitalize the first letter when referring to "the" Internet.**

The three basic functions of Internet communications are addressing, naming and routing.

❑ An Internet address uniquely identifies the **location** of an Internet node. In a sense, an Internet address is like a traditional mailing address. If a node moves to a different network, its address will change. Moves within the same network may, or may not require a change in address. This is similar to moving within a building with un-numbered apartments, versus moving within a neighborhood. It is important to remember that there is no direct mapping between Internet addresses and physical location. We will discuss Internet addressing in greater detail in the next section.

❑ Names provide a location-independent reference to Internet nodes. Unlike Internet addresses that are essentially large integer numbers, names may contain letters and certain symbols making them easier for humans to remember. In order to communicate with an Internet node identified by a name, an application must look up (**resolve**) the Internet address for that name. This operation is similar to using a phone book to look up the number of a person by using his or her name. Unlike printed phone books, the Internet name directory can be changed as often as needed, therefore when a node moves, its name-to-address listing may be updated immediately.

Although the Internet Protocol does not mandate any particular mechanism or protocol for name-to-address resolution, the Domain Name System (DNS) has become the de-facto Internet naming mechanism. We will cover the DNS protocol and operations after discussion of Internet addressing.

❑   Internet nodes forward packets towards their destination address using local **routing** information. Internet nodes used to forward packets between destinations are called **routers**. Routers may be statically configured, or may compute their forwarding table dynamically using one of several dynamic routing protocols. The advantage of computing routes dynamically is that the network can recover from failures by redirecting traffic over alternative paths. Internet routing decisions are hidden from users and can only be modified with administrative privileges, therefore, Internet routing is an advanced topic. We will cover Internet routing in the last section of this chapter.

We illustrate the use of the above three functions by considering the steps involved in accessing a web page. Most Internet users are aware of Internet node names that can be found embedded in URLs such as http://www.wrox.com/ (URLs will be covered in detail in Chapter 12). In this example the name www.wrox.com refers to the Internet node hosting an HTTP service serving the web content of Wrox Press. Before communication can occur, in this example, between the web browser and the Wrox HTTP server, the web browser must resolve the name to an Internet address. This name resolution is performed using the Domain Name System (DNS) protocol. Once the destination address has been resolved, packets can be sent by the web browser towards the Wrox server on a hop-by-hop basis based on the routing information stored in the intermediate Internet routers.

This chapter will detail the structure of Internet addressing and the DNS protocol for performing name-to-address translation, with examples on how to program such access in Java. Internet routes are managed by network administrators so will only be covered here where they relate to addressing.

Internet Addresses

As we described in Chapter 2, Internet addresses are used to identify the location of Internet nodes. All data transmitted over the Internet must be addressed to a single IP address. Typically, that address identifies a single recipient, although in some cases it may identify a group of recipients. For now we will assume a single recipient and will leave discussion of group addressing for Chapter 11.

From the user's perspective, the Internet provides a communications mechanism that moves data segments (packets) from a source node to a destination node using best effort. Each packet is marked with the IP address of the source node as well as the address of the destination node. This behavior is illustrated in the diagram on the next page. On the left, a client host is shown that is an Internet node identified by the IP address 128.59.22.38. On the right-hand side, a server host is shown that is also an Internet node identified by the IP address 204.148.170.161. In the middle of the diagram, we abstract the function of the Internet as a **cloud**. This type of diagram is commonly used when representing networks in order to hide part of the complexity and focus on a particular aspect of network communications. In this case, we focus on the end-to-end packet delivery function of the Internet. The client host sends an IP packet containing the message "Hello!" and addressed to the Internet node located at address 204.148.170.161. The role of the Internet is to deliver that packet to the server using best effort.

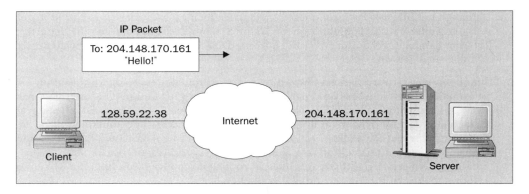

The only guarantee that the Internet Protocol makes is that *if* the packet is delivered to the server, it will have the correct header. The delivered packet may be lost en-route, or may arrive in the server with the correct header, but with a corrupted payload. This type of service is deemed too unreliable for most applications. Other protocols that are built on top of the Internet Protocol, such as UDP and TCP, provide increasingly more reliable services. We will cover these protocols in the next chapters. This chapter will focus on the properties of the Internet Protocol.

In some cases, a single host may be connected to the Internet using multiple addresses. Such hosts act as multiple Internet nodes and are known as **multi-homed**. All routers are by definition multi-homed since they must connect at least two networks and have an address in each network in order to operate. Server hosts may be multi-homed in order to increase their resilience to network failures. Server hosts may also be multi-homed in order to directly offer their services to multiple local networks without router intervention. For example, in the diagram below, the server host is shown connected to the Internet using two Internet addresses. When sending an IP packet to that host, *either* of the two addresses may be used, but not both. Clients may be configured to try one address first and upon failure try the other. Alternatively, the name associated with the server could be resolved to both addresses, and the client may pick one up arbitrarily. The behavior of multi-homed hosts is further discussed in the last section of this chapter covering Internet routing.

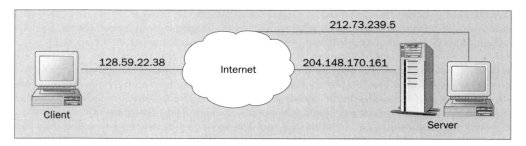

It should be noted that the above discussion provided only a functional description of the Internet. From an operational perspective, most of the interesting functions are hidden in the cloud. The last section on Internet routing will partially uncover the mechanisms used to route packets within this cloud. However, it is important to remember that use of the Internet does not require understanding of its routing mechanisms. The basic model has already been described in this section. The Internet provides a best-effort packet routing mechanism between a source and a destination node.

In order to connect to the Internet a host must be equipped with a **network interface**. A network interface is a hardware device used to provide a link between the host and the Internet access gateway at the link-layer. Popular host network interface types include Ethernet, ISDN, DSL/ADSL, analog modems, and the new wireless IEEE 802.11 standard. Once a network interface has been installed it must be configured with an IP address and other parameters. Typically, each network interface is associated with one IP address, although it is possible to associate multiple addresses with the same interface. It is also possible to use multiple protocol suites over the same network interface. For example, Microsoft Windows host network interfaces are sometimes configured to support IP, as well as the Novell IPX protocol.

IP Version 6 Addressing

The next version of the IP protocol introduces several new features one of which is an enlarged address space. As mentioned in Chapter 2, IP version 4 addresses are 32-bit (four byte) values supporting 2^{32} (over 4 billion) unique addresses. At the time when version 4 of the Internet Protocol was designed, the Internet consisted of a few thousand nodes so this number must have seemed sufficiently large. Today, this address space is nearly exhausted and this problem will be the main driving force behind the deployment of the next version of IP.

IPv6 addresses are 128-bit values supporting 340,282,366,920,938,463,463,374,607,431,768,211,456 (over $3.4*10^{38}$) unique addresses! This is a very large number and could potentially permit a density of $6.6*10^{23}$ hosts per square meter on this planet! In reality, a large percentage of this address space will be wasted because IPv6 addresses will be assigned geographically. Geographic address assignment is desirable because it reduces the amount of state that needs to be maintained in the core Internet routers.

There are three forms for representing IPv6 as strings. Of these, the preferred method is to break the address into 8 hexadecimal numbers each representing a 16-bit value. An example of an IPv6 address represented in this manner is shown below:

```
FEDC:BA98:7654:3210:FEDC:BA98:7654:3210
```

More information on IPv6 addressing can be found in the IETF RFC 2373 (http://www.ietf.org/rfc/rfc2373.txt). Support for IPv6 addressing was added in Java starting with JDK 1.4. This chapter will focus on IPv4 Java programming, but a short section outlining the new features supporting IPv6 programming in JDK 1.4 is included at the end of this chapter. At this point, it is not clear when and if IPv6 will be adopted.

Internet Naming (Domain Name System)

Internet addresses serve to identify location; therefore, they may need to be changed when hosts are moved within the network. Additionally, even when represented in a dotted notation, addresses can be difficult for humans to remember since they don't have any semantic context. For these two reasons, an additional naming mechanism is required to provide location-independent and human-friendly identities to Internet nodes. This section will present the core naming mechanism used in the Internet today called the **Domain Name System** (**DNS**).

In the early experimental days of the Internet (ARPANET) addresses to name mappings were maintained in simple flat file – HOSTS.TXT (IETF RFC 952; http://www.ietf.org/rfc/rfc952.txt). Every night, all Internet hosts would copy the latest version of that file from the Network Information Center (NIC) using the File Transfer Protocol (FTP). There were several problems with this solution. As the number of Internet hosts grew, the bandwidth for file transfers and the load on the FTP servers grew proportionally. Because a single authority controlled the HOSTS.TXT file, individual organizations had to issue an NIC request for every host addition, renaming, or address modification. Changes would only take effect at the time of the file transfer, and there was potential for inconsistent configuration if one or more hosts failed to retrieve the file for some reason. Finally, new naming requirements evolved that could not be addressed by the simple address-to-name mechanism.

Several Internet naming proposals were submitted to the Internet Engineering Task Force (IETF). These proposals evolved into a standard called the Domain Name System (DNS), details of which can be found at http://www.ietf.org/rfc/rfc1034.txt. DNS addressed the problems of the centralized hosts file by creating an extensible distributed hierarchical naming system. DNS defined both a hierarchical data model for Internet name assignment, as well as a protocol for querying the distributed data structure. Interestingly enough, although DNS has become the core naming mechanism of the Internet, it is not strictly part of the Internet Protocol suite but rather an application-layer service. In fact, DNS has been built to support non-IP addressing even though it is primarily used for IP protocol naming.

DNS Namespace

The DNS namespace forms a hierarchical tree structure. Each node in the tree has a **label** of length up to 63 characters (bytes). All nodes except the root node must have a non-empty text label, and all children of a node must have unique labels. Labels preserve the case of their letters, but comparisons must be performed in a case-insensitive manner. A consequence is that sibling nodes may not have labels that only differ in case. Labels must start with a letter and can be followed by a sequence of letters, digits and the hyphen '-' character. In the original specification, letters were restricted to the ASCII character set, but lately an effort has been underway to open the system with support for non-English character sets (see http://www.ietf.org/). This effort has created some controversy and it is not clear when and how alternative characters will be supported.

A **domain name** uniquely identifies a node in the tree. Domain names are created by traversing from any node in the tree up to the root and appending a period '.' between each label. For example, consider the sample DNS namespace shown in the tree figure below. If we traverse the tree from the node labeled www we obtain the domain name for that node "www.wrox.com.". Note the period following the com label is necessary to separate it from the empty root label. The total length of domain names is limited to 255 characters (octets). We could also traverse the tree from the node labeled "wrox". In that case the domain name would be "wrox.com.".

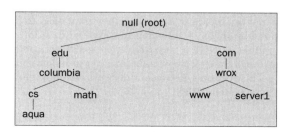

> **Surprised about the terminating period shown? Domain names must be terminated by a period in order to be considered complete (called fully-qualified). As we will show later, when users enter a non-period terminated domain name to a networked application, such as a browser, one of the actions performed is to attempt to add a period to the name in order to fully qualify it.**

DNS Record Types

In addition to labels, each tree node may contain zero or more **resource records** (RR). Resource records contain information about the particular node, such as its Internet address. Unlike other tree structures, DNS permits attributes (resource records) in both nodes with children and leaf nodes. Every resource record must have an owner, class, TTL, and type attribute. The owner is the domain name to which the resource record belongs and the class refers to the protocol family/version of the record. Internet IPv4 records are of type IN. The TTL stands for Time-To-Live and indicates how long (in seconds) the record can be cached before it is discarded (more on that later). Finally, the type attribute characterizes the information stored in the resource record.

For example, an Internet address resource record owned by the domain name "www.wrox.com." will be of type IN (Internet), have a TTL of one week because it is expected to change often (=7*24*60*60 seconds), will be of type A (address), and have an IP address as value (for example, "204.148.170.161"). The example resource record is shown in tabular form in the table below.

Owner	Class	TTL	Type	Value
www.wrox.com	IN	604800	A	204.148.170.161

The core DNS specification specifies the following resource record types:

Type	Description
A	A host address, such as "204.148.170.161".
CNAME	Marks the domain name as an alias for another domain name. When a domain name contains a CNAME resource record, it cannot contain other record types. As a result, alias domains cannot add additional information (resource records). For example, the domain "www.wrox.com." may be used as an alias for the real server host "server1.wrox.com.". Similarly, the domain name "ftp.wrox.com." may also be set as an alias for "server1.wrox.com.".
HINFO	Identifies the CPU and OS used by a host as a string. Typically, this is a space-separated string such as "Pentium Linux". Many sites no longer include an HINFO resource record for security reasons.
MX	Identifies the domain name handling e-mail (SMTP) service for this domain and provides the priority with which it should be used. For example, an MX record may be added to the "wrox.com." domain pointing to the SMTP server host "mail.wrox.com." with priority 100. Another MX record added to "wrox.com." may point to the SMTP server "smtp.some-isp.com." with priority 200. This second entry may point to a backup mail server located on the premises of Wrox's Internet Service Provider.

Table continued on following page

Type	Description
MX (Cont'd)	Mail clients that need to deliver e-mail messages to users at the wrox.com domain (for example, "support@wrox.com") will lookup all the MX resource records for the "wrox.com." domain. Starting with the MX record with the **lowest** priority, they will attempt to establish an e-mail (SMTP) connection with the host identified by resolving the domain name contained in the MX record. In this example, "mail.wrox.com." will first be contacted, if a connection cannot be established, the next server in priority, "smtp.some-isp.com." will be tried. This mechanism is used to increase the reliability of Internet mail delivery.
PTR	Points to another part of the domain space (usually used for supporting reverse lookups, which we will talk about later on).
NS	The authoritative name server for the domain. The concept of authoritative name servers will be presented in the next subsection.

The figure below shows part of the previous DNS domain space example with resource records added. In this example a resource record was added to the "www.wrox.com." tree node with the type CNAME and the value server1. The CNAME record indicates that the domain name is an alias for another domain, in this case the "server1.wrox.com." domain. Looking at the "server1.wrox.com." tree node we find a resource record of type A, which is used to mark the server's network address. So, given this tree, one could resolve the domain name "www.wrox.com." by traversing the tree (. → com → wrox → www) finding the alias entry pointing to the node labeled server1 and then finally obtaining the IP address from the A resource record. The server1 node also has an HINFO type resource-record identifying the CPU and operating system of the server. Note the use of the MX resource type in the wrox node. In this example, a single MX record points to the server1 host.

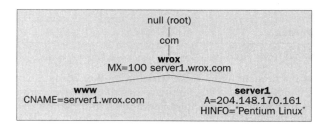

DNS Distributed Architecture

The hierarchical nature of the DNS namespace is a good match for the goal of distributing ownership and storage of domain names. Each node in the tree (domain) can be potentially mapped to a different **name server**. Name servers are programs that hold information about a domain and its children. For example, the domain "wrox.com." will typically be stored in a name server controlled by Wrox Press. Similarly, the domain "columbia.edu." will be stored in a name server controlled by Columbia University. Large organizations, may further delegate storage of subdomains to servers controlled by departments. For example, the "cs.columbia.edu." domain may be delegated to a server controlled by the administrators of the Computer Science department at Columbia University. In order to improve reliability, multiple name servers *must* be assigned to each domain. In order to control change, only one server is considered **authoritative** for a given domain. The remaining servers for that domain are considered as **secondary** and must periodically copy their data from the authoritative server.

Resolvers are client programs that query name servers in order to locate a particular domain name and obtain its resource record information. Resolvers are configured with the IP address of one or more local name servers. In order to improve lookup performance, resolvers cache results of previous lookups for the duration of the resource record TTL. To improve sharing of the cached information, resolvers are typically part of the operating system. This way all programs running on a single host can share the same cache, independent of the language in which they are written. Name servers also cache results to support sharing of lookup results between programs running on hosts. Name servers and resolvers communicate using the DNS protocol via the well-known UDP port 53 or TCP port 53.

DNS defines an algorithm for querying name servers, the operations of which are illustrated in the figure below. For example, a program on the host named "snoopy.wrox.com." invokes the host's DNS resolver to look up the name "aqua.cs.columbia.edu.". The resolver on snoopy has never seen this domain name before so it checks its configuration to find out the *address* of the local DNS name server. The resolver then sends a query (1) to the local name server address conforming to the DNS protocol. In this example, the local name server has never seen that domain name either, so it checks its configuration for the address of one of the **root domain servers** (2).

Root domain servers store the addresses of all second-level domains (such as com, edu, uk) and so form the backbone of the DNS system. In order to improve lookup performance, the root name servers are configured to provide **iterative query** service only.

Iterative queries return partial lookup results by providing the address of the servers for a parent domain of the queried address. In this example, the root server returns (3) the address of the "columbia.edu." name servers (guaranteed to be more than one). The Wrox local name server proceeds to issue a DNS query (4) to one of the Columbia name servers.

Let's assume again that the Columbia server does not act as a secondary server to the Computer Science department server (something unlikely in reality). In that case, the Columbia server will **recursively query** (5) one of the Computer Science name servers that will finally respond (6) with the resource records requested for the "aqua.cs.columbia.edu." domain (in particular the A address record). The Columbia name server will cache the response and reply to the Wrox name server query (7). In the final step the local Wrox name server will cache the result of the query, and return the reply (8) to the resolver on snoopy. This resolver will cache the reply and return the call to the local invoking program.

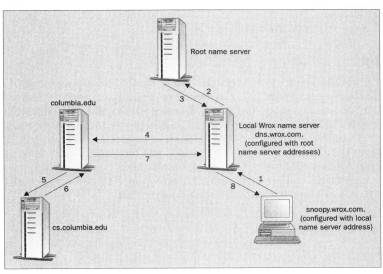

If a program again looks up the same name on snoopy, then the cached value will be returned immediately. Similarly, if any other Wrox host requests the particular host then the local name server will return the result without going through the remaining steps. The local Wrox name server also caches information on the location of the "columbia.edu.", so any subsequent query for any Columbia subdomain will not involve a root server lookup. It now becomes clear why every resource record is associated with a TTL value. All these cached values must be cleared at some time in order to support updates. There is a clear trade-off between DNS lookup overhead and longevity of information. The decision is decentralized and left up to the administrator of each domain via the resource record TTL configuration.

A domain name is called **fully qualified** when it terminates at the root. For example, the domain name "www.wrox.com." is considered fully qualified. The names www, www.wrox, and www.wrox.com are valid domain names, but they are called **relative domain names**. In order to identify the exact node in the tree that they refer to, resolvers must be configured with one or more default domain postfixes. Most resolvers automatically attempt to add the "." root domain to every query. So, if one tried to lookup the www.wrox.com domain, the resolver would create the fully qualified name "www.wrox.com." and use that for its query. In most networks, resolvers are also configured to try the local domain name. For example, within the Wrox network, users can access the web server using just the name "www". The domain name "wrox.com." will be appended to all relative domain name queries in order to perform the lookup.

Domain Name Registration

The owner of the parent domain handles registration of subdomains. Historically, the top-level domains were managed by a single entity, initially SRI, then Government Systems Inc. (Network Solutions). Today, registration of domains has been opened to multiple competing registrars (http://www.icann.org/registrars/accredited-list.html) under the stewardship of the Internet Corporation for Assigned Names and Numbers (ICANN). Top-level domains include the original com, net, org, edu, int, mil and gov, plus two-level country domains based on the ISO 3166 country codes. In the Internet gold rush of the 1990s a large number of second-level domains were pre-registered in anticipation of future business opportunities, or for the purpose of extracting payment from likely users (this was known as domain squatting). As a result, it has become exceedingly difficult to obtain identifiable labels in the non-regulated top-level domains (edu, gov and mil are regulated). In response, ICANN voted on May 2001 to create additional top-level domains. These new top-level domains are aero, biz, coop, info, museum, name, and pro (for more information http://www.icann.org/tlds/

Reverse Lookup

In some cases, it is useful to perform a **reverse lookup** to obtain the domain name of a given IP address. For example, a web server may want to log incoming requests by name in order to facilitate analysis of the log statistics (by domain, country, and so on). Domain name queries use the lookup domain value to determine which name servers to query, so it is not possible to perform reverse queries without additional help. This additional help comes in the form of a special domain called "in-addr.arpa.". A reverse lookup on the address 204.148.170.161 will be performed by looking up the domain name "161.170.148.204.in-addr.arpa.". Owners of address blocks are given ownership of "in-addr.arpa." subdomains and are responsible for providing PTR resource records for the dotted decimal domain names pointing back to the node's domain name.

System vs. IP Interface Name

Most computing systems support the concept of a system name. It is important to remember that the DNS system is used to provide names for IP addresses. Since a system can contain multiple network interfaces, each configured for one or more IP addresses, it is possible to have multiple names resolving to addresses owned by the same system. To make matters more complicated, there is no requirement that the system name match any of the IP address names. This is particularly true in systems that use the Dynamic Host Configuration Protocol (DHCP) to dynamically obtain IP addresses. In such cases, the system will never match the domain name reverse-mapped to the assigned IP address. For example, consider the host pictured to the right with two IP addresses/interfaces. Each address resolves to a different domain name, and the system name matches neither! Clearly this is not an example of good configuration, but it can happen, and programmers must be prepared to handle such cases.

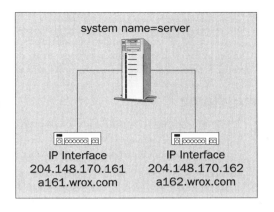

java.net.InetAddress

Now that we have learned the basic concepts behind Internet addressing and naming we can focus on how to manipulate IP addresses and domain names in Java. As we would expect in an object-oriented language, Java encapsulates the concept of an IP address in a class. The class is part of the `java.net` package and is called `InetAddress`. Breaking with most design methodologies, the same class also encapsulates the concept of a DNS resolver. This mixture has the unfortunate effect of creating a weak DNS resolver that can only perform domain name to address, and address to domain name queries. This means that it is not possible to use the `InetAddress` resolver to retrieve other resource record types such as MX, HINFO, and so on. The `InetAddress` class is also missing useful operations for creating addresses out of byte-arrays, obtaining all IP addresses of the local host, and the use of addresses as network masks. Despite these shortcomings, it is an important class that will suffice for most uses. Many of these shortcomings have been addressed in the 1.4 release of JSE.

The diagram on the right highlights the operations provided by the `InetAddress` class. Overall the class has very few methods. They consist of three factory methods used to create new class instances, and four read methods used to query the state of instances. The class does not provide any update methods and is therefore immutable. `InetAddress` was designed to support IPv4 as well as IPv6 addresses, although up to and including the JDK 1.3 series releases, the implementation only supports IPv4 addresses. IPv6 related support issues are briefly discussed at the end of this chapter and fully expanded upon in Chapter 21.

java.net.InetAddress
+getByName() : java.net.InetAddress +getAllByName() : java.net.InetAddress[] +getLocalHost() : java.net.InetAddress +getHostName() : String +getAddress() : byte[] +getHostAddress() : String +isMulticastAddress() : boolean

Factory Methods

The `InetAddress` class employs the factory design pattern and does not provide any public constructors. Three static factory methods are provided, two of which accept a string as an argument that may be either an Internet address in dotted decimal notation, or a domain name. The third factory method does not take any arguments and returns the Internet address of the local host.

getByName

The most commonly used factory method is `getByName` with the following signature:

```
static InetAddress getByName(String host) throws UnknownHostException;
```

The factory method returns an `InetAddress` object encapsulating the result of a DNS lookup on the string domain argument. For example, invoking `getByName("wrox.com.")` will return an `InetAddress` instance storing the domain name `"wrox.com."` as well as the resolved address (at time of print `"204.148.170.161"`). You may remember from the previous discussion that domain names may be mapped to multiple addresses. In case of multiple addresses the method returns one selected in a platform-specific manner.

If the string method argument represents an IP address in dotted decimal notation then the object created will encapsulate the given address. For example, invoking `getByName("204.148.170.161")` will create an `InetAddress` instance encapsulating the address `204.148.170.161`. Because the string argument represents an IP address, the DNS resolver would not normally need to be invoked, however, in order to support reverse lookups, the factory method will attempt to perform a reverse lookup by generating the `"in-addr.arpa."` domain name. If the reverse lookup succeeds, the `InetAddress` object's domain name will be set to that value. For example, the object returned by `getByName("204.148.170.161")` will also store the reverse-resolved `"a161.wrox.com"` domain name. The reverse-resolved name can be invoked using the `getHostName()` method that will be presented later. Note that in this case the reverse-lookup will return the real domain name for that address (`a161`), not the alias (`www`).

Although this is not documented, if the string argument is `null` or zero length, the local loop-back IP address will be returned. The loop-back IP address is a special address that is the same for every Internet host and can only be used for communication within a host. This is useful when running services on hosts that are not connected to the Internet. Loop-back addresses are assigned in the range `127.0.0.0` to `127.255.255.255`. Typically, hosts have at least one loop-back interface configured for IP address `127.0.0.1`.

If the domain name cannot be resolved the `java.net.UnknownHostException` is thrown. Reasons for failed lookups include lack of Internet connectivity, resolver misconfiguration (covered later in this chapter), use of relative domain names when the resolver is not configured with a default domain, or simply use of a domain name that does not exist. The factory method may also throw a runtime `SecurityException` if a Java security manager has been installed, and the code-base has not been given the `resolve` socket permission (see Chapter 7 for coverage on Java security). The following permission should be added to the security policy file when a security manager is installed:

```
grant {
  permission java.net.SocketPermission "*", "resolve";
};
```

The following code snippet illustrates the use of this factory method in resolving a domain name to an address. A reverse lookup example will be shown later on.

```
...
String host = "www.wrox.com.";
java.net.InetAddress address = null;
try {
    address = java.net.InetAddress.getByName(host);
} catch (UnknownHostException e) {
  // throw appropriate application exception
}
...
```

getAllByName

The second factory method is similar to the getByName method with the difference that all lookup results are returned. This method may also throw a runtime SecurityException if a security manager has been installed and the resolve permission has not been granted.

```
static InetAddress[] getAllByName(String host)throws UnknownHostException;
```

Use of this factory method will be demonstrated later in this section when we present a complete lookup example. We delay presentation of the code in order to introduce the accessor methods for the InetAddress class. Readers may choose to read forward to the "*DNS Lookup Example*" section.

getLocalHost

The third and final factory method does not take any arguments and returns an InetAddress object representing the IP address and name of the host executing the JVM. Most modern operating systems support a loop-back network interface that is usually assigned the special IP address 127.0.0.1 and is commonly mapped to the name "localhost". In machines that do not have a real network interface the getLocalHost() method may return an object encapsulating the loop-back address. Preference is given to returning address used for external IP access, as opposed to the loop-back address.

The method may also return the loop-back object *even* if the machine has a non-loopback address, if a security manager has been installed and the resolve permission has not been granted. This quiet failure can become the source of significant frustration! Another potential problem can be caused by the fact that when the loop-back address is returned on a system with no external IP interfaces, its host name will be set to the local *system* name instead of the usual "localhost". As a result, if the programmer attempts to resolve that host name back to an IP address, a failure is likely to occur (that is, the loop address-to-name-to-address is broken). Use of the getLocalHost() method is demonstrated in a complete example later in this chapter.

As with the previous two factory methods, this method may throw the UnknownHostException. In this case the UnknownHostException is used to signal an error in obtaining a local IP address (that is, there is neither a real network interface nor a loop-back interface). Although the Javadoc documentation states that a SecurityException may be thrown by this method, current implementations do not throw it, and it is not clear why it would ever be thrown since failure to obtain the IP address is signaled by an UnknownHostException exception.

```
static InetAddress getLocalHost() throws UnknownHostException;
```

It is unfortunate that a getAllLocalHost() method was not provided to support discovery of all local host network interfaces when more than one is available. In general, there is no way programmers can work around this omission without using native code. In the next chapter on TCP socket programming we will see that it is possible to indirectly discover new interfaces by checking the receipt addresses of incoming requests.

Read Methods

The InetAddress class provides four read methods for querying the state of its instances. The methods do not throw any exceptions since all possible exceptions would have been thrown by the factory methods.

- ❏ String getHostName(): Returns the domain name of this address, for example, www.wrox.com

- ❏ byte[] getAddress(): Returns the address 32-bit value as a 4 byte array in network byte-order (highest order byte is getAddress()[0]), for example,
  new byte[] { (byte) 0xCC, (byte) 0x94, (byte) 0xAA, (byte) 0xA1 }

- ❏ String getHostAddress(): Returns the dotted decimal string representation of this address, for example, 204.148.170.161

- ❏ boolean isMulticastAddress(): Returns true if this is a multicast address (see Chapter 11)

In addition to the above four methods, the InetAddress class overrides the following default java.lang.Object methods:

- ❏ int hashCode(): Returns an integer (32-bit value) representing the IP address

- ❏ boolean equals(Object obj): Returns true if the argument is an InetAddress instance encapsulating the same IP address (the host names are not used in this comparison)

- ❏ String toString(): Returns a string representation of this address. The current implementation returns a string containing both the dotted decimal IP address representation and the host name. Users should use the getHostName() and getHostAddress() methods to obtain the individual string values

It is not possible to construct an InetAddress instance out of a 32-bit (byte[4]) value. Programmers must provide their own translation from binary to dotted-decimal notation. The code snippet below shows how to achieve that:

```
public static String getDottedIPv4Address(byte[] address) {
    if (address == null) {
        throw new NullPointerException("null address argument");
    }

    if (address.length != 4) {
        throw new IllegalArgumentException("Invalid IPv4 address length " +
                                address.length);
    }

    return( (address[0] & 0xFF) + "." +
            (address[1] & 0xFF) + "." +
            (address[2] & 0xFF) + "." +
            (address[3] & 0xFF) );
}
```

DNS Lookup Example

This section will help focus the discussion of the `InetAddress` class by presenting a complete sample program. It is a command-line utility enabling users to perform regular and reverse DNS lookups and it can be found in this chapter's code download at http://www.wrox.com/.

```java
// DNSResolver.java

import java.net.InetAddress;

/**
 * A command-line utility for performing regular and reverse DNS lookups
 */
public class DNSResolver {

  /**
   * Expects single argument containing a domain name or dotted decimal
   * IP address and outputs the domain-address mappings.
   */
  public static void main(String[] args) {
    if (args.length != 1) {
      System.err.println("Usage: DNSResolver [ <name> | <address> ]");
      System.exit(1);
    }

    // Determine if argument is an IP address or a domain name: Since
    // domain names cannot start with a number, check for that.
    boolean isReverseLookup = Character.isDigit(args[0].charAt(0));

    try {
      InetAddress[] addresses = InetAddress.getAllByName(args[0]);

      for (int a = 0; a < addresses.length; a++) {
        InetAddress address = addresses[a];

        if (isReverseLookup) {
          if (address.getHostAddress().equals(address.getHostName())) {
            System.out.println("Could not reverse resolve "
                            + address.getHostAddress());
          } else {
            System.out.println(address.getHostAddress()
                            + " reverse resolves to "
                            + address.getHostName());
          }
        } else {
          System.out.println(address.getHostName() + " resolves to "
                            + address.getHostAddress());
        }
      }
    } catch (java.net.UnknownHostException e) {
      System.err.println("Cannot resolve " + args[0]);
      System.exit(1);
    } catch (java.lang.SecurityException e) {
      System.err.println("A security manager has been installed and the"
                      + "'resolve' java.net.SocketPermission has not"
                      + " been granted");
      System.exit(1);
    }
  }
}
```

The above program takes a single command-line argument, which is expected to be a domain name or an IP address in dotted decimal format. The program invokes the InetAddress getAllByName() method on the string argument. For each address returned, a message is printed reporting the result of the lookup.

The example determines when the lookup involves an IP address (reverse lookup) by checking the first character in the command-line argument. Because domain name labels cannot start with a number character, and valid IP addresses must start with a number, it is sufficient to check the first character. If the lookup fails, due to an unknown host exception, a message is printed for that entry. Reverse lookup failure is not signaled by an exception and must be checked for by comparing the strings representing the address and the name. If they are equal, then the name could not be determined by reverse lookup. If a security exception is thrown then an error message is printed.

Once the class has been compiled we may attempt to resolve a domain name. In this case we attempt to resolve the address of the Wrox web server. Note that the address of the server may change by the time you read this, which is in fact the whole point of using names instead of addresses.

C:\Beg_Java_Networking\Ch08>**java DNSResolver www.wrox.com**
www.wrox.com resolves to 204.148.170.161

We can also try resolving the "www.microsoft.com" domain in the hope of retrieving multiple address records. It should be noted that modern web-server load-balancing architectures no longer rely on multiple address records. Instead, a single entry point is provided pointing to a device that redirects requests to multiple servers with the goal of spreading the load evenly. This means that it is increasingly difficult to find examples of domain names containing multiple address records!

C:\Beg_Java_Networking\Ch08>**java DNSResolver www.microsoft.com**
www.microsoft.com resolves to 207.46.197.100
www.microsoft.com resolves to 207.46.230.218
www.microsoft.com resolves to 207.46.197.102

We now test the reverse lookup function of the resolver by feeding in the IP address of the Wrox Press web server. In this case we note that the reverse mapping does not resolve to the name as we expected. This is because the name www.wrox.com is an alias (CNAME) for the host named a161.wrox.com:

C:\Beg_Java_Networking\Ch08>**java DNSResolver 204.148.170.161**
204.148.170.161 reverse maps to a161.wrox.com

The final invocation example will demonstrate the use of a security policy. We invoke the JVM with a flag enabling the default security manager, and a flag specifying the location of a policy containing the following permission for all codebases:

```
grant {
        permission java.net.SocketPermission "*", "resolve";
};
```

As can be seen, the resolver continues to operate successfully even when a security manager has been installed, thanks to the policy file (the bold user-entry part should be entered as one line):

C:\Beg_Java_Networking\Ch08>**java -Djava.security.manager**
 -Djava.security.policy=policy.resolve DNSResolver www.wrox.com
www.wrox.com resolves to 204.148.170.161

If you remove the policy file flag from the JVM invocation the program will issue a security error message:

C:\Beg_Java_Networking\Ch08>**java -Djava.security.manager DNSResolver www.wrox.com**
A security manager has been installed and the resolve' java.net.SocketPermission has not been granted

Local Host Example

In order to demonstrate the behavior of the getLocalHost() method, we provide a complete example that prints out the result of invoking this method. The program does not take any command-line arguments. It simply invokes the getLocalHost() method and prints the IP address and host name returned.

```java
// LocalHost.java

import java.net.InetAddress;

/**
 * A command-line utility that prints the local host name and address
 * obtained by InetAddress.getLocalHost(), and performs a reverse
 * lookup on the address to obtain the name.
 */
public class LocalHost {

  /**
   * No command-line arguments are used.
   */
  public static void main(String[] args) {

    try {
      InetAddress address = InetAddress.getLocalHost();
      System.out.println("Local address:  " + address.getHostAddress());
      System.out.println("Local hostname: " + address.getHostName());
    } catch (java.net.UnknownHostException e) {
      System.err.println("Cannot determine local host name and address:"
                         + e.getMessage());
      System.exit(1);
    }
  }
}
```

We compile and execute the above program as shown below. Clearly the results will be different since the code will be executed on a different host. In the example below, it should be noted that the name returned is not fully qualified. This behavior is typically observed on Microsoft Windows systems – Unix-based systems typically return a fully-qualified domain name, as long as one has been configured.

C:\Beg_Java_Networking\Ch08>**java LocalHost**
Local address: 128.59.22.229
Local hostname: MANTICORE

Recall that the getLocalHost() method fails quietly when executed with a security manager and no resolve permission. The returned result is the loop-back address and name!

C:\Beg_Java_Networking\Ch08>**java -Djava.security.manager LocalHost**
Local address: 127.0.0.1
Local hostname: localhost

Invoking the JVM with a security policy containing the "resolve" `SocketPermission` can restore the expected behavior. We use the policy file created in the previous example:

C:\Beg_Java_Networking\Ch08>**java -Djava.security.manager**
 -Djava.security.policy=policy.resolve LocalHost
Local address: 128.59.22.229
Local hostname: MANTICORE

As we mentioned, for hosts that do not have any configured interfaces, the `getLocalHost()` method returns the loop-back address with the system name (instead of the usual "loopback"). We demonstrate this behavior by running the example on a system that does not have any *configured* non-loop-back interfaces. Note how this behavior is different from the case when the security manager had been installed without a "`resolve`" permission:

C:\Beg_Java_Networking\Ch08>**java LocalHost**
Local address: 127.0.0.1
Local hostname: MANTICORE

Caching Bug

Recall that DNS resolvers are supposed to cache results of previous lookups in order to reduce the load on the name servers and speed up responses. Resolvers must expire resource records held in the cache past their TTL. Unfortunately, Sun's caching implementation had a serious flaw until JDK1.4. The `InetAddress` lookup cache did not distinguish between positive and negative results. The resource records returned by successful queries were stored and expired as would be expected, however, the resolver also cached failed lookups. Once a lookup for a particular domain failed, subsequent calls would throw an exception without even trying to perform the query. What made this behavior particularly problematic was the fact that these cached failures would never expire in the lifetime of the JVM! Hosts with intermittent connectivity were most affected from this behavior. Consider a host running a JVM without an Internet connection. If the code executing on the JVM performs a DNS query by creating an `InetAddress` object for a particular domain, the factory method will throw an `UnknownHostException` because the DNS server cannot be reached. Even when the host is connected to the network, subsequent invocations of `getByName()` for the same domain will continue to fail because the resolver won't bother to recheck!

Starting with JDK 1.2, Sun added support for a work-around for this bug. Users could set a Sun-specific property called `sun.net.inetaddr.ttl` to configure the maximum time the `InetAddress` resolver would cache results. A positive value of this property sets the number of seconds that addresses are cached. A zero value disables caching, and a −1 value sets the cache duration to forever. So, invoking a JVM with "`-Dsun.net.inetaddr.ttl=0`" will disable all address caching. As this is a Sun-specific solution, which has significant performance implications, it should only be used in environments where JVMs are long-lived.

Although this problem had been known since JDK1.1 it took Sun several years until this problem was truly fixed in JDK1.4. The default behavior in JDK1.4 is not to cache negative responses. Sun also made caching configurable via two properties in the `java.security` file called `networkcache.address.ttl` and `networkcache.address.negative.ttl`. Their values may be −1, indicating cache forever, or a positive number specifying the number of seconds for caching positive and negative results respectively.

JDK 1.4 Changes

JDK 1.4 introduced significant changes to the `InetAddress` class and added support for IP version 6 (IPv6) addresses. Most of the `InetAddress` shortcomings mentioned in this chapter have been addressed through the addition of new methods. A factory method was added for creating an address out of a byte-array. New methods include `getCanonicalHostName()` that attempts to return a fully qualified domain name for the address, and methods for checking if an address is a loop-back address, and if an address belongs to the local-network, as opposed to a remote network. The `InetAddress` class was further subclassed by two new classes called `Inet4Address` and `Inet6Address`, representing IP version 4 and IP version 6 addresses respectively. These methods provide IP version-specific methods. Instances of these two new subclasses are not directly constructed. The static `InetAddress` factory methods actually return one of the two types. Users may check the type of the returned `InetAddress` subclass and typecast if needed.

Advanced Issues

This section discusses advanced topics that can potentially be skipped on a first reading.

Resolver Configuration

The `InetAddress` class does not implement a pure Java resolver. Instead, it relies on the native resolver of the system executing the JVM. It is therefore not possible to configure the `InetAddress` resolver from within a Java program. Native resolvers are typically configured with an ordered list of DNS name server IP addresses, and a list of domain name suffixes used converting partial to fully qualified domain names. For example, the configuration of a Wrox host may be set as shown below. The syntax is generic since the exact labels used and configuration methods are platform specific.

```
NAMESERVER1=198.80.0.6
NAMESERVER2=198.80.0.11
DOMAIN=wrox.com
SEARCH=wrox.com marketing.wrox.com accounting.wrox.com
```

In addition to using DNS for lookups, most systems use a local hosts file. The local hosts file usually contains a single entry mapping the loop-back address 127.0.0.1 to the "localhost" name. Additional mappings may be entered in cases where a system is isolated in a small network and users do not care to install a DNS server. The local hosts file may also be used to work around the problem of `InetAddress.getLocalHost().getHostName()` returning the system name instead of the loop-back interface name when no real IP interfaces have been configured. The work-around is to add the system name to the 127.0.0.1 mappings. A sample hosts file is shown overleaf:

```
127.0.0.1                localhost
```

The following table points to platform-specific files and programs used to configure the system DNS resolver.

OS	Local hosts file	Resolver configuration
Windows 9x	`C:\Windows\HOSTS` (file may not exist; do not use any extension like `.SAM`, `.TXT`)	Control Panel → Network → Configuration Tab → TCP/IP → DNS Configuration Tab
Windows NT/2000	`C:\WinNT\system32\` `   drivers\etc\HOSTS`	Settings → Network and Dial-up Connections → (right click on your network connection and select properties) → highlight Internet Protocol → Properties
Solaris/Linux	`/etc/hosts`	`/etc/resolv.conf`
Mac OSX	NetInfo Manager	`/etc/resolv.conf`

Pure-Java DNS Resolver

Users requiring a fully-functional DNS resolver capable of returning non-address resource records may download Sun's Java Naming & Directory Interface (JNDI) extension. JNDI is a standard Java extension providing a unified interface to multiple naming and directory services. The JNDI extension consists of a core set of interfaces and a number of protocol-specific implementations. These protocol implementations are called service providers. Typically, JNDI is used to access enterprise directory servers using the Lightweight Directory Access Protocol (LDAP) service provider. Sun also provides a separately downloadable DNS JNDI service provider. Despite its name, the DNS service provider is actually a DNS client. At the time of print, the DNS provider was in early access preview. The JNDI extension and service providers are available at http://java.sun.com/products/jndi/.

Internet Address Assignment

As mentioned earlier, an IP address represents the *unique* location of an Internet node. Connecting a networked device to the Internet therefore requires a mechanism for obtaining a globally unique IP address. The role was originally fulfilled by the Internet Assigned Numbers Authority (IANA) and was later assigned to the Internet Corporation for Assigned Names and Numbers (ICANN). ICANN is the organization responsible for coordinating IP address assignment as well as other Internet magic numbers such as protocol numbers, and service port numbers. Originally, IANA directly handled all IP assignment requests, but in recent years it has delegated this task to regional registries and taken the role of coordinating among registries.

Had IP addresses been assigned sequentially, then every Internet router would have had to separately store and compute information on how to reach each of the approximately 4 billion nodes on the Internet. Clearly that would not have been a scalable approach to address assignment. The solution to this problem was to assign IP addresses in blocks.

Every IP address was divided in two parts, with the first part being the **network number** and the second part being the **local address**. In the original Internet specification, addresses were broken down into three standard block sizes called **classes**. The table below lists the format of each class, where the network number bits are marked with the letter 'n' and local address bits marked with the letter 'a'. Local addresses that are all zeros or all ones are considered special addresses and cannot be assigned to nodes. The table does not include addresses starting with 111 (starting with 234.0.0.0) because they were reserved for multicast transmission (see Chapter 11) and future use.

Class	Format	Number of Blocks	Block Size	Range
A	0nnnnnnn aaaaaaaa aaaaaaaa aaaaaaaa	$2^7 - 1$ (=127)	$2^{24} - 2$ (=16m)	1.x.x.x – 127.x.x.x
B	10nnnnnn nnnnnnnn aaaaaaaa aaaaaaaa	2^{14} (=16,384)	$2^{16} - 2$ (=65k)	128.0.x.x – 191.255.x.x
C	110nnnnn nnnnnnnn nnnnnnnn aaaaaaaa	2^{21} (=2,097,152)	$2^8 - 2$ (=254)	192.0.0.x – 233.255.255.x

Organizations were assigned one or more blocks based on their size. For example, Columbia University was assigned block B addresses 128.59.0.0. This permitted the university to internally manage its 2^{16}-2 addresses. More importantly, every router on the Internet could now aggregate routing information for all Columbia hosts into a single entry marking the next hop to reach the Columbia University router.

The advantage of this solution was that routers could now summarize routing information based on the network number. Note that the class-based division works well with the decimal dotted notation for Internet addresses. Local addresses of class A networks consist of the three numbers past the first decimal point, class B of the two numbers past the second decimal point, and class C local addresses consist of the last number. For example, the class B address 128.59.22.38 can be easily broken down into the network number 128.59 and a local address 22.38.

The class-based block assignment scheme created problems as the Internet started to grow in size. Few organizations could take advantage of the class A (16m) or B (65k) blocks they were originally assigned which led to address space fragmentation problems. On the other hand, most organizations needed more than the 254 addresses provided by a class C block. As a result, organizations were assigned multiple C blocks, which led to a proliferation of routes since the multiple class C addresses could not be effectively summarized into a single routing entry. The solution to this problem was to create the **Classless Inter-Domain Routing** (CIDR) scheme.

In Classless Inter-Domain Routing, IP addresses are also divided into a network and local parts, but this time the network address length is **variable** (versus the fixed 8, 16, and 24 bits in class-based blocks). The advantage of this scheme is that addresses can be assigned at finer granularity. Due to this change, a network block can no longer be represented by an address with zeros in the local address. For example, the Columbia University address would now be represented as 128.59.0.0/16 or 128.59.0.0/255.255.0.0. The first representation marks the length of the network address, in this case a 16-bit class B address. The second representation is equivalent, but instead of marking the length of bits in the network address, it uses an IP address with the first 16 bits set to 1 and the remaining bits set to 0. One small disadvantage of the new representation is that determining the local address is no longer trivial using the decimal notation for addresses whose network address length is not 8, 16, or 24.

211

Special Addresses

There are some special addresses that cannot be used for identifying the location of Internet nodes. The all-ones address (255.255.255.255) is used to refer to the limited broadcast address. IP packets sent to this address are broadcast to neighboring nodes according to the rules of the local link-layer protocol. The all-zeros address (0.0.0.0) is sometimes used to refer to the local host. The local address portion of an IP address cannot have any octet with all ones or all zeros (for example, 128.59.0.0, 128.59.0.255). The A block address 127.0.0.0/8 has been assigned to the loop-back interface (local communication).

Certain ranges of addresses have been assigned to private networks. These addresses can be used within IP-based enterprise networks but are not routed within the Internet. Private addresses may be used in a network where hosts do not require access to the Internet at large, or in networks where external requests are handled via gateways (such as proxies, network-address translators, and so on). Lately, private addresses have also been used by enterprises running out of assigned IP addresses. More information can be obtained by reading the IETF RFC 1918 (http://www.ietf.org/rfc/rfc1918.txt). The following table lists the reserved private address blocks:

Address Range	Class Block
10.0.0.0 - 10.255.255.255 (10.0.0.0/8)	Class A private block (not routed)
172.16.0.0 - 172.31.255.255 (172.16.0.0/12)	16 contiguous Class B private networks
192.168.0.0 - 192.168.255.255 (192.168.0.0/16)	256 contiguous Class C private networks

Internet Routing

So far we have explained the structure of IP addresses and noted the fact that IP packets travel on a hop-by-hop basis towards their destination using nodes called routers. The diagram on the next page shows a more concrete example. On the right hand-side, a Wrox client transmits a packet addressed to a Columbia University host with address 128.59.18.5. For now, we will assume that the host is directly connected to the Wrox Press Internet access router. This is not a realistic assumption, and we will later show a more detailed example of how a network may be structured internally. The Wrox Press router will be connected to at least one peer router at some Internet Service provider. In this case, we assume that Wrox is only connected to a single ISP network. In that case, the Wrox router may simply be configured to forward all non-local packets to the peer ISP router A.

In this example, router A is a core router that contains a routing table with entries for publicly accessible networks. One of these entries will point to the Columbia University block 128.59.0.0/16 and list the next-hop router, in this case router B. When router A receives a packet addressed to 128.59.18.5, it will consult its routing table and the network part of the address will match the 128.59.0.0/16 block. As a result, the packet will be transmitted on the outgoing link to router B. The packet will be similarly forwarded from router B to C then to the Columbia University access router and the destination host.

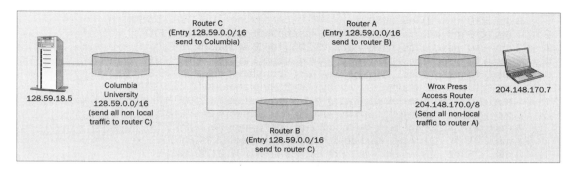

The above example made some simplifying assumptions. As already mentioned, network hosts are not typically directly connected to the access router (a more detailed example will follow). The first ISP router is unlikely to be a core router, instead it is likely to act as a concentrator collecting packets from multiple clients and sending them on using a default route to the ISPs backbone. This is a high-speed network owned and managed by a single entity. ISPs connect to other ISPs in what are called peering points and the ISP market itself is stratified with what are called first-tier, second-tier and third-tier ISPs. In short, the number of hops between the Wrox and the Columbia access routers will be significantly larger than three!

Additionally, the topology shown did not include any firewall devices. Firewalls are used to protect networks by restricting the types of packets admitted by source, destination, and protocol type. With the exception of a few brave (suicidal?) academic networks, all other networks protect from external access using firewalls.

The path between two hosts can be discovered using a utility called traceroute. The traceroute program is typically part of UNIX operating systems and the Microsoft Windows version is called tracert. A sample tracert session showing the path from a Columbia University host to the Wrox web server is shown below. Although the number of hops may appear large, it is actually typical, if not short. Note that the tracert does not actually reach the server. The most likely cause of failure is a firewall.

Based on the router domain names listed, it can be inferred that Columbia is connected to the appliedtheory.net second-tier ISP that appears to be purchasing services from sprintlink.net (Sprint Communications) that is a first-tier ISP. Sprint has a peering connection with bbnplanet.net (Verizon) that is also a first-tier ISP. Based on the bbnplanet.net router names, and some imagination, it can be inferred that they are connected to the interaccess.com second-tier ISP in Chicago, Illinois (USA). It is not possible to infer much about the location of the Wrox web server because of the firewall. The times listed show the round-trip time of each probe (three probes sent per intermediate destination).

C:\Beg_Java_Networking\Ch08>**tracert www.wrox.com**

Tracing route to www.wrox.com [204.148.170.161]
over a maximum of 30 hops:

```
  1  <10 ms  <10 ms <10 ms  vortex-gw.net.columbia.edu [128.59.16.1]
  2   20 ms   20 ms <10 ms  nyser-gw.net.columbia.edu [128.59.1.4]
  3  <10 ms  <10 ms <10 ms  at-gsr1-nyc-10-3-OC3.appliedtheory.net [169.130.253.133]
  4  <10 ms  <10 ms <10 ms  sl-gw18-nyc-7-0.sprintlink.net [144.232.235.153]
```

```
 5  <10 ms  <10 ms  <10 ms  sl-bb21-nyc-12-1.sprintlink.net [144.232.13.162]
 6  <10 ms  <10 ms  <10 ms  sl-bb21-nyc-8-0.sprintlink.net [144.232.7.110]
 7  <10 ms  <10 ms  <10 ms  ms144.232.18.206 [144.232.18.206]
 8  <10 ms  <10 ms  <10 ms  p7-0.nycmny1-br1.bbnplanet.net [4.24.6.229]
 9  <10 ms  <10 ms  <10 ms  p5-0.nycmny1-nbr1.bbnplanet.net [4.24.10.81]
10  <10 ms  <10 ms  <10 ms  p15-0.nycmny1-nbr2.bbnplanet.net [4.24.10.210]
11  <10 ms  <10 ms  <10 ms  p9-0.phlapa1-br1.bbnplanet.net [4.24.10.177]
12   23 ms   22 ms   23 ms  p9-0.iplvin1-br1.bbnplanet.net [4.24.10.182]
13   21 ms   21 ms   21 ms  so-6-0-0.chcgil2-br1.bbnplanet.net [4.24.9.57]
14   21 ms   21 ms   21 ms  p1-0.chcgil2-cr7.bbnplanet.net [4.24.8.106]
15   23 ms   25 ms   23 ms  chi1-ds3.interaccess.com [207.227.0.186]
16   25 ms   25 ms   24 ms  207.208.27.30 [207.208.27.30]
17  *
```

Subnetting

As we hinted earlier, most networks connecting to the Internet have their own internal structure. Consider the Internet network diagram below showing parts of the Columbia University network. Columbia's address space of 65,000 thousand addresses is too large to form a single network. Instead, Columbia internally divides its address space and assigns variable size blocks to various departments. Networks created by further dividing a network address block are known as **subnets**. For example, the Computer Science department was assigned the block 128.59.16.0/21. This block provides $2^{(32-21)} = 2^{11} = 2,048$ addresses in the range (a dash separates the network from the address portion):

```
10000000 00111011 00010 - 000 00000000 =  128.59.16.0
10000000 00111011 00010 - 111 11111111 = 128.59.23.255
```

Internally, the Computer Science department further partitions its address space into groups of 256 addresses (reminiscent of class C addresses). The diagram shows two such networks labeled "Unix student lab" and "PC student lab" subnets. Consider an external host (non Columbia) trying to access a PC student lab host with the address 128.59.18.5. All core Internet routers contain a routing entry for 128.59.0.0/16 with the next hop for reaching the Columbia University router. Once the packet arrives at the main Columbia University router, it will be matched to the local routing table. In this case, the destination address will match the Computer Science network 128.59.16.0/23 and the packet will be forwarded to the Computer Science router (128.59.18.1). Finally, the Computer Science router will match the packet to the PC lab network 128.59.18.0/24 and will transmit using the link-layer Ethernet connection to the destination host.

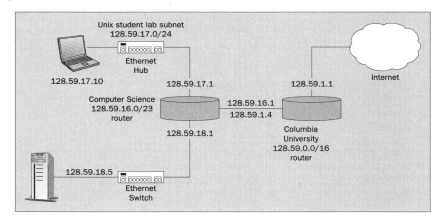

Dynamic Route Computation

One issue we will not be covering in this text is how IP routes are maintained. Due to the complexity and dynamic nature of the Internet (links fail, new networks keep getting added), Internet routers maintain state dynamically using protocols for path discovery. There are two types of routing algorithms. One type is used within individual administrative domains (intra-domain) and another is used to establish routes between administrative domains (inter-domain). The most common intra-domain routing protocol is OSPF (Open Shortest Path First) and the most common inter-domain routing protocol is BGP4 (Border Gateway Protocol version 4).

Summary

This chapter has introduced the basic concepts behind Internet addressing and naming:

❑   The current Internet uses version 4 of the Internet Protocol

❑   IPv4 addresses are 32-bit values and are used to identify the location of Internet nodes – the dotted decimal quad (for example, `128.59.16.1`) is a common representation of IPv4 addresses

❑   IP addresses specify location so they are not useful in identifying hosts over time (due to relocation, or network renumbering)

❑   The Domain Name System (DNS) is a distributed application-layer standard created to support scalable and extensible naming of Internet resources

❑   DNS consists of a hierarchical (tree) data model, a communications protocol (using well-known ports), and an algorithm for performing distributed name resolution

❑   The DNS data model associates resource records with nodes in the tree. Resource records may contain information such as network address, host description, or even application-specific data.

❑   DNS resolvers implement the DNS query algorithm and communicate with name servers using the DNS protocol

Java models Internet addresses as instances of the `java.net.InetAddress` class. The same class also acts as a limited DNS resolver supporting name-to-address and address-to-name lookups. `InetAddress` class instances are created using the factory design pattern. Two complete examples demonstrating a command-line DNS resolver and a utility for obtaining the address and name of the local host were shown.

TCP Programming

Most users think of the Internet in terms of its services. Examples of popular Internet services include e-mail, web browsing, file transfer, and peer-to-peer exchange services. As network programmers, we must have a more detailed understanding of network operations. Previous chapters have introduced the layered approach to network modeling. In particular, we have learned that the Internet is linked by a network layer protocol called IP (Internet Protocol). The Internet Protocol provides a connectionless, unreliable end-to-end packet service between Internet nodes. This model reflects the uncertainty in transmitting bits over physical links, as well as the dependence on intermediate routing nodes that may fail or become saturated. Most applications, on the other hand, would like to obtain access to a reliable connection-oriented channel for data exchange. The **Transport Control Protocol** (**TCP**) bridges this gap.

TCP is a transport layer protocol that builds a reliable end-to-end channel over an unreliable connectionless protocol. Additionally, TCP provides two very important network functions called **flow-control** and **congestion-control**. Flow control is used to prevent fast senders from overwhelming slower receivers, and congestion control is used to provide fair sharing of resources. Nearly all current Internet services make use of the TCP protocol, comprising 90% of all Internet traffic. In fact it would be fair to say that the Internet today is a TCP/IP network. Therefore, TCP will be the first transport layer protocol that we will be covering.

The chapter will begin by introducing the TCP protocol and outlining the mechanisms used to provide reliable connection-oriented transmission over the unreliable IP protocol. This chapter will next introduce a very important programming abstraction called a **socket**. A socket represents the end-point of a network communication. Sockets are protocol-and language-independent abstractions and may be used to program at the network or the transport layer.

After covering the TCP protocol and sockets at the conceptual level, the chapter will introduce the classes used to effect socket-based TCP communications in the Java language. The two main classes will be introduced, and their methods will be presented by operation type (constructors, accessors, and so on). Two in-depth examples for a network time client and server will then be presented to bring the previous discussion to focus, and demonstrate some common network design patterns.

Due to the popularity of the TCP protocol, and the wide use of sockets as programming abstractions this is the *core* chapter for readers wanting to program at the transport layer. By the end of this chapter readers should be able to create network clients and servers that implement existing protocols, as well as design their own protocols. The in-depth TCP examples will provide an opportunity to create clients and servers that interoperate with currently deployed Internet services. Securing such communications, however, will be dealt with in Chapter 14.

Transmission Control Protocol (TCP)

The **Transmission Control Protocol (TCP)** is a transport layer protocol supporting reliable end-to-end streaming communications. TCP enables two network entities to establish a bi-directional communications channel for reading and writing sequences of bytes. For example, a web browser will communicate with a web server over TCP in order to send a request for a particular page and receive the contents of that page. As shown in the diagram below, the TCP protocol provides the web browser and server with a **reliable** byte-pipe in each direction. The protocol guarantees that bytes will be delivered to the recipient in the **order** written by the sender, if at all. This guarantee simplifies the coding of applications since they only have to deal with complete loss of connectivity, as opposed to partial, corrupted or out-of-order delivery of data. TCP only provides a bi-directional byte-stream, and therefore it is up to the applications to agree on the contents of their conversation. The structure and meaning of the bytes exchanged is typically defined by an application-layer protocol. In the web browser example, the bytes transmitted conform to the **Hyper-Text Transfer Protocol (HTTP)**.

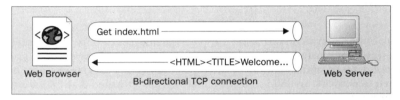

In addition to providing a reliable bi-directional communications channel between two entities, TCP also performs an important Internet "community" service. In most networks, the collective maximum rate in which network participants can pump data into the shared network, greatly exceeds the network's data carrying ability (bandwidth). It is therefore important to provide some mechanism for controlling the sharing of the network's transmission capabilities. This problem is known as **congestion**. The Internet Protocol's approach to congestion control is very simple: don't do anything to prevent it! The Internet's transmission model is best effort, so when links get congested, Internet routers simply drop packets that cannot be queued for transmission. This approach may simplify the work of Internet routers, but ultimately someone must perform congestion control in order to reduce the wasting of network resources (each dropped packet consumed resources to arrive at the router where it was dropped).

The Internet answer is to leave congestion control to the edge-nodes (end-nodes) to be performed by transport-layer protocols. TCP performs congestion control by controlling the rate with which data is written to the network in response to network conditions. The distributed algorithm used guarantees that competing TCP streams will get a "fair share" of the network's bandwidth.

TCP performs an additional service called **flow control**. In any stream-based communication, it is possible for one side to send data at a rate that exceeds the receiver's capability to process that data. This is a different problem from congestion control, because it does not involve a limitation in the network's data carrying ability, but a limitation in the receiver's processing capabilities. The TCP protocol performs flow control by allowing the receiving end of each unidirectional channel to control the rate in which the sender writes data.

The **Transmission Control Protocol (TCP)** is defined in the IETF standard RFC 793 (available at http://www.ietf.org/rfc/rfc0793.txt) with clarifications published as RFC 1122 (http://www.ietf.org/rfc/rfc1122.txt). Although it is not strictly required for the purposes of programming, we will briefly outline the major features of the protocol. This is not meant to be an exhaustive discussion, just a broad description of the protocol's operations. Some readers may prefer to skip this subsection on TCP operations and go straight to the next section on *socket programming*.

TCP Operations

TCP is built on top of the Internet Protocol (IP) that provides an unreliable, best-effort packet transmission infrastructure. As discussed in Chapter 8, IP packets may be lost en route to their destination, arrive out of order, or may even have their payload (but not header) corrupted. How can a reliable stream be built on top of such an unreliable packet-based network? The main issues that TCP must address are:

❑ **Stream segmentation**: Because the IP protocol only supports transmission of limited size byte arrays (packets/datagrams), TCP must break the stream into segments for transmission. In order to amortize the cost of transmitting the IP and TCP headers, it is preferable to transmit packets containing the largest possible payload.

The difficulty lies in deciding when to send a packet that has not been filled to capacity. Since the TCP implementation does not know when and if the application is going to write more data into the stream, it must make a best guess on when to send an unfilled packet. The tradeoff is between network efficiency and application responsiveness. By default, TCP implementations use a timer to decide when to transmit packets. Applications can disable such buffering and request immediate transmission of bytes as they are written to the stream.

❑ **Stream reassembly**: The TCP stream segments that are transmitted as IP packets may arrive at the destination in different order than the one sent. TCP must be able to handle out-of-order delivery and still reassemble the data in the order transmitted. TCP addresses this problem by counting the number of bytes transmitted in the stream and identifying each TCP/IP packet by the index of the first stream byte it carries. The advantage of this approach, as opposed to numbering the packets, is that retransmitted packets may contain additional data written to the stream since the packet was previously sent (retransmission due to packet loss is discussed next).

❑ **Packet loss handling**: IP packets carrying segments of the stream may be lost en route to the destination. TCP must be able to detect the fact that a packet has been lost and arrange for retransmission. This statement hides all sorts of complicated questions, such as how does the sender know that a packet has been lost? How long before a sent packet is considered lost, and what happens if the retransmit request itself is lost?

TCP supports packet loss detection by positive receiver acknowledgements. When a TCP packet arrives, the receiver's TCP protocol implementation will send a TCP packet to the sender acknowledging receipt. If the sender fails to receive an acknowledgement by a certain deadline, it will retransmit the packet.

The deadline is determined by a round-trip estimation that the sender maintains, using a formula that takes into account previous measurements of the time between packet transmission and receipt acknowledgement. Receivers may "piggyback" acknowledgements by storing them in traffic traveling on the reverse path, towards the sender.

❑ **Data corruption detection**: The IP protocol only protects its own header and does not make any guarantees on the payload contents. It is therefore possible that one or more bits in the payload may be corrupted due to transmission errors. How can TCP protect from such data corruption?

The answer is to compute a summary of the TCP packet's payload and store it in the packet's TCP header. An important characteristic of this summary must be that if the data is modified in certain ways, the computed summary must be different. The receiver of the packet can then independently compute the summary of the data received, using the same algorithm and compare it to the summary stored in the streaming header. The IP, TCP and UDP protocols use a summary algorithm called a **checksum**. The algorithm used protects against all 1-bit errors and some, but not all, multiple-bit errors.

❏ **Throughput efficiency**: The design of a reliable streaming channel is further complicated by the requirement for efficiency. For example, one could design a simple reliable channel in which the sender transmits the next packet of data every n-milliseconds until an acknowledgement is received. If any packets can get through, eventually both the data packet will arrive at the receiver, as well as the acknowledgement will arrive back with the sender.

The problem with this **stop-and-wait** design is that even when no packets are lost, the maximum throughput (packets per second) is limited by the communications round-trip overhead. This overhead includes the time to transmit the bits over the physical medium, the time to copy the packet from the transmission medium to the network interface of every node in the hop-path, the time to make routing decisions, and so on.

TCP addresses the problem by using a technique called **sliding-window**. In this approach, the receiver instructs the sender on the maximum number of unacknowledged bytes that can be transmitted (the window). Once the sender has transmitted a window-size full of data, he/she must wait for a receiver acknowledgement. When an acknowledgment has been received, the sender can send out as much data as was acknowledged. This mechanism increases the concurrency of operations as well as enables receivers to control the flow of transmission.

In order to support the above functions the two ends of a TCP connection must maintain various timers and counters. The state of some of these counters requires coordination between the two communicating entities. The two ends exchange control information using a fixed-size TCP header that is appended to every IP packet carrying TCP protocol data.

The TCP header structure is shown below. The TCP header contains information about the source and destination port of the TCP transmission (explained later), a sequence number identifying the position of the first data byte in the stream sequence, a "piggybacked" acknowledgement of data received, the TCP packet type (control bits), header and data checksum, and the sliding-window size. The fixed-size 20-byte TCP header may by followed be a variable size number of TCP options. The length of the variable-size portion is specified by the data-offset header value. Options are used to pass additional information that is not really covered in this book, but readers may refer to the RFC 793 standard.

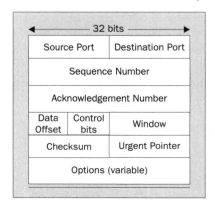

To support stream reassembly and packet acknowledgement, the two ends of a TCP connection must agree on the **initial sequence numbers**. The reason the two sides cannot just start counting from zero, is to prevent packets sent on a previous connection between the two ports from being mistaken as part of an existing connection. For this reason initial sequence numbers must change over time (typically every 4 microseconds).

The diagram below illustrates the TCP connection establishment process. The process starts when the client sends a TCP/IP packet with a header control-bit marking it is a SYN (synchronization) request (called active open). The SYN packet does not carry any data but contains the client's initial sequence number as well as other TCP header information such as windowsize.

Upon receipt, the server sends its own SYN packet containing its initial sequence number and an acknowledgement of the client's SYN request (called passive open).

Finally, the client sends an acknowledgement of the server's SYN message. If no packets are lost, this process involves three messages and it is therefore known as the TCP **three-way handshake**. The most important thing to remember about TCP's connection establishment is that it is expensive: no matter what will be transmitted in the course of the TCP connection, just establishing it will cost one and a half round-trip time.

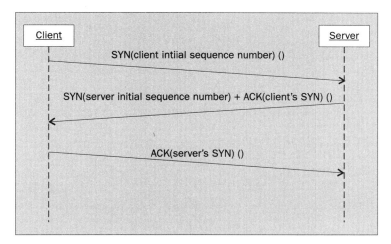

For transmission purposes, the stream is broken down into IP segments. Users typically do not control the segmentation process, but they can force the flushing of all pending bytes in a stream. Every segment transmitted includes the IP header, followed by a TCP header and the payload data.

Looking at the diagram below, we can see that processes transmit data as a byte stream. The TCP protocol segments the data based on a timer. In this example, the characters 'a', 'b', and 'c' were written to a stream followed by a pause. The TCP protocol implementation decided to transmit them by creating an IP packet containing the TCP header and the actual data. Subsequently, the characters 'd', 'e', 'f' were written to the stream, followed by a smaller pause and the character 'g'. In this case, all characters were placed on the same IP packet and sent towards their destination. Each packet sent causes an overhead in transmission of IP and TCP header information, so it is more efficient to send large packets. Programmers can increase performance by writing data in large blocks (up to the maximum IP packet size).

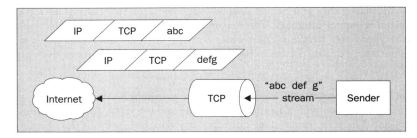

TCP connections are terminated by independently closing each side of the connection. Either side can initiate termination so there is no concept of a client or a server. In the diagram below, host A decides to close its output to the bi-directional channel, by sending a TCP packet marked with the FIN control bit to host B. Host B must acknowledge receipt of the FIN request. When host B decides to close its own output to the now one-directional channel, it will also send a FIN request to host A, which must be further acknowledged. In principle, this is a four-way handshake. In practice, the host A will set the FIN control bit on its last data packet, and host B will likely respond by closing the connection right away by acknowledging the FIN received and sending its own FIN in the same packet.

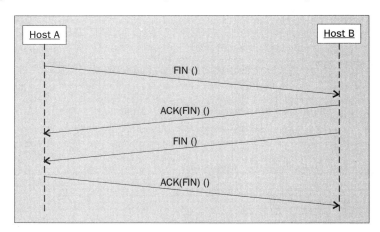

Socket Programming

Java programs communicate through a programming abstraction called a **socket**. A socket represents the end-point of a network communication. The socket abstraction is roughly analogous to the familiar file programming abstraction. Data may be stored in different file-system formats in different locations and storage devices. However, most applications do not care how or where the data is stored. Applications just use a string (filename) to identify the data, and then read or write it as a sequence of bytes. The file abstraction hides all these details from the programs providing a simple functional programming interface.

Similarly, most applications do not care how data is actually transmitted in the network. As in files, applications identify the address of the peer entity and then use the sockets interface to read and write data from and to the peer. Sockets encapsulate the implementation of network and transport layer protocols, providing applications with a simple read/write interface.

The diagram below provides a high-level view of sockets use. Programs create socket objects using the sockets API. Once created, socket objects can be configured for protocol-specific options, and used for network communications. The actual protocol used is typically selected by the application at socket creation time. As in the file object abstraction, applications don't need to know the details of the protocol implementation.

Notice that the diagram only shows a socket on one side of a network connection. Because sockets are just *programming* abstractions for network protocols, the other side of the connection does not have to use them. For example, the network program on the right side of this example may be coded in an exotic system that does not use the socket abstraction. That is, sockets don't use any additional communications mechanism other than that provided by the encapsulated protocol.

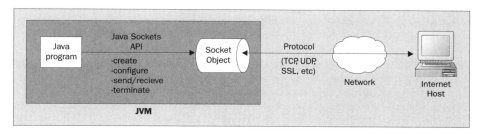

The socket abstraction was developed in the first networked version of UNIX developed at the University of California at Berkeley by Bill Joy (also of Java/Jini fame). Those sockets are, therefore, also known as Berkeley Sockets. The socket abstraction was later adopted by other operating systems including Microsoft Windows (WinSock). Traditionally, sockets were an Operating System concept. Java adapted the sockets abstraction as a core language library feature in order to support portable, cross-platform network programming.

Datagram vs. Stream

There are two basic abstractions of network communication: **connectionless** (datagram/packet), and **connection-based** (stream). We covered connectionless communications in the previous chapter when discussing the Internet Protocol (IP). In the connectionless model, data that needs to be sent to a network peer is first broken down into limited size datagrams, each of which is independently routed towards its destination. Usually, connectionless communications are unreliable, meaning that datagrams may be lost or delivered out of order. An alternative model is the connection-based model. In this model, prior to actual communication, the two entities establish a connection and agree to exchange data as a reliable ordered stream. TCP is an example of such a connection-based protocol.

The difference between these two communications models is also reflected in the design of the socket interfaces. Sockets encapsulating connectionless (datagram) protocols provide methods for sending and receiving byte arrays of restricted size. On the other hand, sockets encapsulating connection-based (stream) protocols provide methods for writing and reading data as a stream. This chapter will present sockets for effecting connection-oriented communications using the streaming abstraction. The following two chapters will cover sockets for connectionless communications using datagrams for one-to-one as well as one-to-many transmission (multicast).

Ports

In the previous chapter we discussed Internet addressing and naming. As we have learned, every Internet node must be assigned a unique IP address identifying its network location. In order to connect to a network service running on an Internet host we must therefore have the IP address of that host. What happens when multiple services are operating on the same network host? In such cases, we need some kind of a de-multiplexing mechanism. De-multiplexing is the task of splitting content that has been aggregated for delivery into multiple different destinations.

For example, mail addressed to residents of a multi-dwelling building will have the same mail delivery address but will be distinguished by apartment number. The postal service employee performs a de-multiplexing operation when delivering letters to the building's mailboxes based on apartment number. Similarly, network applications serving content on a computer identified by an IP address must somehow be distinguished to support individual message delivery.

One mechanism that is commonly used by network protocols, and in particular the Internet transport-layer protocols, is **port** addressing. Every network service is associated with (bound-to) one or more ports on one or more IP interfaces of its host device. Typically, integer numbers are used to identify different ports. In order to contact a network service, it is therefore necessary to provide both the IP address of its host, as well as the port number it is using (listening-to).

The Internet Protocol does not in itself support port addressing. Therefore, it is up to each individual transport layer protocol to provide its own de-multiplexing mechanism. As it happens, both of the popular Internet transport protocols (UDP & TCP) use 16-bit integer port numbers in the range 1 to 65535 for local de-multiplexing. Because ports are a transport layer Internet service, the port numbers used by each protocol are independent of each other. For example, UDP port 80 is unrelated to TCP port 80. Therefore the address of an application may be properly thought of as the triplet "address, protocol, port".

The use of port numbers is illustrated in the diagram below. The diagram shows a networked host with a single IP interface and two network services (processes). The services are an HTTP service bound to TCP port number 80 and a DNS name service bound to UDP port 53 (we will explain later how these numbers are selected). A client performing a DNS query will send an IP/UDP datagram address to port 53 of the name-server's host IP address (204.148.170.161). The datagram is routed on the Internet and (hopefully) will be delivered to the host's IP interface. At that point, the host's operating system looks at the protocol type of the datagram and passes it on to the UDP protocol handler. The local UDP protocol handler consults its port-to-process bindings and finds out that the DNS service process has bound to port 53. At that point, the UDP protocol handler will pass the contents of the datagram to the actual process (using the socket's API).

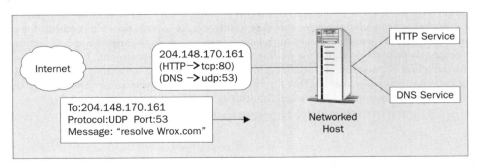

Recall that networked hosts may be configured with multiple IP interfaces. In such cases, network applications may bind to port numbers on all or a subset of the available interfaces. The context of a port number is a single IP interface. Therefore, applications may bind to different port numbers on different interfaces.

The diagram shows a networked host with two IP network interfaces and three network services (processes). Every network service is bound to one or more IP interfaces. For example, the HTTP service is bound to both interfaces using TCP port number 80. Each interface protocol port assignment is independent, so the HTTP service could in principle have bound itself to different TCP port numbers on each interface.

We also show a user service that is bound to one interface at the UDP port 4567, and an FTP service bound to UDP port 21 of the 128.59.16.1 interface. In this example, TCP connections to port 80 of either interface will connect to the HTTP service of this host. However, the FTP service may only be reached by sending UDP packets to port 21 of the 128.59.16.1 address. If an FTP client tries to contact the FTP service on UDP port 21 of the 128.59.22.38 address, it will receive a **service not available** message.

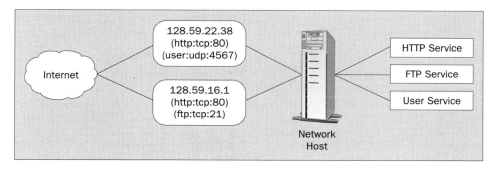

Port Assignment

Mapping services to port numbers may solve the de-multiplexing problem but it creates a new problem of its own. How can we find out the port number of a service? Is there some kind of a port-service directory? For example, I would like to know the port number or numbers of the HTTP service on a particular interface of a host. The Internet answer to that question is that there is no such directory. Instead, published protocols are assigned what are called **well-known port numbers**.

The advantage of this solution is that an additional port-directory mechanism is not needed. The main inconvenience is that every standard Internet application must request a port number from the **Internet Assigned Numbers Authority** (**IANA**; http://www.iana.org/). The table below lists the port numbers of some well-known protocols. Note that some protocols, such as DNS, support access through multiple protocols (TCP and UDP). In such cases port numbers must be reserved in the port-numbering space of both protocols. It is customary to assign the same port number across protocols for such multi-protocol applications. Thus, the DNS protocol is associated with UDP port 53 as well as TCP port 53. Conversely, although TCP and UDP port numbers are independent, IANA avoids assigning different applications the same port number on different protocols.

Protocol	Description	Protocol:Port
FTP	File transfer	`tcp:21`
TELNET	Remote console access	`tcp:23`
SMTP	Mail transfer	`tcp:25`
SNMP	Network management	`udp:161`
DNS	Domain name system	`udp:53, tcp:53`
HTTP	Hypertext transfer	`tcp:80`

How about user-defined services? IANA reserves ports 1 – 1023 for well-known services such as the ones listed above. Less popular or platform-specific services can still request registration of ports in the range 1024 – 49151. If a service is meant for internal deployment, then users can just pick up a port number that is not already assigned. The latest port assignments can be obtained at the URL http://www.iana.org/assignments/port-numbers. Both the client and the server must then be configured to connect to and bind to the given port. Finally, ports in the range 49152 – 65535 are typically used for ephemeral port assignment.

In some operating systems, well-known port numbers are considered special, and processes must be provided with additional rights in order to bind to these ports. For example, most UNIX-based operating systems, like Solaris, Linux, AIX, Mac OS X, etc., restrict port numbers in the range 1 – 1023 to services executing with "root" (system) privileges. Microsoft Window's operating systems do not restrict port usage.

Some platforms also support a proprietary service port directory. For example, the **Sun Network Information System (NIS)**, formerly known as Sun Yellow Pages (YP), permits services to bind to an arbitrary available port and then publish their port address through the directory service. In such systems, clients must first consult the directory service to look up the current port number of a service, before sending datagrams or establishing a connection. Use of such services is not portable across systems, and requires additional Java library support, so they will not be covered in this book. Readers are referred to Sun's Java Naming & Directory Interface (JNDI) core extension for system-specific directory access (http://java.sun.com/products/jndi).

Stream Sockets

The diagram below illustrates the use of sockets to establish two-way byte-streaming communication. On the left-hand side of the diagram is a Java client program wishing to connect to the server on the right. In order to receive remote connections, the server program must first create a **server socket**. A server socket is a receiver of incoming connection requests. Each protocol has its own server socket type.

In this example:

1. The server program creates a TCP server socket **bound** to port 4567.

2. At this point the server invokes the accept() method on the server socket and blocks waiting for the first client connection.

3. On the right side of the diagram, a Java client program creates a regular **socket** with the name or address of the server host (see Chapter 8) as well as the port number of the server program. The protocol type of client socket must match the protocol type of the server socket (TCP in this case).

4. Upon creation, the socket object attempts to establish communications with its peer using the TCP protocol.

5. Once the TCP handshake is complete (more on that later), the server socket creates a socket to model the server's side of the TCP communication.

6. This is returned as the result of the blocked `accept()` call.

At this point, the client and the server are each in possession of a socket object. The asymmetry caused by the connection establishment phase is gone, and the two sides can now converse over a symmetric bi-directional link. In order to transmit information, both the client and the server must obtain an input and an output stream from the socket object (Steps 8 and 9). The content of the conversation is application specific. To round off the example we show a simple request-response exchange of the client requesting a latte with skim milk, and the server responding with a challenge-request for payment. The main emphasis of this chapter will be to demonstrate how to design and implement such application-specific protocols.

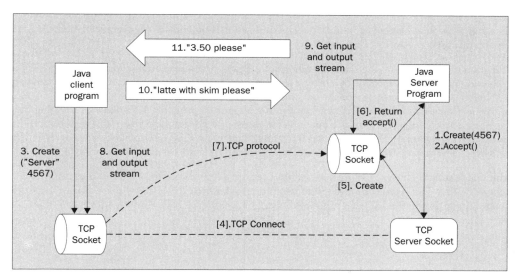

We should not concern ourselves with the details of these examples. We will be introducing the Java stream socket libraries in detail later in the chapter.

On the client side, the sequence of steps is:

❑ Create a socket object with the host name and port of the server (establishes the TCP connection)

❑ Get the socket's output stream and wrap it in a `BufferedWriter`

❑ Write the message and close the connection

On the server side, the sequence of steps is:

- ❏ Create a server socket binding to a specific port
- ❏ Loop forever accepting connections
- ❏ For each connection, wrap the socket's input stream into a `BufferedReader` and read a line of text

> **So far we have only talked about ports associated with server sockets. In fact, client sockets are also associated with port numbers. Client socket ports are assigned at connection time to an arbitrary available port (known as an** ephemeral **port). They are used by the operating system to determine the destination of each incoming TCP/IP packet in an established connection. Most applications do not care what these client port numbers are. The Sockets API provides methods for querying the port number of a client socket if needed.**

Java TCP Programming

The Java language supports TCP programming through the `java.net.Socket` and `java.net.ServerSocket` socket classes. Java clients connect to TCP servers by creating instances of the `java.net.Socket` class. Similarly, Java servers listen for incoming TCP connections by creating instances of the `java.net.ServerSocket` class. Connections are configured through accessor methods of these two classes. Actual network communications, however, are performed using the `java.io` package streaming classes.

The diagram below illustrates the main operations of the Java streaming socket classes. The Java TCP server, on the right, accepts TCP connections by creating a `java.net.ServerSocket` instance bound to a particular port. When a `ServerSocket` establishes a connection with a TCP client, it creates a `java.net.Socket` instance encapsulating that connection and returns it to the server program. It should be noted that the `java.net.Socket` object returned is bound to an ephemeral port number that is different from the one the `ServerSocket` is listening to (most applications don't care about that port number). The server retrieves the socket's input and output streams and effects communication by implementing some protocol.

On the client side, TCP connections are established through instances of `java.net.Socket` associated with a TCP server on the given host and port. Once the client `Socket` has established a TCP connection, retrieving the socket's input and output stream effects communication.

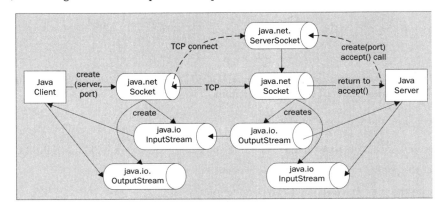

java.net.Socket: TCP Client Socket

So far, we've talked about sockets as abstract end points of communication that encapsulate a communications protocol. Ideally, Java should have defined generic interfaces for streaming and datagram sockets, and then provided some factory mechanism to generate implementations for particular protocols (such as TCP).

Although Java does define a class representing a streaming socket, it is not as abstract as one would expect. The class `java.net.Socket` represents an endpoint of a connection-oriented protocol, however it is strongly related to TCP, since the class defines methods for querying and setting TCP-specific protocol options. Some of these methods make sense for other protocols that are very similar, or built upon on TCP, but may not make sense in others. This is not so much a problem, because most applications will end up using either TCP, or a protocol layered over TCP, such as the **Secure Socket Layer (SSL)** protocol discussed in Chapter 14.

Socket Construction

In order to establish a connection with a network server one must have the address of the server's host, as well as the port number to which the server is bound. The `java.net.Socket` class provides a constructor, which takes an IP address and a port and attempts to establish a connection. By default, the JVM will establish a TCP connection unless the `setSocketImplFactory()` has been invoked to override the default `Socket` class behavior. We will be discussing this behavior at the end of this section.

```
Socket(InetAddress address, int port) throws IOException;
```

The constructor returns only after the connection has been established, that is, once the TCP three-way handshake has been completed. Hence, the constructor must signal errors in establishing the connection. Throwing the `java.io.IOException` exception signals such a communication error.

A connection attempt may fail for multiple reasons. For example, the remote IP address may not be reachable due to network failure or firewall protection. The IP address may be reachable, but the server may not be bound to the specified port on the given address. Although the signature of the constructors only declares the `java.net.IOException`, users wishing to programmatically determine the reason for the connection failure, can try to catch the following `java.net.IOException` subclasses:

Exceptions

`java.net.NoRouteToHostException`	There is no route to the IP address provided. This may indicate that the client or the server host is not connected to a network, or that there is no path from the client's network to the server's network due to some failure.
`java.net.ConnectException`	The network of the remote server can be reached, but either no host has been assigned the specified address, or a host is reachable but no application is listening to the specified port on this address for the protocol used.

Additionally, the constructor may throw the runtime exception `java.lang.SecurityException` if a security manager has been installed, and the `connect` action has not been provided for the target IP address and port. Readers should refer back to the `java.net.SocketPermission` discussion in Chapter 7.

A similar constructor is provided for use with host names, or IP addresses represented as strings. The signature is shown below. This constructor may also throw an additional `IOException` subclass called `java.net.UnknownHostException` if the host name cannot be resolved, or the string representation of the IP address is invalid. The remaining exceptions (`IOException` and `SecurityException`) are thrown for the same reasons as in the previous constructor.

```
Socket(String host, int port) throws IOException;
```

Note that this is a convenience constructor since it is equivalent to using the previous constructor as shown below:

```
new Socket(InetAddress.getByName(host), port);
```

The following complete code example demonstrates construction of a socket. To simplify the code, the name and port number of the target host were hard-coded. Notice that most of the code involves error handling. Because network communications may fail at any point, error handling is a significant part of writing network clients and servers. The example constructs a `Socket` object in order to connect to the target host and port using TCP (shown in bold). Once the connection has been established, a message is printed, and then the connection is closed (the close method is discussed later in this section). Errors are handled by issuing an appropriate error message. Real applications would use exception information to decide on how to handle the failure.

```java
//SimpleSocketCreate.java

import java.io.IOException;
import java.net.Socket;
import java.net.UnknownHostException;

public class SimpleSocketCreate {
  public static void main(String[] args) {
    String host = "localhost";   // hard-coded host
    int port = 4000;             // hard-coded port

    try {
      System.out.println("Attempting to connect to a TCP service on "
                          + host + ":" + port + " ...");
      Socket socket = new Socket(host, port);
      System.out.println("Connection established !");

      // Normally this is where we'd perform communications
      socket.close();

    } catch (UnknownHostException e) {
      System.err.println("Could not resolve host name: " + e.getMessage());

    } catch (IOException e) {
      System.err.println("A communications error occured: "
                          + e.getClass().getName() + ": " + e.getMessage());
```

```
        } catch (SecurityException e) {
          System.err.println("The security manager refused permission to "
                        + "connect to the remote TCP service: "
                        + e.getMessage());
        }
    }
 }
```

The above example may be compiled and executed as shown below (included as `SimpleSocketCreate.java` in the code directory). Note that unless we happen to be running a TCP service bound to port 4000 on our computer, execution will result in an error message indicating a connection failure since no one will be listening. Further on, we'll describe the equivalent trivial server example, and we will rerun this example to show a successful connection.

Compile the example. There is no need to put any particular files in our classpath, as this only needs access to the JDK.

C:\Beg_Java_Networking\Ch09>**java SimpleSocketCreate**
Attempting to connect to a TCP service on localhost:4000 ...
A communications error occured: java.net.ConnectException: Connection refused: no further information

As you may recall from Chapter 8, Internet hosts may have more than one IP address. In some cases, it may be possible to connect to a remote host through more than one of these interfaces. The previous two constructors left the decision on which interface to use up to the system. This is by far the most common approach to constructing socket instances. In some *rare* cases, users may want to explicitly specify the outgoing interface to be used; for example, if one interface is connected to a more secure network. The two interfaces shown below allow users to specify the address of the outgoing interface in addition to the destination address, or hostname, and port.

```
Socket(InetAddress address, int port,
       InetAddress localAddr, int localPort) throws IOException;
Socket(String host, int port,
       InetAddress localAddr, int localPort) throws IOException;
```

Note that the above two constructors also require users to supply a local port argument. As noted earlier, the client socket is associated with a local port number that is usually arbitrarily assigned by the operating system at creation time. In some cases, users may want to specify the local port number used by the client socket. The reasons for needing to specify the port number used by the client socket are quite exotic. Usually, they involve some kind of restrictive firewall configuration.

In the above two constructors it is possible to set the `localAddr` to `null`, in which case the `Socket` implementation will bind to all interfaces (default behavior). The default behavior can also be requested by passing the special IP address 0.0.0.0 that is interpreted as matching all available interfaces. It is not possible to indicate a "don't care" option in the `localPort` argument (zero will not work) and therefore use of these constructors requires users to identify an available local port number.

Socket Input and Output

Connection-oriented sockets are an abstraction for a byte-stream communication between two network programs. Therefore the most important methods of the Socket class are the ones that permit users to actually use instances for communication. The Socket class provides two methods, one for obtaining an input stream for reading bytes from the peer program, and one for obtaining an output stream for writing bytes to the output stream. The streams are represented as java.io.InputStream and java.io.OutputStream instances encapsulating the communications stream (see Chapter 5). A java.io.IOException will be thrown if the socket is not in a connected state, that is, it has been closed.

```
java.io.InputStream getInputStream() throws IOException;
java.io.OutputStream getOutputStream() throws IOException;
```

Once the input and output streams for the Socket have been obtained, it is up to the application to determine the contents of the communication. The chapter will cover issues in designing such protocols. On some platforms, requesting an input stream from a socket may block until the sender transmits some information. It is recommended that the getInputStream() method be called just before the first read. We will demonstrate use of these methods in our in-depth examples later in this chapter.

Socket Information

Connection-oriented sockets encapsulate a connection to a network peer or remote host, therefore, they may be characterized by the set:

```
<local_address, local_port, remote_address, remote_port>.
```

Consider the previous CreateSocket example. The peer address of the socket object will be the address for the hostname localhost, and the port will be 4000. The local socket address will be the interface used to reach the localhost address, and the port number will be an arbitrarily chosen client port. The four methods for querying the Socket local and remote address and port numbers are shown below. (Note that there is an imbalance in the method naming – for example, getPort() is used instead of getRemotePort()).

```
InetAddress getInetAddress() throws IOException;
int getPort() throws IOException;
InetAddress getLocalAddress() throws IOException;
int getLocalPort() throws IOException;
```

Socket Termination

Similarly to file objects, socket objects consume finite operating system resources. An open socket keeps a local port busy, and in most cases uses at least one native operating system file handle. Both port numbers as well as file handles are limited and therefore it is very important to explicitly close sockets when the connection is no longer needed. Depending on the Java garbage collector to free up resources is almost guaranteed to lead to trouble, such as failure to create new client or server sockets, or even opening files! The close() method requests *asynchronous* termination of the socket connection (the performance of the TCP termination handshake).

Note that the close() method will return *immediately*, even if data written before invocation has not completed transmission. The default semantics of the method invocation are that delivery of data written before invocation will continue to be attempted until successfully delivered. It is possible to limit the maximum duration of pending data delivery using the setSoLinger() method as described later in this section.

```
void close() throws IOException;
```

Once a socket has been closed, the input and output streams may no longer be used. An attempt to read data from the input stream, or write data to the output stream will result in an IOException. An alternative way to close a socket is to invoke the close() method on either the input or output streams.

The TCP protocol supports a **half-close** of a bi-directional TCP connection. The half-close feature can be used to close only the input or only the output direction of the connection. Some network protocols were designed to use this feature. For example, a simple request-reply protocol could have a client writing an arbitrary number of requests followed by a termination of the output stream. The server would keep reading requests until it detected an input stream termination, at which point it would start processing the requests and writing them to the output stream. The two methods for effecting such behavior are shown below.

```
void shutdownInput() throws IOException;
void shutdownOutput() throws IOException;
```

Socket Configuration

In some cases, users may need to configure the operations of a socket. Some operations are protocol-independent while others are tied to the specifics of the TCP protocol:

```
int getSoTimeOut() throws SocketException;
void setSoTimeout(int timeout) throws SocketException;
```

The input stream returned by the getInputStream()Socket method will block indefinitely on a read() invocation when no data has been sent by the communicating peer. In some cases, programs may want to specify a time period after which, if no data has been received, the read() method should throw an exception. This can be achieved by using the setSoTimeout(int) method. Invoking the method with a zero value sets the maximum blocking timeout to be infinite (default), while a value greater than zero sets the maximum number of milliseconds to block.

The java.io.InterruptedIOException will be thrown by the read() InputStream method if the specified timeout has expired. This exception does not change the state of the Socket. Programmers may invoke read() right away or more likely perform some internal checks perhaps deciding to query the other party on its status. The current timeout may be obtained by invoking the getSoTimeOut() method.

```
int getReceiveBufferSize()throws SocketException;
void setReceiveBufferSize(int size) throws SocketException;
int getSendBufferSize()throws SocketException;
void setSendBufferSize(int size) throws SocketException;
```

Recall, that the Internet Protocol only supports packet-based communications. TCP builds a streaming abstraction on top of this packet-based network, but ultimately, bytes read from or written to each stream must be segmented into packets for transmission.

If performance has not been an issue, applications never need to know anything about how the streams are segmented. However, applications can significantly improve communications performance by taking this issue into consideration. The above methods enable programmers to query and set the sizes of the input and output stream buffer used by the operating system. The input buffer is used to copy data from the application memory space into kernel memory space for network transmission. The output buffer is used to copy data from the kernel network interface driver into the memory space of the application.

Querying the input and output buffer sizes is a good way for applications to find out the most efficient way to read and write data. For example, if an application has to transfer a large amount of data, it will be more efficient to write getSendBufferSize() bytes at a time to the output stream (using the OutputStream write(byte[]) method). Similarly, if an application is expecting to receive a large amount of data it will be more efficient to read getReceiveBufferSize() number of bytes at a time (using the InputStream read(byte[]) method).

Setting the receive and send buffers will also affect performance. A large receive or send buffer will speed up large transfers, but slow down small transfers. Note that setting the buffer size is treated as a hint to the system, which means that it may be ignored. We will cover efficient streaming communications in greater detail later in this chapter. All methods may throw a java.net.SocketException if the buffer size value cannot be read or modified.

```
boolean getKeepAlive() throws SocketException;
void setKeepAlive(boolean on) throws SocketException;
```

Once a TCP connection is established using the initial handshake, it is kept open until either side explicitly requests its termination. The design goal was to preserve the bandwidth that would otherwise be needed to verify connectivity, as well as to prevent unnecessary connection terminations in case of network failures when there was no data being exchanged.

The disadvantage of this design is that failed clients (due to a system or network failure) tie up resources (port numbers and file handles) on servers. Thus, many protocols introduced their own connectivity verification. The KeepAlive option was added to permit applications to modify this default TCP behavior. Setting the KeepAlive to true results in TCP control messages being exchanged periodically to verify connectivity. As a result, failures can be detected and an exception can be thrown to code blocked in a stream read operation.

```
int getSoLinger() throws SocketException;
void setSoLinger(boolean on, int linger) throws SocketException;
```

The SoLinger option controls socket behavior in cases when the close() method has been invoked before all streamed data could be transmitted. The default behavior is for close() to return immediately with the data remaining being delivered by the system asynchronously.

In some cases, users may want to set an upper bound on the outstanding data delivery time. This decision can have an effect on how quickly resources are freed for other network connections (especially under denial-of-service attacks). The boolean attribute controls the switch between the default behavior (false) and the time-bound behavior (true). The linger attribute sets the maximum number of seconds and can be an integer number up to 65535. A zero linger argument will result in a **hard close** that immediately terminates the connection.

```
boolean getTcpNoDelay()throws SocketException;
void setTcpNoDelay(boolean on) throws SocketException;
```

In most TCP protocol stacks, a byte written to an output stream is not transmitted immediately. Usually, the protocol implementation will wait for a small amount of time for other data to be written, before sending out the next IP packet. The goal is to amortize the TCP/IP header overhead and reduce the routing load in the intermediate nodes. While this mechanism works well for most TCP transfers, it presents a problem for interactive connections.

Consider a remote terminal access application (UNIX users may be familiar with Telnet). In a remote terminal application, users type characters that are transmitted to the remote server and treated as if typed on the server's keyboard. Users expect to see the result of their typing by receiving the echoed character from the server, and when pressing the enter key expect the command to be evaluated. The delay introduced by the TCP stack is not acceptable in such situations. It is therefore desirable to disable the buffering of written bytes and request that data be transmitted immediately. Control of this behavior is effected using the `getTcpNoDelay()` and `setTcpNoDelay()` Socket methods.

Custom Socket Factories

By default, `java.net.Socket` instances establish connections using the TCP protocol. It is possible for users to replace that default behavior by setting alternative socket factories. A socket factory is used to override the default TCP `Socket` implementation with another streaming protocol implementation. For example, later in this chapter we will be covering a protocol providing secure network streaming connections. In some cases, it may be desirable to dictate that all sockets created by the application must be secure sockets. The `setSocketImplFactory()` method may be used to effect this behavior.

```
static void setSocketImplFactory(SocketImplFactory fac) throws IOException;
```

Creation of custom socket factories is an advanced topic that will not be covered in this book.

java.net.ServerSocket: TCP Server Socket

In order to accept network connections a Java program must create an instance of `java.net.ServerSocket`. Server sockets are not directly used to perform any network communication. Instead, they act as factories that create a `java.net.Socket` object for every incoming TCP connection request. As was illustrated in earlier stream socket discussion, the usage pattern for server sockets is simple: programs create the server socket, bind to a specific port on one or more interfaces, and then invoke the blocking `accept()` method. The `accept()` method blocks until an incoming TCP connection successfully negotiates the handshake phase, and then returns a `java.net.Socket` object encapsulating the streaming connection. It is up to the server program to invoke the `accept()` method again in order to handle the next incoming connection. A common design pattern involves having a thread that loops on `accept()` and then spawns off a thread for each `java.net.Socket` returned.

Server Socket Construction

The basic server socket constructor takes a single argument, the TCP port number used in binding. If the constructor returns without throwing an exception then the server socket has successfully bound to the requested TCP port. The constructor may fail due to an I/O error, or due to a security error.

```
ServerSocket(int port) throws IOException, SecurityException;
```

Because ports are used as unique mailboxes identifying a single receiver, it is not permissible to have more than one process listening to the same port. Therefore, if any process has created a socket bound to the specified port an IOException will be thrown. Note that all processes running on a single host for a given interface share the port address space, independent of the language in which they were written. In other words, port assignment is an operating system service versus a language or library service.

Some operating systems restrict certain port number ranges to "special" processes. For example, UNIX-based operating systems do not allow user-privileged processes to bind to ports lower than 1024 (Microsoft Windows does not impose any restrictions). Additionally, operating systems reserve some ports for system services, in addition to ports used by standard services such as HTTP, FTP, and DNS. Although this is not documented, the java.net.BindException will be thrown if the requested port is already in use (a subclass of IOException). The IOException may also be thrown if the operating system was unable to allocate resources for the request. This can occur if some scarce resource, such as a file descriptor, is not available.

A SecurityException will be thrown if a security manager has been installed, and the listen action has not been supplied for localhost. Server socket and client socket permissions are discussed in the java.net.SocketPermissions section later in this chapter.

An additional constructor, shown below, permits users to specify the size of the connection backlog queue. Recall that the server socket generates a java.net.Socket object for an incoming connection in response to an accept() call. Server programs usually loop around the accept() call, spawning threads to process each connection. Because client connection requests happen asynchronously, it is possible that new requests will be received before the server program has been able to invoke the accept() method. What happens in such cases?

The answer is that the requests are placed in a queue, and retrieved on subsequent accept() invocations. No matter how fast a server operates, if the rate of incoming connections exceeds its capacity to serve, the queue can continue to grow infinitely. The clients queued will have to wait for a long time to receive service.

The solution to this problem is to set an upper bound on the queue length. Once the queue fills, new connection requests will be rejected. This will assure that clients receive prompt feedback of service denial, and that holding too many TCP connections open doesn't deplete the server's resources. At this point we may be curious as to the queue size if one uses the single argument constructor. The Java network library designers arbitrarily chose the number 50. This constructor throws the same exceptions as the basic constructor (IOException and SecurityException).

```
ServerSocket(int port, int backlog) throws IOException, SecurityException;
```

The third and final constructor permits users to bind to a particular local network interface. Recall that port numbers are assigned per protocol and per interface. The previous two constructors attempt to bind the program to the specified port on all available interfaces.

In some rare cases, it may be desirable to limit the exposure of the program on a multi-homed host (see Chapter 8 for definition). For example, consider a corporate server that is connected both to the Internet, as well as to the corporate network. If the service provided is to be restricted to internal hosts only, then the server socket should bind to the corporate IP interface. This can provide additional security, in addition to a security policy restricting accept actions from internal hosts. Given that it is currently impossible to discover, using the Java APIs, the addresses of all the host's network interfaces, a program would have to be externally provided (configured) with the required address.

```
ServerSocket(int port, int backlog, InetAddress bindAddr)
           throws IOException, SecurityException;
```

Accepting Socket Connections

The main task of a server socket is to receive incoming connection requests and generate a `java.net.Socket` object that encapsulates each request. As was explained earlier, incoming connections are queued until the program retrieves them one at a time by invoking the `accept()` method. The `accept()` method takes no arguments, and returns the next connection in the queue encapsulated as a `java.net.Socket` object.

If no connection requests are pending then the method blocks until a request is made, or the optionally specified connection timeout has expired (set using `setSoTimeout()` as will be shown later). The method may throw an `IOException` if the server socket has been closed, or a communications error is encountered (for example, the client host became inaccessible for some reason). The method may also throw a `SecurityException` if the incoming connection originated from a host/port not covered by an accept socket permission (for more information, see the discussion on socket permissions in Chapter 7).

The `accept()` method signature is shown below:

```
Socket accept() throws IOException, SecurityException;
```

The example below demonstrates a simple server application that accepts TCP connections and then immediately closes them without reading or writing any data. As in the earlier simple client example, most of the code involves error handling. The program first attempts to create a TCP server socket bound to port `4000`. If that operation is successful, the program enters an infinite loop in which the blocking `accept()` method is invoked to process each incoming connection.

Once `accept()` returns the connection as a `Socket` object, the program prints out the hostname and port of the connecting client and then closes the socket. All exceptions thrown during the processing of an incoming connection are caught within the loop in order to assure continued operation of the server.

```java
//SimpleServerSocketCreate.java

import java.io.IOException;
import java.net.ServerSocket;
import java.net.Socket;

public class SimpleServerSocketCreate {
  public static void main(String[] args) {
    ServerSocket server = null;
    int port = 4000;    // hard-coded port number

    try {
      System.out.println("Attempting to bind to TCP port " + port + " ...");
      server = new ServerSocket(port);

    } catch (IOException e) {
      System.err.println("Error binding to port: " + e.getClass().getName()
                         + ": " + e.getMessage());
      System.exit(1);
```

```
      } catch (SecurityException e) {
        System.err.println("The security manager refused permission to "
                          + "bind to port " + port + " was denied: "
                          + e.getMessage());
        System.exit(1);
      }

      System.out.println("Created socket bound to "
                        + server.getInetAddress().getHostName() + ":"
                        + server.getLocalPort());

      while (true) {
        System.out.println("Listening for connections ...");

        try {
          Socket socket = server.accept();
          System.out.println("Connection from "
                            + socket.getInetAddress().getHostName() + ":"
                            + socket.getPort());

      // Normally this is where we'd spawn a thread to perform communications

          socket.close();

        } catch (IOException e) {
          System.err.println("A communications error occured while "
                            + "waiting for, or establishing a TCP "
                            + "connection: " + e.getMessage());

        } catch (SecurityException e) {
          System.err.println("Unauthorized client connection: "
                            + e.getMessage());

        } catch (Throwable e) {
          System.err.println("Unexpected exception: "
                            + e.getClass().getName() + ": "
                            + e.getMessage());
        }
      }
    }
  }
}
```

A similarly simple example was shown earlier for client sockets, in a class called `SimpleSocketCreate`. We take a small break from our API discussion to execute these two small examples.

Once the source code has been compiled, invoking the JVM with the server's class will start the simple server. The special IP address `0.0.0.0` is used to indicate that the server socket has bound to the specified port on all available IP interfaces (addresses).

C:\Beg_Java_Networking\Ch09>**java SimpleServerSocketCreate**
Attempting to bind to TCP port 4000 ...
Created socket bound to 0.0.0.0:4000
Listening for connections ...

The server will block, waiting for an incoming connection, so in a different window or shell we can execute the simple client. Recall that the simple client had hard-coded the host name (`localhost`) as well as the port number (`4000`). This is why we must start the client on the same host. The client simply connects to the server, prints a message informing the user of success, and then closes the connection.

```
C:\Beg_Java_Networking\Ch09>java SimpleSocketCreate
Attempting to connect to a TCP service on localhost:4000 ...
Connection established !
```

Switching back to the command line window we are running `SimpleServerSocketCreate` in, we should see a message logging the connection similar to the one shown below (obviously the host name will differ based on individual environments):

```
Connection from MANTICORE:3182
Listening for connections ...
```

Server Socket Information

Server socket objects have two identifying attributes: the port number and the Internet address they are bound to. The `java.net.ServerSocket` class provides methods to query these two values. The `getInetAddress()` method returns the IP address of the interface to which the server socket is bound. Recall that the simple `ServerSocket` constructor binds the server socket to the requested port on all available interfaces. In such cases, the `getInetAddress()` method returns the special IP address `0.0.0.0` which should be interpreted as a wildcard (bound to all IP addresses).

Obtaining the port the server socket is bound to involves a simple invocation of the `getLocalPort()`.

```
InetAddress getInetAddress();
int getLocalPort();
```

Server Socket Configuration

Server sockets have a single configurable property, the socket timeout. The socket timeout is used to control the blocking behavior of the `accept()` method. By default, `accept()` blocks until a connection is received, resulting in a value returned or exception thrown, or the server socket is closed. In some applications, programmers may want to perform some action if no connection has been received for a given interval.

Although it would be possible to use a timer thread, the simple solution is to set the `SoTimeout` property to the maximum number of milliseconds that an `accept()` method invocation should block. The default behavior (infinite) is restored by invoking `setSoTimeout()` with a zero timeout. If the property is set to a non-zero value and the timeout expires, the `accept()` method will throw the `java.io.InterruptedIOException` exception. It is up to the programmers to distinguish this exception from the general `IOException` indicating a connection error. Both the `set()` and `get()` methods may throw a `SocketException`.

```
int getSoTimeout() throws SocketException;
void setSoTimeout(int timeout) throws SocketException;
```

Here is a code snippet illustrating use of the server socket timeout feature (the complete example can be found in the chapter code in the file `ServerSocketTimeout.java`).

```
//ServerSocketTimeout.java

. . .
```

```
ServerSocket server = ... // one of the constructors
    int timeoutMillis = 5000;

    try {
      server.setSoTimeout(timeoutMillis);

    } catch (SocketException e) {
      System.err.println("Error setting server socket timeout: "
                          + e.getMessage());
      System.exit(1);
    }

    while (true) {
      try {
        Socket s = server.accept();
        s.close();

      } catch (java.io.InterruptedIOException e) {
        System.out.println("No connections in the past " + timeoutMillis
                            + " milliseconds");

      } catch (java.io.IOException e) {
        System.err.println(e.getClass().getName() + ": " + e.getMessage());
      }
    }
```

Server Socket Termination

A server socket may be terminated simply by invoking the no-argument close() method. Closing the server socket will not affect connections that have already been returned by an accept() invocation. If the accept() method is invoked on a closed socket then a java.net.SocketException will be thrown with a message indicating that the socket has been closed. There is no way to query a server socket to find out if it has been closed, which creates a problem in interpreting accept() exceptions (an isClosed() method has been added in JDK 1.4). It should be noted that some methods, such as setSoTimeout() still succeed even if the server socket has been closed in current implementations.

```
void close() throws IOException;
```

Server Socket Factories

Similarly to the java.net.Socket class, the default java.net.ServerSocket behavior of listening to TCP connections can be changed, using the method shown below. The primary use of this method is to override the default server socket type created by applications. For example, an application coded to use TCP sockets can be switched to using secure socket layer (SSL) sockets by a single invocation of this method. SSL sockets are covered in Chapter 14.

```
static void setSocketFactory(SocketImplFactory fac) throws IOException;
```

Creation of custom server socket factories is an advanced topic that will not be covered in this book.

java.net.SocketPermission

Creating client and server sockets is a security-sensitive operation. Connecting to a remote host is sensitive because it may be used to launch an attack on a remote service, or provide information about the execution environment to a remote host. Creating server sockets is also a sensitive operation since it can be used to disseminate illegal/compromising content, as well as abuse network resources such as bandwidth.

The Java 2 security model is discussed in detail in Chapter 7.

RFC 868 – Time Protocol Implementation

Having covered the classes used on the network client side (Socket), as well as the network server side (ServerSocket), it is time to develop our new skills by creating a simple Java client-server network application. We will be implementing an old Internet (ARPANET) standard used to obtain the current time from a network server. This standard is defined as IETF RFC 868 and is included in the chapter code directory as rfc868.txt and may also be retrieved online at the URL http://www.ietf.org/rfc/rfc868.txt.

The time protocol is extremely simple. A client connects using TCP to a time protocol server on port number 37. On the server side, an incoming connection is interpreted as a request for the current time, which is handled by writing four bytes to the TCP stream and then closing the connection. The client knows in advance that the server will be writing four bytes into the stream and therefore after opening the connection it just blocks until they become available, or the connection is closed signaling an error.

The connection is closed from the server's side right after the 4-bytes are written, and from the client's side once the 4-bytes are read, or after detection of a server close (due to some error). The four bytes exchanged represent a 32-bit integer number counting the number of seconds since an arbitrarily chosen epoch, which is January 1st, 1900 at 0:0:0 hours UTC (otherwise known as GMT). The standard also defines a connectionless protocol using UDP, which we're not going to implement at this point. The time protocol operations are illustrated in the diagram below.

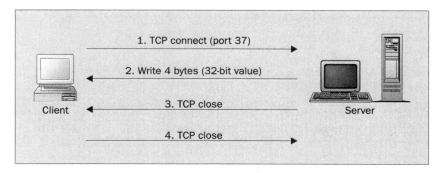

It should be noted that the RFC 1305 Network Time Protocol (NTP) has mostly replaced the RFC 868 Time Protocol. Due to the use of a 32-bit value to count seconds since 1/1/1900, the Time Protocol can only represent times up to year 2036 (the binary equivalent of the year 2000 problem). Moreover, in the days when network delays are counted in milliseconds, the second-order accuracy of RFC 868 is no longer sufficient for most applications. Finally, the RFC 868 protocol does not provide any server discovery mechanism and assumes that clients are configured with the address of the time server(s). The NTP protocol addresses these shortcomings and significantly expands the capabilities by defining a distributed architecture for time synchronization.

We begin implementation of the RFC 868 Time Protocol by defining a class containing time protocol constants. This will enable us to share values between our client and server implementations. It should be noted that this is a software implementation design and does not imply our client and server implementations will communicate via any external mechanism to the protocol.

We call this class `TimeProtocolConstants`. It contains two constant static values, one specifying the standard TCP port for the protocol (37), and another storing the number of milliseconds between January 1st, 1900, 0:0:0 UTC, and January 1st 1970, 0:0:0 UTC. This value will be needed in order to convert between the protocol epoch and the JVM epoch. The JVM epoch derives from the traditional UNIX epoch which is January 1st, 1970, 0:0:0 UTC.

Instead of hard-coding the number of milliseconds, we evaluate it at class-loading time by using a static code block. The static block computes the offset by using the `java.util.Calendar` class. A `Calendar` class instance is created for the UTC time zone, and the date/time is set to the time protocol epoch. The long-value representation of that time is then extracted, which expresses the time in milliseconds as on offset from the Java epoch. Because the Java epoch is later than the time protocol epoch, this will be a negative number, so we use the `java.lang.Math` static method `abs(int)` to obtain the absolute value of that number. A private no-argument constructor is provided to prevent users from creating instances of the class since it is only used to store static constant values.

```java
// TimeProtocolConstants.java

package com.wrox.timeprotocol;

import java.util.Calendar;

public class TimeProtocolConstants {

  // Prevent instantiation
  private TimeProtocolConstants() {}

  //  The time protocol TCP port defined in RFC 868
  public static final int TCP_PORT = 37;

  public static final long EPOCH_OFFSET_MILLIS;

  // Computes the epoch offset
  static {
    Calendar calendar =
      Calendar.getInstance(java.util.TimeZone.getTimeZone("UTC"));
    calendar.set(1900, Calendar.JANUARY, 1, 0, 0, 0);
    EPOCH_OFFSET_MILLIS = Math.abs(calendar.getTime().getTime());
  }
}
```

Time Protocol Client

The role of a network client may be used by different entities. In our time protocol, for example, the client role may be adopted by the operating system at network connection time in order to synchronize the system clock with an authoritative time source (for example, a server with a Global Positioning System (GPS) receiver). Alternatively, the client role may be adopted by a distributed game that needs to have a synchronized view of time for multiple game participants without actually modifying their system clocks. In our case, we will be developing a simple client that uses the time protocol to report the time returned by a server.

Our first decision will involve the user interface used by the client. The three major options in Java are use of a console application, a graphical application, or a graphical applet. We opt to create a console (text) application because we want to focus on network programming, and graphical applications tend to be longer since they have to handle asynchronous events (such as clicking).

We further simplify our client interface, by restricting it to a single request per invocation. In our interface design, users supply the time server's host name or address in the command line invocation of the client, and the result is printed to the standard output stream. In order to permit users to connect to time servers running on non-standard ports, we will allow an optional second argument specifying a port number to be used. If the optional port argument is omitted, then the standard port 37 will be used.

Having designed our client user interface, we continue with the design of the programmatic interface. Ideally, the protocol implementation should be separate from the client interface, to permit use by multiple different user interfaces. Because the time protocol does not maintain state, we have two options in designing the programmatic interface.

One option is to define static methods that return the result of the time protocol request, while the other option is to define operations on instances of a class. The advantage of the static method is that programmers are not forced to create an object just to invoke a single method. The disadvantage of static methods is that they require all the state as arguments at invocation time, or that the static method makes assumptions about those parameters, thereby limiting the flexibility of the method.

In our example, if the instance approach were taken, the constructor would take a host name or address and optional port number and store them as object state. Subsequent query method invocations would thereby not require specification of the host name or address and port. Many times, these two approaches can be used together, supporting both paradigms. In our sample implementation, we will be using static methods only.

Both the client console user interface and the programmatic protocol interface are defined in a single class (for compactness) called TimeProtocolClient. In most cases the two functions would be separated into different classes, especially if a graphical interface was used. Because we use static methods, the TimeProtocolClient class only has one private constructor that prevents instantiation. The programmatic interface consists of two static methods called getSecondsSinceEpoch() and getDate().

```
// TimeProtocolClient.java

package com.wrox.timeprotocol;

import java.io.*;
import java.net.*;
import java.util.*;
```

```
public class TimeProtocolClient {

    private TimeProtocolClient() {}
```

The getSecondsSinceEpoch() method takes two arguments, the IP address of the RFC 868 server, and the port number it is listening to. The method returns a long value representing the raw protocol result, that is, the number of seconds since January 1ˢᵗ, 1900 at 0:0:0 UTC. Because this is a network operation, it may throw a java.io.IOException to signal a communications failure. One of the subtle points in class design is deciding which exceptions should be thrown by its methods. In some cases, it may make sense to create an application-specific exception.

For example, the java.net.InetAddress class throws a java.net.UnknownHostException exception if the host name could not be resolved. In this case, because the time protocol does not have any significant error reporting capability, we either get the time or not, it is acceptable to propagate the java.io.IOException that may be thrown by the underlying socket and stream operations. In the case that the server accepts our connection but does not transmit any data, or transmits fewer than four bytes before closing the connection, we throw the java.io.EOFException to signal an unexpected end-of-file (EOFException is a subclass of IOException).

We can make a more formal analysis of the time protocol client state by using a **finite state machine** (**FSM**). Finite state machines are used to model applications with a finite number of states and a finite number of transitions between these states. The diagram below shows an FSM for a client participating in the time protocol. Initially, the client is in the "Started" phase where no operations have occurred, marked by the empty arrow. At that point, the client will attempt to connect to the server by creating a socket.

 If that operation succeeds, then the client moves to the "Connected" state. Otherwise, if the operation fails, the client moves to the "Failed" state. The "Failed" state is a final state, marked by a double circle. In the "Connected" state, the client must read four bytes from the server. If that operation succeeds, then the machine transitions into the "Completed" state, otherwise if an IOException (including an end-of-file) is encountered, the machine moves to the "Failed" state.

Because all 32-bit values are valid, there are no additional states for checking the value received. Note that besides the standard start, success, and fail states, this protocol only has one state, due to the fact that it is so simple. The main advantage of expressing a protocol participant's state using a FSM is that it forces us to think of all possible transitions. For example, we have to consider the possibility of an I/O exception at every state in the diagram.

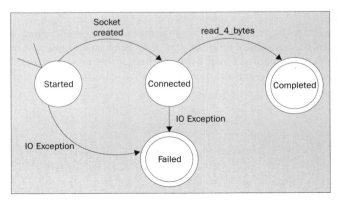

We will now walk through the `getSecondsSinceEpoch()` method implementation. The first action is to create a TCP socket connection to the requested server address on the given port number. This action may throw an I/O or a security exception, both of which we don't try to catch since they will be propagated to the caller.

Once the connection has been established, all operations are performed within a `try` block in order to guarantee that the socket is closed in the `finally` clause, before any subsequent exceptions are propagated. This is an important design pattern to prevent resource exhaustion due to unterminated socket connections. Within the `try` block, we create a buffered input stream on top of the socket input stream. Buffered streams significantly improve I/O performance, especially on certain platforms such as Linux, by reducing the calls to the low-level socket drivers. We use the socket's receive buffer size to set the `BufferInputStream` buffer size (clearly this is not much of an issue for reading 4 bytes, but we wanted to demonstrate an important socket programming pattern).

Once the stream has been buffered, we proceed by reading the four bytes representing the 32-bit time value. Usually, it is not efficient to read data one byte at a time due to the method invocation overhead. Therefore, in most cases the `java.io.InputStream int read(byte[] buffer)` method is used. In this case, we chose to read one byte at a time because there are only four bytes, and to avoid the complexity introduced by the fact that the `read()` method may return before filling the whole buffer. The `InputStream read()` method we are using reads one byte at a time, but returns an integer representation of this value in the range `0 - 254` with `-1` signaling the end-of-file.

This is convenient since we're going to have to turn them into integers in any case in order to join them together into an integer value. It is possible that one or more of the values read were invalid, in other words that they represented the special end-of-file value. We therefore check to see if any of the values was less than zero. In such a case the `EOFException` is thrown.

In the final part of the method, we construct the integer value representing the number of seconds elapsed since the epoch. The bit-shifting process is shown in the diagram below. Each byte value is stored as a 32-bit integer value that has the first 24 bits (left to right) as zeros, followed by the 8-bits storing the byte value. We need to create a single integer value that has the first byte value as its first 8 bits (from the left), followed by the next byte value, etc.

The reason we go from left to right is because Java stores values starting with the most significant bit (big-endian), which is also the convention of how multi-byte values are transmitted in the Internet protocols (network byte order). This is due to the fact that the Internet protocols were developed on UNIX machines which historically used processors that were big-endian. (Intel chips are typically little-endian.) The required assembly is achieved by using the left-bit shift operator (<<).

For example, the first byte needs to be shifted 24 bits to the left:

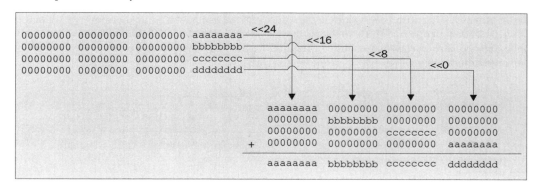

The new integer is created by adding all the shifted values. There is one small caveat, however. Java stores integer numbers in a format called two's complement, where the most significant bit is used as the sign bit. In order to support time specification up to 2036, the time value must be treated as an unsigned number in the range zero to four billion. Therefore, we need to tell Java not to use the leftmost bit as a sign bit. Because Java does not support unsigned numbers, we promote the first byte value into a long value (which is guaranteed to be 64 bits on all platforms).

```java
public static long getSecondsSinceEpoch(InetAddress address, int port)
        throws SecurityException, IOException {

  Socket socket = new Socket(address, port);
  long result;

  try {
    BufferedInputStream bis =
      new BufferedInputStream(socket.getInputStream(),
                              socket.getReceiveBufferSize());

    int b1 = bis.read();
    int b2 = bis.read();
    int b3 = bis.read();
    int b4 = bis.read();

    if ((b1 | b2 | b3 | b3) < 0) {
      throw new EOFException("Server did not provide a 4-byte value");
    }

    result = (((long) b1) << 24) + (b2 << 16) + (b3 << 8) + b4;
  }
  finally {
    socket.close();
  }

  return (result);
}
```

The value returned by getSecondsSinceEpoch() is not likely to be useful for most Java programs. The Java language expresses time as an instance of the java.util.Date class. It is therefore useful to add a static method that returns the time from the server as a java.util.Date object. This method is shown below. The getDate() method takes the same arguments as the previous method, and starts by invoking the getSecondsSinceEpoch() method. The result is then shifted into the Java epoch by subtracting the constant.

Finally, a new java.util.Date object is created from the computed Java offset. One issue to be aware of when dealing with time values is the effect of time zones. We must therefore verify that the java.util.Date constructor understands that we are passing it a UTC (GMT) time value. As it happens, the constructor used does indeed require the time to be expressed in UTC so we don't have to make any additional conversions.

```java
public static Date getDate(InetAddress address, int port)
        throws SecurityException, IOException {

  long millis = ((long) getSecondsSinceEpoch(address, port)) * 1000;
  return (new Date(millis - TimeProtocolConstants.EPOCH_OFFSET_MILLIS));
}
```

An actual implementation would likely add convenience methods that do not require specification of a port number, but use the default one. They have not been included in this example to save space.

Our final task will be to program the client interface. The design calls for a command line invocation interface, so we define a `static void main(String[])` method for this class. The first task will be to parse the command line arguments. The program expects one argument specifying the host name or address of the time server, followed by an optional argument specifying the server's port number. Because the programmatic interface expects an IP address, the host name or address string must be converted into a `java.net.InetAddress` object. This operation may throw an exception if the host name cannot be resolved, or the address is invalid. In addition, if a second argument has been provided, then it must be converted to an integer. This conversion may also fail if the user did not provide a valid integer number as an argument.

Once the command line arguments have been parsed, and the server address and port have been determined, the `main()` method invokes the static `getDate()` method and prints out the result to the standard output stream. Most of the work involves issuing appropriate error messages to the user for exceptions that can possibly be thrown.

```java
public static void main(String[] args) {

  // Parse command-line arguments
  InetAddress address = null;
  int port = TimeProtocolConstants.TCP_PORT;

  try {
    if (args.length == 1) {
      address = InetAddress.getByName(args[0]);
    } else if (args.length == 2) {
      address = InetAddress.getByName(args[0]);
      port = Integer.parseInt(args[1]);
    } else {
      System.err.println("Usage: TimeProtocolClient <server> {<port>}");
      System.exit(1);
    }
  } catch (UnknownHostException e) {
    System.err.println("TimeProtocolClient: unknown host "
                        + e.getMessage());
    System.exit(1);

  } catch (NumberFormatException e) {
    System.err.println("TimeProtocolClient: Invalid port number: "
                        + e.getMessage());
    System.exit(1);

  } catch (SecurityException e) {
    System.err.println("TimeProtocolClient: permission to resolve host "
                        + "name denied: " + e.getMessage());
    System.exit(1);
  }

  // Retrieve current time from server and print to standard out
  try {
    System.out.println(getDate(address, port));

  } catch (java.net.UnknownHostException e) {
    System.err.println("Could not resolve host name: " + e.getMessage());
    System.exit(1);
```

```
    } catch (java.net.ConnectException e) {
      System.err.println("TimeProtocolClient: the time protocol server "
                   + "is not running on " + address.getHostName()
                   + ": " + port);
      System.exit(1);

    } catch (java.io.IOException e) {
      System.err.println("A communications error occured: "
                   + e.getClass().getName() + ": " + e.getMessage());
      System.exit(1);
    } catch (SecurityException e) {
      System.err.println("The security manager refused permission to "
                   + "connect to the remote TCP service: "
                   + e.getMessage());
      System.exit(1);
    }
  }
}
```

Executing the Time Client

Testing the network client will require a running time server. Since we have not coded one yet, we will try to use publicly available time servers (see http://www.boulder.nist.gov/timefreq/service/time-servers.html).

To run this example it is necessary to be connected to the Internet. If the network is using a firewall that requires user authentication this example will not work – ending up in a TimeProtocolClient: unknown host time message. Readers that don't have Internet access will have to wait until the next section, when we have coded the server, in order to test the client.

Compilation and sample executions of the client are shown below. Some of these servers may no longer be available by the time you are reading this. Note that although the date is printed in a localized manner (in this case Eastern Standard Time), not in the UTC, this is a feature of the java.util.Date toString() method which uses java.util.Calendar to localize the UTC time it stores.

If you're using a UNIX system that has been configured to offer the RFC 868 Time Protocol service, you can try using localhost as a username. Not all Microsoft Windows operating systems currently support this service. It is interesting to note that these public servers are most likely written in the C language, and hence this is an example of how network protocols enable interoperation between multiple platforms (Java versus C/UNIX or C/Microsoft Windows).

C:\Beg_Java_Networking\Ch09>**javac com\wrox\timeprotocol\TimeProtocolClient.java**

C:\Beg_Java_Networking\Ch09>**java com.wrox.timeprotocol.TimeProtocolClient time-a.nist.gov**
Tue Jun 12 20:13:00 EDT 2001

If your host is behind a firewall that does not permit outgoing TCP connections, the client will fail to connect to the public Time Protocol servers. Some firewalls can be asked to relay TCP connection requests using a protocol called SOCKS. If your firewall supports unauthenticated SOCKS proxy requests, you can execute the client as shown next (using the name of your own SOCKS proxy):

C:\Beg_Java_Networking\Ch09>**java -DsocksProxyHost="socks.mynet.com"**
com.wrox.timeprotocol.TimeProtocolClient time-a.nist.gov
Tue Jun 12 20:13:30 EDT 2001

The above example used a JVM without security. The client performs two security-sensitive network operations:

❑   The server name is resolved to an IP address

❑   A TCP connection is attempted to the server's address

Time Protocol Server

Servers are typically written as command line applications to enable their execution without a graphical environment, or before one is available. In some cases, separate graphical tools are provided to simplify the task of configuration, but they are usually executed as a separate process and communicate with the server through a network protocol or shared files. Similarly to the time client, the time server example will be coded as a console application. The single configuration parameter supported will be the overriding of the default port, by specifying an alternative at the command line. A production implementation could also provide additional configuration options, such as binding to specific interfaces, and time-shifting from the current system clock.

The server's programmatic interface will be a class representing an instance of the time service bound to a specified port. It will thus be possible for a program to start multiple time servers, if so required. Placing the server code in a class will also support easy sharing between different user interface implementations. The main task of the time server will be to wait for connections and serve each incoming request as defined in the protocol specification.

When designing a server in Java there are a few design decisions that have to be considered. The first decision is where to include the code that binds to the specified port by creating a java.net.ServerSocket instance. It is usually best to perform the binding operation as part of the constructor, in order to propagate I/O exceptions to the invoking code. Another decision involves the use of threads. Due to the blocking behavior of the java.net.ServerSocket.accept() method, every network service must have at least one separate thread that accepts connections. This behavior can be achieved by extending the java.lang.Thread class in the server object, and adding the accept() loop in the overridden void run() method. Typically, the constructor invokes its own thread start() method to simplify usage.

The second thread design decision involves the handling of incoming requests. In nearly all cases, incoming requests should be handled in a separate thread. The main reason is that even if the processing task is trivial, if the server has to read some data from the client, then a slow or misbehaving client can tie up the main thread for an indefinite period of time. By using multiple threads, the speed in which the clients operate becomes less of an issue. Of course, threads are a finite resource, so if a client wanted to attack the server it could open multiple connections until no more threads could be generated. As was discussed in Chapter 6, thread creation is an expensive operation, so the use of thread pools becomes necessary in production servers.

The finite state machine for the time server implementation is shown below. Initially, in the started state, the server attempts to bind to the specified port number. Binding may fail due to an IOException (port is already taken), or a SecurityException (security policy denies binding to the specific port). In that case, the machine transitions to the final failed state (the object will not be constructed).

If the binding succeeds, then the server enters into its accept() loop thread in which it listens for incoming requests. Each request is handled in the same thread by entering the responding state and transmitting the current time as a four-byte value. If the write is successful, the connection is closed and the machine returns to the listening state.

What happens if an error occurs while communicating with the client? In this case, the connection is closed, and then the machine returns to the listening state. In other words, a client failure should not result in a server failure. An interesting issue arises with error handling in the main thread loop. How should an error be handled in the accept() call itself? The error may signal that the server socket has failed, or that the client has failed. It is difficult to distinguish between the two in a Java program, because the accept() method only throws a single exception (IOException). In our design, we will assume that all accept() IOExceptions are client-caused and will remain in the listening state. Finally, the listening state is exited once a termination request has been detected by the accept() thread.

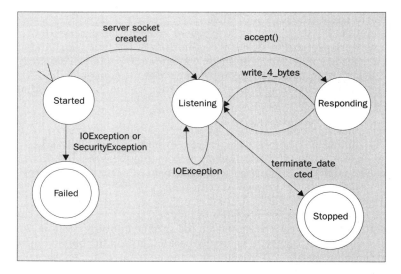

It should be noted, that a single finite state machine can represent the server only because it is single threaded. If a separate thread had been used to handle each client then it would not have been possible to use a single machine, unless the maximum number of threads had been bound. In such cases, one machine is used to model the bind-listen states, and another is used to model the state for each processing thread.

We predictably name the time server class TimeProtocolServer. The class extends the java.lang.Thread class so that it can have its own thread of execution. There are three instance variables, the use of which will become clearer once we cover the constructor and accessor methods. The core instance variable is the server socket object that is assigned in the constructor and used in the server accept() thread.

> **The reason for making every TimeProtocolServer instance a thread is that we would like to support multiple instances of the class offering RFC 868 service on different ports. In this particular application, the thread is not really needed because we will only create a single instance from the main thread. However, it is best to design protocol clients and server in a way that will support multiple different uses.**

The current Java language semantics do not support clean termination of threads, so it is the responsibility of every thread to provide a method for clean termination. One way to achieve this behavior is by controlling the execution of the main ServerSocket.accept() loop using an instance variable. In this case we define a boolean variable called isActive and set its initial value to true. The main loop will then be written in the form:

```
while(isActive){ … }
```

Because the ServerSocket.accept() method is blocking, and the loop decision is only made between client connections, a request to terminate the thread will only succeed following the next client connection. This is not likely to be acceptable behavior, so the implementation will set a finite timeout for the ServerSocket.accept() invocation. The value of this timeout is a tradeoff between termination response and unnecessary looping. In this example the socket timeout value is arbitrarily set to 5 seconds.

```java
// TimeProtocolServer.java

package com.wrox.timeprotocol;

import java.io.*;
import java.net.*;
import java.util.*;

// A network time server supporting RFC-868 over TCP.
public class TimeProtocolServer extends Thread {

    // The TCP server socket used to receive connection requests
    protected ServerSocket server = null;

    // Used to control termination of the accept thread
    protected boolean isActive = true;

    // Server socket timeout milliseconds (used to check termination)
    protected int socketTimeoutMillis = 5000;
```

Two constructors are defined for the TimeProtocolServer class. The first constructor takes no arguments and creates a time protocol server instance bound to the standard port 37. The second constructor permits users to override the port number used.

Predictably, the first constructor simply delegates construction to the second one by providing the standard port number as argument. Both constructors may throw a java.io.IOException as well as a java.lang.SecurityException due to errors in binding to the requested port.

The three actions in the constructor are to:

❑ Create a new server socket

❑ Configure the socket's timeout to support clean thread termination

❑ Start the thread that accepts connections

There is no particular need to define application-specific exceptions since the only errors that can occur are server socket creation or configuration errors.

```
public TimeProtocolServer() throws SecurityException, IOException {
  this(TimeProtocolConstants.TCP_PORT);
}

public TimeProtocolServer(int port)
       throws SecurityException, IOException {
  server = new ServerSocket(port);
  server.setSoTimeout(socketTimeoutMillis);
  start();
}
```

Most network servers execute without direct user supervision. It is therefore important that errors are logged in some way that can facilitate future analysis. Another reason to perform logging in network servers is to support analysis of security or performance problems.

Due to the importance of a standard logging facility, Sun has added a logging package to JDK 1.4 called `java.util.logging`. Users of previous versions must either provide their own facilities or use third-party libraries. Although it may seem trivial, designing a logging system that is flexible as well as efficient is not a simple matter. A popular third-party Java logging library is the IBM/Apache Log4J (http://jakarta.apache.org/log4j/).

In this example, in order not to force readers to download an additional library, two simple logging methods are provided. As noted, real server applications should use a complete logging solution.

```
// Logs an error to System.err
public void error(String message, Throwable e) {
  System.err.println(new Date() + ": TimeProtocolServer("
                  + server.getLocalPort() + "): error: " + message
                  + ": " + e.getClass().getName() + ": "
                  + e.getMessage());
}

// Logs an information message to System.out
public void info(String message) {
  System.out.println(new Date() + ": TimeProtocolServer("
                  + server.getLocalPort() + "): info: " + message);
}
```

The time server may be terminated asynchronously by invoking the `terminate()` method. The method itself does not send any signals, but simply sets the value of the `isActive` instance variable. The next time the thread loops through its `ServerSocket.accept()` method, the check will fail and the thread will terminate. It should be noted that, although the `terminate()` invocation will be made from a different thread, there is no race condition since this is the only location where the value is set. In the worst case, the setting of the value will interleave with the check in the main loop, which may succeed, but will fail the next time through.

```
// Requests asynchronous termination of the server
public void terminate() {
  isActive = false;
}
```

Even in the simplest protocols, such as the time protocol, it is best to separate the processing of a network connection to a separate method. This way the `accept()` loop code can be cleanly separated from the protocol processing code. In this case, the protected `process()` method is defined to be invoked with a `java.net.Socket` object for each new TCP client connection. The method does not throw any exceptions – all communications errors are logged instead.

As was done in the client, all socket operations are performed within a `try` block. In this case, the `try` block is used to both catch I/O exceptions, as well as to assure that the socket is closed before the method returns. After logging the connection, the method creates a buffered output stream that will be used to write the current time in the protocol format. Use of buffered output streams is essential for server output performance.

The next step is to determine the number of seconds since the time protocol epoch, by adding the offset to the current Java time and converting from milliseconds to seconds. Note that a long variable (64-bit) is used to store the result, because it must be unsigned and Java does not support unsigned integers (32-bit). The result is then written one byte at a time to the output stream, with the most significant byte transmitted first. Only the lower 32-bits of the long value are transmitted in a procedure that is the reverse of the one used in the client. The idea is to shift each 8-bit (byte) value to the right and then clear the remaining bits by performing a binary AND with the hexadecimal value FF, as demonstrated in the figure below.

In most cases, writing one byte at a time is not recommended for top performance, but the small number of bytes and the use of the buffered output stream permit it in this case. Because the output stream is buffered, it is very important to use the `flush()` or `close()` methods to push the data to the network once it has been written. If this operation is not performed, and the socket is closed, the buffered data will never be sent. This can lead to unexplained failures, so it is always good practice to flush or close the input buffer before closing the socket.

```
protected void process(Socket socket) {
    if (socket == null) {
        return;
    }
    try {
        info("Connection from " + socket.getInetAddress().getHostName() + ":"
            + socket.getPort());

        BufferedOutputStream bos =
            new BufferedOutputStream(socket.getOutputStream(),
                                     socket.getSendBufferSize());

        // number of seconds since January 1, 1900 0:0:0 UTC
```

```
      long resultSecs =
        ((System.currentTimeMillis()
              + TimeProtocolConstants.EPOCH_OFFSET_MILLIS)
         / 1000);

      bos.write((int) ((resultSecs >> 24) & 0xFF));
      bos.write((int) ((resultSecs >> 16) & 0xFF));
      bos.write((int) ((resultSecs >> 8) & 0xFF));
      bos.write((int) (resultSecs & 0xFF));

      bos.close();    // very important; needed to flush stream contents
    } catch (java.io.IOException e) {
      error("I/O Error", e);
    }
    finally {
      try {
        socket.close();
      } catch (IOException e) {
        error("Error closing socket", e);
      }
    }
  }
```

The `TimeProtocolServer` thread is a simple loop that accepts incoming connections, and then invokes the `process()` method to handle them. Most of the code involves error handling. Because the server socket's timeout has been set to a non-infinite value, the `java.io.InterruptedIOException` must first be caught. This exception does not really signal an error, just the fact that the timeout has expired. In that case, no action is taken except to go back to the top of the loop where the check for termination is made. Both I/O and security exceptions are caught and logged, since there is really not much the server can do.

Note the `catch` clause for `Throwable` exceptions. It is possible that the `process()` method will throw some runtime exception such as `NullPointerException`. Although such an exception is typically caused by some internal error, it may not be desirable to stop the server. It may be best to log the error, and continue attempting to accept connections.

There can be some argument about whether this is the right way to deal with errors such as `java.lang.OutOfMemoryError`. Applications must decide how to handle such resource exhaustion errors, possibly by reducing the number of server processing threads (when those are used). The main point here is that servers are supposed to be long-lived processes, therefore programmers must assure that they are resilient to implementation errors.

```
public void run() {
  info("Accepting connections on TCP port " + server.getLocalPort()
       + "...");

  while (isActive) {
    Socket socket = null;

    try {
      socket = server.accept();
      process(socket);
    } catch (java.io.InterruptedIOException e) {

      // Used to periodically check for termination
```

```
        } catch (IOException e) {
          error("I/O Error", e);

        } catch (SecurityException e) {
          error("An unauthorized client has attempted to connect", e);

        } catch (Throwable e) {
          error("Unexpected exception", e);
        }
      }

      try {
        server.close();
      } catch (IOException e) {
        error("Error closing server socket", e);
      }

      info("server thread terminated");
    }
```

The server's `main()` method is similar to the client's main method. The first step is to parse the optional command line argument specifying the port number for the server. The second step is to create a `TimeProtocolServer` instance. Unlike the client, the command-line invocation will not return until the server is terminated. This behavior is made explicit by having the main thread join the `TimeProtocolServer` thread. Because the time protocol thread had not been made a daemon thread, the `join()` is optional. One small difference with the client is that the command-line usage must be printed in two locations so the message is placed in a separate method. Again, most of the code involves conversion of program exceptions into meaningful user error messages:

```
    public static void usageExit() {
      System.err.println("Usage: TimeProtocolServer { <port> }");
      System.exit(1);
    }

    public static void main(String[] args) {

      // Parse command-line arguments
      int port = 0;

      if (args.length == 0) {
        port = TimeProtocolConstants.TCP_PORT;
      } else if (args.length == 1) {
        try {
          port = Integer.parseInt(args[0]);
        } catch (NumberFormatException e) {
          usageExit();
        }
      } else {
        usageExit();
      }

      // Start time protocol server

      TimeProtocolServer server = null;
      try {
        server = new TimeProtocolServer(port);

      } catch (java.net.BindException e) {
```

```
              System.err.println("The server could not bind to port " + port
                              + " (port may already be used): "
                              + e.getMessage());
              if (port < 1024) {
                System.err.println("Warning: On UNIX systems user-level "
                              + "processes cannot bind to ports below 1024");
              }
          } catch (java.io.IOException e) {
              System.err.println(e.getMessage());

          } catch (SecurityException e) {
              System.err.println("Permission to bind to port " + port
                              + " denied (check the java.security.policy): "
                              + e.getMessage());
          }

          if (server == null) {
              System.exit(1);

              // Join the server thread since we don't have anything else to do

          }
          try {
              server.join();
          } catch (InterruptedException e) {
              System.err.println("Error while joined to server thread: "
                              + e.getMessage());
              System.exit(1);
          }
      }
  }
```

Time Server & Client Execution

Starting the server involves compiling the sample code and invoking the JVM with the appropriate arguments as shown below:

C:\Beg_Java_Networking\Ch09>**java com.wrox.timeprotocol.TimeProtocolServer**
Thu Jun 14 12:18:48 EDT 2001: TimeProtocolServer(37): info: Accepting connections on TCP port 37...

We can first test our server using the client we developed earlier as shown below. Because the server process did not terminate, we need to start a new console window.

C:\Beg_Java_Networking\Ch09>**java com.wrox.timeprotocol.TimeProtocolClient localhost**
Thu Jun 14 12:37:38 EDT 2001

Checking up on the server console, we see that it has logged the connection from our client:

Thu Jun 14 12:37:38 EDT 2001: TimeProtocolServer(37): info: Connection from 127.0.0.1:1768

Depending on the platform being used, the above server invocation may fail due to port restrictions. UNIX-based operating systems typically restrict ports below 1024 to processes executing with system (root) privileges. Microsoft Windows users do not face such restrictions. One solution for UNIX users is to execute the JVM as a root user. This is acceptable in native UNIX programs written in C because they can relinquish their system privileges after binding to the restricted port. This functionality, however, is not supported in Java. Therefore, the whole JVM must execute with system privileges, something that is probably too risky for most real applications.

The solution is to either use native code to relinquish privileges, or to bind to a port above `1023`. If you would like to deploy a production Java application using a privileged port on a UNIX system, we recommend using one of several Java/UNIX JNI-based interfaces (such as the XeNoNSoFT Java Unix Extension API). For the purposes of testing this server, we recommend that users specify a different port as follows (we pick port `4523` arbitrarily):

C:\Beg_Java_Networking\Ch09>**java com.wrox.timeprotocol.TimeProtocolServer 4523**
Thu Jun 14 12:25:19 EDT 2001: TimeProtocolServer(4523): info: Accepting connections on TCP port 4523...

Users who have specified a non-standard server port number can provide an additional argument to the client as shown:

C:\Beg_Java_Networking\Ch09>**java com.wrox.timeprotocol.TimeProtocolClient localhost 4523**
Thu Jun 14 12:38:53 EDT 2001

The true test for a server implementing a standard protocol is interoperation with third-party clients. Some platforms provide a native time protocol client. Microsoft Windows operating systems do not provide a standard Time Protocol client. Solaris and Linux systems have a shell utility called `rdate` that can be used to query time protocol servers.

Unfortunately, both versions do not support specification of alternative ports. Users who want to test their server must execute it with root privileges, or execute it on non-UNIX systems. Sample use of the Linux native `rdate` client is shown below. The Linux host is called `aqua` and the server is running on a Microsoft Windows host called `manticore`.

 # rdate manticore
[manticore]   Thu Jun 14 12:48:20 2001

The connection is logged on our server running on host `manticore`:

C:\Beg_Java_Networking\Ch09>**java com.wrox.timeprotocol.TimeProtocolServer**
Thu Jun 14 12:48:18 EDT 2001: TimeProtocolServer(37): info: Accepting connections on TCP port 37...
Thu Jun 14 12:48:20 EDT 2001: TimeProtocolServer(37): info: Connection from aqua:33492

Application-Layer Protocol Design and Implementation

The first step in designing an application-layer protocol is deciding if such a low-level approach is appropriate. Even assuming a reliable channel, application-layer protocol design can become quite complex once all possible error conditions have been accounted for. A lot of effort has been placed for the past decades in industry as well as academia to develop tools that simplify application layer network interface construction. These tools are generally known as **middleware**.

Remote objects are one of the most popular middleware technologies in use today. The basic idea is to model remote communications as method invocations on objects that reside outside the current process space (the JVM). The task of network programming is thus reduced to the design of standard interfaces exporting the required functionality. The details on how method arguments and results are encoded and transmitted are hidden by the remote object middleware infrastructure. Additional services provided may include object discovery, transactional and persistent storage services, as well as load-balancing and fault-tolerance services. Chapter 16 and 17 cover RMI and CORBA respectively, two popular object-based middleware technologies. Enterprise JavaBeans (EJB) is another popular Java-based server-side component middleware technology (see http://java.sun.com/products/ejb).

One compelling reason to use application-layer protocols is to implement an existing standard. The time protocol is really not a representative example of standard application-layer protocols. Most protocols are significantly more complex and tend to grow significantly between versions. For example, the HTTP protocol when first defined was a simple stateless request-reply protocol. In its current version, the protocol has quadrupled both in length as well as complexity, by becoming stateful. Standards can be broken down into three categories:

❑ **Simple binary standards**: Many IETF standards define protocol exchanges in terms of bit-based masks. Such protocols tend to be efficient to transmit, and sometimes process, but they can be tedious to encode and decode.

❑ **Text-based standards**: These include ASCII keyword-based protocols – for example the Simple Mail Transfer Protocol (SMTP; RFC 2821). Their main advantage is that they tend to be a lot more flexible than binary standards. They are also easy to test and debug using a remote terminal access program (for example Telnet). Their main disadvantage is that they can be inefficient to process, since parsing functions can be more expensive than byte processing.

❑ **ASN.1 based binary standards**: ASN.1 is a standard defining an architecture-and language-independent binary encoding of types. It can be used to store basic types, such as integers, enumeration types, real numbers, and strings placing restrictions on their size. Additionally, it can be used to define classes of more complex structures such as sets and sequences. The ASN.1 standard was part of the OSI model presentation layer developed by the OSI. Its use has been adopted by a few Internet standards, however, such as SNMP and **Lightweight Directory Access Protocol (LDAP)**.

In cases when an application layer protocol is necessary, there are a few design guidelines that can improve portability, expandability, and scalability of the protocol:

❑ Document the protocol using a formal finite state machine representation. Make sure the FSM includes all possible transitions, including errors that may occur. Many ambiguities that can be hidden in natural language descriptions are exposed when applying formal models.

❑ Use stateless servers whenever possible to improve the scalability and reliability of an application. Stateless servers do not store connection state in between client requests. In such protocols, clients provide all the information necessary to provide the requested service as part of the request. Stateful servers incur overhead because of the need to store state in some sort of persistent storage (disk file/database record). Such servers also reduce the ability to distribute requests between servers since the state stored in Server 1 most likely may not be accessible to Server 2, or may require additional data sharing mechanisms.

❑ Minimize round-trip exchanges. End-to-end latency is bound by the speed of light, which is not expected to change any time soon. On the other hand, bandwidth is currently increasing exponentially thanks to rapid advances in optical transmission. Moreover, the emerging optical networking technologies favor large data transfers.

In light of these changes in network technologies, some of the current protocol designs are no longer making much sense. For example, after a web browser retrieves an HTML (web) page from an HTTP server, it will make individual requests for all the images and applets embedded in that page. In the emerging optical networks, it would make more sense to retrieve all the files in a single request. Such an approach saves the cost of multiple request/response roundtrips at the cost of some possibly wasted bandwidth.

❑ The client and server should negotiate supported protocol versions in the initial handshake. Most protocols evolve, and it may not be realistic to expect that all clients and servers will be upgraded concurrently. At the very least, the protocol version negotiation will detect and terminate incompatible connections. More advanced uses include coding of servers that can communicate in multiple versions.

❑ Don't assume that the host address you are talking to is the real one. Many networks use **Network Address Translation (NAT)** gateways that rewrite addresses between the public network and the internal network. Application layer protocols that pass source or destination addressing information cause serious problems to such gateways (such as the FTP protocol).

❑ Encode information in a platform-independent way and explicitly state all the encoding characteristics. Ideally, standard encoding mechanisms such as ASN.1 should be used to exchange data values.

❑ Leave room for expansion. Use of version numbers is one mechanism. Especially in bit-based protocols, do not overly constrain the size of the data exchanged. For example, if our current protocol has 10 operations, we would not store the operation type as a 4-bit value (permitting only 16 operations maximum).

Some implementation suggestions may also be useful:

❑ Separate the application line protocol code as much as possible from the application code. This isolates all byte-stream encoding/decoding so that error tracking and protocol documentation/verification can be simplified. It also isolates the application from changes to the underlying line protocol, and eases swapping of line-protocol versions.

❑ Make sure that protocol documentation tracks the current implementation. New languages and systems may be deployed requiring future implementation in other languages. Reverse engineering protocols without documentation can be a difficult task even when source code is available.

❑ Validate all received data. Buffer overruns in network programs are the leading cause of remote break-ins. Java is safer than most traditional languages since it performs array-bounds checking. However, the language cannot prevent applications from going into an invalid and potentially compromising state by assuming that the received data are valid in terms of the application.

❑ If the protocol is expected to see wide deployment, it may be useful to adopt some packet-sniffing software and provide a module that can convert raw protocol packets into meaningful string messages. This can be useful in debugging strange protocol or application behavior by tapping into the core of the network.

JDK 1.4 TCP Socket Library Changes

The above presentation of the Java sockets library was based on the 1.3 version of the Java Standard Edition. Version 1.4 introduces significant new features to the Java network libraries. Major additions include IP version 6 support, and built-in **Secure Socket Layer (SSL)** support (discussed in the next section), as well as the new non-blocking Java I/O architecture. Both `Socket` and `ServerSocket` objects support access through the new non-blocking I/O API (`java.nio`). Non-blocking I/O should help Java scale to new levels in server performance. Minor changes to the `java.net.Socket` class include support for TCP urgent data (out of sequence delivery of urgent data), TCP traffic types for type (quality) of service, and checking of socket connection status. Another minor addition is inclusion of factory interfaces for `Socket` and `ServerSocket` instance creation (in `javax.net`). These issues are further expanded in Chapter 21, which deals with JDK 1.4.

Summary

Most network programming languages model network communications using the socket abstraction. Sockets are end-points of communications wrapping the underlying transmission protocol in a byte streaming or datagram abstraction. The TCP protocol provides reliable streaming services with distributed flow and congestion control over an unreliable packet-based network. Stream sockets provide programmatic access to the transmission services of the TCP protocol. Port numbering is used to de-multiplex incoming TCP protocol requests to support multiple services per IP address.

The two main classes used to effect TCP network programming in Java are `java.net.Socket` and `java.net.ServerSocket`. Clients connect to servers using instances of the `Socket` class. Servers accept incoming connections using instances of the `ServerSocket` class. Once a TCP connection has been established, both sides are considered peers in a bi-directional communications stream. `Socket` and `ServerSocket` methods are used to configure the connection properties. Actual communications are performed using the `java.io` stream classes.

Designing and coding network services is a lot more involved than just learning how to use the `Socket` and `ServerSocket` classes. Streams are completely unstructured and therefore protocol design is a creative and complex process. Coding resilient network clients and servers is a difficult task because failures can occur at any point during communication.

This chapter introduced two realistic applications, a standards-compliant time server and client, as well as a non-standard secure file server and client. Several design and programming patterns were introduced in these examples.

In the next chapter, we will be covering a different communications model based on unreliable packet-based transmission.

UDP Programming

Although 90% of Internet traffic consists of Transmission Control Protocol (TCP) over IP, the TCP reliable streaming model does not necessarily suit all applications. TCP incurs a certain communications overhead in establishing and tearing down connections. As was explained in Chapter 9, TCP connection establishment requires a three-way handshake between client and server. Additionally, TCP requires that both sides in a connection maintain various timers and counters. These overheads may not be appropriate for applications making small exchanges, such as the time protocol implemented in Chapter 9.

TCP also guarantees that data will be received in the order transmitted by the sender, as long as there is some connectivity. However, because TCP is implemented over the unreliable, best-effort IP protocol, it can make no guarantees on delivery timing. This behavior may be desirable for applications that deal in time-insensitive exchanges, such as file transfers, but can be a bad fit for real-time applications, such as audio streaming. If there is a deadline beyond which data delivery is no longer useful, any attempt to retransmit past the deadline is wasted effort. Moreover, the TCP model of delivering data in the order transmitted means that the expired data will unnecessarily delay delivery of the remaining data.

This chapter will introduce the second major Internet transport layer protocol called the **User Datagram Protocol (UDP)**. UDP provides applications with a connectionless, best-effort datagram transport service. UDP is implemented as a very thin layer on top of IP providing application port addressing, and datagram payload integrity verification. Applications using UDP trade off the lack of control in TCP streaming for the increased control, but also add complexity in dealing with lost and out-of-order datagrams. UDP may be used to send datagrams to single or multiple destinations. This chapter will focus on the use of UDP for single destination transmission. Chapter 11 will cover multiple destination transmission (called multicast).

The chapter will contrast the appropriate uses of TCP versus UDP. Three important UDP-based application protocols will be presented along with a summary of application features for which the UDP protocol is appropriate. Next the chapter will introduce the main Java classes supporting UDP programming with appropriate small examples. A larger example implementing a UDP-based Internet standard protocol will then be presented to highlight common UDP application programming patterns.

The chapter will conclude with an overview of transport and application layer protocols, extending UDP to support shared functions of real-time applications.

By the end of this chapter we should understand how UDP operates, and when to use it. The examples shown demonstrate complete uses of datagram sockets and will provide valuable exposure to design patterns arising in UDP client and server creation. The discussion on real-time communication protocols will offer a direction to readers interested in designing and implementing real-time multimedia applications.

The User Datagram Protocol (UDP)

As you may recall from previous discussion, the Internet Protocol (IP) provides an unreliable, best-effort datagram delivery service. An IP datagram originates in an Internet host and may contain up to 65516 bytes of payload data (practical restrictions limit the typical size of IP packets as will be discussed later). The IP datagram sent by the Internet host is then forwarded (routed) toward its destination over a network of devices called routers. Each IP datagram begins with a fixed header storing the IP address of the sender and the recipient, a checksum used to verify the integrity of the header in case of data corruption during transmission, and additional information used in making routing decisions.

Although in principle applications could directly use the IP protocol to perform network communications, there are three significant limitations in doing so:

❑ IP does not verify the **integrity** of the datagram data payload; only the IP header is protected. As a result, it is possible that delivered IP datagrams will have their payload data corrupted due to errors in link-layer transmission. Nearly all networked applications would not want to receive such corrupted data and would prefer to be relieved of the verification task.

❑ The destination of an IP datagram is identified by an IP address. Upon delivery to its destination, an IP datagram is further classified based on its protocol number (for example, TCP). As was explained in the previous chapter, an Internet host typically executes multiple network applications using the same protocol. Arriving IP datagrams addressed to the host must somehow be delivered to the right application (HTTP, FTP, DNS and so on), therefore, a mechanism for protocol-specific **application addressing** is needed. In Chapter 9 we explained that TCP uses port addressing for this purpose.

❑ Allowing applications access to raw IP transmission is considered dangerous from a **security** standpoint. If an application can create an arbitrary IP packet then it can fake the packet's source address and protocol identifier. This capability can be used to inject data into TCP streams, and perform difficult to trace denial of service attacks. For this reason, most server operating systems restrict raw IP transmission to privileged applications ("root" in UNIX, "Administrator" in Microsoft Windows 2000). Personal operating systems such as Microsoft Windows 9x/ME typically do not support multiple user accounts and therefore permit all applications to send raw IP packets.

The **User Data Protocol** (**UDP**) was created to address the above limitations. UDP provides applications with a connectionless, best-effort datagram transport service, and is specified in IETF RFC 768 (available at http://www.ietf.org/rfc/rfc768.txt). UDP is a very thin layer on top of IP, providing three additional functions:

❑ **Destination port addressing:** UDP datagrams are marked with a destination port address, this is in addition to the destination IP address. When a UDP/IP datagram is delivered to its destination address, the protocol stack consults the UDP destination port value to decide which application should receive this datagram. As was the case in TCP, UDP port numbers are 16-bit port integer values in the range [0-65535]. The use of ports for de-multiplexing was discussed in Chapter 9.

Although both the UDP and TCP protocols employ ports in the same range as a common de-multiplexing mechanism, their actual use is independent of one another. It is perfectly permissible for the same port number to be used by a TCP application and a UDP application, or by other protocols for that matter. This is possible because the IP protocol performs an initial de-multiplexing based on protocol type, so UDP and TCP packets are separately identified and treated.

❑ **Data payload integrity verification:** UDP associates a 16-bit checksum with each datagram sent. A checksum is a summary of the datagram contents computed using an algorithm agreed upon between the sender and the receiver. Before transmitting the UDP datagram, the sender computes this checksum summary and stores it in the UDP header. Upon delivery, the recipient also independently computes the checksum for the datagram and then compares it to the checksum stored in the UDP header. If they are the same, the datagram integrity is considered verified.

Because a checksum is only a summary, different messages may have the same checksum value. The trick is to select a checksum computation algorithm that catches the most likely errors. UDP employs an algorithm called one's complement that catches all single bit-errors and many multiple-bit errors (odd-number errors are more likely to be detected). In principle, it is possible that a datagram may be corrupted in a manner that does not affect its checksum, but this is extremely unlikely in practice because datagrams are rarely corrupted, and when they are, they are typically 1-bit errors.

❑ **Source port identification:** UDP stores the port number of the datagram socket used to transmit a datagram. In combination with the IP header's source IP address, they provide a return address for UDP datagram receivers. Recall that IP and UDP are connectionless protocols and therefore when a datagram is delivered there is no backward channel to send the response to. The solution is to store the sender's address and port in each UDP datagram to provide a unique return address.

The structure of a UDP datagram is shown in the diagram below. UDP is layered over IP, so a datagram begins with the IP header. That IP header includes the packet's source and destination addresses, length, header checksum, time-to-live, and other IP options. The fixed part of the IP header has a length of 20-bytes, while the variable options part can be of length up to 40-bytes; therefore the maximum IP header may have a length of 60-bytes. The UDP header follows with the information required to provide the added port de-multiplexing, payload integrity, and source port identification functions. It consists of two 16-bit (0-65535) values identifying the source and destination port, followed by the 16-bit length of the UDP packet (including the header) and a 16-bit checksum of the UDP header and payload data. The actual data payload is appended after the end of the UDP header.

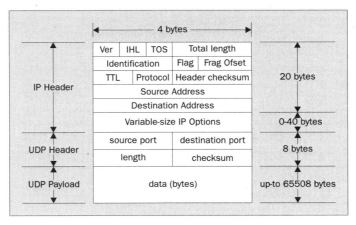

Note that both the IP as well as the UDP headers carry a length field. This duplication is redundant, since the length is specified in the IP header is sufficient. It has been claimed that John Postel, the UDP standard RFC 768 editor, has attributed this redundancy to a historic "glitch".

IP Fragmentation

As shown above, a UDP datagram consists of the IP header (minimum 20 bytes, maximum 60 bytes), and a fixed-length UDP header (8 bytes), followed by the payload data. Both IP and UDP headers maintain packet length as a 16-bit value, therefore the largest UDP data payload can be $(2^{16}-20-8)=65508$ bytes. However, most link-layer protocols do not support such large packets sizes; link protocols typically have their own **Maximum Transfer Unit (MTU)**. The MTU specifies the largest **frame** (link-layer packet) that can be transmitted over a specified link technology, for example, Ethernet frames can carry up to 1500 bytes of data. When an IP router needs to transmit an IP packet that exceeds the MTU of the next-hop link, it may either drop the packet, or perform what is known as IP **fragmentation**. In IP fragmentation, a single IP datagram is broken into multiple smaller IP datagrams that are re-assembled at the destination.

The diagram below shows an example of IP fragmentation. Router A is shown transmitting an IP datagram over an Ethernet link to Router B. Router B reads the destination of the IP datagram from the header and determines based on its routing table that the next hop is Router C. The link to Router C uses a PPP/Modem connection that has an MTU of 576 bytes, but because the payload length of the datagram is 800 bytes, it cannot be transmitted over the link as it is. Router B has the option of either dropping the datagram, or fragmenting it. In this example, Router B is configured to support fragmentation and will split the payload into two fragments, one carrying 512 bytes and another carrying the remaining 288 bytes. The fragmented packets will be re-assembled at the destination (128.59.22.38), not the next hop (Router C). As separate IP packets, fragments may arrive at the destination out of order, and some may even be lost. If any fragment is lost, then the destination will be unable to reassemble the original IP datagram so will drop it.

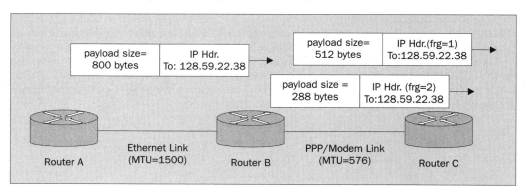

The Internet Protocol standard RFC 791 (http://www.ietf.org/rfc/rfc791.txt) specifies that, at a minimum, every IP gateway must be able to forward datagrams of a total length 576 bytes (arbitrarily chosen as allowing "a reasonable sized data block"). Therefore, UDP datagrams with a data payload of a size up to (576-60-8)=508 should be handled by all networks. Due to another one of these historic peculiarities, most UDP applications actually limit their transmission to 512 bytes (largely attributed to a misreading of RFC 791) – because IP packets rarely, if ever, contain 40 bytes of options, the missing 4 bytes (512-508) do not create a problem in practice. Packet fragmentation is no longer supported in IPv6, and has been replaced by an end-to-end maximum transfer unit discovery mechanism.

IP fragmentation imposes a significant load on routers, and for this reason may sometimes be disabled in router configuration. Applications should not send UDP datagrams with payload size greater than 508, unless they can verify that all the link layers traversed support larger datagram sizes.

UDP Operations

The operations of the UDP protocol are illustrated in the diagram below. A UDP time client application running on host A (pictured on the left) decides to query the UDP time-server application running on host B (pictured on the right). The client application creates a UDP datagram to be delivered to the IP address of host B (139.52.12.2) and port number of the server (37). The query is stored in some application-specific byte-array format (in this example shown as a string). Before sending the UDP datagram, host A will write its own IP address and the port number of the sending application in the header. The UDP/IP datagram will then be routed towards its destination as any other IP datagram. If all goes well, it will then be delivered to host B who will then use the port number to determine that it should be passed on to the server application bound to port 37. Typically, the server application will process the request and send its response to the client application as identified by the source address (128.59.22.38) and port (4321) of the received datagram. Both the query as well as the response may be lost en route and it is up to the application to detect and handle such loss.

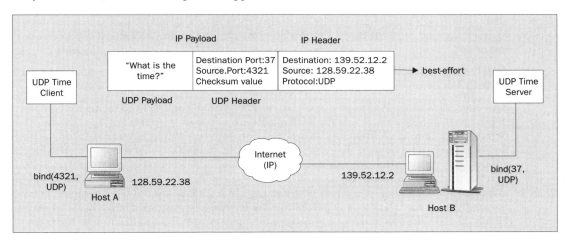

UDP vs. TCP

When designing an Internet application, a choice must be made on the transport protocol that will be used. As we explained in Chapter 9, the Internet transport protocols may be too low-level for the task at hand and use of middleware technologies such as CORBA and RMI may be preferable.

This section will focus in differentiating the uses of UDP from the uses of the TCP protocol. We begin by re-listing the main functions of the TCP protocol:

❑ **Packet ordering:** TCP delivers IP packets in the order transmitted, through sequencing

❑ **Reliable transmission:** Lost packets are detected and recovered through retransmission

❑ **Streaming abstraction:** The TCP protocol can support the abstraction of a continuous bi-directional communications byte-stream between two entities because data packets are delivered reliably and in the order transmitted

❑ **Flow control:** The receiver can slow down the server if data is received at a rate that exceeds the receiver's processing capacity

❑ **Congestion control:** TCP implements a distributed congestion control algorithm that slows down individual stream transmission if packet loss is detected. The algorithm is tuned to provide fair sharing of network resources among TCP streams.

TCP provides a useful service to applications that need to exchange relatively large amounts of data in a reliable manner and without real-time delivery constraints. On the other hand, the UDP protocol provides a less reliable, packet-based service without support for flow or congestion control. It is therefore suitable for applications fitting different criteria:

❑ **Small requests and replies:** If the client's request and the server's reply require less than 508 bytes, then they can be certainly fitted into a single UDP datagram. In such cases, the TCP connection handshake and server state setup overheads become disproportionate.

❑ **Read-only/re-entrant servers:** When a UDP client does not receive a response to a request, it cannot determine whether the request or the response datagram was lost. If the request did not modify server state, or did so in a way that resending the request would have the same effect (that is, the request processing is idempotent) then the response loss can simply be handled through retransmission. Otherwise, if the number of times a request is processed is important, the application must support more complicated status check functionality.

❑ **Stateless servers:** If the protocol server does not need to maintain per-connection state, then requests can be more easily split into multiple independent UDP datagram operations.

❑ **Real-time streaming:** Multimedia applications playing live content need to stream data over the Internet. It may appear that the TCP model is a better fit for streaming application requirements, due to its streaming abstraction, loss recovery through retransmission, as well as flow and congestion control. The problem with TCP, however, is that it does not provide applications with control over its functions. For example, if a packet is lost it only makes sense to request retransmission if the round-trip latency is smaller than the time in which it will need to be played. Additionally, if a part of the stream (in a packet) has not been received in time, the application may want to skip part of the stream and keep reading from what is available. Finally, the application may need to receive flow and congestion notification, in order to adjust its transmission quality.

For these reasons, many real-time applications do not use the TCP protocol. Lacking an alternative, many such applications have built proprietary protocols over UDP. Lately, a new transport protocol called the Real Time Protocol (RTP) has been adopted for such purposes. RTP will be covered at the end of this chapter.

Common UDP-based Applications

UDP is used by several common Internet applications. This section will briefly present three such applications and outline how their protocols make use of the UDP services. As will become apparent, UDP-based application protocols are relatively simple and consist of a basic query-response mechanism.

Domain Name System (DNS)

The most widely used UDP-based application is the **Domain Name System (DNS).** The function and operations of the DNS protocol were covered in Chapter 8. Briefly, the DNS standard defines a hierarchical distributed namespace for associating attributes (resource records) with nodes in the tree (domains), and a protocol for querying the distributed database.

The requirements of the DNS protocol match many of the stated UDP use requirements. Typical DNS queries are small; for example a request to resolve a domain name into an address. The original DNS protocol did not provide update capabilities; therefore submitting the same query multiple times does not change the result of the operation. Domain name servers do not store per-connection state, so requests can be broken down into multiple independent UDP datagram queries. The DNS protocol also supports queries over TCP. By default, resolvers send queries using UDP, and only switch to using TCP if the server's response could not fit in 512 bytes (marked by the application in the UDP response).

The DNS protocol over UDP uses the same data format for both queries as well as responses.

Every datagram is broken into a fixed-header (12-bytes). The fixed header identifies the type (`request` or `response`), provides flags characterizing the datagram, and includes the record count in each variable field.

It is followed by four variable fields:

- ❑ **Question**: Contains the DNS query type (for instance, A for address, MX for mail-exchange), and the domain name to be resolved

- ❑ **Answer**: Contains the resource records for the queries

- ❑ **Authority records**: Contains the records of authoritative servers discovered, and the additional section may contain records that the server deems likely to be also needed

- ❑ Additional "volunteered" information

The diagram below shows a typical DNS query. On the left, a DNS client (`resolver`) sends a UDP datagram to port 53 of its configured DNS server (128.59.16.20). The UDP payload of the UDP datagram contains a DNS header pointing to an address (A) resource record query (`question`) for the domain name "wrox.com". Upon receipt, the DNS server will consult its cache and, if the answer is not stored there, will use the DNS protocol to retrieve the answer as shown in Chapter 8. If the resolution process succeeds, the DNS server will return the answer to the DNS client (`resolver`) by sending a UDP datagram addressed to the datagram's source address and port. The response data payload again will begin with a UDP response header pointing to an answer record containing the address for the domain. The server may provide additional resource records, such as the mail-exchange (MX) for the domain, which the resolver may need to answer future queries.

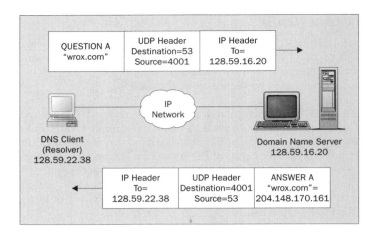

Simple Network Management Protocol (SNMP)

The **Simple Network Management Protocol (SNMP)** is another popular UDP-based protocol. SNMP is used to read, and less commonly set, network device management information. Management information is exported in the form of hierarchical structures called **Management Information Bases (MIBs)**. Various standard MIBs have been defined, exporting device configuration (for example, network hosts, routers, and switches), as well as application/service configuration (such as HTTP server).

Version 1 of the SNMP protocol uses a simple request-response mechanism. SNMP clients create a UDP datagram with a list of `get` or `set` requests for the server encoded using ASN.1 (see Chapter 9). Every datagram also includes authentication and protocol version information. Due to its simple design, the protocol became widely adopted by device manufacturers. The protocol's stop-and-wait design, however, does not support bulk data transfers efficiently, and its security features are too weak. Subsequent versions have addressed these issues; however, version 1 is still widely deployed.

For more information on SNMP, visit http://www.ietf.org/rfc/rfc1157.txt.

Trivial File Transfer Protocol (TFTP)

The **Trivial File Transfer Protocol (TFTP)** is another UDP-based application protocol used in non-authenticated file transfers. Diskless networked devices typically use the TFTP protocol as part of their boot procedure. Device network booting is performed by firmware, that is, software stored in Read Only Memory (ROM), or some type of rewritable persistent storage such as Flash memory. Many times, in order to keep down size and complexity, the firmware's operating system does not support higher-level transport protocols such as TCP, or complex application-layer protocols such as FTP. The TFTP protocol fills this niche by providing a simple (trivial) non-authenticated transfer service.

TFTP clients send a UDP packet with a TFTP request for a specific file name. Two request operations are supported: read and write. TFTP servers receiving a read request begin transmitting the contents of the requested file by sending the first 512 bytes in a datagram preceded by a 2-byte block number identifying the segment in the sequence. Clients must acknowledge each datagram received by sending the received block-number back to the sender. If no acknowledgement has been received in a certain amount of time, the server retransmits the outstanding block.

This is an example of a stop-and-wait protocol, which is extremely inefficient because it slows down transmission to a function of latency (as discussed in the previous chapter). Since the TFTP protocol is typically used in a Local Area Network environment with low latency, its use is deemed acceptable for the specific task of booting diskless devices.

Designing UDP-based Application Protocols

As is evident from the above discussion, UDP-based application protocols tend to have a very simple request-reply format. Ideally, each request can be fitted into a single UDP packet (data <508 bytes). If larger requests are required, they are typically performed using TCP. This approach avoids the use of a sequencing mechanism. UDP-based clients that fail to receive a response to their query typically retransmit based on some application-protocol specific timing mechanism.

Sometimes, it may be tempting to build more complex protocols, ones that provide a subset of the TCP protocol functions. This *ad hoc* approach can quickly lead to designs that closely resemble TCP but have not been put through the same rigorous analysis and testing of TCP. Designing protocols with a large number of states, multiple timers, and shared state is a complex task. User applications built on top of UDP should try to keep the state machines small, and focus on providing loss handling through retransmission on one side only (client or server).

One final word of warning concerns the use of network resources in UDP-based applications. Because UDP does not perform any flow or congestion control, rogue applications can cause significant network performance degradation.

One possible way to reduce error retransmission is to send every packet several times, however, this approach will only work if used by a small number of users. Its success depends on the fact that the remaining users, who are presumably using TCP, will back off until they fairly share the remaining bandwidth of the network between themselves. It serves everyone to play fairly by using TCP-style congestion control mechanisms.

Java UDP Programming

The Java language supports UDP network programming through two main classes: `java.net.DatagramPacket` and `java.net.DatagramSocket`. Unlike stream (TCP) sockets, no differentiation exists between server and client datagram (UDP) sockets. Every datagram socket can be used both for sending as well as receiving datagrams. The reason for this difference is that stream sockets are associated with a single stream, while datagram sockets do not support a streaming abstraction and can be used to send and receive to and from multiple destinations.

In place of the `java.io` stream classes, Java datagram sockets use instances of the `DatagramPacket` class. `DatagramPacket` instances are used similarly to standard mail envelopes, containing a destination or source address as well as a message of a certain maximum size (in principle 65508 bytes, in practice 508 bytes). `DatagramPacket` instances may only be used with `DatagramSocket` instances, and cannot be used with TCP `java.net.Socket` instances.

The diagram overleaf illustrates the typical use of the `DatagramPacket` and `DatagramSocket` classes.

1. The Java UDP server creates a `DatagramSocket` instance bound to a UDP port (specific, or arbitrarily chosen)

2. The server creates a `DatagramPacket` instance that will be used to store the next datagram received

3. The server then invokes the blocking `DatagramSocket receive()` method, passing the datagram created

4. The Java UDP client also creates a `DatagramSocket` instance, typically not bound to a particular port

5. The client next creates a `DatagramPacket` marked for delivery to the server's address and port, with the application-determined payload

6. The datagram is then transmitted using the `DatagramSocket`'s `send()` method

7. The header is created in transmission

8. If the network manages to transmit the UDP packet to the other end (server) without corrupting the headers or the payload, the data will be copied into the server's `DatagramPacket` instance and returned by unblocking the `receive()` call. If a `receive()` call has not been made by the application, the `DatagramPacket` instance will be buffered until it is retrieved by the application. The checksum verification is performed by the system's UDP implementation and applications can assume that delivered `DatagramPacket` instances do not contain corrupted data

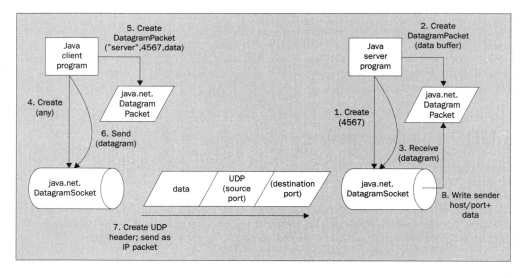

java.net.DatagramPacket

The `java.net.DatagramPacket` class stores the header and data content of a UDP datagram. Instances are used in sending as well as receiving UDP datagrams.

The three main attributes of the `DatagramPacket` class are:

❑ IP address

❑ UDP port

❑ The payload data stored in a byte-array

When `DatagramPacket` instances are used for UDP transmission, the IP address and port specify the destination; when used for receiving UDP datagrams, they specify the source IP address and port.

Constructors

There are four ways to construct a `DatagramPacket` instance. The first two constructors are typically used when reading UDP datagrams, the other two are typically used when transmitting UDP datagrams. These uses are characterized as typical because the class provides update methods allowing programmers to supply missing arguments after construction.

The simplest constructor creates a `DatagramPacket` instance that uses the byte array argument as buffer, and the integer argument as the maximum buffer length to be used.

```
DatagramPacket(byte[] buf, int length)
```

An `IllegalArgumentException` will be thrown if the buffer size of the array provided at constructor execution time is smaller than the specified length. At first, it may appear strange that the `DatagramPacket` class expects users to provide its internal data storage. In fact, this design goes contrary to the usual object-modeling goal of hiding internal data representation. The main reason for exposing the internal data representation in such a manner is efficiency. The design reduces unnecessary data copying, and permits applications to use internal knowledge to predict the size of the required buffer.

The constructor, and in fact every `DatagramPacket` method, does not throw an I/O exception since it does not perform any communication in itself. Communications only occur through `java.net.DatagramSocket` method invocations, as will be discussed in the next subsection. If the application cannot predict the buffer size it expects to receive it should provide the maximum UDP size of 65508 bytes (unfortunately this value is not provided as a constant by the Java UDP classes).

The second constructor adds support for offsetting writes to the byte buffer. In the previous constructor, the `DatagramPacket` created used data stored in buffer indices [0...length-1]. In this constructor, the instance created will use indices [offset...offset+length-1]. This behavior may be appropriate in applications that want to append the data received into an array containing other data, or want to send part of the data stored in an array. An `IllegalArgumentException` will be thrown if the buffer size is smaller than (offset+length).

```
DatagramPacket(byte[] buf, int offset, int length)
```

The remaining two constructors also accept the byte array, length and optional offset arguments, but also support specification of the packet's destination address and port. Note that the destination address and port are only used when sending the packet using the `java.net.DatagramSocket send()` method (presented later on). It is also possible to use `DatagramPacket` instances to receive UDP datagrams, in which case the address and port values are overridden with the sender's address and port. An `IllegalArgumentException` will be thrown if the buffer size is smaller than the specified length, plus the optional offset. No I/O exceptions are thrown because the class does not perform any communications, and the host is described by an IP address, not a name that would need to be resolved. Applications will typically be better able to predict the outgoing buffer size.

As was noted in the UDP introduction, hosts should not send more than 508 bytes of data unless they have somehow discovered that the network will support larger datagrams.

```
DatagramPacket(byte[] buf, int length, InetAddress address, int port)
DatagramPacket(byte[] buf, int offset, int length,
               InetAddress address, int port)
```

Methods

The `DatagramPacket` class supports read operations for accessing its three basic attributes: `address`, `port`, and data buffer (including buffer `offset` and `length`). No exceptions are thrown because the methods operate on local data.

The `getAddress()` method returns the destination or source address for this packet. Similarly, the `getPort()` method returns the destination or source port number. It is up to the application to remember if this packet had been constructed, or received, in order to treat the address and port number values accordingly. These methods are typically invoked on received datagrams in order to determine where the reply should be sent.

```
InetAddress getAddress()
int getPort()
```

Three methods are provided to access the `DatagramPacket` payload:

```
byte[] getData()
int getOffset()
int getLength()
```

The `getData()` method returns the actual buffer, while the `getOffset()` and `getLength()` methods return the range of buffer indices containing payload data. Note that the `getLength()` does not return the length specified in the constructor, but the actual length of the data received. Of these methods, the `getLength()` is most commonly used to determine how much data was received. If no offset has been specified, the `getOffset()` method returns zero.

In addition to the above read operations, `DatagramPacket` provides nearly equivalent write methods.

- ❑   `void setAddress(InetAddress address)`: This method may be used to change the destination of the packet.

- ❑   `void setPort(int Port)`: This method may be used to change the destination port of the packet.

Note that the `DatagramPacket` does not effect any communications, so setting the destination address and port will only change behavior once the `java.net.DatagramSocket` `send(DatagramPacket)` method is invoked with the changed object as its argument.

It is also possible to change the data buffer of the `DatagramPacket` by invoking one of the two `setData()` methods:

```
void setData(byte[] buf)
void setData(byte[] buf, int offset, int length)
```

The first `setData()` method takes as argument a byte array that will henceforth be used as the packet's data storage. Unlike the constructor, this method does not require a length argument. The method specification states that the previously set length will be used, unless it is greater than the new buffer length, in which case the buffer length is used. This appears, at least to the author, somewhat arbitrary, so readers should try to remember the special semantics. If the intended use of the `setData(byte[])` method invocation was to also reset the length to the size of the new buffer, then a separate call to `setLength()` must be made.

The `setLength()` method permits users to change the number of bytes from the byte array buffer that are considered to hold valid data. If the length specified exceeds the current buffer's length, an `IllegalArgumentException` will be thrown.

The second `setData()` method takes a byte array buffer, an integer offset and an integer length as arguments and sets the datagram's payload as described in the constructor of the same signature. As in the constructor, an invalid offset (less than `zero`, or greater than `length`), or invalid length (`offset+length>buffer.size`) will throw an `IllegalArgumentException`. This second `setData()` method permits users to move the window on an existing buffer by passing the same byte array with a different offset and potentially with a different length.

java.net.DatagramSocket

As we have already discussed, instances of the `java.net.DatagramSocket` class can serve both as client as well as server datagram sockets. By default, such instances encapsulate UDP sockets, although in principle this behavior could be changed by invoking `setDatagramSocketImplFactory()` that will be presented later on. In practice, there is no real replacement for the UDP protocol.

Unlike stream sockets, datagram sockets do not have a protocol peer (there is a minor caveat to this rule that will be covered in the `setHost()` and `setPort()` discussion), therefore, the same socket instance may be used to send datagrams to any host/port destination, as well as receive datagrams from any host/port source. To consider a practical analogy: stream/TCP sockets are similar to a dedicated phone line, say between a factory and the town office, and datagram/UDP sockets are similar to a postal mailbox, which can be used to reach anyone in the world.

Constructors

Because every `DatagramSocket` instance can be used to receive datagrams it must be associated with a unique UDP port on the local host. To simplify use when the specific port number assigned is not important, a no-argument constructor has been provided, whose behavior is to pick an available UDP port (known as an ephemeral port).

A `java.net.SocketException` may be thrown at construction time if no free port is available (unlikely), or due to some underlying operating system failure (such as file handle exhaustion, or UNIX port restrictions). In addition, a runtime `SecurityException` may be thrown if the "`listen`" permission has not been granted. Network permissions are protocol independent; therefore users are referred to the Chapter 7 presentation of `java.net.SocketPermission`. Note that the `SecurityException` is a runtime exception and is not formally part of the method's signature. However, it is a method that may be thrown so it has been added for clarity.

```
DatagramSocket() throws SocketException, SecurityException
```

The other two `DatagramSocket` constructors permit users to specify the port and optionally the particular interface used for binding. Both constructors may throw a `SocketException` if the port is in use, or could not be assigned due to some operating system failure. Similar to the no-argument constructor, the runtime `SecurityException` may be thrown if the `"listen"` socket permission has not been granted. An additional error condition may occur in the second constructor if an IP address that does not belong to the local host is provided. A `SocketException` is also used to signal this error.

```
DatagramSocket(int port) throws SocketException, SecurityException
DatagramSocket(int port, InetAddress address) throws SocketException,
               SecurityException)
```

Operations

The main role of the `DatagramSocket` is to send and receive datagrams. Datagrams may be sent by invoking the `send()` method with a `DatagramPacket` instance. The destination host and port cannot be specified in the `send()` method invocation, therefore they must be set in the `DatagramPacket`. This can be achieved by either passing the destination address and port during `DatagramPacket` instance construction, or invoking the `DatagramPacket` `setAddress()` and `setPort()` methods.

```
void send(DatagramPacket packet)
     throws IOException, SecurityException, IllegalArgumentException;
```

Invocation may fail for a number of reasons:

❑ Sun's JDK 1.3/1.4 implementations throw a runtime `NullPointerException` if the packet's address and port attributes have not been configured, as the `send()` method will not know where to forward it to

❑ An `IOException` may be thrown if the packet could not be successfully transmitted by the system, if the socket has been closed, or if the packet exceeds the maximum size supported by the system

❑ A runtime `SecurityException` may be thrown if the `"connect"` `SocketPermission` has not been granted for the target address and port

❑ An `IllegalArgumentException` may be thrown if the socket has been restricted to a single destination through a `connect()` call (described later), and the packet address and port do not match the configured destination address and port

Datagrams may be received by invoking the blocking `receive()` method. The `receive()` method does not return a result, instead it operates by side-effect (again, the `SecurityException` is not formally declared, but shown here for clarity).

```
void receive(DatagramPacket) throws IOException, SecurityException
```

Invocation requires a `DatagramPacket` instance as an argument that will be used to store the next datagram received. Any data previously held in the `DatagramPacket` instance will be overwritten.

> **It is the responsibility of the invoker to assure that the length of the `DatagramPacket` instance provided is long enough to store any datagram received – if a larger datagram is received, it will be truncated. In general, there is no reliable method to detect truncation. Either the buffer size must be set to the maximum (65508) or the application layer protocol must store the length as part of the data (for instance, in an application-layer header).**

The method may throw an IOException if the socket has been closed, or a communication error occurs. The runtime SecurityException may also be thrown if the "accept" SocketPermission has not been granted to the host and port that sent this UDP datagram. By default, the receive() method blocks until a datagram is received, or the socket is closed. If the socket has been configured using the setSoTimeout() method (described later), a java.io.InterruptedIOException may be thrown to signal a timeout.

Because DatagramSocket instances tie up operating system resources, such as UDP ports and file handles, it is necessary to explicitly close a datagram socket before the object is garbage collected. Once the close() method has been invoked the send() and receive() operations will fail.

```
void close()
```

Methods

All DatagramSocket instances may be used for receiving datagrams, and therefore must be associated with a UDP port and a network interface. Depending on the constructor used, the port number and interface address may be user selected, or system assigned.

```
int getLocalPort()
```

The getLocalPort() method returns the UDP port this datagram socket is bound to. Current implementations return the port number even if the datagram socket has been closed, so users should not depend on this method to check socket termination.

```
InetAddress getLocalAddess()
```

The getLocalAddress() method returns the address of the interface used in binding. The default DatagramSocket behavior is to bind to all interfaces represented by the special IP address 0.0.0.0.

Both methods do not throw an exception because they are not dependent on the state of the socket. These methods should not be confused with the similarly named getPort() and getInetAddress() methods which are described shortly.

Earlier, we stated that DatagramSockets may be used to send to and receive from any Internet address/UDP port combination. This behavior is due to the connection less nature of the UDP protocol. In some cases, however, it may be desirable to configure a DatagramSocket instance to send packets to a single destination only. This is a programmatic concept, and does not alter the underlying connection less protocol model.

There are two main advantages in coding the destination in the DatagramSocket as opposed to the DatagramPacket. The first advantage is that the code producing the DatagramPacket instance does not need to know the recipient. The second advantage is that the security check for the "connect" SocketPermission only needs to be performed once: at the time the datagram socket is configured to the destination.

The connect() method shown below configures the socket to transmit datagrams only to the destination specified. The method naming is a little misleading; a better name could have been restrict(). An IllegalArgumentException will be thrown if the address or port arguments are invalid. Invoking connect() results in a security check for "connect" permission to the specified address and port. If the security check fails, a SecurityException will be thrown.

```
void connect(InetAddress address, int port)
    throws SecurityException, IllegalArgumentException
```

DatagramSocket instances restricted to a single destination may be reverted to the default unrestricted state by invoking the disconnect() method. It is safe to invoke disconnect() even if the socket has not been configured using a connect() invocation.

```
void disconnect()
```

Two methods are provided to query the restriction/connection state of a DatagramSocket.

The getInetAddress() method returns the destination address to which the datagram socket has been restricted, or null if it is in the default unconnected state.

```
InetAddress getInetAddress()
```

Similarly, the getPort() method returns the destination port to which the datagram socket has been restricted, or -1 if the port is in the default unconnected state.

```
int getPort()
```

As was just mentioned, it is important to distinguish these methods from the similar getLocalAddress() and getLocalPort() methods that return the local socket configuration.

Datagram sockets share some common configuration attributes with stream sockets. The blocking behavior of the receive() method may be controlled by invoking the setSoTimeout() method.

```
void setSoTimeout(int timeout) throws SocketException
int getSoTimeout() throws SocketException
```

A non-zero argument configures the datagram socket receive() method to throw a java.io.InterruptedIOException if a packet has not been received after the given number of milliseconds. This method is particularly useful because datagrams may be lost and, therefore, the application could block indefinitely, therefore most applications will need to set a timeout. A zero argument to setSoTimeout() reverts to the default infinite blocking receive() behavior.

The DatagramSocket class provides methods to query the protocol stack's current send and receive buffer size. As is the case for streaming sockets, the buffer size only affects performance (that is, will not cause datagram truncation). UDP datagrams exceeding the getSendBufferSize() can still be sent, and datagrams exceeding getReceiveDataSize() can still be received. The values only affect the number of bytes copied from/to the low-level operating system sockets at a time. Applications that can predict datagram packet sizes, can use the setReceiveBufferSize() and setSendBufferSize() methods to assist the low-level protocol stack in reading packets efficiently.

```
void setSendBufferSize(int size) throws SocketException
int getSendBufferSize() throws SocketException
void setReceiveBufferSize(int size) throws SocketException
int getReceiveBufferSize() throws SocketException
```

Factories

The `DatagramSocket` API supports replacement of the default protocol implementation (UDP) with a user-supplied implementation. This method is rarely used, as there are no other significant datagram protocols deployed in the Internet today, with exception of the RTP protocol covered at the end of this chapter. Potentially, this capability may also be used to monitor application performance, by introducing a wrapper class that performs logging before invoking the actual UDP implementation.

```
void setDatagramSocketImplFactory(DatagramSocketImplFactory factory)
    throws IOException
```

Use of `DatagramSocket` factories is an advanced topic that will not be covered in this text.

Simple UDP Example

A simple example of a UDP client and server in one is shown below. The example program creates a datagram socket bound to a specific port, and sends a datagram to its own socket. The datagram contains the byte encoding of a Java string using the default platform Unicode-to-byte conversion.

Once the packet is sent, the program invokes the `receive()` method on the datagram socket. In the extremely unlikely case that the datagram was lost while traveling in the local loop-back interface, the `receive()` method will time out because the `DatagramSocket` has been configured to do so after five seconds. Otherwise, if the datagram is received, the Java String object is recreated using the default byte-to-Unicode conversion and printed out to the screen.

The sample code does not perform any error checking, just propagates the exceptions to the user. In the next section, we will show a complete example with separate client and server programs that handle errors appropriately.

The only subtle programming point in this example involves the reuse of the `DatagramPacket` instance. The datagram data buffer is changed in order to support the minimum UDP datagram packet size. This is not strictly required in this case, since we know what we will receive, but is provided for generality. Unless the length is also changed, however, the `DatagramPacket` will only use the previous buffer's length. This is why we include the `setLength(512)` invocation.

```java
// SimpleUDPExample.java

import java.net.*;


    // Simple example that sends and receives a UDP datagram

public class SimpleUDPExample {

  public static void main(String[] main)
        throws UnknownHostException, SocketException,
              java.io.IOException {
    int port = 5264;    // hard-coded for simplicity

    // create datagram socket
    DatagramSocket socket = new DatagramSocket(port);
```

```
      socket.setSoTimeout(5000);

      // create datagram payload + set destination to self
      String outMessage = "Hello UDP world!";
      byte[] data = outMessage.getBytes();
      DatagramPacket packet =
        new DatagramPacket(data, data.length,
                            InetAddress.getByName("localhost"), port);

      // send datagram (to ourself)
      System.out.println("Sending message: " + outMessage);
      socket.send(packet);

      /* prepare to receive datagram: because we reuse the DatagramPacket
         instance we must reset its length even though we replace its data
         buffer! */
      packet.setData(new byte[512]);
      packet.setLength(512);

      // receive datagram (may time out)
      System.out.println("Waiting for datagram ...");
      socket.receive(packet);

      // print result
      String inMessage = new String(packet.getData(), 0, packet.getLength());
      System.out.println("Received message: " + inMessage);

      socket.close();
    }
  }
```

The above program, which has also been provided in the chapter's code directory, can be compiled and executed as follows (please note that the working directory must be in your classpath):

C:\ Beg_Java_Networking\Ch10>**java SimpleUDPExample**
Sending message: Hello UDP world!
Waiting for datagram ...
Received message: Hello UDP world!

If a security manager had been assigned to the JVM the following permissions file
simple_policy.txt) would need to be provided, otherwise program execution would fail.

```
  grant {
    permission java.net.SocketPermission "localhost", "connect, accept";
  };
```

The example can then be executed with the security manager and policy flags as shown below:

C:\Beg_Java_Networking\Ch10>**java -Djava.security.manager**
                -Djava.security.policy=simple_policy.txt SimpleUDPExample
Sending message: Hello UDP world!
Waiting for datagram ...
Received message: Hello UDP world!

UDP Echo Service

We demonstrate use of the `java.net` package `DatagramPacket` and `DatagramSocket` classes by implementing a client and a server program for the IETF RFC 862 `Echo` protocol (see http://www.ietf.org/rfc/rfc862.txt). The `Echo` protocol is another old Internet (ARPANET) standard, of the same era as the Time protocol implemented in the previous chapter. Echo protocol servers receive datagrams from clients on a well-known port, and simply send them back to the client. Through this service, clients may determine if a host is live or not, as well as collect performance measurement information.

Two versions of the Echo protocol are defined: one over TCP and another over UDP. We will be implementing the UDP version of the Echo protocol in this chapter.

The UDP Echo protocol operations are very simple. The UDP Echo protocol server waits for UDP datagrams arriving on port 7. Because every UDP datagram is marked with the sender's address and port, no application-layer header is required. The Echo server uses the UDP header information to send the packet back to the sender with the same data payload. The protocol operations are shown in the diagram below.

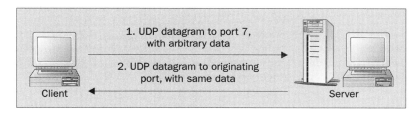

1. UDP datagram to port 7, with arbitrary data

2. UDP datagram to originating port, with same data

Client

Server

Echo Protocol Client

We begin with the design and implementation of the Echo protocol client. Our client will send a UDP datagram to an Echo server, and if it is received back will let the user know that the server is active. Because UDP datagrams may be lost en route, either the request, or the response datagram may not be delivered. Therefore, the client will attempt to send multiple echo requests before deciding that the service is not available or reachable. Readers may modify the example to perform additional services, such as network latency discovery.

For simplicity, the client will be coded as a console application with a simple command line based user interface. Client command line invocation will require a host name or address pointing to the Echo protocol server, with an optional second argument used to override the default echo UDP port.

Programmatically, there are two basic designs for supporting Echo protocol requests. The first approach is to use a static method that creates a `DatagramSocket` instance on each invocation, uses it to send a datagram to the server, and waits for a response. This is a simple solution, however it has a disadvantage in that it creates a new datagram socket for each invocation. If the static method happens to be invoked frequently, as would be the case in latency discovery, or monitoring applications, the socket creation overhead could become significant.

The second approach is to define a class encapsulating a `DatagramSocket` instance Instances of that class would be used to provide Echo protocol services over the shared datagram socket instance. This approach spreads the cost of datagram socket creation over multiple uses, but keeps an open datagram socket in between requests. If instances of this class must support concurrent invocations from multiple threads, then implementation becomes significantly more complex. To accommodate such concurrent functionality, the client implementation must handle responses in a separate thread, determine which thread is the recipient and perform thread blocking and notification.

We will be implementing our Echo client using the static method design in order to focus on the networking code. Echo protocol requests will be made through invocation of a static method of the class `EchoUDPClient`. Our client will have a single static method called `echo()` that will accept the following arguments:

❑　　The address and UDP port number of the Echo protocol server

❑　　The number of echo requests sent before declaring failure. Recall that UDP datagrams may be lost en-route, and therefore the lack of a response to a UDP Echo request cannot be conclusively attributed to the Echo server being unreachable. The solution is to perform multiple requests with the idea that if the server is available, one of the attempts will succeed in reaching the server and receiving back the response.

❑　　How long to wait for the response to an Echo request before giving up on it. Once a UDP Echo datagram is sent, the method will wait for the server's response. However, that response may never arrive for the reasons listed above. It is therefore necessary to set a deadline after which the response will no longer be expected.

The `EchoUDPClient` class implementation is listed below. In the first part, we define some constant static class attributes that will be used by the `echo()` and `main()` methods. The constant values include the well-known Echo protocol UDP port number, the default number of Echo attempts, and the default response expiration time. The default values selected are 3 for the number of tries and 2000 (milliseconds=2 seconds) for the response. It is very unlikely that three consecutive requests will fail due to lost UDP packets. Typical Internet round trips are in the order of 1-600 milliseconds, so a 2000 millisecond wait is considered reasonable without being overly conservative. The maximum UDP datagram size that applications should send is also specified since it is not defined in the Java datagram socket implementation.

```
// EchoUDPClient.java

package com.wrox;

import java.net.*;
import java.io.*;

    // Static methods implementing the RFC 862 UDP echo protocol client
public class EchoUDPClient {

    // Standard UDP echo service port defined in RFC 862 (port=7)

  public static final int STANDARD_ECHO_PORT = 7;


    //  Default number of tries to receive an echo response from a server
```

```
    public static final int DEFAULT_TRIES = 3;

    // Default polling expiration in milliseconds
    public static final int DEFAULT_EXPIRE_MILLIS = 2000;


    //  Maximum UDP payload size to be sent or received
    public static final int MAX_UDP_BUFFER_SIZE = 508;
```

In addition to the above constant (final) class attributes, the implementation defines a single non-constant class variable. The `nextRequestID` static variable will be used by the static `echo()` method implementation to generate a unique request for each invocation. Because UDP is connectionless, when a `DatagramSocket` is used to receive a datagram, it may be passed a response to a previous request. Given our use of a different `DatagramSocket` per request, this is a highly unlikely event (ports assigned to ephemeral sockets are typically incrementally different). Nonetheless, it is an event that can be detected by including a unique value in every Echo request sent. The `echo()` method will read the `nextRequestID` value and increment its value in an atomic manner at every invocation.

```
    //Counter used to generate unique Echo requests
    protected static int nextRequestID = 0;
```

Since our class will only offer static methods, we define a single private constructor to prevent instantiation by classes that are not part of the same package.

```
    //Prevent instantiation (only static methods offered)
    private EchoUDPClient() {}
```

The static `echo()` method accepts the four arguments mentioned earlier: server IP address, server UDP port, the number of Echo requests sent before giving up, and the number of milliseconds before considering a specific request lost or unanswered. The decision on what exceptions to throw is a little tricky in this case. Because we are checking for connectivity, we would not normally want to throw any I/O related exceptions. A connectivity error would normally be signaled by the return of a `false` value; however, it is possible that the attempt to create a UDP datagram socket or the attempt to send the datagram will fail. In such cases, it would be misleading to return `false` since the Echo request would never actually be made. Therefore, the method declares that the `IOException` will be thrown only if it is not possible to send the request. Sending or receiving the Echo request may also trigger a `SecurityException` if a security manager has been installed and the appropriate permissions have not been granted. Again, we chose to propagate this exception because it signals an unusual condition.

```
    public static boolean echo(InetAddress address,
                               int port,
                               int tries,
                               int pollExpireMillis)
        throws IOException, SecurityException {
```

Upon invocation the method generates a unique request number by reading the `nextRequestID` value and incrementing it. Atomicity of the read and increment actions is maintained by synchronizing on the class object; since this is a static method it is not possible to use `synchronize(this)`.

```
    if (address == null) {
        throw new NullPointerException("null echo server address argument");
```

```
    // Generate a unique request ID
  }
  long outValue;
  synchronized (EchoUDPClient.class) {
    outValue = nextRequestID;
    nextRequestID++;
  }
```

The next step is to create a byte array containing the long value that will be the Echo UDP datagram payload. Although it is possible to use bit-shifting to convert a long to a sequence of bytes, as shown in the previous chapter, we will use the `java.io.DataOutputStream` class instead. The `DataOutputStream` class provides methods for writing primitive Java types and string instances into a byte stream. In combination with the `java.io.ByteArrayOutputStream` class, that stores a stream in a byte array, we can use this function to convert the long into a byte array. Note that this usage is inefficient since it generates several temporary objects. It is shown here because it can be useful in situations where multiple primitive or `String` values need to be stored in a byte array.

```
    // Create request packet payload (write current time to byte array)
    ByteArrayOutputStream byteOut = new ByteArrayOutputStream();
    DataOutputStream dataOut = new DataOutputStream(byteOut);
    try {
      dataOut.writeLong(outValue);
      dataOut.close();
    } catch (IOException e) {
      throw new RuntimeException("Unexpected I/O exception:" + e);
    }
```

Given the byte array stored in the `ByteArrayOutputStream` instance, it is now possible to generate the `DatagramPacket` instance that will be sent to the Echo server. The example also creates another `DatagramPacket` instance that will be used to receive the server's response. Next, the method creates a `DatagramSocket` and sets its timeout to the `pollExpireMillis` method argument value. The socket construction and configuration may both throw an `IOException`, which will be propagated to the caller.

```
    DatagramPacket outPacket =
      new DatagramPacket(byteOut.toByteArray(),
                         byteOut.size(),
                         address, port);

    DatagramPacket inPacket = new DatagramPacket
      (new byte[MAX_UDP_BUFFER_SIZE], MAX_UDP_BUFFER_SIZE);

    DatagramSocket socket = new DatagramSocket();
    socket.setSoTimeout(pollExpireMillis);
```

The method has now completed its preparations and is ready to send the Echo UDP datagram to the sender. The sending loop is placed inside a `try-finally` block to assure that the datagram socket will be closed even if an exception is thrown. The `socket.send()` invocation is used to transmit the `DatagramPacket` constructed. The `send()` method may throw an `IOException` or a `SecurityException` both of which will be propagated to the caller (that is, not caught).

Once the datagram has been sent, the method will block to receive the Echo response. If the response is not received within `pollExpireMillis`, the `InterruptedIOException` will be thrown. In such a case, the request will be considered to have failed and the execution will resume at the top of the loop. Similarly, an `IOException` will also be ignored and execution will resume at the top of the loop. The `socket.receive()` method may also throw a `SecurityException` runtime exception. In this case, the exception is propagated to the user because it signals an unusual condition in which the security manager does not permit the server's reply.

```
try {
  /* Loop "tries" times sending the UDP packet and waiting for
     notification of receipt, or expiration of the poll time. */
  for(int i=0; i<tries; i++) {
    // Send packet to the world (IOException propagated to caller)
    socket.send(outPacket);

    // Block for reply, or timeout (as InterruptedIOException)
    try {
      socket.receive(inPacket);
    } catch (InterruptedIOException e) {
      // ignore (loop back to try again)
      continue;
    } catch (IOException e) {
      // receive I/O errors are not propagated to the caller
      continue;
    }
```

When execution has reached this point, a UDP datagram has been received via the datagram socket. Before declaring success, we must verify that the contents of the datagram match what we have sent. One approach would be to compare the byte array of the received datagram with the byte array of the sent datagram. This would be the most efficient approach. However, in order to illustrate the corresponding use of the `DataInputStream` class, we chose to attempt to read the long value that we expect to be stored in the received byte array. If the attempt to read the long value fails, or the value read does not match the one sent, the datagram is considered invalid and the code will loop back. Otherwise, if the extracted value matches the one sent, the method returns `true` (success).

The only subtle point involves the resetting of the `inPacket` length. When we loop back, we will potentially use the same `DatagramPacket` instance to receive another datagram. Due to an unfortunate feature of the `DatagramPacket` class, even though the buffer assigned at construction time may be large, the length of the last datagram received is used as the maximum length that the instance can store. To prevent the truncation of the next datagram received, we reset the length of the `inPacket` instance to the length of the array it was originally assigned.

```
// Convert byte-array reply into a Java Unicode string
ByteArrayInputStream byteIn =
  new ByteArrayInputStream(inPacket.getData(),
                           0, inPacket.getLength());
DataInputStream dataIn =
  new DataInputStream(byteIn);

try {
  long inValue = dataIn.readLong();

  // Verify that the values match
  if (outValue == inValue) {
    return(true);
```

```
          }
      } catch (IOException e) {
        // message was not a long value (loop back to try again)
      }

      /* We're looping back so reset the inPacket buffer length
         (we must do so every time we reuse a DatagramPacket
         instance for a DatagramSocket.receive() invocation) */
      inPacket.setLength(MAX_UDP_BUFFER_SIZE);
    } // for (each try)
  } finally {
    try { socket.close(); } catch (Throwable e) { }
  }
```

Once all Echo attempts have failed, the conclusion is that the service is not available, and the method simply returns `false`.

```
    return(false);
  } // echo()
```

The main method accepts two command line arguments: the name or address of the Echo server host, and an optional port number used to override the well-known Echo protocol port. After parsing the command line arguments, the static method simply invokes `echo()` with the default values for the number of tries and Echo request timeout.

```
public static void main(String[] args) {
  if ((args.length == 0) || (args.length > 2)) {
    System.err.println("Usage: EchoUDPClient <host> {<port>}");
    System.exit(1);
  }

  InetAddress address = null;
  try {
    address = InetAddress.getByName(args[0]);
  } catch (UnknownHostException e) {
    System.err.println("EchoUDPClient: unknown host " + args[0]);
    System.exit(1);
  }

  int port = STANDARD_ECHO_PORT;
  if (args.length > 1) {
    try {
      port = Integer.parseInt(args[1]);
    } catch (NumberFormatException e) {
      System.err.println("EchoUDPClient: invalid port number " + args[1]);
      System.exit(1);
    }
  }

  try {
    if (echo(address, port, DEFAULT_TRIES, DEFAULT_EXPIRE_MILLIS)) {
      System.out.println("Echo service active on " + address);
    } else {
      System.out.println("No echo reply from " + address);
    }
    System.exit(0);
  } catch (Throwable e) {
```

```
        System.err.println("EchoUDPClient: " + e);
        System.exit(1);
    }
  }    // main
}      // EchoUDPClient
```

In the previous chapter, we were able to test our Time protocol client against publicly available servers. Unlike the Time protocol, there are not many public Echo protocol servers. One reason for the protocol's demise is the use of the Internet Control Messaging Protocol (ICMP) to establish host liveness. The popular `ping` and `traceroute` applications (see Chapter 8) use the newer ICMP protocol as opposed to the older Echo protocol.

Security is another reason for disabling Echo protocol servers. If an attacker could somehow inject IP/UDP packets with fake information, they could create an endless Echo loop between two servers. This attack would rapidly consume server, bandwidth, and routing/switching resources. Even without packet spoofing, the service could be used for a distributed denial of service attack, with multiple clients sending very large UDP packets to be echoed by the server.

For these reasons, most operating systems disable the Echo protocol service. In some configurations, Windows 2000 hosts appear to be an exception, so if you have such a host in your network, you could try to execute the client as shown below (`manticore` is a Windows 2000 Professional host with the Echo service enabled). Obviously you will need to substitute the host name `manticore` with the name of your local Windows 2000 host configured to offer the Echo protocol. Readers may also elect to wait until the Echo server has been coded to test the client.

C:\Beg_Java_Networking\Ch10>**java com.wrox.EchoUDPClient manticore**
Echo service active on manticore/128.59.22.229

If the client is invoked with the name or address of a host that does not offer the Echo service then the following error will be printed:

C:\Beg_Java_Networking\Ch10>**java com.wrox.EchoUDPClient sutton**
No echo reply from sutton/128.59.22.38

Echo Protocol Server

We now turn to the design and implementation of the UDP Echo Protocol server. Programmatically, we model an echo server as an instance of the `EchoUDPServer` class. An Echo protocol server just sends back any datagrams received without performing any extra processing. Because datagram sockets are connectionless and deliver packets asynchronously, and requests require no processing, a single thread can serve all incoming requests.

The `EchoUDPServer` class extends the `java.lang.Thread` class so that it can spawn off the datagram receiver/sender thread. We chose to implement the server in a separate thread in order to support multiple instances concurrently serving processes on different ports.

Constant values are defined for the standard UDP Echo port, the default termination check (receive time out), and the maximum UDP payload. The class has only two instance variables: the `DatagramSocket` used to receive and send UDP datagrams, and a boolean variable controlling execution of the receive/send loop.

```
// EchoUDPServer.java

package com.wrox;

import java.net.*;
import java.io.*;

// Server implementing the RFC 862 UDP echo protocol
public class EchoUDPServer extends Thread {

    // Standard UDP echo service port defined in RFC 862 (port=7)
    public static int STANDARD_ECHO_PORT = 7;

    // Default number of milliseconds between termination checks
    public static int DEFAULT_TERMINATION_CHECK_MILLIS = 5000;

    // The maximum UDP data length possible (in bytes)
    public static int MAX_UDP_DATA_LENGTH = 65508;

    // UDP socket used to receive echo requests
    protected DatagramSocket socket;

    // Controls execution of the datagram receive thread
    protected boolean isActive;
```

A single constructor has been provided which simply creates the `DatagramSocket`, configures the `receive()` method time out, initializes the activation state, and starts the receiver thread. Errors in datagram socket creation are propagated to the callers.

```
    /* Constructs an RFC 862 UDP Echo Protocol server
       @param port - the UDP port number used for binding
       @exception SocketException - if the UDP datagram socket creation fails
       @exception SecurityException - if permission to accept connections
                                      is refused by the security manager.*/
    public EchoUDPServer(int port) throws SocketException {
      super("EchoServer(" + port + ")");

      socket = new DatagramSocket(port);
      socket.setSoTimeout(DEFAULT_TERMINATION_CHECK_MILLIS);
      isActive = true;

      start();
    }

    // Requests asynchronous termination of the receiving thread
    public void terminate() {
      isActive = false;
    }
```

The receive/send thread creates a new `DatagramPacket` that will be used in every socket `receive()` invocation, then enters a loop whereby a packet is received and then sent right back to the sender. Due to the design of the `DatagramSocket` class, no processing on the packet itself is necessary, since the attributes used to mark the address and port of the sender are interpreted as the address and port of the destination when the packet is sent. The `receive()` method may throw an `IOException` if an I/O error occurs, a `SecurityException` if the source host/port is not allowed to send us information by the security policy, or an `InterruptedIOException` if the timeout has expired. All errors are simply ignored; non-reliable services don't need to try hard!

```java
    /* Main thread receives and immediately sends back any data received.
       <p>
       Loop termination controlled by the terminate() method. */
    public void run() {
      System.out.println("Echo server bound to port " +
                            socket.getLocalPort());

      DatagramPacket receivePacket =
        new DatagramPacket(new byte[MAX_UDP_DATA_LENGTH],
                            MAX_UDP_DATA_LENGTH);

      while(isActive) {
        try {
           // Reset the receivePacket length to the byte array length
           receivePacket.setLength(MAX_UDP_DATA_LENGTH);

           // Wait to receive echo request (may also time out)
           socket.receive(receivePacket);

           /* We just send the packet back to the sender (already marked in
             the packet by the receive method) */
           socket.send(receivePacket);
        } catch (InterruptedIOException e) {
           // ignore (used to check for termination)
        } catch (Throwable e) {
           // ignore
        }
      }
      try { socket.close(); } catch (Throwable e) { }
    }
```

A simple command line interface is provided to support non-programmatic UDP Echo protocol server invocation. An optional argument may be provided to override the default port the server will bind to. After the server is created, the main thread joins the `EchoUDPServer` thread, since in this example the program has nothing else to do.

```java
    // Command line utility for performing UDP echo requests.
    public static void main(String[] args) {
      if (args.length > 1) {
        System.err.println("Usage: EchoUDPServer { <port> }");
        System.exit(1);
      }

      int port = STANDARD_ECHO_PORT;
      if (args.length == 1) {
        try {
          port = Integer.parseInt(args[0]);
        } catch (NumberFormatException e) {
          System.err.println("EchoUDPServer: invalid port number " + args[0]);
          System.exit(1);
        }
      }

      try {
        EchoUDPServer server = new EchoUDPServer(port);
        server.join();
      } catch (Throwable e) {
        System.err.println("EchoUDPServer: " + e);
```

```
        System.exit(1);
      }
    }
  }
```

The Java source code for the sample Echo protocol client and server is available in the chapter's code directory. The two classes may be compiled by typing:

C:\Beg_Java_Networking\Ch10>**javac com\wrox*.java**

We first attempt to start the Echo protocol server. Recall that the server's command line invocation accepts an optional port number used to override the default Echo protocol port (7). In this case, the example is executed in a Microsoft Windows 2000 host. The invocation fails because in our configuration the Windows 2000 operating system is already running its own echo service on that port.

C:\Beg_Java_Networking\Ch10>**java com.wrox.EchoUDPServer**
EchoUDPServer: java.net.BindException: Address in use: Cannot bind

A similar error may occur if the server is started in a UNIX-based operating system environment, such as Linux or Sun Solaris. In this case, the operating system will refuse the user-level process the right to bind to a privileged port (below 1024):

C:\Beg_Java_Networking\Ch10>**java com.wrox.EchoUDPServer**
EchoUDPServer: java.net.BindException: Permission denied

We work around both of these potential problems by starting the server in a special port. Arbitrarily, we select port number 7777. The server code issues a message verifying successful binding to the requested port and waits to receive UDP datagrams.

C:\Beg_Java_Networking\Ch10>**java com.wrox.EchoUDPServer 7777**
Echo server bound to port 7777

Next, we invoke our Echo protocol client providing both the server's hostname, and the special port we selected to execute our server. The client should report success. If a different port number had been used that was not bound to an Echo protocol server, the client would report that the server could not be reached (after three attempts, two seconds apart).

C:\Beg_Java_Networking\Ch10>**java com.wrox.EchoUDPServer localhost 7777**
Echo service active on localhost/127.0.0.1

The above invocations did not install a Java security manager. Due to the connectionless nature of the UDP protocol, both client and server processes must be given the connect permission. Therefore, the two programs can share the same policy file listed below (saved as echo_policy.txt):

```
grant {
  permission java.net.SocketPermission "*", "connect, accept";
};
```

C:\Beg_Java_Networking\Ch10>**java -Djava.security.manager**
                -Djava.security.policy=echo_policy.txt com.wrox.EchoUDPServer 7777
Echo server bound to port 7777

C:\Beg_Java_Networking\Ch10>**java -Djava.security.manager**
      -Djava.security.policy=echo_policy.txt com.wrox.EchoUDPClient localhost 7777
Echo service active on localhost/127.0.0.1

Real-Time Communication Protocols

As was argued in the first section of this chapter, the TCP model is not appropriate for applications with real-time constraints. On the other hand, the UDP protocol is too low level for these applications. Use of UDP forces real-time applications to perform their own sequence numbering, payload identification, flow control, as well as congestion control. This gap was filled by a new transport protocol called RTP: A Transport Protocol for Real-Time Applications, published as IETF standards track IETF 1889 (more information available at http://www.ietf.org/rfc/rfc1889.txt).

The RFC 1889 real-time application transport protocol really consists of two protocols: **RTP** (**Real-Time Protocol**) and **RTCP** (**Real-Time Control Protocol**). The RTP protocol provides end-to-end unreliable datagram transport with features useful for real-time applications. Although RTP is defined independent of the lower-level protocol, RTP packets are typically carried over IP/UDP. The RTP protocol does not provide any support for resource reservations, flow or congestion control. These functions are assigned to the second protocol called the RTP Control Protocol (RTCP). Participants in a real-time session use RTCP to share monitoring and control information.

The RTP protocol header describes the contents of the real-time datagram. The main header fields are:

❑ Payload type

❑ Sequence number

❑ Timestamp

❑ Synchronization source

❑ Contributing source identifiers

The data payload type characterizes the content of the datagram, for example MPEG-1 layer 3 (mp3) compressed audio data. Receivers use the sequence number to detect and correct delivered out-of-order. Unlike the TCP protocol, RTP delegates sequencing to the application. The timestamp field marks the time when the first byte in the RTP packet was sampled. The source identifier is used to uniquely describe the real-time stream source (for instance, a specific microphone). RTP supports the concept of mixers and translators operating on one or more RTP datagram sequence.

For example, a translator may lower the encoding of an audio datagram sequence to enable transmission over a slower network. Mixers and translators affecting an RTP packet store their identifiers in the contributing sources header field (up to a limit of 15). RTP supports both unicast point-to-point transmission, as well as multicast (point-to-multipoint) transmission. Multicast is introduced in Chapter 11.

Participants in a real-time transmission session periodically exchange performance and control data using the RTCP protocol. RTCP is used to send reception statistics such as a count of lost or delayed packets, as well as available bandwidth estimates. These receptions statistics are used to perform flow and congestion control. The TCP protocol performs flow control by changing the rate in which packets are injected into the network, but not the data itself. Real-time applications are capable of, and many times forced to, react to lower bandwidth availability by modifying the data sent, for example, by using a lower bit-per-second encoding.

Further up-to-date information on the RTP and RTCP protocols may be obtained at the URL http://www.cs.columbia.edu/~hgs/rtp/.

The **Real-Time Streaming Protocol (RTSP)** is a related, but higher-level, protocol. RTSP is a proposed IETF standard published as RFC 2326 (http://www.ietf.org/rfc/rfc2326.txt). RTSP is an application-layer protocol, similar to HTTP, which permits clients to remotely control media servers. For example, RTSP can be used to start, pause and tear down a media stream, as well as synchronize multiple video streams (such as audio and video). RTSP is a control protocol that is orthogonal to the transmission protocol, although typically it is combined with RTP over UDP.

RTSP defines a URL encoding for describing media streams. For example, the URL rtsp://media.acme.com:554/demo can be used by a client to establish an RTSP connection, query the available streams, such as audio and video, and selectively start playing. RTSP requests and media content may be carried over different protocols, for example TCP, as opposed to RTP/UDP.

Java support for real-time communication protocol has not been integrated into the main distributions (standard or enterprise editions). The **Java Media Framework (JMF)** extension provides support for the RTP (and RTCP) protocol. The library may be downloaded from http://java.sun.com/products/java-media/jmf/. The relevant packages are `javax.media.rtp`, `javax.media.rtp.event`, and `javax.media.rtp.rtcp`.

JDK 1.4 Changes

JDK 1.4 does not introduce many changes to Java datagram support. The `java.net.DatagramPacket` and `java.net.DatagramSocket` classes added support for the new `java.net.SocketAddress` class that combines an IP address and a port number in one. The `DatagramSocket` class provides additional configuration methods used to check if the socket is bound, if it has been closed, and if it is in a connected (restricted destination) mode. UDP datagrams can be configured to act as broadcasts on the local link layer (such as the Ethernet).

`DatagramSocket` instances, set to the connected state, can now receive ICMP port unreachable messages. Finally, the UDP datagram traffic class can be set for each `DatagramSocket`. Chapter 21 covers JDK-1.4 networking changes.

Summary

The User Datagram Protocol (UDP) provides an end-to-end unreliable datagram service. UDP is implemented as a thin layer over IP, adding support for port-based de-multiplexing, packet payload integrity checking, and datagram source port identification. UDP does not provide any flow control or congestion control services.

Although UDP packets payload can be of a size of 65508 bytes, most applications use up to 512 bytes to avoid IP packet fragmentation. Typically, UDP is employed in applications exchanging small amounts of data (less than 512 bytes), with idempotent receiver semantics. Most UDP-based application layer protocols are based on a simple request-reply scheme, with the transmitting party responsible for packet-loss detection and retransmission.

The two main Java classes used in performing UDP programming are `java.net.DatagramPacket` and `java.net.DatagramSocket`. `DatagramPacket` instances store the UDP datagram destination or source address and port, as well as the payload data. Users create instances of the `DatagramPacket` class both for sending and receiving UDP datagrams. Instances of the `DatagramSocket` class act as datagram mailboxes. Unlike stream sockets (found in TCP), there is no distinction between client and server `DatagramSocket` sockets: all `DatagramSocket` instances may be used to send or receive datagrams.

The `DatagramSocket` `receive()` method blocks until the next datagram is received. This behavior is typically modified to detect possible datagram loss after a certain interval.

TCP is not appropriate for real-time applications because it does not expose control over payload type, sequencing, retransmission, flow and congestion control. On the other hand, UDP is too low-level for such applications. This gap has been filled by a new transport protocol called RTP. RTP is an unreliable end-to-end datagram protocol providing sequencing, time stamping, and data-source information. RTP session participants periodically exchange information used to perform flow and congestion control through the RTP Control Protocol (RTCP). Due to the real-time nature of these applications, flow and congestion control are application-specific, and are typically performed by changing the data encoding. RTSP is an application-layer protocol, similar to HTTP, which is used to provide remote-control type services to multimedia applications.

Both TCP and UDP provide a one-to-one transport service. Chapter 11 will present the Internet Multicast protocol used to transmit data from one-to-many.

Multicasting

This chapter will introduce the IP multicast protocol that is used to for one-to-many transmission on the Internet. IP multicast is a network-layer protocol, unlike TCP and UDP that are transport layer protocols. The chapter will:

- ❏ Outline how the multicast protocol works
- ❏ Explain how to control the scope of multicast transmissions
- ❏ Introduce the Java support for UDP/IP multicast programming

Because IP multicast is a network service, it requires support by the operating system and the local network. Platform-specific pointers are provided and a small Java program is introduced that can be used to check local multicast availability. The chapter concludes with an in-depth multicast example that builds a graphical group chat application.

Why Use Multicasting?

In the previous two chapters, we have demonstrated the use of TCP and UDP for effecting communication between two parties. This model of communication is described as **one-to-one** (also known as **unicast**) because one specific Internet host is the recipient of every communication. Although the one-to-one model is a good fit for many applications, it is not appropriate for others.

Consider a live Internet video service. In the one-to-one model, every video client will have to establish a separate stream with the video server. All these streams will be carrying the same payload information and will just differ in their destination address. As a result, multiple copies of the same information are likely to traverse the same Internet link, en route to different destinations. It would make more sense to send a single copy of the sampled video and deliver this to all receivers, duplicating it as necessary in the course of the routing process. This is the **one-to-many** transmission model (also known as **multicast**).

Multicast is becoming increasingly important in a variety of applications – besides its obvious utility for live streaming applications, multicast is being used to create dynamic systems, such as Jini federations. The Jini technology from Sun Microsystems uses IP multicast to support automated service discovery. Other companies are experimenting with multicast delivered software updates. Unlike the unicast Internet protocols, IP multicast is still not universally available. It is expected that multicast will increasingly be used within individual organization networks. Unfortunately, it is not clear when and if IP multicast will become available as a global Internet-wide service.

The One-to-One Model – Unicast

So far, we have identified one type of end-to-end communication, called **one-to-one**. In one-to-one communications, an IP datagram originates in a single Internet host, and is marked for delivery to an IP address identifying the unique location of another Internet host. The diagram below illustrates this one-to-one model:

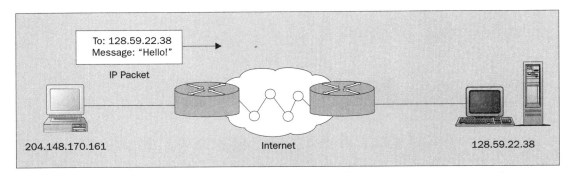

The one-to-one model is appropriate for many types of applications. For example, remote access involves a single user connecting to a specific remote service. Electronic mail is also typically a one-to-one service, unless the message is addressed to multiple users. Web access and file transfer, two essentially similar services, can also be considered as one-to-one applications under certain conditions. If the content transferred, such as a web page or a file, is customized for each user then the end-to-end model is appropriate. Even if the content is not customized for each user, if multiple requests are not likely to coincide in time, then individual transmission may be appropriate.

As we have already seen the one-to-one model is not appropriate for many types of application. The problem of multiple instances of identical data traveling over the same connection is illustrated below:

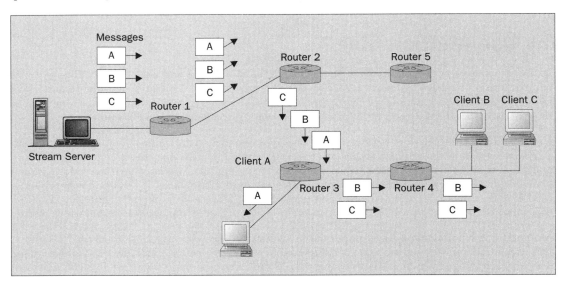

The stream server, on the left, creates a byte-stream by sampling some video source. Consider the case when three clients need to receive the video stream. In the classic IP model, the stream server must transmit three copies of the sampled data over a UDP/IP datagram or a TCP/IP segment – these copies are shown as packets A, B, C in the diagram. The server network's access router (Router-1) will then route these packets to the Internet Service Provider's network. In this example, the packets continue traveling in the same path after the second routing step (Router-2). In the third step, the packet destined for client A is delivered on the local network via Router-3, and the remaining two copies for clients B and C are forwarded to Router-4 for local delivery. Router-5 is not in the path to any of the destinations and hence no datagrams are transmitted on its links.

The One-to-Many Model – Multicasting

How can the one-to-one model be improved? The answer is to use an alternative network model supporting **one-to-many** transmission. In this model, the sender generates a single datagram destined for multiple receivers. In the one-to-many model, it is the responsibility of the network layer to create copies of transmitted datagrams as needed, usually with the goal of optimizing bandwidth usage. Returning to the previous example, the stream server would generate a single packet containing the sampled data. Unlike the one-to-one case, the TCP protocol cannot be used for transport, since there is no single peer with which to negotiate sequencing and retransmission. Hence, some type of connectionless protocol must be used, such as UDP/IP. The one-to many model is illustrated in the diagram below:

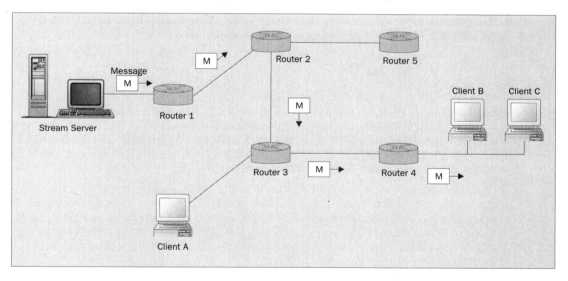

A single copy is transmitted, from Router-1 to Router-2 then to Router-3. Router-3 notices that the packet must be sent in two outgoing links, towards client A, as well as towards clients B, C. The solution is to copy the packet into both outgoing links. One copy is then delivered to client A, and another via Router-4 to clients B, and C. Because Router-5 is not on the path to any of the destinations, no traffic crosses its links.

In the above example, data originated from a single source and was sent to multiple destinations. In other types of applications, such as group conferencing, it is desirable to support **many-to-many** transmission. This model is similar to the one-to-many model with the difference that any receiver may also transmit data to all other receivers.

Implementing Multicast Applications

The idea of transmitting a single packet to multiple receivers may sound simple and intuitive, but its implementation involves several challenges:

❑   **Addressing**: Internet addresses identify a unique location in the network (see Chapter 8). When multiple hosts must be identified, a meaningful way for addressing the group must be devised. A simple solution would be to include all the destination addresses in each packet. However, this solution would not scale as the number of hosts increase. Not only would the data portion grow disproportionately smaller, but also at some point, a single packet would not even be able to fit all addresses (due to the limited IP packet size)! An alternative solution would be to use a unique **group** identifier to represent the multiple destination hosts. In such an approach, the network would be responsible for maintaining the mapping between the unique group identifier and the group members. This latter approach is used in Internet one-to-many communications. A certain range of IP addresses has been reserved to identify groups of Internet hosts, instead of the location of a single Internet host.

❑   **Membership**: The use of group identifiers for addressing creates the need for a network-layer membership mechanism. In one-to-one transmissions, it is the responsibility of the sender to identify the location of the recipient by storing the destination address in the datagram header. In multicast transmissions, the destination address stored in the multicast datagram no longer identifies a location; instead it identifies a group. Therefore, the network layer must maintain knowledge of the group's member addresses. For this purpose, applications must be provided with a protocol for communicating their group join and leave requests to the network layer. Membership is closely tied to routing which is discussed next.

❑   **Routing**: One approach to handling packets with multiple destinations is to send such packets to every possible recipient. This approach is also known as **broadcasting**. All members in a network, without distinction, receive broadcasted packets. Besides the obvious security implications, the primary limitation of broadcasting is scalability. Broadcasting is typically applied only in local area networks because they are usually small, and many times the physical medium itself is shared, so every frame (link-layer packet) is broadcasted anyway. On the Internet, broadcasting would mean that all IP hosts would receive IP packets destined to multiple hosts. Clearly that would not be a scalable solution, as every Internet link would have to handle the world's entire broadcast bandwidth!

The answer is to provide a **multicast** service. In multicasting, packets destined for multiple addresses are only sent to router nodes that are on the path to one of the target recipients. In a sense, multicast is like a smart broadcast in which only the routers required are involved. How can this be accomplished? The answer is by supporting multicast routing at the network layer. Using the information established by multicast membership protocols, routers can decide how to handle packets destined for multiple hosts.

❑   **Reliability**: The TCP protocol supports reliable data transmission between two Internet hosts. This reliable service is built on top of an unreliable network by requiring data recipients to acknowledge packets received (positive acknowledgement). Both sides in the reliable connection must maintain state for unacknowledged packets to permit retransmission in case of loss detection. This mechanism could ostensibly be used in one-to-many transmissions. However, this approach is almost never used due to its scalability limitations. Positive acknowledgement would nullify many of the advantages of multicast since they would create a flood of acknowledgement packets towards the sender, and would require per-receiver maintenance of state in the sender. Scalable reliable multicasting is a difficult problem that is still the subject of research. The current Internet multicasting protocol provides an unreliable service.

IP Multicasting

The current Internet multicasting protocol was introduced in 1991, and published as IETF RFC 966 & RFC 988. These were superceded by RFC 1112, which is available at http://www.ietf.org/rfc/rfc1112.txt). The IP multicast protocol takes a minimalist approach to multicast service. In terms of the four challenges previously described (addressing, membership, routing, reliability) the IETF IP multicast design can be described as using:

- ❑ **IPv4 class D group addressing**: Host groups are identified by class D IP addresses starting with binary "1110", in the range 224.0.0.0-239.255.255.255. This range was allocated in the original IP specification for this use. Unlike unicast addresses, which are uniquely assigned to each organization, most IPv4 multicast group addresses are not allocated to particular organizations (some exceptions to this will be covered later in the chapter). Any Internet node can attempt to send as well as receive datagrams to any group address using any IP-based protocol. The IP multicast layer does not provide any address allocation support; it is the responsibility of multicast applications to coordinate temporary allocation of group addresses.

- ❑ **Dynamic membership**: Hosts may join and leave groups at any time. Group membership is not restricted in location or size. Hosts may belong to more than one group at a given time. Group membership is not required for datagram transmission. That is, a host can send datagrams to a group without being a member.

- ❑ **Multiple routing protocols**: The original IP multicast specification focused on Internet host multicast support. The specification did not state how routers communicate to maintain the multicast service at the core of the network. Instead, the specification defined the protocol used for communication between a multicast-enabled host and its immediately neighboring router. As a result, multiple standard multicast routing protocols have been defined for router-to-router multicast support.

- ❑ **Unreliable delivery**: Multicast packets are delivered with the same "best-effort" reliability as regular unicast IP packets. A multicast datagram may be delivered to all, some, or none of the members in a group. Multicast datagrams may arrive in different ordering at each receiver, and receivers may see a different subset of the datagrams sent due to loss. No standard reliable multicast transport protocol was defined.

Although the IP multicast protocol has been around for about 10 years, it has yet to become universally available. Some people may even choose to characterize it as a failure. To be fair, the problem of providing a scalable universal multicast service is significantly harder than that of providing unicast service. There have been several significant roadblocks to the wide adoption of the IP multicast protocol:

- ❑ **Deployment**: IP multicast is a network-layer service. In contrast, most Internet protocols are transport-or application-layer services. An important difference is that network-layer services must be deployed on *all* Internet nodes, while transport-and application-layer services need only be deployed on *some* of the edge nodes. For example, when the WWW was first conceived it only required the installation of an HTTP server on a host, and some HTTP/HTML clients on one or more other hosts. This is simple, whereas to get all core Internet service providers to install experimental software on their prized routers is a lot more difficult. In fact it might not even be possible as most routers are dedicated proprietary devices and not programmable by general users.

❏ **Scalability**: the original multicast routing protocols were based on a flat network topology. Because IP multicast group addresses were allocated in an arbitrary manner, the size of the multicast routing tables increased proportionally with the number of groups. A new generation of hierarchical multicast routing protocols was developed to address this issue but its deployment has been slow.

❏ **Unpredictability**: the engineering of IP networks is a difficult task due to the lack of traffic reservation or admission policy mechanisms, which would allow you to control the flow of data. Every Internet host is typically free to pump as much data as its Internet access link will allow. This creates a nightmare situation for Internet Service Providers (ISP) who would like to assure customers that their access is not severely affected by the behavior of other customers. For this reason, ISPs usually overprovision their backbone networks, and then limit the bandwidth in the access points to prevent any single source from flooding the backbone.

Perversely, even though multicast was created to improve network efficiency, its deployment on ISP backbones is currently deemed as too risky. This mostly stems from the scalability problems, and the immaturity of cross-domain multicast protocols (discussed later). Some Internet Service Providers have addressed this problem by creating a separate backbone dedicated to multicast transmission.

Due to the above-mentioned problems, many networks participating in the Internet do not carry external IP multicast traffic. Even though they may not be routing IP multicast externally, most of these networks support multicast internally. There are many advantages to using IP multicast even within a single administrative network. Besides the typical multicast streaming applications, such as internal conferencing and shared-whiteboard/design applications, multicast can also be useful for resource discovery. Consider a mobile work force that moves frequently within a single administrative network (for example, a corporate network). When users move to a new location, they would ideally like to discover and use the local resources, such as printers, scanners, etc. If all printers would listen to a given multicast group, then the user could multicast a request query in order to discover the locally available resources. The Jini technology from Sun Microsystems generalizes this idea to provide dynamic discovery of network services using multicast.

Multicast Backbone (MBONE)

To combat the seemingly insurmountable deployment problem, the IETF created a semi-permanent IP multicast network called the **MBONE** (**Multicast Backbone**). The MBONE is a **virtual network** that uses the transmission facilities of the Internet to create **virtual links** between nodes. Multicast datagrams traverse virtual links by being encapsulated into unicast datagrams addressed to the virtual link end-point. For example, consider a university whose routers support IP multicasting. We will assume that the university is connected to the Internet via an Internet Service Provider that is not part of the MBONE. The university can join the MBONE by creating a virtual link with another network that is part of the MBONE. The end-points of this virtual link will be routers that are configured to wrap every multicast datagram in a unicast datagram addressed to the other side of the link.

An example of how such a virtual topology operates is shown in the diagram below. Two networks supporting multicast would like to exchange multicast traffic. Unfortunately, they are connected via one or more legacy routers that do not support multicast routing. The solution is to establish a virtual link, also known as a **tunnel**, between the multicast routers A and B. Multicast datagrams that must be transmitted over this virtual link are encapsulated in a unicast datagram that is addressed to the IP address of the other router.

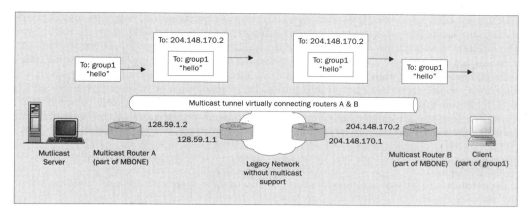

For example, the multicast server on the left sends a datagram to all members of a particular group (called group1 for clarity; in reality it will be a class-D IP address). Upon receipt of the multicast datagram, router A consults its multicast routing table and finds out that the packet must be sent to router B. Because router B is connected over a tunnel, router A creates a new IP datagram destined for router B with the complete datagram packet (IP header + data) as payload. The legacy network then routes the unicast packet just like any other and attempts to deliver it to router B. Upon receipt, router B looks at the packet and figures out that it is tunnel traffic, so it extracts its payload and uses the payload's IP header to transmit the multicast datagram as if directly received from router A.

One of the biggest problems in maintaining a large virtual network, such as the MBONE, is ensuring that the virtual links (tunnels) are created efficiently. Ideally, multiple tunnels should never be layered over a single physical link. In practice, assuring such efficient allocation is difficult, because the physical topology of the Internet is not fixed, and new networks are constantly added to the MBONE. A mapping of the virtual network that made sense at creation time may no longer be efficient due to changes in physical topology.

Although the MBONE has increased in size over the years, its members continue to be mostly research and education organizations. Commercial organizations have not adopted the MBONE largely due to the lack of support by major Internet Service Providers.

> **It is important to distinguish the IP multicast protocols from the multicast backbone (MBONE). Due to the aforementioned problems, IP multicast is not universally routed on the Internet today. Many corporate networks support IP multicast internally, but do not connect to the global MBONE network. Therefore developers cannot assume that any two Internet hosts can communicate using IP multicast.**

IP Multicast Addressing

Unicast IP addresses in the range `0.0.0.0 - 223.255.255.255` uniquely identify the location of an Internet host. In order to support scalable routing, these addresses are allocated in blocks characterized by a shared prefix, as described in Chapter 8. Each block may be further subdivided, for example, an ISP will divide its blocks amongst its customers, who may further subdivide them internally. Using this hierarchical approach, backbone routers can aggregate routing information using shortest prefix summarization, with each organization free to manage its own assigned addresses. If a host is assigned an address outside the allotted blocks, then that host will not be reachable from outside the organization's network.

Unlike unicast IPv4 addresses, IPv4 multicast addresses are not assigned hierarchically. Every multicast address in the range `224.0.0.0 - 239.255.255.255` can be used as a group identifier by any multicast-enabled application anywhere in the world. Clearly, this creates a problem in that no application can be assured exclusive access to an IP multicast group. Because the IP multicast model permits all hosts to join a multicast group, and even allows hosts to send multicast IP packets without joining, every multicast transport or application-layer protocol must be able to detect "foreign" traffic. That is, multicast applications must have a mechanism for identifying traffic conforming to their protocol and session. The main disadvantage of having two multicast applications using the same group address is unnecessary propagation of multicast traffic.

Session Discovery

One problem caused by this arbitrary multicast group address assignment is session discovery. If clients are to discover the current multicast group of a well-known service, a shared directory mechanism must be used. In the unicast Internet, this role is played by the Domain Name System service (DNS). The DNS system, however, is not well suited for storing highly dynamic information, due to its caching architecture. There are two IP multicast address assignment mechanisms in use on the MBONE today static assignments and dynamic reservation.

Static Assignments

The Internet Corporation for Assigned Names and Numbers (ICANN) will assign permanent multicast addresses to well-known protocols, long-lived multicast sessions and large companies. For example, static addresses have been assigned to Sun Microsystems, one of which was used for the Jini multicast discovery protocol. Jini clients can therefore be hard-coded to use that permanently assigned address. It is the responsibility of other multicast applications not to use permanently assigned addresses.

Dynamic Reservation

For short-lived multicast sessions, a dynamic reservation mechanism was devised. Reservation announcements are multicast to a well-known group address and are formatted using the **Session Announcement Protocol** (**SAP**) (experimental IETF RFC 2974). Announcements can be made for immediate or future multicast group use. Before using a multicast address, applications are supposed to listen to a specific multicast channel for group reservation announcements. This wait period is typically at least 10 minutes long. At the end of this period the application picks a multicast group address that has not been reserved and starts sending its own periodic reservation messages. Clearly, this is not a fail-proof mechanism. Group address conflicts may occur if two applications simultaneously pick the same address, or if reservation announcements are lost. Since group address conflicts only have a performance implication, they can be acceptable for a short period until they can be detected and the applications attempt to switch to using another address.

Session Discovery Tools

The reservation multicast group can also be used as a broadcast schedule guide. In addition to the multicast address used, the reservation protocol carries a user description of the session, as well as information about the session protocol and payload encoding. A user tool called SDR can be used to display scheduled multicast sessions to users. The SDR tool is freely available for several platforms (including Windows, and Linux) at http://www-mice.cs.ucl.ac.uk/multimedia/software/sdr/. At the time of writing, the latest release was version 3; two downloads are available, one for IPv4 and another for IPv6 networks.

A sample SDRv3 session listing on an IPv4 MBONE-connected host is shown below. The main window on the left shows a number of advertised sessions by title. The session window on the right shows details about the "NASA TV" session, including the scheduled transmission time, multicast group address and ports (one for audio and another for video), as well as the audio/video encoding of the transmission. Note that if your host is not on an MBONE-connected network, only local session announcements will be received.

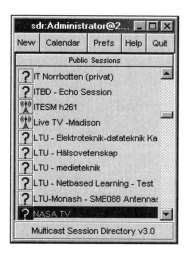 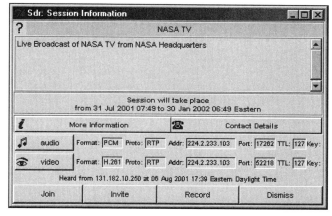

IP Multicast Scoping

Some IP multicast applications may desire to limit the scope of their multicast transmissions. Possible reasons include:

- ❑ Security and privacy

- ❑ Limiting network resources usage (bandwidth/routing load)

- ❑ Avoiding address conflicts

It should be noted that depending on any type of multicast scoping for security or privacy is probably not a very good idea. Currently, there are two mechanisms for scoping multicast transmissions: Time-to-Live scoping (TTL), and administrative scoping.

Time-to-Live Scoping

In TTL scoping the IP time-to-live field is used as the radius of a multicast transmission in terms of the number of hops. Every time an IP packet is forwarded, its TTL value is decreased by one. If the TTL value reaches zero before the destination has been reached, then that packet is discarded. This mechanism was originally introduced to limit the effect of IP routing loops. These occur when packets travel in continuous loops due to redundant links in the routing table.

If you wanted to multicast only on the local area network, then multicast packets could be transmitted with a TTL of one. This value would guarantee that the packet could be picked up by other hosts, but would be discarded by the local router. Using the TTL field to control the extent of transmission propagation can be a difficult task. For example, if one wanted to multicast to all of an organization, then you would need to know the exact topology of the network to determine the TTL. Moreover, unless the server was situated in the middle of the network, then no single TTL would exist that could reach all of the organization's nodes without leaving the network. For example, in the diagram below, a multicast source is connected to a corporate network via a departmental router. The local router is directly connected to the marketing and accounting department routers, as well as the Internet access router. Some departments are further connected to other routers representing internal divisions.

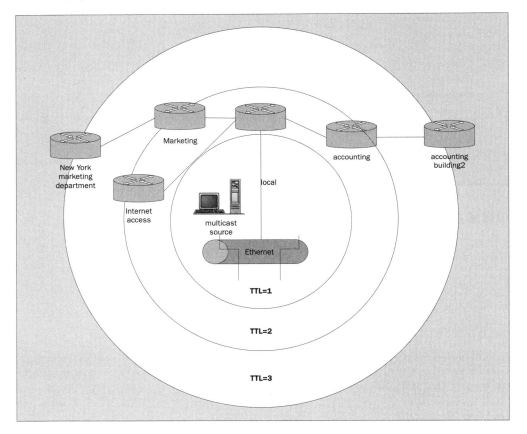

If the multicast source broadcasts a packet with TTL=1, then only the local area network hosts will receive it, that is, it's received by the router, but then discarded because the TTL will have hit zero before getting out "the other side". A packet with TTL=2 will be forwarded to subscribed receivers that are one-hop off. In this case, only routers are one-hop off, so this TTL is not really useful. A TTL=3 will send the packet to all subscribed receivers that are two-hops off. This will include hosts connected to the marketing and accounting departments, but also hosts connected to the Internet access router (oops). In order to reach all organization hosts, in this example, a TTL of 4 is needed, but that will also mean that packets will leak into the Internet.

In order to reduce the guesswork involved in TTL scoping, certain arbitrary values were assigned for specific scopes (called TTL-threshold). The table below shows these assignments:

TTL	Scoping Restriction
= 0	Local host
= 1	Local subnet
<= 32	Site (organization)
<= 64	Region
<= 128	Continent
> 128 (<= 255)	Unrestricted

These assignments are not foolproof as they depend on the correct configuration of the routers involved. For example, if an organization does not configure its Internet access routers to drop multicast packets with TTL less than 32, then these packets will be transmitted on the Internet (up to the specified TTL radius).

Administrative Scoping

The second scoping mechanism is more recent and involves the use of specially assigned IP multicast groups. The range of IP multicast addresses has been further subdivided into blocks. Use of the addresses from each block has implications for the scope of the multicast transmission. This type of scoping is called Administrative Scoped IP Multicast and is defined in IETF RFC 2365 (http://www.ietf.org/rfc/rfc2365.txt). Although the use of administrative scoping may appear to be similar to the use of TTL scoping, it is preferred because TTL scoping interacts negatively with the IP multicast routing protocols. Basically, dropped packets due to TTL expiration interfere with the multicast tree maintenance. To understand why this is the case requires the introduction of several complex topics that are inappropriate here.

IP Range	Scoping Restriction
224.0.0.0 – 224.0.0.255	Link-scope addresses assigned to routing protocols. Addresses in this range are not routed and hence remain local.
224.0.1.0 – 224.0.1.255	Individual addresses assigned to application protocols.
224.0.2.0 – 238.255.255.255	Assigned to companies and applications (global).
239.192.0.0 – 239.251.255.255	Organization-local scope. Not routed outside an organization and therefore can be privately used.
239.255.0.0 – 239.255.255.255	Local-scope. Not routed outside the local scope (further limited from organization-local).

IP Multicast Routing

There are two components to IP multicast routing. The first component is the protocol used by the edge hosts to request multicast group join and leave requests from their first-hop routers. The second component is the IP multicast routing protocol used between routers to efficiently route multicast IP datagrams. The first component is standard for all multicast hosts and is known as the Internet Group Management Protocol (IGMP). The second component is non-standard and is chosen by network administrations.

IP hosts report group membership to immediately neighboring multicast routers using the Internet Group Management Protocol (IGMP). IGMP is defined as part of the "Host Extensions for IP Multicasting" IETF RFC 1112 (http://www.ietf.org/rfc/rfc1112.txt). All Internet hosts that support IP multicast must implement the IGMP protocol. IGMP messages are encapsulated in IP datagrams with a specified binary format. Operationally, there are two types of IGMP messages:

❑ **Host membership query**: Periodically sent by every multicast router to solicit host membership reports (usually no more than once a minute). The query is addressed to the special all-local-hosts multicast group (224.0.0.1) with an IP TTL of 1. Every multicast host is supposed to listen to the 224.0.0.1 group for multicast router membership queries.

❑ **Host membership report**: Hosts send IGMP membership reports in response to a membership query. A separate report is sent for every group for which a local process has requested a join. Each IGMP report is addressed to the joined group and has an IP TTL of 1. In order to prevent an "implosion" of reports, hosts pick a random delay in sending their report. If another host has sent a report for a given group during this delay interval, the report is not sent. This is acceptable since the multicast routers do not need to know how many hosts have joined a group, just that there is at least one.

Version 1 of the IGMP protocol did not provide an explicit group leave message. Multicast routers that have not received a membership report for a specific group after a certain number of queries will simply drop the group from their join-list. Version 2 (IETF RFC 2236 – http://www.ietf.org/rfc/rfc2236.txt) of the IGMP protocol added an explicit leave message in order to support faster pruning of the multicast tree.

Multicast Routing Protocols

The second component to multicast routing is the protocol used between multicast routers. There are multiple multicast routing protocols in use today. They can be roughly divided into two categories: **dense mode** and **sparse mode** multicast protocols. Dense mode protocols perform better when used in a topology densely populated with group members. Their main disadvantage is that they maintain state information for each source at every router in the network. Sparse mode protocols provide better scalability. However, sparse protocols depend on a rendezvous point for synchronization, they typically have a single point of failure. Sparse protocols may also generate non-optimal paths in the multicast tree when routing from the source to the rendezvous point and then to the receivers.

The choice of IP multicast routing protocols is not in the user's control and therefore their coverage is an advanced topic not suitable for this book. The original MBONE routing protocol was called DVMRP (Distance Vector Multicast Routing Protocol) and was a dense mode routing protocol. Newer protocols include PIM (Protocol Independent Multicast) which is a protocol supporting a dense mode, as well as a sparse mode and CBT (Core Based Trees) which is a sparse mode protocol.

Multicast Port Addressing

The Internet Protocol does not support any application-level addressing. IP datagrams may only be addressed to a particular IP address representing a location or a multicast group. For this reason, Internet transport layer protocols such as TCP and UDP add an additional application addressing service using 16-bit port identifiers. TCP cannot be used for multicast transmission since the protocol is built on the assumption that there are only two parties to a streaming connection. Moreover, as discussed in Chapter 10, applications typically do not use raw IP for transmission because it does not detect payload corruption, does not provide application-level addressing and many times is restricted by operating systems due to security considerations. For these reasons, Internet multicast applications typically use the UDP protocol to send datagrams to IP multicast group addresses. In many cases, the UDP datagrams sent contain RTP (Real Time Protocol) formatted data. The RTP protocol was presented at the end of Chapter 10 and is used to provide sequencing and encoding information for real-time streaming.

Multicast UDP applications use port numbers in a different way than unicast UDP applications. In traditional UDP unicast transmissions, port numbers are used to de-multiplex incoming packets for delivery to different applications. In multicast transmission this behavior is not as useful, since different applications typically use different multicast group addresses to avoid sharing traffic. Another important difference is that the semantics of multicast allow for multiple applications to send and receive multicast packets using the same group and port number. Therefore, multiple applications may use the same UDP port for sending and receiving multicast traffic on the same host/address! In other words, multicast UDP ports no longer uniquely identify a single application as a recipient, in the same way that IP multicast group addresses no longer identify a single Internet node as a recipient.

> **It is possible to concurrently bind multiple times to the same multicast port, either in the same or in different processes. The behavior of the multicast protocol stack will be to deliver a copy of each received datagram to all bound sockets. Conversely, every socket may be used to send multicast datagrams marked as originating from the shared port.**

If multicast group addresses are typically used by a single session, why should multicast applications need to use port numbers at all? The main reason is that the single session may transmit datagrams using different protocols and/or different encodings. For example, earlier we showed a multicast session announcement for "NASA TV" that advertised multicast transmission using group address 224.2.233.103 with a PCM-encoded audio stream sent using the RTP protocol to port 17262 and an H.261-encoded video stream sent using the RTP protocol to port 52218 (PCM and H.261 are content encoding standards like WAV and MPEG). When a multicast host joins the 224.2.233.103 group, it will receive both the video and the audio traffic. The different port numbers will enable the client to potentially use different programs for receiving the audio and the video stream. In many cases, a source will transmit the audio and video streams on separate group addresses to enable receivers to join to either or both. For example, a host connected via a slow link may chose to only join the audio multicast group.

Java IP Multicast Programming

IP multicast is a network layer service, and as such, can potentially be used with different transport layer protocols. Of the two popular Internet transport layer protocols, however, only the connectionless UDP protocol is applicable, since the TCP protocol is connection-oriented and synchronizes state between two participants. As a result, nearly all multicast traffic today uses UDP as its transport layer encapsulation. Even real-time streaming applications using the Real Time Protocol (RTP) send data as RTP over UDP over multicast-IP.

The Java network libraries support multicast transmission through instances of the `java.net.MulticastSocket` class. The `MulticastSocket` class extends the UDP `java.net.DatagramSocket` class with multicast-specific operations, such as joining and leaving a multicast group. In the subsequent discussion, it will be assumed that readers are familiar with the coverage of the `DatagramPacket`, and `DatagramSocket` classes in the preceding chapter.

java.net.MulticastSocket

A `MulticastSocket` is a UDP socket with extra support for the IGMP multicast group management protocol. As a UDP extension, multicast sockets instances are also associated with UDP port numbers, but with the different semantics discussed earlier. Most importantly, multiple `MulticastSocket` instances may be bound to the same port!

Constructors

Two constructors may be used in creating `MulticastSocket` instances:

```
MulticastSocket() throws IOException

MulticastSocket(int port) throws IOException
```

The first is a no-argument constructor that creates a multicast socket bound to an arbitrary port. After construction, the local port number used may be retrieved by invoking the `getLocalPort()` method. Similarly to the `DatagramSocket` no-argument constructor, the `java.io.IOException` is used to signal an error in allocating resources for the multicast socket. A `SecurityException` will be thrown if the `checkListen()` `SocketPermission` has not been granted (see Chapter 7). As a runtime exception, the `SecurityException` is not listed in the method's signature but has been added to the text for clarity purposes.

The second constructor is more commonly used and allows invokers to specify the port number used for binding. Although only one port number is typically used per multicast group address, its use must be consistent across all members. Currently, Java does not support arrival notification for all multicast packets destined for a particular group irrespective of the port number. The same exceptions are thrown as in the previous constructor. Unlike the `DatagramSocket(int)` constructor, an `IOException` will not be thrown if this or another local process has already bound to the socket, because the multicast protocol permits such behavior.

> By default, **MulticastSocket** instances are set to transmit datagrams with a time-to-live value of 1. This means that multicast transmissions will be constrained to the local area network. The default TTL value can be changed by invoking the **setTimeToLive()** method as described later in this section.

Methods

The `MulticastSocket` class supports IGMP-based IP multicast membership via two methods. The `joinGroup()` method may be used to request subscription for the specified multicast group from the first-hop (local) router. The method takes an IP address represented as a `java.net.InetAddress` instance as its only argument. The address must represent a multicast address, as defined by the `InetAddress isMulticastAddress()` method, otherwise a `SocketException` is thrown. Due to the nature of the IGMP protocol, the method returns immediately without indication of remote success or failure. Only local failures can be detected, and are signaled by an `IOException` if the IGMP request could not be sent at all, or a `SecurityException` if the "accept, connect" `SocketPermission` permissions have not been granted (as a runtime exception it is not listed in the method signature but shown here for clarity). If the local host does not support IP multicast on any of its interfaces, a `SocketException` may be thrown (platform dependent; discussed later in the multicast host configuration section).

```
void joinGroup(InetAddress mcastaddr) throws IOException
```

After the `joinGroup()` method has been invoked, the `MulticastSocket` will periodically transmit IGMP membership reports, and respond to IGMP membership queries as prescribed by the IGMP protocol. In general, the only way to discover that a multicast router is available is to note the receipt of an IGMP membership query request, however, the Java multicast support does not expose this information. As a result, all Java applications can do is to invoke the `joinGroup()` method and hope that packets start arriving at some point! Note that applications are not required to join a multicast group in order to send multicast datagrams destined for that group. However, in order to receive multicast datagrams addressed to a group the `joinGroup()` method must be invoked.

> **MulticastSocket** instances differ from **DatagramSocket** instances in that datagrams addressed to multicast group addresses for which the **joinGroup()** method has been invoked are also received by the transmitter. This creates a loop-back effect. The "Host Extensions for IP Multicasting" IETF RFC 1112 requires implementations to provide a method to disable local delivery of multicast datagrams; however Java versions prior to JDK1.4 did not comply with this requirement. Therefore, Multicast Java applications executed on earlier versions (including JDK 1.3) cannot disable the loop-back effect and must be prepared to receive their own multicast datagrams.

Applications can request to leave a group by invoking the `leaveGroup()` method. If the application has not previously successfully invoked `joinGroup()` for the same IP group address, the `java.net.BindException` will be thrown. If the multicast socket has been closed the method will throw a `SocketException`. The `SocketException` may also be thrown in response to some underlying communications error. A `SecurityException` will be thrown if the "accept, connect" `SocketPermission` permissions have not been granted. This security check is made to prevent an internal denial-of-service-type attack.

```
void leaveGroup(InetAddress mcastaddr) throws IOException
```

As we explained in Chapter 8, a host may be attached to the Internet through multiple network interfaces, each with its own IP address. By default, the `MulticastSocket` constructor binds the multicast socket to all available interfaces. The effect of this behavior is that the decision of which interface to use is left to the operating system. In nearly all cases, this is the most appropriate approach. In some rare cases a Java multicast program may need to have control over interface selection. For example, a Java program running on a host connected to a corporate network as well as the public Internet may want to restrict its multicast operations to the corporate network interface. The `setInterface()` method takes as a single argument the IP address of one of the local host's interfaces. A `SocketException` will be thrown if the address does not belong to a local interface, or an error occurred while configuring the socket. Invoking the method with the special "0.0.0.0" IP address will restore the default behavior of binding to all sockets. As we discussed in Chapter 8, there was no method prior to JDK1.4 for discovering all interfaces in a host. Therefore, this information would need to be supplied externally. For this reason, the `setInterface()` method was rarely invoked.

```
void setInterface(InetAddress inf) throws SocketException;
```

The `getInterface()` method returns the address of the interface set by the last `setInterface()` invocation, or the special address "0.0.0.0" marking the fact that the multicast socket is not bound to a particular interface. The method may throw a `SocketException` if the multicast socket's configuration cannot be read.

```
InetAddress getInterface() throws SocketException;
```

The IP time-to-live (TTL) field plays a special role in multicast transmission. As was explained earlier in this chapter, the TTL field was originally used to scope the range of multicast transmissions. For example, a TTL of 1 restricts the multicast packet to the local-area network (defined in terms of the LAN broadcast radius), while a TTL less than 32 should restrict the transmission to the local-organization network (depending on router configuration).

The `MulticastSocket` class adds a method for setting and a method for retrieving the default TTL of a multicast socket. The `setTimeToLive()` method deprecates the old `setTTL()` and takes a TTL value as its only argument. The method will throw an `IOException` if the TTL value is invalid, that is not in the range [0..255], or an error occurred while configuring the multicast socket. The `getTimeToLive()` method returns the current TTL value for the socket. The method may also throw an `IOException` if the socket's configuration could not be read.

```
void setTimeToLive(int ttl) throws IOException;
int getTimeToLive() throws IOException;
```

In addition to the `send()` method inherited from `DatagramSocket`, instances of `MulticastSocket` can be asked to transmit a `DatagramPacket` with a specific time-to-live value. This allows applications to temporarily override the current socket TTL for one particular transmission. As in the `DatagramSocket send()` method, a transmission error is signaled by an `IOException` and may be caused by misconfiguration of the `DatagramPacket` (missing address/port), an invalid TTL, or some internal protocol stack error. A `SecurityException` will be thrown if the code-base has not been granted the "accept, connect" permissions. The security requirements are more stringent than those for unicast UDP transmissions, where only the "connect" permission is required. The security requirements also apply for the inherited `send(DatagramPacket)` method.

```
void send(DatagramPacket p, int ttl) throws IOException
```

The `MulticastSocket` class inherits all the methods of the `DatagramSocket` class. Readers should refer to Chapter 10 for coverage of these methods.

Multicast Security Permissions

Multicast operations are security sensitive. In a normal denial of service attack, a single destination is flooded with requests from multiple hosts. Using the multicast protocol, a rogue application can abuse network resources in a much more effective way, flooding a large multicast group from a single host. Using the multiplicative effect of the multicast protocol attackers can cause damage that is disproportionate to their Internet access bandwidth. Even permission to join a group without the right to transmit can be dangerous. An attacking application could simply subscribe to all multicast groups possibly completely overwhelming the local network's Internet access link. Another problem with multicast transmission is that the local security manager cannot determine which hosts will receive the transmission. The IP multicast protocol is distributed and hence no one knows the membership of a group. For these reasons, multicast access should be restricted to trusted applications. That is why Java applets are typically not given multicast access.

The Java `SocketPermission` security model defines four types of operations; their mapping to actual `SecurityManager` methods is shown below:

Operations	Method
Resolving	`checkConnect(host, -1)`
Listening	`checkListen(port)`
Connecting	`checkConnect(host, port)`
Accepting	`checkAccept(host, port)`

Note: there is no `checkResolve(host)` method as you might expect; instead the `checkConnect()` method is used with the invalid port number −1 as an argument (don't ask us why!).

The `MulticastSocket` adds an additional check called `checkMulticast()`:

```
public void checkMulticast(InetAddress maddr)
```

The `checkMulticast()` method is invoked when joining or leaving a group, and when sending a packet to a multicast group address (in addition to `checkConnect()`). You would therefore expect that the `SocketPermission` class would support an explicit "multicast" permission; this is however not the case. Instead, the `checkMulticast(InetAddress)` method is translated into two other calls for `checkAccept(InetAddress)` and `checkConnect(InetAddress)`.

Given the lack of an explicit "multicast" `SocketPermission`, how can we restrict applications from using multicast, but still perform unicast operations? The answer is not to grant permissions to multicast class-D IP addresses (range `224.0.0.0-239.255.255.255`). Unfortunately, the current `SocketPermission` class does not permit use of a network mask in the host argument. Therefore, it is not possible to restrict applications using the default security manager. The answer will be to extend the security manager and override the `checkMulticast()` method to provide the missing functionality.

IP Multicast Host Configuration

Today, most popular computing platforms include support for IP multicast. Multicasting is supported by the 32-bit versions of the Microsoft Windows operating systems family as well as most modern UNIX-based operating systems (Solaris, Linux, MacOS X, AIX). Support however does not imply that multicast will work out of the box. In some cases, some extra configuration may be required. A test program is provided at the end of this section to verify your host's IP multicast configuration.

It will be assumed that the network your host is connected to supports IP multicast. If the network does not support multicast there is not much you can do as a user, except contact your local systems administrators. To find out if your network is connected to the MBONE you can either ask your systems administrators, or download and execute the SDR utility presented earlier in this section.

Configuring Microsoft Windows (32-bit)

The Microsoft Windows 32-bit operating systems support multicast transmission over Ethernet and other popular link-layer protocols by default. No special configuration is required for such "real" interfaces. Unfortunately, Microsoft Windows-based operating systems currently do not support IP multicast transmission over the loopback interface. The loopback interface is a virtual interface used to provide local delivery of IP packets. As a result, standalone Microsoft Windows hosts cannot execute multicast applications! A possible work-around is to install a network interface card and configure it for some specific IP address. Note that it is not sufficient to just install a network interface card; it must be configured as well. Mobile users who use the Dynamic Host Configuration Protocol (DHCP) will need to manually enter an IP address when not connected to the network in order to test multicast applications.

Configuring GNU/Linux

The Linux kernel provides optional support for IP multicast. Nearly all current GNU/Linux distributions ship with IP multicast support. Unfortunately, some distributions, such as RedHat, do not enable multicast support in the IP interface by default, and do not include a default multicast route. You can check the configuration of your interfaces by using the `ifconfig` command as shown below. This example was executed on a host running RedHat Linux, with one Ethernet network interface and a loop-back interface. Users need to look for the MULTICAST flag (shown in bold).

```
$ /sbin/ifconfig -a
eth0   Link encap:Ethernet  HWaddr 00:10:4B:C6:D3:39
       inet addr:128.59.22.27  Bcast:128.59.23.255  Mask:255.255.248.0
       UP BROADCAST RUNNING MULTICAST  MTU:1500  Metric:1
       RX packets:95096460 errors:0 dropped:0 overruns:61 frame:0
       TX packets:18386848 errors:0 dropped:0 overruns:0 carrier:0
       collisions:0 txqueuelen:100
       Interrupt:11 Base address:0x1400

lo     Link encap:Local Loopback
       inet addr:127.0.0.1  Mask:255.0.0.0
       UP LOOPBACK RUNNING  MTU:16436  Metric:1
       RX packets:8340660 errors:0 dropped:0 overruns:0 frame:0
       TX packets:8340660 errors:0 dropped:0 overruns:0 carrier:0
       collisions:0 txqueuelen:0
```

If the MULTICAST flag is missing, pick an interface you want to enable IP multicast transmission on, and then execute the ifconfig utility as root:

/sbin/ifconfig eth0 multicast

You must also verify that a route exists to the multicast interface in the host's routing table. Invoke the route utility as shown:

```
$ /sbin/route
Kernel IP routing table
Destination    Gateway         Genmask        Flags Metric Ref   Use Iface
128.59.16.0    *               255.255.248.0  U     0      0       0 eth0
127.0.0.0      *               255.0.0.0      U     0      0       0 lo
224.0.0.0      *               240.0.0.0      U     0      0       0 eth0
default        vortex-gw.net.c 0.0.0.0        UG    0      0       0 eth0
```

Look for the line listing the 224.0.0.0/240.0.0.0 route (shown in bold). If it is missing you must add it by invoking:

>/sbin/route add –net 224.0.0.0 netmask 240.0.0.0 dev eth0

Replace eth0 with the interface you selected in the previous step.

Testing Your Configuration

The following small program may be used to test your host's multicast configuration. The program creates a MulticastSocket bound to a specific port, and joins a multicast group belonging to the link-local administrative scope. We further guarantee that multicast datagrams will not leave the local network by explicitly setting the TTL to 1 (its default value).

```java
// TestLocalMulticast.java

import java.net.*;

public class TestLocalMulticast {

  public static void main(String[] args)
          throws UnknownHostException, SocketException,
                 java.io.IOException {

    int port = 5265;
    InetAddress group = InetAddress.getByName("239.255.10.10");

    System.out.println("Binding multicast socket to "
                    + group.getHostAddress() + ":" + port + " ...");
    MulticastSocket msocket = new MulticastSocket(port);
    msocket.setSoTimeout(10000);
    msocket.setTimeToLive(1);   // restrict to local delivery

    System.out.println("Requesting multicast group membership ...");
    msocket.joinGroup(group);
```

A `DatagramPacket` instance is then created, and a message is addressed to the multicast group at the specified port. After sending the datagram to the group, the program tries to receive a datagram. Because the multicast datagrams loop-back to the sender, and we have already joined the group, we would expect to receive the datagram that we just sent. Although the multicast service is unreliable, it is extremely unlikely that a datagram would be lost during loop-back delivery. If the datagram is not received within 10 seconds, the socket timeout will expire and an exception will be thrown. Note that o error handling is performed in the program to keep the example simple.

```java
        String outMessage = "Hello multicast world!";
        byte[] data = outMessage.getBytes();
        DatagramPacket packet = new DatagramPacket(data, data.length, group,
                                            port);

        System.out.println("Sending multicast message: " + outMessage);
        msocket.send(packet);

        packet.setData(new byte[512]);
        packet.setLength(512);    // very important!

        System.out.println("Waiting for multicast datagram ...");
        msocket.receive(packet);

        String inMessage = new String(packet.getData(), 0, packet.getLength());
        System.out.println("Received message: " + inMessage);

        System.out.println("Leaving multicast group ...");
        msocket.leaveGroup(group);

        msocket.close();
    }
}
```

On a host correctly configured for at least local IP multicast delivery the above program should produce the output shown below.

C:\Beg_Java_Networking\Ch11>**javac TestLocalMulticast.java**

C:\Beg_Java_Networking\Ch11>**java -classpath . TestLocalMulticast**
Binding multicast socket to 239.255.10.10:5265 ...
Requesting multicast group membership ...
Sending multicast message: Hello multicast world!
Waiting for multicast datagram ...
Received message: Hello multicast world!
Leaving multicast group ...

If an exception is thrown during execution, then the host has not been configured correctly for IP multicast. For example, on a Microsoft Windows host that does not have a real IP interface, the `BindException` will be thrown when attempting to join the multicast group. On GNU/Linux platforms that have not been properly configured the binding and joining requests may succeed, but the datagram receipt will time-out. In such cases, readers should refer to the previous platform configuration discussion and the documentation of the operating system.

In-depth Example: A Group Chat Application

We will develop an in-depth example that will help us highlight some valuable protocol and implementation design patterns. Our goal will be to build a simple group chat application. The application will permit multiple users to join in a chat group and exchange simple string messages. Chat participants will assign themselves nicknames to be used for identification during the session. To simplify the application, no attempt will be made to guarantee uniqueness of nicknames.

Protocol Design

We will use the peer-to-peer paradigm, no single entity will be in control of the chat. As in the multicast model, anyone may join or leave a chat session, and members may send as many messages as they like. In fact, due to the design of the IP multicast protocol, users who have not even joined the group may send messages. Message delivery will not be guaranteed either.

> **Providing scalable reliable multicast is a difficult problem. Reliable multicast is a hot research area but as of today no single proposal has been standardized upon. In the meanwhile, it is advised that multicast be used only for applications that can accept datagram loss.**

Our multicast chat protocol will be simple because we have matched it closely to the IP multicast model. Had our specification required the assignment of unique names, authentication and privacy (encryption) the protocol would have been much more complicated. As it stands, the protocol will use the following three simple PDUs (Protocol Data Units), a.k.a. message-types:

❑ **JOIN PDU**: This is a datagram multicast when a user first joins; includes the user's self-assigned username (string)

❑ **LEAVE PDU**: This datagram is multicast when a user leaves the group; it includes the user's self-assigned username

❑ **MESSAGE PDU**: This datagram is multicast when a user finishes typing a message; it includes the self-assigned username, and a string containing the message

Every multicast application must be capable of coexisting with another application using a different protocol on the same multicast group and port. One simple solution is to begin every datagram sent with a so-called magic number. The magic number can be any binary value whose length makes it highly unlikely that the same value will be picked by two protocol authors. In the multicast chat application we will be using a randomly chosen 64-bit value. Following the magic number, every multicast chat datagram will contain a 32-bit integer value identifying the PDU-type (JOIN, LEAVE, MESSAGE). This is likely overkill in terms of space, but that's what programmers probably thought when deciding not to use a 4-byte year representation (which led to the well-known year 2000 problem).

The above pretty much describes the multicast chat application-layer protocol. No synchronization will be provided, so chat messages may arrive at different receivers in different order. You may think that this can simply be addressed by adding a timestamp to the message, but there is a catch. This is that the clocks are unlikely to be closely synchronized and therefore should not be relied upon for ordering. This is a well-known distributed programming problem that has been studied extensively. Interesting enough, many of the algorithms developed are being replaced today by GPS-based clocks whose synchronization can be guaranteed to an extremely small margin of error.

Implementation

Having completed the group chat protocol design, we proceed to design the programmatic and user interface of our application. As in the previous examples, we would like to separate the two in order to support multiple user interfaces. The programmatic interface will consist of a Java class called `MulticastChat` whose instances will encapsulate the participation in a multicast chat. Users may send messages by invoking the `sendMessage()` method of this class. A group chat is a two-way process so we must design a method for receiving incoming messages. For this purpose, we employ the Java AWT event model by defining the `MulticastChatEventListener` interface. Users of `MulticastChat` instances may subscribe to receive notification of incoming multicast chat events (join, leave, message) by registering an object implementing this listener interface. The listener interface is shown below. We have deviated a little from the AWT event model by not defining a `MulticastChatEvent` class in order to keep the example manageable.

```java
// MulticastChatEventListener.java

import java.net.InetAddress;

public interface MulticastChatEventListener
    extends java.util.EventListener {

    // Invoked when a multicast chat message has been received
    void chatMessageReceived(String username, InetAddress host, int port,
                             String message);

    // Invoked when a multicast participant has joined
    void chatParticipantJoined(String username, InetAddress host, int port);

    // Invoked when a multicast participant has left
    void chatParticipantLeft(String username, InetAddress host, int port);
}
```

As stated, the `MulticastChat` class provides a simple programmatic interface to the multicast chat protocol. The constructor takes the participant's self-selected chat identity, the address of the IP multicast group, the port number, and a listener object as arguments. At construction time, the multicast socket is initialized and the multicast chat JOIN message is sent. An alternative design would be to require users to invoke a `sendJoin()` method, or to send the JOIN message in response to the first `sendMessage()` invocation. The advantage of creating and initializing the multicast socket in the constructor is that any exception can be propagated to the caller. Before returning, the constructor starts a new thread that will be used to perform blocking reads from the multicast socket.

This design is similar to the one used in Chapter 10. The class attribute state requirements are predictable. The class must store the constructor's arguments and the multicast socket instance created. This class is a programmatic interface to a simple peer-to-peer multicast chat protocol. Instances of this class provide an entry-point into a multicast chat characterized by a multicast group address and a port number. Users of `MulticastChat` instances may send multicast chat messages (JOIN, LEAVE, MESSAGE), and subscribe for notification of chat message receipt through the `MulticastChatEventListener` interface.

```java
// MulticastChat.java

import java.io.*;
import java.net.*;
import java.util.*;
```

```
public class MulticastChat extends Thread {

  // Identifies a JOIN multicast chat PDU
  public static final int JOIN = 1;

  // Identifies a LEAVE multicast chat PDU
  public static final int LEAVE = 2;

  // Identifies a MESSAGE multicast chat PDU
  public static final int MESSAGE = 3;

  // Chat protocol magic number (preceeds all requests)
  public static final long CHAT_MAGIC_NUMBER = 4969756929653643804L;

  // Default number of milliseconds between terminations checks
  public static final int DEFAULT_SOCKET_TIMEOUT_MILLIS = 5000;

  // Multicast socket used to send and receive multicast protocol PDUs
  protected MulticastSocket msocket;

  // Chat username
  protected String username;

  // Multicast group used
  protected InetAddress group;

  // Listener for multicast chat events
  protected MulticastChatEventListener listener;

  // Controls receive thread execution
  protected boolean isActive;
```

The MulticastChat constructor expects the following arguments:

❑   group: This is the multicast group used for communications

❑   port: This is the port used to bind the multicast socket

❑   ttl: This defines the time to live value used in multicast transmission and hence determines the multicast radius

❑   listener: This defines the object to receive notification of chat events

The constructor initializes the instance variables of the new object and then creates a multicast socket bound to the port argument number and configured to join the multicast group specified in the group argument. Once the multicast socket has been configured, the constructor starts its thread and sends the multicast JOIN request.

```
public MulticastChat(String username, InetAddress group, int port,
                     int ttl,
                     MulticastChatEventListener listener) throws IOException {

  this.username = username;
  this.group = group;
  this.listener = listener;
```

```
    isActive = true;

    // create & configure multicast socket
    msocket = new MulticastSocket(port);
    msocket.setSoTimeout(DEFAULT_SOCKET_TIMEOUT_MILLIS);
    msocket.setTimeToLive(ttl);
    msocket.joinGroup(group);

    // start receive thread and send multicast join message
    start();
    sendJoin();
}
```

We repeat the thread termination pattern used in the TCP and UDP chapter examples, by defining a `terminate()` method. The method changes the `isActive` instance variable so that the next time, the thread read loop is terminated when the socket read timeout expires, or after the next packet is received. It also sends a multicast chat leave message.

```
    public void terminate() throws IOException {
       isActive = false;
       sendLeave();
    }

    // Issues an error message
    protected void error(String message) {
       System.err.println(new java.util.Date() + ": MulticastChat: "
                          + message);
    }
```

Following are methods for sending and receiving multicast chat PDUs. The `sendMessage()` method is public while the `sendJoin()` and `sendLeave()` methods are protected to assure that they will only be called by the constructor and the `terminate()` method. All receive methods are protected because they should only be invoked internally by the class instance thread. The send and receive methods are paired to facilitate protocol verification.

PDUs are written and read using the `DataOutputStream` and `DataInputStream` I/O utilities. Their encoding is well defined and could in principle be replicated by non-Java applications. Every send method begins by writing the multicast chat protocol magic number, and the PDU ID. The receive methods do not reciprocate because the magic number and PDU ID have already been read by the de-multiplexing read loop thread.

```
    // Sends a multicast chat JOIN PDU
    protected void sendJoin() throws IOException {
       ByteArrayOutputStream byteStream = new ByteArrayOutputStream();
       DataOutputStream dataStream = new DataOutputStream(byteStream);

       dataStream.writeLong(CHAT_MAGIC_NUMBER);
       dataStream.writeInt(JOIN);
       dataStream.writeUTF(username);
       dataStream.close();

       byte[] data = byteStream.toByteArray();
       DatagramPacket packet = new DatagramPacket(data, data.length, group,
                                                  msocket.getLocalPort());
       msocket.send(packet);
```

```
    }

    // Processes a multicast chat JOIN PDU and notifies listeners
    protected void processJoin(DataInputStream istream, InetAddress address,
                               int port) throws IOException {
      String name = istream.readUTF();

      try {
        listener.chatParticipantJoined(name, address, port);
      } catch (Throwable e) {}
    }

    // Sends a multicast chat LEAVE PDU
    protected void sendLeave() throws IOException {

      ByteArrayOutputStream byteStream = new ByteArrayOutputStream();
      DataOutputStream dataStream = new DataOutputStream(byteStream);

      dataStream.writeLong(CHAT_MAGIC_NUMBER);
      dataStream.writeInt(LEAVE);
      dataStream.writeUTF(username);
      dataStream.close();

      byte[] data = byteStream.toByteArray();
      DatagramPacket packet = new DatagramPacket(data, data.length, group,
                                                 msocket.getLocalPort());
      msocket.send(packet);
    }

    // Processes a multicast chat LEAVE PDU and notifies listeners
    protected void processLeave(DataInputStream istream, InetAddress address,
                                int port) throws IOException {
      String username = istream.readUTF();

      try {
        listener.chatParticipantLeft(username, address, port);
      } catch (Throwable e) {}
    }

    // Sends a multicast chat MESSAGE PDU
    public void sendMessage(String message) throws IOException {

      ByteArrayOutputStream byteStream = new ByteArrayOutputStream();
      DataOutputStream dataStream = new DataOutputStream(byteStream);

      dataStream.writeLong(CHAT_MAGIC_NUMBER);
      dataStream.writeInt(MESSAGE);
      dataStream.writeUTF(username);
      dataStream.writeUTF(message);
      dataStream.close();

      byte[] data = byteStream.toByteArray();
      DatagramPacket packet = new DatagramPacket(data, data.length, group,
                                                 msocket.getLocalPort());
      msocket.send(packet);
    }

    // Processes a multicast chat MESSAGE PDU and notifies listeners
    protected void processMessage(DataInputStream istream,
                                  InetAddress address,
```

```
                                   int port) throws IOException {
  String username = istream.readUTF();
  String message = istream.readUTF();

  try {
    listener.chatMessageReceived(username, address, port, message);
  } catch (Throwable e) {}
}
```

After studying the earlier TCP and UDP examples, the main read loop should be familiar now. While a terminate() request has not been made, the next datagram packet is read from the multicast socket. The DataOutputStream is used to verify the multicast chat protocol magic number and determine the PDU ID. To keep the example simple, any errors are silently ignored.

```
// Loops receiving and de-multiplexing chat datagrams
public void run() {
  byte[] buffer = new byte[65508];
  DatagramPacket packet = new DatagramPacket(buffer, buffer.length);

  while (isActive) {
    try {

      // DatagramPacket instance length MUST be reset before EVERY receive
      packet.setLength(buffer.length);
      msocket.receive(packet);

      DataInputStream istream =
        new DataInputStream(new ByteArrayInputStream(packet.getData(),
            packet.getOffset(), packet.getLength()));

      long magic = istream.readLong();

      if (magic != CHAT_MAGIC_NUMBER) {
        continue;

      }
      int opCode = istream.readInt();
      switch (opCode) {
      case JOIN:
        processJoin(istream, packet.getAddress(), packet.getPort());
        break;
      case LEAVE:
        processLeave(istream, packet.getAddress(), packet.getPort());
        break;
      case MESSAGE:
        processMessage(istream, packet.getAddress(), packet.getPort());
        break;
      default:
        error("Received unexpected operation code " + opCode + " from "
            + packet.getAddress() + ":" + packet.getPort());
      }

    } catch (InterruptedIOException e) {

    /**
     * No need to do anything since the timeout is only used to
     * force a loop-back and check of the "isActive" value
     */
    } catch (Throwable e) {
```

```
        error("Processing error: " + e.getClass().getName() + ": "
            + e.getMessage());
      }
    }

    try {
      msocket.close();
    } catch (Throwable e) {}
  }
}
```

Our programmatic interface implementation is now complete. The advantage of using the peer-to-peer model is that there are no separate client and server implementations!

The User Interface

The final step will be to develop a user interface for our group chat application. In the previous chapters, we made use of simple command line interfaces. Due to the asynchronous nature of the multicast protocol – messages can arrive while the user is typing – a console-based interface is not really appropriate. Instead, we will develop a simple Swing-based graphical interface. We will assume that readers are familiar with Swing-based GUI development. For those who are not, we recommend looking at *Beginning Java 2 JDK 1.3 Edition, Wrox Press, ISBN 1861003668*. The next section will include complete instructions on how to execute the client.

The user interface will consist of a window containing a large message-log area in the center, and a small message-entry area in the bottom. The Swing JTextArea class will be used to display incoming messages, and the JTextField will be used to support user message entry. Users may signal message completion by pressing the *ENTER* key, or by clicking on a *Send* button provided. The MulticastChatFrame class extends the Swing JFrame to encapsulate the graphical interface. The nesting of the Swing components is shown in the diagram below.

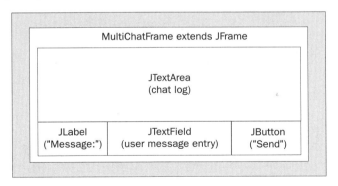

At construction time, the Swing components are initialized, but the group chat session is not initialized. This can be achieved by invoking the join() method with the username, IP multicast group, and port to be used. The join() method then creates a MulticastChat instance passing its own parameters and the MulticastChatFrame object as a listener. After this initialization, all operations are asynchronous. Either a message arrives, signaled by a MulticastChatEventListener method invocation, or the user sends a message. Typically, the interface would provide a menu-based system for parameter entry, but to keep the example small, we read that information from the command line and invoke the join() method from the main() method.

> The Java Swing classes are not thread safe! Once a Swing component has been displayed, all its methods must be invoked from within the Swing event thread. In our application, **MulticastChatEventListener** methods are invoked in the **MulticastChat read()** thread. Therefore, we cannot directly log messages received by invoking methods on the **JTextArea** object. Instead, we use the **SwingUtilities.invokeLater()** method to queue the operation on the Swing event thread. Care must also be taken when performing blocking operations from within the Swing event queue. If the Swing event queue blocks, then the Swing components will "freeze". Because our application uses a non-blocking protocol for sending, we do not have to worry about this problem. Had this not been the case, the *send* **JButton** action would have needed to use a thread to invoke the **MulticastChat.send()** method.

The code for the user interface class is shown below:

```java
// MulticastChatFrame.java

import java.io.IOException;
import java.net.InetAddress;
import java.awt.*;
import java.awt.event.*;
import javax.swing.*;
import javax.swing.text.*;

// A swing-based user interface to a MulticastChat session

public class MulticastChatFrame extends JFrame implements ActionListener,
        WindowListener, MulticastChatEventListener {

  // The multicast chat object
  protected MulticastChat chat;

  // Text area used to log chat join, leave and chat messages received
  protected JTextArea textArea;

  // Scroll pane used for the text area (used to auto-scroll)
  protected JScrollPane textAreaScrollPane;

  // The text field used for message entry
  protected JTextField messageField;

  // Button used to transmit messageField data
  protected JButton sendButton;

  // Constructs a new swing multicast chat frame (in unconnected state)
  public MulticastChatFrame() {
    super("MulticastChat (unconnected)");

    // Construct GUI components (before session)
    textArea = new JTextArea();
    textArea.setEditable(false);
    textArea.setBorder(BorderFactory.createLoweredBevelBorder());

    textAreaScrollPane = new JScrollPane(textArea);
    getContentPane().add(textAreaScrollPane, BorderLayout.CENTER);
```

```
        JPanel messagePanel = new JPanel();
        messagePanel.setLayout(new BorderLayout());

        messagePanel.add(new JLabel("Message:"), BorderLayout.WEST);

        messageField = new JTextField();
        messageField.addActionListener(this);
        messagePanel.add(messageField, BorderLayout.CENTER);

        sendButton = new JButton("Send");
        sendButton.addActionListener(this);
        messagePanel.add(sendButton, BorderLayout.EAST);

        getContentPane().add(messagePanel, BorderLayout.SOUTH);

        // detect window closing and terminate multicast chat session
        addWindowListener(this);
    }

    // Configures the multicast chat session for this interface
    public void join(String username, InetAddress group, int port,
                     int ttl) throws IOException {
        setTitle("MulticastChat " + username + "@" + group.getHostAddress()
                + ":" + port + " [TTL=" + ttl + "]");

        // create multicast chat session
        chat = new MulticastChat(username, group, port, ttl, this);
    }
```

The protected log method is used internally to write a message in the chat text area, and scroll the pane to display it in a thread-safe manner (using `invokeLater`). This must be invoked on swing thread since we're invoked from the action listener methods in the context of the `MulticastChat` receive thread.

```
protected void log(final String message) {
    java.util.Date date = new java.util.Date();

    SwingUtilities.invokeLater(new Runnable() {
      public void run() {
        textArea.append(message + "\n");
        textAreaScrollPane.getVerticalScrollBar()
          .setValue(textAreaScrollPane.getVerticalScrollBar().getMaximum());
      }
    });
  }
```

The `actionPerformed` method is invoked by the Swing event queue in response to asynchronous `ActionListener` events. In our program, it will be invoked when the user presses *ENTER* in the `messageField`, or presses the *Send* button.

```
    public void actionPerformed(ActionEvent e) {

      if ( (e.getSource().equals(messageField)) ||
           (e.getSource().equals(sendButton)) ) {

        String message = messageField.getText();
        messageField.setText("");
```

```
      try {
        chat.sendMessage(message);
      } catch (Throwable ex) {
        JOptionPane.showMessageDialog
          (this, "Error sending message: " + ex.getMessage(),
            "Chat Error", JOptionPane.ERROR_MESSAGE);
      }
    }
  }
```

In the constructor we subscribed to receive notification of window events. Several window-related events may be received. Our application is interested in dealing with two of these: when the window is first opened, and when the user clicks on the window close button. In the windowOpen event, we request focus for the user entry messageField so that users do not have to explicitly click in the message area to type. In the windowClosing event that is triggered when the user clicks on the window close button, we request termination of the chat session.

```
// Invoked the first time a window is made visible.
  public void windowOpened(WindowEvent e) {
    messageField.requestFocus();
  }

  // On closing, terminate multicast chat
  public void windowClosing(WindowEvent e) {
    try {
      if (chat != null) {
        chat.terminate();
      }
    } catch (Throwable ex) {
      JOptionPane.showMessageDialog(this,
                          "Error leaving chat: "
                          + ex.getMessage(), "Chat Error",
                          JOptionPane.ERROR_MESSAGE);
    }
    dispose();
  }
  public void windowClosed(WindowEvent e) {}
  public void windowIconified(WindowEvent e) {}
  public void windowDeiconified(WindowEvent e) {}
  public void windowActivated(WindowEvent e) {}
  public void windowDeactivated(WindowEvent e) {}
```

In order to display incoming JOIN, LEAVE and MESSAGE events we subscribed with the MulticastChat object at construction time. The MulticastChat object will invoke one of the three MulticastChatEventListener methods listed below. Recall that these methods will be invoked in the MulticastChat thread. Therefore, all three implementations log the message to the text area using the protected Swing thread-safe log() method listed earlier.

```
// Invoked by the MulticastChat receive thread when a message has arrived
public void chatMessageReceived(String username, InetAddress address,
                                int port, String message) {
  log(username + ": " + message);
}

// Invoked by the MulticastChat receive thread when a user has joined
public void chatParticipantJoined(String username, InetAddress address,
```

```
                                    int port) {
    log("+++ " + username + " has joined from " + address.getHostName()
        + ":" + port);
}

// Invoked by the MulticastChat receive thread when a user has left
public void chatParticipantLeft(String username, InetAddress address,
                                int port) {
    log("--- " + username + " has left from " + address.getHostName() + ":"
        + port);
}
```

The main() method is responsible for parsing the command-line arguments that include the nickname (username) used in the chat session, the multicast group address and port number, as well as an optional time-to-live (TTL) value. In a production client these values would most likely be queried using a graphical interface.

```
// Command-line invocation expecting three arguments
public static void main(String[] args) {
    if ((args.length != 3) && (args.length != 4)) {
        System.err.println("Usage: MulticastChatFrame "
                        + "<username> <group> <port> { <ttl> }");
        System.err.println("       - default time-to-live value is 1");
        System.exit(1);
    }

    String username = args[0];
    InetAddress group = null;
    int port = -1;
    int ttl = 1;

    try {
        group = InetAddress.getByName(args[1]);
    } catch (Throwable e) {
        System.err.println("Invalid multicast group address: "
                        + e.getMessage());
        System.exit(1);
    }

    if (!group.isMulticastAddress()) {
        System.err.println("Group argument '" + args[1]
                        + "' is not a multicast address");
        System.exit(1);
    }

    try {
        port = Integer.parseInt(args[2]);
    } catch (NumberFormatException e) {
        System.err.println("Invalid port number argument: " + args[2]);
        System.exit(1);
    }

    if (args.length >= 4) {
        try {
            ttl = Integer.parseInt(args[3]);
        } catch (NumberFormatException e) {
            System.err.println("Invalid TTL number argument: " + args[3]);
            System.exit(1);
```

```
      }
    }

    try {
      MulticastChatFrame frame = new MulticastChatFrame();
      frame.setSize(400, 150);

      frame.addWindowListener(new WindowAdapter() {
        public void windowClosed(WindowEvent e) {
          System.exit(0);
        }
      });

      frame.show();

      frame.join(username, group, port, ttl);
    } catch (Throwable e) {
      System.err.println("Error starting frame: " + e.getClass().getName()
                         + ": " + e.getMessage());
      System.exit(1);
    }
  }
}
```

Running the Example

The group chat example code should all be stored in the same directory. The first step will then be to compile the Java source as shown:

C:\Beg_Java_Networking\Ch11>**javac MulticastChatEventListener.java MulticastChat.java MulticastChatFrame.java**

We are going to demonstrate use of the group chat client on a single host. It will be assumed that the host supports multicast as discussed in an earlier section. In our demonstration, we will start two instances of the multicast chat program, one for user A. Bell and another for user T. Watson. An arbitrary local administrative scope IP multicast address (239.255.10.11) and UDP port (4000) will be used. In this example, benhi1 is the name of the Microsoft Windows 2000 host used.

We first start the group chat client for user A. Bell (username is "a-bell").

C:\Beg_Java_Networking\Ch11>**java -classpath . MulticastChatFrame a-bell 239.255.10.11 4000**

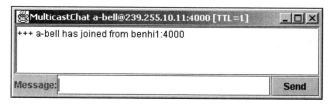

Notice how the chat group JOIN message sent by A. Bell's client is also received by and echoed on the same client (due to the loop-back effect). Next, we start a group chat client for user T. Watson (username is "t-watson").

C:\Beg_Java_Networking\Ch11>**java -classpath . MulticastChatFrame t-watson 239.255.10.11 4000**

A separate client window is started and the chat group JOIN message from T. Watson's client should then be displayed on A. Bell's client as below:

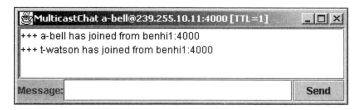

In the next step, we type in a message on A. Bell's client as shown below, and then press the *send* button. The message shown was reportedly the content of the first telephone conversation in history between Alexander Graham Bell and his assistant Thomas Watson.

Mr. Watson come here, I want you.

Once the *Send* button has been clicked (or the *ENTER* key pressed), the message will be sent to the multicast group and will be displayed on both clients.

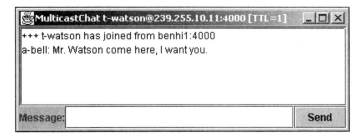

Finally, we demonstrate use of the leave message by closing T. Watson's client window. The multicast chat leave message should be shown on A. Bell's client window as seen below.

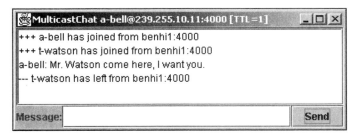

Summary

In this chapter, we have seen that multicasting can offer important reductions in the bandwidth required by a server and backbone networks. Internet applications may effect multicast communications using the IP multicast protocol. Some main points to remember about IP multicasting are:

- In the IP multicast model any host may send a datagram to a group address.

- Groups of Internet hosts are identified by class-D Internet addresses in the range 224.0.0.0 - 239.255.255.255.

- In order to receive multicast datagrams, hosts must request to join one or more groups. The request to join is sent to the first-hop router using the IGMP protocol.

- IP Multicast transmission is unreliable; multicast datagrams are routed with best effort.

- IP multicast transmissions may be scoped using two methods:

    - Using the IP TTL field to restrict the radius of transmission.

    - Administrative scoping which uses a new subdivision of the class-D address space.

Java supports IP multicast programming through the java.net.MulticastSocket class. The MulticastSocket class extends the UDP DatagramSocket class with support for IGMP join/leave operations, the setting of a datagram's TTL, and the binding to a particular network interface.

The Java IP multicast support is dependent on native platform multicast support. All major Java 2 platforms are IP multicast-capable, but may require appropriate configuration. Moreover, in order to send multicast datagrams to other hosts, the network routers must support IP multicast. The chapter concluded with an in-depth multicast example of a group chat application.

Java URL Handler Architecture

Naming and addressing, as we saw in Chapter 8, are core features of network and transport layer protocols. Without a means to identify a destination, by address or by name, it would be impossible to effect network communications. However, networks don't exist for their own sake; they exist to provide services (applications). Popular network services include electronic message exchange, file transfer, database lookup, instant messaging, and so on. In order to access these services, it is necessary to establish a naming scheme for application-layer resources. For example, an Internet standard document may be identified by location (host, retrieval protocol, file name), or by a unique location-independent name (IETF RFC number). This chapter will introduce the core Internet application-layer naming mechanism called the Uniform Resource Identifier (URI).

URIs are used to identify resources by location, unique name, or both. Most readers are familiar with a specific type of these identifiers called URLs – this chapter will explain the differences between the various types of URIs. The bulk of the chapter will be dedicated to coverage of the Java URL class and the Java URL protocol and content handler architecture. This architecture provides a web browser-style plugin mechanism for Java applications. The main advantage of this plugin style approach is that applications can be extended without any code modification; this is similar to a browser being extended with a new document-type viewing capability. The chapter walks through the main classes involved in the architecture and demonstrates the concepts in practice through a number of examples.

The chapter is structured so as to provide most of the essential information early on, with more advanced topics left for the end. The first two sections will give you an introduction to URIs and the Java URL handling architecture, the remaining sections will cover the Java classes involved, starting with the `java.net.URL` entry-point class and navigating from there to the remaining classes. Small complete examples are presented to demonstrate use of the APIs presented and in-depth examples will show you two realistic examples of Java handlers (plugins) for a standard protocol and a popular file format.

Uniform Resource Identifiers (URI)

Chapter 4 introduced the concept of a Uniform Resource Identifier (URI). To summarize that discussion, URIs provide a simple and extensible character-based representation of resources:

❑ Anything that can be identified can be considered as a resource. Examples of resources include complete documents, parts of documents, images, services and collections of other resources. The content of the resource referred to by a URI may change over time. For example, a URI may refer to the current weather report for a particular city.

❑ Resources may be accessed in multiple ways. The URI syntax is intentionally general in order to support multiple protocols, and extensibility over time.

❑ The syntax of URIs is character-based to facilitate exchange over different media (such as print publications). The character set of URIs is purposefully limited to avoid user-transcription problems caused by special characters. Due to historical bias, it is assumed that all user terminals support entry of English language characters.

A Uniform Resource Identifier may be further classified as a **locator**, a **name**, or both. A URI locator, also known as a **Uniform Resource Locator** (**URL**), identifies a resource by specifying its access protocol, network location, and name. For example, the URL http://www.wrox.com/index.asp identifies the resource called index.asp that can be retrieved using the HTTP protocol from the address of the DNS domain www.wrox.com. The URL does not provide any information about the type or content of the index.asp resource. Nearly all URIs in use today are URLs.

A URI name, also known as **Uniform Resource Name (URN)**, provides globally unique and persistent resource identification. For example, urn:ISBN:1-861-00560-1 uniquely describes this book. Unlike a URL, the URN does not directly provide any information on how to obtain the book. An extra step is required to translate a URN into a URL, which for this case would be an ISBN resolution service.

In some cases, a URI may include both a location and a name. Interpretation of such URIs is application-specific, a typical application may first attempt to resolve the name part, and upon failure fall back to the location part. The advantage of using such URIs is that applications can still possibly retrieve the named resource even if they do not have access to a name resolution service for that scheme.

The difference between URI locators and names can be compared to that of IP addresses and DNS domain names. IP addresses identify the location of a host on the Internet. Domain names describe a resource and can be associated with different IP addresses. To be useful, domain names must at some point be resolved, typically using the DNS protocol. Similarly, URLs identify the particular location of a resource, while URNs persistently identify a unique resource without specific reference to its location. URNs must also be resolved using some mechanism to one or more URLs in order to be useful.

There are two types of URIs: **absolute identifiers** and **relative identifiers**. Absolute identifiers are independent of the context in which the URI is used. Relative identifiers identify resources by overriding parts of the current context URI. Relative URIs are meaningless unless evaluated in the context of a base URI. Such relative identifiers are useful in naming resources in a portable manner.

URI Characters

The character set of URIs is restricted to support exchange over multiple media and locale-independent transcription. Of the characters permitted, some are reserved for use in separating URI syntactic components. The following characters may be used in URIs:

❑ Lower and upper case ASCII letters ['a' .. 'z'], ['A' .. 'z']

❑ Number digits ['0' .. '9']

❑ Mark characters: '-' (dash), '_' (underscore), '.' (period), '!' (exclamation-point), "~" (tilde), '*' (star), "`" (single back quote), '(' (left parenthesis), ')' (right parenthesis)

The remaining characters must be escaped by specifying the ASCII hex representation preceded by the '%' (percent) sign; this is known as URL encoding. For example, the space character is not permitted, and therefore has to be escaped as %20 (hexadecimal 20 = 32 decimal, which is the ASCII code for the space character). In case you are wondering why the space character is not allowed, the decision was made to support easier transcription since it is difficult to estimate the number of spaces when URIs are read from a printed source. Some of the reserved characters may be released for use by specific URI schemes. These are characters that are not used as URI separators and are not expected to confuse gateways. For example, the URI HTTP scheme permits the use of the plus sign ('+') character to represent the space character (the actual plus character may be only represented in escaped form).

In the current standard, URI characters are 8-bit entities. Therefore, Unicode characters cannot be used in URIs even in escaped form, however, it is possible to use one of the ISO 8859-* character sets that extend the US ASCII standard with characters in the range [128..255].

Java URL String Encoding and Decoding

The Java network libraries provide support for converting a string to a URL-safe representation, and back again using the java.net.URLEncoder and java.net.URLDecoder classes. These are very simple classes, each providing a single static method. The URLEncoder class has a static method called encode() that accepts a string argument and returns its URL-safe representation. Similarly, the URLDecoder class has a single static method called decode() that takes an argument containing a URL encoded string, and returns its un-escaped content. The URLEncoder uses the HTTP URL conventions, such as use of the plus '+' character for space, and unescaped use of the dash '-', underscore '_', period '.', and star '*' characters.

The small Java program below demonstrates use of the Java URL string encoding and decoding functionality. The program takes a single command-line argument, encodes it in a URI-safe manner and then immediately decodes it. The source code for this and all other complete examples is included in this chapter's code directory.

```java
// URLEncodeDecode.java

import java.net.URLEncoder;
import java.net.URLDecoder;

public class URLEncodeDecode {
  public static void main(String[] args) {
    if (args.length != 1) {
      System.err.println("Usage: URLEncodeDecode <string>");
      System.exit(1);
    }

    System.out.println("Original:" + args[0]);
    String encoded = URLEncoder.encode(args[0]);
    System.out.println("Encoded :" + encoded);
    String decoded = URLDecoder.decode(encoded);
    System.out.println("Decoded :" + decoded);
  }
}
```

The above example can be executed as shown below. We demonstrate encoding by providing the program with a filename containing spaces and other URI-reserved characters. Make sure to type the quotes so that the shell interprets the name as a single argument.

C:\Beg_Java_Networking\Ch12>**java URLEncodeDecode "Spaces & reserved-characters_in+file.txt"**
Original:Spaces & reserved-characters_in+file.txt
Encoded :Spaces+%26+reserved-characters_in%2Bfile.txt
Decoded :Spaces & reserved-characters_in+file.txt

You will see that the URL encoder converted the space characters to the '+' character, escaped the ampersand '&' (%26), and '+' plus (%2B) characters, but did not escape the minus '-', underscore '_' and period '.' characters. The decoded string was identical to the original string argument.

Java URL Handling Architecture

The Java network class libraries have provided some support for URIs since the first release of the language. Until JDK 1.4, Java supported only URI locators (URLs) using the class `java.net.URL`. The constructor of the `java.net.URL` class parses and stores the components of a hierarchical URL. For example, users may create a new URL object as shown below:

```
java.net.URL url = new java.net.URL("http://www.ietf.org/rfc/rfc2396.txt");
```

The constructor will verify the syntactical validity of the URL and throw an exception if the string argument does not represent a syntactically valid URL. Once created, the object may be queried for its components such as the `authority` (`host`, `port`, `username`), `path`, and `query`. As we will explain later in this chapter, the actual parsing of the URL string is delegated to a scheme-specific class. For example, a class specializing in HTTP scheme URLs will be used to parse the above `http` protocol URL. For this reason, instances of the `java.net.URL` class cannot represent arbitrary protocol URLs (for example, `myprotocol://wrox.com`). JVMs include support for parsing popular URL schemes such as `http`, `ftp`, `gopher`, `mailto`, and so on. Programmers may extend this built-in support with additional protocols, as we will demonstrate later in this chapter.

There is a lot more to the `java.net.URL` class than simple URL string parsing, however. It is an entry point into an extensible architecture for protocol-transparent resource retrieval and content interpretation. Instances of the URL class can be used to retrieve the resource identified as a byte-stream independent of the protocol used (`http`, `ftp`, and so on). In this manner, network applications can be separated from application-layer protocol implementations, similarly to the way the file abstraction separates applications from the details of how bytes are stored on a disk. The classes encapsulating such protocol-specific streaming are known as **stream handlers**.

Applications may also request the parsing (interpretation) of the stream identified by a URL. Thus, instead of treating the resource as a raw stream of bytes, applications can obtain an object-level representation of the resource. For example, an application may prefer to retrieve a URL identifying a GIF image as an object of type `java.awt.Image` instead of as a raw byte-stream. By delegating the parsing of the byte-stream to another class, the Java application does not have to encapsulate GIF-processing code. Moreover, the application can potentially be transparently extended to support new image types, as long as they can be represented as instances of `java.awt.Image`. The classes used to parse streamed resources are known as **content handlers**.

Consider two different Java-based applications: a web mirror (copy) application and a web browser. Both of these applications need to retrieve resources identified by URLs. Thanks to Java's stream handlers neither application needs to implement any of the popular web protocols such as HTTP, FTP, or Gopher. Instead, both applications simply create `java.net.URL` instances and use these objects to retrieve the content as a byte-stream or as higher-level Java objects. In the diagram below, the web mirror application uses the URL streaming function to retrieve the content of an HTTP URL. The web mirror application will then just write the contents of that stream into some file, without caring about its content. On the other hand, the browser does care about the content because it must display it to the user. For this reason, the browser will prefer to retrieve the content in the more useful form of an AWT Image object. The object can readily be displayed on any AWT or Swing graphical panel. Note that neither application has to worry about the application protocol used to retrieve the resource.

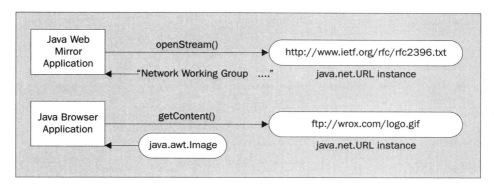

> **The Java URL stream (protocol) and content handlers are similar to the popular web-browser plugins. Their main difference is that plugins are browser and operating system-specific while handlers are only language-specific (Java-specific). The advantage of generalizing at the language level is that all applications handling URLs get to benefit from the added functionality (plus they are cross-platform thanks to Java).**

Stream (Protocol) Handlers

The Java URL class supports transparent protocol access by allowing programs to treat URLs as input streams. As shown below, an application can retrieve the resource identified by a URL instance using a single method invocation. Once an input stream for the URL identified resource has been obtained, it can be treated like any other input stream. We will later show how to obtain an `OutputStream` for writing to a resource, for example to perform an HTTP POST.

```
InputStream istream = url.openStream();
```

In order to support such transparent access, the `java.net.URL openStream()` method must implement the protocol identified in the URL object. Had network protocols been few and static, the `java.net.URL` class could simply include support for all known protocols. In reality, there are many network protocols, some of which are rarely used or are proprietary, and new protocols keep getting introduced. Therefore, it is not reasonable to expect the `java.net.URL` class to implement all known protocols and track the evolution of new ones (including some that may be proprietary). For this reason, the `java.net.URL` class supports an extensible architecture for delegating the implementation of protocols and their representation as byte streams.

This extensible URL protocol architecture is illustrated in the diagram below. When a Java program invokes the openStream() method on an instance of the URL class, the method implementation uses the scheme type (http, ftp) to identify a class implementing the particular protocol (details on that later). The role of this class, known as a **stream handler** (or **protocol handler**) is to retrieve the resource as a stream of bytes.

In this example, the URL instance encapsulates an HTTP protocol URL and therefore the URL openStream() implementation will delegate the streaming request to the HTTP stream handler. The HTTP stream handler will use the HTTP protocol to connect to the web server running on www.ietf.org and request retrieval of the /rfc/rfc2396.txt file. If the connect operation succeeds, the stream handler can return an InputStream to the URL openStream() method which will return it to the Java application. As will be shown later, the stream handler can also be used to stream data (post) to the resource identified by the URL.

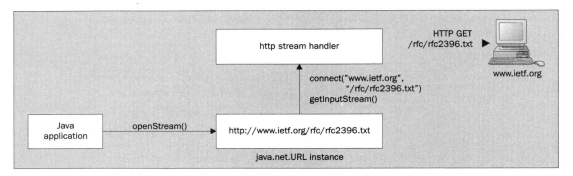

We will defer discussion of stream handler details for later in this chapter. The important point that should be taken from the above discussion is that Java supports an extensible architecture for streaming resources identified by URLs. This architecture enables applications to delegate application-layer protocol implementation to the JVM. Programmers may extend the basic JVM protocol support by providing additional stream handlers.

Content Handlers

Instead of requesting the URL resource as a stream of bytes using the openStream() method, Java applications may request the resource as a Java object using the getContent() methods. The no-argument getContent() method, shown below, returns a Java object representing the resource. The type of object returned is the choice of the content handler, or may be null if no content handler has been defined for the given content type. Applications are required to check the type of the object returned by querying its class.

```
Object object = url.getContent();
```

Alternatively, the application may request that the resource be represented as one of several specific classes. In the example below the getContent() method is passed an array of Class objects with one element of type java.awt.Image. The result of the method will either be an Image instance or null if the content could not be represented as such. The methods below will be discussed in detail later in this chapter.

```
Image image=(Image)url.getContent(new Class[]{Image.class});
```

Content handlers are used by the `java.net.URL` class to convert the stream of bytes retrieved by the stream handler into a Java object. For example, in the diagram below a Java application invokes the `getContent()` method on a URL instance containing an HTTP URL pointing to the file `/logo.gif`. The URL class will first identify the HTTP protocol stream handler and will verify that the resource can be retrieved. As part of that process, the stream handler will also attempt to query the content type of the identified resource. Note that even though the file ends in a `.gif` extension, it is best to rely on the server to determine its true type and not attempt to guess based on name. In this case, the HTTP stream handler will identify the content type as a GIF image. Once the content type has been identified, the URL class will look for a content handler for that type (we will explain how later on). In this example, we show that this content handler is found and its `getContent()` method is invoked, with the stream handler as argument. The content handler will then read the bytes from the stream handler and construct the object to be returned to the application (if possible).

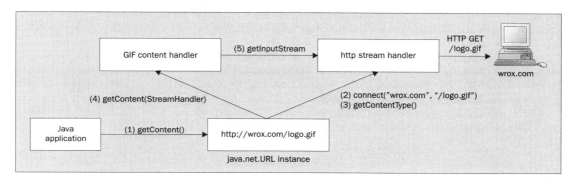

Note that the content handler operates on a stream and is independent of the protocol used to retrieve the resource. Therefore, the same content handler may be used to parse a particular content type (GIF images) independent of the protocol used to retrieve the content (HTTP, FTP). We will return to provide more detailed coverage of how content handlers may be used. The main point is that applications can interface through the URL class to obtain a Java object representation of a resource independent of the protocol or encoding used. Clearly, the possible types of object returned must somehow be known in order to enable applications to use these objects. As we will discover, this is a significant problem that has not been properly addressed so far in Java.

Java Stream and Content Handler Classes

The Java URL stream and content handling architecture uses the following Java classes:

- ❑ `java.net.URL`: This is the entry point class to the connection and content handling architecture. Instances of the class are constructed by parsing a string representing a URL. The class supports an API for querying information about the identified resource, obtaining an input stream for reading data from the resource, or obtaining a Java object providing additional information about the identified source and supporting more complex operations. All operations are delegated to the respective protocol and content handlers.

- ❑ `java.net.URLStreamHandler`: This is an abstract class whose subclasses encapsulate protocol handlers. Instances are used by the `java.net.URL` class to parse the string representation of a URL and for optionally establishing a streaming connection with the resource (returned as a `java.net.URLConnection` instance).

337

❑ `java.net.URLConnection`: This class encapsulates streaming connections created by the `URLStreamHandler` subclasses. In addition to providing access to the `InputStream` and `OutputStream` for the connection, the `URLConnection` object supports protocol-specific queries such as content-type and length retrieval. Instances are not directly created but obtained through the `java.net.URL` class `openConnection()` method.

❑ `java.net.ContentHandler`: This is an abstract class whose subclasses act as content handlers. Each subclass is responsible for converting the byte-stream representation of a single type, such as HTML, GIF, PDF, into an appropriate Java language object. Instances are generated by the `URLConnection` `getContent()` method for each new contents-type encountered.

The overall design of the Java class library URI support is shown in the UML class diagram below. The four main classes are shown including some of their most important methods. The `java.net.URL` class stores the components of a URL. The class may only represent URL schemes for which a `java.net.URLStreamHandler` instance has been assigned. The `URLStreamHandler` is an abstract class that is used to parse scheme-specific URL strings and generate `java.net.URLConnection` instances. `URLConnection` instances are used to configure and create a connection with the service described in the URL. Additionally, in protocols such as HTTP where the server provides meta-information about the connection in the form of headers, the `URLConnection` class may be used to retrieve such header information. `ContentHandler` is an abstract class whose subclasses are used to parse the streaming content of a `URLConnection` to obtain a Java object representation. The next sections will cover these classes in detail.

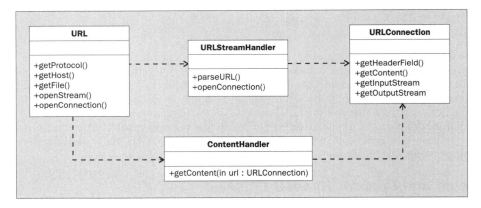

The Java network library designers decided to require protocol handler support for every URL represented by a **java.net.URL** instance. That is, it is not possible to create an instance of the **java.net.URL** class for a scheme that is not natively supported by the JRE, or has been previously installed by the program. The advantage of this approach is that **java.net.URL** instances can be treated as data streams, abstracting from the underlying transmission protocol. The main disadvantage is that one cannot represent arbitrary URLs that are not supported by the system. In JDK 1.4, the **java.net.URI** class was added to support URNs as well as arbitrary URIs.

Java Handler Architecture Use Case

The UML use case diagram below shows a typical use of the Java URL protocol and content handler architecture. In this use case, a user (top left) inputs the URL magic://wrox.com/index.pdf to a Java web browser. Let's assume that browser itself does not directly support the magic protocol, and does not know how to interpret PDF documents. Normally, the application would give up at this point with an appropriate error message. However, if the application makes use of the Java URL handler architecture, it can attempt to retrieve and display the document by delegating the respective tasks (assuming that Java knows about the magic protocol and how to handle PDF content). As explained earlier, the browser will create an instance of the java.net.URL class and then invoke the getContent() method in order to obtain a Java object encapsulating the content of the resource. That is, if the object returned is of a type that can be displayed, for example an instance of java.awt.Component that can be directly embedded in the browser's frame. Otherwise, the browser may fall back to obtaining the resource as a stream and offering the user to save the contents in a file.

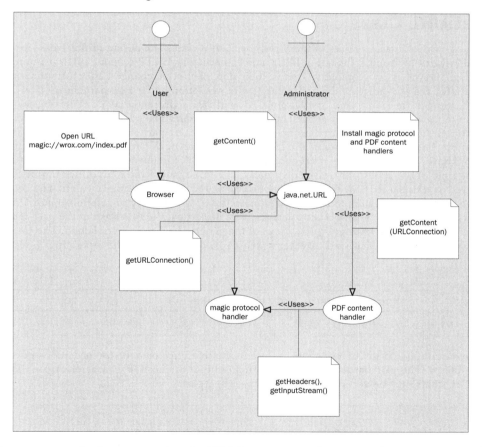

In this use case, we further assume that the JVM does not natively support the magic protocol (since it is of our own invention), and the JVM does not provide an Adobe PDF content handler. Both of these shortcomings may be addressed prior to use through the installation of additional handlers. In this use case, we show an administrator (top-right), who could be the same person as the user, installing a magic protocol handler, and a PDF content handler prior to the open URL request.

When the browser receives the open URL request, it creates a `java.net.URL` instance for the specified URL. The `java.net.URL` instance checks the installed protocol handlers for one supporting the `magic` protocol and uses it to parse the URL and to open a connection. We will assume that as part of its connection establishment, the `magic` protocol retrieves the content type of the resource identified by the URL (`/index.pdf`).

Given the content type of the resource, the URL class will identify the installed PDF content handler and invoke its `getContent()` method with the `URLConnection` object generated by the `magic` protocol handler. At that point, the PDF content handler will use the `URLConnection` object to retrieve the resource as a byte-stream and possibly inquire further about its attributes. If the bytes read from the stream can be correctly parsed, the PDF content handler will create an appropriate Java object and will return it to the URL class. The URL class will simply return that object to the browser as the result of the `getContent()` request.

java.net.URL Class

Java represents URLs as instances of the `java.net.URL` class. The design of the `java.net.URL` class is geared towards hierarchical location URIs, and in particular HTTP scheme URLs. Instances of the `java.net.URL` class are immutable, that is, their state cannot be changed after instantiation. The parts of a Java URL are shown in the diagram below (with exception of the `ref` part shown later). As can be observed, some of these parts are overlapping. All parts are represented as `String` objects with the exception of the `port` part that is represented as an `int` value. The `protocol` part contains the string description of the URI scheme (`http`, `ftp` ...). The `userInfo` part contains the optional user specification. The `host` part contains the DNS domain name or dotted IP address representation of the authority's host. The integer `port` part contains the optional port specification, or −1 if not specified (implying used of the protocol's well-known port). The three parts (`userInfo`, `host`, `port`) may also be accessed as a single string with the separating characters as the `authority` part. The `path` part stores the slash-separated path to the resource up to the optional query or reference part. Unlike the previous cases where the '@' and ':' characters where discarded, the first slash of the path is kept since it is significant. Finally, the optional `query` part of the generic URI may be obtained. The `path` and `query` parts may also be accessed together as the `file` part, including the separating '?' character.

http://anonymous@wrox.com:80/search/lookup.cgi?name=beginning+java					
protocol	userInfo	host	port	path	query
	authority			file	

The above example did not demonstrate the use of the reference part. Its use is demonstrated in the example below. The `ref` part includes the information past the hash '#' character. Again, both `path` and `ref` contents may be accessed together as the `file` part.

http://anonymous@wrox.com:80/index.html#contents					
protocol	userInfo	host	port	path	ref
	authority			file	

Constructors

The most commonly used `java.net.URL` constructor accepts a string representation of a URL, identifies the URL scheme and locates the `URLStreamHandler` for the specified protocol in order to parse the rest of the string. At a minimum, the string must contain a URI scheme (protocol) terminated by the colon (':') character. For example, the string `http:` represents a valid URL, alas not a very useful one. If the URL is not valid syntactically, the `java.net.MalformedURLException` will be thrown. Even if the URL is syntactically valid, a `MalformedURLException` may be thrown if no content handler is available for the protocol. For example, the URL `ldap:` is valid syntactically but will result in a `MalformedURLException` because the protocol is unknown (it is not supported by default in the JVM). Note that the constructor does not throw a `java.net.UnknownHostException` because it does not attempt to resolve the optional host part of the URL string.

```
URL(String spec) throws MalformedURLException
```

A sample use of the URL string constructor is shown below. We will discuss the default protocol and content handler support in JVMs later in this section.

```
URL url = null;
try {
 url = new URL("http://wrox.com/");
} catch (MalformedURLException e) {
 // notify user of error
}
```

Because the above constructor requires specification of a URI scheme (protocol) it may only be used to parse absolute URLs. Because every `java.net.URL` instance must be capable of retrieving the identified resource, every instance must represent an absolute URL. To simplify conversion of a relative URL into an absolute URL a constructor is provided that takes a `java.net.URL` instance as context, and a string representation of a relative URL. The context is used to convert the string into an absolute URL. If the context is `null`, use of this constructor is equivalent to use of the previous constructor. If the string represents an absolute URL then the context is not used at all.

```
URL(URL context, String spec) throws MalformedURLException
```

The following table lists pairs of parameters and the resulting URL created. Note that the terminating slash ('/') in a URL is important as it conveys the fact that the last path component is empty (that is, the next-to-last component is a directory).

URL argument	String argument	Result
http://wrox.com/a	help.html	http://wrox.com/help.html
http://wrox.com/a/	help.html	http://wrox.com/a/help.html
http://wrox.com/a/i.html	help.html	http://wrox.com/a/help.html
http://wrox.com/a/i.html	/help.html	http://wrox.com/help.html
http://wrox.com/a/b/i.html	../help.html	http://wrox.com/a/help.html
http://wrox.com/a/	ftp:help.txt	ftp:help.txt

In some cases, the URL's components may be separately known to an application. Instead of joining them together into a string, the application can pass them individually to the `java.net.URL` class constructor. Two constructors are provided that accept the `protocol`, `host`, `port` and `file` components separately. Their difference is that one requires the optional definition of the `protocol` port. No constructor is provided for URLs whose file component is further broken down into a `path` and `reference` or `path` and `query` components. In such cases, the `path`, `reference`, and `query` components must be provided as a single string, separated by the standard URI characters. The same applies to the `authority` component (note that the JavaDocs label the second parameter as `host`, which is not accurate).

```
URL(String protocol, String authority, String file) throws MalformedURLException

URL(String protocol, String authority, int port, String file) throws
MalformedURLException
```

The following code snippet demonstrates use of such a constructor:

```
URL url = null;
try {
 url = new URL("http",
                "anonymous@wrox.com",
                "lookup.jsp?query=java");
} catch (MalformedURLException e) {
 // notify user of error
}
```

The two remaining constructors allow users to specify the `URLStreamHandler` instance responsible for parsing the string URL and for obtaining the scheme (protocol) stream. In our previous discussion we implied that non-standard protocol and content handlers must be installed for global JVM use. This was not entirely accurate, as an application may request a specific protocol handler if required, but for maximum flexibility it is best that the protocol handler be installed globally, as will be demonstrated later. The first constructor takes a `java.net.URL` instance as context, a string specifying an absolute or relative URL and the protocol (stream) handler to be used. For absolute string URL representations, the context may be `null`. The second constructor takes a `protocol`, `host`, `port`, `file` and `stream` handler as arguments. Passing −1 as a port value may specify the default port. Both constructors throw the `MalformedURLException` due to a parsing error, or if the protocol handler passed is not appropriate for the URL represented by the string. If the handler argument is `null` the behavior is similar to the previous constructors, that is, the installed constructors are looked up. Overriding the default protocol handler is a security-sensitive operation. A `SecurityException` will be thrown if the `java.net.NetPermission specifyStreamHandler` permission has not been granted.

```
URL(URL context, String spec, URLStreamHandler handler) throws
MalformedURLException

URL(String protocol, String host, int port, String file, URLStreamHandler handler)
throws MalformedURLException
```

Accessing URL Parts

The `java.net.URL` class has methods for querying every part of the URL it represents. The names correspond to the URL components discussed in the introduction of this section. To repeat, every URL has a mandatory scheme (protocol) part, followed by an optional `authority` part, and an optional `file` part. When present, the `authority` part can be further decomposed into the `user-info`, `host` and `port` subparts. All three of these sub-parts are optional. The file part can also be decomposed into the `path`, `query` and `ref` sub-parts. All three of these subparts are also optional. The following methods may be used to query the values of the parts and subparts for a `java.net.URL` instance. All the methods return a `String` value, with the exception of the `getPort()` method that returns a primitive integer value. If a part or subpart is not provided in the URL represented, the `null` value is returned by these methods. Again, the `getPort()` method is an exception because it returns a primitive type and cannot return a `null` value. Instead, `getPort()` returns the invalid port number value of −1. This behavior may surprise some users who would expect `getPort()` to return the default port number for the protocol. Unfortunately, even though the default port may be obtained by querying the `URLProtocolHandler`, there is no simple way for obtaining a reference to that object. None of the methods throw an exception since the parsing of the URL string is performed at construction time.

```
String getProtocol()
String getAuthority()
String getUserInfo()
String getHost()
int getPort()
String getFile()
String getPath()
String getQuery()
String getRef()
```

The complete string representation of the URL represented by the `java.net.URL` instance can be obtained by invoking the `toExternalForm()` method. The `java.lang.Object toString()` method also returns the same result. Implementation of the method is delegated to the `URLStreamHandler` for the given protocol.

```
String toExternalForm()
```

Comparing URL Files

Because the `java.net.URL` class is immutable, no methods are provided for modifying the attributes of an instance. The `sameFile()` method may be used to compare two URLs without considering their `query` and `ref` parts.

```
boolean sameFile(URL other)
```

The following table compares the result of invoking the `sameFile()` method versus the result of invoking the `java.lang.Object equals()` method. Note that the `sameFile()` method is not intelligent enough to determine that the host name `localhost` and the IP address `127.0.0.1` refer to the same host. The `java.net.URL` class delegates implementation of this method to the `URLStreamHandler` for the specified protocol. Therefore the behavior of the method may not be the same for other URL protocol schemes.

url1	url2	sameFile()	equals()
`http://localhost/i.html#a`	`http://localhost/i.html#b`	true	false
`http://localhost/i.html#a`	`http://localhost/i.html?b`	true	false
`http://localhost/i.html#a`	`http://127.0.0.1/i.html#b`	false	false

Opening an Input Stream

Applications that just want to read the resource identified by a `java.net.URL` instance as a stream without obtaining any other information about it may invoke the `openStream()` method. The method returns an `InputStream` for reading the resource content as a byte stream. It is up to the application to interpret the content of this stream. Because the method requires the establishment of a remote connection, the `IOException` may be thrown to signal a communications error. An example of using this method will be shown later in this section.

```
InputStream openStream()throws IOException
```

In some cases, the stream may not contain the resource but some error message. For example, when accessing a web page that is not available, the web server may return an HTML page to describe the problem. This behavior can make it difficult for users of `openStream()` to determine when an error has occurred. For this reason it is preferable to use the `openConnection()` method that will be described next.

The `URL` class implements the `openStream()` method by delegating connection establishment to the `URLStreamHandler` for the specific scheme.

Creating a Connection

Applications that want to write to as well as read from the identified resource, or need to query/modify the connection configuration need to obtain a `URLConnection` object. The `openConnection()` method will return a `URLConnection` object supporting such functionality. Because the implementation of this method is delegated to the `URLStreamHandler` for the given protocol, its behavior may vary. The JavaDoc documentation states that the `openConnection()` method opens a network connection to the remote host. As a result, the method may throw the `IOException`. This statement is a little misleading as most `URLStreamHandlers` do not perform any I/O at this point in order to allow applications to configure the initial connection parameters in the `URLConnection` object.

```
URLConnection openConnection() throws IOException
```

For example, the default FTP and HTTP stream handlers supplied in Sun's JRE version 1.3.1 do not even check if the host name in the URL can be resolved at this point, and obviously don't try to connect to the remote service. Therefore users should not assume that if an `openConnection()` invocation succeeds that the resource is retrievable. We will later show that the `URLConnection` class provides a `connect()` method to perform the actual connection. Perhaps a better name for the method would be `prepareConnection()`. Note that the returned object may be an instance of a subclass of the `URLConnection` class. For example, the default HTTP `URLStreamHandler` implementation returns an `HttpURLConnection` instance, which provides additional support for HTTP-specific operations. This behavior is discussed in greater detail in the default handlers section.

Retrieving Content As an Object

Applications that only care for the byte-stream representation of the URL's content may invoke the `openStream()` or `openConnection()` methods. In some cases, applications may want to make use of the installed content handlers to obtain a Java-object representation of the identified content. This behavior is effected by invoking one of the two `getContent()` methods. Both methods return a generic Java object representing the resource, and may throw an `IOException` or a `SecurityException` if an error occurs while attempting to read or parse the stream. The `UnknownServiceException` runtime exception will be thrown if no content handler has been installed for the given content type.

In order for these methods to be useful, the invoking application must know how to use the type of object returned. For example, if the URL represents a JPEG encoded image, the content handler may return an instance of the `java.awt.Image` class. The invoking application will need to check the type of the object returned using the `instanceOf` keyword or the Java reflection APIs. In some cases, the content handler may support generation of different Java object representations.

```
Object getContent() throws IOException, UnknownServiceException
```

If the application knows the supported types, it can state its preferences by invoking the second `getContent()` method with an array of classes as argument. The class array specifies the preferences of the application. If the content handler does not support any of the types specified a `null` value will be returned. An example demonstrating the use of this method is included in the next subsection.

```
Object getContent(Class[] classes)
        throws IOException, UnknownServiceException
```

The `java.net.URL` class looks up `URLStreamHandler` instances by consulting the default object implementing the `URLStreamHandlerFactory` interface. New protocol handlers may be installed by either completely replacing that factory object, or by configuring the existing factory object. The former may be achieved by invoking the static `setURLStreamHandlerFactory()` method. We will postpone discussion of this method until we have presented the `URLStreamHandlerFactory` interface.

```
static setURLStreamHandlerFactory(URLStreamHandlerInterface fac)
        throws IOException
```

URL Examples

This section demonstrates use of the `openStream()` and `getContent()` methods of the `java.net.URL` class. To execute most of these examples you must be connected to the Internet or install a web server on your host. If your host is behind a firewall that does not permit outgoing TCP connections, you will need to set `-DsocksProxyHost="my_socks_hostname"` as described in Chapter 9.

Reading Raw Byte Content

The example overleaf demonstrates the use of the `openStream()` method for reading the raw byte content identified by a URL. The console program takes a string representing a URL as its only argument and first attempts to create a `java.net.URL` instance. If the URL is syntactically incorrect, or a stream handler for it does not exist, an error will be issued to the user. Otherwise, the `java.net.URL` `openStream()` method will be invoked.

At invocation time, the URLStreamHandler will attempt to resolve the host name in the URL and establish a HTTP connection with the remote server, as identified in the authority field. Any of these steps can potentially fail, signaled by the throwing of the java.io.IOException exception. Although this is not documented in the JavaDocs, the openStream() method may also throw a SecurityException if a security manager has been installed and the remote connection is not authorized.

To keep the example simple, we will assume that the resource identified is a text file and will use a BufferedReader instance to print it one line at a time. If the resource is not a text file, many bytes will be interpreted as terminal-control characters and are likely to wreak havoc with your terminal window!

```java
// URLDump.java

import java.net.*;
import java.io.*;

public class URLDump {
 public static void main(String[] args) {
  if (args.length != 1) {
   System.err.println("Usage: URLDump <url>");
   System.exit(1);
  }

  URL url = null;
  try {
   url = new URL(args[0]);
  } catch (MalformedURLException e) {
   System.err.println("Malformed URL argument: " + e.getMessage());
   System.exit(1);
  }

  BufferedReader reader = null;
  try {
   reader = new BufferedReader
    (new InputStreamReader(url.openStream()));

   String line = reader.readLine();
   while(line != null) {
    System.out.println(line);
    line = reader.readLine();
   }
  } catch (IOException e) {
   System.err.println("Error reading URL stream: " + e.getMessage());
   System.exit(1);
  } finally {
   try { reader.close(); } catch (Throwable e) { }
  }
 }
}
```

The example may be executed as shown below. Users should be warned that the URI RFC document is very long so only the top section is displayed below. Any other URL may be used instead; preferably referring to a text document.

C:\Beg_Java_Networking\Ch12>**java URLDump http://ietf.org/rfc/rfc2396.txt**

Network Working Group   T. Berners-Lee
Request for Comments: 2396   MIT/LCS

Updates: 1808, 1738
Category: Standards Track

R. Fielding
U.C. Irvine
L. Masinter
Xerox Corporation
August 1998

Using the getContent() Method

Next, we demonstrate use of the `getContent()` method. This example takes a URL as its argument, creates a `java.net.URL` object for it, and invokes the `getContent()` method on that instance. Users may optionally follow the URL argument with one or more strings describing Java class names. The program will convert these strings to `java.lang.Class` objects and pass them to the `getContent(Class[])` method.

The program prints out the class of the object returned as well as all its superclasses and interfaces. The reason for printing that additional information is to try to determine what standard classes and interfaces the object encapsulating the content extends or implements. Because the `java.lang.Class` class does not provide a single method for obtaining a recursive listing of all super classes and interfaces, we provide a simple static recursive method for doing so. The method takes a single argument representing a class, prints out its name and then recursively invokes itself for all interfaces implemented by the argument, and the argument's superclass.

```java
// URLGetContentExample.java

import java.net.*;
import java.io.*;

public class URLGetContentExample {

  /* Recursively prints all the classes extended and
     all the interfaces implemented by the class argument */
  public static void printClassInfo(Class c) {
   if (c == null) return;

   if (c.isInterface()) {
    System.out.println(" interface " + c.getName());
   } else {
    System.out.println(" class " + c.getName());
   }

   Class[] ifs = c.getInterfaces();
   for(int i=0; i<ifs.length; i++) {
    printClassInfo(ifs[i]);
   }

   printClassInfo(c.getSuperclass());
  }

  /* Retrieves the URL specified as the first argument and
     displays its content type. Optionally users may request
     specific content types. */
  public static void main(String[] args) {
   if (args.length < 1) {
    System.err.println("Usage: URLGetContentExample <url> " +
            "{ <class> <class> ... }");
    System.exit(1);
   }
```

```
    URL url = null;
    try {
     url = new URL(args[0]);
    } catch (MalformedURLException e) {
     System.err.println("Malformed URL argument: " + e.getMessage());
     System.exit(1);
    }

    Class[] contentClasses = new Class[args.length - 1];
    for(int i=1; i<args.length; i++) {
     try {
      contentClasses[i-1] = Class.forName(args[i]);
     } catch (Exception e) {
      System.err.println("Cannot find Class object for " +
               args[i] + ": " + e.getMessage());
      System.exit(1);
     }
    }

    try {
     Object content = null;

     if (contentClasses.length == 0) {
      content = url.getContent();
     } else {
      content = url.getContent(contentClasses);
      if (content == null) {
       System.err.println("Content handler does not support" +
                " the specified classes");
       System.exit(1);
      }
     }

     System.out.println("Content handler returned an object " +
                "of the type: " +
                content.getClass().getName());
     System.out.println("\nThe object may be type-cast as:");
     printClassInfo(content.getClass());
    } catch (IOException e) {
     System.err.println(e.getClass().getName() + ": " + e.getMessage());
     System.exit(1);
    }

    System.exit(0); // required because we can't close the connection
   }
  }
```

In this sample execution we request retrieval of a GIF image identified by a particular URL. Notice that
the result is of an undocumented class. However, that object implements the
java.awt.image.ImageProducer interface and therefore can be accessed through that published
API. Any other URL can replace the one used, even if it does not identify an image. It is possible that
the particular URL will no longer be valid by the time you read this.

C:\Beg_Java_Networking\Ch12>**java URLGetContentExample**
http://wrox.com/Includes/images/newwroxlogo.gif
Content handler returned an object of the type: sun.awt.image.URLImageSource

The object may be type-cast as:
  class sun.awt.image.URLImageSource
  class sun.awt.image.InputStreamImageSource
  interface java.awt.image.ImageProducer
  interface sun.awt.image.ImageFetchable
  class java.lang.Object

Using the ImageProducer interface to display an image is not a simple matter because it is too low-level. Instead we will retry retrieving the content of the URL, but this time we will request that a java.awt.Image object be returned. We are not guaranteed that the content handler supports such a representation, but it does not hurt to try. As it turns out, a class extending java.awt.Image is indeed returned. As we will explain later, there is no documentation concerning the standard Java content handlers and the type of objects they will return.

C:\Beg_Java_Networking\Ch12>**java URLGetContentExample**
http://wrox.com/Includes/images/newwroxlogo.gif java.awt.Image
Content handler returned an object of the type: sun.awt.windows.WImage

The object may be type-cast as:
  class sun.awt.windows.WImage
  class sun.awt.image.Image
  class java.awt.Image
  class java.lang.Object

java.net.URLConnection Class

An instance of the URLConnection class stores the information required to access a remote resource. Access may involve reading as well as writing to the resource using a byte stream abstraction. In addition, the URLConnection object may be used to query meta-information about the remote resource, and set up the type of connection to be created. Instances of the java.net.URLConnection class are obtained by invoking the openConnection() method on a java.net.URL instance. Under the hood, the java.net.URL class uses a factory object to identify and cache the URLStreamHandler object that is actually going to create the object. We will defer discussion on how the object is really created until later, for now, we will pretend that the URLConnection instance is created by the java.net.URL instance.

For example, obtaining a URLConnection from a java.net.URL object representing an HTTP URL enables users to access the HTTP request headers, such as preferred language, as well as the HTTP response headers, such as server info, content type and length. The URLConnection object does not preclude applications from reading resources as byte streams, or using a content handler for obtaining an object content representation. The class provides additional capabilities, such as writing to a resource and configuring the connection parameters.

Instances of the URLConnection class created using the java.net.URL openConnection() method are initially in a setup state. This behavior enables users to set up the request parameters prior to connection establishment. Once the connect() method is invoked on an instance it moves into the connected state. Some class methods may be invoked in only one of the two states. The UML state-chart diagram overleaf shows the URLConnection class states and transitions.

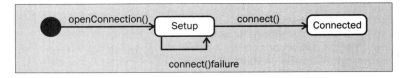

Unfortunately, because the URLConnection has many capabilities and must accommodate any URL scheme, it ends up being one of those Java classes with many methods. There is no need to be intimidated; you are unlikely to need all the methods. Our presentation will group methods by type of function so that the flow will be more natural.

Constructors

The URLConnection class does not have any public constructors. Instances are typically obtained by invoking the openConnection() method on a java.net.URL instance.

Setup Methods

By default, URLConnection objects are set up to support reading (input) of the remote stream resource, but not writing (output). This behavior can be modified prior to invoking the connect() method. The setDoInput() method is used to set up support for input and the setDoOutput() method set up support for output. An IllegalAccessError exception will be thrown if the connect() method has already been invoked (starting with JDK 1.4 the more appropriate IllegalStateException is thrown). Note that invoking these methods does not guarantee that the input or output will succeed, only that it will be enabled or disabled. The setup of the connection can be queried at any point using the getDoInput() and getDoOutput() methods. As stated, the default behavior is to enable input and disable output.

```
void setDoInput(boolean doinput)
void setDoOutput(boolean dooutput)
boolean getDoInput()
boolean getDoOutput()
```

Instances of the URLConnection class are configured prior to connection using key-value pairs assigned using the setRequestProperty() method. The key and value types are dependent on the underlying protocol. This design is largely due to the influence of the HTTP protocol in the design of the class. For example, the HTTP protocol defines the "accept-language" key whose value is a comma-separated list of ISO language identifiers. Before connecting, a user could invoke setRequestProperty("Accept-Language", "fr") to request that the document be served in the French language. We cover some of the HTTP protocol headers in a subsequent section, no protocol-independent keys are defined so there is not much to discuss at this point. An IllegalAccessError exception will be thrown if the setRequestProperty() method is invoked after the connect() method has been invoked. The getRequestProperty() method may be invoked at any point to query the value associated with a request key.

```
void setRequestProperty(String key, String value)
String getRequestProperty(String key)
```

Some protocol handlers may cache the result of previous queries to improve performance. Users may disable this feature by invoking the setUseCaches() method with a false value as an argument before connect() has been invoked. An IllegalAccessError exception will be thrown if the connect() method has already been invoked. The caching setup of a connection may be queried at any point using the getUseCaches() method. In current implementations, most protocol handlers return true by default, even if they do not support caching. Users assuming that a protocol handler does not perform caching are advised to invoke setUseCaches() with a false value, just to be safe.

```
void setUseCaches(boolean usecaches)
boolean getUseCaches()
```

In some cases, accessing a resource identified by a URL may require additional user interaction. For example, retrieving a file identified by an HTTP URL may require the user to authenticate. Depending on the protocol handler, it may be possible to provide that information programmatically. However, if the additional information is not supplied, the protocol handler may prompt the user through some kind of user interface (in fact the Sun stream handlers do not prompt the user and simply fail). Interactive programs may want to enable this feature since they are most likely executed with direct user supervision. The behavior of a single URLConnection instance may be modified using the setAllowUserInteraction() method before the connection has been established. As before, the IllegalAccessError exception will be thrown if the connect() method has already been invoked. The user interaction setup of an instance may be queried using the getAllowUserInteraction() method.

```
void setAllowUserInteraction(boolean allowuserinteraction)
boolean getAllowUserInteraction()
```

Some protocols support the filtering of resources based on the last modification time. For example, the HTTP protocol may be used to retrieve multiple resources in the same connection. A web-mirroring program may only want to retrieve resources that have changed since the last mirroring operation. This behavior can be requested by invoking the setIfModifiedSince() method. A zero argument disables the feature, resulting in the download of all resources. A non-zero argument represents a date as an offset from the Java epoch (see the documentation for System getCurrentTimeMillis(). This property must be configured before the connection is established, otherwise an IllegalAccessError exception will be thrown. The value may be queried at any point using the getIfModifiedSince() method.

```
void setIfModifiedSince(long timeMillis)
long getIfModifiedSince()
```

The URL from which the URLConnection instance has been created can be retrieved at any state by invoking the getURL() method.

```
URL getURL()
```

State Transition Methods

As shown in the UML state-chart diagram earlier, the URLConnection object may be in two states: setup, and connected. The setup state is automatically entered at instantiation time. The connect() method may be used to transition from the setup to the connected state. The transition does not have to be explicit. Methods requiring the object to be in a connected state will automatically invoke connect(). Therefore users must be careful not to invoke any such methods before setup is complete. It is safe to invoke connect() multiple times but it will only actually establish a connection once. The connect() method will attempt to resolve the host name into an IP address and establish a connection in a protocol-specific manner. An IOException will be thrown to signal failure of any of these steps. If a security manager has been installed, a SecurityException may be thrown if the connect permission has not been granted to the remote host.

```
abstract void connect() throws IOException, SecurityException
```

The exact behavior of connect() is dependent on the URLConnection setup. For example, invoking connect() on an HTTP URLConnection will issue an HTTP GET by default. If the setDoOutput() method has been invoked with a true value, an HTTP POST request will be made instead. Notice that the method is declared as abstract in the URLConnection class. This is because its implementation is protocol-specific and therefore should be handled by the particular subclass generated by the URLStreamHandler. We will cover this issue in detail when discussing how to create custom handlers.

It should be noted that there is no closed state. Unlike the java.net.Socket class, a URLConnection does not represent a single connection. It is possible to use the same connection to retrieve a resource multiple times, even without using caching, hence there is no close() method. However, it is the responsibility of the application to close any streams obtained by the URLConnection using getInputStream() and getOutputStream() (covered later).

Connected Methods

The methods listed in this section access the URLConnection object in its connected state. If the explicit connect() call has not been previously made, these methods will indirectly invoke it.

Accessing Headers Describing Resource Content

Information about the remote resource may be obtained by accessing key-value pairs. This is similar to the connection properties set using setRequestProperty() to control the connection establishment, only this time they are part of a response header providing information about the remote resource. Obviously, header information can only be provided after a connection has been established. For that reason, any request to read the content of a header implies a request to connect() if one has not been made already.

The simplest way of reading a key-value pair is by invoking the getHeaderField() method with the name of the key. The method returns the value for the field, or null if there is no such key in the header. Two convenience methods are also provided. The getHeaderFieldInt() method is used when the value is expected to be of an integer type. The method takes a key name and a default value as arguments. If the string value for the key is defined and can be parsed as an integer then it is returned, otherwise the default value specified is returned (and no exception is thrown). The getHeaderFieldDate() method operates similarly in converting a standard string representation of a date into a long value offset from the Java epoch (as in System.getCurrentTimeMillis()).

```
String getHeaderField(String name)
int getHeaderFieldInt(String name, int default)
long getHeaderFieldDate(String name, long default)
```

The second way of reading key-value pairs is to iterate through all the pairs in the header. This is useful when the program does not know in advance what headers will be provided. Of course, if the program does not know about a header, it is limited in its ability to interpret it. Each key-value pair is associated with a unique index in sequence. Two methods are provided that take an integer as argument and return the key or value for the pair identified. The getHeaderFieldKey() method returns the name of the nth key, while the getHeaderField() returns the nth value. If the pair does not exist then the null value is returned by both methods. The JavaDoc documentation does not state at what index number counting starts. Historically, Java counting starts at zero (for example, primitive arrays, Vectors, and so on). The default handlers exhibit a strange and undocumented behavior: the first pair (at index zero) has a null key and a non-null value sometimes containing the result code (this is the case for Sun's HTTP stream handler implementation). Therefore, when iterating one should start from zero and count upwards until both key and value are null. Readers may refer to the URLInfo code in the examples subsection for a header key-value pair iteration example.

```
String getHeaderField(int n)
String getHeaderFieldKey(int n)
```

Standard Header Methods

The URLConnection class also supports retrieval of well-known header key types. These methods may be viewed as convenience functions since their values could also be retrieved using the getHeaderFieldKey() method. The getContentType() method returns a String containing the MIME description of the next resource's type, for example text/html. The length in bytes of the stream content may be obtained by invoking getContentLength(). The getContentEncoding() returns additional encoding information about the type, for example gzip if the content has been compressed using the gzip algorithm. The getDate() method returns the time in which the header was originated according to the server's clock. The getExpiration() method returns the time after which the content should no longer be cached (server-controlled expiration). Finally, the getLastModified() method returns the time when the retrieved resource was last modified.

```
int getContentLength ()
String getContentType()
String getContentEncoding()
long getDate()
long getExpiration()
long getLastModified()
```

Obtaining the Content and I/O Streams

As you may recall from the java.net.URL discussion, the content identified by a URL may be retrieved as an object provided by a content handler. The same two methods are also available from within the URLConnection class. In fact, the java.net.URL methods are just convenience methods that create a URLConnection object and invoke the getContent() or getContent(Class[]) method.

To review our previous discussion, the getContent() method returns an object representation of the content, if a content handler for the given content type is available. If no content handler is available the UnknownServiceException is thrown. The getContent(Class[]) method may be used to request particular object representations of the content. If none of the requested object class representations are supported, the method will return null. Invoking this method will imply a connect() request if one has not already been made. The main problem with this generic architecture is that the application must have some way of predicting what types will be returned or can be requested. We will discuss this issue in the section covering the default protocol and content handlers.

```
Object getContent() throws IOException, UnknownServiceException
Object getContent(Class[] classes)
        throws IOException, UnknownServiceException
```

The URLConnection class may also be used to read and write the raw-byte content of the identified resource. The getInputStream() and getOutputStream() methods return an input and an output stream respectively for reading from and writing to the resource. In order to use each, the setDoInput() or setDoOutput() must be set to true, or default to true. Both methods may throw an IOException or SecurityException if a connect() has to be made implicitly.

```
InputStream getInputStream() throws IOException
OutputStream getOutputStream() throws IOException
```

Static Methods

It is possible to modify the default caching behavior for all URLConnections created. Invoking the setDefaultUseCaches() method will change the caching behavior of all new URLConnection instances created by any URLStreamHandler. It is important to remember that the behavior only affects instances created **after** the method has been invoked! Strangely, the method is not declared to be static, so in order to modify the default behavior, an instance must be created. Not only that, but the behavior of the instance on which the setDefaultUseCaches() method is invoked is not affected! A method is also provided to query the default caching behavior of URLConnection instances for the given protocol (again non-static).

```
void setDefaultUseCaches(boolean defaultusecaches)
boolean getDefaultUseCaches()
```

As in the case of caching configuration, the default user interaction setup can be configured for all URLConnection instances created. Invoking the static setDefaultAllowUserInteraction() method will affect the default behavior of all URLConnection instances created after invocation. The individual behavior of instances may still be modified using the setAllowUserInteraction() method. The default user interaction behavior may be queried using the static getDefaultAllowUserInteraction() method.

```
static void setDefaultAllowUserInteraction(boolean allowuserinteraction)
static boolean getDefaultAllowUserInteraction()
```

There are two methods for installing additional content handlers. One is to replace the factory object used to look up content handler instances, and another is to configure the existing factory object. The setContentHandlerFactory() method may be used to effect the first method; its details will be discussed in the section covering creation of custom content handlers.

```
static void setContentHandlerFactory(ContentHandlerFactory fac)
```

Sometimes, a remote server may not return a header value for the content type, or may return an incorrect MIME type. In such cases, the static guessContentTypeFromStream() method may be used to ask the URLConnection class or subclass to deduce the content type by its binary encoding. The method will return null if the content type cannot be deduced. The method rewinds the input stream passed so that it does not chew off part of the content.

```
static String guessContentTypeFromStream(InputStream is) throws IOException
```

The URLConnection may also try to guess the type of a resource by its filename. Users may provide an alternative type-guessing algorithm by supplying an object implementing the java.net.FileNameMap interface. The existing type-guessing algorithm may be retrieved as well using the getFileNameMap() method.

```
static FileNameMap getFileNameMap()
static void setFileNameMap(FileNameMap map)
```

Retrieving URL Headers Using URLConnection

The examples for using the getContent() and openStream() methods in the java.net.URL class also apply for the URLConnection class. The getContent() methods are identical, and the openStream() method is renamed to getInputStream(). The only difference is that we can set up the connection before actually performing the request. However, because the setup examples are particular to a specific transport protocol (for example, HTTP), we will defer these examples until our HTTP URLConnection discussion.

The following example uses a generic URLConnection to retrieve and print the header information. It is included to show the correct way of iterating through the header key-value pairs. Note that this example is not efficient when used with the HTTP protocol because it retrieves both the headers as well as the content. The HTTP protocol supports a request for the headers only. We will demonstrate this HTTP-specific functionality in another example.

```java
// URLHeaders.java

import java.net.*;

// Prints the header information of a URL connection
public class URLHeaders {
 public static void main(String[] args) {
  if (args.length != 1) {
   System.err.println("Usage: URLHeaders <url>");
   System.exit(1);
  }

  URL url = null;
  try {
   url = new URL(args[0]);
  } catch (MalformedURLException e) {
   System.err.println("Malformed URL argument: " + e.getMessage());
   System.exit(1);
```

```
    }

    try {
    URLConnection connection = url.openConnection();
    connection.connect();

    int n=0;
    while((connection.getHeaderFieldKey(n) != null) ||
        (connection.getHeaderField(n) != null)) {
      System.out.println(connection.getHeaderFieldKey(n) + ": " +
              connection.getHeaderField(n));
      n++;
    }
    } catch (java.io.IOException e) {
      System.err.println(e.getClass().getName() + ": " + e.getMessage());
      System.exit(1);
    }

    System.exit(0);
  }
}
```

The first line in the output for this example has a `null` header key name and a value containing the HTTP response of the server. This behavior is particular to Sun's HTTP protocol handler implementation and is not documented. We will later show a standard method for obtaining the HTTP response. The output provides interesting information that web browsers typically don't make available. For example, the HTTP Server header identifies the product name and version of the server used by the W3C consortium. We can also notice that the page expiration is set to ten minutes, by comparing the Date header with the Expires header.

C:\Beg_Java_Networking\Ch12>**java URLHeaders http://www.w3c.org/**
null: HTTP/1.1 200 OK
Date: Thu, 16 Aug 2001 13:11:05 GMT
Server: Apache/1.3.6 (Unix) PHP/3.0.11
P3P: policyref="http://www.w3.org/2001/05/P3P/p3p.xml"
Cache-Control: max-age=600
Expires: Thu, 16 Aug 2001 13:21:05 GMT
Last-Modified: Tue, 14 Aug 2001 16:39:37 GMT
ETag: "d419f-4a60-3b795449"
Accept-Ranges: bytes
Content-Length: 19040
Keep-Alive: timeout=15
Connection: Keep-Alive
Content-Type: text/html; charset=us-ascii

Standard Java Handlers

Sun's Java 2 JREs include several different protocol and content handlers. The following issues limit their utility:

❑ The required protocol and content handlers for the Java 2 platform are not specified. Therefore, any application depending on such a handler may not be portable across JVM implementations.

❑ The types supported by content handlers are not specified. For example, an application reading a resource whose content type is text/html does not know what type of object the getContent() method will return. Although it is possible to discover what the default Sun handlers return, dependence on their behavior will not be portable.

In general, it is easier to use unknown protocol handlers since they all provide a simple byte-streaming service. In contrast, content handlers are more difficult to use because the type of Java object they will return cannot be easily predicted (unless documented).

In the Sun JRE implementation, protocol handlers are placed in the sun.net.www.protocol package. The Sun Standard Edition JRE 1.3.1 supports the following protocols: doc, file, ftp, gopher, http, jar, mailto, netdoc, systemresource, verbatim. Of these protocols some are standard, and some are Sun-proprietary. Of the supported protocols, only two are documented in any significant manner: http and jar. The public Java 2 APIs include two abstract subclasses of the URLConnection class, these are called HttpURLConnection and JarURLConnection.

java.net.HttpURLConnection Class

The java.net.HttpURLConnection class extends URLConnection with support for HTTP-specific stream operations. In particular the HttpURLConnection object permits users to:

❑ Specify the HTTP request method: one of GET, POST, HEAD, OPTIONS, PUT, DELETE, TRACE

❑ Obtain the HTTP response code: there are several different response codes listed in the HttpURLConnection class. These include the HTTP_OK (100) code and the HTTP_NOT_FOUND (404)

❑ Specify behavior when receiving a redirect response

❑ Request disconnection if further requests are not expected

❑ Check if the protocol handler is using a proxy

An instance HttpURLConnection is obtained by invoking the openConnection() method on a java.net.URL instance encapsulating an HTTP URL, and then type-casting the returned value. An example of such usage is shown in the code fragment to follow.

An HTTP-scheme URL object is first created. Then the openConnection() method is invoked, but instead of assigning the result to a URLConnection variable, it is type-cast into an HttpURLConnection variable. This way, we can invoke the special HTTP-related methods. In this example, we show how a Java program can verify that an HTTP URL refers to a resource that actually exists.

The HttpURLConnection setRequestMethod() is first used to instruct the stream handler to retrieve only the response headers, not the actual data. Since we only care to check about the existence of the resource, we can be efficient and prevent unnecessary downloading of the contents. Next, the code fragment explicitly invokes the connect() method. This is not necessary since the next method will invoke connect() anyways, but it helps in the readability of the code (it makes the transition change explicit).

Finally, we invoke the HttpURLConnection getResponseCode() method to identify the server's response to our request. If the resource exists, the server should return the HTTP_OK constant, otherwise it will return an error code whose description we will print out. Note that if the server requires authentication, an error code will be returned as well.

357

```
// HttpURLVerify.java

import java.net.*;

// Verifies that a resource identified by a HTTP URL is available

public class HttpURLVerify {
  public static void main(String[] args) {
    if (args.length != 1) {
      System.err.println("Usage: HttpURLVerify <url>");
      System.exit(1);
    }

    URL url = null;
    try {
      url = new URL(args[0]);
      if ((!url.getProtocol().equalsIgnoreCase("http"))
              && (!url.getProtocol().equalsIgnoreCase("https"))) {
        System.err.println("URL argument must use the HTTP protocol");
        System.exit(1);
      }
    } catch (MalformedURLException e) {
      System.err.println("Malformed URL argument: " + e.getMessage());
      System.exit(1);
    }

    try {
      HttpURLConnection connection =
        (HttpURLConnection) url.openConnection();

      connection.setRequestMethod("HEAD");   // just the headers (no data)
      connection.connect();

      int code = connection.getResponseCode();
      if (code == HttpURLConnection.HTTP_OK) {
        System.out.println("Verified URL " + url);
        System.exit(0);
      } else {
        System.out.println("Error verifying URL " + url + ": "
                            + connection.getResponseMessage());
        System.exit(1);
      }
    } catch (java.io.IOException e) {
      System.err.println(e.getClass().getName() + ": " + e.getMessage());
      System.exit(1);
    }
  }
}
```

C:\Beg_Java_Networking\Ch12>**java HttpURLVerify www.wrox.com**
Malformed URL argument: no protocol: www.wrox.com

C:\Beg_Java_Networking\Ch12>**java HttpURLVerify http://www.wrox.com**
Verified URL http://www.wrox.com

HTTP POST

The next HttpURLConnection example will demonstrate the use of the HTTP POST operation. The following sequence of steps must be:

1. Determine the URL for the POST resource (typically a CGI script or a Servlet)

2. Create an HttpURLConnection and configure it to send a POST request, enable output so that the POST arguments can be written, and set the POST content type

3. Write the POST content, and close the output stream

4. Read the server's response (terminated by the end-of-file)

The type of data written to POST server-side program depends on the application. Many times, the data is written in a URL-encoded form of attribute=value pairs, separated by an ampersand '&' character.

The program example below demonstrates coding of an HTTP POST operation. The target of the POST operation is a CGI program made available at Sun's Java site for demonstration of HTTP POST requests. The server-side program expects a URL-encoded content with a single attribute called string whose value is to be reversed. The URL for the POST operation is hard-coded into the program, but the actual data sent is taken as a single command line argument.

```java
// HttpPost.java

import java.net.*;
import java.io.*;

// Demonstrates an HTTP POST operation (hard-coded to URL)
public class HttpPOST {
  public static void main(String[] args) {
    if (args.length != 1) {
      System.err.println("Usage: HttpPOST <message>");
      System.exit(1);
    }

    try {

      // Point to Sun's demo backwards POST URL
      URL url = new URL("http://java.sun.com/cgi-bin/backwards");
      String message = args[0];
```

Our program creates an HttpURLConnection to the CGI program's URL, and configures that connection for a POST operation, output, and the appropriate content type (MIME URL encoded type). Once the connection has been configured, the program invokes the connect() method to explicitly move into the connected state. The connect method may fail if the HTTP server cannot be reached, or the URL identified does not exist or does not support a POST operation (for example it is not executable).

```java
HttpURLConnection connection =
        (HttpURLConnection) url.openConnection();

    connection.setRequestMethod("POST");
    connection.setDoOutput(true);
    connection.setRequestProperty("content-type",
                        "application/x-www-form-urlencoded");
    connection.connect();
```

Once the connection has been established we write the attribute (`string`) followed by the equals `'='` sign and the URL-encoded message (using the `java.net.URLEncoder` utility). The output stream must also be closed in order to signal completion to the server-side program.

```
PrintWriter writer =
        new PrintWriter(new OutputStreamWriter(connection
        .getOutputStream()));
    try {
      writer.print("string=" + URLEncoder.encode(message));
    }
    finally {
      writer.close();
    }
```

After writing the `POST` content we can reads-back the server's response. As shown before, we also check the response code to differentiate between an operation response and an error message.

```
if (connection.getResponseCode() != HttpURLConnection.HTTP_OK) {
        System.err.println("POST Error: "
                          + connection.getResponseMessage());
        System.exit(0);
    }

    // Read the response
    BufferedReader reader =
      new BufferedReader(new InputStreamReader(connection
        .getInputStream()));

    try {
      String line = reader.readLine();
      while (line != null) {
        System.out.print(line);
        line = reader.readLine();
      }
    }
    finally {
      reader.close();
    }
  } catch (java.io.IOException e) {
    System.err.println(e.getClass().getName() + ": " + e.getMessage());
    System.exit(1);
    }
  }
}
```

The program may be executed on an Internet connected host as shown:

```
C:\Beg_Java_Networking\Ch12>java HttpPOST "hello world"
hello world reversed is: dlrow olleh
```

java.net.JarURLConnection Class

The `java.net.JarURLConnection` class extends `URLConnection` with support for Java Archive (JAR) stream operations. The JAR format is used to store and compress multiple files in a Windows Zip-compatible format. Some of the JAR files are known as manifest and provide meta-information about the archive such as its digital signatures. A JAR URL is of the format:

```
jar:<hierarchical-url>!<spec>
```

For example, `jar:http://wrox.com/java/begin.jar!/chapter12/URLHeaders.class`
refers to a file `/chapter12/URLHeaders.class` in the JAR file available as
`http://wrox.com/java/begin.jar`. The `JarURLConnection` methods may be used to obtain
the attributes, entries and certificates of the JAR file, as well as its content represented as an instance of
`java.util.jar.JarFile`.

Providing Additional Handlers

Extensibility is the core design goal of the Java URL protocol and content handler architecture. Users
may provide additional handlers and/or replace existing handlers. To understand how this can be
accomplished, we need to present a more detailed diagram of the Java URL classes. In the UML class
diagram below, we show two additional Java interfaces called `URLStreamHandlerFactory` and
`ContentHandlerFactory`. Each of these two interfaces has a single method taking a string
description of the protocol or content type and returning a handler object (if available). When the
`java.net.URL` class is first presented with a URL for a new protocol, it uses the
`URLStreamHandlerFactory` interface to request a `URLStreamHandler` instance for the protocol.
Similarly, when the `URLConnection` object is asked to provide the content of the remote resource,
using the `getContent()` method, it uses the `CreateHandlerFactory` interface to retrieve a
`ContentHandler` for the MIME-type of the content.

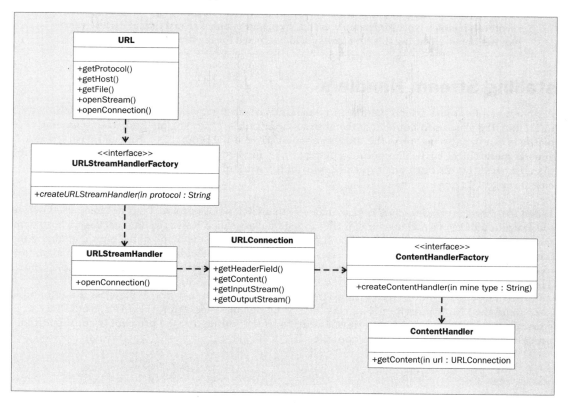

In order to add or replace one or more handlers it is necessary to alter the behavior of the protocol and content factories. There are two options:

❑ **Configure the default factory objects**: Although the Java API does not define any standard implementations of the protocol and content factory interfaces, it does specify two special properties that can be used to configure the default implementations. The default URLStreamHandlerFactory is configured using the property java.protocol.handler.pkgs. Similarly, the default ContentHandlerFactory is configured using the java.content.handler.pkgs property. We will discuss the details of their use later.

❑ **Replace the default factory objects with custom implementations**: The java.net.URL class has a static method called setURLStreamHandlerFactory() that can be used to completely replace the URLStreamHandlerFactory object used to obtain URLStreamHandler instances for specific protocols. Similarly, the URLConnection class has a static method called setContentHandlerFactory() that can be used to completely replace the ContentHandlerFactory implementation used to obtain ContentHandler instances for particular MIME types. An example of this approach will also be shown later on.

Typically, it is preferable to configure the default factory objects since it is the simplest approach. It also is more flexible since the configuration can be provided at the command-line. Replacing the default factory objects requires special security permissions and does not really add any new capabilities.

> **WARNING: the java.net.URL class will only perform a single lookup for each scheme (protocol) handler type (for example, http, ftp, and so on). The instance of each stream handler obtained during this first lookup will be cached for the life of the JVM.**

Installing Stream Handlers

A stream handler must extend the URLStreamHandler abstract class, either directly or indirectly. At a minimum, the class must implement the abstract openConnection() method. The remaining methods can be inherited from the URLStreamHandler if the protocol's URL can be parsed as a generic hierarchical URL. The openConnection() method returns an instance of a class extending the abstract URLConnection. Typically, most of the work of a stream handler is left to the class extending URLConnection.

When the java.net.URL class is instantiated with a URL whose protocol has not been used before in the execution of the virtual machine, it tries to load a class called Handler in a package whose name matches the protocol. For example, if the URL protocol is http the name of the class containing the handler must be http.Handler. The class name may be preceded by a default package name, for example, in the Sun JRE the protocol handlers are placed in the package sun.net.www.protocol. Thus, when creating an http URL the java.net.URL class tries to load the sun.net.www.protocol.http.Handler class and create an instance. If the class is not found, does not extend the URLStreamHandler class, or has no default constructor, the java.net.URL constructor will throw a MalformedURLException to indicate that the protocol is not supported. This process is illustrated in the diagram opposite.

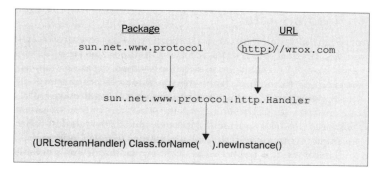

New handlers may be installed by configuring additional package prefixes. The `java.protocol.handler.pkgs` property may be used to specify one or more additional package name prefixes. Prefix values must be separated by the bar ('|') character. The `java.net.URL` class will first try to obtain a protocol handler instance by pre-pending each user-supplied prefix in order. The default prefix is tried if none of the user-supplied prefixes match a class.

For example, in order to add support for the time protocol introduced in Chapter 9, we could create a class called `wrox.protocol.time.Handler` and add the `wrox.protocol` prefix to the handler package path. When first creating a time protocol URL, such as time://time-a.nist.gov, the `java.net.URL` would try to obtain the class for the string "`wrox.protocol + . + time + .Handler`" and attempt to create an instance. The byte code for the class must be in the classpath, and the class must extend the `URLStreamHandler` interface and have a default constructor. We will demonstrate use of this mechanism later when we develop a protocol handler for the `WHOIS` protocol.

The advantage of this naming convention is that many protocols may be supported with minimal configuration. For example, when adding `wrox.protocol` to the package prefix list, any number of protocols may be supported as long as they are placed in that package as specified above. The main disadvantage is that protocol implementations from different packages cannot be mixed in arbitrary order. For example, if `wrox.protocol` contained support for `http` and `ftp` it would not be possible to use the `http` protocol handler and defer to the default handler for the `ftp` protocol. Another minor disadvantage is that every handler class must be called `Handler` for this mechanism to work.

The Java property value may be set at the command line invocation of the JVM, or may be set programmatically. To set at the command line, use the `-D` flag as shown below:

```
java -Djava.protocol.handler.pkgs="wrox.protocol|acme.protocol"
```

In order to set the property programmatically, you must invoke the `java.lang.System` `setProperty()` method as shown below:

```
System.setProperty("java.protocol.handler.pkgs",
                   "wrox.protocol|acme.protocol");
```

If a security manager has been installed, the `write` property permission must be granted in a policy file as shown below:

```
grant {
 permission java.util.PropertyPermission "java.protocol.handler.pkgs",
                   "write";
};
```

Using URLStreamHandlerFactory

The alternative approach is to install a URLStreamHandlerFactory object by invoking the java.net.URL setURLStreamHandlerFactory() method. The first time a new URL protocol is encountered, the java.net.URL class will consult the installed stream factory object invoking the createURLStreamHandler() method. If the stream factory object supports the given protocol, then it should return a URLStreamHandler instance, otherwise it should return null. The returned URLStreamHandler instance should be one creating URLConnection objects capable of performing remote operations using the protocol specified. Although this is not stated in the documentation, Sun's JRE java.net.URL implementation will still use its internal handler lookup mechanism if the installed factory returns null. Therefore, it is not possible to cleanly uninstall Sun's default stream handlers, for example, completely removing support for HTTP.

Implementing URLStreamHandlerFactory

A trivial implementation of the factory interface that always returns null to create requests is shown below:

```
// NullURLStreamHandlerFactory.java

import java.net.*;

// A minimal stream handler factory supporting no protocols
public class NullURLStreamHandlerFactory
 implements URLStreamHandlerFactory {

// Returns the URLStreamHandler for the requested protocol, or null
public URLStreamHandler createURLStreamHandler(String protocol) {
  return(null);
 }
}
```

The above stream handler factory can be installed as shown below:

```
URL.setURLStreamHandlerFactory(new NullURLStreamHandlerFactory())
```

A URLStreamHandlerFactory may only be installed once in the lifetime of a JVM. A second attempt will throw a java.lang.Error exception. Setting the stream handler factory also requires special security permission. The java.lang.RuntimePermission with target name setFactory must be provided if a security manager has been installed. Readers should be warned that this property also grants code the ability to set the various socket factories. The ability to set socket factories can be exploited to deny service, or monitor all network transmissions, and should therefore not be granted to untrusted code.

Installing Content Handlers

A content handler must extend the ContentHandler class, either directly or indirectly. At a minimum, the handler must implement the getContent() method. This method uses the URLConnection to read the content as raw bytes, and then parses the data and constructs an appropriate Java object. It is the responsibility of the URLConnection to invoke the right content handler for the type of the resource identified by the URL.

Content handlers are identified by MIME type – a separate content handler class must be provided for each MIME type. MIME types have a top-level type and a sub type, for example, the MIME type for a regular text file is `text/plain`, where `text` is the **top-level type** and `plain` is the **sub type**. MIME types may also have additional parameters but they will be ignored in selecting the content handler.

The base `URLConnection` method uses a mechanism for selecting content handlers that is similar to that of the `URLStreamHandler` class. If a `getContent()` request is made on a URL resource whose type is `text/plain`, the default content handler will look for a class called `plain` in a package called `text`. As before, a package prefix may be added before the name; for example, the Sun JRE stores its content handlers in a package called `sun.net.www.content`. It will therefore look for the `text/plain` content handler by looking up the **class** name `sun.net.www.content.text.plain`. The content handler naming mechanism is illustrated below.

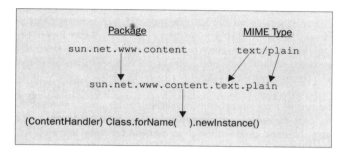

Note that because Java is case-sensitive, the MIME top-level type and sub type must be used in lower-case. This choice breaks the traditional Java convention of naming classes with a capital first letter. The `URLConnection` lookup mechanism differs from the `URLStreamHandler` lookup mechanism in that part of the MIME sub type is used as a class name, as opposed to the fixed `Handler` class name used in the `URLStreamHandler` lookup.

New content handlers may be installed by providing additional package prefixes using the `java.content.handler.pkgs` property and multiple prefixes must be separated by the bar ('|') character. As before, the property may be set at the command line, or programmatically. Readers should refer to the earlier stream handler installation discussion for examples on setting properties in the command line and within programs. A complete content handler for the Comma Separated Value (CSV) format will be shown in the in-depth examples section.

Unlike stream (protocol) handlers there is no method for installing content handlers that will guarantee their use. Because the `URLConnection` class is abstract, a stream-protocol specific class must always extend it. Therefore, it is possible that a stream handler may decide to use an alternative mechanism for content handler selection. In practice, this is not much of a problem since most stream handlers defer to the base `URLConnection getContent()` method implementation.

Using ContentHandlerFactory

The alternative approach is to install a `ContentHandlerFactory` object by invoking the `URLConnection setContentHandlerFactory()` method. The first time a new MIME type is encountered, the `URLConnection` class will consult the installed content factory object invoking the `createContentHandler()` method. If the content factory object supports the given MIME type, then it should return a `ContentHandler` instance, otherwise it should return `null`. Although this is not stated in the documentation, Sun's JRE `URLConnection` implementation will still use its internal handler lookup mechanism if the installed factory returns `null`.

MIME Header Problems

The Java content handler architecture is dependent on the correct assignment of MIME types to resources. If a resource is mistyped then the wrong handler will be used, probably resulting in a `null` object being returned. For example, an HTML file has a MIME type of `text/html`, however, it can also be thought of as a text file with MIME type `text/plain`. If the server reports its type as `text/plain`, the receiving application may open it in a text editor instead of an HTML-editor. Similarly, a GIF image has a MIME type of `image/gif` but may also be considered a binary file and reported as `application/octet-stream`.

In more rare cases, the server may completely mislabel content, for example due to a filename extension conflict. The only defense against such problems is to try to guess the data type by looking at the stream. Some binary formats, such as image and audio formats, are well suited for such guessing due to their standard format. Text encodings such as HTML whose standards are less strictly enforced are typically more difficult to deduce. The `URLConnection` class supports content deduction through the static `guessContentFromStream()` method. If the resource is read from a file, it is also possible to try to guess the content by the filename extension. The `URLConnection` class supports this through the protected `guessContentTypeFromName()` method.

In-Depth Examples

In this section we will show in-depth examples of a stream and a protocol handler. The stream handler will provide support for the `WHOIS` protocol. The `WHOIS` protocol is a query/response protocol used to access the directory services of Internet name and address registrars. The protocol handler will support parsing of Comma Separated Values (CSV) resources. CSV is a popular format for exchanging tabular information generated programs such as spreadsheets and address organizers.

A WHOIS Protocol Stream Handler

The `WHOIS` protocol is an old Internet (ARPANET) query/response protocol used to access the databases of the Internet address and naming registrars. Because the Internet is administered by multiple entities a central directory is required to facilitate problem resolution. For example, if an administrator detects a security attack from an external IP address, he/she must somehow identify to whom that address belongs. Although it is possible to resolve the DNS name for the address, not all addresses can be reverse-resolved. In a similar example, consider a company that wants to use a particular domain name that is already registered. One approach would be to contact the owner in order to negotiate a possible sale. It is therefore useful to be able to identify an e-mail or physical address for a DNS domain owner. Although there are alternative directory protocols today, such as `LDAP`, the `WHOIS` protocol continues to be used largely for historical reasons.

The WHOIS protocol is standardized as IETF RFC 954 (http://www.ietf.org/rfc/rfc954.txt). It is a very simple protocol. Clients connect to a WHOIS server at a well-known port (43), and write zero or more characters terminated by the special ASCII <CR> (Carriage Return) and <LF> (Line Feed) control characters. The server then writes a response back as characters and closes the connection. The structure of the query string is unspecified. The special ?<CR><LF> query may be used to obtain help on the service's use.

A stream handler must extend the URLStreamHandler class. Because we will be installing the stream handler by configuring the default stream handler, we must comply with the naming requirements. The handler class is therefore named Handler and placed in the whois package. We use the com.wrox package prefix, but any other valid package prefix could be used. At a minimum, the stream handler must implement the openConnection() method. In this case, the openConnection() method simply creates a new instance of the WhoisURLConnection class that we will show right after. The class implementation also overrides the getDefaultPort() method, returning the well-known WHOIS protocol port (43).

```
// Handler.java

package com.wrox.whois;

import java.io.IOException;
import java.net.*;

// WHOIS RFC 954 URL stream handler
public class Handler extends URLStreamHandler {

  // Well-known WHOIS protocol TCP port
  public static final int WHOIS_PORT = 43;

  // Returns a WhoisURLConnection in an unconnected state
  public URLConnection openConnection(URL u) throws IOException {
    return (new WhoisURLConnection(u));
  }

  // Returns the default WHOIS protocol port
  protected int getDefaultPort() {
    return (WHOIS_PORT);
  }
}
```

The code that actually performs the WHOIS protocol is placed in the WhoisURLConnection class. When designing a URLConnection sub class the most important decision is when to perform the actual transfer of information. One option is to use the connect() method to send the request and receive the response. In this approach, the response is cached locally and returned as a byte-array based input stream when getInputStream() is invoked. The advantage of this approach is that network connections are opened and closed in the same method, thereby avoiding leaving connections open and thus typing up system resources until the objects are garbage collected. Another advantage is that network connections are kept as short as possible (good for servers). Simple protocol stream handlers that do not support any exchange of header information typically take this approach.

The other approach is to retrieve header information at `connect()` time, but leave data retrieval up to the `getInputStream()` method. This approach is more difficult to implement because the `URLConnection` class allows for multiple invocations of the `getInputStream()` method. At each `getInputStream()` invocation, the returned stream must point to the beginning of the data. This requirement makes connection management more complex. The approach is typically taken by more complex protocols, such as HTTP, where multiple requests can be made per connection. In our implementation, we will use the first approach of reading and caching all the data at `connect()` time.

```
package com.wrox.whois;

import java.io.*;
import java.net.*;

// Represents a communication link with an RFC 954 WHOIS server
public class WhoisURLConnection extends URLConnection {
```

Most of the `URLConnection` functionality can be inherited. Two additional instance variables are provided to store the cached data and the headers. The WHOIS query response is stored as an array of bytes in the `data` instance variable. The headers are stored in a two dimensional string array called `headers`. The `headers` array has dimension `[n] [2]` where n is the number of headers. For any header i (where 0<i<n) the header attribute name is in `[i] [0]` and the header value is stored in `[i] [1]`.

```
protected byte[] data = null;
protected String[][] headers = null;
```

Although the WHOIS protocol does not provide any headers, we add HTTP-style `content length`, `type`, and `encoding` headers to assist content handlers. The constructor first invokes the super-class constructor because we depend on a lot of inherited functionality. The constructor further restricts the URL from having a query or a reference part.

```
public WhoisURLConnection(URL url) throws IOException {
    super(url);    // don't forget!

    if (url.getHost() == null) {
      throw new UnknownHostException("URL has null host value");
    }

    if ((url.getQuery() != null) || (url.getRef() != null)) {
      throw new MalformedURLException("whois URL cannot contain query "
                                + "or reference parts");
    }
  }
}
```

The `connect()` method checks the value of the inherited connected instance variable and returns if it has already been set. The first time `connect()` is invoked, the check will evaluate to `false` and the private `cacheData()` method will be invoked. The `cacheData()` method is the one actually performing the WHOIS query. The functionality was separated so that the cache can also be renewed by the `getInputStream()` method if caching has been disabled. All methods in the implementation are declared as synchronized because there are possible race conditions in our caching design. For example, if the `connect()` method is invoked by one thread and the `getInputStream()` by another, it is possible that the content will not be fully retrieved . The simple solution is to synchronize all methods.

```
public synchronized void connect() throws IOException {
    if (connected) {
      return;
    }
    cacheData();
    connected = true;
  }
```

The `cacheData()` method creates a TCP connection with the WHOIS server identified by the URL at the URL's port, if specified, otherwise at the well-known port. The query string is extracted from the URL by retrieving the file part, removing the leading slash ('/') character, and converting any URL encodings into regular characters. For example, for the URL whois://server/Wrox+Press, the file part is /Wrox+Press and will be converted into the string Wrox Press. An empty query string is interpreted as a help request and is converted into a "?" query.

Using the socket's output stream (buffered), the query string is written out followed by the Carriage-Return ('\r') and New-Line ('\n') control characters. Because the WHOIS standard does not specify the encoding of non-ASCII characters (whose value is greater than 127), the default platform encoding is used. Once the query has been sent, the method starts reading the response (blocking read) and copying it into a ByteArrayOutputStream. This type of stream stores all data written and permits their extraction as a byte-array. Once the copying is complete, the data is stored in the cache instance variable and the fake headers are generated containing its length, and hard coding the type and encoding.

```
// Performs the WHOIS query and caches the data
  protected synchronized void cacheData() throws IOException {
    Socket socket;
    if (url.getPort() == -1) {
      socket = new Socket(url.getHost(), Handler.WHOIS_PORT);
    } else {
      socket = new Socket(url.getHost(), url.getPort());
    }

    try {

      // Write whois request
      BufferedWriter writer =
        new BufferedWriter(new OutputStreamWriter(socket
          .getOutputStream()));

      // Query will be preceeded by the '/' character
      String query = url.getFile();

      if ((query == null) || (query.length() < 2)) {
        writer.write("?\r\n");
      } else {

        // Decode any special characters encoded in the URL
        query = URLDecoder.decode(query.substring(1, query.length()));
        writer.write(query + "\r\n");
      }

      writer.flush();

      // Copy data from socket input stream into a byte-array buffer
      ByteArrayOutputStream byteStream = new ByteArrayOutputStream();
      BufferedInputStream inStream =
        new BufferedInputStream(socket.getInputStream());
```

```
      byte[] buffer = new byte[4096];
      int len = inStream.read(buffer);
      while (len != -1) {
        byteStream.write(buffer, 0, len);
        len = inStream.read(buffer);
      }

      // Store the cached data and set the headers
      data = byteStream.toByteArray();

      headers = new String[][] {
        {
          "content-type", "text/plain"
        }, {
          "content-length", Integer.toString(data.length)
        }, {
          "content-encoding", "iso-8859-1"
        }
      };
    }
    finally {
      try {
        socket.close();
      } catch (Throwable e) {}
    }
  }
```

The getInputStream() method implementation is quite simple. The first action is to verify that we are in the connect state, by invoking the connect() method. It is always safe to call connect() since it only operates once. If the user has disabled caching for this URLConnection, the cacheData() method is invoked again to retrieve the latest value from the server. Finally, the method returns a ByteArrayInputStream object that is an InputStream backed by a byte-array.

```
public synchronized String getHeaderField(String name) {
    try {
      connect();
    } catch (IOException e) {
      return (null);
    }

    for (int i = 0; i < headers.length; i++) {
      if (headers[i][0].equalsIgnoreCase(name)) {
        return (headers[i][1]);
      }
    }
    return (null);
}

// Returns the value of the n-th header, or null if fewer headers exist
public synchronized String getHeaderFieldKey(int n) {
    try {
      connect();
    } catch (IOException e) {
      return (null);
    }

    if (n >= headers.length) {
```

```
        return (null);
      } else {
        return (headers[n][0]);
      }
    }

    // Returns the key of the n-th header, or null if fewer headers exist
    public synchronized String getHeaderField(int n) {
      try {
        connect();
      } catch (IOException e) {
        return (null);
      }

      if (n >= headers.length) {
        return (null);
      } else {
        return (headers[n][1]);
      }
    }
  }
```

Testing the WHOIS Stream Handler

Our coding of the WHOIS protocol stream handler is not complete. In order to test the handler, we will need to create a simple program that takes a URL as an argument and prints out its contents to standard-out. In fact, we have already written such a program earlier in this chapter called URLDump. The beauty of the Java stream handler architecture is that we can turn that program into a WHOIS client without changing a line of code!

The instructions required for compiling the protocol handler and URLDump example are shown below. The JVM is invoked with an argument setting the value of the java.protocol.handler.pkgs attribute to com.wrox. Recall that the full name of our handler is com.wrox.whois.Handler and therefore the prefix is com.wrox. We demonstrate the client by querying the Network Solutions WHOIS database for information about the wrox.com domain. Network Solutions is one of several private DNS domain registrars. Note the large notice on use statement – in the past, network mail spammers have used information harvested from this database to build their address databases.

C:\Beg_Java_Networking\Ch12>**javac URLDump.java com/wrox/whois/*.java**

C:\Beg_Java_Networking\Ch12>**java -Djava.protocol.handler.pkgs=com.wrox URLDump whois://whois.networksolutions.com/wrox.com**
The Data in Network Solutions' WHOIS database is provided by Network
Solutions for information purposes, and to assist persons in obtaining
information about or related to a domain name registration record.
Network Solutions does not guarantee its accuracy. By submitting a
WHOIS query, you agree that you will use this Data only for lawful
purposes and that, under no circumstances will you use this Data to:
(1) allow, enable, or otherwise support the transmission of mass
unsolicited, commercial advertising or solicitations via e-mail
(spam); or (2) enable high volume, automated, electronic processes
that apply to Network Solutions (or its systems). Network Solutions
reserves the right to modify these terms at any time. By submitting
this query, you agree to abide by this policy.

Registrant:
Wrox Press, Inc. (WROX-DOM)
  2710 W. Touhy Ave.
  Chicago, IL 60645

  Domain Name: WROX.COM

  Administrative Contact, Technical Contact:
    Hostmaster, InterAccess (DNS353) hostmaster@INTERACCESS.COM
    InterAccess Co
    168 N Clinton, 2nd Floor
    Chicago, IL 60661
    (312) 496-4650 (FAX) (312) 496-4499
  Billing Contact:
    Controller (IA-BILL) controller@INTERACCESS.COM
    InterAccess Co.
    168 N. Clinton, 3rd Floor
    Chicago, IL 60661
    US
    (312) 496-4400
    Fax- (312) 496-4499

  Record last updated on 11-Jun-2001.
  Record expires on 12-Jun-2003.
  Record created on 11-Jun-1995.
  Database last updated on 16-Aug-2001 00:56:00 EDT.

  Domain servers in listed order:

  NS1.INTERACCESS.COM   198.80.0.6
  NS2.INTERACCESS.COM   198.80.0.11

A CSV Content Handler

Our second in-depth example will present a content handler for the Comma Separated Value (CSV) format. The CSV format is used to represent tabular data with column values separated by a comma, and row values separated by new-line character. This format is sometimes used to exchange data between different spreadsheet, and other programs storing tabular information. There is no real standard for this format; however, most programs dealing with CSV data use similar conventions:

❑   Values that contain comma (',') characters as data are written in double-quotes ('"')

❑   Values containing double-quotes ('"') are themselves quoted and the actual double-quotes characters are written twice in sequence. For example, the single value he said "hello" will be stored as "he said ""hello""". Empty values are never quoted so the ambiguity is removed.

❑   Lines may be separated by a New-Line (UNIX), or a Carriage-Return followed by a New-Line (Microsoft Windows/DOS)

❑   Sometimes the first line may contain headers describing each column, but because this is not always the case, we will assume all lines contain actual data

A content handler must extend the `ContentHandler` class. Because we choose to install our content handler by configuring the default content handler factory, we follow the MIME-based naming conventions. The MIME type for the CSV type is `text/csv`. Therefore we need to name the content handler class `csv` and place it in a package called `text`. Again, we use the package prefix `com.wrox` so that we can identify the path in the property. Remember that we have to ignore the Java class naming convention and name our handler class in all lower-case letters.

When designing a content handler, one must decide on the Java object representation of the parsed data. As a tabular format, the CSV contents could be represented as a two-dimensional array, a list of lists (rows/columns), a Swing table model, or an XML tree structure. A content handler may support multiple representations, one of which must be the default. It is very important that these representations be documented, otherwise use will be difficult. In this example we will support two representations; the default representation will be a `Vector` containing other vectors as elements representing rows, with each of the row Vectors containing Strings representing the column values. The second representation will be a Swing Table model (`javax.swing.table.TableModel`).

As a minimum, a content handler must implement the `getContent(URLConnection)` method. Because we want to support multiple representations, we will also have to implement the `getContent(URLConnection, Class[])` method.

```
// csv.java

package com.wrox.text;

import java.io.*;
import java.net.*;
import java.util.Iterator;
import java.util.Vector;
import javax.swing.table.DefaultTableModel;
import javax.swing.table.TableModel;

public class csv extends ContentHandler {
```

The `getContent()` method takes a `URLConnection` as argument and returns the default object representation of a CSV stream as a Vector of Vectors. The contents of the stream are accessed through an `InputStream` obtained by the `URLConnection` argument. The stream contents are in raw-byte format. Because we will be treating the bytes as characters, we need to convert them from 8-bit values into 16-bit Unicode values. This presents a problem for the non-ASCII codes in the range `127-255`. Without any additional information, we defer to the default platform conversion performed by the `BufferedReader`.

Most of the method code involves parsing of the CSV data. Due to the unconventional quoting escape mechanism used in this format, we cannot use the standard `StreamTokenizer` class and are forced to perform our own parsing (which can be messy). Basically, when reading a character we need to treat it differently based on the state we are in: regular, or in-string. In the regular state commas are treated as column separators. In the in-string state, commas are treated as normal value characters. We also need to worry about escaped quotes, which we detect by looking ahead to see if another quote immediately follows.

```
public Object getContent(URLConnection urlc) throws IOException {
    BufferedReader reader =
        new BufferedReader(new InputStreamReader(urlc.getInputStream()));

    Vector rows = new Vector();
```

```
        Vector columns = new Vector();

        StringBuffer buffer = new StringBuffer();

        String line = reader.readLine();
        while (line != null) {
          boolean inString = false;

          for (int i = 0; i < line.length(); i++) {
            char c = line.charAt(i);
            if ((c == ',') && (!inString)) {
              columns.add(buffer.toString());
              buffer.setLength(0);
            } else if ((c == '"') && (!inString)) {
              inString = true;
            } else if ((c == '"')
                        && ((i + 1 == line.length())
                            || (line.charAt(i + 1) != '"'))) {
              inString = false;
            } else if (c == '"') {
              buffer.append(c);
              i++;    // skip second string character
            } else {
              buffer.append(c);
            }
          }

          columns.add(buffer.toString());
          buffer.setLength(0);

          rows.add(columns);
          columns = new Vector();

          line = reader.readLine();
        }

        return (rows);
      }
```

The second getContent() method takes a URLConnection as argument as well as an array of Java object classes. The classes specify the type of object that must be returned in the order of preference. The sample implementation supports the two class representations: Vector and TableModel. If the user does not include one of the two in the array, the method will return null.

The implementation simply loops sequentially through the class-array argument and checks to see if one of the two supported has been included. The first supported class-type found in the ordered search is returned by delegating the parsing to either the default getContent() method (for Vector) or the protected getContentAsTableModel() method (for TableModel).

```
    public Object getContent(URLConnection urlc,
                             Class[] classes) throws IOException {

        if (classes == null) {
          return (getContent(urlc));
        }

        for (int c = 0; c < classes.length; c++) {
```

```
       if (classes[c].equals(Vector.class)) {
         return (getContent(urlc));
       } else if (classes[c].equals(TableModel.class)) {
         Vector vector = (Vector) getContent(urlc);
         return (getContentAsTableModel(vector));
       }
     }
     return (null);
   }
```

The `getContentAsTableModel()` takes the already parsed `Vector` of `Vectors` representation of the CSV stream and creates a `javax.swing.table.DefaultTableModel` instance. The `DefaultTableModel` object conveniently takes a `Vector` of `Vectors` as argument for the table data. Due to a restriction that all rows have the same number of columns, the method first identifies the maximum column number and then expands all rows up to that column with empty string values. The `DefaultTableModel` also requires specification of the column names (as a `Vector`), so the method numbers the columns sequentially.

```
   protected TableModel getContentAsTableModel(Vector vector) {

       // Figure out maximum number of columns in a line
       int maxColumn = 0;
       for (Iterator iter = vector.iterator(); iter.hasNext(); ) {
         Vector line = (Vector) iter.next();
         maxColumn = Math.max(maxColumn, line.size());
       }

       // Expand all lines to the maximum number of columns
       for (Iterator iter = vector.iterator(); iter.hasNext(); ) {
         Vector line = (Vector) iter.next();
         while (line.size() < maxColumn) {
           line.add("");
         }
       }

       // Create names for the headers
       Vector headers = new Vector(maxColumn);
       for (int i = 0; i < maxColumn; i++) {
         headers.add(Integer.toString(i));
       }

       // Return a mutable model backed by the values read
       return (new DefaultTableModel(vector, headers));
     }
   }
```

Testing the CSV Content Handler

In order to test our content handler we need to write a program that will try to read the content of a URL as a Swing Table model and then display it in a window. To demonstrate our program, we will use a `file` URL, since it is not easy to find published (that is, permanent) web URLs identifying a CSV formatted document.

```
   // ShowCSV.java

   import java.io.*;
```

375

```
import java.net.*;
import java.awt.*;
import javax.swing.*;
import javax.swing.table.*;

public class ShowCSV {

  public static final String CSV_MIME_TYPE = "text/csv";

  public static void main(String[] args) {
    if (args.length != 1) {
      System.err.println("Usage: ShowCSV <url>");
      System.exit(1);
    }

    URL url = null;
    try {
      url = new URL(args[0]);
    } catch (MalformedURLException e) {
      System.err.println("Malformed URL argument: " + e.getMessage());
      System.exit(1);
    }
```

The program is complicated by the fact that the CSV MIME type is not configured by default in the Sun JREs. As a result, the stream handler reports the type `text/plain` and our content handler is never invoked. We work around the problem by adding a mapping between the `.csv` extension and the `text/csv` MIME type. This is accomplished by installing a `FileNameMap` instance that only checks for the `.csv` extension and defers all other requests to the default `FileNameMap`.

```
final FileNameMap defaultMap = URLConnection.getFileNameMap();

    URLConnection.setFileNameMap(new FileNameMap() {
      public String getContentTypeFor(String filename) {
        if (filename.toLowerCase().endsWith(".csv")) {
          return ("text/csv");
        } else {
          return (defaultMap.getContentTypeFor(filename));
        }
      }
    });
```

Using the `java.net.URL` object created, we invoke the `openConnection()` method so that we can access the content-type for the resource. If the content-type of the resource is not `text/csv`, we know that our work-around was not successful and that our CSV handler is not going to be invoked. In such a case we issue an error. The main reason for this failure would be the retrieval of the resource from a remote server that provided the wrong MIME type. Unlike the local file system that provides no MIME type, and therefore the `FileNameMap` is consulted, an incorrect MIME type cannot be worked-around for text formats. Binary formats can correct the type by looking at the unique header, however text files (plain versus CSV) cannot be distinguished in principle.

```
URLConnection urlc = null;
    try {
      urlc = url.openConnection();
      urlc.connect();
    } catch (IOException e) {
```

```
        System.err.println(e.getClass().getName() + ": " + e.getMessage());
        System.exit(1);
      }

      if (!CSV_MIME_TYPE.equalsIgnoreCase(urlc.getContentType())) {
        System.err.println("Error: URL MIME type reported as "
                          + urlc.getContentType() + ": expected "
                          + CSV_MIME_TYPE);
        System.exit(1);
      }
```

Once the MIME type has been verified we proceed by invoking the `getContent()` method of the `URLConnection` object with an explicit request for the `javax.swing.table.TableModel` representation.

```
      TableModel model = null;
      try {
        model = (TableModel) urlc.getContent(new Class[] {
          TableModel.class
        });
      } catch (IOException e) {
        System.err.println(e.getClass().getName() + ": " + e.getMessage());
        System.exit(1);
      }
```

If the object returned is non-null we know that the URL resource was a valid CSV file and we can proceed to display the `TableModel` in a `JTable` component embedded in a `JFrame` window.

```
      if (model == null) {
        System.err.println("Error retrieving CSV content: "
                          + "verify content handler installation");
        System.exit(1);
      }

      // Display content
      JFrame frame = new JFrame(url.toString());
      JTable table = new JTable(model);
      JScrollPane pane = new JScrollPane(table);
      frame.getContentPane().add(pane);
      frame.setSize(400, 150);
      frame.show();
    }
  }
```

Executing ShowCSV

We test the CSV content handler and viewer using the following test file (saved as `example.csv`). The file includes commas in quotes, and quotes in quotes to test our CSV parser.

```
a csv,file, example
"comma, in quotes","""quote start end""","quote "" in data"
```

The CSV content handler and CSV viewer can be compiled as shown below. The viewer is started in a Java Virtual Machine with the `java.content.handler.pkgs` property set to our package prefix `com.wrox`, and the data is referenced using a `file` URL. Both the compilation as well as the execution must be performed in the directory containing the `ShowCSV.java` file (on UNIX systems use the forward slash '/' to separate the path in the `javac` invocation).

C:\Beg_Java_Networking\Ch12>**javac ShowCSV.java com\wrox\text*.java**

C:\Beg_Java_Networking\Ch12>**java -Djava.content.handler.pkgs=com.wrox ShowCSV file:example.csv**

The CSV parsed data should then show up in a window as shown in the screenshot below:

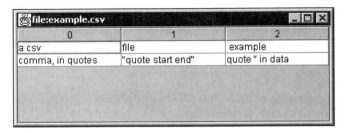

JDK 1.4 Changes

JDK 1.4 introduced a new class called `java.net.URI`; this class can be used to represent any URI that is compliant with RFC 2396 (http://www.ietf.org/rfc/rfc2396.txt). Unlike the `java.net.URL` class, instances of the URI class do not have to be associated with a content handler. Obtaining a `URLConnection` from a URI is a two-step process, requiring conversion of the URI to a URL object. Small changes were made to the `URLConnection` object to supply some convenience for headers and properties. With the addition of standard SSL support in JDK1.4, an `HttpsURLConnection` class was added to support access to SSL connection configuration. No standard content handlers have been provided. More information on JDK 1.4-related changes can be found in Chapter 21.

Summary

Resources on the Internet may be identified using the Uniform Resource Identifier (URI) naming scheme. The basic URI has the simple format `<scheme>:<scheme-specific-part>`. Because many URIs represent hierarchical information, a default hierarchical URI scheme-specific-part has been defined in the format of `<scheme>://<authority><path>?<query>`. There are two types of URIs: URLs that identify by location, and URNs that identify by unique name. URNs require an additional resolution mechanism. Although URNs are more flexible, due to the lack of a global directory infrastructure, URLs continue to prevail.

The Java URL handler architecture provides an extensible protocol and content plugin mechanism for Java applications. Because the plugin interface is at the language level, every Java application benefits from the additional protocol and content support. The entry point for this architecture is the `java.net.URL` class. The `java.net.URL` class constructor uses the scheme (usually protocol) part of the URL to locate a stream handler. The stream handler is responsible for parsing the scheme-specific-part of the URL, and for providing the resource as a byte-stream. Due to this dependence, only URLs for which stream handlers have been installed can be instantiated.

Content handlers are used to transform the raw byte-stream representation of a resource into a type-dependent Java object representation. There can be multiple Java representations of a resource, and applications may request for particular ones, as long as the content handler supports them.

Due to the generic nature of the Java handler architecture, and the general lack of documentation, many of its features are difficult for applications to use. In general, stream handlers are simpler because they provide a uniform byte-stream interface. Use of content handlers is more dependent on documentation since the result is an arbitrary Java object.

Users may install their own stream and content handlers, making them available to every Java application. Installation involves configuration, either at the command line, or programmatically. Two in-depth examples of a WHOIS protocol stream handler, and a Comma Separated Values (CSV) content handler were shown to illustrate the handler design and installation process.

Implementing an HTTP Server

In this chapter, we will implement a practical example of an HTTP 1.0- and CGI-compliant HTTP server. While HTTP 1.0 is a large protocol, HTTP 1.1 is even larger. HTTP 1.1 primarily focuses on improving performance by introducing persistent connections and better cache validation commands. It also more than doubles the number of HTTP response codes. Since HTTP 1.1 is fully compatible with HTTP 1.0, the example in this chapter can be easily expanded to HTTP 1.1. However this would also double the lines of source code and many HTTP servers don't need all these features.

We will first analyze a number of operation details of both standards (HTTP 0.9 and HTTP 1.0), with which we need to comply. Then we will design the classes that we need and implement them.

We will investigate the following:

- ❑ How to use the classes of the `java.io` and `java.net` packages to process HTTP GET, HEAD and POST requests
- ❑ How to prepare the environment and execute a CGI program
- ❑ How to design a class hierarchy that models an HTTP server

All of this will give the reader a lot more practice in writing larger Java networking applications.

The Quintessential HTTP Server

Our simple HTTP server prototype will only respond to GET requests and will simply return the request information as plain text in its response. It consists of two classes: the main application class SimpleHTTPServer and the class HTTPRequest, which handles incoming requests.

SimpleHTTPServer

Here is the source code for the SimpleHTTPServer class. Like all the classes we will be looking at in this chapter, it is available in the code package that can be downloaded from http://www.wrox.com/ for this chapter:

```
//SimpleHTTPServer.java

package com.wrox.simplehttpserver;

import java.net.*;

class SimpleHTTPServer {
```

The `main()` method creates a server socket that listens on port `1234` for incoming connections. While HTTP servers typically run on port 80, we choose port `1234` to avoid interference with other HTTP servers that might be running on your system. Port numbers between `1` and `1023` are reserved for well-known services such as FTP, Telnet and HTTP. On Linux or UNIX systems, you must run a process as the `root` user, to receive data on one of these ports. On Microsoft Windows, any user may use these ports without special privileges.

```
public static void main(String[] args) {
    ServerSocket server;
    Socket clientconnection;
    HTTPRequest request;

    try {
        server = new ServerSocket(1234);
```

Once a client (which is typically a browser) has connected, a socket for communicating with the client is returned. A new `HTTPRequest` object is constructed and the method `process()` is called to handle the request, after which the server continues to wait for the next connection.

```
        while (true) {
            clientconnection = server.accept();
            request = new HTTPRequest(clientconnection);
            request.process();
        }
    } catch (Exception e) {
        System.err.println("Unable to start SimpleHTTPServer: "
                            + e.getMessage());
        e.printStackTrace();
    }
  }
}
```

HTTPRequest

The `HTTPRequest()` constructor saves the socket that will communicate with the client in a variable called `clientconnection`.

Here is the source code for the `HTTPRequest` class:

```
// HTTPRequest.java

package com.wrox.simplehttpserver;

import java.net.*;
import java.io.*;
```

```
import java.util.*;

class HTTPRequest {
  private Socket clientconnection;
  public HTTPRequest(Socket clientconnection) {
    this.clientconnection = clientconnection;
  }
```

The `process()` method constructs a `PrintStream` object called `os` to print character lines to the client and a `BufferedReader` object called `br` to read character lines from the client.

```
public void process() {

  // Obtain the client connection's input and output streams
  try {
    PrintStream os = new PrintStream(clientconnection.getOutputStream());
    BufferedReader br =
      new BufferedReader(new InputStreamReader(clientconnection
        .getInputStream()));

    // Read the HTTP request line
    String request = br.readLine().trim();
```

We use a `StringTokenizer` object called `st` to parse the request method and the relative URI from the request line. Our server only processes `GET` requests. If it encounters a request for another method, it responds with the following line:

```
HTTP/1.0 501 Not Implemented
```

In the case of a `GET` request, it continues to read the request header lines until it encounters an empty line, which indicates the end of the request.

```
    // Parse the requested method and resource from the request line
    StringTokenizer st = new StringTokenizer(request);

    // Read in the method
    String header_method = st.nextToken();

    // Check if we support the method
    if (!header_method.equals("GET")) {
      os.print("HTTP/1.0 501 Not Implemented\r\n");
      os.flush();
      return;
    }

    // Read in the uri
    String header_uri = st.nextToken();

    // Read the header lines
    StringBuffer responseDocument = new StringBuffer();
```

After it returns a success response, the concatenated request strings and some additional remarks are printed out as our response entity-body.

```java
            // Create response
            responseDocument
              .append("If I were a real HTTP server and you asked me to send you "
                      + header_uri + "\r\n");
            responseDocument
              .append("(which is stored relative to my document root)
                       and you told me about\r\n");
            responseDocument
              .append("yourself with the following header lines:\r\n");

            String line = null;

            // Read the rest of the header until we encounter an empty line
            while ((line = br.readLine().trim()) != null && line.length() > 0) {
              responseDocument.append(line + "\r\n");
            }

            responseDocument
              .append("then I would open the file, read the bytes
                       and send them right back to you.\r\n");

            // Now we return the response
            os.print("HTTP/1.0 200 OK\r\n");
            os.print("Content-length: " + responseDocument.length() + "\r\n");
            os.print("Content-type: text/plain\r\n\r\n");
            os.print(responseDocument);
            os.flush();
        } catch (Exception e) {

            /* Normally we would catch the specific
             * exceptions to provide better error handling.*/
            System.err.println("Unable to process HTTPRequest: "
                               + e.getMessage());
            e.printStackTrace();
        }
```

The `finally` clause makes sure that the `clientconnection` socket is closed.

```java
        finally {
          try {
            clientconnection.close();
          } catch (IOException e) {
            // Ignore this
          }
        }
      }
    }
  }
```

Place the two files `SimpleHTTPServer.java` and `HTTPRequest.java` in a directory called `com\wrox\simplehttpserver`. To compile them, type the following command:

C:\Beg_Java_Networking\Ch13>**javac com\wrox\simplehttpserver*.java**

Enter the following command to start up the server:

C:\Beg_Java_Networking\Ch13>**java com.wrox.simplehttpserver.SimpleHTTPServer**

Enter the following URL in your browser:

http://localhost:1234/index.html

You should get the following response:

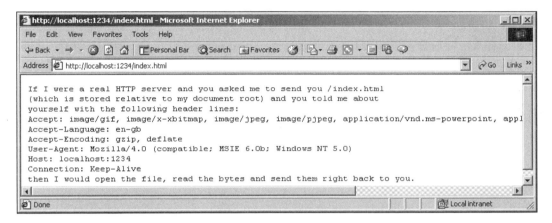

We use this prototype to explore and understand the basics of HTTP operation. A full-blown HTTP server requires better exception and error handling.

HTTP 1.0 Compliance

To be HTTP 1.0 compliant, our `SimpleHTTPServer` application still lacks the following:

❑   All message header strings should be encoded as **ISO 8859-1** characters. This encoding should be specified when the `InputStreamReader` is constructed and the `PrintStream` object should be replaced with a `BufferedWriter` object accordingly. **ISO** stands for **International Organization for Standardization**. The ISO provides a **catalog** of their standards at http://www.iso.ch/iso/en/ISOOnline.openerpage. An excellent introduction to the ISO 8859 character sets can be found at http://czyborra.com/charsets/iso8859.html and is called **The ISO 8859 Alphabet Soup**)

❑   An HTTP 1.0 compliant server must always respond in the HTTP version of the request, which may be HTTP 0.9 or HTTP 1.0. `HTTPRequest` should check for the existence of a version number in the request. If none exists, HTTP 0.9 may be assumed. This version does not use headers.

❑   The HEAD and POST request methods (which will be explained in detail in the next section) need to be implemented.

Apart from compliance, an HTTP server should also implement the following:

❑ Parallel processing of incoming requests in threads

❑ Logging of both errors and successful requests

❑ Return of the requested entity-body (typically an HTML document that was specified in the URL) and response entity-body headers describing its content (unless the server responds to an HTTP 0.9 request)

❑ Directory listings

❑ Secure connections – we will discuss these in further detail in Chapter 14

HTTP 1.0 Operation Details

We will now look at some of the major methods implemented in HTTP 1.0.

The HEAD Method

The HEAD method is used to test if a document on a server still exists, and if it has been modified recently. An important response entity header is Last-Modified which contains the timestamp for when the requested entity was last modified. HTTP 1.0 recommends the use of the following format for any timestamps in HTTP messages:

```
Sun, 06 Nov 1994 08:49:37 GMT
```

GMT indicates Greenwich Mean Time, which is used to eliminate problems with different time zones, so that the Last-Modified timestamp of documents can be compared regardless of the geographic location and time zone setting of the server it is requested from.

Let's use a telnet client as a web browser and send a HEAD request directly to an HTTP server (this is also useful to check if an HTTP server is up and running).

On a command line, enter:

C:\Beg_Java_Networking\Ch13>**telnet www.w3.org 80**

The screen will go utterly blank, with a single flashing cursor, but persevere, even though what is entered will not appear on the screen. Now type the following:

HEAD / HTTP / 1.0

Be careful to include the spaces. Press *Enter* twice so that the server knows your HEAD request is complete. The following result will be displayed on screen:

HTTP/1.1 200 OK
Date: Tue, 14 Aug 2001 14:18:47 GMT
Server: Apache/1.3.6 (Unix) PHP/3.0.11
P3P: policyref="http://www.w3.org/2001/05/P3P/p3p.xml"

Cache-Control: max-age=600
Expires: Tue, 14 Aug 2001 14:28:47 GMT
Last-Modified: Fri, 10 Aug 2001 18:08:04 GMT
ETag: "13c488-49c0-3b742304"
Accept-Ranges: bytes
Content-Length: 18880
Connection: close
Content-Type: text/html; charset=us-ascii

Please note that the server responds to an HTTP 1.0 request with an HTTP 1.1 response. Unlike HTTP 1.0, HTTP 1.1 only requires the server to respond in the same major version used by the client.

The POST Method

The POST method is used to send requests that contain a request entity-body, such as the parameters of an HTML form and the corresponding request entity headers that describe its contents.

Here is an HTML file from an example we will be running later in the chapter. Don't worry about implementing it now, as full instructions will be given later when the server is up and running. This example, however, demonstrates how such a POST request would work:

```
<HTML>
<HEAD>
  <title>Basic Form</title>
</HEAD>
<BODY>
  <H1>Basic Form</H1>
  <FORM METHOD=POST ACTION="http://localhost:1234/cgi-bin/form.pl">
    Enter your name:
    <INPUT TYPE="TEXT" NAME="NAME" SIZE="40"><P>
    Enter your e-mail address:
    <INPUT TYPE="TEXT" NAME="E-MAIL" SIZE="40"><P>
    <INPUT TYPE="SUBMIT">    <INPUT TYPE="RESET">
  </FORM>
</BODY>
</HTML>
```

This example uses a Perl script, form.pl – we could run it if we had Perl installed on our machine, which we will do later on. In order to run this however, it would be necessary to set the directory information for this script so that it was relative to the root document. It is easy enough to follow the logic in any case. This HTML form should display in your browser as follows, regardless of whether Perl is installed or not. Fill in the information with your own name and e-mail address:

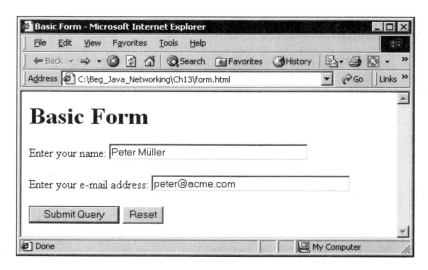

When the **Submit Query** button is clicked, the following POST request is made from Microsoft Internet Explorer 6.0:

```
POST /cgi-bin/form.pl HTTP/1.1
Accept: image/gif, image/x-xbitmap, image/jpeg, image/pjpeg, */*
Referer: http://localhost/form.html
Accept-Language: de
Content-Type: application/x-www-form-urlencoded
Accept-Encoding: gzip, deflate
User-Agent: Mozilla/4.0 (compatible; MSIE 6.0b; Windows NT 5.0)
Host: localhost
Content-Length: 40
Connection: Keep-Alive
Cache-Control: no-cache

NAME=Peter+M%FCller&E-MAIL=peter@acme.com
```

The first line requests the Perl CGI script form.pl to be executed.

The following lines are request header fields that inform the server about the capabilities and preferences of the browser, and provide information about the attached request entity-body:

❑ The Accept header indicates a list of media ranges, which are acceptable as a response to the request

❑ The Referer header field allows the client to specify the URI of the resource from which the request URI was obtained

❑ The Accept-Language header field restricts the set of natural languages that are preferred as a response (de requests a German response)

❑ The Content-Type header indicates the media type of the request entity-body

❑ Accept-Encoding restricts the sort of content-coding values that are acceptable in the response

❑ The `User-Agent` contains information about the user-agent (the HTTP browser) originating this request. This header has been introduced for statistical purposes, for tracing of protocol violations, and for automating responses tailored to known limitations or features of a browser

❑ The `Host` header field specifies the Internet host and port number of the resource being requested

❑ The `Content-Length` header field indicates the size of the request entity-body

❑ The `Connection` header field indicates that the browser wants to keep the connection open for subsequent requests

❑ The `Cache-Control` header indicates that the response to the request should not be derived from cache

The request entity-body is an `urlencoded` string of the form variables. Please note that all non-ASCII characters, such as the German umlaut ü used in this name, are encoded. If the HTML form had specified `GET` as the `FORM ACTION`, pressing the **Submit Query** button would have resulted in the following `GET` request:

```
http://localhost/cgi-bin/form.pl?NAME=Peter+M%FCller&E-MAIL=peter@acme.com
```

The URL is followed by the `urlencoded` query string. URLs do not allow blanks, so URL encoding replaces a blank with a + sign. The + sign itself would be encoded as `%2b`. The `GET` method should be used when queries are made. This makes good sense, because it is also possible to bookmark such URLs for later use. The `POST` method should be used when the request causes a permanent change of state of a resource on the server. Typically a `POST` method is used to submit form data that will be stored in a database (for example a banking transaction, or a purchase).

When the `GET` method is used to execute a CGI program, the query string is passed as an environment variable to the CGI program. Since some operating systems restrict the length of environment variables, it is a good idea to keep the query string short (less than 200 characters is a safe working limit).

CGI Execution

When the HTTP server translates the relative URI from the request line, it is responsible for recognizing whether a CGI program or a file resource is requested. A CGI program typically processes user input from an HTML form, acts upon it accordingly and returns a corresponding response in an HTML document. CGI programs are commonly stored in the path /cgi-bin/.

Preparing the CGI Environment

CGI 1.0 requires the following list of variables to be passed as environment variables to the executing CGI program. In our example application, most of these will be set in `HTTPConstants`. It is worth having a glance through them now, to acquaint ourselves with their names and potential values:

SERVER_SOFTWARE	The name and version of the HTTP server
	Format: name/version
SERVER_NAME	The server's hostname, DNS alias or IP address, as derived from the host part of the script URI

Table continued on following page

GATEWAY_INTERFACE	The revision of the CGI specification to which this server complies
	Format: CGI/revision
SERVER_PROTOCOL	The name and revision of the information protocol used for this request
	Format: protocol/revision
SERVER_PORT	The port number to which the request was sent
REQUEST_METHOD	The method with which the request was made ·
PATH_INFO	The extra path information, as given by the client, which is everything that follows the virtual pathname
PATH_TRANSLATED	The server-provided translation of PATH_INFO to a physical path
SCRIPT_NAME	The virtual path to the script
QUERY_STRING	The information that follows a question mark ? in the URL
REMOTE_HOST	The hostname making this request
REMOTE_ADDR	The IP address of the remote host making the request
AUTH_TYPE	The protocol-specific authentication method used in case the script was protected
REMOTE_USER	The user name if the user has been authenticated
REMOTE_IDENT	The remote user name if the server supports RFC 931 identification (http://www.ietf.org/rfc/rfc0931.txt). This should be used for logging purposes only
CONTENT_TYPE	The content type of request entities
CONTENT_LENGTH	The content length of request entities
HTTP_ACCEPT	The list of MIME types the client accepts
HTTP_HOST	The HTTP general-header field Host
HTTP_PRAGMA	The HTTP general-header field Pragma
HTTP_REFERER	The HTTP general-header field Referer
HTTP_USER	The HTTP general-header field User

When a secure connection is used, security relevant environment variables are also passed to the CGI program. These variables are prefixed by HTTPS (for example HTTPS_CLIENT_CERT).

The HTTP server typically executes the CGI program in a separate process as if the CGI program was started from the command line. The request entity-body (if present) is passed to the CGI program's **standard input**. The HTTP server usually writes the HTTP response line containing the status code and general response headers, such as SERVER_SOFTWARE. Then it directs the CGI program's **standard output** to the browser to write the response entity headers and a response entity-body (which is optional).

Compatibility with Older HTTP Versions

The HTTP 1.0 specification mandates backward compatibility with HTTP 0.9. We need to make sure that our HTTP server does the following:

❑ Recognizes the format of the request line for HTTP 0.9 and HTTP 1.0 requests

❑ Understands any valid request in the format of HTTP 0.9 or HTTP 1.0

❑ Responds appropriately with a message in the same protocol version used by the client

Fortunately, HTTP 0.9 is very simple, as it only defines GET requests. It does not use headers or MIME types. For practical reasons, we will make sure that our HTTP server also accepts HTTP 1.1 requests, as modern browsers such as Microsoft Internet Explorer 6.0 and Netscape Navigator 6 use this version. Since HTTP 1.1 is fully backward compatible, we can safely accept HTTP 1.1 requests and simply ignore HTTP 1.1-specific request headers.

Designing a Class Hierarchy

We will now have a look at the sort of files we need to accomplish this project. Don't worry too much about how the hierarchy will look – for now it is a good idea to concentrate on the relationships.

In the next section, we will go through each of the required files in turn.

Describing the Required Objects

We will call our main application class HTTPServer.

We will call our HTTP server configuration HTTPConfig, which will contain parameters such as the **document root** and the **port**. When an error occurs in reading the configuration file which initializes the HTTPConfig object, a ConfigFileException will be thrown. HTTPConfig will be initialized in the HTTPServer constructor.

Our HTTP server will also have a logging facility called HTTPLog to log successful requests and errors. The name of the log file will be stored in HTTPConfig. HTTPLog will be initialized in the HTTPServer constructor.

We will have a MIME type converter called MimeConverter to ascertain the file type based on the file extension of the requested document. MimeConverter will read in a file defining MIME types when it is initialized. When an error occurs while reading in this file, a ConfigFileException will be thrown. MimeConverter will be initialized in the HTTPServer constructor.

The three utility classes, HTTPConfig, HTTPLog and MimeConverter, should be independent of all other classes. They will be initialized once when the server starts up and they will be referenced from other classes that use them (for instance, errors can be logged from problems occurring in many classes).

HTTPServer constructs HTTPRequest objects to process incoming requests. Please note that in a real-world example, we would create a number of threads and reuse them since constructing objects frequently places a burden on the Java garbage collector and will inevitably lead to performance and memory problems.

The HTTPRequest object will parse the request headers and store them in an HTTPMessageHeaders object. All information relevant to CGI execution will be stored in an HTTPInformation object. Based on the HTTP method, HTTPRequest will create an HTTPGetHandler, HTTPHeadHandler or HTTPPostHandler object to handle the particular request.

HTTPGetHandler, HTTPHeadHandler and HTTPPostHandler will be derived from HTTPHandler.

The HTTPHandler will construct an HTTPResponse object and initialize it. The corresponding method object will construct the HTTPObject that is requested by the relative URI, which will be either an HTTPFileObject or an HTTPProcessObject (in the case of a CGI program). The constructed HTTPObject will add response entity headers such as Content-type to the HTTPResponse object (if required) and will then send it the client as the response entity.

Non-locale dependent constants such as HTTP header keywords that will be used by more than one class will be stored in an abstract class, HTTPConstants, that will be extended by all classes using the constants. Keeping all constants in one place makes it easier to maintain them.

The following diagram displays the most important classes and how they interact with each other:

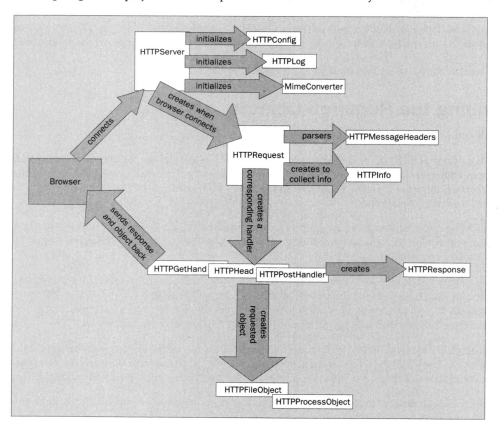

The HTTPServer Application

The source code for this application can be found in the code download for this chapter. When the Java files are installed, they should be run from the `C:\Beg_Java_Networking\Ch13\com\wrox\httpserver` directory.

HTTPConstants

All locale-independent application constants need to be defined in this abstract class, including low-level error messages and HTTP header strings. These constants are typically used in more than one class. All classes that use these constants, such as `HTTPRequest` and `HTTPResponse`, extend this class. It is good coding practice to maintain application constants like this to make maintenance easier. Constants that are only used in a single class (such as the `MIN_PORT` and `MAX_PORT` constants that are used when the port number is validated in the configuration class `HTTPConfig`) are declared as private static final variables in the corresponding class.

```java
// HTTPConstants.java

package com.wrox.httpserver;

abstract class HTTPConstants {

  // Resource error string
  protected static final String RESOURCE_ERROR =
    "Unable to read properties.";
  protected static final String VMVERSION_ERROR =
    "This application must be run with a 1.3.0 or higher version JVM.";

  // HTTP protocol constants
  protected static final String SERVER_SOFTWARE = "HTTPServer/1.0";
  protected static final String GATEWAY_VERSION = "CGI/1.1";
  protected static final String MIME_VERSION = "1.0";
  protected static final String DEFAULT_MIME_TYPE = "text/plain";
  protected static final String HTTP_09 = "HTTP/0.9";
  protected static final String HTTP_10 = "HTTP/1.0";
  protected static final String HTTP_11 = "HTTP/1.1";
  protected static final String HTTP_ENCODING = "8859_1";
  protected static final char HTTP_HEADER_FIELD_SEPERATOR = ':';
  protected static final String METHOD_GET = "GET";
  protected static final String METHOD_POST = "POST";
  protected static final String METHOD_HEAD = "HEAD";

  // Request and response header fields

  // General headers
  protected static final String HEADER_FIELD_DATE = "Date";
  protected static final String HEADER_FIELD_PRAGMA = "Pragma";

  // Header fields
  protected static final String HEADER_FIELD_CONTENTLENGTH =
    "Content-Length";
  protected static final String HEADER_FIELD_CONTENTTYPE = "Content-Type";
  protected static final String HEADER_FIELD_REFERER = "Referer";
  protected static final String HEADER_FIELD_USERAGENT = "User-Agent";
```

```
    protected static final String HEADER_FIELD_SERVER = "Server";

    // Additional header fields
    protected static final String HEADER_FIELD_ACCEPT = "Accept";
    protected static final String HEADER_FIELD_MIMEVERSION = "MIME-Version";

    // Buffer, backlog and timeouts
    protected int BUFFER_SIZE = 8192;
}
```

HTTPServer

In HTTPServer.java we define one class of variables – resources – which will hold all locale-specific messages for this class. We need to define this variable as static, since it is used in the static main() method. We have one file called httpserver.properties, which contains English messages used in this class. We could translate this file into another language and store it with a corresponding locale suffix in the same directory as the default English message file. The constructor of the HTTPLocalizedResources class expects the directory and file name (without the file extension) of the properties file to be loaded. separated by a '.'.

We check the version of the JVM in the static block. When the user starts up the server, the static block gets executed before the main() method. We need to make sure that the server runs with a 1.3.0 or higher version JVM, because we use an overloaded version of the Runtime.exec() method in the HTTPProcessObject class, and this has only been available since JDK 1.3. If we detect a lower JVM version, we print a corresponding error message and terminate the program.

```java
// HTTPServer.java

package com.wrox.httpserver;

import java.io.*;
import java.net.*;
import java.util.*;

public class HTTPServer extends HTTPConstants implements Runnable {

  // Localized messages and the application itself
  private static HTTPLocalizedResources resources;
  // Check if we run with the right JVM and read resources
  static {
    String vers = System.getProperty("java.version");
    if (vers.compareTo("1.3.0") < 0) {
      System.err.println(VMVERSION_ERROR);

      // Exit the JVM
      System.exit(1);
    }

    try {

      // Load locale-specific messages
      resources = new HTTPLocalizedResources("msg.httpserver");
    } catch (MissingResourceException mre) {
      System.err.println(RESOURCE_ERROR);
      System.exit(1);
    }
  }
```

The HTTPServer constructor expects the configuration file name as its only parameter. We are then able to run multiple instances of the server (such as one secure and one non-secure instance) on a single machine using different configuration files. We use this parameter to construct our HTTPConfig object. If the construction (that is, the parsing of the configuration file) fails, a ConfigFileException is thrown and we terminate the JVM, indicating abnormal termination. The MimeConverter object and the HTTPLog objects are constructed in a similar way.

```
public HTTPServer(String[] args) {
  if (args != null && args.length == 1) {
    try {
      HTTPConfig.initializeConfig(args[0]);
    } catch (ConfigFileException e) {

      /* An error occurred while reading the information       */
      /* A locale-specific error message is retrieved and displayed */
      System.err.println(resources.getResourceString("ERROR_HTTP_CONFIG")
                         + e.getMessage());
      exit(ABNORMAL_TERMINATION);
    }
  } else {

    // Write usage information and terminate
    System.err
      .println(resources.getResourceString("ERROR_INVALID_ARGUMENT"));
    exit(ABNORMAL_TERMINATION);
  }

  // Initialize MIME converter
  try {
    MimeConverter.initializeConverter(MIME_TYPES_FILES);
  } catch (ConfigFileException e) {

    // An error occurred while reading the mime types
    System.err.println(resources.getResourceString("ERROR_MIME_CONFIG")
                       + e.getMessage());
    exit(ABNORMAL_TERMINATION);
  }
```

The configuration has been read, so now we can initialize the logger, reporting any errors that may occur.

```
  try {
    HTTPLog.initializeLogger(HTTPConfig.config.getLogfile());
  } catch (IOException e) {

    // An error occurred while reading the mime types
    System.err.println(resources.getResourceString("ERROR_OPEN_LOGFILE")
                       + e.getMessage());
    exit(ABNORMAL_TERMINATION);
  }
}
private void exit() {
  exit(NORMAL_TERMINATION);
}
private void exit(int status) {
  System.exit(status);
}
```

When the server starts up, it creates an `HTTPServer` object, starts it as a thread and displays the server console. In the `main()` method, we construct our application object and assign it to `theApp`.

```java
public static void main(String[] args) {

    // Create an application instance
    HTTPServer theApp = new HTTPServer(args);

    // Start the server
    Thread server = new Thread(theApp);
    server.setDaemon(true);
    server.start();

    // Display console to allow the user to gracefully shut down the server
    BufferedReader br =
      new BufferedReader(new InputStreamReader(System.in));
    BufferedWriter bw =
      new BufferedWriter(new OutputStreamWriter(System.out));

    while (true) {
      try {
        bw.write(resources.getResourceString("CONSOLE_PROMPT"));
        bw.flush();
        String input = br.readLine();

        if (input != null && input
                .compareToIgnoreCase(resources
                .getResourceString("CONSOLE_QUIT_COMMAND")) == 0) {

          // The user requests to shut down the server
          theApp.shutdown();
          theApp.exit();
        }
      } catch (Exception e) {

        // Shutdown when a console exception occurs
        theApp.shutdown();
        theApp.exit(ABNORMAL_TERMINATION);
      }
    }
}
```

This section runs the server and listens for incoming requests using a `while` loop. We create a `Thread` object to start executing the `run()` method in a separate thread. We do this so that we can present a console that prompts the user for commands. The locale-specific console prompt is retrieved from the `resources` that we previously loaded using the method `getResourceString()` which will be explained later in this chapter. We only recognize the letter q currently as a command (which is also locale-specific) to shut down the server, but we could implement many other useful commands here, including refreshing the configuration or displaying runtime load statistics.

The `run()` method should look familiar to you already. We construct a server socket to listen either at all IP addresses of our machine or just at one specific IP address. To process incoming requests, we construct an `HTTPRequest`, passing the socket to communicate with that client, start the `HTTPRequest` and let it take care of the rest as the server continues to listen for the next incoming request.

```java
public void run() {
    ServerSocket server = null;
```

```
    try {

      // Get port to listen at for incoming requests
      int port = HTTPConfig.config.getPort();

      // Create socket and listen for incoming connections

      if (HTTPConfig.config.getBindAddress() == null) {
        server = new ServerSocket(port);
      } else {
        server = new ServerSocket(port, DEFAULT_BACKLOG,
                                  HTTPConfig.config.getBindAddress());
      }

      // Set an infinite timeout
      server.setSoTimeout(0);

      while (true) {
        Socket socket = server.accept();

        Thread request = new Thread(new HTTPRequest(socket));
        request.setDaemon(true);
        request.start();
      }
    } catch (Exception e) {
      System.err.println(resources.getResourceString("ERROR_HTTP_SERVER")
                         + e.getMessage());
      exit(ABNORMAL_TERMINATION);
    }
    finally {
      try {
        if (server != null) {
          server.close();
        }
      } catch (IOException e) {

        // Ignore this exception
      }
    }
  }
  public void shutdown() {

    // Closes the log
    HTTPLog.logger.close();
  }

  private static final int ABNORMAL_TERMINATION = 1;
  private static final int DEFAULT_BACKLOG = 50;

  // Class constants
  private static final String MIME_TYPES_FILES = "mime";
  private static final int NORMAL_TERMINATION = 0;
}
```

HTTPLocalizedResources

The `HTTPLocalizedResources` class helps us to separate text strings from the actual source code.

```java
// HTTPLocalizedResources.java

package com.wrox.httpserver;

import java.util.*;

class HTTPLocalizedResources {
```

The constructor uses the `static` method `ResourceBundle.getBundle()` to get an object of the appropriate `ResourceBundle` subclass. Since we specify a properties file as the parameter, we will get an object of the `PropertyResourceBundle` class and save it in an instance variable called `resources`. The only reason why we implement a class of its own and not use `ResourceBundle` directly, is that we want to provide a safe version of `getString()` called `getResourceString()` that does not throw a `MissingResourceException` when the key cannot be found.

```java
  private ResourceBundle resources;

  public HTTPLocalizedResources(String propertiesFile)
          throws MissingResourceException {

    // Load the localized messages from the properties file
    resources = ResourceBundle.getBundle(propertiesFile);
  }

  public String getResourceString(String res) {
    String str;
    try {
      str = resources.getString(res);
    } catch (MissingResourceException mre) {
      str = null;
    }
    return str;
  }
}
```

httpserver.properties

The `httpserver.properties` file contains all the messages that we use in the `HTTPServer` class. This file and the other message files all live in the `msg` directory in the code download, and supply the user with messages concerning exceptions and failures:

```
# httpserver.properties 1.0
# Resource strings for locale specific HTTPserver messages

# Application error messages
ERROR_INVALID_ARGUMENT=Usage: java com.wrox.httpserver.HTTPServer httpd.properties
ERROR_HTTP_CONFIG=HTTPServer configuration error:
ERROR_MIME_CONFIG=MIME configuration file error:
ERROR_HTTP_SERVER=HTTP server error:
ERROR_OPEN_LOGFILE=Error opening log file:
CONSOLE_PROMPT=HTTPServer - enter Q or q to quit>
CONSOLE_QUIT_COMMAND=q
```

This leads to an interesting digression, for while English is understood by most system administrators, there could be a requirement to provide localized messages for system administrators who do not speak English. The `ResourceBundle` mechanism makes it very easy to implement localized messages. In order to provide German messages when the application is run on a system with a German language locale (for example, Austria, Germany or Switzerland), the following `httpserver_de.properties` file would have to be placed in the same directory as `httpserver.properties`.

```
# httpserver_de.properties 1.0
# Resource strings for locale specific HTTPserver messages in German

# Application error messages
ERROR_INVALID_ARGUMENT=Verwendung: java com.wrox.httpserver.HTTPServer
httpd.properties
ERROR_HTTP_CONFIG=Fehler beim Einlesen der HTTPServer Konfigurationsdatei:
ERROR_MIME_CONFIG=Fehler beim Einlesen der MIME Konfigurationsdatei:
ERROR_HTTP_SERVER=HTTPServer Fehler:
ERROR_OPEN_LOGFILE=Fehler beim Öffnen der Log-Datei:
CONSOLE_PROMPT=HTTPServer - Geben Sie Q oder q ein um den Server zu stoppen>
CONSOLE_QUIT_COMMAND=q
```

The `getBundle()` call in the `HTTPLocalizedResources` constructor uses the system locale to look for a matching properties file. If no matching properties file can be found, the default properties file without a locale-specific name extension is loaded.

HTTPConfig

To avoid having to write the source code to parse a configuration file, we put our HTTP server configuration parameters into a properties file. This file, `httpd.properties`, contains some very important information, namely:

- ❏ The document root
- ❏ The log file name and address
- ❏ The CGI path

We will need all of these to be set correctly to run our example. If you decide to run this code in a different package structure than the one outlined, you will need to alter these values in order for the server to run.

Here is our default `httpd.properties` file:

```
# httpd.properties 1.0
# Configuration file for HTTPServer
# Where filenames are specified, you must use forward slashes.

#####################
# Mandatory settings #
#####################
# Port at which HTTPServer listens for incoming requests (default 80)
Port=1234

# The directory out of which you will serve your documents
```

```
DocumentRoot=C:/Beg_Java_Networking/Ch13

# Default document that is looked for when a directory is requested
DirectoryIndex=index.html

# Log file where errors and accesses are logged
LogFile=C:/Beg_Java_Networking/Ch13/httpserver.log

# Directory on server where CGI scripts are stored
CGIPath=C:/Beg_Java_Networking/Ch13/cgi-bin

#####################
# Optional settings #
#####################
# Bind address for multi-homed host so that the server will only accept connect
requests
# to one of its addresses (the loopback address 127.0.0.1 is not allowed here)
#BindAddress=
```

Here is the source code for the `HTTPConfig` class that reads the properties file and checks the validity of all parameters.

```java
// HTTPConfig.java

package com.wrox.httpserver;

import java.util.*;
import java.io.*;
import java.net.*;

class HTTPConfig extends HTTPConstants {

  // Class constants
  private final static int MAX_PORT = 65535;
  private final static int MIN_PORT = 0;

  // Convenience config object
  public static HTTPConfig config = null;

  // Error messages
  private HTTPLocalizedResources resources;

  // Configuration settings
  private HTTPLocalizedResources httpConfig;
  private int port;
  private String documentRoot;
  private String directoryIndex;
  private File logfile;
  private String cgiPath;
  private InetAddress bindAddress;

  protected HTTPConfig(String configFile) throws ConfigFileException {

    // Read in message resources
    try {
      resources = new HTTPLocalizedResources("msg.httpconfig");
    } catch (MissingResourceException mre) {
```

```
        // The resource is missing, throw exception with error message
        throw new ConfigFileException(resources
          .getResourceString(RESOURCE_ERROR));
    }

    // Read in configuration file
    try {
      httpConfig = new HTTPLocalizedResources(configFile);
    } catch (MissingResourceException mre) {

      // The resource is missing, throw exception with error message
      throw new ConfigFileException(resources
        .getResourceString("ERROR_UNABLE_TO_READ_CONFIG_FILE"));
    }
```

If the configuration file could be correctly read, the instance variables are now initialized and the port parsed.

```
    try {
      port = Integer.parseInt(httpConfig.getResourceString("Port"));
    } catch (NumberFormatException nfe) {

      // The port was not a valid integer value
      throw new ConfigFileException(resources
        .getResourceString("ERROR_INVALID_PORT"));
    }

    // Check the range of the port value
    if (port < MIN_PORT
            || port > MAX_PORT) {   // The port value is out of range
      throw new ConfigFileException(resources
        .getResourceString("ERROR_INVALID_PORT"));
```

Let us take a look at how we check that the document root directory parameter is an existing directory. The getResourceString() method returns null if the DocumentRoot parameter cannot be found (it catches the MissingResourceException and handles it by returning null). To check whether documentRoot is a valid directory, we put all the source code into a try-catch block where we catch all exceptions. We do not care what exception is thrown – whether it is a NullPointerException because the configuration parameter could not be found in the properties file, or whether it simply is not a directory, in which case we explicitly throw an Exception. We catch all exceptions and throw a ConfigFileException with a message that indicates a problem with the documentRoot parameter.

```
        // Get document root
    }
    documentRoot = httpConfig.getResourceString("DocumentRoot");

    // Check if this is a valid and existing directory
    try {
      File dir = new File(documentRoot);
      if (!dir.isDirectory()) {
        throw new Exception();
      }
    } catch (Exception e) {
```

```
    // Invalid document root directory
    throw new ConfigFileException(resources
      .getResourceString("ERROR_INVALID_DOCUMENTROOT"));
}
```

This section gets the `CGIPath` pathname, where all CGI programs are stored. It determines whether the path is a valid and an existing directory. It does this with all the values in the properties file in turn.

```
cgiPath = httpConfig.getResourceString("CGIPath");

// Check if this is a valid and existing directory
try {
  File dir = new File(cgiPath);
  if (!dir.isDirectory()) {
    throw new Exception();
  }
} catch (Exception e) {

  // Invalid document root directory
  throw new ConfigFileException(resources
    .getResourceString("ERROR_INVALID_CGIPATH"));
}

// Get directory index
directoryIndex = httpConfig.getResourceString("DirectoryIndex");

// The directory index must not be null and not empty
if (directoryIndex == null || directoryIndex.length() == 0) {
  throw new ConfigFileException(resources
    .getResourceString("ERROR_INVALID_DIRECTORYINDEX"));

  // Get log file
}
String logfilename = httpConfig.getResourceString("LogFile");

// The log file must be a valid file we can append entries to
try {
  logfile = new File(logfilename);
  if (!logfile.exists()) {

    // Create log file
    FileOutputStream fos = new FileOutputStream(logfile);
    fos.close();
  }

  // Check if the logfile is a file and we can write to it
  if (!logfile.isFile() ||!logfile.canWrite()) {
    throw new Exception();
  }
} catch (Exception e) {
  throw new ConfigFileException(resources
    .getResourceString("ERROR_INVALID_LOGFILE"));
}
```

The following lines get the optional `BindAddress` parameter. This must be a valid IP address for this host, or else an empty `String`.

```
            String strBindAddress = httpConfig.getResourceString("BindAddress");
            if (strBindAddress != null && strBindAddress.length() > 0) {

                // The bind address must be a valid IP address for this host
                // or an empty string
                strBindAddress = strBindAddress.trim();
                try {
                    int i = 0;
                    InetAddress[] localAddresses =
                        InetAddress
                            .getAllByName(InetAddress.getLocalHost().getHostName());
                    if (localAddresses.length > 0) {
                        String localIPAddresses[] = new String[localAddresses.length];
                        for (i = 0; i < localAddresses.length; i++) {
                            if (localAddresses[i].getHostAddress().compareTo(strBindAddress)
                                    == 0) {
                                break;
                            }
                        }

                        // This will throw an exception when we have not found the address
                        bindAddress =
                            InetAddress.getByName(localAddresses[i].getHostAddress());
                    } else {
                        throw new Exception();
                    }
                } catch (Exception e) {
                    throw new ConfigFileException(resources
                        .getResourceString("ERROR_INVALID_BINDADDRESS"));
                }
            } else {
                bindAddress = null;
            }
        }

        public InetAddress getBindAddress() {
            return bindAddress;
        }

        public String getCGIPath() {
            return cgiPath;
        }
```

The following method returns the `DirectoryIndex` parameter, which is the default file that is requested when the requested URI points to a directory rather than a file.

```
        public String getDirectoryIndex() {
            return directoryIndex;
        }

        public String getDocumentRoot() {
            return documentRoot;
        }

        public File getLogfile() {
            return logfile;
        }

        public int getPort() {
```

```
      return port;
  }

  public static void initializeConfig(String configFile)
        throws ConfigFileException {
    config = new HTTPConfig(configFile);
  }
}
```

We follow correct coding guidelines and perform all parameter-validity and range checking in the constructor, so that, once we have constructed the object, we know all the parameter variables have been correctly initialized or a `ConfigFileException` containing a corresponding error message would have been thrown.

Here is the `httpconfig.properties` file that contains all of these error messages. Again, this lives in the `msg` folder:

```
# httpconfig.properties 1.0
# Resource strings for locale specific HTTPConfig messages

# Error messages while reading in configuration file
ERROR_UNABLE_TO_READ_CONFIG_FILE=Unable to read configuration file.
ERROR_INVALID_PORT=Invalid Port number.
ERROR_INVALID_DOCUMENTROOT=Invalid DocumentRoot entry.
ERROR_INVALID_DIRECTORYINDEX=Invalid DirectoryIndex entry.
ERROR_INVALID_BINDADDRESS=Invalid BindAddress entry.
ERROR_INVALID_CGIPATH=Invalid CGIPath entry.
ERROR_INVALID_LOGFILE=Invalid LogFile entry.
```

ConfigFileException

The `ConfigFileException` class extends `Exception` and can only be constructed by passing an error message.

```
// ConfigFileException.java

package com.wrox.httpserver;

class ConfigFileException extends Exception {

  public ConfigFileException(String msg) {
    super(msg);
  }
}
```

MimeConverter

The `MimeConverter` class is used to translate file name extensions such as `.html` or `.gif` into their corresponding MIME types such as `text/html` or `image/gif`. We need to provide the MIME type in our response to the browser, so that the browser knows how to render a returned resource.

Objects of this class cannot be created using new, because the constructor is defined as `protected`. The class contains a public static MimeConverter object called `converter`, which is constructed using the static method `initializeConverter()`. This enables the stand-alone use of this class. This also saves us from the problem where we would have stored an object of this type, since it really does not belong to any object we create.

```
// MimeConverter.java

package com.wrox.httpserver;

import java.util.*;
import java.io.*;

class MimeConverter extends HTTPConstants {
```

The constructor reads the localized error messages for this class from the `mimeconverter.properties` file, which is stored in the `msg` directory.

```
// Convenience converter object
public static MimeConverter converter = null;

// Stores the messages
private HTTPLocalizedResources resources;

// Stores the mime types
private HTTPLocalizedResources mimeTypes;
```

Next, it reads the defined MIME types from the `mime.properties` file. We do not need to declare resources or mimeTypes as static class variables, because we will only create a single object of this class anyway (unlike the error messages in the HTTPRequest class which are saved in a static class variable, so that the file is not read in whenever a new HTTPRequest object is constructed). The method `getContentType()` extracts the extension of the filename passed as parameter and searches the Hashtable for a matching MIME type. If it cannot find a matching MIME type, `text/plain` is returned.

```
protected MimeConverter(String mimeFile) throws ConfigFileException {

    // Read in message resources
    try {
      resources = new HTTPLocalizedResources("msg.mimeconverter");
    } catch (MissingResourceException mre) {

      // The resource is missing, throw exception with error message
      throw new ConfigFileException(resources
        .getResourceString(RESOURCE_ERROR));
    }

    // Read in mime type properties file
    try {
      mimeTypes = new HTTPLocalizedResources(mimeFile);
    } catch (MissingResourceException mre) {

      // The resource is missing, throw exception with error message
      throw new ConfigFileException(resources
        .getResourceString("ERROR_UNABLE_TO_READ_MIME_PROPERTIES"));
    }
```

```
    }
    public String getContentType(String filename) {

      // Get file extension first
      int index = filename.lastIndexOf('.');

      // Index of first character of file extension
      int extensionIdx = index + 1;

      if (index != -1 && (extensionIdx < filename.length())) {

        // The filename has an extension
        String extension = filename.substring(extensionIdx);
        String mimeType = mimeTypes.getResourceString(extension);

        if (mimeType != null && mimeType.length() > 0) {
          return mimeType;
        }
      }

      return DEFAULT_MIME_TYPE;
    }
    public static void initializeConverter(String mimeFile)
          throws ConfigFileException {
      converter = new MimeConverter(mimeFile);
    }
}
```

The message file for the `MimeConverter` class contains only one message:

```
# mimeconverter.properties 1.0
# Resource strings for locale specific MimeConverter messages

# Error messages while reading in mime.properties file.
ERROR_UNABLE_TO_READ_MIME_PROPERTIES=Unable to read mime.properties.
```

HTTPGMTTimestamp

An object of the class `HTTPGMTTimestamp` represents an immutable, current timestamp.

```
// HTTPGMTTimestamp.java

package com.wrox.httpserver;

import java.text.*;
import java.util.*;
```

The constructor creates a `Date` object that represents the current timestamp.

```
class HTTPGMTTimestamp {

  // Instance variable
  private Date currentTime;
```

The `SimpleDateFormat` object `formatter` is created as a static variable, because there is no need to construct it every time an `HTTPGMTTimestamp` object is created.

```java
    // Class variable
    private static SimpleDateFormat formatter =
      new SimpleDateFormat("d MMM yyyy hh:mm:ss 'GMT'", Locale.US);

    public HTTPGMTTimestamp() {
      currentTime = new Date();
    }
```

The only method in this class is `toString()` which returns a string representation of the timestamp in the HTTP 1.0 required format.

```java
    public String toString() {
      return formatter.format(currentTime);
    }
  }
```

HTTPLog

The `HTTPLog` class uses a single file for logging both errors and successful requests.

```java
  // HTTPLog.java

  package com.wrox.httpserver;

  import java.io.*;
  import java.util.*;

  class HTTPLog extends HTTPConstants {
```

Objects of this class cannot be constructed using `new`, because the constructor is defined as `protected`. The class contains a public static `HTTPLog` object called `logger`, which is constructed using the static method `initializeLogger()`.

```java
    // Convenience logger object
    public static HTTPLog logger = null;

    // Localized messages
    private HTTPLocalizedResources resources;
```

The `HTTPLog` constructor creates a `BufferedWriter` called `logfileWriter` that will be used to append entries to the log file.

```java
    // Instance variables
    private BufferedWriter logfileWriter;

    protected HTTPLog(File logfile) throws IOException {
      try {
        resources = new HTTPLocalizedResources("msg.httplog");
      } catch (MissingResourceException mre) {
```

```
        // The resource is missing, throw exception with error message
        throw new IOException(resources.getResourceString(RESOURCE_ERROR));
    }

    // Initialize instance variables, append to the logfile
    this.logfileWriter =
        new BufferedWriter(new FileWriter(logfile.toString(), true));
}

public void close() {
    try {
        logfileWriter.flush();
        logfileWriter.close();
    } catch (IOException e) {

        // Ignore exceptions when closing the logfile

    }
}

public static void initializeLogger(File logfile) throws IOException {
    logger = new HTTPLog(logfile);
}
```

The `log()` method writes the log entry. It is important to put the code that writes to the log file into a `synchronized` block. Synchronized blocks should always be as short as possible to enable maximum concurrency. If the method cannot write to the log file, it has to write an error message to the console, so that the system administrator is informed about the problem.

```
public void log(HTTPInformation info) {
    String logMessage = info.remoteAddr + "-[" + new HTTPGMTTimestamp()
                        + "]-" + info.requestString + "-" + info.status
                        + "\r\n";
    synchronized (logfileWriter) {
        try {
            logfileWriter.write(logMessage);
        } catch (IOException e) {

            /* The log could not be written, write out at least */
            /* a warning message to the console so that the     */
            /* user is informed of the problem                  */
            System.err
                .println(resources.getResourceString("ERROR_WRITING_LOG"));
        }
    }
}
```

The information we log includes the following:

❑   The client's numeric IP address

❑   The GMT timestamp

❑   The request line

❑   The HTTP status code

The message file for the `HTTPLog` class contains only one message:

```
# httplog.properties 1.0
# Resource strings for locale specific HTTPLog messages

# HTTP log error messages
ERROR_WRITING_LOG=Unable to write to the log file.
```

The JDK 1.4 provides sophisticated logging and tracing support in its `java.util.logging` package. The `HTTPLog` and all other utility classes including `MimeConverter` and `HTTPConfig` are modeled after the `Logger` class in that package.

HTTPException

`HTTPException` requires an `HTTPStatus` code and a message for construction, so that the exception handler in the `HTTPRequest` class `handleException()` can respond to the client accordingly and can append a meaningful log entry.

```java
// HTTPException.java

package com.wrox.httpserver;

class HTTPException extends Exception {

  // HTTP status code
  private int status;

  public HTTPException(String msg, int status) {

    /* Calls the superclass constructor to construct an Exception */
    /* with the specified detail message                          */
    super(msg);

    // Initialize instance variables
    this.status = status;
  }

  public int getStatus() {
    return status;
  }
}
```

HTTPStatus

The `HTTPStatus` class encapsulates all HTTP status codes defined by HTTP 1.0 as public class variables.

```java
// HTTPStatus.java

package com.wrox.httpserver;

import java.util.*;

class HTTPStatus {
```

```
/* Informational 1xx                                         */
/* HTTP/1.0 does not define any 1xx status                   */

/* Successful 2xx                                            */
/* This class of status code indicates that the client's request */
/* was successfully received, understood, and accepted       */

public final static int OK = 200;
public final static int CREATED = 201;
public final static int ACCEPTED = 202;
public final static int NO_CONTENT = 204;

/* Redirection 3xx                                           */
/* This class of status code indicates that further action needs to be */
/* taken by the user agent in order to fulfill the request   */

public final static int MULTIPLE_CHOICES = 300;
public final static int MOVED_PERMANENTLY = 301;
public final static int MOVED_TEMPORARILY = 302;
public final static int NOT_MODIFIED = 304;

/* Client error 4xx                                          */
/* The 4xx class of status code is intended for cases in which the */
/* client seems to have erred                                */

public final static int BAD_REQUEST = 400;
public final static int UNAUTHORIZED = 401;
public final static int FORBIDDEN = 403;
public final static int NOT_FOUND = 404;

/* Server error 5xx                                          */
/* Response status codes beginning with the digit "5" indicate cases in */
/* which the server is aware that it has erred or is incapable of */
/* performing the request                                    */

public final static int INTERNAL_ERROR = 500;
public final static int NOT_IMPLEMENTED = 501;
public final static int BAD_GATEWAY = 502;
public final static int SERVICE_UNAVAILABLE = 503;

// Status strings: Informational 1xx not used

// Successful 2xx
private final static String OK_STRING = "OK";
private final static String CREATED_STRING = "Created";
private final static String ACCEPTED_STRING = "Accepted";
private final static String NO_CONTENT_STRING = "No Content";

// Redirection 3xx
private final static String MULTIPLE_CHOICES_STRING = "Multiple Choices";
private final static String MOVED_PERMANENTLY_STRING =
  "Moved Permanently";
private final static String MOVED_TEMPORARILY_STRING =
  "Moved Temporarily";
private final static String NOT_MODIFIED_STRING = "Not Modified";

// Client Error 4xx
private final static String BAD_REQUEST_STRING = "Bad Request";
private final static String UNAUTHORIZED_STRING = "Unauthorized";
```

```java
    private final static String FORBIDDEN_STRING = "Forbidden";
    private final static String NOT_FOUND_STRING = "Not Found";

    // Server Error 5xx
    private final static String INTERNAL_ERROR_STRING =
      "Internal Server Error";
    private final static String NOT_IMPLEMENTED_STRING = "Not Implemented";
    private final static String BAD_GATEWAY_STRING = "Bad Gateway";
    private final static String SERVICE_UNAVAILABLE_STRING =
      "Service Unavailable";

    /* The hashtable is used to store the strings that describe an http    */
    /* status code under the key of the http status so that it can be used */
    /* for logging                                                         */

    private static Hashtable strings;

    static {
      strings = new Hashtable();

      // Informational 1xx: not used

      // Successful 2xx
      strings.put(new Integer(OK), OK_STRING);
      strings.put(new Integer(CREATED), CREATED_STRING);
      strings.put(new Integer(ACCEPTED), ACCEPTED_STRING);
      strings.put(new Integer(NO_CONTENT), NO_CONTENT_STRING);

      // Redirection 3xx
      strings.put(new Integer(MULTIPLE_CHOICES), MULTIPLE_CHOICES_STRING);
      strings.put(new Integer(MOVED_PERMANENTLY), MOVED_PERMANENTLY_STRING);
      strings.put(new Integer(MOVED_TEMPORARILY), MOVED_TEMPORARILY_STRING);
      strings.put(new Integer(NOT_MODIFIED), NOT_MODIFIED_STRING);

      // Client error 4xx
      strings.put(new Integer(BAD_REQUEST), BAD_REQUEST_STRING);
      strings.put(new Integer(UNAUTHORIZED), UNAUTHORIZED_STRING);
      strings.put(new Integer(FORBIDDEN), FORBIDDEN_STRING);
      strings.put(new Integer(NOT_FOUND), NOT_FOUND_STRING);

      // Server error 5xx
      strings.put(new Integer(INTERNAL_ERROR), INTERNAL_ERROR_STRING);
      strings.put(new Integer(NOT_IMPLEMENTED), NOT_IMPLEMENTED_STRING);
      strings.put(new Integer(BAD_GATEWAY), BAD_GATEWAY_STRING);
      strings.put(new Integer(SERVICE_UNAVAILABLE),
                  SERVICE_UNAVAILABLE_STRING);
    }
```

Since we need the corresponding text description of an HTTP status code in our response line (this is optional but it is common practice to include it), we use a method getString() that returns the description of an HTTP status. To accomplish this, we will store the description strings in a static Hashtable (which is initialized in the static block) with the status code as the key (the HTTP 1.0 status codes and descriptions are according to RFC 1945 – http://www.ietf.org/rfc/rfc1945.txt).

```java
    public static String getString(int status) {
      return (String) strings.get(new Integer(status));
    }
}
```

HTTPRequest

The `HTTPRequest` class processes an HTTP request. For every accepted connection, the `HTTPServer` `run()` method constructs an `HTTPRequest` object and passes the socket that was obtained from the `accept()` call as a parameter, which serves as the communication endpoint for the server to talk to the browser. After constructing the `HTTPRequest` object, the `run()` method calls `start()`, so that the request processes in a concurrently running thread. This allows the `run()` method in the `HTTPServer` class to continue immediately and wait for a new incoming connection.

```java
// HTTPRequest.java

package com.wrox.httpserver;

import java.net.*;
import java.io.*;
import java.util.*;

class HTTPRequest extends HTTPConstants implements Runnable {

  // Localized messages
  private static HTTPLocalizedResources resources;

  // Read message resources
  static {
    try {
      resources = new HTTPLocalizedResources("msg.httprequest");
    } catch (MissingResourceException mre) {
      System.err.println(RESOURCE_ERROR);
      System.exit(1);
    }
  }

  // Instance variables
  private Socket socket;
  private BufferedOutputStream bos;
  private HTTPBufferedInputStream bis;
  private HTTPHandler handler;
  private HTTPMessageHeaders headers;
  private HTTPInformation info;
  private String header_method;
  private String header_uri;
  private String header_protocol;

  public HTTPRequest(Socket socket) {

    // Initialize instance variables
    this.socket = socket;
```

As we need to read both character strings and then later, in case of a `POST` request, also bytes, we need a special input stream that can do both.

The `HTTPRequest` constructor creates the I/O streams that we need to communicate with the client. Any error that occurs while constructing the streams is processed by the exception handler `handleException()`, which makes sure that an adequate response is returned to the browser and that the error is logged. We construct an empty `HTTPMessageHeaders` object called `headers`, which we will use to store the request headers when we parse them. We also construct an `HTTPInformation` object called `info` where we will store all data that is relevant in the context of this request for logging or for CGI execution.

```
    try {

      bis = new HTTPBufferedInputStream(socket.getInputStream(),
                                   BUFFER_SIZE, HTTP_ENCODING);
      bos = new BufferedOutputStream(socket.getOutputStream(), BUFFER_SIZE);
    } catch (Exception e) {
      HTTPException httpre =
        new HTTPException("ERROR_HTTP_GET_STREAMS" + e.getMessage(),
                          HTTPStatus.INTERNAL_ERROR);
      handleException(httpre);
    }

    headers = new HTTPMessageHeaders();
    info = new HTTPInformation();
  }
```

The following getHeaders() method parses the request lines until an empty line is encountered:

```
private void getHeaders() throws HTTPException {
    String line;
    boolean firstLine = true;

    try {

      // Read the request headers, line by line
      while ((line = bis.readLine()) != null && line.length() > 0) {
        if (firstLine) {

          // Store request string for logging
          info.requestString = line;

          // Parse the HTTP request line to determine the request method
          parseRequestLine(line);

          if (header_protocol.equalsIgnoreCase(HTTP_09)) {

            // No more headers, so just continue
            return;
          }

          // The first line has been processed
          firstLine = false;
        } else {
          parseHeaderLine(line);
        }
      }
    } catch (IOException e) {
      throw new HTTPException(resources
        .getResourceString("ERROR_HTTP_READ_REQUEST"), HTTPStatus
        .INTERNAL_ERROR);
    }
  }
```

All exceptions that occur during the processing of an HTTPRequest are handled by the following method:

```
private void handleException(HTTPException e) {
  int status = e.getStatus();
  info.status = status;

  try {

    // Return relevant information to the browser
    String statusString = HTTPStatus.getString(status);

    if (statusString == null) {

      // Unrecognized status
      status = HTTPStatus.INTERNAL_ERROR;
      statusString = HTTPStatus.getString(status);
    }

    // Create HTTP response
    HTTPResponse response = new HTTPResponse();
    response.getHeaders().addHeader(HEADER_FIELD_CONTENTTYPE,
                                    DEFAULT_MIME_TYPE);
    response.printStatus(bos, info.serverProtocol, status);
    response.printHeaders(bos);

    // Build status message and return HTML error information
    String statusMessage = new Integer(status).toString() + " "
                         + statusString;
    StringBuffer message = new StringBuffer();
    message.append("<html>\n<head>\n<title>" + statusMessage
                 + "</title>\n</head>");
    message.append("<body>\n<h1>" + statusMessage + "</h1>\n");
    message.append(e.getMessage() + "\n</body>\n</html>\n");
    byte bytes[] = message.toString().getBytes(HTTP_ENCODING);
    bos.write(bytes);
    bos.flush();
  } catch (Exception exception) {

    // The exception handler throws an exception, ignore
  }

  // Log the error
  HTTPLog.logger.log(info);
}
```

The following method, `parseHeaderLine()`, parses the header line and adds a header to the request

```
private void parseHeaderLine(String header) {

  // Trim any whitespace characters
  header = header.trim();
  try {
    int colonIndex = header.indexOf(HTTP_HEADER_FIELD_SEPERATOR);
    if (colonIndex > 0) {
      String fieldName = header.substring(0, colonIndex);
      String fieldValue = header.substring(colonIndex + 1);
      headers.addHeader(fieldName, fieldValue);
    }
  } catch (Exception e) {

    // Bad header line, ignore it or write to error log
  }
}
```

414

The following method, `parseRequestLine()`, parses the first line of the request to determine the URI, the protocol and the HTTP request method of this request.

```java
private void parseRequestLine(String request) throws HTTPException {

  // Remove any whitespace from both ends
  StringTokenizer st = new StringTokenizer(request.trim());

  try {

    // Read the method
    header_method = st.nextToken();

    // Read the URI
    header_uri = st.nextToken();
    header_uri = URLDecoder.decode(header_uri);
    if (header_uri.endsWith("/")) {

      // Add the default document when the URI points to a directory
      header_uri = header_uri + HTTPConfig.config.getDirectoryIndex();
    }

    if (!st.hasMoreTokens()) {

      // When the protocol is missing, we assume it is HTTP/0.9
      header_protocol = HTTP_09;
      return;
    } else {
      header_protocol = st.nextToken();
    }
  } catch (Exception e) {

    // An error occurred while parsing the request
    throw new HTTPException(resources
      .getResourceString("ERROR_HTTP_PARSE_REQUESTLINE"), HTTPStatus
        .BAD_REQUEST);
  }
}
```

The `process()` method reads the request, consisting of the request line and optional request headers, using the helper method `getHeaders()`. The `getHeaders()` method initializes the variables `header_protocol` and `header_method`.

```java
private void process() throws HTTPException {

  // Read in the request headers
  getHeaders();

  // Check that we have a supported protocol
  if (!(header_protocol.equalsIgnoreCase(HTTP_09)
        || header_protocol.equalsIgnoreCase(HTTP_10)
        || header_protocol.equalsIgnoreCase(HTTP_11))) {

    // Invalid request
    throw new HTTPException(resources
      .getResourceString("ERROR_HTTP_INVALID_PROTOCOL"), HTTPStatus
        .BAD_REQUEST);
  }
```

The following code segment gets all the variables required for method processing and checks that the request method is supported.

```
InetAddress address = socket.getInetAddress();

// Check if we support the request method
if (header_method.equals(METHOD_GET)) {
  handler = new HTTPGetHandler(info, header_uri, headers, address,
                             header_protocol, bis, bos);
} else if (header_method.equals(METHOD_POST)) {
  handler = new HTTPPostHandler(info, header_uri, headers, address,
                             header_protocol, bis, bos);
} else if (header_method.equals(METHOD_HEAD)) {
  handler = new HTTPHeadHandler(info, header_uri, headers, address,
                             header_protocol, bis, bos);
}

if (handler == null) {

  // Unsupported method
  throw new HTTPException(resources
    .getResourceString("ERROR_HTTP_INVALID_PROTOCOL"), HTTPStatus
      .NOT_IMPLEMENTED);
}

// Process method
handler.process();

// Log request
HTTPLog.logger.log(info);
}
```

After constructing an `HTTPRequest` object, the `HTTPServer` starts processing the request in a separate thread, so that it can continue to listen for incoming requests. The `run()` method executes the `process()` method and makes sure that the exception handler properly handles any exception.

Next, we check whether we support the client protocol or not. After this check, we construct a handler object corresponding to the request method and pass all relevant parameters to it. Then we call `process()` on the handler to handle the request and log it accordingly.

```
public void run() {
  try {
    process();
  } catch (HTTPException e) {
    handleException(e);
  }
```

The `finally` block makes sure that the browser output stream (bos) is flushed and closed and that the socket to communicate with the browser is closed as well. Closing the output stream and socket indicates to the browser that the request is complete (the browser will read from the stream until it is closed by the server).

```
finally {
  try {
    bos.flush();
```

```
            bos.close();
            socket.close();
        } catch (IOException e) {
        handleException(new HTTPException(
                        resources.getResourceString(
                                "ERROR_HTTP_REQUEST_SHUTDOWN")
                        + e.getMessage(), HTTPStatus.INTERNAL_ERROR));
        }
    }
    }
    }
}
```

Let us now look at the private helper methods we use in detail.

The getHeaders() method reads lines that are sent by the browser until an empty line is encountered. The first line is the request line. It is parsed using the helper method parseRequestLine(). All other lines are request header lines by definition and parseHeaderLine() will take care of parsing them and will save them in our headers object. All error conditions result in an HTTPException being thrown. We could be a little bit more specific here and indicate whether the error was caused by an invalid request or an internal server problem. In order to keep things simple, we just make the server respond with an internal server error.

If the request indicates that the browser uses HTTP 0.9, we return immediately after the first line, because we do not expect any header information.

The parseRequestLine() method uses a StringTokenizer to parse the method, the relative URI and the protocol from the request line. We use the static URLDecoder.decode() method to decode the URI into a string. The URI passed in a request line always represents either a relative path or a relative file name. The standard specifies that a path has to be delimited by a forward slash. If we detect that the requested relative URI is a request for a path, we will append the default directory index document name to it. This directory index file name is usually called index.html. When there is no protocol token on the request line, we may assume it is an HTTP 0.9 request.

The parseHeaderLine() method expects a field name and a field value separated by a colon ':'. The parsed header fields will be stored in the headers variable.

The handleException() method is called whenever an error occurs while processing an HTTP request. It constructs a response containing the HTTPStatus code stored in the exception and returns an HTML error message as the response entity-body. Since we use a BufferedOutputStream to talk to the browser, we cannot use a method such as writeLine(). We first use the getBytes() method using ISO 8859-1 encoding to convert the message string into bytes. Then we use write() to write the bytes to the browser.

Here is the httprequest.properties file that contains all the error messages used in the HTTPRequest class:

```
# httprequest.properties 1.0
# Resource strings for locale specific HTTPRequest messages

# HTTP Request error messages
ERROR_HTTP_GET_STREAMS=Unable to get request input and output streams.
ERROR_HTTP_PARSE_REQUESTLINE=Error while parsing request line.
```

```
ERROR_HTTP_READ_REQUEST=Error while reading request.
ERROR_HTTP_INVALID_PROTOCOL=Invalid protocol.
ERROR_HTTP_REQUEST_SHUTDOWN=Error while connection shutdown.
ERROR_SOCKET_EXCEPTION=A socket exception occurred.
```

HTTPBufferedInputStream

In this file, the code reads the header information of an HTTP request line by line, until it encounters an empty line, which indicates the end of the request header and, in the case of a POST request, the beginning of the request entity-body sent with the request. We also know that the request header information is ISO 8859-1 encoded. The most convenient way to read lines of character data using a specific encoding would be to use the following statement, which chains a BufferedReader and an InputStreamReader:

```
BufferedReader br = new BufferedReader(new InputStreamReader
                         (socket.getInputStream, HTTP_ENCODING);
```

Unfortunately this does not help us. The problem is that after we have read the last header line, we need to read the request entity-body as bytes and send them to the CGI program's standard input (it could be a GIF file, for instance).

If at that time, we constructed a DataInputStream to continue reading from the socket, data would already have been read ahead into the internal buffer of the BufferedReader object. However, there is no unbuffered input stream class in JDK 1.3 that allows reading lines. The readLine() method in DataInputStream is deprecated because the character-encoding issues were not well understood and supported, which led to a redesign of the way character data was read and written in JDK 1.1.

> **The reason why lines can only be read using a buffer has to do with the way lines are delimited on different platforms. If you look at the definition in the readLine() method of BufferedReader, it will specify that a line is terminated by a new line '\n' or a carriage return '\r' or a carriage return followed immediately by a new line '\r\n'. So when readLine() reads a carriage return '\r' it needs to read ahead. If a '\n' follows it is ignored. If any other character follows, it is already part of the next line.**

Ideally, we would like to have a buffered input stream that allows reading a String (encoded in ISO 8859-1) and that also allows reading bytes when necessary. This is exactly what HTTPBufferedInputStream does.

```
// HTTPBufferedInputStream.java

package com.wrox.httpserver;

import java.io.*;

class HTTPBufferedInputStream extends BufferedInputStream {

  // Class constants
  private final static int BUFFER_SIZE = 8192;

  // Instance variables
```

```
    private String encoding;

    public HTTPBufferedInputStream(InputStream in, int size,
                                   String encoding) {
      super(in, size);
      this.encoding = encoding;
    }
```

Reads a line from the stream in ISO 8859-1 encoding. A character set overview can be found at http://www.htmlhelp.com/reference/charset/.

```
    public String readLine()
          throws UnsupportedEncodingException, IOException,
                 IndexOutOfBoundsException {
      byte[] buffer = new byte[BUFFER_SIZE];
      int index = 0;

      /* Read until a line feed '\n' (as defined in RFC 1945 as the end */
      /* of a line) or until -1 or until an exception is encountered    */

      while (true) {
        buffer[index] = (byte) read();

        // Check for end of stream
        if (buffer[index] == -1) {

          // The end of the stream has been reached
          if (index == 0) {
            return null;
          } else {
            String result = new String(buffer, 0, index, encoding);
            return result.trim();
          }
        } else if (buffer[index] == '\n') {

          // The end of the line has been reached
          String result = new String(buffer, 0, index, encoding);
          return result.trim();
        }

        // Check whether the buffer size needs to be increased
        index++;
        if (index >= buffer.length) {

          /* Allocate new, larger buffer, initialize with current buffer */
          /* contents and continue                                       */

          byte[] new_buffer = new byte[buffer.length * 2];
          for (int i = 0; i < buffer.length; i++) {
            new_buffer[i] = buffer[i];
          }
          buffer = new_buffer;
        }
      }
    }
  }
```

Our `HTTPBufferedInputStream` class extends `BufferedInputStream` that already has a `read()` method to read bytes. All we need to do is to add a `readLine()` method. Fortunately for us, HTTP is very specific about the end of a line being '\r\n'. This makes our life much easier. The `readLine()` method reads one `byte` at a time into a buffer until it encounters a new line character. Then it converts the buffer into a `String`, trims any white-space characters such as '\r' from both ends and returns the `line`. In the very unlikely case our buffer gets too small, we allocate a buffer that is twice as large as before.

Since we deal with primitive byte data, it is a good idea to implement our buffer as a simple array, so that we have little overhead. Typically we would choose a class such as `StringBuffer` if we dealt with strings or a class from the collections framework such as `Hashtable` or `Vector`, that grows automatically if we had dealt with objects rather than bytes.

Let's take a look at the classes we will use to encapsulate message headers, `HTTPMessageHeaders`, and the class that will likewise cover our general HTTP information, `HTTPInformation`.

HTTPMessageHeaders

HTTP headers consist of a field name and a value. It makes good sense to extend the `Hashtable` class to store them, since a `Hashtable` implements almost everything we need already and we can use the inherited method `keys()`, which we will need in the `HTTPResponse` class to enumerate all our headers (when we print the response headers).

```
// HTTPMessageHeaders.java

package com.wrox.httpserver;

import java.util.*;

class HTTPMessageHeaders extends Hashtable {

  public HTTPMessageHeaders() {

    // Create a hashtable
    super();
  }

  public void addHeader(String key, String value) {
    if (key != null && value != null) {
      put(key.toLowerCase(), value);
    }
  }

  public String getHeader(String key) {
    return (String) get(key.toLowerCase());
  }
}
```

The `addHeader()` method stores the key value pair by converting the key to lower-case to avoid capitalization conflicts. Headers are in mixed case by definition, but we should be tolerant here, as many HTTP clients do not implement this according to the standard. The `getHeader()` method retrieves the header value already cast to a `String`.

HTTPInformation

The implementation of the `HTTPInformation` class is an exception to good coding practice that recommends to use accessors to access variables. In this particular case, it would not be practical to do so because of the large number of variables and also because we just use basic types such as `int` and `Strings` so we really do not have to hide implementation details.

```java
// HTTPInformation.java

package com.wrox.httpserver;

import java.io.*;
import java.util.*;

class HTTPInformation extends HTTPConstants {

  // Instance variables
  public String serverSoftware;
  public String serverName;
  public String gateway;
  public String serverProtocol = HTTP_10;
  public int serverPort;
  public String requestMethod;
  public String pathInfo;
  public String translatedPath;
  public String scriptName;
  public String queryString;
  public String remoteHost;
  public String remoteAddr;
  public String authType;
  public String remoteUser;
  public String remoteIdent;
  public String contentType;
  public String contentLength;
  public String documentRoot;
  public String accept;
  public String host;
  public String pragma;
  public String referer;
  public String userAgent;
```

The `serverProtocol` variable needs to be initialized with a value even before we read the request string, because we use it in our error response in the `handleException()` method of the `HTTPRequest` class. If an error occurs before or while reading this line, we need to make sure that we return a default HTTP protocol version.

The request string and HTTP status are stored for logging purposes:

```java
  public String requestString;
  public int status;

  // CGI 1.0 required environment variables
  private final static String env_serverSoftware = "SERVER_SOFTWARE";
  private final static String env_serverName = "SERVER_NAME";
  private final static String env_gateway = "GATEWAY_INTERFACE";
  private final static String env_serverProtocol = "SERVER_PROTOCOL";
```

```
private final static String env_serverPort = "SERVER_PORT";
private final static String env_requestMethod = "REQUEST_METHOD";
private final static String env_pathInfo = "PATH_INFO";
private final static String env_translatedPath = "PATH_TRANSLATED";
private final static String env_scriptName = "SCRIPT_NAME";
private final static String env_queryString = "QUERY_STRING";
private final static String env_remoteHost = "REMOTE_HOST";
private final static String env_remoteAddr = "REMOTE_ADDR";
private final static String env_authType = "AUTH_TYPE";
private final static String env_remoteUser = "REMOTE_USER";
private final static String env_remoteIdent = "REMOTE_IDENT";
private final static String env_contentType = "CONTENT_TYPE";
private final static String env_contentLength = "CONTENT_LENGTH";
private final static String env_docRoot = "DOCUMENT_ROOT";

// Important HTTP header lines
private final static String env_accept = "HTTP_ACCEPT";
private final static String env_host = "HTTP_HOST";
private final static String env_pragma = "HTTP_PRAGMA";
private final static String env_referer = "HTTP_REFERER";
private final static String env_userAgent = "HTTP_USER_AGENT";
```

In the `HTTPInformation` constructor, we initialize the variables that we know at the time, such as the server software and the gateway version. The constructor creates an HTTP header information object and initializes known header fields:

```
public HTTPInformation() {

  // Initialize known header fields
  serverSoftware = SERVER_SOFTWARE;
  gateway = GATEWAY_VERSION;
  serverPort = HTTPConfig.config.getPort();
  documentRoot = HTTPConfig.config.getDocumentRoot();
}
```

We will execute CGI programs using the `Runtime.exec()` method, to which we can pass environment variables as a `String[]` array. To accomplish this, we implement a method called `getCGIEnvironment()`. This method uses a `Hashtable` to store all the information, and then it builds an array of environment parameters.

```
public String[] getCGIEnvironment() {
  Hashtable env = new Hashtable();

  // Add everything to a hashtable first
  put(env, env_serverSoftware, serverSoftware);
  put(env, env_serverName, serverName);
  put(env, env_gateway, gateway);
  put(env, env_serverProtocol, serverProtocol);
  put(env, env_serverPort, new Integer(serverPort).toString());
  put(env, env_requestMethod, requestMethod);
  put(env, env_pathInfo, pathInfo);
  put(env, env_translatedPath, translatedPath);
  put(env, env_scriptName, scriptName);
  put(env, env_queryString, queryString);
  put(env, env_remoteHost, remoteHost);
```

```
      put(env, env_remoteAddr, remoteAddr);
      put(env, env_authType, authType);
      put(env, env_remoteUser, remoteUser);
      put(env, env_remoteIdent, remoteIdent);
      put(env, env_contentType, contentType);
      put(env, env_contentLength, contentLength);
      put(env, env_docRoot, documentRoot);
      put(env, env_accept, accept);
      put(env, env_host, host);
      put(env, env_pragma, pragma);
      put(env, env_referer, referer);
      put(env, env_userAgent, userAgent);
```

Here, we construct a string array to contain the environment elements:

```
    String cgi_env[] = new String[env.size()];

    int i = 0;
    for (Enumeration e = env.keys(); e.hasMoreElements(); ) {
      String key = (String) e.nextElement();
      StringBuffer sb = new StringBuffer(key);

      sb.append("=");
      sb.append((String) env.get(key));

      cgi_env[i++] = sb.toString();
    }

    return cgi_env;
```

The helper method put() places an environment field into the Hashtable. If either the key or the value is null, the header is invalid. The HTTP 1.0 specification recommends that servers should tolerate non-severe HTTP client errors.

```
  private void put(Hashtable env, String key, String value) {
    if (key != null && value != null) {
      env.put(key, value);
    }
  }
}
```

HTTPHandler

The process() method of the HTTPRequest class creates an object called handler that corresponds to the request method. HTTPHandler is an abstract class that contains the common variables and methods that all specific HTTP method classes use. The specific variables and processing requirements of each HTTP method are implemented in the corresponding subclasses.

```
  // HTTPHandler.java

  package com.wrox.httpserver;

  import java.io.*;
```

```java
import java.net.*;

abstract class HTTPHandler extends HTTPConstants {

    // Instance variables
    protected HTTPResponse response;
    protected HTTPMessageHeaders headers;
    protected BufferedInputStream bis;
    protected BufferedOutputStream bos;
    protected String uri;
    protected HTTPInformation info;

    public HTTPHandler(HTTPInformation info, String uri,
                       HTTPMessageHeaders headers, InetAddress address,
                       String protocol, BufferedInputStream bis,
                       BufferedOutputStream bos) {

        // Initialize instance variables
        this.headers = headers;
        this.info = info;
        this.bis = bis;
        this.bos = bos;
        this.uri = uri;

        // Create an HTTP response
        response = new HTTPResponse();

        // Set up information
        info.serverProtocol = protocol;
        info.accept = headers.getHeader(HEADER_FIELD_ACCEPT);
        info.contentLength = headers.getHeader(HEADER_FIELD_CONTENTLENGTH);
        info.contentType = headers.getHeader(HEADER_FIELD_CONTENTTYPE);
        info.pragma = headers.getHeader(HEADER_FIELD_PRAGMA);
        info.referer = headers.getHeader(HEADER_FIELD_REFERER);
        info.userAgent = headers.getHeader(HEADER_FIELD_USERAGENT);
        info.remoteAddr = address.getHostAddress().toString();
        info.remoteHost = address.getHostName();
    }
    public abstract void process() throws HTTPException;
}
```

The HTTPHandler constructor saves the data passed as a parameter and adds further information to the HTTPInformation object. It also creates an HTTPResponse object, which will be used to store the response headers and print the response line. We declare an abstract method process() that needs to be implemented by the corresponding subclasses, as each method handler will process a request in a slightly different way.

HTTPGetHandler

Here is the source code that implements the specific handling of an HTTP GET request:

```java
// HTTPGetHandler.java

package com.wrox.httpserver;

import java.io.*;
```

```
import java.net.*;

class HTTPGetHandler extends HTTPHandler {

  // Requested object (file or process)
  private HTTPObject httpObject;

  public HTTPGetHandler(HTTPInformation info, String uri,
                        HTTPMessageHeaders headers, InetAddress address,
                        String protocol, BufferedInputStream bis,
                        BufferedOutputStream bos) {
    super(info, uri, headers, address, protocol, bis, bos);
  }

  public void process() throws HTTPException {
    info.requestMethod = METHOD_GET;

    // Get HTTPObject that is addressed by the URI and process it
    httpObject = HTTPObject.getHTTPObject(response, info, uri, bos, bis);
```

According to RFC 1945 (http://www.ietf.org/rfc/rfc1945.txt) we need to be backwards compatible with HTTP 0.9, so we only print response headers if the client request was not made using HTTP 0.9.

```
    if (!info.serverProtocol.equalsIgnoreCase(HTTP_09)) {
      info.status = HTTPStatus.OK;
      response.printStatus(bos, info.serverProtocol, info.status);
      if (httpObject.isHeadersGenerated()) {
        response.printHeaders(bos);
      }
    }

    /* The headers have been written, now let the object do the rest */
    /* and retrieve the data in an object-specific way               */
    httpObject.retrieve();
  }
}
```

The `process()` method stores the selected request method in the info variable. A GET requests either a file or a CGI program. We let the static `HTTPObject.getHTTPObject()` factory method worry about this. If HTTP 1.0 or higher is used, we print a status line and any response entity headers that might have been added by the `HTTPObject`. Then we return the response entity-body of the object by calling its `retrieve()` method.

HTTPHeadHandler

The HTTP HEAD method is almost identical to the HTTP GET method, with the exception that no response entity-body is returned. It is also not necessary to check for HTTP 0.9 because HTTP 0.9 does not define a HEAD method.

```
// HTTPHeadHandler.java

package com.wrox.httpserver;

import java.io.*;
import java.net.*;
```

```
class HTTPHeadHandler extends HTTPHandler {

  // Requested object (file or process)
  private HTTPObject httpObject;

  public HTTPHeadHandler(HTTPInformation info, String uri,
                         HTTPMessageHeaders headers, InetAddress address,
                         String protocol, BufferedInputStream bis,
                         BufferedOutputStream bos) {
    super(info, uri, headers, address, protocol, bis, bos);
  }
```

The following method, process(), processes a HEAD method by creating the requested object and returning the requested status information.

```
public void process() throws HTTPException {
  info.requestMethod = METHOD_HEAD;

  // Get HTTPObject that is addressed by the URI and process it
  httpObject = HTTPObject.getHTTPObject(response, info, uri, bos, bis);

  // For a HEAD method we only return header information
  info.status = HTTPStatus.OK;
  response.printStatus(bos, info.serverProtocol, info.status);
  if (httpObject.isHeadersGenerated()) {
    response.printHeaders(bos);
  }
}
}
```

HTTPPostHandler

The HTTP POST method is almost identical to the HTTP GET method, with the only difference that, again, we do not need to worry about HTTP 0.9 as HTTP 0.9 does not define a POST method.

```
// HTTPPostHandler.java

package com.wrox.httpserver;

import java.net.*;
import java.io.*;

class HTTPPostHandler extends HTTPHandler {
```

This class implements the POST method. The POST method sends the entity-body that is enclosed in the request to the process object and returns the output of the process object in its response.

```
private HTTPObject object;

public HTTPPostHandler(HTTPInformation info, String uri,
                       HTTPMessageHeaders headers, InetAddress address,
                       String protocol, BufferedInputStream bis,
                       BufferedOutputStream bos) {
  super(info, uri, headers, address, protocol, bis, bos);
}
```

The following method processes a POST method by creating the requested object and returning the requested status information, as well as retrieving the entity-body from the process object.

```java
public void process() throws HTTPException {
   info.requestMethod = METHOD_POST;

   // Get HTTPObject that is addressed by the URI
   object = HTTPObject.getHTTPObject(response, info, uri, bos, bis);

   /* HTTP/0.9 doesn't know about POST so we don't need to check */
   /* the version                                                */
   info.status = HTTPStatus.OK;
   response.printStatus(bos, info.serverProtocol, info.status);
   if (object.isHeadersGenerated()) {
     response.printHeaders(bos);

     // The headers have been written, now let the object do the rest
   }
   object.retrieve();
 }
}
```

HTTPObject

HTTPObject is an abstract class that represents a response entity and its corresponding headers. It implements the common methods and variables that are used when either a file or a CGI program is requested. The subclasses HTTPFileObject and HTTPProcessObject implement specific methods and variables.

```java
// HTTPObject.java

package com.wrox.httpserver;

import java.io.*;
import java.util.*;

abstract class HTTPObject extends HTTPConstants implements Runnable {

   // Class constants
   private static final String HTTP_CGIPATH = "/cgi-bin/";

   // Resource object streams
   protected BufferedInputStream objectbis;
   protected BufferedOutputStream objectbos;

   // Browser input and output streams
   protected BufferedInputStream browserbis;
   protected BufferedOutputStream browserbos;
```

The headersGenerated variable indicates whether the response generated any headers (only used when file resources are returned, as CGI programs generate their own header information).

```java
protected boolean headersGenerated;

// Request information that is primarily relevant for CGI execution
protected HTTPInformation info;
```

```
protected HTTPObject(HTTPInformation info, BufferedOutputStream bos,
                     BufferedInputStream bis) {

    // Initialize instance variables
    this.info = info;
    this.browserbis = bis;
    this.browserbos = bos;
}
```

This method, `getHTTPObject()`, returns the requested HTTP object based on the request URI and path translation. The static `HTTPObject` method `getHTTPObject()` creates and returns an `HTTPFileObject` or `HTTPProcessObject` based on the relative URI passed as a parameter. This is very convenient, because we do not have to parse the data outside of the class and then make a decision as to what kind of HTTP object we need to construct.

> **Static methods that parse a passed parameter string and create corresponding objects are common throughout the JDK. A good example is the JDBC `DriverManagers.getConnection()` method, where a database URL is passed that indicates the type of database (DB2, Informix , Oracle) for which a connection is requested.**

First `getHTTPObject()` checks whether a query string exists (which starts after a question mark '?') and saves it. If a relative URI starts with `/cgi-bin/`, we know that a CGI program is requested.

```
public static HTTPObject getHTTPObject(HTTPResponse response,
                                       HTTPInformation info, String uri,
                                       BufferedOutputStream bos,
                                       BufferedInputStream bis)
                       throws HTTPException {

    // First check if there are any query parameters and save them
    String requestedPath = uri;
    String queryString = "";

    int question = uri.indexOf('?');
    try {
      if (question >= 0) {
        requestedPath = uri.substring(0, question);
        if (question < uri.length() - 1) {
          queryString = uri.substring(question + 1);
        }
      }
    } catch (StringIndexOutOfBoundsException e) {

      // The URI is not correctly formatted
      requestedPath = uri;
      queryString = "";
    }

    // Save them in info, they are important for CGI execution
    info.scriptName = requestedPath;
```

```
          info.queryString = queryString;

          // Translate the path from the URI to the actual path on the server
          String translatedPath;

          // Check if the requested path is a CGI script
          if (requestedPath.startsWith(HTTP_CGIPATH)) {
```

We build the absolute path to the executable script or program using the CGI path configuration parameter that we get by calling getCGIPath().

```
            // A process object is to be created
            StringBuffer fileName =
              new StringBuffer(HTTPConfig.config.getCGIPath());

            // Find the actual executable name relative to the CGIPath
            fileName.append(requestedPath.substring(HTTP_CGIPATH.length() - 1));

            // Change the separator characters
            translatedPath = fileName.toString().replace('/', File.separatorChar);
```

Next, we create an HTTPProcessObject and pass the translated path to it. We do almost the same for requested files, but we start from the document root directory and create an HTTPFileObject instead.

```
            // Store the translated path
            info.translatedPath = translatedPath;
            return new HTTPProcessObject(translatedPath, info, bos, bis);
          } else {

            // A file object is to be created
            StringBuffer fileName =
              new StringBuffer(HTTPConfig.config.getDocumentRoot());

            // Change all forward slashes to the appropriate separator chars
            fileName.append(requestedPath);
            translatedPath = fileName.toString().replace('/', File.separatorChar);
            info.translatedPath = translatedPath;
            return new HTTPFileObject(translatedPath, info, response, bos);
          }
        }
```

isHeaderGenerated() returns true if headers have been generated.

```
        public boolean isHeadersGenerated() {
          return headersGenerated;
        }
```

We will also have to deal with one common task regardless of the HTTP object, which is transferring bytes between the browser and the HTTP server. The following figure shows how this works for an HTTP POST request:

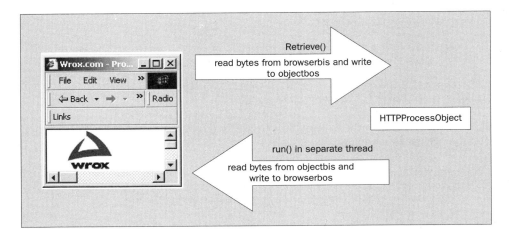

To achieve the best performance when responding to a request, it is a good idea to write data from the browser to the object and to write data back from the object in concurrent threads, though not all requests will require data to be written both ways. For example, the HEAD method will not require any data to be written, the GET method for a file object will not require data to be sent to the object and only a GET request for a process object and a POST request will require bytes to be written in both directions.

To write data in both directions, we implement the Runnable interface and put the source code that will execute in parallel to our retrieve() method into the run() method. However, which part of the data writing should we implement in the parallel method?

> **Reading from or writing to a stream object from different threads should be avoided because it causes unpredictable results, including unexpected Socket exceptions. It is a very common error made by programmers beginning Java network programming and is difficult to trace.**

Since we have already read data from the browser input stream, we will read the request entity in the retrieve() method within the same thread. We will put the data writing from the object to the browser into the run() method, where every byte read from the object will simply be written to the browser until the end of the stream is detected.

The retrieve() method starts the run() method in a separate thread, and only if browserbis and objectbos have been created will we enter a while loop to write data from the browser to the object. However, here we have to implement non-blocking reading. If we tried a blocking read from the browser until the browser closed the input stream and sent this data to objectbos, we would wait forever, as the browser will very likely hang on to its connection and thus not close the input stream.

```
public void retrieve() {
```

retrieve() starts the thread that will write data from the object to the browser.

```
Thread writer = new Thread(this);
writer.setDaemon(true);
writer.start();
```

The `writer` writes data from the browser to the object in the same thread where the input stream was created and read from. The `BufferedInputStream` and `BufferedOutputStream` variables that are passed to the constructor are saved in the variables `browserbis` and `browserbos`. We will use them to read from or write to the browser. We also need a set of matching `objectbis` and `objectbos` variables to read from the HTTP object and write to it. The constructor of the `HTTPProcessObject` and `HTTPFileObject` classes will take care of this for us.

```
if (browserbis != null && objectbos != null) {
  byte[] buffer = new byte[BUFFER_SIZE];

  int bytesRead = 0;
  try {
    do {
```

This has to be non-blocking as the browser does not close its output stream and we would wait here forever. By using the `available()` method, we can find out the number of bytes that can be read from the `browserbis` stream without blocking.

On the other side, after the HTTP object has closed its output stream, there is no point in waiting for incoming data from the browser anymore. We use the `available()` method to check whether or not data is available, and then we use the `isAlive()` method to check whether our background thread is still alive or has completed already. If it has, we can close our streams and return.

```
      int bytesavailable = browserbis.available();
      if (bytesavailable > 0) {
        bytesRead = browserbis.read(buffer, 0, bytesavailable);

        if (bytesRead != -1) {
          objectbos.write(buffer, 0, bytesRead);
          objectbos.flush();
        }
      }
      if (!writer.isAlive()) {
        browserbis.close();
        objectbos.close();
        bytesRead = -1;
      }

    } while (bytesRead != -1);
  } catch (IOException ioe) {
  }
}
```

We will ignore this `IOException` and continue; incomplete input should be handled by the CGI program.

```
try {
  writer.join();
} catch (InterruptedException ie) {

  // Ignore and continue
}
}
```

It is safe to ignore the InterruptedException here, because it would only be thrown if the writer thread was interrupted by the interrupt() method in the Thread class. Since we do not use this method, we may ignore this exception because it will never be thrown. However as it is derived from the Exception class, we need to catch it. The run() method writes bytes from the resource object to the browser for rendering.

```java
public void run() {
  byte[] fileBuffer = new byte[BUFFER_SIZE];

  int bytesRead = 0;
  try {
    do {
      bytesRead = objectbis.read(fileBuffer);

      if (bytesRead != -1) {
        browserbos.write(fileBuffer, 0, bytesRead);
        browserbos.flush();
      }
    } while (bytesRead != -1);
  } catch (IOException ioe) {

    /* We can ignore this from the server side, the user will notice */
    /* and will reload the page                                      */
  }
}
}
```

HTTPFileObject

The HTTPFileObject class extends HTTPObject, and does the specific processing tasks required to return a file as an entity in an HTTP response by providing the proper entity headers and the byte contents of the file itself.

```java
// HTTPFileObject.java

package com.wrox.httpserver;

import java.io.*;

class HTTPFileObject extends HTTPObject {

  public HTTPFileObject(String fileName, HTTPInformation info,
                        HTTPResponse response,
                        BufferedOutputStream bos) throws HTTPException {
```

We do not have a browser input stream since a file object is only returned for a GET request, and does not require additional input from the browser. The HTTPFileObject constructor calls the super class constructor.

```java
super(info, bos, null);

// Determine if the file exists and set up response header information
try {
  File file = new File(fileName);
```

```
                    // The file must exist and must be readable
                    if (!(file.exists() && file.canRead())) {
                      throw new FileNotFoundException();

                      // Only create an input stream if the HTTP method is not HEAD
                    }
```

Next, the constructor opens the file, creates a `BufferedInputStream` object and saves this in the `objectbis` variable. The `objectbos` variable is not needed and is explicitly set to `null` which is not required (as it is automatically initialized with `null` anyway). However in this case it increases the legibility of the code, as the `retrieve()` method of the `HTTPObject` class explicitly checks whether `objectbos` is not equal `null` to start writing data from the browser to the object which is not required when a file object is retrieved.

```
                  if (!info.requestMethod.equalsIgnoreCase(METHOD_HEAD)) {
                    objectbis = new BufferedInputStream(new FileInputStream(fileName),
                                                 BUFFER_SIZE);
                    objectbos = null;
                  }
```

Then the constructor adds the entity headers `Content-type` and `Content-length` to the response headers, and indicates that headers have been generated by setting the `headersGenerated` variable to `true`.

```
                  // Setup response headers Content-length and Content-type
                  response.getHeaders().addHeader(HEADER_FIELD_CONTENTLENGTH,
                                             Long.toString(file.length()));
                  response.getHeaders()
                    .addHeader(HEADER_FIELD_CONTENTTYPE,
                              MimeConverter.converter.getContentType(fileName));
                  headersGenerated = true;
```

Any exception means that we cannot retrieve the file or file information.

```
              } catch (Exception e) {

                /* Any exception means that we cannot retrieve the file or */
                /* file information                                        */
                throw new HTTPException(e.getMessage(), HTTPStatus.NOT_FOUND);
              }
            }
          }
```

HTTPProcessObject

The `HTTPProcessObject` class is similar to `HTTPFileObject`. However, instead of opening a file and reading it, the `HTTPProcessObject` constructor executes a file.

```
    // HTTPProcessObject.java

    package com.wrox.httpserver;

    import java.io.*;
```

```
class HTTPProcessObject extends HTTPObject implements Runnable {
  private Process proc;

  public HTTPProcessObject(String fileName, HTTPInformation info,
                           BufferedOutputStream bos,
                           BufferedInputStream bis) throws HTTPException {
    super(info, bos, bis);

    // We need to determine whether or not the file exists
    try {
      File file = new File(fileName);

      // The file must exist and must be readable
      if (!(file.exists() && file.canRead())) {
        throw new FileNotFoundException();

        /* Run the executable or script in its directory      */
        /* This is recommended as the CGI script might create files */
      }
      File pathName = file.getParentFile();

      // Get the CGI execution environment variables
      String[] env = info.getCGIEnvironment();
```

Check if this is a script file which has a first line indicating the absolute path to the interpreter such as `#!C:\Perl\bin\Perl.exe`.

```
      HTTPBufferedInputStream execbis =
        new HTTPBufferedInputStream(new FileInputStream(fileName),
                                    BUFFER_SIZE, HTTP_ENCODING);
      byte[] scriptToken = new byte[2];
      if (scriptToken.length
              != execbis.read(scriptToken, 0, scriptToken.length)) {
        throw new Exception();

      }
      if (scriptToken[0] == '#' && scriptToken[1] == '!') {

        // We assume this is a script file
        String[] args = new String[2];
        args[0] = execbis.readLine();
        execbis.close();
        args[1] = fileName;
        proc = Runtime.getRuntime().exec(args, env, pathName);
      } else {

        // We assume this is an executable
        execbis.close();
        proc = Runtime.getRuntime().exec(fileName, env, pathName);
      }

      // Get the process STDIN and STDOUT      streams
      objectbis = new BufferedInputStream(proc.getInputStream(),
                                          BUFFER_SIZE);
      objectbos = new BufferedOutputStream(proc.getOutputStream(),
                                           BUFFER_SIZE);
```

The CGI program will generate its own headers. We do not know what type of content it sends back.

```
        headersGenerated = false;
    } catch (FileNotFoundException fnfe) {
        throw new HTTPException(fnfe.getMessage(), HTTPStatus.NOT_FOUND);
    } catch (Exception e) {

        // Any exception during execution
        throw new HTTPException(e.getMessage(), HTTPStatus.INTERNAL_ERROR);
    }
  }
}
```

Executing a program always needs special attention and consideration even in Java. A CGI program could be an executable or it could be a script file (such as a Perl script) that needs to be executed using an interpreter. Determining this by looking at the file extension would not necessarily work across platforms. For example under UNIX, executables do not have a specific file extension, but rather a corresponding execute file attribute.

We use a technique here that is used in UNIX shells (such as the Korn and Bourne shells) and also works on Microsoft Windows platforms (the Apache HTTP server uses the same technique to determine whether a CGI program is a script file or an executable). These shells read the first two bytes of a file, which the user wants to execute. If they encounter the character string '#!', then they assume that this is a script file and that the absolute path to the interpreter will follow on the same line.

Once we know the absolute path name of the executable or script file interpreter, we use `Runtime.exec()` to start it in a separately running process. We specify the directory where the CGI program resides as the working directory, so that if the CGI program creates files, they will be created in the same directory as the CGI program.

After starting the process, we use the `getInputStream()` and `getOutputStream()` methods to initialize the corresponding `objectbis` and `objectbos` variables. Since it is the responsibility of the process to write the response entity headers, we will indicate that we have not generated headers. We actually do not know whether the process will write an image file, a text file or (more likely) an HTML file response or how long it is.

HTTPResponse

We have already used the `HTTPResponse` class a number of times. The first time we used it was in the `HTTPRequest` exception handler when we simply returned an HTML error response. The `HTTPResponse` class encapsulates an HTTP response, which includes the status line and response headers. The response entity-body itself is retrieved from the requested `HTTPObject`.

```
// HTTPResponse.java

package com.wrox.httpserver;

import java.util.*;
import java.io.*;
```

The `HTTPResponse` constructor adds general response headers required for any HTTP response (such as the `MIME` version, the server name and the date), which is recommended (but not mandated) by the HTTP specification.

```
class HTTPResponse extends HTTPConstants {
  private HTTPMessageHeaders headers;

  public HTTPResponse() {

    // Construct and add message headers required for the response
    headers = new HTTPMessageHeaders();
    headers.addHeader(HEADER_FIELD_MIMEVERSION, MIME_VERSION);
    headers.addHeader(HEADER_FIELD_SERVER, SERVER_SOFTWARE);

    // The browser expects date strings in a special format
    headers.addHeader(HEADER_FIELD_DATE, new HTTPGMTTimestamp().toString());
  }

  public HTTPMessageHeaders getHeaders() {
    return headers;
  }
```

The printHeaders() method prints the response headers to the browser and adds an empty line at the end to indicate that the entity-body will follow.

```
public void printHeaders(OutputStream os) throws HTTPException {
  try {

    // Print all the fields and values that are set
    for (Enumeration e = headers.keys(); e.hasMoreElements(); ) {
      String type = (String) e.nextElement();
      String header = type + ": " + headers.getHeader(type) + "\r\n";
      byte bytes[] = header.getBytes(HTTP_ENCODING);
      os.write(bytes);
      os.flush();
    }

    // Print an additional line break
    String lineBreak = "\r\n";
    byte bytes[] = lineBreak.getBytes(HTTP_ENCODING);
    os.write(bytes);
    os.flush();
  } catch (Exception e) {

    // All possible exceptions are rethrown as an HTTPRequest exception
    throw new HTTPException(e.getMessage(), HTTPStatus.INTERNAL_ERROR);
  }
}
```

The printStatus() method prints the HTTP response line for HTTP 1.0 or HTTP 1.1 requests using ISO 8859-1 encoding. As defined by HTTP 1.0, we add carriage return and new line to indicate the end of the line. We always respond using the HTTP protocol version that was requested.

```
public void printStatus(OutputStream os, String protocol,
                        int status) throws HTTPException {
  String line = protocol + " " + status + " "
                + HTTPStatus.getString(status) + "\r\n";
  try {
    byte bytes[] = line.getBytes(HTTP_ENCODING);
    os.write(bytes);
    os.flush();
```

```
    } catch (Exception e) {

      // All possible exceptions are rethrown as an HTTPRequest exception
      throw new HTTPException(e.getMessage(), HTTPStatus.INTERNAL_ERROR);
    }
  }
}
```

Installing and Running HTTPServer

`HTTPServer` consists of a number of source code files, message and configuration files that need to be placed in the right directories.

Directory Structure

Let us assume we are working in Microsoft Windows and have created a directory called `/Beg_Java_Networking/Ch13/com/wrox/httpserver` on our `C:` drive. This is where the HTTP server source code from the code download has been saved to.

If you download the chapter files from http://www.wrox.com, the files and directories will be in the following structure:

```
C:\Beg_Java_Networking\Ch13>dir
 Volume in drive C has no label.
 Volume Serial Number is 3803-B844

 Directory of C:\Beg_Java_Networking\Ch13

15/08/2001  17:25    <DIR>         .
15/08/2001  17:25    <DIR>         ..
15/08/2001  17:25    <DIR>         cgi-bin
15/08/2001  17:25    <DIR>         com
15/08/2001  09:01           359    form.html
15/08/2001  17:40           940    httpd.properties
11/07/2001  22:18            90    index.html
08/07/2001  00:51           855    mime.properties
15/08/2001  17:25    <DIR>         msg
             4 File(s)      2,244 bytes
             5 Dir(s)   5,898,158,080 bytes free
```

The `cgi-bin` directory contains the following Perl script:

```
form.pl
```

The `form.pl` file will work on Microsoft Windows platforms, if `Perl.exe` is installed in the `C:\Perl\bin` directory, and this directory is also in the classpath. If you use the `form.pl` script on a different platform, you will have to modify the first line of the script accordingly. A Perl interpreter for many platforms including Linux, Sun Solaris and Microsoft Windows can be downloaded from http://www.activestate.com/.

If you are running this application on Windows, just download the `ActivePerl.msi` file and click on it to install all the correct files to the right places in your directory, and add `C:\Perl\bin` to your `PATH` variable. You will probably have to put it in your classpath manually, however. Enter the following before you run the server:

`C:\Beg_Java_Networking\Ch13>`**set classpath=%classpath%;.;C:\Perl\bin**

The `msg` directory contains all the message properties files:

```
httpconfig.properties
httplog.properties
httprequest.properties
httpserver.properties
httpserver_de.properties
mimeconverter.properties
```

The `com\wrox\simplehttpserver` directory contains all the `.java` source files for our first example in this chapter:

```
HTTPRequest.java
SimpleHTTPServer.java
```

The `com\wrox\httpserver` directory contains all the `.java` source files:

```
ConfigFileException.java
HTTPBufferedInputStream.java
HTTPConfig.java
HTTPConstants.java
HTTPException.java
HTTPFileObject.java
HTTPGetHandler.java
HTTPGMTTimestamp.java
HTTPHandler.java
HTTPHeadHandler.java
HTTPInformation.java
HTTPLocalizedResources.java
HTTPLog.java
HTTPMessageHeaders.java
HTTPObject.java
HTTPPostHandler.java
HTTPProcessObject.java
HTTPRequest.java
HTTPResponse.java
HTTPServer.java
HTTPStatus.java
MimeConverter.java
```

To compile all of your Java files in the `C:\Beg_Java_Networking\Ch13\com\wroxhttpserver\` directory, you type the following command:

`C:\Beg_Java_Networking\Ch13>`**javac com\wrox\httpserver*.java**

To run the server, simply enter the following:

`C:\Beg_Java_Networking\Ch13>`**java com.wrox.httpserver.HTTPServer httpd**

This displays the HTTP server console prompt:

HTTPServer – enter Q or q to quit>

It is as simple as that. If something is wrong with your httpd configuration, MIME types file or the log file, the server will tell you via the HTTPConfig.properties messages.

Configuration File

The default httpd.properties file should be sufficient for all of these examples, provided that the code package is deployed in the same way as we have demonstrated here. The only entries you should edit and adapt for your system are the entries that point to absolute path names that must exist on your system.

```
DocumentRoot=C:/Beg_Java_Networking/Ch13
LogFile= C:/Beg_Java_Networking/Ch13/httpserver.log
CGIPath=C:/Beg_Java_Networking/Ch13/cgi-bin
```

If the log file does not exist, it will be created. Do not forget to use forward slashes, as they will be converted into system-specific directory separator characters at a later point. If you use backward slashes, it will work as well in Microsoft Windows, but it is not recommended for portability of your configuration file.

Testing the Example

To find out if everything works, let's put a file called index.html with the following contents in our document root directory (C:\Beg_Java_Networking\Ch13):

```
<HTML>
  <HEAD>
    <TITLE>hello, world</TITLE></HEAD>
  <BODY>
    hello, world
  </BODY>
</HTML>
```

You should now be able to enter the following URL in your browser:

http://localhost:1234/

This should cause the following response to be displayed:

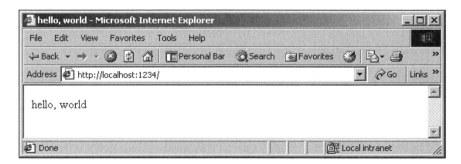

Now stop the server, and take a look at the log file. It should contain an entry like this:

```
127.0.0.1-[16 Jun 2001 03:45:45 GMT]-GET / HTTP/1.1-200
```

Let's see if form processing also works. If you have downloaded the code from the chapter, the file form.html should be in your C:\Beg_Java_Networking\Ch13 directory already, as well as the following Perl script file form.pl in C:\Beg_Java_Networking\Ch13\cgi-bin:

```perl
#!C:\Perl\bin\Perl.exe

use CGI qw(:standard);
use CGI qw(param);

# query request parameters
my $name = param("NAME");
my $e-mail = param("E-MAIL");

# print document header
print header();

# print confirmation
print "<html><body>Thanks for your name <b>$name</b> and address <b>$e-
mail</b><body></html>\n";
```

We should now be able to enter the following URL into the browser:

http://localhost:1234/form.html

The following form will be displayed:

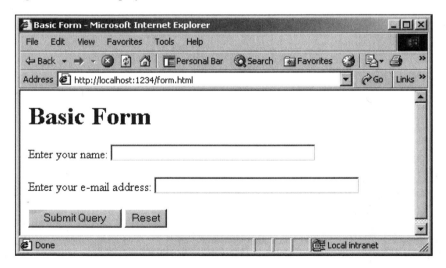

Enter your name and e-mail address and press Submit Query. If everything has been installed correctly, we should get a response similar to this:

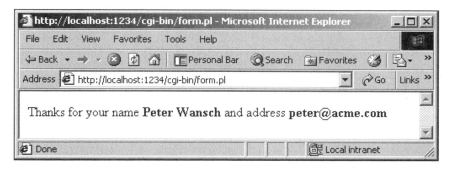

Now stop the server and take a look at the log file. It should contain the following entries:

```
127.0.0.1-[11 Jul 2001 10:35:28 GMT]-GET / HTTP/1.1-200
127.0.0.1-[11 Jul 2001 10:42:53 GMT]-GET /form.html HTTP/1.1-200
127.0.0.1-[11 Jul 2001 10:46:48 GMT]-POST /cgi-bin/form.pl HTTP/1.1-200
```

Adding Features To HTTPServer

While our `HTTPServer` provides most of the functionality required by a fully-fledged HTTP server, there is certainly room for improving it. Here are a few features that you might want to think
about adding:

❑   **Pooling and reusing HTTPRequest and HTTPHandler objects:** Frequently constructing new objects will inevitably lead to performance problems and puts a strain on the garbage collector. Create and use corresponding object pool classes which manage a collection of reusable objects.

❑   **Improved error checking and handling:** For instance, if a CGI program hangs in execution, this means that the corresponding `HTTPRequest` thread waits forever. This could potentially crash your server. It is better to time out CGI execution instead.

❑   **A more user-friendly server administration interface:** A GUI interface instead of our austere command line interface or an HTML-based administration interface that you can use through a browser would improve the usability (especially when managing your configuration files becomes more complex). IBM has added an HTML-based administration interface to the Apache server in its own free Apache distribution called IBM HTTP Server to make the configuration task easier. This can be downloaded from http://www.ibm.com/software/webservers/httpservers/download.html.

❑   **A servlet engine:** If you understand the principles of CGI program execution, with a little research you can easily implement a servlet engine into `HTTPServer`. We have not included it here, as it is beyond the scope of this book and would not really give you any more insight into developing a well-designed, larger Java networking program. Note that a number of free and commercial products exist to do the job.

❑   **Support for Server-Side Includes:** This is a technology that an HTTP server with a servlet engine can use to convert a section of an HTML file into an alternative dynamic portion each time the document is sent to the browser. Pages that use this technology often have the extension `.shtml`.

❑   **Support for multiple document roots:** so that individual users can have their own sites

❑   **Support for virtual hosts:** Service providers on the Internet often serve thousands of web sites from different companies from one physical machine. This is accomplished not necessarily by installing thousands of different IP addresses on a physical machine, but by using virtual servers.

   For example, www.company1.com and www.company2.com can resolve to the same IP address. The user would still see different pages when requesting either the one or the other through a browser. This is accomplished by using the Host: request header field as a parameter for path translation.

❑   **Caching response entities:** You could make your web server considerably faster by caching recently and frequently accessed resources in memory.

❑   **URL redirection:** Implementing URL redirection can be very useful. Imagine that a company has changed its name or been bought by another company, but people still go to its old web site. Instead of putting up a message telling people where they have to go now, it would be nice if they were automatically redirected to the new site. Redirection in HTTP is very simply. When the path translation has detected a URI for a resource that needs to be redirected, it sends back the following status string:

```
HTTP/1.0 301 Moved Permanently

Location: http://www.newsite.com/newdocument.html
```

   It is recommended to also send an HTML document with your redirection response that includes the link to the new site because there are some browsers that do not support redirection. POST methods must not be automatically redirected. The HTTP standard recommends user confirmation in this case.

❑   **Basic User Authentication**: This will be covered in Chapter 14

❑   **Support for secure connections**: This will be covered in Chapter 14

Summary

In this chapter we have discussed the basics of HTTP operation and CGI program execution. Additionally, we saw how to implement a well-designed HTTP server in Java and how to tackle all the networking issues involved.

We discussed the following important points:

❑   The relevant details about the HTTP protocol and how a GET, HEAD and POST request works

❑   The details that the CGI standard entails and how CGI programs can be used to create dynamic HTTP responses

❑   The difference between the existing HTTP versions and what you have to consider when you implement a server

❑   How to implement an HTTP 1.0- and CGI-compliant server

❑   Features to extend this HTTP server, including caching and URL redirection

Making Network Applications More Secure

Security and cryptography play an important role in today's networked world. Confidential data is often being sent over public networks such as the Internet. Restricted services are made available over such networks. Even where private networks are being used, the physical security of the network is often insufficiently guaranteed. When developing networked services, you *must* assume that an unauthorized party will eventually attempt to access your services or try to intercept confidential data. Cryptography and authentication are essential for a much broader range of applications than the proverbial e-commerce shops that merely take credit card details.

In this chapter, we will explore the Java **Cryptography Architecture** and its extensions. In particular, you will learn to:

❑   Understand the basics of cryptography, including encryption and digital signatures

❑   Work with the provider-based Java Cryptography Architecture framework

❑   Authenticate and protect your data using digital signatures

❑   Securely send data over an insecure medium such as the Internet using encryption

❑   Authenticate users, and authorize them to access your services, in a flexible and extensible way

❑   Access secure (HTTPS) web servers

❑   Create secure web servers and other services that use socket-level SSL security

We will start the chapter with a brief introduction to encryption. Armed with this background, we will tackle the Java Cryptography Architecture (JCA) and its three extensions: **Java Authentication and Authorization Services (JAAS)**, **Java Cryptography Extension (JCE)**, and **Java Secure Sockets Extension (JSSE)**.

Cryptography

Most of the Java libraries discussed in this chapter are based directly on cryptographic concepts. The Java Cryptography Architecture supports digital signatures. Java Authentication and Authorization Services rely on certificates. The Java Cryptography Extension revolves around symmetric and asymmetric encryption. Finally, the **Secure Socket Layer** in JSSE uses a baroque mix of virtually all the cryptography discussed in this chapter.

Many of these concepts are related to each other, and this section aims to introduce you to some encryption basics before we descend into the nitty-gritty detail of Java cryptography support.

Encryption and Decryption

Cryptography, a field with a long and venerable history, is often used to send a message (the **plaintext**) safely over insecure methods of transport. This was necessary for ancient emperors attempting to send news of troop movements through battle lines, and it is even more necessary today with credit card details and other confidential information being sent over the Internet every second. The idea behind encryption is that when a third party intercepts the encrypted **ciphertext** message, it is incomprehensible to that party. When an encrypted message arrives, the receiver can have some confidence that it is genuine.

To be precise, encryption (and cryptography in general) can be used for four purposes:

❑   **Confidentiality**: The message is only readable by the person to which it is sent.

❑   **Integrity**: The message cannot be modified during transmission. Any tampering will be detected.

❑   **Authentication**: The identity of the sender can be verified.

❑   **Non-repudiation**: The sender of the message cannot deny that he or she has sent it.

There are various ways to send messages employing some form of cryptography, depending on which of these four purposes is the most important to the situation at hand. We will examine them in the remainder of this chapter. Finally, we will take a first look at Java cryptography support. Do not worry if you cannot absorb it all at once; you can refer back to the introductory sections as you go through the APIs in the remainder of the chapter.

Secret Key Cryptography

The earliest known encryption algorithms were **secret key** algorithms. Secret key or **symmetric** encryption relies on a single, secret key shared by both the sending and the receiving party.

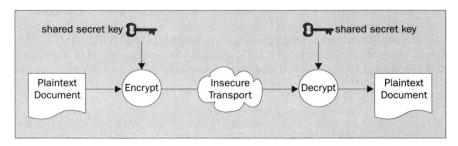

The **key** is a mathematical value used for encryption and decryption; without exactly the right key, decryption is impossible. It should be very hard to guess and obviously remain secret. Apart from that, the security of encryption – any type of encryption – crucially depends on the **cipher** (also referred to as the *algorithm*). One of the most famous early examples of encryption, the Caesar cipher, simply shifts the letters in the alphabet by three positions – for instance, A becomes D, B becomes E, X becomes A, and so forth. The Caesar cipher could be improved somewhat by interchanging the letters of the alphabet in a more complex way. To decode the message, the recipient would need information indicating how the letters are mapped to each other; this information forms the key necessary for decryption.

However, even such an improved cipher would be highly insecure. For all human languages, the frequency with which letters occur in a text has a very characteristic distribution. For example, in the English language the letter "e" occurs more frequently than any other. Some simple statistic analysis on the encrypted text will reveal how the "e" and other letters are mapped to each other. The algorithm becomes even weaker if the attacker knows part of the plaintext, for example a name or a stock phrase. This known piece of text can be compared to the encrypted text and immediately produces part of the cipher.

These general principles are still true for a lot of far more sophisticated algorithms known today. Clever analysis and mathematical shortcuts can crack many encryption methods, and known plaintext weakens almost any algorithm. Algorithms that are highly resistant against such attacks, so much so that in the foreseeable future hardware will not be powerful enough to break them, are called **cryptographically secure**. We will encounter a number of cryptographically secure encryption algorithms, but always remember that cryptography is an evolving field and today's secure algorithm can become weak overnight after a mathematical or computational breakthrough. In the race between code makers and code breakers, the code makers are currently ahead, but that has not always been the case.

The problem of secret key encryption is that all parties involved in the communication need to have the same secret key. This has two consequences.

❑ The secret key has to be communicated between the parties using a secure communication channel. For us, as for ancient emperors, the only absolutely secure channel is a face-to-face meeting (and even there we might be cheated).

❑ Because all parties have the same key, all can encrypt messages. Given an encrypted document, any one in possession of the secret key could be the author. Secret key cryptography has weaknesses in the areas of authentication and non-repudiation.

Both problems are solved by **public key encryption**, discussed below. This does not mean that secret key encryption is obsolete – far from it. There are many applications where the two problems quoted above are irrelevant, like automated teller machines. Secret key cryptography is also often combined with public key cryptography, because secret key encryption is a good deal faster and simpler, and offers far stronger security for a given key size.

Password-Based Encryption

There are cases where the secret key is actually a password or passphrase that has to be remembered by a person. The problem of **password-based encryption** is that even hard to guess passwords are comparatively weak because they tend to be both relatively short and not very random. There is only so much a human being can remember.

A common approach is to transform the password to a suitable secret key by mixing it with a large random number, the **salt**. The salted password is then used to encrypt the plaintext; the salt is transmitted together with the ciphertext so that the receiving end has all the information it needs to reconstruct the key from the password and decipher the message. The salt and the transformation make password-based encryption a good deal less vulnerable to attack.

Public Key Cryptography

Public key encryption is a relatively recent development dating back to the 1970s. In public key encryption, two different but mathematically related keys are generated as a pair: the **public key** and the **private key**. The public key is made widely known; others can use it to encrypt a document, but it cannot be used to decrypt the document again. Only we can decrypt the message again using our private key, which must be kept secret.

This type of encryption is also called **asymmetric encryption**, because if you know the public key with which a document has been encrypted, that does not make it easy to decrypt it again. The symmetry between encryption and decryption that exists in secret key algorithms has gone.

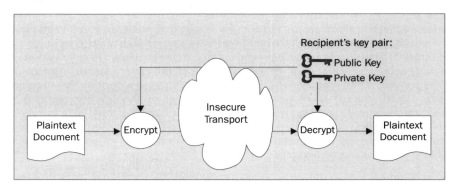

How is it impossible to decrypt a message even though you know the (public) key with which it was encrypted? Public key cryptography relies heavily on **one-way functions**, functions for which it is extraordinarily difficult to find the corresponding inverse function, preventing information from retracing its steps and being decrypted using the public key. At the same time, the function has a **trapdoor** allowing easy decryption by anyone in possession of the private key. The mathematics behind such functions is fascinating, but unfortunately well outside the scope of this discussion.

The asymmetry of public key algorithms has important implications.

❑ The need for a secure communication channel for the key is removed. The public key can be shared freely, because possession of the public key does not enable attackers to decrypt the text.

❑ Authentication is possible if the sender encrypts the plaintext message using his own private key instead of the recipient's public key:

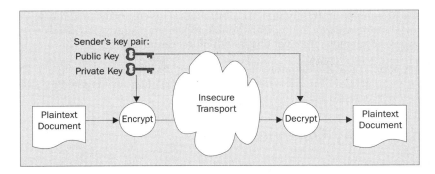

Anyone can then decrypt the ciphertext using the sender's public key; if the original plaintext appears, you managed to **authenticate** the sender. After all, only the legitimate sender has the private key necessary to produce a ciphertext that decodes with his public key. The message can be said to have a **digital signature**.

Unfortunately for Caesar, public key cryptography is so computationally intensive that it has become conceivable only with the advent of computers. You need far larger keys to achieve an acceptable level of security – ignoring a truckload of ifs and buts, 512-bit RSA asymmetric encryption can be compared to 56-bit symmetric DES encryption.

Session Keys

One of the problems of asymmetric encryption is that it is a good deal slower than symmetric encryption. A commonly used technique to address this problem works as follows:

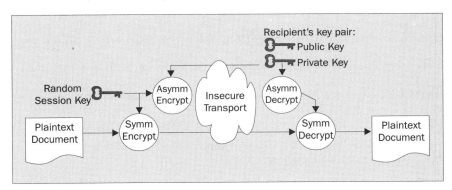

First, a secret **session key** is randomly generated and used to encrypt the plaintext using a fast, symmetric cipher. The ciphertext is sent to the receiver. This corresponds to the lowest line in the diagram above. Obviously, the receiver will need the session key to decrypt the message. The trick is now to encrypt and send the session key using normal public key cryptography; the top half of the diagram is identical to the previous section's first diagram.

In many respects, this approach combines the advantages of symmetric and asymmetric encryption.

❏ The plaintext, typically the bulk of the message, is transmitted using fast and efficient symmetric encryption. For a given key size, it gives far greater cryptographic strength.

❑   Public key encryption is only used to transmit a relatively small session key; this session key is completely random data and not susceptible to known plaintext attacks. Not only the speed has improved, but also the overall strength of the set-up.

This is the most popular way to use public-key encryption. For example, the popular **PGP (Pretty Good Privacy)** encryption package uses fast symmetric IDEA encryption for the plaintext, and asymmetric RSA encryption for the session key.

Java Cryptography Overview

Java has an extensive set of standard APIs supporting the cryptography constructs discussed above. They aim to be as algorithm-neutral as possible and provide a similar interface for substantially different implementations.

Moreover, the cryptography APIs are based on a **provider architecture**. The JCA is merely a set of abstract classes and interfaces defining, but not implementing, the API. The actual implementation is delivered by a **provider**, which can be a third party or indeed Sun itself. This architecture ensures that similar libraries can be used interchangeably and best-of-breed solutions can be adopted. The same approach has been taken, for example, in the JDBC API where any database vendor can implement a JDBC driver for his product.

The most important APIs you will encounter in Java cryptography are the following:

❑   **Java Cryptography Architecture** (**JCA**), encompassing key pair generation, signatures, message digests, and certificates (in fact, certificate support that predated JCA, but we will discuss it as part of JCA). It also provides the provider-based infrastructure that the security extensions build on.

The JCA has been part of the Java platform since JDK v1.1. It is used by the security API discussed in Chapter 7.

In addition, there are three APIs available as optional packages for the Java 2 platform:

❑   **Java Authentication and Authorization Service** (**JAAS**) dealing with user authentication and authorization. It can be downloaded for J2SE 1.2 and 1.3 to give these platforms, among other things, the `Principal`-driven security settings of JDK 1.4 (http://java.sun.com/products/jaas/).

❑   **Java Cryptography Extension** (**JCE**) providing public-key and secret-key encryption facilities (http://java.sun.com/products/jce/).

❑   **Java Secure Socket Extension** (**JSSE**) extending normal Java sockets to provide a secure SSL transport layer (http://java.sun.com/products/jsse/).

All of these optional packages have been integrated into the core Java platform as of J2SE version 1.4 – if you are running an earlier version, they can be downloaded as optional modules.

The Sun JCE implementation in J2SE 1.4 has been crippled to satisfy some countries' cryptography regulations, but if you live in a country without such restrictions you can download unrestricted policy files from http://java.sun.com/j2se/1.4/index.html#jcepolicyfiles. Be sure to obtain it when you want to use Sun's cryptography provider classes for production purposes. These files are *not* needed for the optional modules.

The provider-based architecture means there are really *two* sets of APIs: one for developers who wish to develop applications using the Java security APIs, and a **Service Provider Interface** (**SPI**) for those who need to code a provider for the security framework. As you are reading a Java networking book, not a Java cryptography book, we will not concern ourselves with the SPI classes (usually distinguished by the Spi suffix) and other purely provider-facing APIs.

Java 2 Platform Cryptography Support: JCA

The core Java platform has featured basic cryptography support since version 1.1. Its functionality is split up in a number of packages:

❑ java.security: This package comprises of the basic security and cryptography building blocks for the JDK, including the Java 2 language security model. Many of the classes related to that model have already been discussed in Chapter 7 and will mostly be ignored below.

❑ java.security.acl: This package contains the **Access Control Lists**, supporting Principal-based resource access. In J2SE 1.2, classes in the java.security package have superseded this package. See also the section on JAAS.

❑ java.security.cert: This includes classes and interfaces for generic and X.509 certificate support.

❑ java.security.interfaces: These are interfaces for generating and representing RSA and DSA key pairs.

❑ java.security.spec: This package deals with algorithm parameters and key specifications.

Providers

In the introduction, it was already mentioned that the Java cryptography architecture is **provider-based**, with the providers supplying the actual implementation of services based on the JCA API. Each implementation installed on the machine is represented by an instance of the Provider class.

The JCA services implemented by a provider can be one or more of:

❑ Digital signature algorithms

❑ Message digest algorithms

❑ Key generation algorithms

❑ Key factories

❑ Keystores

❑ Algorithm parameter management and/or generation

❑ Certificate factories

❑ Random number generator

It is not limited to this, as the Provider class is completely generic – it does not only represent JCA providers, but the providers for all the Java security extensions as well. The JDK ships with a Sun provider with basic cryptography support.

The `java.security.Security` class keeps track of the providers. It exposes methods to add, remove, and retrieve lists of installed providers. This class is initialized using the security settings file discussed below. All its functionality is implemented using static methods; a `Security` object cannot be instantiated any more than you can instantiate `java.util.Collections` or `java.lang.Math`.

Installing a Provider

To install a provider, two things need to be done.

❏ The JAR files with the provider classes either need to be in the `CLASSPATH`, or installed in the `${java.home}/lib/ext/` system directory, so that they can be found by the JVM.

   If the provider JARs are installed in `${java.home}/lib/ext`, they are treated as system libraries and will automatically have full security permissions. If they are installed in the `CLASSPATH`, the provider's documentation should specify what security settings to use in case the application runs under a security manager.

❏ The provider needs to be *registered*.

   a. This can be done by adding a line specifying the provider class to the `${java.home}/lib/security/java.security` file. There is no fixed guideline for the name and package of this class; it should be specified in the provider's documentation. The `java.security` file specifies (among other things) the security providers installed, in order of preference:

   ```
   security.provider.1=sun.security.provider.Sun
   security.provider.2=cryptix.provider.Cryptix
   ```

   b. Alternatively, the same provider can be registered dynamically at runtime using the `Security` class that manages the providers.

   ```
   Security.addProvider(new cryptix.provider.Cryptix());
   ```

Obviously, you will only be able to use dynamic registration if the security policy allows it (this is governed by the `java.security.SecurityPermission`). The advantage of this is that you, as a developer, have more control over the implementations used, and no changes to the system security file have to be made by your customer.

When an attempt is made to instantiate a JCA service, the installed providers will be queried in order of preference. The first one that provides a suitable implementation of the service will be used. If none of the installed providers has an implementation, an exception is thrown.

Using a Provider

To use a provider, you create the service you need using one of the **engine classes**. There is one engine class per service type, for example `Signature` for signatures or `KeyFactory` for keys. An engine class exposes a static `getInstance(String type)` method to get a service implementation for the specified type or algorithm:

```
Signature sig = Signature.getInstance("SHA1withDSA");
```

This will request an object capable of generating signatures using an SHA1 message digest encrypted using the DSA algorithm. If a specific provider needs to be enforced, there also is a second, overloaded getInstance() method taking an additional provider specification String.

```
Signature sig = Signature.getInstance("SHA1withDSA", "Sun");
```

JCA cryptographic classes are *never* instantiated with the new operator, but always with getInstance().

> *The JCA is a treasure trove of creational design patterns. The* getInstance() *method is an example of the Factory Method pattern, while the provider could be regarded as an Abstract Factory.*

Services differ slightly in the way they are provided. The code above instantiates a signature object, but the KeyFactory provided by KeyFactory.getInstance(String) is not the certificate object itself, but a **factory object** that is used to instantiate the actual keys. Factories such as these instantiate objects from existing encoded material. **Generators**, on the other hand, generate completely new instances, for example the KeyPairGenerator.

A newly instantiated service may need to be initialized in some way using a set of init() or initialize() methods:

```
Cipher cipher = Cipher.getInstance("DES");
cipher.init(Cipher.ENCRYPT_MODE, key);
```

This will instantiate a cipher (encryption/decryption engine) for DES encryption, and initializes it with the secret key. Whether initialization is necessary, and what parameters the initialization takes, depends again on the type of service provided.

Provider and Service Properties

The Provider class is primarily a table holding whatever properties the provider wants to expose. It is a subclass of java.util.Properties. In addition, there are methods to retrieve the provider's name (getName()), version (getVersion()), and a human-readable description (getInfo()).

To find out the provider of a service implementation created by getInstance(String type), you can use the getProvider() method of the object returned. Similarly, getAlgorithm() or getType() (depending on the service) return the algorithm or type implemented, and match the type argument given to getInstance().

The Sun Provider

The Sun JDK (v1.1 and later) comes with a default provider named "SUN". It provides:

- ❑ An implementation of the **Digital Signature Algorithm (DSA)**
- ❑ An implementation of the MD5 and SHA-1 message digest algorithms, which calculate a secure hash code for a message
- ❑ A key pair generator for generating a pair of public and private keys for the DSA algorithm
- ❑ A DSA algorithm parameter generator
- ❑ A DSA algorithm parameter manager

453

- ❑ A DSA key factory
- ❑ An implementation of the proprietary SHA1PRNG random number generator
- ❑ A certificate factory for X.509 certificates and Certificate Revocation Lists
- ❑ A keystore implementation for the **Java Key Store (JKS)** format, proprietary to Sun

These implementations provide the Sun Java 2 platform with support for cryptographic signing and authentication, but none for encryption and decryption.

Manipulating Keys

The terms **Key** and **key pair** played quite a prominent role both in the chapter on the Java security model and the introduction to this chapter, and it will probably not surprise that they are part of the basic cryptography support in the `java.security` classes.

Three different services are related to keys and key management:

- ❑ **Key factories** instantiating objects from existing encoded keys
- ❑ **Key pair generators**
- ❑ In-memory key databases called **keystores**

In Java, a key can have two different types of representation: it can be **transparent**, giving immediate access to the material that constitutes the key. Generally, transparent keys are used to access encoded key material on disk, the network or elsewhere. There is also an **opaque** representation giving direct access only to some generic key properties; opaque keys are used when working with cryptographic algorithms.

Reading and Converting Keys

In general, keys for cryptographic algorithms have three properties: the **algorithm** they are intended for, a standard **encoding** for external representation such as exporting to a file, and the **format** giving the name of the standard (primary) encoding, such as X.509.

Opaque Keys

The `java.security.Key` interface represents **opaque keys**. It gives access to the generic attributes of a key (`getAlgorithm()`, `getFormat()`, `getEncoded()`) and nothing more. There are two sub-interfaces, `PublicKey` and `PrivateKey`. They do not add any methods, but provide type-safety and act as markers for public and private keys in asymmetric algorithms.

For example, the following code might be used to write a DSA public key to a file in its default encoding, which happens to be X.509 encoding:

```
OutputStream out = new FileOutputStream("key");
out.write(myPublicDSAKey.getEncoded());
out.close();
```

Key Specifications

Physically, keys may be specified in a number of different ways. They can be specified by whatever parameters their algorithm takes; they can be part of an *X.509 certificate* or have another type of encoding; they might even exist on a hardware device. The `java.security.spec.KeySpec` interface encapsulates such a *transparent key specification*. Subclasses of `KeySpec` are used to read or specify keys, or to access key properties.

To read the X.509 encoded key specification written out above back from disk:

```
File keyFile = new File("key");
byte[] buffer = new byte[(int)keyFile.length()];
InputStream in = new FileInputStream(keyFile);
in.read(buffer);
in.close();
X509EncodedKeySpec myPublicDSAKeySpec = new X509EncodedKeySpec(buffer);
```

Alternatively, a key may be specified in terms of its algorithm parameters. For example, a DSA key takes four parameters, called `y`, `p`, `q` and `g`. We will not worry here what these parameters mean; given the parameters, the code to create the DSA public key specification would be:

```
DSAPublicKeySpec myPublicDSAKeySpec =
    new java.security.spec.DSAPublicKeySpec(y, p, q, g);
```

Only opaque keys can be used in the JCA cryptographic services. A **key factory** will convert between key specifications and opaque keys. The two code snippets above used two completely different representations (`X509EncodedKeySpec` and `DSAPublicKeySpec`) of what might well be the very same key. In that case, they will convert to the same opaque key.

The Key Factory

A **key factory** for asymmetric keys, implemented by a provider-supplied subclass of `java.security.KeyFactory`, can perform three types of key conversions.

❑   Convert a **transparent** key specification to an opaque public or private key with `generatePrivate(KeySpec)` and `generatePublic(KeySpec)`.

❑   Convert an opaque key to a transparent key specification with the methods `getKeySpec(Key, Class)`. As the key may be specified in a number of ways, the method needs the `Class` to be used for the key specification. This may be one of the classes from `java.security.spec`, for example `DSAPublicKeySpec`, or a provider-supplied class. The class needs to be appropriate for the given key.

❑   Translate a key from one opaque `Key` representation to another using `translateKey(Key)`. This may be used, for instance, to translate a `Key` implementation from an untrusted provider to an equivalent opaque `Key` implemented by a known and trusted one.

Key factories are, of course, provider-based as usual in the Java Cryptography Architecture. To retrieve a factory for a specific algorithm you need to call one of the static `getInstance()` methods in the `KeyFactory` class.

For example, to provide the `DSAPublicKeySpec` from the previous section to an opaque public key:

```
X509EncodedKeySpec myPublicDSAKeySpec = new X509EncodedKeySpec(buffer);
KeyFactory keyFactory = KeyFactory.getInstance("DSA");
PublicKey myPublicDSAKey = keyFactory.generatePublic(myPublicDSAKeySpec);
```

This opaque key can then be used, for example, to digitally sign data. The factory will also perform conversions to other way around, from opaque keys to key specifications.

Generating Keys: KeyPairGenerator

In public-key cryptography, keys are always generated in pairs. One of the keys will be a `PrivateKey` to be kept secret at all times, the other a `PublicKey` to be freely disseminated. Data encrypted by one key can only be decrypted by the other.

Generating a key pair is done, unsurprisingly, using a `KeyPairGenerator`, a provider-based generator class. To generate a 512-bit DSA key pair, we could use the following code:

```
KeyPairGenerator kpg = KeyPairGenerator.getInstance("DSA", "SUN");
kpg.initialize(512);
KeyPair keyPair = kpg.generateKeyPair();
PublicKey myPublicDSAKey = keyPair.getPublic();
PrivateKey myPrivateDSAKey = keyPair.getPrivate();
```

As apparent in the code above, generation of the pair takes three steps.

1. As with any provider-based generator or factory, the class is not instantiated using `new` but with a call to `getInstance()`, specifying the algorithm for which we need a key, and optionally the provider name. In this case, we specifically want the DSA key implementation provided by Sun. The algorithm names known to this method are listed in the table below.

2. The next step is to initialize the generator. The `initialize()` method needs two things: parameters telling it what kind of key to generate, and a random number generator. The latter is optional; if no random number generator is specified, it will be obtained from one of the installed providers.

There are actually two different sets of `initialize()` methods, **algorithm-dependent** and **algorithm-independent** ones. The former take a set of algorithm parameters, the latter merely the key size, usually in bits. Usually, the `KeyPairGenerator` is used to generate a fresh key pair of a given strength using simple algorithm-independent initialization: in the sample code above, the `initialize(512)` call asks for a 512-bit key pair. We don't specify a random number generator, so the highest-preference provider that implements a random number generator will supply one.

3. Finally, one or more key pairs are generated by calling `generateKeyPair()`. Confusingly, there also is a `genKeyPair()` method that works exactly the same. You can use either. The full-length name is preferred because it is clearer and more consistent with the `generate…()` functions in the other JCA factories.

The key pair generation method returns a `KeyPair` object encapsulating a `PublicKey` and a `PrivateKey`, returned by `getPublic()` and `getPrivate()`, respectively. A table outlining the possible algorithms and describing them is shown later.

Message Digests and Signatures

In the introduction to this chapter, we have looked at the four goals of encryption: confidentiality, integrity, authentication and non-repudiation. We also examined how secret- and public-key encryption can be used to address these aims. The issue of **integrity** was only partially addressed however. If an encrypted message is changed, this will show up as garbage in the decrypted plaintext. A human eye would be immediately able to see that the message has been tampered with, but this is far more difficult for a computer to do. To guard the integrity of a message so that a computer may check it, you can calculate a **message digest**, also known as a **hash**. This is a highly condensed "fingerprint", typically a large number, derived from the entire plaintext using a **one-way function**. Even the smallest change in the plaintext message should lead to a completely different digest, so that tampering or other corruption can be reliably detected.

Popular cryptographic hash functions are MD5 (Message Digest algorithm 5) and SHA (Secure Hash Algorithm). There are many more hash functions in common use, such as the CRC checksum used in many places to protect data integrity and the functions used to implement the `Object.hashCode()` method in Java, but they are cryptographically weak – it is too easy to tweak the input to yield a certain hash – and unusable for security purposes.

By combining the message digest with public-key encryption, we get a **digital signature**. The sender encrypts the digest with his private key. The recipient calculates the message digest at his end, and uses it together with the sender's public key to verify the encrypted digest.

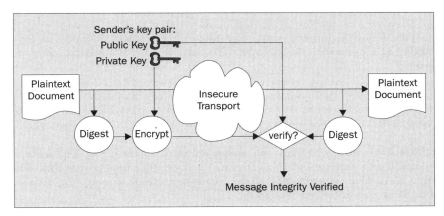

If the digest is successfully verified, the recipient can be sure of both the integrity and the authenticity of the message; encryption and verification of the relatively small message digest is also much faster than encryption and decryption of the entire message would be. Finally, it is impossible for the sender to deny that the message is his, as only he possesses the private key used to encrypt the digest (non-repudiation). These are exactly the properties associated with an ordinary handwritten signature.

Common digital signature algorithms are DSA (Digital Signature Algorithm) and RSA (Rivest, Shamir and Adleman).

The following table shows the keypair generation algorithm names and their descriptions:

Algorithm	Description
DSA	Digital Signature Algorithm (NIST FIPS 186) – produces a key pair. The key length must be a multiple of 64 bits. Common lengths are 512, 768 and 1024 bits.
RSA	The Rivest, Shamir and Adleman algorithm (PKCS#1) – key length must be a multiple of 8 bits, minimum length is 512.
	The SunRsaSign provider implements keypair generation for digital signatures, but no RSA encryption.

Calculating a Message Digest

The `java.security.MessageDigest` class provides the ability to calculate a digest from a byte array. As usual in the JCA, it is an abstract service to be implemented by one or more providers.

```
byte[] message = ... // get message
MessageDigest md = MessageDigest.getInstance("MD5");
md.update(message);
byte[] messageDigest = md.digest();
```

The basic steps to calculate a digest are:

1. Instantiate a new `MessageDigest` using the `getInstance()` method with the desired algorithm and, optionally, the provider. You can find a list of algorithm names in the table below.

2. Call the `update()` methods zero or more times, processing the data block by block. This is an overloaded method with three different sets of parameters; all of them essentially take `byte` primitives.

3. Finally, call `digest()` to finish processing and calculate the digest. This method is overloaded with versions that take a `byte[]` array to do a final update with. The latter version is especially convenient if all the data is in memory anyway –the code snippet above could just as well have been written as:

```
byte[] message = ... // get message
MessageDigest md = MessageDigest.getInstance("MD5");
byte[] messageDigest = md.digest(message);
```

The length of the array returned by `digest()` depends on the algorithm. The `getDigestLength()` method can be called to find out the digest length in bytes.

After calculating the digest, the `MessageDigest` will reset its internal state. This means that if you subsequently call `update()` again, you will start a *new* digest calculation, not continue the old one. Should you need to calculate the digest so far and continue, use `clone()` to create a copy of the digest and call `digest()` on the clone. Beware that digest implementations may not support this and throw a `CloneNotSupportedException` instead.

The following table shows the message digest algorithm names and descriptions:

Algorithm	Description
SHA	SHA-1 Secure Hash Algorithm (NIST FIPS 180-1) – produces a 160-bit digest
MD2	Message Digest 2 algorithm (defined in RFC 1319) – produces a 128-bit digest
MD5	Message Digest 5 algorithm (defined in RFC 1321) – produces a 128-bit digest (this algorithm was designed to be more secure than its predecessor, MD4)

Calculating the Digest of a Stream

The `MessageDigest` interface can be a bit awkward to work with. It is block-based, not stream-based, and only takes `byte` primitives for input. Fortunately, there are `InputStream` and `OutputStream` wrappers that calculate a stream's `MessageDigest` on the fly. This makes integrating a digest calculation into existing code that reads from or writes to a stream very simple indeed:

```
MessageDigest md = MessageDigest.getInstance("MD5");

// open a digest-calculating network stream
OutputStream out =
    new DigestOutputStream(
        new BufferedOutputStream(socket.getOutputStream()),
        MessageDigest.getInstance("SHA")));

// now write data to the network stream as usual

// retrieve the digest for the data written so far
byte[] messageDigest = md.digest();
```

This is usually the most transparent way to calculate a digest. The `DigestInputStream` and `DigestOutputStream` classes are very straightforward to use, the only thing worth noting here is that you can switch the digest calculation on and off at will using `on(boolean)`. This is important if the data written to the stream consists of a number of parts (for instance a header, a message, an encrypted digest and a certificate), only some of which need digest functionality.

Calculating and Verifying a Digital Signature

It is only a small step from digests to signatures. A signature is after all little more than a digest encrypted with the sender's private key. In fact, using the `java.security.Signature` class that provides signatures is remarkably like using `MessageDigest`. The main difference is that it needs a cryptographic key to work with, which adds a step to the initialization:

1. Instantiate a new `Signature` using the `Signature.getInstance()` method. The table overleaf lists possible algorithm names.

2. Initialize the signature for signing with `initSign(PrivateKey)`, or for verification with `initVerify(PublicKey)`.

3. Call `update()` one or more times. The `Signature` class has a set of three `update()` methods that are identical to those in `MessageDigest`.

4. Finally, call `sign()` to calculate the signature. This method is overloaded with a version that takes a `byte[]` array, an offset and a length to write the signature to. If the length parameter is too small to hold the signature, a `SignatureException` is thrown.

Like a `MessageDigest`, the internal state of the `Signature` is reset once you call `sign()` or `verify()`. To preserve the calculated digest and continue working, you can `clone()` the object and use the clone to generate the signature.

Calculating a Signature

The code to calculate a signature is almost identical to that of calculating a digest, with one additional line to initialize the signature with the private key:

```
byte[] message = ...   // get message
PrivateKey mykey = ... // retrieve the private key
Signature sig = Signature.getInstance("SHA1withDSA");
sig.initSign(mykey);   // going to sign with the given private key
sig.update(message);
byte[] signature = sig.sign();
```

Verifying a Signature

Signature verification is much like signing, except for the initialization and, of course, the call to `verify()`:

```
byte[] message = ...   // get message
byte[] signature = ... // get signature
PublicKey hisKey = ... // retrieve the sender's public key
Signature sig = Signature.getInstance("SHA1withDSA");
sig.initVerify(hisKey);// this signature is going to be used for signing
sig.update(message);
boolean verified = sig.verify(signature);
```

There is an overloaded `initSign()` method taking a **certificate** containing a public key instead of a "bare" public key. As we will see, a certificate is usually included as part of the signature.

Signatures and Streams

One might hope that there were `SignatureInputStream` and `SignatureOutputStream` classes to help calculating signatures on the fly, but this is unfortunately not the case. If you look at Sun's source for `DigestInputStream` and `DigestOutputStream`, it is trivial to come up with equivalent classes for signatures.

The following table shows the main digital signature algorithm names and descriptions:

Algorithm	Description
SHA1withDSA	The SHA-1 digest algorithm with DSA signatures (FIPS PUB 186)
MD2withRSA	The MD2 digest algorithm with RSA signatures (PKCS #1)
MD5withRSA	The MD5 digest algorithm with RSA signatures (PKCS #1)
SHA1withRSA	The SHA1 digest algorithm with RSA signatures (PKCS #1)

Certificates

The section on public key cryptography almost entirely ignored the distribution of public keys. Yet, unless you can afford to organize face-to-face meetings to exchange public keys, there are many security problems associated with the distribution of such keys. If you get e-mail with a public key and information whose key it is, how do you know you can trust it? It may be an elaborate attempt by a hacker to tap into your secure communications. And when you finally have a public key you dare trust, what happens when the owner lets the private key get into someone else's hands?

Certificates provide the answers to these questions. A **certificate** contains the **public key** belonging to a person or entity, together with information about the owner's **identity** (the **subject**), a limited **validity period**, and possibly the key's domain of applicability and other information. The certificate is digitally signed, that means that it comes with an encrypted digest of itself, so it is authenticated and tamper-proof.

The simplest certificates are **self-signed certificates**, such as those generated by the Java keytool -genkey command. They are signed using the private key associated with the public key that is contained inside the certificate. Such self-signed certificates are little more trustworthy than plain public keys; the only assurance you get is that the person who owns the private key professes to have the name mentioned in the certificate.

Things are looking up when a party you can trust, a **Certificate Authority** (**CA**), signs the certificate. Assuming that you know the authority's public key and are so able to convince yourself of the validity of their signature, and provided that you can rely upon the authority to check the validity of a certificate before signing it, it is the next best thing after a face-to-face meeting to exchange public keys. Of course this requires you to be in the possession of the authority's public key, which brings us back to the original issue: you need a trusted channel to get it in the first place. There is no way around this. A chain of trust has to start somewhere. This "somewhere" is the self-signed certificate of a **root Certificate Authority**.

Examples of public certificate authorities are VeriSign (http://www.verisign.com), Entrust (http://www.entrust.com), GTE CyberTrust (http://www.gte.com) and Thawte (http://www.thawte.com). Companies establishing a security infrastructure can also institute their own authorities. The only important criterion is that users of the certificates are prepared to trust the authority, or that their software can be set up to trust it.

There are several standards for digital certificates, such as PGP and SDSI, but the most popular is the X.509 set of standards, which is the type of certificate best supported by the Java core libraries and used by key applications such as SSL (secure sockets).

Giving certificates limited validity is only part of the answer to the problem of ensuring certificate validity. **Certificate revocation lists** are the other part. CRLs are timestamped lists of revoked certificates, regularly issued by the authority in much the same way that a credit card issuer publishes lists of lost or stolen credit cards. Most certificates issued today include information about the **CRL Distribution Point**, usually a web URI, where the appropriate CRL can be found.

Certificate Chains

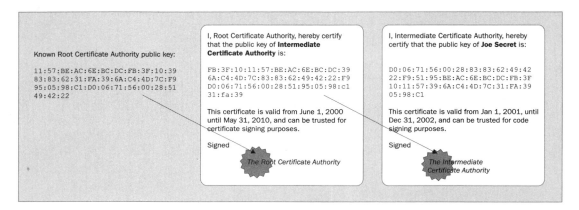

A certificate signed by a Certificate Authority is the simplest example of a **certificate chain**. Suppose that the authority issued a certificate to us stating that certificates signed by *ourselves* can be trusted. Then, by virtue of that certificate, we can be trusted as an intermediate CA by anyone who trusts in the good judgment the original authority. There would be a certificate chain leading from the root authority via ourselves to the certificates signed by us.

This idea can be arbitrarily extended; a certificate chain can have any length. When you receive a signed document, you go back up the certificate chain until you encounter a certificate you know you can trust. At that point, you can stop searching. This will often be the root certificate, but that does not necessarily have to be the case.

The JCA Certificate Framework

The classes in the `java.security.cert` package provide Java with the ability to read and verify certificates. Three classes make up the core of the certificate framework: the `Certificate` class to represent certificates, the `CRL` class for revocation lists, and `CertificateFactory`, whose job it is to generate instances of the first two classes.

The framework is best introduced by an example where we read an X.509 certificate, instantiate it, and display some of its attributes. The following is a listing of an application called `ReadCert.java`.

```
// ReadCert.java

import java.io.*;
```

```java
import java.net.*;
import java.util.*;
import java.security.cert.*;

public class ReadCert {

  public static final String CRL_DISTRIBUTION_POINT_OID = "2.5.29.31";

  public static void main(String args[]) {
    InputStream in = null;
    try {

      // Instantiate an X.509 certificate factory
      CertificateFactory cf = CertificateFactory.getInstance("X.509");

      // Read the certificate
      in = new BufferedInputStream(new FileInputStream(args[0]));
      X509Certificate cert = (X509Certificate) cf.generateCertificate(in);

      // Print certificate information
      System.out.println("Subject: " + cert.getSubjectDN().getName());
      System.out.println("Validity: " + cert.getNotBefore() + " - "
                         + cert.getNotAfter());
      System.out.println("Issuer: " + cert.getIssuerDN().getName());
      System.out.println("Signature Algorithm: " + cert.getSigAlgName());

      // Print the CRL Distribution Point if there is one
      byte[] crlDP = cert.getExtensionValue(CRL_DISTRIBUTION_POINT_OID);
      if (crlDP != null) {
        URL crlUrl = extractURL(crlDP);
        if (crlUrl != null) {
          System.out.println("CRL Distribution Point: " + crlUrl);
          CRL crl = cf.generateCRL(crlUrl.openStream());
          System.out.println("Certificate revoked: " + crl.isRevoked(cert));
        }
      }
    } catch (Exception e) {
      e.printStackTrace();
    }
    finally {
      if (in != null) {
        try {
          in.close();
        } catch (Exception e) {

          // do nothing
        }
      }
    }
  }

  public static URL extractURL(byte[] bytes) throws MalformedURLException {
    String s = new String(bytes);
    int urlOffset = s.lastIndexOf("http");
    return (urlOffset >= 0) ? new URL(s.substring(urlOffset)) : null;
  }
}
```

We also need a certificate to print. You may have a personal certificate in your e-mail application, either your own or someone else's, that you can export in X.509 format. Alternatively, you can generate a certificate using the Java keytool discussed in Chapter 7:

C:\Beg_Java_Networking\Ch14> **keytool -genkey -keystore JCA.keystore -alias certkey**

Answer the prompts (when asked for a password, enter, for example, secret) and the tool will generate a key pair called certkey. Now export the certificate containing the public key:

C:\Beg_Java_Networking\Ch14> **keytool -export -keystore JCA.keystore -alias certkey -file certkey.cer**

Compile the application, then run it using the following command:

C:\Beg_Java_Networking\Ch14> **java ReadCert certkey.cer**

This will read the certificate and display its subject, validity period, who issued it, and the algorithm with which it was signed. If there is a CRL Distribution Point web address, it will display that too, download the CRL and check if the certificate is in the list. For a VeriSign digital certificate, the output would look something like the following:

```
Subject: EmailAddress=joe@secret.com, CN=Joe Secret,
OU=Digital ID Class 1 - Microsoft Full Service, OU=Persona Not Validated,
OU="www.verisign.com/repository/RPA Incorp. by Ref.,LIAB.LTD(c)98",
OU=VeriSign Trust Network, O="VeriSign, Inc."
Validity: Sat Sep 02 01:00:00 BST 2000 - Mon Sep 03 00:59:59 BST 2001
Issuer: CN=VeriSign Class 1 CA Individual Subscriber-Persona Not Validated,
OU="www.verisign.com/repository/RPA Incorp. By Ref.,LIAB.LTD(c)98",
OU=VeriSign Trust Network, O="VeriSign, Inc."
Signature Algorithm: MD5withRSA
CRL Distribution Point: http://crl.verisign.com/class1.crl
Certificate revoked: false
```

If you are using a HTTP proxy, you will have to add -Dhttp.proxyHost=*host* -Dhttp.proxyPort=*port* arguments to the command line, indicating the location of the proxy, for CRL downloading to work.

The Certificate Factory

As with other provider-based objects, you do not generally instantiate a Certificate yourself. Instantiating certificates is a two-step process. First, you retrieve a **certificate factory** that knows how to instantiate the type of certificate you need. In the example, this was done by the following code:

```
// Instantiate an X.509 certificate factory
CertificateFactory cf = CertificateFactory.getInstance("X.509");
```

It is very well possible that there are multiple installed providers which can provide a given certificate type. If you need to force a particular choice of provider, there is a second version of this method taking an additional provider string.

Second, you use the factory to create certificates and revocation lists from an InputStream with an encoded certificate or list. As usual for JCA factory objects, you cannot use it to create a completely new certificate or CRL.

```
in = new BufferedInputStream(new FileInputStream("mykey.cer"));
X509Certificate cert = (X509Certificate)cf.generateCertificate(in);
```

X.509 is the certificate defined in X.509, consisting of an X.500 distinguished name (DN), a public key, and possible extensions.

The generateCertificate() method reads a single encoded certificate from the InputStream. If there are multiple certificates in the stream, for example because you are reading an entire certificate chain, use the generateCertificates(InputStream) which reads the entire stream and returns a Collection of the certificates it finds. The generateCRL() and generateCRLs() methods do the same for revocation lists. If the certificates are expired or not yet valid, the InputStream could not be parsed, or if there was another error, the factory methods throw an appropriate subclass of CertificateException.

Certificate

The abstract java.security.cert.Certificate class provides a basic representation of the properties common to certificates in general. You will recognize these properties from the discussion of certificates above.

❑   A certificate encapsulates a public key, which can be retrieved using getPublicKey()

❑   A certificate is *signed* by some trusted entity. If you are in the possession of the public key of the signer, the certificate can be verified using the verify(PublicKey) method.

There is a second, overloaded form of this method which enables you to specify which provider you want to use in the verification process. This is relevant only if you have installed multiple providers capable of verifying the certificate's signature.

❑   The certificate type can be retrieved by calling getType(). This is the standard to which the certificate conforms (for example, X.509).

In addition, with getEncoded(), an encoded form of the certificate is retrieved for external representation, such as transmission to a remote host or exporting to a file. The encoding is specific to the certificate type; the assumption is that there is just one standard encoding per type.

The Sun provider provides support for X.509 certificates, represented by the X509Certificate abstract class. The additional properties of an X.509 certificate include:

❑   Information about the **validity period** for the certificate

```
System.out.println("Validity: " + cert.getNotBefore() +
                   " - " + cert.getNotAfter());
```

❑   A **Distinguished Name** (**DN**) for both issuer and subject (DNs usually, but not necessarily, uniquely identify the issuer and subject)

```
System.out.println("Subject: " + cert.getSubjectDN().getName());
```

❑   **Critical extensions** and **non-critical extensions**, provided through the X509Extension interface

```
byte[] crlDP = cert.getExtensionValue(CRL_DISTRIBUTION_POINT_OID);
```

Critical extensions *must* be acted upon, but non-critical ones may be ignored. If an application cannot parse a critical extension, it should reject the certificate. A good example of a critical extension is `KeyUsage` specifying what uses the certificate is valid for (authentication, code signing, etc). If an application does not understand the value of `KeyUsage`, then the only safe assumption is that the key should not be used for that particular application. The CRL Distribution Point is an example of a non-critical extension.

Certificate Revocation List

Certificates can be stolen, or slip through a CA's identity verification process. Certificate authorities publish regular **revocation lists** with revoked certificates to prevent these certificates from being abused. The `CRL` class represents such a list; `isRevoked(Certificate)` returns a `boolean` indicating whether the given certificate is in the list. The location of the relevant list for a certificate depends on the issuer; many issuers specify this location as part of the certificate itself. For example, for an X.509 certificate the distribution point may be incorporated as an extension (Object ID `"2.5.29.28"`; see http://www.ietf.org/rfc/rfc2459.txt).

Remembering Keys and Certificates: The Key Store

For cryptography to work, we need a place to store our private keys, plus certificates containing public keys for all entities to whom we need to send encrypted messages or from whom we need to authenticate signatures. These are stored in a `KeyStore`. `KeyStore`s are again provider-based, so we may have support for any number of different stores of different types, dependent on the providers we have installed on our system..

The Sun provider shipping with the JDK provides a proprietary JKS-type `KeyStore`:

```
// instantiate a JKS keystore
KeyStore ks = KeyStore.getInstance("JKS");
```

JKS (Java Key Store) is a proprietary format. It is the default format used by `keytool` and the other JDK cryptography tools. Neither keystores in general nor the tools (with the exception of `keytool`) are limited to file-based stores, however. Keystores may be based on networked directories, databases, and any other place where you can store information.

Before a keystore can be used, the information that is to go into the store needs to be loaded.

```
// load the JKS keystore contents from the "keystore" file on disk
String keystoreFilePath = "keystore";
String keystorePassword = "secret";
ks.load(new FileInputStream(keystoreFilePath), keystorePassword);
```

The `load()` method will throw an exception if there was an I/O problem (`IOException`), if there is no provider for the algorithm used to verify keystore integrity (`NoSuchAlgorithmException`), or if a certificate could not be loaded (`CertificateException`). Passing `null` for the `InputStream` argument creates an empty `KeyStore`. This is used to create a brand new keystore, or to start creating a keystore from a source that cannot be exposed as an `InputStream`. The `load()` method *must* be called before a `KeyStore` can be used.

Every entry in the `KeyStore` class is known by an identifying string, its **alias**. Every entry in the store can contain two types of entries:

❑ A key, usually a private key paired with a certificate chain containing the corresponding public key. Private keys are used for signing and decrypting ciphertext. Because they are very security sensitive, they are stored in encrypted form using password-based encryption.

To retrieve a key, use `getKey(String alias, char[] password)`. If there is no key entry with that alias, the method returns `null`. A `SecurityException` is thrown if the keystore has not been loaded, there is no provider for the key's algorithm, or if the password is wrong.

The `setKeyEntry(String alias, Key key, char[] password, Certificate[] chain)` method is used to set a key. The `chain` argument should give the certificate chain associated with the private key. If the alias already exists, its entry is overwritten.

❑ A trusted certificate or certificate chain containing information about an entity, together with their public key. Certificates are used to authenticate other parties and to encrypt data to be sent. As they are not particularly security sensitive, they are stored in unencrypted form.

Certificates are retrieved using the `getCertificate(String alias)` method. To get the entire certificate chain, you can use `getCertificateChain(String alias)`. Both methods return `null` if the alias is not associated with a certificate, and throw a `KeyStoreException` if the keystore has not been loaded.

The `setCertificateEntry(String alias, Certificate cert)` sets a trusted certificate entry. An existing entry with the same alias will be overwritten.

Searching the list of trusted certificates in the keystore for a particular certificate is facilitated by `getCertificateAlias(Certificate cert)`. It returns the alias if the given certificate was found in the store, or `null` otherwise.

The passwords arguments are `char[]` arrays, not `Strings`, so that you can erase them from memory after use. Strings are immutable and will linger in memory until they have been garbage collected and their memory reused.

To continue the code example, the following would attempt to retrieve the `mykey` private key from the loaded keystore:

```
try {
    // retrieve "mykey" from the keystore
    String keyPassword = keystorePassword;
    Key mykey = ks.getKey("mykey", keyPassword);
    // ... use the key ...
}
catch (UnrecoverableKeyException e) {
    System.out.println("Could not retrieve key, wrong password?\n" + e);
}
catch (GeneralSecurityException e) {
    System.out.println("Problems retrieving key: " + e);
}
```

Further `KeyStore` methods dealing with managing and querying keystore entries are:

❑ `aliases()` returns an `Enumeration` of all aliases in the keystore

❑ `deleteEntry(String alias)` deletes the entry with the given alias

❑   containsAlias(String alias) returns a boolean indicating if a key or certificate with a given alias is in the store; isCertificateEntry(String alias) and isKeyEntry(String alias) additionally check if the entry is a certificate or a key, respectively.

Finally, the keystore can be written back to a file, network connection, or elsewhere in much the same way it was loaded, using store(OutputStream stream, char[] password).

The following table shows the type names and descriptions for keystores.

Type	Description
JKS	Java KeyStore, a proprietary implementation provided by the SUN provider – the default type for the JDK security tools (keytool, policytool, jarsigner)
JCEKS	JCE KeyStore, a proprietary keystore type: JCEKS uses strong encryption for private keys stored in the keystore *This keystore is provided by the SunJCE provider that ships with JCE.*
PKCS12	A transfer syntax for personal identity information (PKCS#12) *The SunJSSE provider that ships with JSSE implements this type of keystore.*

Secure Random Numbers

There are a number of places in Java cryptography in need of a good **random number generator**. When generating key pairs, for instance: if you are generating more than one key pair, you would not want the loss of one pair to a malicious third party to enable that party to calculate what the subsequent pairs might have been.

The normal random number generator, java.util.Random, uses a simple linear formula to generate pseudo-random numbers. This is very fast and surprisingly effective for most purposes, but far too weak to be useful for cryptography. The internal state of the generator is contained in a 48-bit seed; a few random numbers are enough to calculate its value and predict all subsequent numbers.

The java.util.SecureRandom class is a subclass of Random that preserves its interface, but provides a cryptographically secure **pseudo-random number generator (PRNG)**. Unlike most provider-based services, this is *not* an abstract class. You can instantiate it with new SecureRandom() like any other class; this will give you an implementation from the highest-preference provider that has a PRNG in the offering. Alternatively, you can call getInstance() with the algorithm and an optional provider name, as usual.

```
SecureRandom random = SecureRandom.getInstance("SHA1PRNG");
```

SHA1PRNG, or the pseudo-random number generator based on the SHA1 hash algorithm. It concatenates a large seed with a 64-bits counter, and then calculates the SHA1 hash of the whole.

The `SecureRandom` class adds a constructor and a `setSeed()` method allowing you to set a longer seed than the 64-bit `long` used by `Random`. If you create `SecureRandom` without supplying a seed either in the constructor or immediately after it, a seed will be generated automatically. Re-seeding the generator – calling `setSeed()` after the initial seeding – does not replace the current state but rather supplements it with the new seed. If you need reproducible random numbers, you have to start out with a new `SecureRandom` instance every time so you can seed it from a pristine state.

`SecureRandom` is very secure, but a good deal slower than the normal `Random` class.

Identifying People: JAAS

The **Java Authentication and Authorization Service** (**JAAS**) provides an infrastructure for authenticating users, and setting code permissions based on the authenticated user executing it. As discussed in Chapter 7, this capability is completely integrated with the core Java platform as of version 1.4. For versions 1.2 and 1.3 of the JDK, JAAS is an optional package that can be downloaded and installed separately from http://java.sun.com/products/jaas/; installation can be as simple as putting `jaas.jar` in the classpath.

For the purposes of our examples, if we are running JDK 1.3 or lower, we will install `jaas.jar` in the `%JAVA_HOME%\jre\lib\ext` directory. This way, we can keep our classpath freed up for classpath instructions that appear in any other JAR manifests we create.

JAAS is distributed over a number of packages:

- ❑ `javax.security.auth` contains the main JAAS classes and interfaces
- ❑ `javax.security.auth.callback` contains the callbacks used during the interactive login procedure
- ❑ `javax.security.auth.login` provides login support
- ❑ `javax.security.auth.spi` contains the `LoginModule` Service Provider Interface used to write login modules

There are two parts to JAAS. *Authentication* provides the infrastructure to establish the identity of users and other entities in a large number of ways, from a simple password-based login prompt to a hardware key. *Authorization* extends the Java 2 security framework to support code permissions based on the authenticated user running the code, in addition to the usual criteria of where the code was loaded from and who signed it.

Authentication

JAAS implements stacked, pluggable authentication. **Stacked**, because multiple forms of authentication can be activated for a single application, either as alternatives or in combination. **Pluggable**, because new forms of authentication (login modules) can be plugged into the framework at will. A configuration file controls the authentication setup for one or more JAAS-aware applications. In the next few sections, we will examine the way users and entities are represented in JAAS, look at a detailed example, and finally discuss the API in detail.

Keeping Track: Subject, Principal and Credentials

The `javax.security.auth.Subject` class represents a **subject**: usually a person or an entity such as a corporation. Every subject has one or more identities called **principals**. The relation between subjects and principals is best illustrated by taking an everyday example: you (the *subject*) probably possess multiple, independent forms of identification, each of them giving you certain rights. Your driving license allows you to drive a car (corresponding to a "car driver" type principal). Your passport allows you to travel ("citizen" type principal). You may also have a pass giving access to the company premises ("employee" type principal).

Similarly, in a complex information system a single subject may very well have a number of different kinds of principal associated with it, representing identities or roles in different parts of the system.

Principals are represented by the `Principal` interface; they are actually not part of JAAS, but include the JDK. The whole thing is a very generic concept, and correspondingly the `Principal` interface is extremely lightweight. The only property it defines is the name, returned by `getName()`. Other than that, principals can only be tested for equality (`equals`). The core JAAS platform does not have any public `Principal` implementations.

The `Subject` class keeps track of:

❑ All the principals associated with the subject, contained in a `Set` returned by `getPrincipals()`. To query, add or remove principals, you simply use this `Set`.

❑ Public and private **credentials** associated with the subject. Any security-related object can be a credential; possible examples are certificates (which would be a public credential), private keys (which would be private), and application-specific classes.

The `getPublicCredentials()` and `getPrivateCredentials()` methods each return the corresponding credential `Set`. Usually, though, you are not interested in a full list but only credentials of a particular type, for example `PrivateKey`. There are overloaded versions of the `get...Credentials` methods that take a `Class` argument:

```
Set privateKeys = subject.getPrivateCredentials(PrivateKey.class);
```

These methods return all the credentials that are assignable to the given type. For example, the code given above will return *all* private keys of any type since every private key will implement the `PrivateKey` interface.

A `Subject` can be marked read-only by calling `setReadOnly()`. Once it has been marked read-only, neither the principal nor the credential `Set`s can be modified anymore. The remaining `Subject` methods deal with authorization and will be discussed in the *Authorization* section below.

Logging In: LoginContext

Authenticating a `Subject` takes three distinct steps.

❑ Instantiating a `LoginContext`. The `LoginContext` uses the login `Configuration` to load the **login modules** that have been configured for the application. If the module(s) need to prompt the user for information, such as a username and password, the `LoginContext` constructor must be supplied with a **callback handler** for these prompts.

❑ Call the `login()` method on the `LoginContext`.

> ❑ Each loaded `LoginModule` will be called to attempt to authenticate the subject.

> ❑ If all required login modules were successful, each `LoginModule` will be called again to associate the relevant principals and credentials with the `Subject`. If not, each module is called to clear the information assembled during the previous step.

> The `LoginContext` throws a `LoginException` if authentication was unsuccessful.

❑ The application can now retrieve the authenticated `Subject` from the `LoginContext`.

The `LoginModule` interface is responsible for much of the flexibility of the authentication framework. Its implementations can use any method of authentication. Usernames and passwords, certificates, smart cards, hardware keys, fingerprints – all may be implemented as a `LoginModule`.

The login module concerns itself only with the actual authentication procedure. Yet, it may need to display instructions, prompt for information, or interact with the user in other ways. The problem is that the module may be used in a variety of environments: a text-based application, a graphical application, a proprietary server, and so forth. To isolate the module from the environment, JAAS uses the *callback handler* for all user interaction. It is up to the application to implement the callbacks, and every application can realize these in the way most appropriate to it.

> *This callback approach is quite an important pattern for a programmer to become familiar with. It is used in many situations where you want to plug in some custom, situation-specific behavior into a generic engine. For example, SAX XML parsers handle the intricacies of XML parsing yet call back the user program for the handling – also known as the rendering – of each element.*

An Authentication Example

Before we take a closer look at login contexts, modules, and callbacks, we will work through an example that illustrates the entire authentication procedure. The example will implement a login module that uses the Java keystore to authenticate its users, and a test application with a simple callback handler for text-based alias and password prompts. It is fairly long, but worth studying because it pulls together quite a bit of the material discussed up to now.

This example assumes that you are either using JDK 1.4, or have installed JAAS as an installed extension. In this case, this merely involves copying it into `${java.home}/lib/ext`. The following code is the "application", with the `main()` method and a simple callback handler. Save it as `Login.java`.

```
// Login.java

import javax.security.auth.*;
import javax.security.auth.login.*;
import javax.security.auth.callback.*;
import java.io.*;

public class Login implements CallbackHandler {
```

`Login` is a simple application using the JAAS framework to authenticate a user. It first instantiates a `LoginContext`, passing the application name (`Login`) and a callback handler. The `LoginContext` will at this point read the `Login.config` configuration file and find the login module for the `Login` application (the code for `Login.config` is shown below).

The `SampleLoginModule` handles this application's authentication needs and is required to log in, and it is this class that `Login.config` points to.

```java
public static void main(String args[]) throws Exception {
    LoginContext loginContext = new LoginContext("Login", new Login());
```

Next, the application starts the authentication procedure by calling `login()`. The `LoginManager` interacts with the configured login module(s) to do the actual authentication. The `login()` method will throw some flavor of `LoginException` if unsuccessful. In particular, a `FailedLoginException` is thrown if the credentials supplied by the user are wrong, so it is usually a good idea to catch this exception and retry the login procedure a few times before giving up by calling `login()` again.

Once authentication is successful, the application retrieves the `Subject` constructed by the `LoginContext` and dumps its contents, in this case a single `Principal`.

```java
    loginContext.login();
    System.out.println("Login successful.");
```

```java
    System.out.println(loginContext.getSubject());
```

When `logout()` is finally called, the `LoginContext` interacts with the modules to remove all principals and credentials that have been associated with the `Subject`.

```java
    loginContext.logout();
}
```

The following method implements the `CallbackHandler` interface. There are many types of possible callbacks defined in the `javax.security.auth.callback` package, but this implementation just supports a `NameCallback` and a `PasswordCallback`. Any other type of callback will throw an exception.

Callbacks are discussed in more detail below.

```java
public void handle(Callback[] callbacks)
        throws IOException, UnsupportedCallbackException {
    for (int i = 0; i < callbacks.length; i++) {
        if (callbacks[i] instanceof NameCallback) {

            // prompt the user for a username
            NameCallback nc = (NameCallback) callbacks[i];
            nc.setName(prompt(nc.getPrompt()));
        } else if (callbacks[i] instanceof PasswordCallback) {

            // prompt the user for sensitive information
            PasswordCallback pc = (PasswordCallback) callbacks[i];
            pc.setPassword(prompt(pc.getPrompt()).toCharArray());
        } else {
            throw new UnsupportedCallbackException(callbacks[i],
                                            "Unsupported Callback: "
                                            + callbacks[i]);
        }
    }
```

```
      }
    }
    private String prompt(String prompt) throws IOException {
      System.out.print(prompt);
      System.out.flush();
      BufferedReader input =
        new BufferedReader(new InputStreamReader(System.in));
      return input.readLine();
    }
  }
```

The next step is to configure a login module. The sample module that comes with JAAS, in `jaas1_0\doc\samples`, will do fine for a start; copy `SampleLoginModule.java` and `SamplePrincipal.java` into `C:\Beg_Java_Networking\Ch14\com\wrox\sample`. In JDK 1.4, these sample files are hiding in the `jdk1.4\docs\guide\security\jaas\samples` directory.

The **login module configuration file** is used to configure what login modules need to be used for a given application. Save the following as `C:\Beg_Java_Networking\Ch14\Login.config`:

```
Login {
    com.wrox.sample.SampleLoginModule required;
};

other {
    // no authentication configured for other apps
};
```

Compile the application then run it using the following command lines:

C:\Beg_Java_Networking\Ch14>**javac Login.java**

C:\Beg_Java_Networking\Ch14>**javac com\wrox\sample*.java**

C:\Beg_Java_Networking\Ch14>**java -Djava.security.auth.login.config=Login.config Login**

Enter testUser for the username, testPassword for the password, as these are hardwired in the `SampleLoginModule`. The application should respond with:

SampleModule username: **testUser**
SampleModule password: **testPassword**
Login successful.
Subject:
      Principal: SamplePrincipal: testUser

Any other username or password will throw a `FailedLoginException`.

Handling User Interaction

Whenever user interaction is necessary, the login modules will use the callback handler we pass to the `LoginContext` constructor. Objects from the `javax.security.auth.callback` package are used to represent the individual callbacks. In the example above, the `handle(Callback[])` method is called with two callbacks: the alias prompt, and the password prompt. These are the only ones implemented by the application. Generally, you implement a complete handler only if you cannot make any assumptions about authentication; otherwise, you just code the necessary.

The `CallbackHandler` interface consists of a single method, `handle(Callback[] callbacks)`. The array is a list of `Callback` objects to be processed in sequence. To process a callback, you need to determine what type (class) it is, cast it to its proper type, and write code to implement the interaction.

There are different implementations of `Callback`, which can be configured to perform the following:

- `ChoiceCallback`: The callback displays a list of choices, and allows the user to pick one (or more than one if `allowMultipleSelections()` returns `true`).

- `ConfirmationCallback`: The callback displays a confirmation dialog box with one or more options, such as Ok and Cancel, or Yes, No and Cancel. Predefined constants in the class, such as `OK_CANCEL_OPTION` and `YES_NO_CANCEL_OPTION`, correspond to the possible options.

- `LanguageCallback`: The callback retrieves the current `Locale` (language setting). This is usually not implemented as a user interaction, but retrieved from the environment.

- `NameCallback`: The callback prompts the user for a name.

- `PasswordCallback`: The callback prompts the user for a password or other sensitive information. If `isEchoOn()` returns `false`, user input should not be echoed to the screen.

- `TextInputCallback`: The callback prompts the user for generic text information.

- `TextOutputCallback`: The callback displays information to the user. The `getMessageType()` method returns a value determining the type of message box that should appear. The value returned is equal to one of the constants in this class, `ERROR`, `INFORMATION`, or `WARNING`.

- A login module may add its own `Callback` classes if desired; the callback handler would have to cater for these. It is also possible to add new options to the `ConfirmationCallback` class.

If you think the `ConfirmationCallback` looks a bit odd, it may be useful to compare it to the `javax.swing.JOptionPane` class.

The Login Module Configuration File

The default configuration file implementation reads its information from the file specified by the `java.security.auth.login.config` system property. In addition, it can read from a number of default locations, determined by `login.config.url.n` system properties in the `java.security` file.

For example, you could set:

```
login.config.url.1=file:${java.home}/lib/security/java.configuration
login.config.url.2=file:${user.home}/.java.configuration
```

The login module configuration file itself consists of one entry per application, and any number of login modules per entry:

```
Login {
    com.wrox.sample.SampleLoginModule required;
};

other {
    // no authentication configured for other apps
};
```

The `other` entry applies to applications that don't have their own entry in any of the configuration files. Login module lines have the format:

```
login.module.class flag options
```

The `flag` determines how the success or failure of the login module impacts the success of the authentication procedure as a whole:

❑ `Requisite`: The module *has* to succeed; if it fails, further modules from the list will not be processed but the failure to log in will be communicated to the application immediately.

❑ `Required`: The module *has* to succeed; if it fails, the remainder of the modules will still be processed but authentication will fail.

❑ `Sufficient`: The module is *not* required to succeed. If it is successful, control will return immediately to the application and the remainder of the list will be skipped. If it fails, the remainder of the list will be processed. This is useful to implement a number of alternative means of authentication: if the smart card module fails, continue with the login/password module.

❑ `Optional`: The module is *not* required to succeed. The remainder of the list will be processed regardless of whether the module succeeded or not. This flag can be used when the module does not affect the ability to log in but merely assigns additional privileges.

Overall, authentication is considered successful only if at least a single login module was successful and no `required` or `requisite` module failed.

The `options` in the login module line consist of one or more `key=value` pairs. The possible options and their meaning depend on the login module in question. For example, the `KeyStoreLoginModule` presented below requires a single option, the keystore file location.

Available Login Modules

Unfortunately, there are no login modules implemented as part of the JAAS core. If you downloaded and installed the JAAS module packages in addition to JAAS itself, Windows NT, Solaris and JNDI modules are available in the `com.sun.security.auth.module` package. For example, the following configuration will use NT authentication for the Login application:

```
Login {
    com.sun.security.auth.module.NTLoginModule required;
};
```

Since the Sun modules are not part of the core platform, their future availability and compatibility are not guaranteed. The Solaris login module is a case in point; in JDK 1.4 it has been deprecated in favor of a generic UNIX login module.

The following table shows the names and descriptions for the JAAS Login Modules in `com.sun.security.auth.module`:

Name	Description
JndiLoginModule	Authenticates using a directory service accessed through JNDI (Java Naming and Directory Interface), such as NIS or LDAP
NTLoginModule	Windows NT authentication
SolarisLoginModule	Login module for the Sun Solaris operating system *Deprecated and replaced by* `UnixLoginModule` *in JDK 1.4*
UnixLoginModule	Generic Unix authentication module *JDK 1.4*
Krb5LoginModule	Kerberos authentication *JDK 1.4*
KeyStoreLoginModule	Keystore authentication – a Java keystore implementation is used as a user database *JDK 1.4*

Please refer to Sun's documentation for more information on how to use these login modules.

Authorization

With the JAAS user authentication framework, the Java 2 security model can be enhanced by `Principal`-based permissions in addition to the normal `CodeSource`-based ones. In other words, permission can be granted to execute privileged operations based on *who executes* the code, rather than *who signed* it and *where* the code was loaded from. The JAAS optional package uses a separate policy for these permissions, but the JDK 1.4 integrates them completely with the main security policy file.

In order to get the most out of this discussion of JAAS Authorization, you should be familiar with the Java 2 security model covered in Chapter 7.

The JAAS Security Policy

The policy file used for the JAAS optional package configures the `Principal`-based security permissions. Much like the normal security policy, its location is specified by a system property, `java.security.auth.policy`. In addition, there are a number of default locations where policy information is read from, determined by the `auth.policy.url.n` system properties in the `java.security` file.

For instance:

```
auth.policy.url.1=file:${java.home}/lib/security/auth.policy
auth.policy.url.2=file:${user.home}/.security.auth.policy
```

The file consists of `Principal`-based grant entries that are exactly like those of the normal security policy file:

```
grant Principal sample.SamplePrincipal "testUser" {
    permission java.io.FilePermission "/private/-", "read, write";
    permission java.net.SocketPermission "*.wrox.com", "connect";
};
```

This entry gives any `Subject` that has the `SamplePrincipal` **testUser** associated with it, permission to read and write files in the `/private` directory hierarchy, and open network connections to the wrox.com domain. Multiple principals may be specified, separated by commas.

A `Subject` needs to be associated with *all* the listed principals in order to acquire the listed privileges. This can be used, for instance, to grant permission based on both the user and the group (such as granting permission to both `SolarisNumericGroupPrincipal` and `SolarisPrincipal`). `CodeBase`, `SignedBy` and `Principal` can be freely combined.

The special principal name `"*"` matches all principals of the given type. This can be used, for instance, to grant access to a privileged facility to all users who have been authenticated as a `SamplePrincipal`:

```
grant Principal sample.SamplePrincipal "*"{
```

For the JAAS add-on to JDK 1.3, every entry in the JAAS policy *must* specify a `Principal`; other entries must go in the main security policy. In JDK 1.4, on the other hand, the JAAS grants are part of the normal security policy file and this restriction no longer applies.

Performing a Privileged Operation

Naively, it might be expected that once the user had been authenticated, `Principal`-based permissions would "just work" in the same way that `CodeSource`-based permissions do. This is not the case. When the application starts, authentication has still to be done. The very first protection domain, that of the `main(String[])` method, does not have any principals associated with it. With the way the Java 2 security model works, this means that none of the `Principal`-based permissions are granted to the application, or any code called by the application.

This is actually quite similar to the situation we encountered when the `CheckPassword` class from Chapter 7 needed to access the password file, an operation denied to the application itself. The class used a `AccessController.doPrivileged(PrivilegedAction)` call to perform the action subject to the `CheckPassword` protection domain only, disregarding that of the application itself.

What we need in this case is a way to execute a `PrivilegedAction` in such a way that the `Principal`-based permissions the subject might have are added to the action's protection domain. The `Subject.doAs()` and `Subject.doAsPrivileged()` static methods do exactly that. We will explore them using an example.

Principal-Based Permissions Example

This example builds on the previous one, which authenticated a user and wrote the generated `Subject` to the screen. This version will attempt to write this information to a disk file under a security policy that allows only **testUser** to do this. The action needs to be encapsulated in a `PrivilegedExceptionAction`; this type of action has been discussed in Chapter 7.

```
// PrivilegedAction.java

import java.security.*;
import javax.security.auth.*;
import java.io.*;

public class PrivilegedAction implements PrivilegedExceptionAction {
  private final String toDump;
  private final String filename;

  public PrivilegedAction(String toDump, String filename) {
    this.toDump = toDump;
    this.filename = filename;
  }

  public Object run() throws IOException, SecurityException {
    PrintWriter out = new PrintWriter(new FileWriter(filename));
    try {
      out.println(toDump);
    }
    finally {
      try {
        out.close();
      } catch (Exception e) {

        // do nothing
      }
    }
    return null;
  }
}
```

The JAASAction.java application is identical to Login.java from the previous example, with a number of modifications and additions, highlighted in the listing below:

```
// JAASAction.java

import com.wrox.sample.*;
import java.security.*;
import javax.security.auth.*;
import javax.security.auth.login.*;
import javax.security.auth.callback.*;
import java.io.*;

public class JAASAction implements CallbackHandler {

  public static void main(String args[]) throws Exception {
    if (System.getSecurityManager() == null) {
      System.setSecurityManager(new SecurityManager());
    }

    LoginContext loginContext = new LoginContext("Login", new JAASAction());
    loginContext.login();
    System.out.println("Login successful.");

    // perform the privileged operation
    writeSubjectToFileAs(loginContext.getSubject(), "subject.txt");

    loginContext.logout();
  }
```

```
    private static void writeSubjectToFileAs(Subject subject, String filename)
            throws IOException, SecurityException {
      try {
        Subject.doAs(subject,
                     new PrivilegedAction(subject.toString(), filename));
      } catch (PrivilegedActionException e) {
        Exception actionException = e.getException();
        if (actionException instanceof IOException) {
          throw (IOException) actionException;
        } else {
          throw (RuntimeException) actionException;
        }
      }
    }
  }
  ...
```

The remainder of the class, from the `handle()` method onwards, does not need to change in any way. The effect of the changes above is that the `PrivilegedAction` is called with the identity of the authenticated `Subject`. Also, the application now ensures that it is running under a security manager. The login module, application, and sample action all need to be packaged in JARs so that permissions can be set up. The main JAR gets the following manifest file, `JAASAction.manifest`, to set up the classpath and the application entrance point:

```
Class-path: Privileged.jar SampleMod.jar
Main-class: JAASAction
```

Make sure that the end of the manifest ends in a carriage return, or the JAR will not load. A copy of this file is available in the code download for this chapter, anyway. Compile the classes, then run the following three commands from your working directory:

C:\Beg_Java_Networking\Ch14> **jar cf SampleMod.jar com\wrox\sample*.class**

C:\Beg_Java_Networking\Ch14> **jar cf Privileged.jar PrivilegedAction.class**

C:\Beg_Java_Networking\Ch14> **jar cfm JAASAction.jar JAASAction.manifest
JAASAction.class**

The login configuration file from the last example will take care of logging in, but the security policies still need setting up. Save the following in `JAASAction.security.policy`:

```
grant CodeBase "file:JAASAction.jar" {
    permission javax.security.auth.AuthPermission "createLoginContext";
    permission javax.security.auth.AuthPermission "doAs";
    permission java.io.FilePermission "subject.txt", "write";
};

grant CodeBase "file:SampleMod.jar" {
permission javax.security.auth.AuthPermission "modifyPrincipals";
};
```

This gives the `JAASAction` application access to the `doAs()` method and the privilege to write to the subject file. The `PrivilegedAction` gets permission to write to the file only if the user is **testUser**; so save the following in `JAASAction.auth.policy`:

```
grant CodeBase "file:Privileged.jar", Principal com.wrox.sample.SamplePrincipal
"testUser" {
   permission java.io.FilePermission "subject.txt", "write";
};
```

If you are using JDK 1.4, you don't need a separate authorization policy, but can simply concatenate the two listings into a single `JAASAction.security.policy` file. With all these preparations out of the way, the demo can now be run (finally!):

C:\Beg_Java_Networking\Ch14>**java -Djava.security.policy=JAASAction.security.po licy -Djava.security.auth.policy=JAASAction.auth.policy -Djava.security.auth.log in.config=Login.config -jar JAASAction.jar**
SampleModule username: **testUser**
SampleModule password: **testPassword**
Login successful.

As always, the command has been spread over multiple lines for legibility; you need to type all of this in one line or, even better, put it in a batch file or shell script. If you are using JDK 1.4, you should have a single policy file and don't need to enter the -Djava.security.auth.policy=Action.auth.policy argument.

Log in as **testUser**, password **testPassword**. The application writes a file called `subject.txt` to the current directory. Change the username in the `SamplePrincipal` grant entry and try again. Authentication should still succeed, but a security exception is thrown and no file is written because the **testUser** no longer has writing privileges. You can continue along these lines by commenting out permissions, modifying the code base entry, amongst other things – you can also try out the appropriate Sun authentication module for your platform instead of the sample module.

Login Module Security

The security policies used in the example above divide the code into three protection domains:

❑ The domain `SampleMod`, the login module, allows the module to modify the subject's principals. This security-sensitive operation is now denied to normal application code.

❑ The domain `JAASAction`, the main application, allows it to create a login context and to execute `doAs()` in order to run the privileged action. Write access to the `subject.txt` file is also granted.

❑ The domain `Privileged`, the privileged action, gives write access to `subject.txt`, *provided that* the authenticated user is **testUser**. For any other user, access to this file would be denied.

We have seen in Chapter 7 that under normal circumstances, `SampleMod` would not have permission to modify principals because it is ultimately called by `JAASAction`, which doesn't have this permission. However, whenever the `LoginContext` calls the keystore login module, it uses `doPrivileged()` which liberates `SampleMod` from `JAASAction`'s restrictions.

Limiting Permissions: doAs()

When the application calls our `PrivilegedAction` using the static `doAs()` method:

```
Subject.doAs(subject, new PrivilegedAction(subject.toString(), filename));
```

The method combines the normal permissions for the `Privileged` domain (none whatsoever) with the permissions assigned to the `Subject`. If the subject is a `SamplePrincipal` called **testUser**, permission is granted to write to the `subject.txt` file. Otherwise, an attempt to write to this file will throw a `SecurityException`. It is worth noting that, given the policy files used, the *only* security-sensitive operation the `PrivilegedAction` is allowed to perform is writing to this file; it cannot even read what it has written.

Enhancing Permissions: doAsPrivileged()

Glancing over the example's policy files, it may have struck you that the application (`JAASAction`) has permission to write to the `subject.txt` file, even though it does not need this. In a security-conscious environment, code gets exactly those permissions it needs to work and you would immediately want to remove it:

```
grant CodeBase "file:JAASAction.jar" {
    permission javax.security.auth.AuthPermission "createLoginContext";
    permission javax.security.auth.AuthPermission "doAs";
    permission java.io.FilePermission "subject.txt", "write";
};
```

This won't quite work; a `SecurityException` is thrown and no file is written. The reason is that in the action, there are two protection domains in the call chain, `Privileged` and `JAASAction`. Recall from Chapter 7 that the access controller allows an action only if *all* protection domains in its call chain have the required permission. By revoking the permission from `JAASAction`, the `Privileged` code can no longer write to the file as long as `JAASAction` is in the call chain.

We might think that granting the required permission through a `Principal`-based policy entry would work:

```
grant CodeBase "file:JAASAction.jar"
        Principal sample.SamplePrincipal "testUser" {
    permission java.io.FilePermission "subject.txt", "write";
};
```

In fact, it does not – try it! Even though the Java documentation appears to suggest otherwise, the `Principal`-based grants are not retrofitted into pre-existing protection domains. If there is a need to avoid giving the `FilePermission` to the application itself, we have to use `doAsPrivileged()` to insert a "barrier" in the call chain and isolate the action's protection domain from the application's.

```
private static void writeSubjectToFileAs(Subject subject, String filename)
throws IOException, SecurityException {
  try {
    Subject.doAsPrivileged(subject,
        new PrivilegedAction(subject.toString(), filename), null);
  }
    catch (PrivilegedActionException e) {
```

After changing the target of `javax.security.auth.AuthPermission` in the security policy to:

481

```
grant CodeBase "file:JAASAction.jar" {
    permission javax.security.auth.AuthPermission "createLoginContext";
    permission javax.security.auth.AuthPermission "doAsPrivileged";
    permission java.io.FilePermission "subject.txt", "write";
};
```

The `subject.txt` file should be written again and no exceptions thrown.

Authorization and Authentication Permissions

The JAAS optional package introduced a new permission, `AuthPermission`. The table below summarizes its most important targets; you can find a complete list in the javadocs for this class.

Target	Description
doAs	Allows calling the `Subject.doAs()` methods.
doAsPrivileged	Allows calling `Subject.doAsPrivileged()`. This is a security-sensitive method like `doPrivileged()`, as it allows code to ignore the protection domains in the call chain.
getSubject	Allows retrieving the subject related to the current `Thread`. This does not affect the ability to call `LoginContext.getSubject()`.
createLoginContext	Allows the instantiation of a `LoginContext` in order to authenticate users.

Protecting from Eavesdropping: JCE

Much of the introduction was spent discussing encryption, and a lot of the material discussed so far uses encryption, such as digital signatures, or deals with the generation and distribution of keys. Yet encryption itself has been curiously absent – from the core Java platform as well as our discussion. The problem with encryption is that some countries' laws regulate the dissemination and use of strong cryptography. Traditionally, United States export laws were a major stumbling block, but these have been relaxed and after some reworking Sun was able to release the **Java Cryptography Extension** (**JCE**) version 1.2.1 almost worldwide, complete with a `SunJCE` provider, and even to integrate it into version 1.4 of the JDK.

The JCE limitations are as follows:

❑ Because of export regulations, only approved, digitally signed providers will install in Sun's JCE 1.2.1 framework.

❑ **Jurisdiction policies** were introduced that impose key size restrictions on all applications. **Exemption mechanisms** allow applications to escape these restrictions.

a. The normal, global distributions for JCE 1.2.1 and above ship with policy files that allow unlimited cryptography to be used. Citizens of countries whose governments impose strength restrictions on cryptography should install appropriate jurisdiction policies.

> **b.** The JCE version that is part of JDK 1.4 ships with policies imposing crippling key size restrictions. To use truly strong cryptography, you need to download and install unlimited policy files from http://java.sun.com/j2se/1.4/index.html#jcepolicyfiles. These policy files should be copied to ${java.home}/lib/security.

The JCE builds upon the Java Cryptography Architecture (JCA) and encompasses a provider-based framework for symmetric and asymmetric encryption, secret key generation and conversion, message authentication codes, and key agreement. It is comprised of the following packages:

- ❑ `javax.crypto` contains the main JCE classes and interfaces
- ❑ `javax.crypto.interfaces` defines the interfaces for Diffie-Hellman keys
- ❑ `javax.crypto.spec` defines key specifications and algorithm parameter specifications

The four main areas to be discussed are encryption, key manipulation, key agreement, and **message authentication code** (**MACs**). The exemption mechanisms are irrelevant to most of us and will not be discussed.

The SunJCE Provider

The Sun Java Cryptography Extension comes with a default provider named `SunJCE`. It provides:

- ❑ An implementation of DES, Triple-DES and Blowfish symmetric encryption
- ❑ A password-based encryption (PBE) implementation using the MD5 hash algorithm with DES/CBC symmetric encryption
- ❑ An implementation of the HMAC-MD5 and HMAC-SHA1 message authentication code (MAC) algorithms
- ❑ Key generators for DES, Triple-DES, Blowfish, HMAC-MD5 and HMAC-SHA1
- ❑ Key factories for DES, Triple-DES, and PBE (Password-Based Encryption) keys
- ❑ An implementation of the Diffie-Hellman key agreement protocol, with implementations of a DH key pair generator, key factory, and algorithm parameter generator
- ❑ Algorithm parameter managers for DES, Triple-DES, Blowfish, PBE, and Diffie-Hellman
- ❑ `PCKS#5` padding
- ❑ A keystore implementation for the proprietary JCEKS keystore; this is a drop-in replacement for the normal JKS keystore. It provides better security using strong cryptography.

Most of the above, except for the Diffie-Hellman and algorithm parameter managers, will be discussed in the remainder of this section.

Encrypting and Decrypting Data

The core of JCE is the `Cipher` class representing a cryptographic algorithm. Implementations of `Cipher` can encrypt data, decrypt data, and also wrap and unwrap keys. Of course there are accompanying classes to generate and convert secret keys, similar to the ones manipulating key pairs we have already seen in the JCA. Further supporting classes add features such as stream-based encryption and decryption.

When you need to send confidential information, for example credit card details, over an untrusted network such as the Internet, you will be using these classes. We will start with a practical example sending encrypted traffic over a network connection.

An Encrypted Network Transmission Example

We are going to send an encrypted message over the network using symmetric encryption. This means that both sender and receiver need to have the same secret key at their disposal, stored in a file. This example assumes that both the JCE framework and the SunJCE provider have been installed as system extensions; see the installation instructions that come with JCE. If not, ensure that the JCE libraries are on the classpath and add the following code snippet at the start of all the main() methods:

```java
Security.addProvider(new com.sun.crypto.provider.SunJCE());
```

The first ingredient we need is a small application to generate the secret key and write it to a file called key. The secret key file is then copied to both the sending and the receiving end – using a secure communication channel, of course, perhaps personal delivery on a floppy disk. The source is saved to the CryptKey.java file.

```java
// CryptKey.java

import java.io.*;
import javax.crypto.*;
import javax.crypto.spec.SecretKeySpec;
import java.security.spec.KeySpec;

public class CryptKey {

  public static final String ALGORITHM = "DESede";

  public static final String KEY_FILENAME = "key";

  public static void main(String[] args) throws Exception {
    int keysize = Integer.parseInt(args[0]);

    // Create a secret key
    System.out.println("Generating key, size " + keysize + "...");
```

The example generates a new secret key of the given size. It then writes it to disk in its primary encoding. Given the discussion of key specifications and factories in the JCA section, it would be reasonable to expect the readSecretKey() method to use a key specification to read the key from disk, and a factory to convert that to an opaque representation:

```java
    KeyGenerator kg = KeyGenerator.getInstance(ALGORITHM);
    kg.init(keysize);
    SecretKey key = kg.generateKey();

    // Write the key out to a disk file
    System.out.println("Writing to disk...");
    OutputStream os = new FileOutputStream(KEY_FILENAME);
    try {
      os.write(key.getEncoded());
    }
    finally {
      try {
```

```
        os.close();
      } catch (Exception e) {

        // do nothing
      }
    }
  }
```

Because both sender and receiver will need to read the key from disk, it makes sense to put this code in a shared place; and what class would be more fitting than the one that wrote the key to disk in the first place? That is why CryptKey implements a readSecretKey() method as well:

```
public static SecretKey readSecretKey() throws Exception {

  // Read the secret key
  System.out.println("Reading key...");
  byte[] keyBuffer = new byte[(int) new File("key").length()];
  InputStream is = new FileInputStream("key");
  try {
    is.read(keyBuffer);
  }
  finally {
    try {
      is.close();
    } catch (Exception e) {

      // do nothing
    }
  }

  // Use a generic key spec to represent the spec as an opaque key
  System.out.println("Creating opaque key...");
  return new SecretKeySpec(keyBuffer, ALGORITHM);
  }
}
```

Compile the class and run it:

C:\Beg_Java_Networking\Ch14> **java CryptKey 112**

The output should be:

Generating key, size 112...
Writing to disk...

This will generate a 112-bit triple-DES (DESede) secret key. The algorithm is specified by the ALGORITHM constant defined in this class. The example should work with all symmetric algorithms supported by JCE. Be warned that it can take a little while for the key to be generated; this is partly due to the time it takes for the secure random number generator to initialize itself.

In the JCA section, we discussed the two representations of cryptographic keys: *opaque* and *transparent*. Key factories are used to convert between them; key generators are used to create new keys. The basic JCA framework only provides engine classes and generators for (asymmetric) key pairs, the JCE adds equivalent KeyGenerator, SecretKeyFactory and supporting classes for symmetric keys that work in exactly the same way. They are part of the javax.crypto package.

485

The `Encrypt.java` encryption application prompts the user for the plaintext message, reads the shared secret key, encrypts the message and transmits it over the network to the decryption application.

```java
// Encrypt.java

import java.io.*;
import java.net.*;
import java.security.spec.KeySpec;
import javax.crypto.*;

public class Encrypt {

  public static void main(String args[]) throws Exception {
    String plaintext = prompt("Plaintext: ");

    // Read the shared secret key
    SecretKey key = CryptKey.readSecretKey();

    // Encrypt the message with the secret key
    System.out.println("Encrypting message...");
    Cipher cipher = Cipher.getInstance(CryptKey.ALGORITHM);
    cipher.init(Cipher.ENCRYPT_MODE, key);
    byte[] ciphertext = cipher.doFinal(plaintext.getBytes());

    // Send the ciphertext over the network
    Socket s = new Socket(Decrypt.DECRYPTION_HOST, Decrypt.DECRYPTION_PORT);
    try {
      DataOutputStream os = new DataOutputStream(s.getOutputStream());
      os.writeInt(ciphertext.length);
      os.write(ciphertext);
      os.close();
    }
    finally {
      try {
        s.close();
      } catch (Exception e) {

        // do nothing
      }
    }
  }

  public static String prompt(String prompt) throws IOException {
    System.out.print(prompt);
    System.out.flush();
    BufferedReader input =
      new BufferedReader(new InputStreamReader(System.in));
    String response = input.readLine();
    System.out.println();
    return response;
  }
}
```

Finally, here is the decryption application. It reads the secret key file, creates a server socket and waits for the encryption application to send the ciphertext. The ciphertext is decrypted and displayed. Save this as `Decrypt.java`.

```
// Decrypt.java

import java.io.*;
import java.net.*;
import java.security.spec.KeySpec;
import javax.crypto.*;

public class Decrypt {

  public static final String DECRYPTION_HOST = "localhost";

  public static final int DECRYPTION_PORT = 1220;

  public static void main(String args[]) throws Exception {

    // Read the shared secret key
    SecretKey key = CryptKey.readSecretKey();
    byte[] ciphertext = null;

    // Receive ciphertext from the network
    System.out.println("Listening for ciphertext...");
    ServerSocket ss = new ServerSocket(DECRYPTION_PORT);
    try {
      Socket s = ss.accept();
      try {
        DataInputStream is = new DataInputStream(s.getInputStream());
        ciphertext = new byte[is.readInt()];
        is.read(ciphertext);
      } finally {
        try {
          s.close();
        } catch (Exception e) {

          // do nothing
        }
      }
    }
    finally {
      try {
        ss.close();
      } catch (Exception e) {

        // do nothing
      }
    }

    // Decrypt the received ciphertext using the secret key
    System.out.println("Decrypting message...");
    Cipher cipher = Cipher.getInstance(CryptKey.ALGORITHM);
    cipher.init(Cipher.DECRYPT_MODE, key);
    System.out.print(new String(cipher.update(ciphertext)));
    System.out.println(new String(cipher.doFinal()));
  }
}
```

The DECRYPTION_HOST constant is used by the encryption application to determine where to send the ciphertext to. If you are running the applications on a single machine, the given values should be just fine. Otherwise, please change the value of DECRYPTION_HOST to match the actual location.

Compile all classes, open two command prompts and run the decryption application in the first one:

```
C:\Beg_Java_Networking\Ch14>java Decrypt
Reading key...
Creating opaque key...
Listening for ciphertext...
```

And the encryption application in the second:

```
C:\Beg_Java_Networking\Ch14>java Encrypt
Plaintext: Hello World!

Reading key...
Creating opaque key...
Encrypting message...
```

If you go back now to the window you are running `Decrypt` in, you should see the following output:

```
Decrypting message...
Hello World!
```

If you are running the applications on different machines, you will need to ensure the key file generated by `CryptKey` is present on both. Enter a message when prompted. The message will be Triple-DES encrypted and sent over the network. After a short pause while `Decrypt` decrypts the message, it should be printed in the decryption window.

In the next few sections, we will explore in depth how this example works and use it to illustrate the JCE API.

Manipulating Secret Keys

The `SecretKeySpec` class is both a provider-independent secret key specification *and* an opaque key class. It implements `KeySpec` as well as `SecretKey`. With this class, there is no need to rely on provider-dependent key specification classes; also, it can be used directly in cryptographic objects that only work with opaque keys.

`SecretKeySpec` can also be useful for algorithms for which no key factory or key specification class has been provided, for example, Blowfish. There is no `BlowfishKeySpec` class or Blowfish key factory to retrieve the secret key from the encoded key material. We have to use the `SecretKeySpec` instead:

```
SecretKey key = new SecretKeySpec(encodedKeySpec, "Blowfish");
Cipher cipher = Cipher.getInstance("Blowfish");
cipher.init(Cipher.DECRYPT_MODE, key);
byte[] plaintext = cipher.doFinal(ciphertext);
```

Although `SecretKeySpec` does not provide the flexibility, for example with hardware-based keys, that normal key specifications and opaque keys do, it can be more intuitive and straightforward to work with.

The following table names and describes some of the more common secret key generation algorithms:

Algorithm	Description
DES	Digital Encryption Standard (FIPS PUB 46-2). The key size must be 56 bits.
DESede	Triple-DES – performs three passes of DES, providing twice the cryptographic strength of normal DES. The SunJCE default key size is 112 bits; the only other allowed size is 168.
The SunJCE provider implements generators but no factories for the following three types:	
Blowfish	Block cipher conceived by Bruce Schneier as a stronger alternative for DES. The SunJCE default key size is 56 bytes, but the size can be any multiple of 8 from 32 to 448 bytes inclusive.
HMAC-MD5	Hash MAC using the MD5 message digest algorithm (RFC 2104). The SunJCE default key size is 64 bytes.
HMAC-MD1	Hash MAC using the SHA1 message digest algorithm (RFC 2104). The default key size is 64 bytes.

Cipher

The Cipher is the core of the JCE framework. It is the engine providing encryption services. A cipher is obtained by calling getInstance(), as usual, with the name of the desired transformation and an optional provider. The **transformation** is characterized by three parameters:

❑ The **algorithm,** such as DESede (Triple-DES) in the example.

❑ The **feedback mode** – if the cipher is a **block cipher**, encoding fixed-size blocks worth of data at a time, we can simply chop up the data in blocks of that size and encode them one by one. This is known as **Electronic Code Book (ECB)** mode. The problem with ECB is that some of the structure of the plaintext could show up in the blocks, and a third party can interchange or substitute blocks at will. **Feedback modes** such as CBC and CFB address this by combining a block with the previous one in various ways.

❑ The **padding scheme,** which is again relevant only for block ciphers: what to do if the plaintext does not fit into an integral number of blocks? It needs to be padded in some way. The padding scheme tells how. The JCE supports either a scheme called PCKS5Padding or, for algorithms or feedback modes that don't need it, NoPadding.

The transformation name passed into the getInstance() method can specify all three, separated by a slash: *algorithm/mode/padding*. For example, in order to use Triple-DES in Cipher Feedback (CFB) mode without padding, simply write:

```
Cipher cipher = Cipher.getInstance("DESede/CFB/NoPadding");
```

Mode and padding are generally optional, and unless some external system expects a specific format it is safe to stick with the defaults. For this reason, we will not discuss them in any more detail.

Before the cipher can be used, we'll first need to initialize it. There are eight different init() methods available; all take an integer determining the mode, a key specification in the form of a Key or a Certificate, and optionally algorithm parameters and/or a random number generator.

We'll take a closer look at the encryption and decryption modes.

Encrypting Data

The Encrypt example uses a Cipher to encrypt the plaintext. Instantiating and using one takes up to five distinct steps:

1. Instantiate the cipher using Cipher.getInstance(String algorithm).

```
Cipher cipher = Cipher.getInstance(CryptKey.ALGORITHM);
```

2. Initialize the new cipher with the encryption key. This usually means calling init(Cipher.ENCRYPT_MODE, key) with a secret or private key. In Encrypt:

```
cipher.init(Cipher.ENCRYPT_MODE, key);
```

3. Feedback modes (such as any mode other than ECB) combine each block of data with the previous one, as discussed above. The very first block is combined with a randomly generated block called the **initialization vector (IV)**. The same IV needs to be used in decryption, so the generated IV is retrieved by calling getIV() and transmitted together with the ciphertext:

```
byte[] iv = cipher.getIV();
```

The example used the default ECB mode, which does not use an initialization vector, so this step could be skipped.

4. Call the update() methods one or more times to feed in blocks of plaintext. This is an overloaded method with three different sets of parameters; all of them essentially take a plaintext byte[] array and return a ciphertext array. This step can be skipped if one of the overloaded doFinal() versions is used, as in Encrypt.

5. Finally, call doFinal() which returns the final ciphertext byte[] array. There are overloaded versions that take a last plaintext block; they can be used in lieu of calling update() and doFinal() separately. This is what Encrypt does:

```
byte[] ciphertext = cipher.doFinal(plaintext.getBytes());
```

The actual encryption is done in one single call to doFinal().

After doFinal(), the cipher is reset to the state it was in just after the call to init, ready for another encryption operation. There are further methods to retrieve such things as the cipher block size, but they are less frequently used.

Decrypting Data

Decryption is analogous to encryption, except that the cipher is initialized in DECRYPT_MODE:

1. Instantiate the cipher using Cipher.getInstance(String algorithm).

```
Cipher cipher = Cipher.getInstance(CryptKey.ALGORITHM);
```

2. Initialize the new cipher with the encryption key. This usually means calling init(Cipher.DECRYPT_MODE, key) with a secret or private key, as in Decrypt:

```
cipher.init(Cipher.DECRYPT_MODE, key);
```

If the data was encrypted using a feedback mode other than ECB, we will need to pass the initialization vector used during encryption:

```
AlgorithmParameterSpec ivSpec = new IvParameterSpec(iv);
cipher.init(Cipher.DECRYPT_MODE, key, ivSpec);
```

3. Call the update() methods zero or more times with the ciphertext data blocks.

```
System.out.print(new String(cipher.update(ciphertext)));
```

4. Finally, call doFinal() or one of its overloaded variants.

```
System.out.println(new String(cipher.doFinal()));
```

After the last step, the cipher is reset to its initial state and ready to decrypt the next document.

Password-Based Encryption

In the introduction for this chapter, we saw that password-based encryption can be implemented by combining the password with randomly generated salt, then using the result as the secret key for a symmetric algorithm. The PBEWithMD5AndDES algorithm implements password-based encryption based on DES in Cipher Block Chaining mode.

```
// Encapsulate the password in a secret key using a secret key generator
KeySpec pbeKeySpec = new PBEKeySpec(password);
SecretKeyFactory skf = SecretKeyFactory.getInstance("PBEWithMD5AndDES");
SecretKey secretKey = skf.generateSecret(pbeKeySpec);

// Create the cipher
Cipher cipher = Cipher.getInstance("PBEWithMD5AndDES");
cipher.init(Cipher.ENCRYPT_MODE, secretKey);

// Retrieve salt and iteration count, and encode them for transfer
byte[] encodedSaltAndCount = cipher.getParameters().getEncoded();

// Encrypt the plaintext byte array
byte[] ciphertext = cipher.doFinal(plaintext);
```

To decrypt, the salt and iteration count parameters used by the algorithm are retrieved together with the ciphertext:

```
// Encapsulate the password in a secret key using a secret key generator
PBEKeySpec pbeKeySpec = new PBEKeySpec(password);
SecretKeyFactory skf = SecretKeyFactory.getInstance("PBEWithMD5AndDES");
SecretKey secretKey = skf.generateSecret(pbeKeySpec);

// Retrieve the algorithm parameters used during encryption
AlgorithmParameters saltAndCount =
    AlgorithmParameters.getInstance("PBEWithMD5AndDES");
params.init(encodedSaltAndCount);

// Create the cipher supplying the algorithm parameters
Cipher cipher = Cipher.getInstance("PBEWithMD5AndDES");
cipher.init(Cipher.DECRYPT_MODE, secretKey, saltAndCount);

// decrypt the plaintext byte array
byte[] plaintext = cipher.doFinal(ciphertext);
```

Note that there is no real need for us to be aware that this algorithm uses salt and count parameters. All the above code is doing is communicating an abstract `AlgorithmParameters` object together with the ciphertext.

Secure Streams

While discussing the `MessageDigest` facilities available in the basic Java Cryptography Architecture, we found that it is often more convenient to plug the digest into an existing stream. The same is true for encryption and decryption: we often have an `InputStream` or `OutputStream`, perhaps retrieved from a `Socket`, and would like to plug our cryptographic transformation in that stream with a minimum of fuss.

The `CipherInputStream` and `CipherOutputStream` classes provide exactly that. They are normal stream filter objects that take a `Cipher` in the constructor:

```
// Create the cipher to be used
Cipher cipher = Cipher.getInstance("DESede");
cipher.init(Cipher.ENCRYPT_MODE, secretKey);

// Construct the encrypting output stream using the cipher
OutputStream out = new CipherOutputStream(socket.getOutputStream(),
                                          cipher));
```

The above output stream could be decrypted using the following input stream at the receiving end:

```
// Create the cipher to be used
Cipher cipher = Cipher.getInstance("DESede");
cipher.init(Cipher.DECRYPT_MODE, secretKey);

// Construct the decrypting input stream using the cipher
InputStream in = new CipherInputStream(socket.getInputStream(), cipher));
```

Other than digest streams, there are no methods to retrieve the cipher or to switch encryption on and off. All data filtered through the cipher stream is encrypted (or decrypted).

One caveat when using `CipherOutputStream` with block ciphers: the `flush()` method only flushes bytes that have already been processed. Any information that has not yet been processed by the cipher because it does not make up a full block cannot be flushed. Only the `close()` method, which calls `doFinal()` on the cipher, is guaranteed to process all buffers and write them to the underlying stream.

The Null Cipher

There are applications where encryption may need to be disabled. Instead of duplicating a lot of code or inserting `if (encrypting) ... else` constructs that choose between the two modes, we can simply use a `NullCipher`. The `NullCipher` performs no encryption at all – the ciphertext is identical to the plaintext.

> *The `NullCipher` is an example of the `Null` Object design pattern. It provides an alternative to using `null` to indicate the absence of an object performing an operation, which would necessitate checking for `null` everywhere. Instead of this, the `Null` Object pattern uses a reference to an object that doesn't do anything.*

Authenticating Messages

In the JCA section, we have examined digital signatures, message digests encrypted using public-key encryption. The same can be done using secret-key encryption; this is called a **message authentication code (MAC)**.

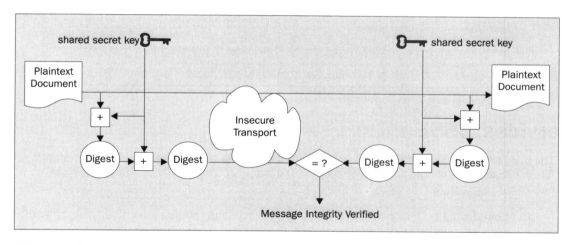

If both sender and receiver share a secret key, a digest that cannot be forged can be sent with the text. The most commonly used algorithm calculates a digest for the combination of plaintext document and secret key, then combines the digest with secret key again and calculates a digest of the combination. This second digest, the **Hash MAC (HMAC)**, is sent with the message. The recipient can use its own copy of the key and the received plaintext to repeat the procedure. If the result matches the MAC that was sent with the message, both its integrity and its authenticity have been verified. Without the secret key, it is impossible for a third party to have calculated the MAC of a new or modified text.

Calculating a MAC

The `Mac` class is the message authentication code engine. Its use is virtually a carbon copy of that of the `MessageDigest` class, with the addition of an initialization step to set the secret key.

```
byte[] message = ... // get message
Mac mac = Mac.getInstance("HmacMD5");
mac.init(secretKey);
mac.update(message);
byte[] messageAuthCode = mac.doFinal();
```

The basic steps to calculate a MAC are:

❑ Instantiate a new `Mac` using the `getInstance()` method with the desired algorithm and, optionally, the provider.

❑ Initialize the new `Mac` with the secret key by calling `init(Key)`. There is a second version that takes an algorithm parameter specification.

❑ Call the `update()` methods zero or more times; they all essentially take `byte` primitives.

❑ Finally, call `doFinal()` to calculate the MAC, which will be returned in a `byte[]` array. This method is overloaded with versions that take a `byte[]` to do a final update with.

The length of the MAC returned by `doFinal()` depends on the algorithm. To find out the length, call `getMacLength()`. As with `MessageDigest`, use `clone()` to calculate an interim value for the MAC.

The following table contains some common Message Authentication Code algorithm names and their descriptions:

Algorithm	Description
HmacMD5	Hash MAC using the MD5 message digest algorithm (RFC 2104)
HmacSHA1	Hash MAC using the SHA1 message digest algorithm (RFC 2104)

Services: JSSE

The need for security in web services is easily illustrated by the ubiquitous e-commerce example. Assume that we are conducting a credit card transaction over the web. To do this safely, there are a number of requirements that should be met.

❑ **Confidentiality**: Our credit card details must remain fully confidential. If an attacker has installed a packet sniffer on the network, the details should remain secure.

❑ **Integrity**: It should be impossible to tamper with the transaction without detection. Otherwise, it might be easy, for example, for an attacker to have the items delivered to a different address.

❑ **Authentication**: We must be confident that the server we are sending our order to be bona fide, and not a fake storefront set up by a malicious third party.

These are actually three out of the four purposes of encryption mentioned in the introduction to this chapter. The **Secure Socket Layer** (**SSL**) standard and its successor **Transport Layer Security** (**TLS**) are TCP socket-level protocols that use cryptography to meet all three requirements. The fourth objective of cryptography, non-repudiation, is not supported. If non-repudiation is required, we will have to digitally sign our messages using a mechanism outside SSL.

The applications of SSL are by no means restricted to e-commerce. Usually, companies and individuals want their data to remain confidential. Companies sometimes expose web services that should not be accessible by just about anyone. Both can be achieved using the JCE framework, but in many cases, secure sockets provide a more convenient alternative.

The **Java Secure Socket Extension** (**JSSE**) is a pure-Java framework supporting SSL versions 2.0 and 3.0 and TLS version 1.0. It is comprised of the following packages:

- ❑ `javax.net` contains abstract factories for sockets and server sockets

- ❑ `javax.net.ssl` contains the main SSL classes, including abstract socket and socket factory classes for SSL sockets

- ❑ `javax.security.cert` provides classes and interfaces for generic and X.509 certificate support. They are not to be confused with the virtually identical classes in `java.security.cert` that are part of JCA. X.509 is the only type of certificate currently supported in JSSE.

JSSE 1.0.2 can be downloaded from http://java.sun.com/products/jsse/ for versions 1.2 and 1.3 of the JDK. In JDK 1.4, JSSE 1.1 is an integral part of the JDK and does not need to be downloaded separately. Download this now, as we will be using it in coming examples.

In addition, there are a number of support and implementation classes in `com.sun.net.ssl`. Formally, they are not part of JSSE and their stability across versions is not guaranteed. Preferably, they should not be used directly, but this can sometimes be difficult to avoid. Many of these classes have been moved into the core framework in version 1.4 of the JDK.

The SunJSSE Provider

The Sun Java Secure Socket Extension ships with a default provider named SunJSSE. It provides:

- ❑ Reference implementations of SSL 3.0 and TLS 1.0 using RSA, RC4, DES, and Triple-DES ciphers, and Diffie-Hellman key agreement

- ❑ A protocol handler for HTTP over SSL, the HTTPS protocol

- ❑ A PKCS#12-compatible key store implementation

The cryptographic export restrictions that blighted early versions of JCE also affected JSSE. From version 1.0.2 onwards, they have largely been lifted; the only restriction on the global version of JSSE is that the `SocketFactory` and `ServerSocketFactory` implementations cannot be changed.

Accessing HTTPS URLs

One of the nice things about JSSE is that in its most basic form, using it takes almost no effort; you don't have to know how it works any more than you need to know how exactly a socket works. It has been mentioned that SSL is often used with HTTP; this is called **HTTPS (secure HTTP)**. HTTPS URLs look like https://*servername.domain*[:*sslport*]. The default port number for HTTPS is 443, but you can use any other port.

It takes just one statement to add HTTP support to any application that uses the `java.net.URL` class for its communication:

```
System.setProperty("java.protocol.handler.pkgs",
                    "com.sun.net.ssl.internal.www.protocol");
```

This system property tells the URL class where to look for **protocol handlers**; JSSE implements a HTTPS protocol handler in the `https` subpackage of the package given above. Any URL that starts with https:// will now be processed using the JSSE handler. The `java.protocol.handler.pkgs` property can also be set on the Java command line using the `-D` option.

A Secure URL Example

To explore HTTPS support using the URL class, we will look at a little application to download the contents of a possibly secure URL and display them on the screen. In this and subsequent examples, if you are running these examples with less than version 1.4 of the JDK, it is assumed that you have configured JSSE as an installed system extension; see the instructions that come with JSSE. Install the JAR files into your `JAVA_HOME\lib\ext` directory, and edit your `JAVA_HOME\lib\security` file with the following entry:

```
security.provider.3=com.sun.crypto.provider.SunJCE
security.provider.4=com.sun.net.ssl.internal.ssl.Provider
```

Should you prefer to run JSSE from the command-line, ensure that the JSSE libraries are on the `CLASSPATH` and add the following line of code to the `main()` function:

```
Security.addProvider(new com.sun.net.ssl.internal.ssl.Provider());
```

Similar modifications will have to be made to all other example code in this section. Since JSSE has been fully integrated in J2SE v1.4, you don't need to set either the system property or the provider to enjoy SSL support if you are using this version.

If you are confused, consult the earlier section concerning the installation of providers.

The listing below is of a small application called `URLGrab.java`. It grabs the contents of a URL and dumps it, together with some information such as the content type and the properties of the HTTPS connection, if any.

```
// URLGrab.java

import java.io.*;
import java.net.*;
import javax.security.cert.Certificate;
import com.sun.net.ssl.HttpsURLConnection;     // J2SDK 1.3

// import java.net.ssl.HttpsURLConnection;     // J2SDK 1.4

public class URLGrab {

  private static final String PROTOCOL_HANDLERS =
    "com.sun.net.ssl.internal.www.protocol";

  public static void main(String args[]) throws Exception {
    System.setProperty("java.protocol.handler.pkgs", PROTOCOL_HANDLERS);

    if (args.length != 2) {
```

```
        System.out.println("Please give a URL and a filename.");
      } else {
        URLConnection urlConn = new URL(args[0]).openConnection();
        urlConn.connect();                    // connect to the server
        displayProperties(urlConn);           // display connection properties
        writeContents(urlConn, args[1]);      // write URL contents to file
      }
  }

  private static void writeContents(URLConnection urlConn,
                                    String filename) throws IOException {
    InputStream in = urlConn.getInputStream();
    OutputStream out = new FileOutputStream(filename);
    try {
      byte[] buffer = new byte[512];
      int bytesRead;
      while ((bytesRead = in.read(buffer)) > 0) {
        out.write(buffer, 0, bytesRead);
      }
    }
    finally {
      try {
        out.close();
      } catch (Exception e) { /* do nothing */
      }
      try {
        in.close();
      } catch (Exception e) { /* do nothing */
      }
    }
  }

  private static void displayProperties(URLConnection urlConn) {
    System.out.println("Content Length: " + urlConn.getContentLength());
    System.out.println("Content Type: " + urlConn.getContentType());
    System.out.println("Content Encoding: " + urlConn.getContentEncoding());
    if (urlConn instanceof HttpsURLConnection) {
      displaySecureProperties((HttpsURLConnection) urlConn);
    }
  }

  private static void displaySecureProperties(HttpsURLConnection urlConn) {
    System.out.println("Cipher Suite: " + urlConn.getCipherSuite());
    Certificate[] chain = urlConn.getServerCertificateChain();
    for (int i = 0; chain != null && i < chain.length; i++) {
      System.out.println("Certificate #" + (i + 1) + ":\n" + chain[i]);
    }
  }
}
```

Most of the listing is not different from what you'd normally expect: instantiate a URL object, get a connection and use it to get the contents of a URL.

Compiling this application and running the URLGrab application using:

C:\Beg_Java_Networking\Ch14> **java URLGrab https://www.verisign.com verisign.html I more** will then retrieve the VeriSign homepage via the secure server, connecting to the default port for HTTPS, 443, and write out the contents to verisign.html. It will also print information about the connection on the screen. The bulk of the information consists of the server certificates sent by the secure VeriSign server, starting with:

```
Content Length: -1
Content Type: text/html
Content Encoding: null
Cipher Suite: SSL_RSA_WITH_RC4_128_MD5
Certificate #1:
[
[
  Version: V1
  Subject: CN=www.verisign.com, OU=Production, O="VeriSign, Inc.", L=Mountain Vi
ew, ST=California, C=US
  Signature Algorithm: MD5withRSA, OID = 1.2.840.113549.1.1.4
...
```

If you have to connect to a HTTP proxy in order to get through the firewall, you need to find out where the proxy is located and start the application using two additional options:

C:\Beg_Java_Networking\Ch14> **java –Dhttps.proxyHost=*host* –Dhttps.proxyPort=*port* URLGrab https://www.verisign.com verisign.html | more**

Virtually all SSL-specific code in URLGrab concerns the display of connection properties. If the connection is a secure one, URL.openConnection() returns a HttpsURLConnection, a subclass of the normal URLConnection. HttpsURLConnection gives access to some SSL-specific connection properties, such as the cipher suite and the server certificate chain.

```
System.out.println("Cipher Suite: " + urlConn.getCipherSuite());
Certificate[] chain = urlConn.getServerCertificateChain();
```

Beware of the different locations of this class in JSSE (com.sun.net.ssl) and J2SE version 1.4 (java.net.ssl).

How SSL Works

The Secure Socket Layer sits between the application layer (such as HTTP or RMI) and the transport layer (usually TCP). It provides encryption, authentication, and session management services to the application layer.

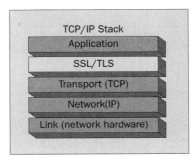

The figure above shows its position in the TCP/IP four-layer model. SSL is most often associated with HTTP (the ubiquitous HTTPS protocol) but by no means limited to this. Virtually all common Internet protocols – Telnet, SMTP (mail transport), NNTP (news), FTP (file transfers), LDAP (Lightweight Directory Access Protocol), etc. – can be used with secure sockets. SSL is an Internet standard first developed by Netscape in 1994. The Internet Engineering Task Force (IETF) has more recently taken over SSL development and renamed it **Transport Layer Security** (**TLS**). TLS version 1.0 is a minor development of SSL 3.0 (the protocol in fact identifies itself as SSL 3.1 during the negotiation phase).

The output from the URLGrab application above tells us a lot about the way the secure connection works. The **cipher suite** SSL_RSA_WITH_RC4_128_MD5 gives us the cryptographic ciphers used to establish and maintain the connection:

❑ The connection is of the Secure Socket Layer (SSL) type.

❑ It uses **data encryption** using the RC4 secret-key cipher. Encryption is done with a randomly generated session key, which is exchanged using RSA public-key encryption. This protects the confidentiality of the data.

❑ It ensures **data integrity** using MD5 message digests.

The remote server has also sent us its **certificate chain** to authenticate itself.

❑ The server's hostname is checked against the certificate, making it very difficult for an attacker to use a trusted certificate on a different web server even if he could have acquired the corresponding private key. The server is thereby authenticated as belonging to VeriSign.

By default, JSSE uses the ${java.home}/lib/security/cacerts keystore file to check the server certificate. The default cacerts ships with a VeriSign certificate entry, which is why the connection was successfully established.

SSL Handshaking

Setting up secure communication between client and server takes quite a bit of setting up. The encryption and authentication parts of SSL are optional, and a number of ciphers can be used for each. This cipher suite needs to be negotiated, and then key information and (optionally) digital certificates exchanged. **SSL handshaking** takes care of all this when the SSL connection is first established.

1. The client sends a hello message to the server. This incorporates information about the highest SSL version the client supports and a list of supported cipher suites.

2. The server sends its response back to the client:

a. A hello message, incorporating information about the highest version of SSL and the best cipher suite supported by both client and server.

b. Optionally, a certificate chain if the server wishes to authenticate itself to the client.

c. Optionally, a certificate request if the server wants to authenticate the client. This is more often used in special applications and intranet environments than in the Internet world, but is likely to become more important as e-business develops.

d. The **server public key** is sent unless a certificate with a suitable public key has already been transmitted.

499

e. A hello finished message to indicate that the response is finished.

3. The client then checks the certificate chain sent by the server. If the client is a web browser and it cannot trace the chain back to a known, trusted Certificate Authority, a message like the following will come up prompting the user about whether they want to proceed:

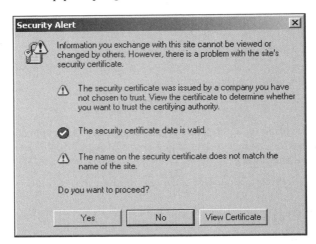

If the browser accepts the certificate chain, the client will respond with:

a. A certificate chain if the server requested it.

b. A session key encrypted with the server's public key. The session key is randomly generated for each SSL session, and used for symmetric encryption of data. If no RSA public-key cipher is available, Diffie-Hellman may be used for key agreement instead.

c. Optionally, a **certificate verify** message. The client sends the server some signed information; the server can then use the client certificate to verify that the client is in the possession of the private key corresponding to the certificate's public key. This option is rarely used in the Internet world.

d. A **change cipher spec** message indicating that the server should switch to encrypted mode. The client selects the strongest cipher supported by both parties.

e. A **finished** message to indicate that the response is finished.

4. The server checks the client's certificate chain (if any), decrypts the session key and finally responds to the information sent by the client with:

a. A change cipher spec message indicating that the client should switch to encrypted mode.

b. A finished message to indicate that the SSL handshaking process is finished.

At this point, the **SSL session** is established and encrypted data can be exchanged between client and server. For all data, a HMAC message authentication code is calculated to guarantee data authenticity and integrity. If the client is a browser, it will indicate that the connection is secure by displaying a key symbol (Netscape) or a lock symbol (Internet Explorer) in its status line.

Making HTTPServer Secure

SSL can also be used at the socket level. To explore this, we will concentrate on using JSSE to add HTTPS support to the HTTP server from the previous chapter. With a secure HTTPServer, even credit card details could be entered in a form and safely transmitted over the Internet without having to worry about the risk of potential criminal interception. As with the URL example above, we will only need to add a few lines of source code to our HTTPServer class to make it secure. We will implement server authentication only, which is fine for most web applications.

The highlighted source code below is code that we need to change or add to the HTTPServer class to make it secure:

```java
// HTTPServer.java

package com.wrox.httpserver;

import java.io.*;
import java.net.*;
import java.util.*;
import java.security.KeyStore;
import javax.net.*;
import javax.net.ssl.*;
import com.sun.net.ssl.*;    // remove if you're using JDK 1.4
import javax.security.cert.X509Certificate;

public class HTTPServer extends HTTPConstants implements Runnable {
```

Insert the following right after the main() method, and make the indicated modifications to run():

```java
  private static HTTPLocalizedResources resources;

  // Check if we run with the right VM and read resources
  static {
    String vers = System.getProperty("java.version");
    if (vers.compareTo("1.3.0") < 0) {
      System.err.println(VMVERSION_ERROR);

      // Exit the VM
      System.exit(1);
    }

    try {

      // Load locale-specific messages
      resources = new HTTPLocalizedResources("msg.httpserver");
    } catch (MissingResourceException mre) {
      System.err.println(RESOURCE_ERROR);
      System.exit(1);
    }
  }

  public HTTPServer(String[] args) {

    /* Check if the correct application parameters have been provided, we */
    /* expect the name of the properties file                            */
    if (args != null && args.length == 1) {
```

```
      try {
        HTTPConfig.initializeConfig(args[0]);
      } catch (ConfigFileException e) {

        /* An error occurred while reading the information          */
        /* A locale-specific error message is retrieved and displayed  */
        System.err.println(resources.getResourceString("ERROR_HTTP_CONFIG")
                           + e.getMessage());
        exit(ABNORMAL_TERMINATION);
      }
    } else {

      // Write usage information and terminate
      System.err
        .println(resources.getResourceString("ERROR_INVALID_ARGUMENT"));
      exit(ABNORMAL_TERMINATION);
    }

    // Initialize MIME converter
    try {
      MimeConverter.initializeConverter(MIME_TYPES_FILES);
    } catch (ConfigFileException e) {

      // An error occurred while reading the mime types
      System.err.println(resources.getResourceString("ERROR_MIME_CONFIG")
                         + e.getMessage());
      exit(ABNORMAL_TERMINATION);
    }

    // The configuration has been read, now we can initialize the logger
    try {
      HTTPLog.initializeLogger(HTTPConfig.config.getLogfile());
    } catch (IOException e) {

      // An error occurred while reading the mime types
      System.err.println(resources.getResourceString("ERROR_OPEN_LOGFILE")
                         + e.getMessage());
      exit(ABNORMAL_TERMINATION);
    }
  }

  private void exit() {
    exit(NORMAL_TERMINATION);
  }

  private void exit(int status) {
    System.exit(status);
  }

  public static void main(String[] args) {

    // Create an application instance
    HTTPServer theApp = new HTTPServer(args);

    // Start the server
    Thread server = new Thread(theApp);
    server.setDaemon(true);
    server.start();
```

```
        // Display console to allow the user to gracefully shut down the server
        BufferedReader br =
          new BufferedReader(new InputStreamReader(System.in));
        BufferedWriter bw =
          new BufferedWriter(new OutputStreamWriter(System.out));

        while (true) {
          try {
            bw.write(resources.getResourceString("CONSOLE_PROMPT"));
            bw.flush();
            String input = br.readLine();

            if (input != null && input
                    .compareToIgnoreCase(resources
                      .getResourceString("CONSOLE_QUIT_COMMAND")) == 0) {

              // The user requests to shut down the server
              theApp.shutdown();
              theApp.exit();
            }
          } catch (Exception e) {

            // Shutdown when a console exception occurs
            theApp.shutdown();
            theApp.exit(ABNORMAL_TERMINATION);
          }
        }
      }
```

First, an SSLContext is created, using the static getInstance() method, to which we pass the actual secure protocol implementation that we want to use. Objects of this class represent a secure socket protocol implementation that acts as a factory for secure socket factories (objects that create secure sockets). Because certificates are in a specific standard such as ISO X.509, we need a key manager factory that is able to handle keys in this format. We create a key manager factory using the static method getInstance().

```
        private ServerSocketFactory getServerSocketFactory(boolean secure) {
          if (secure) {
            SSLServerSocketFactory ssf = null;
            try {

              // Set up a key manager to do server authentication
              SSLContext ctx;
              KeyManagerFactory kmf;
              KeyStore ks;
              char[] passphrase = "secret".toCharArray();

              ctx = SSLContext.getInstance("TLS");
              kmf = KeyManagerFactory.getInstance("SunX509");
              ks = KeyStore.getInstance("JKS");
```

Now, we need the actual certificate that will be used for negotiating an SSL connection with a connecting client. JSSE wraps a collection of keys and certificates into a KeyStore. We create a KeyStore object and load the supplied key file testkeys (which needs to be in the directory from which the application is started) with the required password ("passphrase") into the keystore. The key manager factory is now initialized with the key in keystore, and the SSL manager is initialized with a list of the supported key managers. Now we are ready to create and return a server socket factory using getServerSocketFactory(). The rest of the source code stays unchanged.

```
            ks.load(new FileInputStream("httpd.keystore"), passphrase);
            kmf.init(ks, passphrase);
            ctx.init(kmf.getKeyManagers(), null, null);

            ssf = ctx.getServerSocketFactory();
            return ssf;
        } catch (Exception e) {

            // Ignore the exception and return null
            return null;
        }
    } else {
    return ServerSocketFactory.getDefault();
    }
}
public void run() {
    ServerSocket server = null;

    try {

        // Get port to listen at for incoming requests
        int port = HTTPConfig.config.getPort();

        // Create socket and listen for incoming connections


        // Request a server socket factory that constructs secure sockets
        ServerSocketFactory ssf = getServerSocketFactory(true);

        if (HTTPConfig.config.getBindAddress() == null) {
          server = ssf.createServerSocket(port);
        } else {
          server = ssf.createServerSocket(port, DEFAULT_BACKLOG,
                                     HTTPConfig.config.getBindAddress());
        }

        // Set an infinite timeout
        server.setSoTimeout(0);

        while (true) {
          Socket socket = server.accept();

          Thread request = new Thread(new HTTPRequest(socket));
          request.setDaemon(true);
          request.start();
        }
    } catch (Exception e) {
        System.err.println(resources.getResourceString("ERROR_HTTP_SERVER")
                        + e.getMessage());
        exit(ABNORMAL_TERMINATION);
    }
    finally {
      try {
        if (server != null) {
          server.close();
        }
      } catch (IOException e) {

        // Ignore this exception
      }
```

```
      }
    }

    public void shutdown() {

      // Closes the log
      HTTPLog.logger.close();
    }

    private static final int ABNORMAL_TERMINATION = 1;
    private static final int DEFAULT_BACKLOG = 50;

    // Class constants
    private static final String MIME_TYPES_FILES = "mime";
    private static final int NORMAL_TERMINATION = 0;
}
```

The code above has been compiled and tested with JDK1.3 and JSSE 1.02. If you want to use JDK 1.4 to enable SSL security for the `HTTPServer` class, you will have to comment out the following import statement. The rest of the source code remains unchanged:

```
//import com.sun.net.ssl.*; // remove if you're using JDK 1.4
```

Now we generate the server certificate using Sun's `keytool` by typing the following and answering the prompts (for a refresher on the `keytool` utility, refer back to Chapter 7):

C:\Beg_Java_Networking\Ch14> **keytool -genkey -keystore httpd.keystore -alias serverkey -keyalg RSA -keypass secret -storepass secret**

When we connect to our secure server by requesting https://localhost:1234/secure.html, a security alert like the one shown under *SSL Handshaking* above will pop up. The reason is that the certificate that we have created for `HTTPServer` has not been issued by a company that the browser trusts. Browsers only trust well-known CAs such as VeriSign by default, and for production purposes you would want to acquire your certificate from them.

The user can now decide to trust you for this session and the SSL handshake continues. The result is shown in the following screenshot:

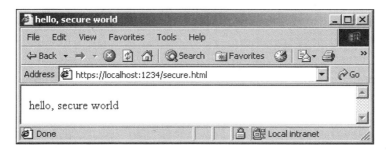

Please note that we explicitly have to provide the port number `1234` in the URL since we do not use the default HTTPS port. The lock in the status line at the bottom of the browser window indicates that a secure connection has been established.

The good thing about SSL is that even before the first request header line is transferred, the communication is already secured. Our setup, however, is currently only a one-way-trust mechanism. If someone stole Mary's credit card, he or she could still connect to our secure HTTP server and buy things using Mary's credit card.

There are also situations where the web server needs to make sure the user is who he or she claims to be. Imagine that the FBI had a web site with secret files that could be accessed over the Internet by special agents. They would certainly not only be concerned about encrypting data, but also about authenticating the requestor. There are two commonly used methods to accomplish that:

❑   We can use basic authentication to challenge the user to enter a username and password. This works because all data that is being sent in HTTP headers is encrypted.

❑   Or we can use client authentication, which requires the client to have a certificate installed in the browser, which the server can reject or accept.

Client authentication could be enabled very easily in our secure `HTTPServer` by adding the following line of source code after the server socket has been created:

```
((SSLServerSocket)server).setNeedClientAuth(true);
```

For high-security sites, a combination of a certificate on a chip card as well as a password is very likely the best solution. This means that a system cannot be broken into, even if someone loses their chip card or someone looks over a user's shoulder to get the password.

For more information on SSL, try: http://developer.netscape.com/docs/manuals/security.html#SSL.

Summary

In this chapter, we discussed cryptography, the Java Cryptography Architecture (JCA), and three of its extensions, the Java Authentication and Authorization Service (JAAS), the Java Cryptography Extension (JCE), and the Java Secure Socket Extension (JSSE). We covered:

❑   The basics of cryptography; which included symmetric and asymmetric encryption, message digests and digital signatures, and certificates and the role of Certificate Authorities

❑   The mechanics of instantiating and initializing services in the JCA provider-based framework, including the creation of factories and generators, the two types of services in the JCA framework

❑   The construction of (X.509) certificates

❑   The generation and manipulation of both transparent and opaque keys for a variety of symmetric and asymmetric ciphers

❑   The encryption and decryption of data using a cryptographic `Cipher`

❑   The authentication of a message using a HMAC algorithm

❑   The storing of keys and certificates in the Java keystore

❑   The importance of secure random number generators, and how to instantiate them

❑   The calculation of a message digest and the digital signing of a document or other data using a given algorithm

❑ The setting up of authentication in the JAAS framework, including handling callbacks

❑ The configuration and enforcing of JAAS authorization rules, and the performance of privileged operations

❑ The basics of the Secure Socket Layer (SSL) protocol

❑ The accessing of secure HTTP servers using the URL class with the HTTPS protocol handler

❑ The fundamentals of network communication using SSL sockets in the context of a secure web server

Most of the cryptographic services you are likely to need when implementing networked applications have been examined in this chapter.

Object Serialization

Serialization is the process of converting the state of objects into byte streams and restoring objects from those byte streams. Once an object's data is converted to a byte stream, we can use the various byte stream classes in the `java.io` package to **persist** the objects state to a file, pipe it to another thread, or send the object's data over a network connection to another host.

Here's a quick list of the topics we will cover in this chapter:

- ❑ How serialization works
- ❑ Working with object streams
- ❑ How to create a serializable class
- ❑ Customizing the serialization process
- ❑ Versioning
- ❑ Practical applications

How Serialization Works

In most object-oriented programming languages serialization is a moderately difficult task. A programmer needs to write two routines. The first iterates through the properties of an object and then writes them out so that the object can later be reconstructed. A second routine is needed to reconstruct the object later; this process is called **deserialization**. If the object's class structure is modified, those changes are also likely to ripple through the serialization routines. Hence, the two routines for serializing the object will need to be modified.

For non-trivial classes, writing code to serialize objects can become very involved and tedious. It can become especially complicated when a class includes references to other classes. Serializing one object's state might also require serializing the state of lots of objects. If an object depends on the state of other objects, restoring that object also means restoring the state of those collaborating objects. Otherwise, the object relationships would be broken.

Serialization in Java

Java makes serialization a relatively easy task. You can serialize nearly any class in Java, even your own classes, without writing custom methods to save and restore object data. An object whose class implements the `java.io.Serializable` interface can be transformed into a stream of bytes or restored from a stream of bytes without adding any extra code to the class. Only in rare instances do you need to write custom code to save or restore the state of an object.

The `Serializable` interface is an **empty interface** – meaning that it includes no methods that you must implement. Here's the complete definition of the `Serializable` interface:

```
package java.io;
public interface Serializable {
   // there's nothing in here!
} ;
```

The `Serializable` interface exists merely to signal to the Java virtual machine that the class is eligible for serialization. Sometimes, this is referred to as a tagged interface. Declaring that a class implements the `Serializable` interface is a necessary condition for serializing an object. From the programmer's perspective, most of the serialization work is done automatically. You just add `implements Serializable` to your class declaration, like this:

```
public class MySerializableClass implements Serializable {
}
```

Adding an interface reference to `Serializable` is not sufficient for serializing every Java class. There are some Java classes for which serialization makes no sense, for instance those involving threads are intricately tied to a particular VM. JDBC connections are another good example; it makes no sense to pass an object containing database connection information from one server to another, as each new connection will be different.

The Mechanism of Serialization

Serialization breaks down into two main parts: **Serializing** and **Deserializing**.

❑　Serializing is the first part of the process. It breaks data down into a byte stream so it can be stored in a file or transmitted over a network connection. An `int`, for example, is converted into a four-byte high-order byte stream. However, serializing does more than just convert Java primitive data types into simple byte streams. It also provides enough information for the object to be reconstructed later, perhaps even on a different machine.

❑　Deserializing, just as the name suggests, is the opposite of serializing. It unpacks the byte stream and reconstructs the object.

You're already familiar with the mechanism Java uses for serializing and deserializing primitive data types. We discussed the `DataOutputStream` and `DataInputStream` classes in Chapter 5. `DataOutputStream` uses binary representations that are common for Internet protocols: big-endian values for integer types, IEEE-754 for floats and doubles, UTF-8 for Unicode characters. `DataOutputStream` is well suited for sending Java primitives like `int` or `char` across a network to another host. `DataInputStream` is used to read previously serialized Java primitives.

Objects are usually composed of multiple data types. Some are likely to be Java primitives. Others might be references to other objects. This makes the serialization of objects a lot more complicated than Java primitives. The `java.io` package includes two classes for serializing and deserializing objects. We'll have more to say about `ObjectOutputStream` and `ObjectInputStream` in the next section.

Once an object is serialized, we can use the various byte stream classes in `java.io` to work with it. We might want to store the serialized data in a file. Or send it across a network to a remote host.

A game is a good example of using serialization. Let's assume we are designing a computer game based on a board game. A player might want to save the board position and move history so they can come back and finish the game later.

- ❏ The game program can use `ObjectOutputStream` to serialize the game object

- ❏ The serialized byte stream for the game object can be passed to a `FileOutputStream` instance, which stores the byte stream in a file

- ❏ Later, when the player wants to restore the game, the game program can use an instance of `FileInputStream` to retrieve the serialized byte stream from the file

- ❏ `ObjectInputStream` can be used to restore the instance of the game object

We can extend our game example to be a network game, with players participating over a TCP/IP network. Instead of sending the byte stream to an instance of `FileOutputStream`, we could instead send the byte stream to a network socket. In network applications it is desirable to have objects that are distributed across disparate machines work together. The main framework for this is Remote Method Invocation (RMI). In Chapter 16, we'll see that object serialization is an important part of how RMI works.

Serializing an object involves more than converting primitive data types into byte representations. At some point, the data will need to be restored. Restoring data requires an object instance to restore the data into. The serializing process in `ObjectOutputStream` attaches a header to the byte stream that includes the object type and version information. When deserializing takes place, the JVM uses the header information to create an object instance and then copies the data in the object byte stream to the object's data members.

> The header for an object byte stream includes a number of elements – full details of which are beyond the scope of this book. The complete specification can be found in Java documentation under "Java Object Serialization Specification". You can find it on the Sun Microsystems web site:
> http://java.sun.com/j2se/1.3/docs/guide/serialization/spec/serialTOC.doc.html

Controlling Serialization

Declaring a data member as `transient` prevents the serializing process from adding it to the object's byte stream. No data is sent for `transient` data members. When the data is later deserialized, the data member will be recreated (it is, after all, part of the class definition) but it will contain no data.

It sometimes makes good sense to mark a data member as `transient`, even if it could be serialized. Objects that represent the current date or the current time are classic examples. The reconstructed object needs to include the data member, but we can set these data members explicitly, rather than relying on the automatic behavior when a class is marked `Serializable`.

Java allows us to declare a class `Serializable`, so we get the benefits of automatic serialization for most of the class and still take manual control over those data members that are marked `transient`. We can include `readObject()` and `writeObject()` methods to properly initialize a data member when the object is recreated.

The Externalizable Interface

In some cases, it may be necessary to completely take over control of the serialization process. Another interface `Externalizable` is provided which enables you to do this. The `Externalizable` interface extends the `Serializable` interface and signals to the JVM that our class will manually handle its own serialization. When using the `Externalizable` interface it is necessary to implement two further methods `readExternal()` and `writeExternal()`, which gives the class complete control over the form of the input and output streams.

Now that we have a high-level understanding of serialization, let's take a closer look at some of the details.

Working with Object Streams

The `java.io` package includes two classes for serializing objects. `ObjectOutputStream` is responsible for writing out an object to a byte stream and `ObjectInputStream` reconstructs objects from a byte stream.

Working with `ObjectOutputStream` and `ObjectInputStream` is no more difficult than it would be using any of the other byte stream classes in `java.io`. `ObjectOutputStream` chains to another subclass of `OutputStream`; `ObjectInputStream` does the same with a subclass of `InputStream`. Both these classes can persist object hierarchies as well as primitive data types. This process is illustrated in the diagram below:

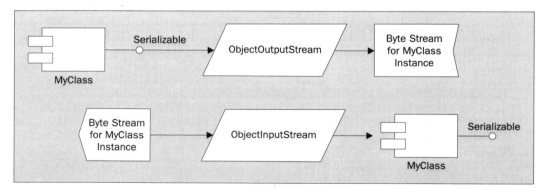

The ObjectOutputStream Class

The `ObjectOutputStream` class extends the `DataOutput` interface. `DataOutputStream` also implements the `DataOutput` interface. The methods in `ObjectOutputStream` mirror the eleven public methods in `DataOutputStream` used to write Java primitive data types.

Constructors

The `ObjectOutputStream` class includes two constructors, one is `public` and the other is `protected`. Unless you wish to create your own subclass of `ObjectOutputStream` (which is beyond the scope of this book), you can only use the provided `public` constructor.

```
public ObjectOutputStream(java.io.OutputStream stream)
        throws IOException
protected ObjectOutputStream()
           throws IOException, SecurityException
```

Methods

In addition to the methods in `DataOutputStream`, the `ObjectOutputStream` class includes several methods directly related to serializing objects:

```
public void defaultWriteObject() throws IOException
public PutField putFields() throws IOException
public void reset()throws IOException
public void useProtocolVersion(int version) throws IOException
public void writeFields()throws IOException
public final void writeObject(Object obj) throws IOException
```

The `writeObject()` method is the most important method as it's the one used to serialize an object. If an object contains references to other objects, the `writeObject()` method recursively serializes those objects, too. Each `ObjectOutputStream` maintains a reference list of the objects it has serialized. It does this to keep from sending multiple copies of the same object. Because `writeObject()` can serialize an entire set of cross-referencing objects, it can easily happen that the same `ObjectOutputStream` instance can inadvertently be asked to serialize the same object. When this happens, a back-reference is serialized instead of writing the object's byte stream a second time. The `reset()` method restores the `ObjectOutputStream` to its initial state. A subsequent call to `writeObject()` to serialize the same object will generate a fresh copy of the object to the `ObjectOutputStream` instead of a back-reference.

The `useProtocolVersion()` method is rarely used. Later changes of the JDK have introduced some incompatible changes in the protocol for serializing objects. The `useProtocolVersion()` method specifies the protocol version to use for the output stream. This can be helpful in client-server settings when objects have been compiled with different versions of JDKs. The current default is `ObjectStreamConstants.PROTOCOL_VERSION_2`.

The `defaultWriteObject()` method is used to take some control over the serialization process. We'll have more to say about this method in our section on customizing the serialization process. When a custom `writeObject()` method is added to a class to handle the details of writing an object to a byte stream, the first method call in the custom `writeObject()` method is usually to `defaultWriteObject()`. This lets the custom `writeObject()` method take advantage of the logic built into automatic serialization. The custom `writeObject()` method then appends any additional information to the byte stream after the call to `defaultWriteObject()`.

The `ObjectOutputStream` class includes an inner class called `PutField`. This inner class is used when default serialization is replaced with custom serialization. The `putFields()` method is used to obtain an instance of `PutField`. The `PutField` object can be initialized with a list of data member names and the values to serialize. The `writeFields()` methods then writes those data members to the byte stream.

JDK 1.2 introduced another mechanism for declaring which fields to serialize. A class can declare a static array of `java.io.ObjectStreamField` objects named `serialPersistentFields`. Only the fields specified in the array will be serialized. This is not the usual way to do things but it is useful when extra control is required over which fields to serialize.

Using ObjectOutputStream

Let's start with a basic example. The simplest serialization task that you'll want is persisting an object instance to a file. In this case the class has two data members: a `String` object and a `Date` object.

```java
// SimpleSerialize.java

import java.io.*;
import java.util.*;

public class SimpleSerialize
{
    public static void main(String[] args) throws IOException
    {
        // Serialize the current date to a file


        File myfile = new File("data.dat");
        myfile.createNewFile();

// This version of the FileOutputStream() method allows the file to be
// appended to rather than overwritten
        FileOutputStream oFileOutputStream = new
                FileOutputStream("data.dat", true);
        ObjectOutputStream oObjectOutputStream = new
                ObjectOutputStream(oFileOutputStream);

        oObjectOutputStream.writeObject("Today");
        oObjectOutputStream.writeObject(new Date());

        // Flush and close the output stream.
        oObjectOutputStream.flush();
        oObjectOutputStream.close();
    }
}
```

When you run this class:

C:\Beg_Java_Networking\Ch15>**java SimpleSerialize**

The `String` and DATE objects are serialized to a file called `data.dat`, which is stored in the same directory that the example was run from. The contents of this file is only partially human readable as it contains binary data along with the header information and object types. We will see how to deserialize this data when we get to the `ObjectInputStream` class.

There are no problems here because `String` and `Date` objects expose the `Serializable` interface. They are, therefore, automatically serializable. All we have to do is pass them, in turn, to the `writeObject()` method of `ObjectOutputStream`. This will serialize each of the objects.

In the example above, the objects are simple. If we instead serialize an object with multiple data members, `writeObject()` would send all of the data members, whether they are declared `public`, `protected`, or `private`. The only data members not serialized are those declared `transient` or `static`.

What happens if we try to serialize an object that does not implement the Serializable interface? The writeObject() method will throw a NotSerializableException.

Example: Serialization Across a Network

Sending our object to a TCP network socket is not much harder. We've left out most of the exception handling from the snippet below to make the mechanics of serializing an object over a network connection more evident:

```java
// SerializeOverSocket.java

import java.io.*;
import java.util.*;
import java.net.*;

public class SerializeOverSocket {
  public static void main(String[] args) throws IOException {

    Socket oSocket = new Socket("SomeHost", 1234);
    OutputStream oOutputStream = oSocket.getOutputStream();

    // Create the object output stream. Chain the output stream to it.
      ObjectOutputStream oObjectOutputStream =
        new ObjectOutputStream(oOutputStream);

    // Write the objects to the network stream
    oObjectOutputStream.writeObject("Today");
    oObjectOutputStream.writeObject(new Date());

    // Flush and close the output stream.
    oObjectOutputStream.flush();
    oObjectOutputStream.close();
  }
}
```

Obviously if you want to run this example the code below must refer to a real host and an accessible socket number.

```java
    Socket oSocket = new Socket("SomeHost", 1234);
```

As you can see only a few alterations are needed. All we have to do is create a new Socket and then create an OutputStream for it.

The ObjectInputStream Class

The ObjectInputStream works like the ObjectOutputStream. ObjectInputStream extends the DataInput interface, which is also implemented by the DataInputStream class. The methods in ObjectInputStream mirror the public methods in DataInputStream that are used to read serialized Java primitive data types.

Constructors

There are two constructors, one public and one protected. As with ObjectOutputStream you can only use the public one unless you wish to create your own subclass of ObjectInputStream.

```
public ObjectInputStream(java.io.OutputStream stream)
        throws IOException, StreamCorruptedException
protected ObjectInputStream()
            throws IOException, SecurityException
```

Methods

In addition to the methods in `DataInputStream`, `ObjectOutputStream` includes several methods that are related to reading and serializing objects:

```
public void defaultReadObject()
        throws IOException, ClassNotFoundException, NotActiveException
public GetField readFields()
        throws IOException, ClassNotFoundException, NotActiveException
public readObject()
        throws OptionalDataException, ClassNotFoundException, IOException

public void registerValidation(ObjectInputValidation validator,
                               int priority)
```

The `readObject()` method deserializes an object from a byte stream. Each call to `readObject()` returns the next `Object` in the stream. Object byte streams do not transmit the bytecode for the class. The stream instead includes the class name and its signature. When an object is received by `readObject()`, the JVM tries to load the class named in the header. If it cannot find the class, `readObject()` will throw a `ClassNotFoundException`. If you do need to transfer both object data and byte code you can use the RMI framework, which is covered in Chapter 16.

The remaining private methods for `ObjectInputStream` are used to customize the deserialization process. When the serialization process used by `ObjectOutputStream` is customized, the deserialization process for `ObjectInputStream` must also be customized. The `defaultReadObject()` method is used to supplement automatic serialization. You need to call `defaultReadObject()` before trying to read any data added to the output stream by the `defaultWriteMethod()` method.

The `ObjectInputStream` class also includes an inner class. The inner class is named `GetField`, and it is used to read data members serialized by the `writeFields()` method of `ObjectOutputStream`. The `GetField` instance is populated by the `getFields()` method. The individual data members can then be read from the `GetField` instance. We'll cover all of this in more detail in our section on customizing the serialization process.

Reconstructing a Serialized Object

In a previous example we serialized `String` and `Date` objects to a file, `data.dat`. The code to reconstruct our `String` and `Date` objects from the byte stream is also easy to write and understand.

```java
// SimpleDeserialize.java

import java.io.*;
import java.util.*;

public class SimpleDeserialize {
  public static void main(String[] args) throws Exception {

    // Deserialize a string and date from a file.
```

```
        FileInputStream oFileInputStream =
          new FileInputStream("data.dat");
        ObjectInputStream oObjectInputStream =
          new ObjectInputStream(oFileInputStream);

        String sDate = (String) oObjectInputStream.readObject();
        Date dtDate = (Date) oObjectInputStream.readObject();

        System.out.println(sDate);
        System.out.println(dtDate);

        // Close the input stream.
        oObjectInputStream.close();
    }
  }
```

If you run the code above after first running `SimpleSerialize` you should get this result:

C:\Beg_Java_Networking\Ch15>**java SimpleDeserialize**
Today
Wed Aug 01 15:11:54 BST 2001

Obviously the time will reflect when you originally serialized the objects to `data.dat`.

Again, there are no surprises in the code snippet above. The `readObject()` method returns an `Object` instance for the next object in the byte stream. It is the programmer's responsibility to cast the object correctly upon its return.

```
        String sDate = (String) oObjectInputStream.readObject();
```

Trying to cast an object to the wrong type will result in `java.lang.ClassCastException`. If we know to expect a Java primitive, such as an `int` value, we can use a more specific read method, such as `readInt()` and avoid the cast.

Creating a Serializable Class

If the classes you create need to be serializable you need to take into account the following rules:

❑ You can only serialize a class if it exposes the `Serializable` interface. It can do that in several different ways:

   ❑ Declaring `Implements Serializable`

   ❑ Declaring `Implements Externalizable`

   ❑ The class could subclass another class that exposes the `Serializable` or `Externalizable` interface

❑ Serialization is only possible if every data member is serializable or declared `transient`, or `static`. Most basic Java data types are serializable. The list below is a quick rundown of common serializable data types (their subclasses are also serializable):

   ❑ `java.lang.Character`

   ❑ `java.lang.Boolean`

517

❏   `java.lang.String`
❏   `java.lang.StringBuffer`
❏   `java.lang.Throwable`
❏   `java.lang.Number`
❏   `java.util.Hashtable`
❏   `java.util.Random`
❏   `java.util.Vector`
❏   `java.util.Date`
❏   `java.util.BitSet`
❏   `java.io.File`
❏   `java.net.InetAddress`
❏   Arrays of Java primitives
❏   Most of the AWT and Swing components

❏ Only `public` classes are serializable. This is because the object stream must contain enough information to create another instance of the same class and put it into the same state as the serialized instance, even if the serialized instance exists on another JVM.

❏ If a class implements the `Serializable` interface and its immediate superclass does not, the superclass must provide a constructor that takes no arguments. The subclass will have to implement custom serialization in order to serialize any data members for the superclass. Classes that implement `Externalizable` must also implement a no-argument constructor.

That's it for the basic rules of serialization. Declaring that a class implements the `Serializable` interface is easy. We already mentioned that `Serializable` is an empty interface, also known as a marker or tagged interface.

Customizing the Serialization Process

There are cases when you might want to customize the serialization process. It is the programmer's responsibility to decide which data members should be serialized. By default, every data member will be serialized, except those declared `static` or `transient`. In some cases you will want to declare a data member `transient` but still serialize it, for instance the current time.

You think of declaring a variable `transient` as signaling to the JVM that we will assume responsibility for serializing the variable. Remember deserialization creates a completely new instance of a class and then copies data from the byte stream to put the new instance in the same state as the serialized instance. That means `transient` data members will receive the default values for the class unless we override the behavior with `readObject()` and `writeObject()` methods. They are both declared `private`, and they both take an object stream as a parameter.

```
private void writeObject(java.io.ObjectOutputStream out)
        throws IOException
private void readObject(java.io.ObjectInputStream in)
        throws IOException, ClassNotFoundException
```

Take a very simple serializable class, with just two data members, one of them `transient`:

```
public class MySerializableClass implements Serializable{

    String sToday = "Today: ";
    transient Date dtToday = new Date();
}
```

The class above contains the current date and a simple string. As written, deserialization creates an object with a `null` value for the `dtToday` data member. In the next section, we'll see how to add a private `readObject()` method to restore the object with the current date instead of a `null` value.

For our next example we've modified the serialization code – extending it to include a `static` data member, two `transient` data members, and an ordinary data member. We also added some simple property accessor and mutator methods.

Just a quick reminder, the object streams do not serialize `static` or `transient` data members. Our class has to include custom `writeObject()` and `readObject()` methods in order to handle those data members. When we use `writeObject()` and `readObject()`, we also need to be careful to read those data members in the same order they were written.

```
// MySerializableClass.java

import java.io.*;
import java.util.*;
import java.net.*;

public class MySerializableClass implements Serializable {
    private static int iGlobalID;
    private transient int iID;
    String sToday = "Today: ";
    private transient Date dtToday = new Date();
    private transient Socket oSocket;

    public MySerializableClass() {
        iID = getID();

        try {
            oSocket = new Socket("SomeHost", 1234);
        } catch (IOException e) {}
    }
    private synchronized static int getID() {
        return iGlobalID++;
    }

    private void writeObject(ObjectOutputStream outputStream)
            throws IOException {

        // perform automatic serialization of serializable data members.
        outputStream.defaultWriteObject();

        // Perform custom serialization of the socket object.
        outputStream.writeObject(oSocket.getInetAddress());
        outputStream.writeInt(oSocket.getPort());
    }

    private void readObject(ObjectInputStream inputStream)
            throws IOException, ClassNotFoundException {

        // Perform automatic serialization of serializable data members.
```

```
    inputStream.defaultReadObject();

    // Perform custom serialization of the socket object.
    InetAddress oAddress = (InetAddress) inputStream.readObject();
    int iPort = inputStream.readInt();
    oSocket = new Socket(oAddress, iPort);

    // Perform custom serialization of the data members
    iID = getID();
    dtToday = new Date();
  }
}
```

> **Although this class will compile, it is only an example of how to code `readObject()` and `writeObject()` methods. Running this class at the command line will generate an error, as it has no `main()` method.**

Our class is, admittedly, a catch-all collection of data members. A `Date` value is used to hold the current date. It's marked `transient`, because the date could change between the time the class is serialized and deserialized – perhaps the host is a remote server in a different time zone. The `int` for the `iID` data member is declared `transient` because it needs to be globally unique on the host where the class runs. The `Socket` object is not serializable, so it has to be marked `transient`. New sockets, JDBC connections, and the like are easily created when the object is restored from a byte stream.

```
    outputStream.defaultWriteObject();

    // Perform custom serialization of the socket object.
    outputStream.writeObject(oSocket.getInetAddress());
    outputStream.writeInt(oSocket.getPort());
```

The `writeObject()` method begins with a call to `defaultWriteObject()`. This takes care of the serialization for all of the data members that are not marked `static` or `transient`. It is strongly recommended that `writeObject()` begin with a call to `defaultWriteObject()`. The only other responsibility for `writeObject()` in our class is to serialize the information so the `Socket` can be restored. The IP address and the port number are written in turn to the object output stream.

```
    inputStream.defaultReadObject();

    // Perform custom serialization of the socket object.
    InetAddress oAddress = (InetAddress) inputStream.readObject();
    int iPort = inputStream.readInt();
    oSocket = new Socket(oAddress, iPort);
```

The `readObject()` method has some additional responsibilities. It begins with a call to `defaultReadObject()`, the recommended beginning for `readObject()`. Then it restores the `Socket` object, retrieving the IP address and port number from the object input stream. Once the socket is re-established, the `readObject()` method initializes the ID and the current date.

Completely Customizing the Serialization Process

If a class is going to be completely responsible for its own serialization, it implements the Externalizáble interface, rather than the Serializable interface. The definition of the Externalizable interface includes two methods writeExternal() and readExternal().

```
public void writeExternal(Java.io.ObjectOutput out)
        throws IOException
public void readExternal(Java.io.ObjectInput in)
        throws IOException, ClassNotFoundException
```

Using these methods you can control exactly how the data members of an object are written out to the byte stream. When a class implements Externalizable, a header is written to the object stream and then the class is completely responsible for serializing and restoring its data members. There is no automatic serialization at all, aside from the header.

Declaring that a class implements the Externalizable interface poses an important security risk. The writeExternal() and readExternal() methods are declared public. A malicious class can use them to read and/or write data to the object through those methods. If the object contains sensitive information, precautions must be taken. These could include using secure sockets or encrypting the entire byte stream. For more information on securing applications see Chapter 14.

In the case of our example in the previous section, it's only a trivial amount of extra work to implement the Externalizable interface. For a large, complicated class, implementing Externalizable can be a lot more work than if you rely on the automatic serialization that comes when implementing Serializable. The only changes needed for MySerializableClass have been highlighted in the code shown below:

```java
// MyExternalizableClass.java

import java.io.*;
import java.util.*;
import java.net.*;

public class MyExternalizableClass implements Externalizable {
    private static int iGlobalID;
    private int iID;
    String sToday = "Today: ";
    private Date dtToday = new Date();
    private Socket oSocket;

    public MyExternalizableClass() throws IOException
    {
        iID = getID();

        try
        {
            oSocket = new Socket("SomeHost", 1234);
        } catch (IOException e) {}
    }

    private synchronized static int getID() {
        return iGlobalID ++;
    }
```

```
public void writeExternal(ObjectOutput outputStream) throws IOException {

    // Perform custom serialization of the socket object.
    outputStream.writeObject(oSocket.getInetAddress());
    outputStream.writeInt(oSocket.getPort());

    // Serialize the basic data members.
    outputStream.writeUTF(sToday);
}

public void readExternal(ObjectInput inputStream) throws IOException
{
    try
    {
        // Perform custom serialization of the socket object.
        InetAddress oAddress = (InetAddress) inputStream.readObject();
        int iPort = inputStream.readInt();
        oSocket = new Socket(oAddress, iPort);

        // Serialize the basic data members.
        sToday = inputStream.readUTF();
        iID = getID();
        dtToday = new Date();
    } catch (ClassNotFoundException e) {}
}
}
```

Although this class will compile, it is only an example of how to code for the
Externalizable interface. Running this class at the command line will generate an
error, as it has no **main()** method.

Data members that were declared `transient` in our earlier example are now declared `private`. The
`static` members are unchanged.

```
private static int iGlobalID;
private int iID;
String sToday = "Today: ";
private Date dtToday = new Date();
private Socket oSocket;
```

A class that implements `Externalizable` must provide a no-argument constructor. The constructor
could be empty, but it must be there. Our example uses the no-argument constructor to initialize the ID
number data member.

```
public MyExternalizableClass() throws IOException {
    iID = getID();
...
}
```

The `writeObject()` and `readObject()` methods in the previous example are replaced by
`writeExternal()` and `readExternal()`. Care needs to be taken to restore objects from the input
stream in exactly the same order as they were serialized to the stream. The `writeExternal()` method
serializes the data members needed to reconstruct the `Socket` instance first and then the `String`
object. The `readExternal()` method restores those data members in exactly the same order.

In our previous example, the `writeObject()` was responsible only for serializing information needed to create a new `Socket` instance. The `writeExternal()` method in our example above has the added responsibility of serializing the `String` object, which it does by calling `writeUTF()`. The `readExternal()` method reconstructs the `Socket` instance and then the `String` object. That's all the information it needs from the object stream. The `readExternal()` method initializes the remaining data members before it returns them.

Versioning

When an object is serialized, version information is included in the header. If you serialize an object and then persist the byte stream or send it over a network connection to another host, it is possible that the version of the class that reads the data will be different from the class that wrote the data. A few common reasons include:

❏ Different hosts with different versions of the class

❏ Upgraded applications

❏ Bug fixes

We've said it before. The Java serialization system tries to copy previously serialized data into a new instance of the class that was serialized. Compatible changes do not affect the contract between a class and its callers. When an object is restored from a byte stream, the version of the class must be type compatible with the version of the class that was written to the byte stream. Incompatible changes mean that the JVM cannot guarantee the two versions are interoperable.

There is another important set of incompatible changes. They involve the order that data members are written to and read from the object byte stream. Data members must be read from the stream (or skipped over) in exactly the same order they were written. The data members are ordered with the Java primitives ordered first in the stream. They're in alphabetical order by name. Java objects follow, also in alphabetical order by name.

Versioning issues are bi-directional. The older class version might be the version of the object that was written to the byte stream, or, it might be the version of the class used to restore the object.

Here's a quick list of the most common incompatibility changes:

❏ Deleting data members. If an earlier class is used to restore the object, the data member will not be found in the object byte stream. The data member will be set to the default value, but this might violate contracts between the earlier version and other classes.

❏ Changing the names of data members. This can cause the sequence of data members in the object byte stream to shift.

❏ Changing member variable data types. Each data member is written to the object byte stream with its specific data type. The data types between the two class versions will no longer match.

❏ Changing a non-`static` data member to `static` or a non-`transient` data member to `transient`. Has the same effect as deleting a data member.

❏ Changing `writeObject()` or `readObject()` so they do (or do not) read/write default values for data members. Default data member values must consistently appear in the object byte stream.

❏   Changing or removing the declaration implementing `Serializable` or `Externalizable`.

Versioning does not prevent classes from evolving. Existing interfaces can be extended. Java classes can read object streams written by older versions of the same class, as long as the new version implements or extends the same interface as the previous version. The assumption is that the evolved class can be used in place of the original version. There should be no loss of data or functionality.

There are some common version changes that are compatible. The JVM will help you with those and attempt to copy the serialized data:

❏   Adding data members. Any new data member gets initialized to its default value.

❏   Changing the access modifier for a data member between `public`, `protected`, `private`, and `package`. None of these affect the ability of the JVM to assign values to the data member.

❏   Changing a `static` data member to non-`static` or a `transient` data member to non-`transient`. Has the same effect as adding a data member.

> **Automatic versioning is only available when a class implements the `Serializable` interface. Classes that implement the `Externalizable` interface are completely responsible for detecting and handling their own version incompatibilities.**

Java serialization uses a 64-bit hashcode to identify each class. The identifier is called an `SUID` (`serialVersionUID`). The JVM computes the hashcode from the signature of the class and the class name. Each version of the class gets its own unique SUID. You can use the SUID to tell the JVM which version of the class the object byte stream is compatible with. The SUID is part of the header for the byte stream.

You can determine the SUID for a class version by running the `serialver` program, which is included with the JDK:

```
C:\Beg_Java_Networking\Ch15>serialver MySerializableClass
MySerializableClass:    static final long serialVersionUID = -3043238012631174796L;
```

Once you identify the SUID, you should include it in a subsequent version of the class. This will inform the JDK that the new version is compatible with the earlier version and guards against classes with the same name being inadvertently identified as different versions of a single class. Declaring the SUID of a compatible class is quite simple. It requires just one declaration. Here's an example:

```
static final long serialVersionUID = -3043238012631174796L;
```

Practical Applications

Object serialization is not the most exciting topic in network programming but it is an important topic, with many practical implications. Firstly, object serialization facilitates distributed objects. The topic of Chapter 16, RMI, relies upon object serialization to run services on remote hosts as if the objects were running on the local machine.

Additionally, Java's implementation of object serialization not only preserves the data for a single object, it also recursively saves the data for every object referenced by a single object. If those objects reference other objects, they too are serialized. An entire object hierarchy can be written out to a byte stream, where it can be persisted in a file or communicated across a network connection. To flesh this argument out, you can persist an entire linked list, just by serializing the initial link. Java's serialization process will follow the chain to its conclusion, serializing every link in turn.

One practical implication that becomes apparent is cloning, that is, creating a new copy of an object using an existing one as a template. This is different from just creating a new instance of a class, as the clone object may contain different data representing its current state. The default cloning behavior in Java is a 'shallow clone', where only the object itself and any object references are cloned. The referenced objects themselves are not cloned.

Using object serialization we can perform a 'deep clone' of an object, as serialization clones the object itself and any other serializable objects it references. If those objects reference objects, those objects will be cloned as well. Serializing a single object can result in an entire series of objects being saved.

The following deep cloning example saves a container object and its contents to a byte array, so it can later be restored. To make this discussion a little more concrete, we'll name the objects `InvoiceItems` and `InvoiceItem`. `InvoiceItems` is nothing more than a `Vector` object that holds instances of `InvoiceItem`.

This is `InvoiceItem.java`:

```java
// InvoiceItem.java

package com.wrox.clone;

import java.io.*;
import java.util.Vector;

public class InvoiceItem implements Serializable
{
  private String m_sDescription;
  private int m_iQuantity;
  private float m_fPrice;

  public InvoiceItem(String sDescription, int iQuantity, float fPrice)
  {
    m_sDescription = sDescription;
    m_iQuantity = iQuantity;
    m_fPrice = fPrice;
  }

  public void printInvoice()
  {
    System.out.println(m_sDescription);
    System.out.println(m_iQuantity);
    System.out.println(m_fPrice);
  }
}
```

This is `InvoiceItems.java`:

```java
// InvoiceItems.java

package com.wrox.clone;

import java.io.*;
import java.util.Vector;

public class InvoiceItems implements Serializable
{
  private Vector m_oInvoiceItems;

  public InvoiceItems()
  {
    m_oInvoiceItems = new Vector();
  }

  public void addInvoice(InvoiceItem oInvoiceItem)
  {
    m_oInvoiceItems.addElement(oInvoiceItem);
  }

  public InvoiceItem getInvoice()
  {
    return (InvoiceItem) m_oInvoiceItems.firstElement();
  }
}
```

This is `CloneInvoices.java`:

```java
// CloneInvoices.java

package com.wrox.clone;

import java.io.*;

public class CloneInvoices {
  public static void main(String[] args) {
    try {
      InvoiceItems oInvoiceItems = new InvoiceItems();

      // Add an invoice;
      oInvoiceItems.addInvoice(new InvoiceItem("Widget", 1, 1.00F));

      // Create a Memory I/O Stream to hold the serialized InvoiceItems object;
      ByteArrayOutputStream oByteArrayOutputStream =
        new ByteArrayOutputStream();

      // Serialize the InvoiceItems object and its contents;
      ObjectOutputStream oObjectOutputStream =
        new ObjectOutputStream(oByteArrayOutputStream);
      oObjectOutputStream.writeObject(oInvoiceItems);

      // Save the byte array stream;
      byte[] bSerializedObject = oByteArrayOutputStream.toByteArray();

      // Release the reference to the InvoiceItems object;
      oInvoiceItems = null;
```

```
        // Create a Memory I/O Stream to restore the serialized
        // InvoiceItems object;
        ByteArrayInputStream oByteArrayInputStream =
          new ByteArrayInputStream(bSerializedObject);

        // Restore the InvoiceItems object and its contents;
        ObjectInputStream oObjectInputStream =
          new ObjectInputStream(oByteArrayInputStream);
        oInvoiceItems = (InvoiceItems) oObjectInputStream.readObject();

        // Write the details to System.out to confirm the clone was restored;
        InvoiceItem oInvoiceItem = oInvoiceItems.getInvoice();
        oInvoiceItem.printInvoice();
      } catch (IOException e1) {}
      catch (ClassNotFoundException e2) {}
  }
}
```

If you run the code, you'll see that the invoice details are written to `System.out` and we get a deep clone of our `CloneInvoices` object:

C:\Beg_Java_Networking\Ch15>javac com\wrox\clone*.java
C:\Beg_Java_Networking\Ch15>java com.wrox.clone.CloneInvoices
Widget
1
1.0

What we're simulating here is the ability to clone the `InvoiceItems` object, including all of its contents. The practical utility is obvious. We could clone an object before we make changes. If a rollback is desired, we just restore the object's serialized byte stream. Otherwise, we just free the reference and let the JVM garbage collect the clone.

The `InvoiceItems` and `InvoiceItem` classes are far from robust implementations. We're only using them to illustrate deep cloning via serialization.

The `InvoiceItem` class is simple; it has a single constructor that accepts invoice details and a single method that writes invoice details to `System.out`. The `InvoiceItems` class has methods to add an invoice item and to read the first element in the `Vector` object.

The real demonstration occurs in the `CloneInvoices` class. Here's what happens:

- ❏ `CloneInvoices` starts by creating an instance of `InvoiceItems` and populating it with an instance of `InvoiceItem`

- ❏ The `InvoiceItems` instance is then serialized and stored in a byte array

- ❏ The reference to the `InvoiceItems` instance is set to `null`, in order to release it

- ❏ The serialized object in the byte array is then restored

- ❏ Restoring the `InvoiceItems` instance automatically restores its contents, an instance of `InvoiceItem`

Summary

We've taken a good, solid look at object serialization; although we have not covered all of the intricacies, the topics we have covered should handle all but the most complicated cases. The important points in this chapter are:

❑   Serialization is the process of writing objects out to byte streams and reading objects from byte streams.

❑   Java makes serialization a relatively easy task. Only in rare instances do you need to write custom code to save or restore the state of an object.

❑   An object whose class implements the `java.io.Serializable` interface, can be transformed into a stream of bytes or restored from a stream of bytes without adding any code to the class.

❑   Not every class is serializable; it makes no sense for some types of class such as those involving threads, which are intricately tied to a particular JVM.

❑   To be serializable, all data members of a class must be serializable or declared as `transient`.

❑   Declaring a data member as `transient` prevents the serializing process from converting it to a byte stream. When the data is later deserialized, the data member will be recreated but it will contain no data, since no data was written to the stream for that particular data member.

❑   While serialization can normally be accomplished automatically, sometimes you might want to control part of the process. Java allows us to declare a class `Serializable` and still take manual control over data members declared `static` or `transient`.

RMI

In the last chapter, we saw how object serialization can be used to our advantage when distributing objects over a network. Java has a built-in, easy-to-use, formalized mechanism for distributed computing that makes extensive use of object serialization. It is called RMI (Remote Method Invocation).

In this chapter, we will examine the basic principles behind RMI. Starting with its predecessor – RPC (Remote Procedure Call), we will appreciate how RMI attempts to improve upon RPC, by having the advantage of hindsight, and leveraging specific features of the Java platform.

Specifically, we will code two versions of a distributed remote school grading system that makes use of RMI extensively. Through this experience, we will become familiar with:

❑   The principles behind RPC

❑   What RMI is and how it is different from RPC

❑   How RMI compares to TCP/UDP socket-based programming, and be able to compare it against CORBA (covered extensively in Chapter 17)

❑   The tools that are used in creating and starting RMI systems

❑   The importance of marshaling and unmarshaling in RMI and RPC

❑   The function of RMI stubs and skeletons

❑   Creation of objects that can be accessed remotely across a network

❑   Creation of client applications that access remote objects

❑   Relevance of exception handling and Java 2 security to RMI

❑   The unique ability of RMI to support behavior/code movement via Java's dynamic class loading

❑   Bootstrapping a distributed system

We will be well-versed in RMI programming by the end of this chapter, and ready to design our own distributed applications using RMI technology.

Distributed Computing and RPC

The concept of performing computation over a network of machinse had been around long before the conception of Java itself. A popular way to distribute work over a network is through RPC (or Remote Procedure Call).

Most programming languages that were popular before Java (Fortran, C, COBOL) are very procedural and less object-oriented. As a result, it was "natural" in these programming languages to think about taking a chunk of work in the form of a procedure (or function, or sub-routine) and having it executed on another machine over a network. The diagram below illustrates this concept.

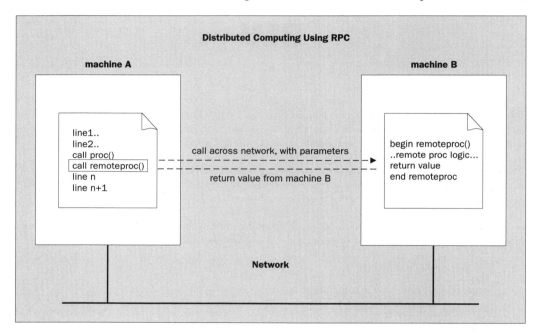

In the figure, we can see that while local procedures are executed on machine A, the remote procedure is actually executed on machine B. The program executing on machine A will wait until machine B has completed the operation of the remote procedure, and then continue with its program logic. The remote procedure may have a return value that the continuing program may use immediately. From the view of the program on machine A, there is little difference between calling a local procedure versus a remote one.

From previous chapters , we can see how we may "roll our own" RPC manually using TCP/IP-based network programming. However, there are some issues that one must consider before taking this labor-intensive route:

❑   Using socket-based programming can require highly repetitive coding, and can often be tedious for performing complex distributed operations

❑   We need to define and implement a mutually agreed upon protocol between the client and the server in order for it to work well (this can be significant work if we do not use one of the existing protocols – HTTP, FTP, and so on)

❑ Any change in the required interaction between the client and the server requires redesign of the protocol underneath

RPC provides a higher-level alternative that addresses these concerns, as we shall see next.

Marshaling and Unmarshaling

RPC alleviates these concerns by leveraging the procedure calling convention "built-in" to most programming languages. In operation, RPC intercepts calls to a procedure, and the following happens:

❑ Packages up the name of the procedures, and arguments to the call, and transmits them over the network to the remote machine where the RPC server is running

❑ The RPC server picks up this transmission, decodes the name of the procedure and the parameters

❑ The RPC server makes the actual procedural call on the server (remote) machine

❑ The RPC server packages the returned value and output parameters (in some programming language) and then transmits it over the network back to the machine that made the call

In fact, the calling machine does not even have to know the procedure is actually performed remotely on another machine.

> **The act of packaging the data involved in a call, and transmitting it over the network is called** Marshaling. **The act of unpacking such data is called** Unmarshaling.

The figure below shows the action of marshaling and unmarshaling during typical RPC operations.

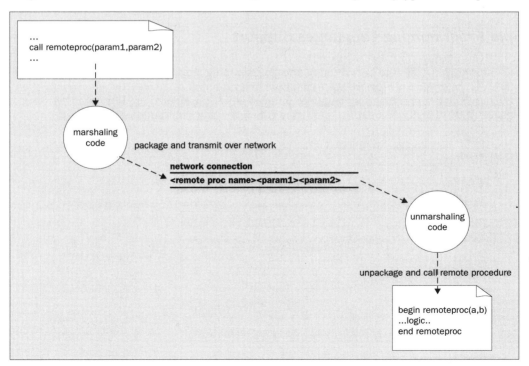

In the figure, we can see how a remote call is actually placed "on the network wire" by marshaling code. On the remote machine, corresponding unmarshaling code will unpackage the data and make the actual call (locally) on the remote machine. Although not shown on the figure for simplicity's sake, a reversed path would typically occur for the return value that is marshaled from the remote machine and unmarshaled back on the local one.

One important thing to note is that steps 1-4 above (marshaling and unmarshaling) are all accomplished for you, either with automatically generated code or by the RPC runtime environment.

The Important Role of Interfaces

RPC over a network cannot work without some prior agreement between the client/server on the data that is transmitted and how it may be used. In socket programming, this is the protocol that we must define and implement. With RPC, it is a programming interface.

Even though it may be expressed differently, an RPC interface serves exactly the same function as an interface in the Java programming language. An interface is a programming contract between a caller and callee as to the set of procedures (methods) that is implemented by the callee – including parameter and return value types.

Once an agreement is reached (that is, the interface is defined), the RPC client can then generate the required marshaling code for the remote procedure call, and the specific unmarshaling code for the return value (and/or output parameters) for the call. The RPC server can also generate the associated unmarshaling code for the procedure call and the marshaling code for the return value.

In essence, the interface describes a high-level protocol, and RPC generates the implementation of this protocol.

Multiple Programming Languages Support

Since RPC is a technology that works across a variety of programming languages (including Java!), it is possible for an RPC client to be written in one programming language while the server is written in another. To cater for code generation in multiple programming languages, the description of an RPC interface is kept in a programming language-independent format called the Interface Description Language (IDL). The figure opposite shows the complete code generation process.

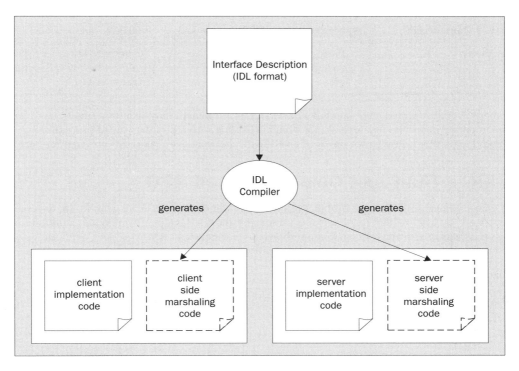

The figure shows how an IDL Compiler, a utility that is part of the RPC toolkit, compiles a programming language-independent IDL file. This compiler will generate client-side marshaling/unmarshaling code, as well as server-side marshaling/unmarshaling code in the specific programming language – in uncompiled source code format. These generated source code files are then compiled with user-written client implementation code, and/or server implementation code (using the appropriate programming language compiler) to form the client or server executable.

The code generation afforded by the IDL compiler saves a lot of tedious network programming work. The following table contrasts the RPC "code generation" approach to distributed computing versus the use of raw TCP/IP sockets coding from scratch.

Area of Comparison	Sockets over TCP/IP	RPC
Design and implementation of protocol	Has to be custom coding unless one makes use of existing protocol (HTTP, FTP, and so on)	Code completely generated from IDL file
Ease of maintenance and modification	Protocol must be redesigned and implementation retested	Make modification to IDL file and regenerate
Dependence on transport	Code can work over any network supporting socket based programming	Code is independent of transport, some RPC runtimes are implemented over non-TCP/IP network that has no socket support

Table continued on following page

Area of Comparison	Sockets over TCP/IP	RPC
Flexibility	Protocol defined can have any custom behavior	Protocol always works in a synchronous call-return manner

We can see from the above table that RPC offers significant benefit in return for a small loss of flexibility in implementing distributed systems. Little wonder that it is such a popular way of programming distributed logic. RMI, Java's own flavor of an RPC mechanism, even takes this one step further.

RMI: More Than Just Object-Oriented RPC

The Java programming language is object oriented and network-ready from ground up; as a result, the object-based RMI (RPC-like) mechanism is built right into the Java platform. When combined with object serialization as a way of distributing objects over a network, RMI provides a unique yet powerful distributed computing model that non-Java platforms simply cannot match.

Just like RPC, RMI has the following features:

- ❑ Enables a client to make a method call to a remote server in the same way as local method invocation

- ❑ Enables the specification of a client/server programming contract based on an interface

- ❑ Automatic generation of marshaling and unmarshaling code

Unlike RPC, RMI:

- ❑ Is a 100% Pure Java mechanism, giving Java programmers a performance advantage over RPC language-specific "bindings". On the flip side, it will only work with Java and does not work with clients or servers created in other programming language (although RMI-IIOP in JDK 1.3 and beyond enable interoperation with CORBA – see Chapter 17 for more details).

- ❑ Supports automatic generation of marshaling and unmarshaling code via introspection of the binary class file from the server object; there are no special IDL files to create and maintain

- ❑ Extends the Java programming model across the machine boundary (and JVM boundary) without requiring any special syntax

- ❑ Enables transfer of behavior (code) simultaneously with data within a single remote method invocation; we will see this in action later when we code our example

Step by Step RMI

Let us turn our attention now to how Java RMI actually works. Essentially, Java RMI enables you to:

- ❑ Specify certain objects to be remotely accessible

- ❑ Prepare server-side objects to accept client calls

- ❑ Automatically generate the client-side marshaling and server-side unmarshaling code

- ❑ Write client code to locate and access the remotely accessible objects over a network

Along the way, we will see how to deal with exceptions in RMI. We will now visit each of these vital steps and take a look at the procedures and tools that are provided by RMI to carry them out.

Making Objects Remotely Accessible

As it is the case in RPC, the unit of distributed work is a "method". The Java RMI runtime requires that any method that may be called remotely to be part of a **remote interface**.

More precisely, a remote interface is an interface that extends java.rmi.Remote interface. If you look up the Javadoc of this interface, you will find that it has no methods. It is used only as a "marker" for the Java runtime to recognize the special property of this interface – ability to be accessed remotely. For example, the interface SchoolGrades below is a remote interface:

```
// SchoolGrades.java

package com.wrox.rmi.simple;

import java.rmi.Remote;
import java.rmi.RemoteException;

public interface SchoolGrades extends Remote {
   int getAverageGrade() throws RemoteException;
}
```

Under Java RMI, any object that implements at least one remote interface is considered a remotely callable object. For example, the GradingService class here can be used to create remotely callable object instances:

```
import java.rmi.RemoteException;
import java.rmi.server.UnicastRemoteObject;
public class GradingService extends UnicastRemoteObject implements SchoolGrades {
      public GradingService() throws RemoteException { super() };
      public int getAverageGrade() { return 0; }
      }
```

The GradingService class above implements the remote SchoolGrades interface, and also extends from java.rmi.server.UnicastRemoteObject (we will discover why we do this in the next section). As part of the obligation of implementing the SchoolGrades interface, it must have a method called getAverageGrade(), which is implemented trivially here.

In the definition of SchoolGrades interface, we notice that the getAverageGrade() method throws a java.rmi.RemoteException. Let's look at why all remote methods of a remote interface will throw this exception.

Exceptions in RMI

RMI provides a simple and structured way of dealing with what is potentially a very large set of exceptions.

Since any remote method call actually transforms to many lower-level network operations, a network error can occur anytime during the invocation. This is the reason why every single method on a remote interface throws a `java.rmi.RemoteException`. `java.rmi.RemoteException` is a subclass of `java.io.IOException`, which in turn is an immediate subclass of `java.lang.Exception` – this implies that all `java.rmi.RemoteExceptions` must be explicitly handled in our code (unlike subclasses of `java.lang.RuntimeException`). This explains all the `try` and `catch` blocks around all the RMI-based activities.

In fact, there are many specialized subclasses of `java.rmi.RemoteException`. These can be used to obtain more detailed information on the exception condition. Interested readers should consult the JDK documentation for more detailed information.

Preparing Server Object for Remote Calls

In our discussion of RMI (and RPC) so far, we have always assumed that an RMI server is somehow ready and waiting to accept a remote call – without specifying how this happens.

Setting up remote objects to accept a remote call is akin to starting a socket based server listening on a `ServerSocket` object. In fact, when the transport is TCP/IP, this is exactly what is happening underneath.

When coding with RMI, however, we do not have to know the details. Under RMI, an object is ready to accept request as soon as it is "exported".

There are two generally accepted ways of exporting a remote object.

❑ Make sure it extends a subclass of `java.rmi.server.RemoteServer`. As of JDK 1.4 (currently a beta version), your choice will be either `java.rmi.server.UnicastRemoteObject` or `java.rmi.Activation.Activatable`.

❑ Explicitly export an instance using the static `exportObject()` method call of `java.rmi.server.UnicastRemoteObject`

Most of the time, you will be using the first alternative and extending `java.rmi.server.UnicastRemoteObject`. The super class will automatically export the instance upon construction. `UnicastRemoteObject`, as the name suggests, enables clients to connect one-to-one with server object instances. This is similar to a TCP based one-to-one connection (see Chapter 9).

`java.rmi.Activation.Activatable` is part of an advanced feature in the JDK enabling RMI objects to be activated "just in time" when a call arrives and to survive multiple system reset. Coverage of `java.rmi.Activation.Activatable` is outside the scope of this chapter. Interested readers should consult the Java 2 documentation and *Professional Java Server Programming J2EE edition, ISBN 1861004656 , Wrox Press.*

Generating Client and Server Side Marshaling Code

When programming in Java, all code is encapsulated in Java `.class` files. The code that is generated by RMI to marshal and unmarshal a remote call is no exception.

> **In RMI, the generated code on the client side to marshal the call parameters and unmarshal the return value is called a Stub. The generated code on the server side to unmarshal the call parameters, make the actual method call, and marshal the return value is called a Skeleton.**

Java RMI provides a command line tool, called `rmic` (RMI Compiler), for generating the Stub and Skeleton code. `rmic` scans the `.class` file of the remote object to generate the Stub and Skeleton code. The diagram below shows how `rmic` works.

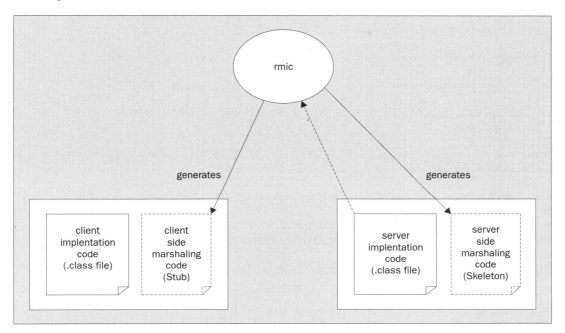

In this figure, we can see that `rmic` works by reading the binary remote object (server) implementation class file. It generates both the client and server side marshaling code (again in binary). These are the stub (on the client side) and the skeleton (on the server side) files. The client and server implementation code, written by the developer, works together with the generated code to form the distributed system. Unlike its RPC counterpart (the IDL Compiler that we have seen earlier), `rmic` does not read source files (IDL files) and does not generate source code. This approach alleviates many maintenance problems associated with generated source files.

> **Since JDK 1.2 and beyond, the generation of skeletons is no longer required. The RMI runtime on the server side will use introspection to dynamically create a skeleton during remote method call. However, all tools – including `rmic` – maintain compatibility with earlier JDK version by defaulting to the creation of pre-JDK 1.2 Skeletons. This is also a safe way of proceeding if you cannot be sure that all clients and servers that you will encounter are all JDK 1.2 or later. In this chapter, we will opt to generate both Stubs and Skeletons for completeness.**

Here is a typical invocation of `rmic`:

```
C:\Beg_Java_Networking\Ch16>javac com\wrox\rmi\simple\*.java
C:\Beg_Java_Networking\Ch16>rmic com.wrox.rmi.simple.GradingService
```

Running this on the trivial `GradingService` class that we have defined earlier, the following files will be generated in the C:\Beg_Java_Networking\Ch16\com\wrox\rmi\simple directory:

```
GradingService_Stub.class
GradingService_Skel.class
```

Notice that there are no corresponding source (.java) files. These are the automatically generated marshaling code that we discussed earlier.

To generate the skeletonless stubs of JDK 1.2+, then this command should be used:

C:\Beg_Java_Networking\Ch16>**rmic -v1.2 com.wrox.rmi.simple.GradingService**

Running this on the trivial class, only the stub is generated, since JDK versions later than 1.2 do not require the skeleton.

Other than the automatic generation of marshaling code, Java RMI also provides utilities to bootstrap a typical distributed application.

Bootstrapping refers to the act of "kick-starting" a system. Since a distributed application may involve many different machines, an "initial connection" must be made between all the machine pairs that will communicate. Translated to RMI-speak, there must be a way for a client to locate an initial remote object. This is provided through the command line RMI Registry utility.

Using rmiregistry To Locate Remote Objects

Exporting objects on the server side makes them accessible remotely, but the client must still somehow get in touch with these remote objects.

The RMI specification does not specify how this must be done. Instead, the JDK distribution provides a utility called the RMI Registry, executed using the rmiregistry command.

The rmiregistry utility maintains a mapping between a text name and a reference to a remote object for remote access (the reference is actually the stub for the remote object, as we shall see shortly).

In the client's coding, the RMI registry can be accessed programmatically via the static lookup() method of the same java.rmi.Naming class. Here's how a client may look up a remote GradingService instance, residing on the host named bigserver. Note the use of the remote SchoolGrade interface in referencing the instance:

```
SchoolGrades gServer = (SchoolGrades)
Naming.lookup("rmi://bigserver:1234/GradingService");
```

The above code assumes that rmiregistry is running on the bigserver machine at the default port of 1234. When the code executes successfully, gServer on the client will be referring to an instance of remote object, in this case an instance of our GradingService object – implementing the SchoolGrades interface.

Through the rmiregistry, we can locate an instance of a remote object via a URL such as:

rmi://bigserver:1234/GradingService

This URL specifies rmi as the protocol. It will attempt to locate the service through the rmiregistry listening at port 1234. Instead of using a hostname like bigserver, we can also use an IP address (such as, 28.122.33.1). The rmiregistry utility must be started on the server where the remote object to be located resides. One can think of rmiregistry as a minimalist naming service.

On the server side, an exported remote object can be registered with the locally running instance of the rmiregistry via the java.rmi.Naming library class. For example, we can use the rebind() method to associate (bind) an instance of a GradingService in gService with the name GradingService.

```
GradingService gService = new GradingService();
Naming.rebind("/GradingService", gService);
```

Note that the argument to rebind() is not the full URL, but only "/GradingService". Since the rmiregistry on the server must be running on the same node, this simplified URL path is accepted. In fact, the code becomes more flexible because the hostname is no longer hard-coded into the URL (as it is with the full URL) – allowing it to run anywhere without modification.

Underneath the rmiregistry Hood

To recap, SchoolGrades is a Java interface, therefore gServer is really a reference to an object instance (local) that implements the SchoolGrades interface. This local object instance is not the actual remote GradingService instance, of course. It is the "local representation" of the remote GradingService. In fact, it is a local instance of the Stub code – GradingService_Stub.class. Recall that the Stub code is the automatically generated client-side marshaling code (generated using rmic).

The diagram below illustrates how the remote object reference actually works:

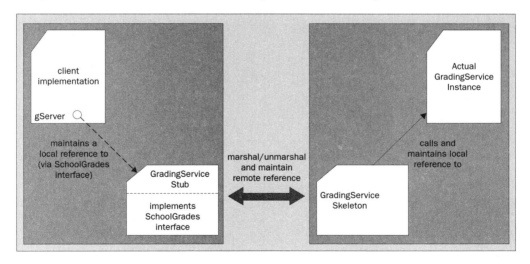

In the figure, we can see that the client implementation maintains a reference to the remote object via the gServer variable. In fact, we can see that the gServer variable is actually a local reference to an object that implements the SchoolGrades interface. This object is the GradingService Stub implementation. This Stub works in conjunction with the Skeleton on the server end to marshal/unmarshal all remote calls through the SchoolGrades interface. Furthermore, the current reference semantics is preserved through a distributed garbage collector (DGC) algorithm to ensure that the remote object is released when no longer referenced.

The DGC works just like the normal garbage collector, freeing up any instances that are no longer referenced, only it works across a set of distributed machines (or JVMs). The `GradingService` Skeleton on the server-side is actually maintaining a reference to an actual `GradingService` object instance – where the calls coming from the remote Stub are being directed to.

For all intents and purposes, we can work with `gServer` as if it is indeed a local instance that implements the `SchoolGrades` interface. The work performed underneath by the stub code makes this relatively transparent.

Distributed System Bootstrapping

We can observe, from the above analysis, two interesting facts:

❑ The RMI registry actually maps textual names to Stubs, and not directly to remote object instances

❑ A remote object reference through its Stub can be used as any regular object reference, and may – amongst other things – be passed in parameters and return values

The second point deserves more detailed examination. When we pass the remote object references to other objects on the client, those objects may in turn make use of the remote object (and be invoking remote methods) without having performed the object location process itself.

On the flip side, a method on the remote object may also pass other remote object references (actually stubs) as return values (acting like a kind of factory of remote object). This allows the client to access other remote objects without referring back to the initial bootstrap mechanism – the registry. This explains the "bootstrap" process: once a single remote object reference is obtained through the bootstrap mechanism, future remote interactions between the client and server need not depend on the mechanism. The "bootstrap" is used only to "kick-start" the system; this is illustrated in the figure opposite:

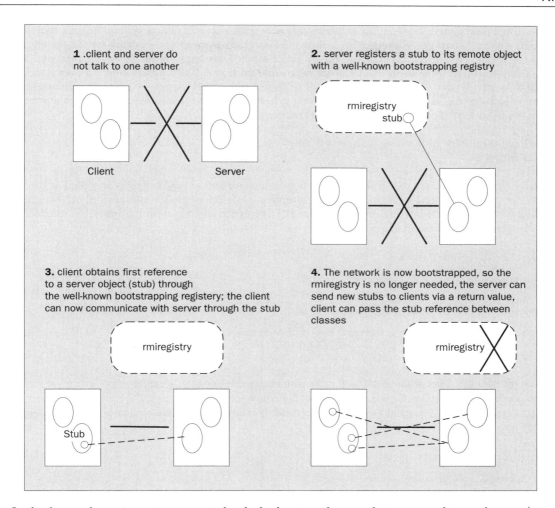

In the figure, the `rmiregistry` is vital only for locating the very first remote object reference (actually a stub that is registered earlier by the server). Once this initial reference is located, the system can be considered bootstrapped. This initial reference can be passed around to other objects within the client, and new remote references (stubs) may be returned from the server through the methods of the remote interface. There can be many other ways one may bootstrap the distributed system (such as, through a corporate directory service instead of `rmiregistry`), but the use of `rmiregistry` is the most straightforward for the purpose of this chapter.

At this point, we should be familiar with all the basic concepts of RMI, so it is a good time to put this new knowledge to work on a simple example.

A Simple School Grading System

This is our first RMI example so we'll keep it simple. Despite its simplicity, we will be able to cover the aspects of RMI interactions that we have discussed thus far.

The distributed system under study is a remotely accessible school grading system. From a remote client, we can obtain-grade average for a student. This grade average is calculated on-the fly when we run the client. The individual score on the different subjects are kept on the server. In practice, they are probably stored in some form of a database accessible through a JDBC connection – a Java standard for connecting to databases. In our case, in order to focus on the RMI aspects, we will artificially use a static integer array to represent the data. The grading system for each subject is assumed to be a number ranging from 0 (pathetic failure) to 10 (perfect score).

We have seen some of the code from this example in our discussions earlier. Here we will present them in its entirety.

First the remote interface that is the contract between client and remote object is specified as the com.wrox.rmi.simple.SchoolGrades interface. Note the single remote method on this interface, called getAverageGrade(), this will return the average grade based on the subject grade data stored on the server at the time of execution.

```java
// SchoolGrades.java

package com.wrox.rmi.simple;

import java.rmi.Remote;
import java.rmi.RemoteException;

public interface SchoolGrades extends Remote {
   int getAverageGrade() throws RemoteException;
}
```

Next, the remote object instance that will be implementing this interface is called com.wrox.rmi.simple.GradingService. Note how it extends java.rmi.server.UnicastRemoteObject and therefore instances of it will be automatically exported upon creation.

```java
// GradingService.java

package com.wrox.rmi.simple;

import java.rmi.Naming;
import java.rmi.RemoteException;
import java.rmi.server.UnicastRemoteObject;

public class GradingService extends UnicastRemoteObject
   implements SchoolGrades {

   static int subjectGrades[];
   static {
     subjectGrades = new int[3];
     subjectGrades[0] = 10;
     subjectGrades[1] = 1;
     subjectGrades[2] = 3;
   }

   public GradingService() throws RemoteException {
     super();
   }

   public int getAverageGrade() {
     System.out.println("GradingService: computing average grade");
```

```
    int numOfSubjects = subjectGrades.length;
    int sumOfAllSubjects = 0;
    for (int i = 0; i < numOfSubjects; i++) {
      sumOfAllSubjects += subjectGrades[i];
    }
    return (sumOfAllSubjects / numOfSubjects);
  }

  public static void main(String args[]) {
    try {
      GradingService gService = new GradingService();

      Naming.rebind("/GradingService", gService);

      System.out.println("GradingService bound in registry");
    } catch (Exception e) {
      System.out.println("GradingService err: " + e.getMessage());
      e.printStackTrace();
    }
  }
}
```

We can also see how the subject grades are trivially implemented in the static `subjectGrades[]` integer array, and initialized using a static initializer. This array simulates a grades database for all the subjects, which is a read-only resource in this example. The remote method `getAverageGrade()` simply calculates the average across subjects. It will also print out a message that indicates the method had been invoked.

Finally, we can find the client code in the `com.wrox.rmi.simple.RemoteGetGrades` class. The hostname, `localhost`, in the `//localhost/GradingService` URL (the `rmi://` protocol is the default with `Naming.lookup()`) should be replaced with the name of the remote host where the actual `GradingService` instance is running.

```
// RemoteGetGrades.java

package com.wrox.rmi.simple;

import java.rmi.Naming;
import java.rmi.RemoteException;

public class RemoteGetGrades {
  static SchoolGrades gServer = null;
  public static void main(String args[]) {
    try {
      gServer = (SchoolGrades) Naming.lookup("//localhost/GradingService");
      System.out.println("Average grade is " + gServer.getAverageGrade()
                         + " out of 10");
    } catch (Exception e) {
      System.out.println("RemoteGetGrades exception: " + e.getMessage());
      e.printStackTrace();
    }
  }
}
```

The client code above will locate the GradingService with the help of java.rmi.Naming and assign the reference to gServer (the SchoolGrades remote interface). It will then invoke the remote method getAverageGrade() and print out the results. Other than the additional exception handling, note how the invocation syntax is identical to calling a local method. This is the programmatic transparency that we referred to earlier. The way RMI handles call parameters and return values (that is, the call semantics) varies slightly from conventional method calls. Let's take a look at the difference now.

Handling Parameters and Return Value in RMI

When a remote method is invoked, it may contain input arguments and may also return values. Unlike other RPC mechanisms, where the caller and callee may be implemented using different programming languages, there is no need to map the types of one programming language to another (or to an intermediate standard). With RMI, the caller and callee are both Java programs, and the types are preserved during any remote call.

However, supporting the standard local parameter passing semantics is not possible for remote calls. Non-primitive types are passed by reference with the standard convention; passing by reference is meaningless when performed across a network or multiple JVMs.

Instead, how RMI handles a specific parameter or return value depends on the following:

❑ The primitive value or object

❑ If it is an object, is it local or remote

As it is with the standard local semantics, all primitive types (int, bool, and so on) are passed by value.

If an object type is passed, and it is not a remote object, pass by value semantics are triggered. In this case, object serialization (see Chapter 15) is used to send the complete object (and all its dependant) across the network. This requires that the object instance being passed (and all its dependants) be serializable. In effect, a non-remote object is passed by reconstituting a copy of the object on the other machine.

If the object being passed is a remote object, only a stub of the object will be passed. This means that the remote object will continue to live on the same machine, while the other machine will now have a stub to interact with the object remotely. This mechanism can readily be used to create a new remote object for client access – without the rmiregistry.

Setting Up for RMI Experimentation

RMI is a built-in feature of the JDK since version 1.1. Therefore, as long as you have a working version of a JDK (1.1 or later) installed and running, you already have RMI ready to go.

If you have a network of two or more machines, you may want to try out the experimentation with this school grading system on two separate physical machines. For our discussions in the chapter, we will assume that we are using a single machine, and simply using basic TCP/IP loopback capabilities to simulate multiple machines.

You should have already compiled the source files for this example when we first introduced stubs and skeletons. If not, you should do so now. Since they are all part of the com.wrox.rmi.simple package, we can use the command line:

C:\Beg_Java_Networking\Ch16>**javac com/wrox/rmi/simple/*.java**

Generating Stubs and Skeletons with RMIC

Next, we will generate the stub and skeleton code with rmic. For this example we opt for JDK 1.1 compatibility and simply use the command line:

C:\Beg_Java_Networking\Ch16>**rmic com.wrox.rmi.simple.GradingService**

Packaging the Client and Server Distributions

With the code compiled, we need to decide what goes to the client distribution and what goes to the server distribution. We will need the following on the client:

File	Description
RemoteGetGrades.class	The actual client logic itself
SchoolGrades.class	The remote interface that the client will use for referencing instances of the remote grading service
GradingService_Stub.class	The marshaling code that is generated by rmic, this is the stub that the client will work with locally to represent the remote instance

That is all that needs to go on the client. There is no need to include the GradingService_Skel.class since it is used on the server side to unmarshal the call. Including GradingService.class is unnecessary, since we wish to call the object remotely.

We can package all of these class files into a RemoteClient.jar file using the command line:

C:\Beg_Java_Networking\Ch16>**jar cvf RemoteClient.jar
com/wrox/rmi/simple/RemoteGetGrades.class com/wrox/rmi/simple/SchoolGrades.class
com/wrox/rmi/simple/GradingService_Stub.class**

If this has worked you should see the following output:

added manifest
adding: com/wrox/rmi/simple/RemoteGetGrades.class(in = 1193) (out= 670)(deflated 43%)
adding: com/wrox/rmi/simple/SchoolGrades.class(in = 233) (out= 176)(deflated 24%)
adding: com/wrox/rmi/simple/GradingService_Stub.class(in = 2952) (out= 1485)(deflated 49%)

On the server, we must install the following code:

File	Description
GradingService.class	The remote object logic itself, implementing the methods of the SchoolGrades interface
SchoolGrades.class	Definition of the remote interface that is used to access the service remotely

Table continued on following page

File	Description
GradingService_Skel.class	The unmarshaling code generated by rmic (not required in JDK 1.2+ only installations), used on server side to handle the remote call
GradingService_Stub.class	This is somewhat of a surprise, as it is client-side marshaling code. However, this is what is passed to the rmiregistry (a stub) when the GradingService registers itself with the registry

We can bundle the above classes into a GradeService.jar archive using the command line:

C:\Beg_Java_Networking\Ch16>**jar cvf GradeService.jar**
com\wrox\rmi\simple\GradingService.class com\wrox\rmi\simple\SchoolGrades.class
com\wrox\rmi\simple\GradingService_Stub.class
com\wrox\rmi\simple\GradingService_Skel.class

which will generate the following output on the screen and place the file GradeService.jar in the current directory.

```
added manifest
adding: com/wrox/rmi/simple/GradingService.class(in = 1342) (out= 788)(deflated 41%)
adding: com/wrox/rmi/simple/SchoolGrades.class(in = 233) (out= 176)(deflated 24%)
adding: com/wrox/rmi/simple/GradingService_Stub.class(in = 2952) (out= 1485)(deflated 49%)
adding: com/wrox/rmi/simple/GradingService_Skel.class(in = 1430) (out= 824)(deflated 42%)
```

This completes all the setup for our first RMI experiment. Now we need to start each of the following in order:

1. The rmiregistry

2. The server

3. The client

Starting the RMIRegistry

From the code directory, you can type in:

C:\Beg_Java_Networking\Ch16>**start rmiregistry**

This will start an instance of the rmiregistry running quietly in its own console window.

Starting the Server

Start the server using the following command:

C:\Beg_Java_Networking\Ch16>**start java -classpath GradeService.jar**
com.wrox.rmi.simple.GradingService

This will start the GradingService. The service will create an instance of the GradingService remote object and register it with the registry. At this time, it is ready for client requests. It will report its progress on the console, which just after starting the service should contain:

GradingService bound in registry

This message is printed by the server once the remote object is exported and waiting for client invocations.

Starting the Client

To start the client service enter the following at the command line:

C:\Beg_Java_Networking\Ch16>**java -classpath RemoteClient.jar com.wrox.rmi.simple.RemoteGetGrades**

At this point, the client will locate the grading service via the rmiregistry, and then make the remote call to calculate the grade average.

The output in the window should be:

Average grade is 4 out of 10

It is important to realize what has happened, the client-initiated grade average calculation is completed on the server then the return value is marshaled back to the client for display. To prove this to yourself, look on the server console window, you should see an indication of the successful call:

GradingService bound in registry
GradingService: computing average grade

The message above, GradingService: computing average grade, is an output from inside the getAverageGrade() method implemented in the server. The remote method invocation from the client has triggered its printing.

Improving the School Grading System

Shortly after our school grading system went online, we discovered that our users in the school require radically different ways of calculating the average grade points. Unfortunately, the existing grading system has the grade point averaging algorithm built right into the server – and cannot be easily changed.

This offers us a chance to show off a versatile feature of RMI, illustrating how we can transfer behavior (code) and data in the same remote method invocation. Using any other RPC technology, our only solution would be to implement multiple algorithms on the server and select between them at the time of the remote call. This is shown overleaf:

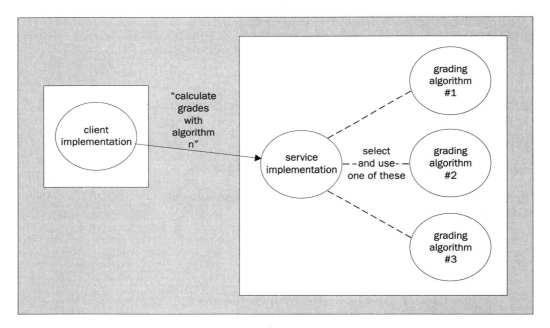

In the figure, the client will request a specific algorithm to be used whenever a grade average computation is required. The client must have full knowledge of the algorithms that are available (and will need to be kept up to date on this list). In addition, all of the algorithms required by the potential client must be kept on the server.

This solution is adequate, but not necessarily the best. For one thing, even algorithms that may only be used for one single time must be coded and maintained on the server. Also, with time, the number of different algorithms that must be maintained with the server may grow to a very large number.

With RMI, however, there is an alternative solution. We can allow the users themselves to supply their own custom grade points calculating algorithms! That is, each and every call to the grading server can use a completely different algorithm to calculate the grade point. This is flexibility in system design that is unique to the 100% Java RMI mechanism, opposed to other RPC mechanisms where multiple programming languages must be catered for. Since both the client and server are running Java, we can take advantage of Java's built-in dynamic class loading capability – and have the server load the required algorithm class during runtime! The figure opposite illustrates this design:

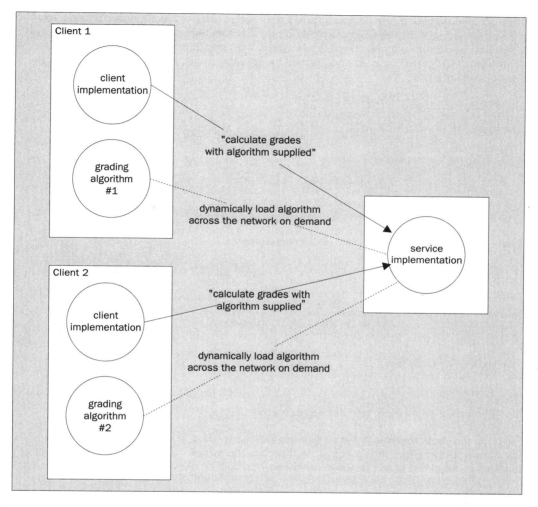

In this figure, both `client 1` and `client 2` have different grading requirements. When a client makes the request to the server, it specifies that it will supply its own grading algorithm. Actually, it will supply an instance of a grading algorithm object that will implement a well-known interface. Once the remote service receives the call, and starts to use the algorithm in computing the grade point, the required code will be dynamically loaded across the network from the client. In this way, the server does not have to maintain any grading algorithm, and the clients have full control over how the grades are calculated – a win/win design.

Let us now modify our Simple Grading System to reflect this new design.

Redefining the Remote Interface

Instead of the `com.wrox.rmi.simple` package, we'll create this new and improved system under its own `com.wrox.rmi.flex` package.

In this upgraded system, the remote interface is `com.wrox.rmi.flex.FlexSchoolGrades`. Note that the `getAverageGrade()` remote method now takes an argument. This is the actual algorithm class that will be used to calculate the average grade. The only thing that this interface specifies is that the algorithm class, passed in as an argument to the `getAverageGrade()` method, will support the `GradeScheme` interface.

```
// FlexSchoolGrades.java

package com.wrox.rmi.flex;

import java.rmi.Remote;
import java.rmi.RemoteException;

public interface FlexSchoolGrades extends Remote {
   public int getAverageGrade(GradeScheme customScheme)
          throws RemoteException;
}
```

And here is the definition of the `GradeScheme` interface:

```
// GradeScheme.java

package com.wrox.rmi.flex;

public interface GradeScheme {
   public int computeAverage(int[] SubjectScores);
}
```

We can see that the interface:

❑   Is not remote

❑   Has only one method; `computeAverage()`

It is important to note that it is not remote, therefore the method `computeAverage()` will be executed on the same machine where it is invoked. In this case, the method will be invoked by the remote object on the server – therefore it will be executed there.

Code Movement Via Dynamic Class Loading

Now, we have defined two different algorithms (or schemes) of computing averages. Each of these schemes is represented by a separate Java class. The first one is called `com.wrox.rmi.flex.AverageScheme`. The actual algorithm used here is identical to the one in the first cut of our grading system.

```
// AverageScheme.java
package com.wrox.rmi.flex;
public class AverageScheme implements GradeScheme, java.io.Serializable {
   public int computeAverage(int[] subjectScores) {
      int numOfSubjects = subjectScores.length;
      int sumOfAllSubjects = 0;
      for (int i = 0; i < numOfSubjects; i++) {
         sumOfAllSubjects += subjectScores[i];
      }
      return (sumOfAllSubjects / numOfSubjects);
```

```
      }
   }
```

Note that object serialization (covered in Chapter 15) will be the mechanism through which an instance of a `GradeScheme` supporting class will be transmitted from the client to the server. This is why any `GradeScheme` supporting class must also implement the `java.io.Serializable` interface.

The other alternative-grading scheme is a weighted average. In this case, the first subject has twice the weight of all the rest of the subjects during the calculation. The code for this algorithm is encapsulated in the `com.wrox.rmi.flex.WeightedScheme` class:

```java
// WeightedScheme.java

package com.wrox.rmi.flex;

public class WeightedScheme implements GradeScheme, java.io.Serializable {

   public int computeAverage(int[] subjectScores) {

      int numOfSubjects = subjectScores.length;
      int sumOfAllSubjects = 0;
      sumOfAllSubjects += 2 * subjectScores[0];
      for (int i = 1; i < numOfSubjects; i++) {
         sumOfAllSubjects += subjectScores[i];
      }
      return (sumOfAllSubjects / (numOfSubjects + 1));

   }
}
```

Note how the first subject is counted twice in the above algorithm. Note also that it is a serializable class and implements the `GradeScheme` interface. As long as the object instance is referred to via the `GradeScheme` interface, `AverageScheme` or `WeightedScheme` instances can be interchanged without affecting the calling code. This is the mechanism that we will take advantage of in our server design.

The actual remote object code is in `com.wrox.rmi.flex.FlexGradingService`:

```java
// FlexGradingService.java

package com.wrox.rmi.flex;

import java.rmi.Naming;
import java.rmi.RemoteException;
import java.rmi.RMISecurityManager;
import java.rmi.server.UnicastRemoteObject;

public class FlexGradingService extends UnicastRemoteObject
   implements FlexSchoolGrades {

   static int subjectGrades[];
   static {
      subjectGrades = new int[3];
      subjectGrades[0] = 10;
      subjectGrades[1] = 1;
      subjectGrades[2] = 3;
   }

   public FlexGradingService() throws RemoteException {
      super();
```

```
        }
    public int getAverageGrade(GradeScheme customScheme) {
        System.out.println("GradingService: computing average grade using "
                           + customScheme.getClass().getName());
        return (customScheme.computeAverage(subjectGrades));
    }

    public static void main(String args[]) {
        if (System.getSecurityManager() == null) {
            System.setSecurityManager(new RMISecurityManager());
        }

        try {

            FlexGradingService gService = new FlexGradingService();

            Naming.rebind("/FlexGradingService", gService);

            System.out.println("FlexGradingService bound in registry");
        } catch (Exception e) {
            System.out.println("FlexGradingService err: " + e.getMessage());
            e.printStackTrace();
        }
    }
}
```

While similar to the structure of the GradingService class, we can note two distinct differences:

❑   The code now installs an RMISecurityManager instance

❑   The logic of the remote method, getAverageGrade(), is significantly different

Let's examine the latter point first. Here is the new getAverageGrade() coding reproduced in isolation:

```
    public int getAverageGrade(GradeScheme customScheme) {
        System.out.println("GradingService: computing average grade using "
                           + customScheme.getClass().getName());
        return (customScheme.computeAverage(subjectGrades));
    }
```

This method no longer contains the algorithm to calculate the average. Instead, the object that contains the algorithm is passed in as an input parameter. The grade point average is computed by calling the computeAverage() method of the incoming algorithm object. All we know about the object passed in is that it supports the GradeScheme interface – therefore assuring that the computeAverage() call is safe.

There is no knowledge in advance what the actual class of the object is. In fact, the class will be dynamically loaded when we call its computeAverage() implementation if the JVM has not yet loaded its definition.

Note also the use of getClass().getName() to print out the class name of the actual object being passed in. We can reliably do this because all object instances in Java are subclasses of the java.Object class (which support the getClass() method).

Before examining the client code, let us take a break and discuss the additional need of the RMISecurityManager in this code.

Java 2 Security Model and RMI

Taking the standpoint of the server, one realizes that it is executing code (such as the `computeAverage()` method of `AverageScheme`) without knowing in advance of what it may do. This is surely a potential security loophole! And indeed it is. But in our specific case, this is exactly what we wanted to happen – potentially a different grade point averaging algorithm on each call.

Under the Java 2 security model, both application and applets are treated uniformly. It is not possible, without setting explicit permission, for an application to download foreign code and execute them.

Maintaining compatibility with the Java 1.x security model, the checking of permission can be performed via an instance of `RMISecurityManager`. In fact, the Java 2 implementation of the `RMISecurityManager` will delegate to the `AccessController` class of the Java 2 security system to check permission.

This is the precise reason that we supply an explicit security policy file (called `flex.policy` in our case) to expressly permit this type of promiscuous execution. Our `flex.policy` file contains the following:

```
grant {
    permission java.security.AllPermission;
};
```

This policy file effectively disables permission checking, by granting all access. This will enable us to proceed without diving into the detailed facets of Java 2 Security (see Chapter 7 for a detailed discussion). Obviously, a more restrictive policy file should be used when working in a production environment.

Computing Grades with a Client-Supplied Algorithm

The new client code can be found in `com.wrox.rmi.flex.FlexGetGrades`. This code will by default supply the `AverageScheme` algorithm unless a `-w` switch is used to tell it to use the `WeightedScheme` algorithm.

```java
// FlexGetGrades.java

package com.wrox.rmi.flex;
import java.rmi.Naming;
import java.rmi.RemoteException;

public class FlexGetGrades {

  static FlexSchoolGrades gServer = null;

  public static void main(String args[]) {
    GradeScheme myCustScheme = null;
    try {
      gServer =
        (FlexSchoolGrades) Naming.lookup("//localhost/FlexGradingService");
      if ((args.length > 0) && (args[0].equals("-w"))) {
        myCustScheme = new WeightedScheme();
      } else {
        myCustScheme = new AverageScheme();
      }
```

```
        System.out.println("Average grade is "
                        + gServer.getAverageGrade(myCustScheme) + "out of 10");
    } catch (Exception e) {
        System.out.println("FlexGetGrades exception: " + e.getMessage());
        e.printStackTrace();
    }
  }
}
```

The client uses the `Naming.lookup()` static method to access the `FlexGradingService` stub that implements the `FlexSchoolGrades` remote interface as before. It then checks for the –w switch. A new instance of the `WeightedScheme` is created if it is found; otherwise, a new instance of `AverageScheme` is created. In either case, the algorithm is passed to the remote object via the `getAverageGrade()` method. Since the algorithm instances are non-remote objects, they will be passed by value. The remote object will then use the selected algorithm to calculate the average grade and the returned average is printed out.

Compiling the Flexible Grading System

Use the following command line to compile the source files, and generate the stub and skeletons:

C:\Beg_Java_Networking\Ch16>**javac com\wrox\rmi\flex*.java**
C:\Beg_Java_Networking\Ch16>**rmic com.wrox.rmi.flex.FlexGradingService**

Next, we need to package up the code for the client, and the server. Here are the files required on the client:

File Name	Description
FlexGetGrades.class	The actual client logic
FlexSchoolGrades.class	The remote interface used in referencing the remote FlexGradingService instance
FlexGradingService_Stub.class	The rmic generated stub for accessing the remote FlexGradingService
GradingScheme.class	Definition of the non-remote interface for algorithms
AverageScheme.class	Algorithm for calculating grade averages
WeightedScheme.class	Alternative algorithm for calculating grade averages

And here are the classes required on the server:

File Name	Description
FlexGradingService.class	The implementation of the server-side remote object logic
FlexSchoolGrades.class	The remote interface definition

File Name	Description
`FlexGradingService_Skel.class`	rmic generated server-side marshaling skeleton code
`FlexGradingService_Stub.class`	rmic generated client-side stub code, used in registration with `rmiregistry`
`GradingScheme.class`	Definition of the non-remote interface for algorithms
`flex.policy`	Security policy file to allow execution of the downloaded code

We can create a `FlexGradeService.jar` file and `FlexRemoteClient.jar` file using the following commands:

```
C:\Beg_Java_Networking\Ch16>jar cvf FlexGradeService.jar
com\wrox\rmi\flex\FlexGradingService.class com\wrox\rmi\flex\FlexSchoolGrades.class
com\wrox\rmi\flex\FlexGradingService_Stub.class
com\wrox\rmi\flex\FlexGradingService_Skel.class com\wrox\rmi\flex\GradeScheme.class
```

```
C:\Beg_Java_Networking\Ch16>jar cvf FlexRemoteClient.jar
com\wrox\rmi\flex\FlexGetGrades.class com\wrox\rmi\flex\FlexSchoolGrades.class
com\wrox\rmi\flex\FlexGradingService_Stub.class com\wrox\rmi\flex\GradeScheme.class
com\wrox\rmi\flex\AverageScheme.class com\wrox\rmi\flex\WeightedScheme.class
```

To make the code/behavior movement more obvious, we will use the HTTP server created in Chapter 13 for servicing the on-demand loading of the grading algorithm classes. The directory where we will be placing the two algorithms, bundled in a JAR archive, is C:\Beg_Java_Networking\Ch13; you can modify the location according to where you may have installed the HTTP server. We can use the following command line:

```
C:\Beg_Java_Networking\Ch16>jar cvf C:\Beg_Java_Networking\Ch13\client-dl.jar
com\wrox\rmi\flex\AverageScheme.class com\wrox\rmi\flex\WeightedScheme.class
```

Testing the Flexible Grading System

To test the new grading system, we must start the following in order:

1. The `rmiregistry`

2. An HTTP server to support code movement

3. The server

4. The client

Starting the rmiregistry

We can start the `rmiregistry` using the command line:

```
C:\Beg_Java_Networking\Ch16>start rmiregistry
```

Starting the HTTP Server To Support Code Movement

Next, we need to start an HTTP server that can be used when the server attempts to download the algorithm from the client. Protocols such as `ftp://` or `file:///` (shared files) are supported, however HTTP is the most frequently used.

Assuming that we have Chapter 13's server file installed in the C:\Beg_Java_Networking\Ch13 directory, we should edit the `httpd.properties` file to set the mandatory paths:

```
# httpd.properties 1.0
# Configuration file for HTTPServer
# Where filenames are specified, you must use forward slashes.

######################
# Mandatory settings #
######################
# Port at which HTTPServer listens for incoming requests (default 80)
Port=1234
# The directory out of which you will serve your documents
DocumentRoot=C:/Beg_Java_Networking/Ch13

# Default document that is looked for when a directory is requested
DirectoryIndex=index.html

# Log file where errors and accesses are logged
LogFile=C:/Beg_Java_Networking/Ch13/httpserver.log

# Directory on server where CGI scripts are stored
CGIPath=C:/Beg_Java_Networking/Ch13/cgi-bin
```

Next, we can start the HTTP server from the C:\Beg_Java_Networking\Ch13 directory (or wherever you may have installed your server) using the command:

C:\Beg_Java_Networking\Ch13>**java com.wrox.httpserver.HTTPServer httpd**
HTTPServer - enter Q or q to quit>

This will start an HTTP server listening at port 1234 and serving the files contained in the C:/Beg_Java_Networking/Ch13 directory. Note that this is where we have placed our `client-dl.jar` file previously, containing the two algorithm implementations.

Starting the Server

Now use the following command to start the server:

C:\Beg_Java_Networking>**start java -Djava.security.policy=flex.policy -classpath FlexGradeService.jar com.wrox.rmi.flex.FlexGradingService**

Note the use of the `java.security.policy` system property to specify the policy file to use. In this case, the `flex.policy` file grants all permissions, including the permission that we need – dynamic class loading from a foreign host.

The server will start in its own console window, which should contain the following line:

FlexGradingService bound in registry

Starting the Client

Finally, we are ready to start the client using the following command:

C:\Beg_Java_Networking\Ch16>**java -Djava.rmi.server.codebase=http://localhost:1234/client-dl.jar -classpath FlexRemoteClient.jar com.wrox.rmi.flex.FlexGetGrades -w**

Note that we are defining the `java.rmi.server.codebase` property. This will set the CODEBASE for the algorithm class that we will be passing from the client to the server. It tells the server where to find the class definition file. In this case, we have pointed it to the HTTP server that we have just set up. You may need to modify the hostname from `localhost` to your own hostname. Also note that we have used the `-w` switch to specify the `WeightedScheme` algorithm. Running the client will result in the display of the weighted average of the subjects, as shown below.

C:\Beg_Java_Networking\Ch16>**java -Djava.rmi.server.codebase=http://localhost:1234/client-dl.jar -classpath FlexRemoteClient.jar com.wrox.rmi.flex.FlexGetGrades -w**
Average grade is 6 out of 10

Let's pause for moment to think about what has happened. The client asked the server to compute the grade average, and passed in an instance of `WeightedScheme`. The server only knows that the object passed in supports the `FlexSchoolGrades` interface, and does not really care if it is a `WeightedScheme` instance. When the server computes the average, it calls a method of the `FlexSchoolGrades` interface, and the underlying `WeightedScheme` class is dynamically loaded across the network (or across two JVMs on the same machine via TCP/IP loopback) from the CODEBASE, which we have set pointed to our HTTP server.

If you look at the server console, you will see that it has indeed computed the average using the `WeightedScheme` algorithm (a class that is not local):

FlexGradingService bound in registry
GradingService: computing average grade using com.wrox.rmi.flex.WeightedScheme

The message from the server clearly indicates that it has used the `com.wrox.rmi.flex.WeightedScheme` to calculate the grade average. This class has been dynamically downloaded from our HTTP server. You can find evidence of this if you look at the log file produced by the HTTP server. In our case, we have specified the log file to be `C:\Beg_Java_Networking\Ch13\httpserver.log`. It should contain a record that shows the `client-dl.jar` file has been downloaded by the server. Note that you may have to quit the HTTP server before you see this record; as the HTTP server may need to flush the log output.

```
127.0.0.1-[21 Aug 2001 01:40:05 GMT]-GET /client-dl.jar HTTP/1.1-200
```

Now, try again using a different algorithm. Use the following command to invoke the client:

C:\Beg_Java_Networking\Ch16>**java -Djava.rmi.server.codebase=http://localhost:1234/client-dl.jar -classpath FlexRemoteClient.jar com.wrox.rmi.flex.FlexGetGrades**

This will calculate the grade average using the `AverageScheme` algorithm, since the `-w` switch is not specified, resulting in an average grade point of only 4:

Average grade is 4 out of 10

You should also check the server console and the HTTP server console to see that indeed the `com.wrox.rmi.flex.AverageScheme` algorithm had been dynamically downloaded and used in the calculation.

Other Distributed Solutions

The Java 2 platform supports distributed computing in many ways. For 100% Java system where the networking code is created from scratch, the use of technologies such as RMI and socket-based programming is more than sufficient. However, in production scenarios where the Java based subsystem coexists with non-Java systems, an alternative approach must be taken. Thankfully, the Java 2 platform supports an industry standard way of communicating with legacy systems – including mainframe computers and other non-Java servers. The next chapter will show how distributed computing may be carried out using Java 2 support for the CORBA standard.

Summary

In this chapter, we have taken a hands-on tour through the world of distributed computing using Java RMI.

We have seen how RPC concepts are fundamental to the operation of RMI. The unit of distributed work is a procedure/method. The client and server-programming contract is based on an interface. The code that performs the low-level marshaling work is automatically generated. We appreciate how this can be superior to lower-level socket-based programming for many applications.

Creating our own RMI based school grading system, we have witnessed how to declare a remote interface, make a server object remote invocation ready, and code a client application to access the remote object. Along the way, we have worked with the `rmic` tool that generates stub and skeleton code for marshaling of calls; as well as the `rmiregistry` utility that enables us to bootstrap a distributed RMI system.

When improving our school grading system for more flexibility, the unique 100% Java nature of RMI enabled us to combine object serialization with remote procedure invocation to create potent new features. Specifically, we upgraded the school grading system to support "behavior transfer". This enables the client to supply the grading algorithm to the server at the time of remote invocation. The ability for code, as well as data, to move across a remote call is unique (currently) to RMI, unmatched by other RPC or RPC-like mechanisms.

CORBA

In the last chapter, we looked at RMI, which enabled us to access objects remotely. As we will see, Common Object Request Broker Architecture (CORBA) provides several benefits not available when using Java's RMI, most notably that client applications and objects can be written in different programming languages. By eliminating the restriction of a pure Java solution, programmers can more easily integrate applications and components into their distributed applications.

In this chapter we will:

- ❏ Give an overview so that programmers new to CORBA can develop an understanding of its fundamental concepts
- ❏ See how the lines between CORBA and Java's native RMI have blurred with the introduction of **RMI-IIOP** (**Remote Method Invocation over Internet Inter-ORB Protocol**)

CORBA Overview

CORBA is a specification for a distributed application framework. Developed by the Object Management Group (OMG), CORBA, along with other OMG specifications such as CORBA's "over-the-wire" protocol, the Internet Inter-ORB Protocol (IIOP), provides a vendor-independent architecture for distributed object computing. At the time of writing, the current specification version is 2.4.2. The complete specifications are available from the OMG at http://www.omg.org/technology/documents/formal/. For more general starting questions, try http://www.omg.org/gettingstarted/corbafaq.htm.

There are a few common misconceptions that tend to make learning and understanding CORBA much more difficult than it needs to be, so let's dispel them right away. Firstly, CORBA is not a programming language like Java or C++. CORBA is a specification, a definition of an application framework that was designed to simplify and standardize distributed object development. When building an application using CORBA, client and object development is still done in your programming language of choice.

There is one restriction: the language you choose must have a mapping defined between itself and the OMG's Interface Definition Language, which we will see shortly.

Secondly, CORBA is not a product of a particular vendor. In fact, it is quite the opposite. The OMG consists of over 800 member companies. Currently, there are both commercial and public domain implementations of CORBA available from many different vendors.

Another popular misconception is that CORBA is strictly a competitor of Java's RMI. As we will see in the final section of this chapter, CORBA and RMI used in combination can provide a more powerful application framework than is achievable using either one on its own.

In general, distributed applications built using the CORBA architecture enjoy several benefits:

- ❏ **Language independence**
  Clients and objects can interact regardless of the programming language used to implement each, provided that the programming languages have defined mappings to the OMG's Interface Definition Language (IDL). Currently the OMG has defined mappings for Java, C, C++, SmallTalk, Ada, Lisp, COBOL, Python, and IDLscript.

- ❏ **Location transparency**
  Clients and objects are not directly aware of each others' locations within the network, allowing relocation of one (or both) with no impact on the other.

- ❏ **Support for heterogeneous networks**
  Due to the platform-independence of the CORBA architecture and support from many different vendors, CORBA-compliant products and frameworks exist for most operating systems and hardware platforms, allowing CORBA applications to span many different types of systems, from small, handheld devices to mainframes.

- ❏ **Interoperability**
  Clients and objects running within different vendors' ORBs can communicate just as if they were located within the same ORB.

Before we discuss the CORBA architecture, let's first consider an object that resides within an application. The object provides access to its functionality through its **interface**. The object's interface is simply the collection of public methods and attributes that the object implements to expose its functionality to clients. Any client that makes use of the object will do so through this interface, by invoking the object's public methods and accessing the object's public attributes:

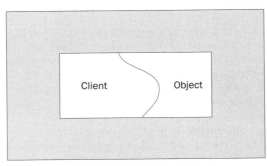

To create distributed objects in an *n*-tier application, we need to separate our objects from the client applications that contain them. Most distributed object frameworks use the same approach to enable this separation, which is based on the object's interface. Using the interface of the object, two new pieces of code are generated:

❏ A **stub** or **client stub** used in place of the object in the client application

❏ A **skeleton** or **server stub** included in a new server-side application that the programmer will create to contain the object

This new code effectively sits between the client and object and passes invocations on the object's interface back and forth between the client application and the new server application:

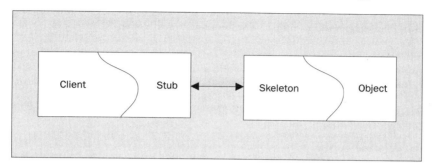

On the client side, the stub exposes the same interface as the original object. As a result, the client is unaware that the object now resides in a different process. When the client interacts with the stub through the interface, the stub takes the details of the interaction (which method was invoked, what parameters were provided, etc.), packages them into a message, called a **request**, and sends it across the network to the skeleton. The stub then waits for a return message, called a **reply**, from the skeleton.

On the server side, the server skeleton receives the request message and extracts the details of the client's interaction with the stub. Once this is complete, the skeleton invokes the correct method on the object, passing the parameters that were extracted from the request message. Any return values or exceptions thrown from the object are packaged into a new message, the reply. The reply is then sent back to the client stub. The client stub extracts the information from the reply message and returns it back to the client application:

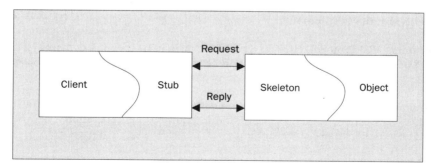

The key to the success of the interaction is that the client stub and the object expose the same interface. This allows the stub and skeleton to process any method invocations that the object can handle, passing the correct parameters. This also allows the skeleton and stub to return the correct return types and possible exceptions that the client is expecting.

CORBA follows basically the same approach with a few modifications. Let's first look at the different parts of the CORBA framework. The CORBA framework consists of three major parts:

❑ The **Interface Definition Language** (**IDL**)

❑ The **Object Request Broker** (**ORB**)

❑ The **Internet Inter-ORB Protocol** (**IIOP**)

The Interface Definition Language (IDL) is a programming-language independent language created by the Object Management Group for defining interfaces of distributed objects. The term 'programming-language independent' means that we can define our interface, using IDL, without being concerned with the programming language used to implement the object or the client(s).

> **In conjunction with IDL, the OMG has defined IDL-to-language mappings, allowing an IDL interface to be mapped into a particular programming language. Once an IDL interface has been defined, the interface is compiled using an IDL-to-language compiler, generally provided by the ORB vendor, to generate the stub and/or skeleton in the target programming language.**

With these mappings, a given IDL interface can be compiled using an **IDL compiler** to generate client stubs and server skeletons in a target programming language. Using IDL compilers for different target languages, interfaces defined in IDL along with the IDL-to-language mappings permit clients written in one programming language to access objects written in different programming languages.

The Object Request Broker (ORB) is the CORBA software product that is used when constructing distributed application components. The ORB's primary responsibility is to facilitate the creation and transmission of request and reply messages that occur between clients and objects (from client stub to server skeleton). The ORB also provides functionality to the client and object directly for manipulating references to remote objects and acquiring references to commonly used services. The ORB is usually implemented as a set of libraries (or packages) included within each distributed application client and object server. In addition, some ORB implementations also include daemon processes (software services that run behind the scenes to support the distributed application) that are used for object location and/or launching of remote server processes. One of the most important properties of an ORB product is the level of CORBA specification compliance that is provided. This level of compliance guarantees the functionality that the ORB provides.

The Internet Inter-ORB Protocol (IIOP) is a protocol, defined by the Object Management Group, which is used by ORBs to send messages back and forth between clients and objects. IIOP is actually the TCP/IP version of a more generic OMG-defined protocol named GIOP, the General Inter-ORB Protocol. All CORBA 2.0-compliant ORBs must have the ability to communicate using IIOP. Since IIOP is a vendor-independent protocol, any two ORB products that are 2.0 compliant can communicate with each other. This feature of the 2.0 specifications, known as **interoperability**, allows a client using one ORB implementation to use objects running within a different ORB product.

Using CORBA as our distributed object framework, our theoretical example presented above would resemble the following:

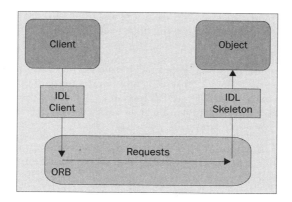

As in the approach described at the beginning of the chapter, the client and object communicate via a stub and skeleton. However, in CORBA, the stub and skeleton are generated from an IDL-defined interface, which provides us with an **IDL stub** and an **IDL skeleton**, commonly referred to as the stub and the skeleton. Also new to our conceptual view is the introduction of the ORB, which sits between the stub and skeleton and is responsible for the transmission of requests and responses as IIOP messages between client and server processes. The ORB also exposes an interface directly to the client and object for ORB initialization, acquiring references of commonly used services such as the Naming Service, and manipulation of CORBA object references, which are described below.

To create a distributed object using CORBA, the object's interface is first defined in IDL. From this IDL definition, the stub and skeleton source code are generated in the client's, and object's, programming language(s). For example, below is a simple interface named `Test` consisting of two methods, `method1()` and `method2()`, each taking two parameters, a `short` named `param1` and a `String` named `param2`. `method1` returns a `short` and `method2` returns a `String`. As you may have noticed, each parameter below is qualified with an 'in' label. We will examine this in detail later:

```
interface Test {
  short method1(in short param1, in string param2);
  string method2(in short param1, in string param2);
};
```

When a client wants to invoke methods on the remote object, it first obtains an **interoperable object reference**, also called an **IOR** or simply an **object reference**, for the remote object, also known as a **CORBA object**. (We discuss how an object reference is obtained in the *Object Location* section.) The object reference will be represented within the client as a local object (an instance of a class in the client's programming language), containing data that is used by the ORB to locate the remote object in the network.

The data contained within the object reference is considered **opaque**, meaning that its format and value is unimportant to the client's application-level code. The actual contents and format of the object reference data is defined by the OMG in the CORBA/IIOP specification to ensure that an object reference is **interoperable**, meaning that an IOR can be used to access the remote object from within any ORB framework, regardless of where the IOR was created. As mentioned above, the actual type of the object reference is defined in the client's programming language within the IDL client stub. The object reference will expose an interface that maps directly to the interface defined in the IDL (using the IDL-to-language mapping).

It may be helpful to think of an object reference as a proxy object for the remote object. Once obtained, the client application can invoke methods on the object reference (proxy object) just as if it was the actual object:

❑ For each invocation on the object reference by the client, the stub-defined object creates a CORBA-defined request object, providing any parameter data that is necessary, and passes the request object to the ORB. The ORB examines the object reference in order to locate the application that contains the remote object, creates an IIOP message, and sends it via the network to the server application.

❑ On the server side, the server application, on startup, creates an instance of the actual object and notifies the ORB that the object exists. The server application's ORB then waits for incoming client requests.

❑ When an IIOP message is received by the server application, the ORB extracts the method invocation data from the message. From the message, the ORB identifies the object that is the target of the method invocation and hands the invocation information to the IDL-generated skeleton of the CORBA object. The skeleton reads the message data, extracting the parameters, and then invokes the correct method, passing the parameters. The skeleton receives any return values or exceptions and creates the reply information including these return types and/or exceptions. This reply information is then returned to the ORB, which creates an IIOP message and sends it back to the client.

❑ The ORB at the client side, upon receiving the reply message, extracts the data from the IIOP message and passes it back to the stub-defined object reference. The stub then extracts the return data or exception from the reply and returns it back to the client application through the original IDL-to-language mapped interface.

We'll look at this in more detail below as we trace through a CORBA method invocation using a simple CORBA object and client.

Object Location

Before we can invoke operations on our CORBA object, our client must first obtain the CORBA object's object reference. The CORBA architecture provides several mechanisms that CORBA objects and their server applications can use to make their object references available to potential clients, namely:

❑ Using an object location service, such as the OMG Naming Service

❑ Recreating an object reference from its `String` form

❑ Receiving an object reference from another CORBA object, commonly referred to as a factory object

To begin with, let's discuss object location services.

Object Location Services

In general, an object location service is a software product that provides the ability to publish and retrieve object references. The most commonly used object location service is the OMG-defined Naming Service.

The OMG has defined a set of object services that are commonly used within distributed object systems. This set of services is called the CORBAServices. One of the most commonly used of these services is the Naming Service.

Simply put, the Naming Service is a repository for storing CORBA object references. When a server application inserts an object reference into the Naming Service, it is required to also provide a name (unique within the Naming Service) that will be used to identify that object reference, similar to registering an EJB within a JNDI service. This object reference-name association is called a **binding**. Once the object reference is bound, client applications can query the Naming Service, providing a name and receiving the associated object reference, if one exists. In the event that an object reference is not associated with the name provided, an exception is returned indicating that the name was not found.

The Naming Service stores its object reference bindings in **naming contexts**. A naming context is a CORBA object that maintains a collection of zero or more object reference bindings and zero or more naming contexts. The recursive nature of the naming context allows the creation of a hierarchy of naming contexts, much like the directory structure of a file system where each directory can contain files and additional directories. By creating new naming contexts within existing contexts, it allows developers to segment the global object namespace, helping to alleviate the problem of name collisions. To begin with, the Naming Service contains a single naming context, called the **root** or **initial context**. When you first obtain an object reference for the Naming Service, it is actually the object reference of the root context. From there, additional contexts and object reference bindings can be added. When querying the Naming Service for an object reference, we will provide a list of names describing the navigation through the hierarchy of naming contexts of names, the last name in the list being the name of the object. We will see this in practice in our CORBA examples.

So, how is an object reference inserted into the Naming Service? Typically, the server application that contains the CORBA object is responsible for inserting it into the Naming Service. To do this, the server application must first obtain the object reference of the Naming Service's root context. It does this using a built-in mechanism of the ORB, namely the `resolve_initial_references()` method. Using this method, the server can obtain object references to several commonly used services, one of which is the Naming Service. The actual object references returned are determined within the configuration of the ORB product.

The client, using the same mechanism as the server, can now obtain the object reference of the Naming Service's root context and look up the object reference of its intended target CORBA object.

CORBA 3 will introduce a new Interoperable Name Service that will provide a URL-based method of accessing defined services on remote hosts. For example, a client application can obtain the object reference for a service, such as the Naming Service, running at http://www.abc.com *by specifying the following URL:* iioploc://www.abc.com/NameService.

Alternatively, queries can be made to a remote Naming Service directly through a second URL format. For example, to obtain the IOR of an object named `CheckingAccount` from the Naming Service running on http://www.abc.com, client applications can specify the following URL: iiopname://www.abc.com/CheckingAccount.

The second method that we can use to publish and retrieve object references is to store our CORBA object's object references in a data store in their `String` form.

Using an Object Reference's String Form

An object reference's `String` form is the contents of its internal data serialized into a string data type. An object reference is made into a `String` using a method in the ORB's interface called `object_to_string()`. Once in the `String` form, the object references can be stored in some form of data storage, such as a database record or file. When adding the object reference to the data store, it should be associated with some sort of a label or primary key, making it possible to retrieve it by querying the data store for that label. When a client needs an object reference, it can obtain the object reference from the data store using the label and reconstruct the object reference from the string using another method of the ORB's interface, `string_to_object()`.

The third mechanism that a client may use to obtain an object reference is to invoke a method on a CORBA object that returns another object reference.

Using Another CORBA Object

This is possible because IDL interfaces can define attributes, parameter types, and return types that are themselves object references. This type of CORBA object, one that provides object references to other CORBA objects, is commonly referred to as a **factory object**, since it appears from the perspective of the client to create objects on demand. Obviously, this mechanism cannot be used unless the client has already obtained the object reference of the factory object, presumably through some other mechanism (as earlier).

In addition to these methods, many CORBA implementations provide their own non-CORBA-compliant object location mechanisms that will provide clients with object references.

A Simple CORBA Object and Client

Let's take a closer look at CORBA by building a simple example. We will then be able to trace the path of a method invocation from the client to the object and back.

There are several steps necessary to build a CORBA object and client. We will begin by examining the steps involved in developing the CORBA object and its containing application.

Defining the Interface

Before we can build the client or server applications, we must first define the IDL interface for the CORBA object. We'll use the simple IDL interface we saw earlier consisting of two methods, `method1()` and `method2()`:

```
interface Test {
  short method1(in short param1, in string param2);
  string method2(in short param1, in string param2);
};
```

To generate the stub and skeleton, we can use the IDL to Java compiler, `idlj`. If you have the 1.3 or above version of the J2SE SDK (JDK1.3 or above), `idlj` can be found in the `%JAVA_HOME%\bin` directory, as an executable file. It does not need to be added to your classpath.

To compile the IDL interface, assuming the file containing the IDL is named `Test.idl`, perform the following:

C:\Beg_Java_Networking\Ch17>**idlj –fall Test.idl**

The option **–fall** instructs the compiler to generate both the client stub and server skeleton. To create only one or the other, use the **–fclient** or **–fserver** options.

Compiling the IDL interface will generate several Java source files (all of which will be stored in the directory containing the `Test.idl` file):

Source File	Description
`Test.java`	This file defines a Java interface, `Test`, which is the object reference of our CORBA object (remote object). As with all CORBA object references in Java, `Test` extends the CORBA object reference base interface, `org.omg.CORBA.Object`. `Test` is an empty interface, but extends the `TestOperations` interface below.
`TestOperations.java`	The `TestOperations` interface defines the IDL-to-Java mapped operations of the IDL interface.
`_TestStub.java`	This represents the client stub. The `_TestStub` class is the actual data type of an object reference in the client application. It extends `org.omg.CORBA.portable.ObjectImpl`, which provides the default implementation for all object references, and implements interface `Test`, described above.
`_TestImplBase.java`	This represents the server skeleton. The `_TestImplBase` class provides an abstract base class for object implementations in the server-side application. Using the `_TestImplBase` base class, the ORB component within the server can directly invoke methods on implementation objects derived from it. This class also implements the `Test` interface, forcing derived classes to provide an implementation for each of the IDL-defined methods.
`TestHelper.java`	This file provides utility-type static methods for objects of type `Test`. Utilities include insertion and removal from CORBA types, input and output streams, etc. Also provides a `narrow()` function which is used for downcasting object references to type `Test`. We'll examine this method later in the chapter.
`TestHolder.java`	This file acts as a container for streaming objects (of type `Test`) to and from input and output streams.

We'll see how this source code is used as we build our client and server applications.

Creating the CORBA Object and Server

Once the IDL skeleton is created, we can build our CORBA object implementation and the application that contains it, namely the CORBA server. Note that there are two common methods for creating object implementations, the `ImplBase` approach and the `Tie` approach.

The `ImplBase` approach involves using an IDL compiler-generated class as the base class of our object implementation.

For instance, given an interface named `Test`, the IDL-to-Java compiler provided as part of the J2SE SDK will generate a class called `_TestImplBase`, an abstract class we can use as the base class of our object implementation. This base class implements a Java interface created from our IDL interface, ensuring that our object will provide an implementation of every method in the CORBA object's interface. Since the `ImplBase` is more commonly used, we will use this approach throughout this chapter.

The `Tie` approach is useful when our intended object implementation already extends another class, since Java does not support multiple inheritance. The `Tie` approach creates a secondary object that extends the skeleton generated class just as the `ImplBase` base class does. By associating this `tie` object with our object implementation, all CORBA invocations are invoked on the `tie` object which in turn delegates these invocations to our actual implementation object. Use the `-ftie` option of the IDL compiler to generate the necessary `Tie` classes.

To create the CORBA object using the `ImplBase` approach:

❑ Create a new class, extending from the `ImplBase` class, `_TestImplBase` that we generated using the IDL compiler

❑ Within our new class, implement each of the methods in the Java interface that was generated by the IDL compiler (in our case, the interface `Test`)

Here is an implementation of the `Test` object:

```java
// TestObject.java

public class TestObject extends _TestImplBase {
  public short method1(short param1, String param2) {
    return param1;
  }

  public String method2(short param1, String param2) {
    return param2;
  }
}
```

Now we must create the server application that will contain the `Test` object. The server implementation is as follows (cross-referenced to the numbered steps below):

```java
// TestServer.java

import org.omg.CORBA.*;                                    // Step 1
import org.omg.CosNaming.*;

public class TestServer {
  public static void main(String args[]) {
    try {

      // Initialize the ORB
      ORB orb = ORB.init(args, null);                      // Step 2

      // Create the Test object
```

```
        TestObject impl = new TestObject();                    // Step 3

        // Connect to the Naming Service
        org.omg.CORBA.Object contextObj =                      // Step 4
            orb.resolve_initial_references("NameService");
        NamingContext rootContext =
            NamingContextHelper.narrow(contextObj);

        // Insert the Test object reference in the Naming Service
        NameComponent name = new NameComponent("Test", "");    // Step 5

        NameComponent path[] = {
          name
        };
        // Show that the server is doing something
        System.out.println("TestServer started;" +
                        "waiting for client contact...");
        rootContext.rebind(path, impl);

        // Wait for incoming requests
        java.lang.Object sync = new java.lang.Object();        // Step 6
        synchronized (sync) {
          sync.wait();
        }

    } catch (Exception e) {
      System.err.println("Exception : " + e);
      e.printStackTrace(System.err);
    }
  }
}
```

The following steps describe how we implemented this server:

1. We imported the packages containing CORBA and Naming Service classes:

```
org.omg.CORBA.*
org.omg.CosNaming.*
```

2. In the `main()` method of the application, we initialized the ORB by calling `ORB.init()`. `ORB.init()` accepts its properties in one of two ways. Using the method's first argument, properties can be sent in the form of a `String` array. This is a convenient way to pass arguments from the command line to the ORB class. Another way to pass the ORB its properties is by passing a `java.util.Properties` object containing the property settings as the second parameter. For completeness, we set the unused parameter to `ORB.init()` to `null`. The following code demonstrates setting the ORB's initialization properties using the command line arguments.

```
public static void main(String args[]) {
    try {

        // Initialize the ORB
        ORB orb = ORB.init(args, null);
```

The most common of these parameters are:

Property Name	Description of Value
`org.omg.CORBA.ORBInitialPort`	The port that the Naming Service is using (defaults to `900`)
`org.omg.CORBA.ORBInitialHost`	The host where the Naming Service is running (defaults to the `localhost`)
`org.omg.CORBA.ORBClass`	The class name of an ORB implementation
`org.omg.CORBA.ORBSingletonClass`	The class name of an ORB implementation that is returned by the `init()` method with no parameters

The last two, `ORBClass` and `ORBSingletonClass` are used to 'plug in' a new ORB implementation in place of the default JavaIDL implementation. We will not be using these two properties within our examples.

To provide the ORB with its properties using the command line, we'll eventually start the server in the following manner:

C:\Beg_Java_Networking\Ch17>**java TestServer -ORBInitialPort 900 -ORBInitialHost localhost**

3. We created an instance of the `Test` object implementation with the server's `main()` method.

4. Then, we used the ORB's `resolve_initial_references()` method, passing in `"NameService"` as a parameter, to obtain an object reference to the Naming Service's initial context.

5. We inserted the CORBA object's object reference into the Naming Service, binding it to a name. In our case we used `"Test"`

6. Now, all we have to do is wait for incoming requests from clients. The following code will allow the server application to remain alive while incoming requests are handled by the ORB:

```
java.lang.Object sync = new java.lang.Object();
synchronized (sync) {
    sync.wait();
}
```

Notice the call to `ORB.resolve_initial_references()` in Step 4. The `String` `"NameService"` causes the method to return the object reference of the root context of the Naming Service. Also notice that the `resolve_initial_references()` method returns as type a basic object reference, namely an `org.omg.CORBA.Object`. In order to use the object reference as a `NamingContext` object, we must narrow the object reference using the `NamingContextHelper`'s `narrow()` method, to yield a `NamingContext` object reference that we can use. Note that using the `narrow()` method is not identical to a simple casting operation and should not be disregarded. The `narrow()` method is discussed in greater detail in the section *'The Anatomy of a CORBA Object Invocation'* later in this chapter.

Once we have a valid `NamingContext` object reference, we must construct an array of `NameComponents` that describe the location of our `Test` object reference in the Naming Service. The reason that an array is required is to allow objects to be bound in the Naming Service in other than the root context that is returned by `resolve_initial_references()`. Each `NameComponent`, with the exception of the last one, identifies another subcontext under which the object will be located. For instance, if a Naming Service contained the following contexts, it would have this structure:

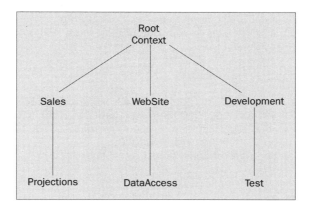

If we needed an object reference to the `Test` object in the `Development` context, we would create an array of `NameComponents` as follows:

```
NameComponent dev = new NameComponent("Development", "");
NameComponent test = new NameComponent("Test", "");
NameComponent path[] = {dev, test};
```

Note that the second parameter of the `NameComponent` constructor is the **kind** parameter, a `String` that can be used to further describe the object. Like the object name, this can be any `String` value that might be of value in identifying objects within the Naming Service. In our examples, we will leave the kind field blank.

We will insert our object reference in the root context. To do that, we will create a `NameComponent` array consisting of one `NameComponent` object that contains the name "Test". After defining the `NameComponent` array, we call the `NamingContext` object's `rebind()` method to insert the object reference. Using `rebind()` will overwrite any existing object reference in the context that has the same name. Alternatively, we could have used the `NamingContext`'s `bind()` method, which would throw an `AlreadyBound` exception in the event that an object reference with the specified name already existed within the context. Since we may want to restart this server several times during testing, we'll use the `rebind` method.

At this point, all that is left to do is to wait for incoming requests, as is done in Step 6.

To build the server, simply compile the classes we created, making sure that the IDL-generated source files are in the `CLASSPATH`.

To start the server, we must first start the Naming Service. To do this, run `tnameserv` from the command line. By default, the Naming Service will run on port 900. If you want (or need) to run the Naming Service on a different port, provide it on the command line like so:

C:\Beg_Java_Networking\Ch17>**tnameserv –ORBInitialPort x**

where x is the new port that you want to use. Note that when providing parameters to the ORB on the command line, it is not necessary to fully qualify them as `org.omg.CORBA.ORBInitialPort`, etc.

Running the Naming Service should result in output similar to the screenshot below. Note that the output contains the string form of the initial Naming Context object reference. This object reference contains the network location of the computer on which our Naming Service is running and therefore will differ from one machine to another, so your output most likely will not match exactly. Also note that the port used (900) is the default:

C:\Beg_Java_Networking\Ch17>**tnameserv**
Initial Naming Context:
IOR:000000000000002849444c3a6f6d672e6f72672f436f734e616d696e672f4e616d696e67436f6e74
6578743a312e30000000000001000000000000005400010100000000000e3139322e3136382e31302e373
4000a5000000018afabcafe00000002400da3e1000000080000000000000000000000000001000000001000
0001400000000000010020000000000001010000000000
TransientNameServer: setting port for initial object references to: 900
Ready.

Once the Naming Service is up and running, start the server by typing:

C:\Beg_Java_Networking\Ch17>**java TestServer -ORBInitialPort 900 -ORBInitialHost localhost**

It is possible, as explained above, to set the port and host accordingly by using the parameters on the command line.

Creating the CORBA Client

The client application is similar to the server application, in that both initialize the ORB and retrieve the root context of the Naming Service from the ORB in the same manner.

Here is the source code for our test client application; again the numbered comments refer to the steps below:

```
import org.omg.CORBA.*;                                    // Step 1
import org.omg.CosNaming.*;

public class TestClient {
  public static void main(String args[]) {
    try {
      ORB orb = ORB.init(args, null);                      // Step 2

      org.omg.CORBA.Object contextObj =                    // Step 3
      orb.resolve_initial_references("NameService");
      NamingContext rootContext =
        NamingContextHelper.narrow(contextObj);

      NameComponent name = new NameComponent("Test", "");
      NameComponent path[] = {
        name
      };

      org.omg.CORBA.Object obj = rootContext.resolve(path); // Step 4
```

```
      Test testObj = TestHelper.narrow(obj);

      short result1 = testObj.method1((short) 1, "Test");        // Step 5
      String result2 = testObj.method2((short) 1, "Test");

      System.out.println("Result 1 is " + result1);
      System.out.println("Result 2 is " + result2);

      testObj._release();                                         // Step 6
    } catch (Exception e) {
      System.err.println("Exception : " + e);
      e.printStackTrace(System.err);
    }
  }
}
```

To create the above CORBA client application:

1. Import the following packages:

```
org.omg.CORBA.*
org.omg.CosNaming.*
```

2. Initialize the ORB by calling `ORB.init()` in the application's `main()` method, just as we did in the server application. Note that here also we set the unused parameter to `null`.

3. Using the ORB's `resolve_initial_references()` method, obtain an object reference to the Naming Service's initial context, just as in the server application.

4. Retrieve the desired CORBA object's object reference from the Naming Service using its bound name, in our case "Test". Be sure to use the `narrow()` method instead of simple casting. (see *The Anatomy of a CORBA Object Invocation* section to follow for more detail on `narrow()`).

5. Invoke methods on the object reference.

6. When finished using the object, call `_release()` on the object reference to indicate to the ORB that we no longer need the object. This allows the ORB to clean up any resources that it is using for that object reference.

The ORB initialization and retrieval of the root `NamingContext` are done exactly as in the server application. In the case of the client, however, we call `resolve()` on the initial `NamingContext`, providing the path necessary to locate the object reference bound to the name "Test". Just as with the `resolve_initial_references()` method, the `resolve()` method returns a basic object reference which we must narrow using the `TestHelper.narrow()` method defined in the `TestHelper` class generated by the IDL compiler.

Once we have a valid object reference, we are free to invoke methods on it. When finished, we should always call `_release()` on the object reference to indicate that we are finished using it, allowing the ORB to clean up any resources dedicated to that object reference.

To run the CORBA client, we do the following (while `TestServer` is still running):

C:\Beg_Java_Networking\Ch17>**java TestClient -ORBInitialPort** *x* **-ORBInitialHost** *host*

where the port and host are set just as in the server application.

The resulting output be as follows: C:\Beg_Java_Networking\Chap17>**java TestClient**
Result 1 is 1
Result 2 is Test

The Anatomy of a CORBA Object Invocation

Now that we have a working example, we are in a position to better understand what happens when we invoke a method on our `Test` object reference. To do this, let's trace the course of a CORBA object invocation from the client's object reference to the object implementation and back. We'll use the invocation of `method1()` as our example.

First, let's take another look at how we obtain the object reference in our client application. When we retrieve an object reference from one of the object location mechanisms discussed above, such as the Naming Service, we receive a generic object reference, in other words it is of type `org.omg.CORBA.Object`. In order to invoke operations defined in our interface, we'll need to downcast, or **narrow**, the object reference from the base `Object` interface to the Java-mapped IDL interface, namely interface `Test` defined in `Test.java`. This is performed using the `narrow()` method of class `TestHelper`.

Let's look at the `TestHelper.narrow()` method and a few related definitions within `TestHelper` to see what happens during the narrow process:

```
/**
 * TestHelper.java
 * Generated by the IDL-to-Java compiler (portable), version "3.0"
 * from Test.idl
 * 24 August 2001 15:56:15 o'clock BST
 */

abstract public class TestHelper
{
  private static String  _id = "IDL:Test:1.0";

  public static void insert (org.omg.CORBA.Any a, Test that)
  {
    org.omg.CORBA.portable.OutputStream out = a.create_output_stream ();
    a.type (type ());
    write (out, that);
    a.read_value (out.create_input_stream (), type ());
  }

  public static Test extract (org.omg.CORBA.Any a)
  {
    return read (a.create_input_stream ());
  }
```

```
      private static org.omg.CORBA.TypeCode __typeCode = null;
      synchronized public static org.omg.CORBA.TypeCode type ()
      {
        if (__typeCode == null)
        {
          __typeCode = org.omg.CORBA.ORB.init ().create_interface_tc
            (TestHelper.id (), "Test");
        }
        return __typeCode;
      }

      public static String id ()
      {
        return _id;
      }

      public static Test read (org.omg.CORBA.portable.InputStream istream)
      {
        return narrow (istream.read_Object (_TestStub.class));
      }

      public static void write (org.omg.CORBA.portable.OutputStream ostream,
          Test value)
      {
        ostream.write_Object ((org.omg.CORBA.Object) value);
      }

      public static Test narrow (org.omg.CORBA.Object obj)
      {
        if (obj == null)
          return null;
        else if (obj instanceof Test)
          return (Test)obj;
        else if (!obj._is_a (id ()))
          throw new org.omg.CORBA.BAD_PARAM ();
        else
        {
          org.omg.CORBA.portable.Delegate delegate =
              ((org.omg.CORBA.portable.ObjectImpl)obj)._get_delegate ();
          return new _TestStub (delegate);
        }
      }
  }
}
```

Examining the conditions in `narrow()` will show us exactly what we retrieve as the object reference in our client application. The four conditions have been labeled in the source code as 1 to 4:

❑ The first condition is straightforward. If a `null` object reference is narrowed, the method simply returns `null`.

❑ The second condition uses the `instanceof` operator to determine if the object passed to narrow is an object that directly implements the `Test` interface. If so, a simple cast is done and the cast object is returned. This allows clients of CORBA objects that are contained within the same application as the CORBA object, to bypass the stub and skeleton and invoke its methods directly.

❑ The third condition uses the `org.omg.CORBA.Object._is_a()` method to ensure that the `obj` parameter is a class that implements the `Test` interface, designated by the `id()` method of `TestHelper`. In the event that the `obj` parameter doesn't implement our `Test` interface, an `org.omg.CORBA.BAD_PARAM` exception is thrown to indicate that the object passed to narrow does not implement the `Test` interface.

❑ The final condition creates a new `_TestStub` object from the `obj` parameter that was passed to `narrow()`. The `Delegate` object reference that is extracted from the `obj` parameter and set into the stub object is for support of vendor-specific object reference implementations and is not important to us here. Note that `_TestStub` implements the `Test` interface, allowing us to invoke any of the methods defined in the `Test` interface (or its base interfaces) on the object returned from `narrow()`.

Now, assuming that our CORBA object is located on a remote host, our client will receive a `Test` interface to a `_TestStub` object from the call to `TestHelper.narrow()`. Below is the code for the `_TestStub` class (at least, the portion we are interested in), as generated by `idlj` earlier:

```
/**
* _TestStub.java
* Generated by the IDL-to-Java compiler (portable), version "3.0"
* from Test.idl
* 24 August 2001 15:56:15 o'clock BST
*/

public class _TestStub extends org.omg.CORBA.portable.ObjectImpl implements Test
{
  // Constructors
  // NOTE:  If the default constructor is used, the
  //        object is useless until _set_delegate (...)
  //        is called.
  public _TestStub ()
  {
    super ();
  }

  public _TestStub (org.omg.CORBA.portable.Delegate delegate)
  {
    super ();
    _set_delegate (delegate);
  }

  public short method1 (short param1, String param2)
  {
    org.omg.CORBA.portable.InputStream _in = null;
    try {
      org.omg.CORBA.portable.OutputStream _out = _request ("method1",
          true);
      _out.write_short (param1);
      _out.write_string (param2);
      _in = _invoke (_out);
      short __result = _in.read_short ();
      return __result;
    } catch (org.omg.CORBA.portable.ApplicationException _ex) {
      _in = _ex.getInputStream ();
      String _id = _ex.getId ();
      throw new org.omg.CORBA.MARSHAL (_id);
    } catch (org.omg.CORBA.portable.RemarshalException _rm) {
```

```
            return method1 (param1, param2);
         } finally {
            _releaseReply (_in);
         }
      } // method1

      public String method2 (short param1, String param2)
      {
         org.omg.CORBA.portable.InputStream _in = null;
         try {
            org.omg.CORBA.portable.OutputStream _out = _request ("method2",
               true);
            _out.write_short (param1);
            _out.write_string (param2);
            _in = _invoke (_out);
            String __result = _in.read_string ();
            return __result;
         } catch (org.omg.CORBA.portable.ApplicationException _ex) {
            _in = _ex.getInputStream ();
            String _id = _ex.getId ();
            throw new org.omg.CORBA.MARSHAL (_id);
         } catch (org.omg.CORBA.portable.RemarshalException _rm) {
            return method2 (param1, param2);
         } finally {
            _releaseReply (_in);
         }
      }    // method2

   // ... remainder truncated

   }    // class _TestStub
```

The stub class _TestStub provides a method for each of the methods defined in the IDL interface. These are the methods that are invoked when the client application uses the object reference returned from TestHelper.narrow(). Let's look at the implementation of method1() to see what occurs when an invocation is made on this object.

```
public short method1 (short param1, String param2){
   org.omg.CORBA.portable.InputStream _in = null;
   try {
      org.omg.CORBA.portable.OutputStream _out =
         _request ("method1",true);                    // Step 1
      _out.write_short (param1);                        // Step 2
      _out.write_string (param2);
      _in = _invoke (_out);                             // Step 3
      short __result = _in.read_short ();               // Step 4
      return __result;                                  // Step 5
   } catch-finally code to end of method
```

So, what happens when this method is called?

❑ At Step 1, the stub object creates an org.omg.CORBA.portable.OutputStream object named _out, and passes it a request object with a method name of "method1". The org.omg.CORBA.portable.OutputStream object is used for marshaling method requests, parameters, exceptions, etc., in a platform-independent manner for transport across platforms.

❏ At Step 2, the parameters passed into the _TestStub method1() method are marshaled into the OutputStream object.

❏ At Step 3, _invoke() is called on the stub object passing the OutputStream object _out as a parameter. _invoke() is implemented by _TestStub's underlying base class, org.omg.CORBA.portable.ObjectImpl. At this point, the ORB takes over, using the OutputStream we've provided to construct an IIOP message. This message is then sent to the remote object using the network location of the remote object contained in the object reference.

❏ At this point, the client blocks waiting for the _invoke() method to return. When it does, the return type of the method1() invocation is unmarshaled from _invoke()'s InputStream return object (Step 4).

❏ Finally, the result is returned back to the caller (Step 5).

On the server side, the ORB will receive the IIOP method that has been sent by the client. When it does, it creates an org.omg.CORBA.portable.InputStream object using the data from the IIOP message. The InputStream object contains the information that our _TestStub object in the client inserted into its OutputStream. The ORB then uses the information in the object reference to locate the correct CORBA object in its application and calls _invoke() on the CORBA object, providing the method name and the InputStream as parameters.

Below is the source code for the Test interface skeleton, _TestImplBase, as created by idlj (the comments for step numbers have been added):

```
/**
* _TestImplBase.java
* Generated by the IDL-to-Java compiler (portable), version "3.0"
* from Test.idl
* 24 August 2001 15:56:15 o'clock BST
*/

public abstract class _TestImplBase extends org.omg.CORBA.portable.ObjectImpl
                implements Test, org.omg.CORBA.portable.InvokeHandler{

  // Constructors
  public _TestImplBase (){
  }

  private static java.util.Hashtable _methods = new java.util.Hashtable ();
  static{
    _methods.put ("method1", new java.lang.Integer (0));
    _methods.put ("method2", new java.lang.Integer (1));
  }

  public org.omg.CORBA.portable.OutputStream _invoke (String method,
                            org.omg.CORBA.portable.InputStream in,
                            org.omg.CORBA.portable.ResponseHandler rh){
  org.omg.CORBA.portable.OutputStream out = null;
  java.lang.Integer __method = (java.lang.Integer)_methods.get (method); //step1
  if (__method == null)
     throw new org.omg.CORBA.BAD_OPERATION (0,
            org.omg.CORBA.CompletionStatus.COMPLETED_MAYBE);

  switch (__method.intValue ()){  //step2
     case 0:  // Test/method1{  //step3
        short param1 = in.read_short (); step4
```

```
                String param2 = in.read_string ();
                short __result = (short)0;              //step5
                __result = this.method1 (param1, param2);   //step6
                out = rh.createReply();              //step7
                out.write_short (__result);          //step8
                break;
            }

        case 1:  // Test/method2{
            short param1 = in.read_short ();
            String param2 = in.read_string ();
            String __result = null;
            __result = this.method2 (param1, param2);
            out = rh.createReply();
            out.write_string (__result);
            break;
        }

        default:
            throw new org.omg.CORBA.BAD_OPERATION (0,
                org.omg.CORBA.CompletionStatus.COMPLETED_MAYBE);
    }

    return out;    //step9
} // _invoke

// Type-specific CORBA::Object operations
private static String[] __ids = {
    "IDL:Test:1.0"};

public String[] _ids (){
    return __ids;
}


} // class _TestImplBase
```

It is important to note here that our CORBA object implementation, TestObject, extends the
_TestImplBase class, so the _invoke() method that is invoked by the ORB is actually part of our
implementation object. Let's trace through the steps that occur in our CORBA object's _invoke() method:

❑ At Step 1, the method name passed to invoke is used to get the ordinal value of the method, as
   defined in the static HashTable variable _methods, defined in _TestImplBase.

❑ This ordinal value, stored in the Integer variable __method, is applied to the switch
   statement in Step 2 to jump to the proper handler code for the specified method. In the case of
   an invocation on method1(), this code begins at Step 3.

❑ At Step 4, the input parameters are unmarshaled from the InputStream object and stored in
   temporary variables param1 and param2.

❑ Step 5 defines a temporary variable, __result, to contain the result of the method invocation.

❑ The invocation of the method takes place at Step 6 as follows:

```
    __result = this.method1(param1, param2);
```

Notice that since our CORBA object is actually the _TestImplBase object, the object invokes the method on itself, passing the parameters it marshaled from the InputStream object, and storing the return value in the temporary __result variable.

❑ At Step 7, the actual method invocation has completed. The skeleton is now beginning to construct the OutputStream for return to the client. First, the skeleton uses the ReplyHandler object passed as a parameter to _invoke() to create the OutputStream, inserting a reply object into it.

❑ At Step 8, the return value is marshaled onto the output stream.

❑ We then break out of the switch statement to Step 9, where the completed OutputStream object is returned to the caller, namely the ORB. The ORB creates the IIOP reply message containing the OutputStream, and sends it back to the client.

When the client receives the message, the ORB creates an InputStream object and populates it with the data from the message. Now the _TestStub object can unmarshal the return value and return it back to the client application, Steps 4 and 5 in the _TestStub object. This completes the round trip of our CORBA method invocation.

An IDL Primer

To make use of CORBA servers, we'll need to invoke methods on their IDL interfaces, so let's now briefly examine the details of the IDL language. We will first look at the data types of the language and then proceed to the definition of interfaces. Note that this is not a complete specification for the language, but an abbreviated description designed to provide you with a good overview of the IDL language. For the complete specification, visit the OMG web site at http://www.omg.org/, where the specifications for the IDL language as well as the IDL-to-Java mapping are available for downloading.

Basic IDL Types

There are several basic data types in IDL that can be used to build up more complex structures in your IDL interface definitions. They include the usual integer and floating point numbers, such as [unsigned] short, [unsigned] long, etc., as we would expect. Non-numeric data types also are much like the Java equivalents, char, bounded and unbounded strings (fixed and non-fixed length), the boolean type and any, a type that allows any IDL-defined data type to be stored in it.

Complex IDL Types

In addition to these simple types, IDL provides a number of complex types.

Structures

A structure is probably the simplest of all the complex types and is much like the struct in C and C++. A structure, declared as struct, is a data type that consists of one or more data elements of other types. Structures are convenient when an operation requires a number of parameters that can be logically grouped into one entity. The syntax for defining a structure is as follows:

```
interface Log{
  struct date
  {
    unsigned short month;
    unsigned short day;
    unsigned short year;
  };

  struct logMessageStruct
  {
    string msg;
    date msgDate;
  };

  void submitLogMsg( in logMessageStruct msg );
};
```

Examining the above IDL definition, you can see that structures can contain not only basic types, but other structures as well. In fact, structures can also contain other types of complex types, enums, sequences, arrays, and even references to other objects.

Enums

An enumerated type, declared as enum, allows the definition of a set of values that can be referenced as a particular type. Once defined, the enumerated type can be used as a parameter or return value type. For example, let's say that we need to add to our previous IDL interface to accept log messages of varying severities. The IDL interface can define an enumerated type that specifies the legal values for the log message severity as follows:

```
enum Severity { INFO, WARNING, ERROR };
```

Unions

A union is another type of data structure, however rather than containing several data elements, it contains only one element. The actual type of the element can be one of several different specified types, as specified in the union's case statement. The actual type is controlled by a variable called a discriminator.

The discriminator, which is referenced after the union name, can be of integer, boolean, character or enum type. Depending on the value of the discriminator, the correct data element will be referenced. We can add a union, named logMessage, to our Log example as follows:

```
interface Log{
  struct date
  {
    unsigned short month;
    unsigned short day;
    unsigned short year;
  };

  enum Severity { INFO, WARNING, ERROR };

  struct logMessageStruct
  {
    string msg;
```

```
      date msgDate;
      Severity msgSeverity;
    };

    union logMessage( short )
    {
      case 0 : string msgString;
      default: logMessageStruct msgStruct;
    };

    void submitLogMsg( in logMessage msg );
  };
```

Arrays and Sequences

Arrays are declared in IDL as containing a fixed number of data elements. Arrays can also be declared as multi-dimensional. When declaring the array, the number specified indicates the total number of elements that can be contained within it. Note that the elements within the array are zero indexed, so an array of 10 elements is accessed as elements 0 through 9. Also note that in order for an array to be passed as a parameter or return type, a `typedef` must be created that identifies the array type and size. Once the `typedef` is defined, it is used in place of the complete array syntax, as seen below:

```
interface Log{
   // ... interface as before

    typedef logMessage logMessageArray[10];

    void submitLogMsg( in logMessage msg );
    void submitLogMsgs( in logMessageArray msgArray );

  };
```

Sequences are similar to arrays in that they define a list of elements. The sequence's elements are zero-indexed, meaning that the first element in the list is accessed as element 0. However, sequences differ from arrays in that they can be defined as **bounded** or **unbounded**. Unbounded sequences can contain any number of elements, constrained only by the available memory, whereas bounded sequences have a fixed number of elements.

First let's demonstrate the use of a bounded sequence by replacing our fixed-size array. As with arrays, a `typedef` must be used to enable it to be passed as a parameter or return type:

```
interface Log{

...

    union logMessage( short )
    {
      case 0 : string msgString;
      default: logMessageStruct msgStruct;
    };

    // Replaced the array with a bounded sequence
    typedef sequence <logMessage, 10> logMessageSeq;
    void submitLogMsg( in logMessage msg );
    void submitLogMsgs( in logMessageSeq msgSeq );
}
```

We could also make use of an unbounded sequence by replacing the highlighted code above with the following:

```
// Replaced the bounded sequence with an unbounded sequence
typedef sequence <logMessage> logMessageSeq;
```

Modules

IDL interfaces may be defined within modules, providing a naming space that contains and isolates any names within it. The syntax of a module in IDL is as follows:

```
module OnlineBroker
{
  interface Account
  {
    // ...
  };

  // Additional interface definitions, if any
};
```

To access the Account interface from outside of the module, it must be scoped using the module name and the scope resolution operator :: similarly to:

```
OnlineBroker:: Account
```

Although using modules is not necessary when defining IDL interfaces, it does provide us with an isolated naming space. In this case, we will prevent any ambiguities with other IDL interfaces that happen to be named Account.

Also note that IDL files can contain comments, denoted by the // symbol just as in Java.

Interfaces

Interfaces define the functionality of an object in a distributed system, and can contain several different types of definitions, each of which we will examine in turn. It is important to note that everything defined in an IDL interface is public. There is no concept of package, protected, or private access modifiers. Let's begin with attributes.

Attributes

Extending our example IDL, we now have:

```
module OnlineBroker{
  interface Account{
    readonly attribute string AccountNumber;
    attribute string AccountHolderName;
  };
};
```

The interface now includes two attributes, namely AccountNumber and AccountHolderName. Each attribute usually has two implied operations associated with it, a get() and a set() operation.

An attribute can, however, be denoted as `readonly`, meaning that its value cannot be altered. Because of this, the `AccountNumber` attribute will have only one operation defined in the IDL client stub, `getAccountNumber()`. In the case of the `AccountHolderName` attribute, two operations, `getAccountHolderName()` and `setAccountHolderName()` will be created. We'll look at the contents of the client stub in more detail later.

Operations

Operations define methods on the remote object that can be invoked by clients. Remember that the only way clients can access the CORBA object is through its interface, so any functionality that the object wants to provide must be exposed through its interface as an attribute or operation.

Extending our example IDL, we have:

```
module OnlineBroker{
   interface Account{
      readonly attribute string AccountNumber;
      attribute string AccountHolderName;

      boolean buy( in string symbol, inout long quantity, out string cusip );
      boolean sell( in string symbol, out string cusip );
   };
};
```

Now we've added two operations, `buy()` and `sell()`, to our interface. These look very similar to methods defined in Java interfaces, however note that the parameters are preceded by a modifier, namely `in`, `out`, or `inout`. These parameter modifiers describe in which direction the parameter is passed:

❑　`in` parameters are set to a particular value by the client and passed to the server. The server receives the value and is free to alter it during the course of its processing, however the client will not receive the updated value upon return of the operation invocation.

❑　`out` parameters work in the reverse manner, the server sets this value during its processing and returns the new value to the client

❑　`inout` parameters allow a client to pass a value to the server object, the server object is capable of altering this value, and the resulting value is returned to the client

One important note about operation names is that they cannot be overloaded, regardless of the operation's signature. Therefore, if you have two operations that have similar functionality but take different parameter types, you are forced to create two separate names for these operations. For example, an interface cannot include the following two operations:

```
void add( long num );
void add( float num );
```

Instead, the operations will require different names, such as `addLong()` and `addFloat()`.

Exceptions

When defining operations for a distributed object, it may be beneficial to define exceptions that can be thrown during the course of processing. Exceptions in IDL can optionally contain data elements, although including data elements is not necessary.

Once defined, the exceptions that an operation can throw are identified in the operation's `raises` clause. Let's define a few exceptions in our example, and in conjunction with this we'll remove the rather vague `boolean` return types from the `buy()` and `sell()` operations and replace them with the current `out` parameters:

```
module OnlineBroker{
   interface Account{
      readonly attribute string AccountNumber;
      attribute string AccountHolderName;

      exception InvalidSymbol()
      {
        string symbol;
      };

      exception ExceededBalance()
      {
        double currentBalance;
        double requiredBalance;
      };

      string cusip buy( in string symbol, inout long quantity )
         raises ( ExceededBalance, InvalidSymbol );

      string cusip sell( in string symbol )
         raises ( InvalidSymbol );
   };
};
```

Now, when the client invokes our `buy()` and `sell()` operations, they will expect that upon success, a `cusip` number will be returned which will identify the transaction. In the event of a problem, an exception will be thrown. When caught, the exception's data items can be examined to gain more information about the error that has occurred. Obviously, this interface would not be acceptable if this were a production system, since we don't want our client blocking during the `buy()` or `sell()` operations, which could possibly take minutes. The purpose of this interface is simply to demonstrate the different parts and syntax of an IDL interface.

A quick note, operations can also be defined as `oneway`, which causes them to be asynchronous: the invocation returns to the client immediately after the request is transmitted to the server. The syntax is as follows:

```
oneway void doSomething( in string abc );
```

As a result of being asynchronous, `oneway` operations have several restrictions; they cannot have a non-void return type, they can only have `in` parameters, and no exceptions can be thrown. Note that without the benefit of a return type or exception, the client application that invokes a oneway method on a CORBA object may not be sure that the method completed successfully.

Inheritance

Just like Java interfaces, IDL interfaces can inherit from other interfaces. In addition, all IDL interfaces implicitly inherit from the `Object` interface, making the `Object` interface the base interface of all CORBA objects. Again extending our example, let's create an interface for a margin account. The syntax for interface inheritance is as follows:

```
   interface MarginAccount : Account
   {
     readonly attribute double margin;
     void requestAdditionalMargin( in double additionalAmt );
   };
```

Multiple Inheritance

Unlike Java, it is also possible when defining an interface in IDL to inherit from more than one interface. This allows the new interface to inherit the attributes, operations, exceptions, etc. from each of its base interfaces. To demonstrate this, lets add an additional interface to our module to describe another type of account, and then create an account interface that inherits from two account types.

```
module OnlineBroker{
   interface Account{
     readonly attribute string accountNumber;
     attribute string accountHolderName;

     exception InvalidSymbol()
     {
       string symbol;
     };

     exception ExceededBalance()
     {
       double currentBalance;
       double requiredBalance;
     };

     string cusip buy( in string symbol, inout long quantity )
       raises ( ExceededBalance, InvalidSymbol );

     string cusip sell( in string symbol )
       raises ( InvalidSymbol );
   };

   interface MarginAccount : Account
   {
     readonly attribute double margin;
     void requestAdditionalMargin( in double additionalAmt );
   };

   interface OptionsAccount : Account
   {
     void call( in string symbol );
     void put( in string symbol );
   };

   interface MarginOptionsAccount : MarginAccount, OptionsAccount
   {
     // some additional operations, attributes, etc.
   };
};
```

RMI-IIOP and CORBA

Up until recently, Java programmers responsible for building distributed systems have had to make a choice between Java's RMI and CORBA. RMI provides a pure-Java programming environment that eliminates the need to learn additional languages or technologies but forces an all-Java solution. CORBA provides the ability to interface with clients and objects written in other programming languages at the expense of learning a new interface definition language.

With the introduction of RMI-IIOP, we can now enjoy the benefits of both RMI and CORBA. Using RMI-IIOP causes RMI clients and objects to communicate by transferring method requests and their associated parameters and return values by passing IIOP messages back and forth instead of using RMI's original transfer protocol, JRMP (Java Remote Messaging Protocol). This alone is not terribly exciting, until you recall that IIOP is also the messaging protocol used by CORBA to transfer its method requests and data. What this means to us is that we can integrate RMI clients with CORBA objects and vice versa because RMI clients, CORBA clients, RMI objects and CORBA objects all transfer their requests 'across the wire' using the same protocol: in a sense, they all speak the same language:

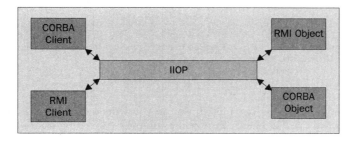

As you will see shortly, there are a few things that we'll need to do to get our RMI clients and objects to use IIOP. To demonstrate, let's start by building a small RMI example in the conventional manner. Then we'll make the necessary adjustments to start using IIOP. And finally, we'll construct a similar CORBA object and client and experiment with using them together.

An RMI Example

To begin our example, let's build a simple RMI application. We are going to build an RMI-based `HelloWorld` program. To keep our interface, server, and client source and class files separated, let's create three subdirectories within your working directory. For example, on a Windows platform if your working directory is `C:\Beg_Java_Networking\Ch17\`, create the following three subdirectories:

```
C:\Beg_Java_Networking\Ch17\RMI1\Client
C:\Beg_Java_Networking\Ch17\RMI1\Interface
C:\Beg_Java_Networking\Ch17\RMI1\Server
```

As always, when building a distributed object we first need to define the object's interface, so let's create a file called `HelloWorld.java` in our `Interface` subdirectory that contains the following interface definition:

```java
// HelloWorld.java

import java.rmi.Remote;
import java.rmi.RemoteException;
```

```
public interface HelloWorld extends Remote {
  String hello() throws RemoteException;
}
```

Since this is an interface for an RMI object, we need to extend the Remote interface. In addition, each method must include RemoteException in its throws clause. Now, we can create an RMI object that implements this interface. This file will be called HelloWorldRMIImpl.java and will be placed in the Server subdirectory.

```
// HelloWorldRMIImpl.java

import java.rmi.*;
import java.rmi.server.*;

public class HelloWorldRMIImpl extends UnicastRemoteObject
  implements HelloWorld {

  public HelloWorldRMIImpl() throws RemoteException {
    super();
  }

  public String hello() throws RemoteException {
    return "Hello from RMI";
  }
}
```

Once we have our implementation completed, we can construct a server application to contain it. As with any RMI server, we need to make this object available by inserting it into the RMI registry. For our RMI version of HelloWorld, we'll give it a name of "/HelloWorldRMI". This file will be called HelloWorldRMIServer.java and will also be placed in our Server subdirectory.

```
// HelloWorldRMIServer.java

import java.rmi.*;
import java.rmi.server.*;

public class HelloWorldRMIServer {
  public static void main(String[] args) {
    try {
      System.out.println("Creating implementation object");
      HelloWorld impl = new HelloWorldRMIImpl();

      String objName = "/HelloWorldRMI";
      System.out.println("Connecting to Naming Service");
      System.out.println("Binding object to naming context "
                      + "with name '" + objName + "'");
      Naming.rebind(objName, impl);

      System.out.println("Ready to accept requests");
    } catch (Exception e) {
      System.out.println("Exception : " + e);
      e.printStackTrace(System.out);
    }
  }
}
```

To build our RMI object and its server, we need to do two things:

❑ Create an RMI stub using the `rmic` compiler

❑ Build our source and the generated source to create our class files

To perform the steps listed above, first of all, set the following directories into your classpath, as we will create the necessary classes using the `rmic` utility:

C:\Beg_Java_Networking\Ch17\RMI1\Server>**rmic -classpath .;C:\..\Interface -d ..\Interface HelloWorldRMIImpl**

C:\Beg_Java_Networking\Ch17RMI1\Server>**javac -classpath .;..Interface *.java**

The first line above uses the `rmic` utility to create the RMI stub and skeleton files needed by the client and server applications. Note that we use the `-d` option to direct `rmic`'s output into the `Interface` subdirectory. The second line above simply compiles the server.

Now that we have our server built, let's turn our attention to the client application. This file, named `HelloWorldRMIClient.java` can be placed in our `Client` subdirectory.

```
// HelloWorldRMIClient.java

import java.rmi.*;

public class HelloWorldRMIClient {
  public static void main(String[] args) {
    try {
      HelloWorld obj =
        (HelloWorld) Naming.lookup("//localhost/HelloWorldRMI");

      String response = obj.hello();
      System.out.println("RMI Client : The response is '" + response
                         + "'\n");
    } catch (Exception e) {
      System.out.println("Exception : " + e);
      e.printStackTrace(System.out);
    }
  }
}
```

As with the server application, be sure to include the directory that contains the `rmic`-generated files when compiling the client application, like so:

C:\Beg_Java_Networking\Ch17\RMI1\Client>**javac -classpath .;..\Interface *.java**

Once the client and server are built, we can test our example. First start the RMI registry. If you choose not to provide a port number, `rmiregistry` will use the default port number `1099`:

C:\Beg_Java_Networking\Ch17\RMI1\Server>**rmiregistry *port***
security properties not found. using defaults.

Assuming the directory structure mentioned earlier, we can run our server application from within the `Server` subdirectory by issuing the following command:

C:\Beg_Java_Networking\Ch17\RMI1\Server>**java -**
Djava.rmi.server.codebase=file:/C:\Beg_Java_Networking\Ch17\RMI1\Interface
-classpath .;..\Interface HelloWorldRMIServer

Running the above command should result in the following output:

```
Creating implementation object
Connecting to Naming Service
Binding object to naming context with name '/HelloWorldRMI'
Ready to accept requests
```

Then, we can run our client application from within the `Client` subdirectory as follows:

C:\Beg_Java_Networking\Ch17\RMI1\Client>**java -classpath .;..\Interface HelloWorldRMIClient**

Compile your client class, again including the `Interface` directory classpath. The output from the client application should appear as follows:

C:\Beg_Java_Networking\Ch17\RMI1\Client>**java -classpath .;..\Interface HelloWorldRM**
IClient
RMI Client : The response is 'Hello from RMI'

Using RMI-IIOP

So far, it's been business as usual for RMI object development. Our next task is to take our new RMI example and make the necessary changes so it will use IIOP instead of RMI.

Before we start, let's create a new working directory for our example – RMI2. In this directory, let's create our three subdirectories as we did in the last example:

```
C:\Beg_Java_Networking\Ch17\RMI2\Client
C:\Beg_Java_Networking\Ch17\RMI2\Interface
C:\Beg_Java_Networking\Ch17\RMI2\Server
```

To convert our server application to use RMI-IIOP, we'll need to do two things:

❑ Our implementation must extend `javax.rmi.PortableRemoteObject` instead of `UnicastRemoteObject`

❑ Replace the use of the RMI registry with the JNDI registry by making the following changes to `HelloWorldRMIImpl`:

```java
// HelloWorldRMIImpl2.java

import java.rmi.*;
import java.rmi.server.*;

public class HelloWorldRMIImpl2 extends javax.rmi.PortableRemoteObject
    implements HelloWorld2 {

  public HelloWorldRMIImpl2() throws RemoteException {
    super();
```

```
      }
    public String hello() throws RemoteException {
      return "Hello from RMI-IIOP";
    }
  }
```

We also need to make changes to HelloWorldRMIServer, as follows:

```
// HelloWorldRMIServer2.java

import java.rmi.*;
import javax.naming.*;

public class HelloWorldRMIServer2 {
  public static void main(String[] args) {
    try {
      System.out.println("Creating implementation object");
      HelloWorld2 impl = new HelloWorldRMIImpl2();
      Context initialNamingContext = new InitialContext();

      String objName = "/HelloWorldRMI2";
      System.out.println("Connecting to Naming Service");
      System.out.println("Binding object to naming context "
                      + "with name '" + objName + "'");
      initialNamingContext.rebind(objName, impl);

      System.out.println("Ready to accept RMI-IIOP requests");
    } catch (Exception e) {
      System.out.println("Exception : " + e);
      e.printStackTrace(System.out);
    }
  }
}
```

For our client, we also need to do two things:

❑ As with the server, we need to make use of the JNDI registry instead of the RMI registry

❑ Since we now use the PortableRemoteObject as our objects base class, we need to alter our casting of the object

Make these changes as follows:

```
// HelloWorldRMIClient2.java

import java.rmi.*;
import javax.rmi.*;
import javax.naming.*;

public class HelloWorldRMIClient2 {
  public static void main(String[] args) {
    if (args.length == 0) {
      System.err.println("Usage : HelloWorldRMIClient2 <objName>");
      System.exit(-1);
    }
```

```
      try {
         Context initialNamingContext = new InitialContext();
         HelloWorld2 helloWorld2Obj =
            (HelloWorld2) PortableRemoteObject
              .narrow(initialNamingContext.lookup(args[0]), HelloWorld2.class);

         String response = helloWorld2Obj.hello();
         System.out.println("RMI-IIOP Client : The response is '" + response
                              + "'\n");
      } catch (Exception e) {
         System.out.println("Exception : " + e);
         e.printStackTrace(System.out);
      }
   }
}
```

Notice one more change that was made to the client. It now takes one command line argument, which it uses to acquire the `objectName`. This change is not related to the IIOP changes, it has been made to make testing our RMI-CORBA interoperability easier later.

That's it for the code changes. The main difference in the process occurs, however, when generating the RMI stubs with the `rmic` compiler. We need to indicate to `rmic` that we want to generate IIOP compatible stubs. We can do this simply by including the `-iiop` command line flag when compiling the interface:

C:\Beg_Java_Networking\Ch17\RMI2\Server>**rmic -iiop -classpath .;C:\..\Interface -d ..\Interface HelloWorldRMIImpl2**

You'll notice a difference in the stub files created depending on the use of this flag. In our conventional sample, `rmic` generated two stub files (plus two other files that aren't of interest right now):

❑   `HelloWorldRMIImpl_Stub.class`

❑   `HelloWorldRMIImpl_Skel.class`

Instead, when using the `-iiop` flag, we get the following class files (as replacements):

❑   `_HelloWorld2_Stub.class`

❑   `_HelloWorldRMIImpl2_Tie.class`

Using these stub files in place of the ones generated in our conventional RMI sample will allow our RMI client and object to communicate using the IIOP protocol rather than the original JRMP protocol.

After compiling our two new applications in the normal manner (remember to include the `Interface` subdirectory in the classpath), we can test them by doing the following:

❑   Start the JNDI Registry using `tnameserv` or starting the `j2ee` server. Be cautious here: `tnameserv` defaults to a port of 900, whereas the JNDI registry in the `j2ee` server defaults to 1050.

❑   Run the server, including both the current and `Interface` directories in the classpath:

C:\Beg_Java_Networking\Chap17\RMI2\Server>**java -classpath .;..\Interface -Djava.
naming.factory.initial=com.sun.jndi.cosnaming.CNCtxFactory -Djava.naming.provide
r.url=iiop://localhost:900 HelloWorldRMIServer2**

This should produce the following results:

```
Creating implementation object
Connecting to Naming Service
Binding object to naming context with name '/HelloWorldRMI2'
Ready to accept RMI-IIOP requests
```

❑ Run the client:

C:\Beg_Java_Networking\Chap17\RMI2\Client>**java -classpath .;..\Interface -Djava.
naming.factory.initial=com.sun.jndi.cosnaming.CNCtxFactory -Djava.naming.provide
r.url=iiop://localhost:900 HelloWorldRMIClient2 HelloWorldRMI2**

Note the addition of the command line argument in the client. The output that you should see is (almost) identical to that of the initial client application:

```
RMI-IIOP Client : The response is 'Hello from RMI-IIOP'
```

That's all there is to it. We are now running RMI over IIOP.

Interaction of CORBA and RMI-IIOP

Our next goal is to demonstrate the interoperability of CORBA and RMI. We are again going to rely on the `rmic` compiler, but this time we're not going to generate stubs of Java source code. By compiling the Java interface with the −idl flag, we can create an IDL interface. This is possible because of two OMG specifications that have been developed:

❑ **The Java-to-IDL mapping**
This specification defines the rules for converting a Java language interface into IDL

❑ **The Objects-by-Value definition**
This defines how to pass objects by value through an IDL interface via IIOP

For more information on these specifications, visit the OMG's web site (http://www.omg.org/).

With that said, let's convert our Java interface into an IDL interface using the `rmic` compiler. By issuing the following command within the `Interface` subdirectory (with the directory on the CLASSPATH):

C:\Beg_Java_Networking\Ch17\RMI2\Interface>**rmic −idl HelloWorld2**

we get the following IDL interface in a file named `HelloWorld.idl` (also in the `Interface` directory):

```
/**
 * HelloWorld2.idl
 * Generated by rmic -idl. Do not edit
 * 24 August 2001 14:37:04  BST
 */
```

```
#include "orb.idl"

#ifndef __HelloWorld2__
#define __HelloWorld2__

    interface HelloWorld2 {

        ::CORBA::WStringValue hello( );
    };

#pragma ID HelloWorld2 "RMI:
#endif
```

> Here's a tip: when compiling the rmic-generated IDL file using the **idlj** compiler,
> always direct the generated files to a different subdirectory than the subdirectory
> containing our **HelloWorld2** Java interface file, **HelloWorld2.java**. Compiling
> the IDL file **HelloWorld2.idl** will generate a new file as part of the object
> reference definition, also named **HelloWorld2.java**, overwriting our existing Java
> interface file and preventing us from recompiling the RMI code later.

Notice the inclusion of the `orb.idl` file. This is located in the `lib` directory of the JDK installation
and will be included during compilation.

To begin writing the CORBA portion of our example, let's create two more subdirectories to contain the
server and client source code, say:

```
\RMI2\CORBAClient
\RMI2\CORBAServer
```

We will begin creating our CORBA source code by compiling the IDL definition created above and
generating our server-side skeleton code and client-side stub code. To avoid confusion as to which files
are generated for the server and which for the client, we will create the skeleton and stub code
separately. For the server, from within our `CORBAServer` subdirectory issue the following command:

C:\Beg_Java_Networking\Chap17\RMI2\CORBAServer>**idlj -fserver -i C:\jdk1.3\lib ..
\Interface\HelloWorld2.idl**

For the client, from within our `CORBAClient` subdirectory issue the following command:

C:\Beg_Java_Networking\Chap17\RMI2\CORBAClient>**idlj -fclient -i C:\jdk1.3\lib ..
\Interface\HelloWorld2.idl**

The above commands assume that your JDK installation is located in the `C:\jdk1.3` directory. Notice
the use of the `-i` option to locate `orb.idl`, and the use of the `-fserver` and the `-fclient` options
to create only server-side skeleton or client-side stub code.

Now that we've compiled our new IDL file, let's write the code for our CORBA example. Here is the
source code for our object implementation, to be saved in the `CORBAServer` directory:

```
// HelloWorldCORBAImpl.java

public class HelloWorldCORBAImpl extends _HelloWorld2ImplBase {
  public String hello() {
    return "Hello from CORBA";
  }
}
```

And here is the server code, also to be saved in the CORBAServer directory:

```
// HelloWorldCORBAServer.java

import org.omg.CORBA.*;
import org.omg.CosNaming.*;
import java.io.*;

class HelloWorldCORBAServer {
  public static void main(String args[]) {
    try {
      ORB orb = ORB.init(args, null);

      System.out.println("Creating implementation object");
      HelloWorldCORBAImpl impl = new HelloWorldCORBAImpl();
      orb.connect(impl);

      System.out.println("Connecting to Naming Service");
      org.omg.CORBA.Object rootContextObj =
        orb.resolve_initial_references("NameService");
      NamingContext rootContext =
        NamingContextHelper.narrow(rootContextObj);

      String objName = "HelloWorldCORBA";
      System.out.println("Binding object to naming context "
                          + "with name '" + objName + "'");
      NameComponent name = new NameComponent(objName, "");
      NameComponent path[] = {
        name
      };
      rootContext.rebind(path, impl);

      System.out.println("Ready to accept requests");
      java.lang.Object syncObj = new java.lang.Object();
      synchronized (syncObj) {
        syncObj.wait();
      }
    } catch (Exception e) {
      System.err.println("Exception caught : " + e);
      e.printStackTrace(System.err);
    }
  }
}
```

Next we have the code for our client, HelloWorldCORBAClient.java, which we save in the CORBAClient directory:

```
// HelloWorldCORBAClient.java

import org.omg.CORBA.*;
import org.omg.CosNaming.*;
```

```
import java.util.GregorianCalendar;
import java.io.*;

class HelloWorldCORBAClient {
  public static void main(String args[]) {
    if (args.length == 0) {
      System.err.println("Usage : HelloWorldCORBAClient <objName>");
      System.exit(-1);
    }

    HelloWorld2 helloWorld2Obj = null;

    try {
      ORB orb = ORB.init(args, null);

      org.omg.CORBA.Object contextObj =
        orb.resolve_initial_references("NameService");
      NamingContext rootContext = NamingContextHelper.narrow(contextObj);

      NameComponent name = new NameComponent(args[0], "");
      NameComponent path[] = {
        name
      };

      org.omg.CORBA.Object obj = rootContext.resolve(path);
      helloWorld2Obj = HelloWorld2Helper.narrow(obj);
    } catch (Exception e) {
      System.err.println(e.getMessage());
      System.exit(-1);
    }

    try {
      String responseStr = helloWorld2Obj.hello();
      System.out.println("CORBA Client : The response is '" + responseStr
                         + "'\n");
    } catch (Exception e) {
      System.out.println("Exception : " + e);
      e.printStackTrace(System.out);
    }
  }
}
```

Note that our CORBA client also takes as its first parameter the name of the object to contact. After building the client and server applications, you should verify that the new client and server work correctly by first running the JNDI registry with tnameserv, and then starting the new CORBA server and client applications. Be sure to indicate to the client and server the correct port number that the Naming Service is running on (900 for tnameserv) and also to provide the correct name, HelloWorldCORBA, to the CORBA client.

Now compile the server classes:

C:\Beg_Java_Networking\Chap17\RMI2\CORBAServer>**javac -classpath .;..\Interface *
.java**

To run the server with a Naming Service port of 900 (as specified by tnameserv):

C:\Beg_Java_Networking\Chap17\RMI2\CORBAServer>**java HelloWorldCORBAServer -
ORBInitialPort 900**

you should see the following output:

Creating implementation object
Connecting to Naming Service
Binding object to naming context with name 'HelloWorldCORBA'
Ready to accept requests

To run the client with a Naming Service port of 900 (as specified by tnameserv):

C:\Beg_Java_Networking\Chap17\RMI2\CORBAClient>**java HelloWorldCORBAClient HelloW
orldCORBA -ORBInitialPort900**

you should see the following output:

CORBA Client : The response is 'Hello from CORBA'

We now have two client applications, one CORBA, one RMI, and two object servers, again one CORBA and one RMI. To see the power of RMI IIOP in action, try each of the client applications with each server by providing the remote objects' names, HelloWorldCORBA and HelloWorldRMI, to each client application. You will see that each of our client applications access and use the objects as if they all resided in the same distributed framework.

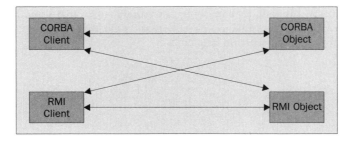

For example, let's attempt to access the HelloWorldCORBA object from our RMI client. To do this, make sure the CORBA server has been started, as we did when testing our CORBA example above. Once the CORBA server is running, run the RMI client application just as we did initially, but this time providing HelloWorldCORBA as the command line parameter, as below:

C:\Beg_Java_Networking\Chap17\RMI2\Client>**java -classpath .;..\Interface -Djava.
naming.factory.initial=com.sun.jndi.cosnaming.CNCtxFactory -Djava.naming.provide
r.url=iiop://localhost:900 HelloWorldRMIClient2 HelloWorldCORBA**

You should see the following results:

RMI-IIOP Client : The response is 'Hello from CORBA'

In the same manner, running the CORBA client to access the RMI object will provide similar results. Start the RMI server as we did earlier, then run the CORBA client, providing HelloWorldRMI as the command line argument as follows:

C:\Beg_Java_Networking\Chap17\RMI2\CORBAClient>**java HelloWorldCORBAClient**
HelloWorldRMI2 -ORBInitialPort900

You should see the following results (here we used the same window in which we'd just run the CORBA client against the CORBA server):

CORBA Client : The response is 'Hello from RMI-IIOP'

Summary

In this chapter, we have examined several aspects of distributed programming with Java and CORBA:

❑ We discussed the principles of the Common Object Request Broker Architecture (CORBA) and discussed how to implement CORBA objects and clients using the JavaIDL ORB included in the Java 2 platform

❑ We walked through a typical CORBA invocation to see what happens within the IDL client stub and IDL skeleton as the invocation passes from one process to another

❑ Finally, we showed how using RMI-IIOP allows our CORBA clients and objects to interoperate with our native Java RMI clients and objects as if they all were built and deployed in a common application framework

Using the information in this chapter, we can build *n*-tier applications where Java and non-Java clients and objects can seamlessly interact. By combining the benefits of CORBA and Java, our *n*-tier applications can now be both accessible to new clients and able to accommodate new distributed objects without concern for their implementation languages.

Servlets

Java has quickly become the language of choice for writing server-side network applications. Its flexibility and its built-in support for networking make writing networked applications if not easy, at least easier than other methods. Java servlets are part of the Java 2 Platform Enterprise Edition (J2EE) suite of technologies for building scalable web-based applications. The J2EE incorporates several important Java technologies including:

- ❑ **Enterprise JavaBeans (EJBs)** – These software components are used to implement business objects and processes. They are deployed into a server-side software component called an EJB container, which provides services such as persistence, transactional integrity, and security.

- ❑ **JDBC** – This is the means by which Java applications access relational databases, CSV files, Excel files and so on. It includes features for generating queries, managing resultsets, and making updates. Most popular databases have JDBC drivers available.

- ❑ **Java Naming and Directory Interface (JNDI)** – JNDI is the network naming service that enterprise Java applications use to look up services

- ❑ **JavaServer Pages (JSP)** – JSP technology builds on servlets, which allows non-Java programmers to create web pages. We'll look more closely at JSPs below.

- ❑ **Java Servlet Technology** – Java Servlets are a way to extend the services of any server using a request-response protocol, most often web servers. You'll recall from Chapter 4, *Web Basics*, that simple HTTP requests and responses can be generated in any Java application. Servlets built on that basic technology simplify more complicated operations like session tracking and form processing.

In this chapter we'll look at the servlet API and compare servlets to other similar technologies.

What Are Servlets?

When web servers were first deployed, they simply read files and sent them to the client browser, which displayed the HTML data (or whatever it happened to be). This was a big step forward over the alternatives for sharing information like FTP, but the data was still **static** – every client got the same page and the only way to change the content was to edit the file on the server.

An important milestone in the evolution of the web was the development of techniques, such as CGI for generating **dynamic** content. That is, content that was customized based on the context of the request. Now every client can get customized pages built using data from many sources, not just files. Now the web server can act as a **web application** rather than just a file server. Java servlets are a technology for generating dynamic content for the web.

Fundamentally, servlets are Java software components (classes) that plug into web servers and respond to requests from clients. These clients are often web browsers, but they might be any other network-aware application. Servlets allow developers to generate dynamic content by simply writing new Java classes and plugging them into the web server.

Servlets often use other J2EE technologies to build their responses. For example, they might use JDBC to read records to build a display for a client. They might use Enterprise JavaBeans to carry out some business processes like summarizing some data. Servlets also often work with JavaServer Pages to generate HTML content that a browser can display.

A class that implements a servlet, implements the `javax.servlet.Servlet` interface. This interface defines the few methods that a servlet must support to process clients' requests. Another class, `javax.servlet.http.HTTPServlet`, implements the `Serializable` interface and includes a few more methods required to handle HTTP requests. The vast majority of servlets are subclasses of `HTTPServlet` and all of the examples that we will see in this chapter are subclasses of `javax.servlet.http.HTTPServlet`. We'll look in detail at how these classes are used below.

In this chapter, we will look at the capabilities of servlets and how to build, deploy, and debug them. For details on installing a common web server servlet container – Apache Tomcat – see Appendix B.

Servlets and Web Servers

When a servlet is deployed into a web server, it appears to a web browser as just another web page. However, because servlets are executable Java code, they can generate web pages on the fly based on the context and any other data available. As such, they are often used as a critical piece of a web-based application. Let's look at how a servlet works.

The software packages that run servlets are called **servlet containers**. They are often implemented as plugins to web servers. For example, the Apache web server can be configured to delegate servlet requests to the Tomcat servlet container. The person who installs the servlets will configure the web server to route certain URL requests to the servlet container. Sometimes any URL with a particular extension is routed to the servlet container, other times any URL with a certain prefix will be redirected. For example, the URL http://somehost.somedomain.com/servlet/ might be configured to redirect to the servlet container.

Once the request is routed to the servlet container, the container must decide which servlet will service the request. To do this, it must map a URL to a servlet class. Again, this mapping can be done by various criteria:

❑ A servlet can be mapped to a particular URL. For example, /dirname/myServlet.html might be mapped to a particular servlet. Servlets usually aren't mapped to names ending with ".html" to avoid confusion with static pages, but they can be mapped to any name.

❑ A servlet can be mapped to all URLs that begin with a particular directory name. For example, a servlet mapped to /myServlet will receive the requests /myServlet/aFile.html and /myServlet/aDir/aFile.html but notably not /myServlet.html. This type of mapping can be useful if you want an entire subdirectory of the URL space to be processed by a single servlet.

❑ A servlet can be mapped to any URL that ends in a particular filename extension. So, if you map a servlet to "*.servlet" any URL filename that ends with ".servlet" will cause the servlet to be invoked. For example, a reference to /myDir/someThing.servlet would be routed to the servlet.

❑ A servlet can be mapped to the special URL /servlet. So a servlet named myServlet can be accessed by the URL /servlet/myServlet. For simplicity, the examples in this chapter assume this mapping. In the figures that follow, the URL display of the web server shows the URL to which the servlet was mapped.

❑ A servlet can be invoked by its class name. So a servlet class named com.domain.myServlet could be invoked by the URL /servlet/com.domain.myServlet. In practice, this is very rarely a good idea as it ties the structure of the web site to the package structure of the servlets.

Once a request is mapped to a servlet, the web server invokes the servlet. This diagram shows the flow of control when a servlet is invoked.

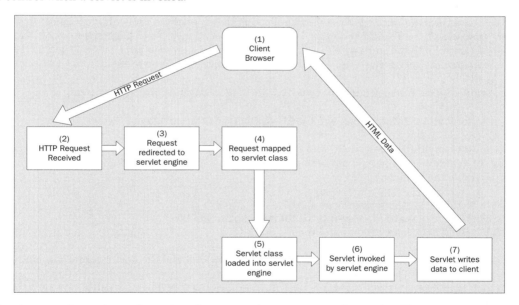

The diagram above shows the order of events in the invocation of a servlet. They are:

1. The client transmits an HTTP request to the web server. This request includes a URL so the web server knows how to handle the request.

2. The request is received by the web server, which parses the URL from the HTTP request

3. The web server uses its configuration information and the URL of the request to determine how to process the request. In this example, the request is routed to the servlet engine.

4. The servlet engine uses its configuration information and the URL of the request to determine which servlet should process the request

5. If necessary, the servlet engine loads the servlet class. If this servlet class has been loaded before, the servlet engine can skip this step and eliminate the time required to find the servlet class and load it. For frequently used servlets, the time saved by this efficiency can be significant.

6. The servlet container invokes the servlet. The container sets up the input and output streams to the client for the servlet. It also manages any session state if the client has already accessed the web application.

7. The servlet parses the URL and session information, generates its response and writes the data back to the client

This process of indirection through the web server and the servlet container allows the web site developer a lot of flexibility in how servlets are deployed. Flexibility is important if the web site is changed frequently, or needs to be able to scale to multiple servers.

Configuring the Tomcat Server for the Code Examples

The code examples are packaged as a web application that is ready to use with the Tomcat servlet server. First, install the Tomcat server as described in Appendix B. Next, place the folder in the code download (`wrox`) into the `webapps` directory. It will create a new web application called `wrox` that will be loaded when the server starts up. Restart the Tomcat server and you're ready to try the examples.

To recompile the examples, go into the `wrox\WEB-INF\classes` directory and run:

```
C:\jakarta-tomcat-4.0-b7\webapps\wrox\WEB-INF\classes>javac *.java
```

If you run into any difficulties, make sure that the following variables are set correctly. To check this, in the case of Windows simply type **set** on the command-line, and they should all be listed. Make sure that yours resemble the following:

```
CATALINA_HOME=C:\jakarta-tomcat-4.0-b7
CLASSPATH= .;C:\jakarta-tomcat-4.0-b7\common\lib\servlet.jar
TOMCAT_HOME=C:\jakarta-tomcat-4.0-b7
```

In case of continued difficulty, go back and consult Appendix B and the documentation again.

If you look in the `wrox\WEB-INF\web.xml` file, you can see that there are entries for a few of the examples in this chapter, but most of them just use the default configuration. We'll look at the specialized entries in `web.xml` as we discuss the examples.

Similar Technologies

There are several ways besides servlets to generate dynamic web content and each has its advantages. Some are more suitable for particular applications or environments; some require skills with particular programming languages or operating environments. We will look at some similar technologies to see how servlets compare.

Common Gateway Interface (CGI)

CGI was one of the earliest ways to extend a web server and generate web pages on the fly. CGI programs are often scripts (especially Perl scripts), but can be any executable program. As described above in the example of a servlet container, web servers can be configured to treat some requests as special and instead of reading a file to send to the client, the web server will run a program that generates the data for the client. In simple applications a URL directory (like http://somehost.somedomain.com/cgi-bin/) will be populated with scripts that can generate some customized web content. The diagram below shows the control flow when a CGI program is invoked.

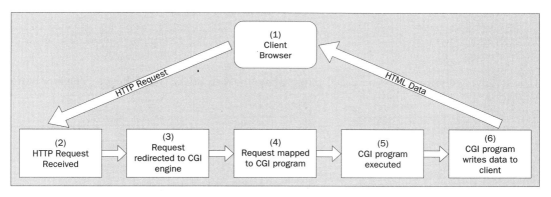

In this example, the flow of events is as follows:

8. The client transmits an HTTP request to the web server. This request includes a URL so the web server knows how to handle the request.

9. The request is received by the web server, which parses the URL from the HTTP request.

10. The web server uses its configuration information and the URL of the request to determine how to process the request. In this example, the request is routed to the CGI engine.

11. The CGI engine maps the request to a CGI program.

12. The CGI program is executed and uses properties of the request, which the CGI engine mapped to environment variables, to generate its response.

13. The CGI program writes its response to the C standard output stream. The CGI engine and web server route this stream to the client.

CGI programs are fairly easy to write and are a popular choice for simple applications, and because they can be written in almost any programming language, they don't impose some of the same skill requirements on developers as other technologies. CGI has some significant limitations, though; because each invocation of a CGI program requires a new process, they can be slower than other techniques. Additionally, because each invocation is a new process, any history of interactions with the client (called **session state**) must be maintained by the CGI programmer. Several improvements have been made in the efficiency and functionality of CGI engines, but in general, CGI is best suited for simple applications.

PHP

PHP is an open source server-side scripting language developed as part of the Apache Project. It has syntax similar to Perl with concepts from C and Java. It supports many common functions required of a web application including database access, regular expression text matching, and e-mail processing.

PHP scripts are snippets of code embedded within an HTML document, which are executed by the PHP interpreter when the page is requested. The PHP code is delimited by special tags that are interpreted by the PHP processor.

The PHP code starts with the <?php" tag and ends at the " ?> tag. Everything outside the tags is passed directly to the client as HTML. The PHP interpreter executes everything between the tags.

PHPs are invoked through an interpreter plugged into the web server. The following diagram illustrates the process:

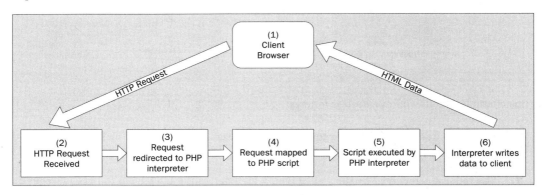

The invocation of a PHP script proceeds as follows:

1. The client transmits an HTTP request to the web server. This request includes a URL so the web server knows how to handle the request.

2. The request is received by the web server, which parses the URL from the HTTP request.

3. The web server uses its configuration information and the URL of the request to determine how to process the request. In this example, the request is routed to the PHP interpreter.

4. The PHP interpreter uses its configuration information and the URL of the request to select the appropriate PHP script.

5. The PHP interpreter reads and interprets the PHP script. HTML output is generated

6. The output of the PHP script is written to the client by the PHP interpreter through the web server

This is a very simple example, but if you're willing to learn a new language, PHP can be a powerful technology for server-side development.

Active Server Pages (ASP)

Like PHP, ASP is a server-side scripting technology. Unlike PHP, ASP is a Microsoft commercial product. As such, it has great support for Microsoft technologies like Component Object Model (COM), but is limited to Microsoft platforms. ASP code snippets can be written in any scripting language that has an Active Script interface – such as VB Script, Jscript or Perl – delimited by <% and %> tags.

The invocation of an ASP page is much like the PHP invocation. The main difference is the language used within the <% %> tags.

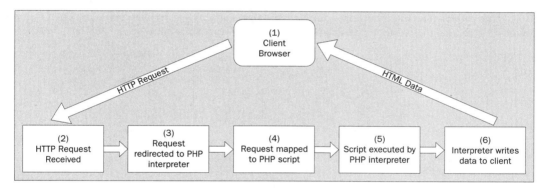

Steps in the invocation of an ASP page are similar to the invocation of a PHP page. The figure above shows the following steps:

1. The client transmits an HTTP request to the web server. This request includes a URL so the web server knows how to handle the request.

2. The request is received by the web server, which parses the URL from the HTTP request.

3. The web server uses its configuration information and the URL of the request to determine how to process the request. In this example, the request is routed to the ASP interpreter.

4. The ASP interpreter uses its configuration information and the URL of the request to select the appropriate ASP script.

5. The ASP interpreter reads and interprets the ASP script. It may utilize COM objects in the generation of its output.

6. The output of the ASP script is written to the client by the ASP interpreter through the web server.

JavaServer Pages (JSP)

JavaServer Pages are an extension of servlet technology and a component of the J2EE suite of technologies. Like PHP and ASP, JSP allows the web developer to embed code snippets in a web document. What distinguishes JSP is that the code snippets are in Java.

As in ASP code, JSP code snippets are delimited by <% and %> tags. Everything outside the tags is treated as verbatim text and sent to the client unmodified. Text between the tags is compiled as Java code and executed by the server. Here's a simple JSP file:

```
<html>
<head><title>A JSP Page</title></head>
<body>
<% out.println("Hello, world!"); %>
</body></html>
```

When the servlet container receives a request for a Java Server Page, the JSP text document is read by a special servlet that converts the page to Java source code. The source code that it generates is exactly a servlet. This code is then automatically compiled and installed into the servlet container. Then the servlet is invoked to service the request. The diagram below shows the control flow when a JSP is invoked.

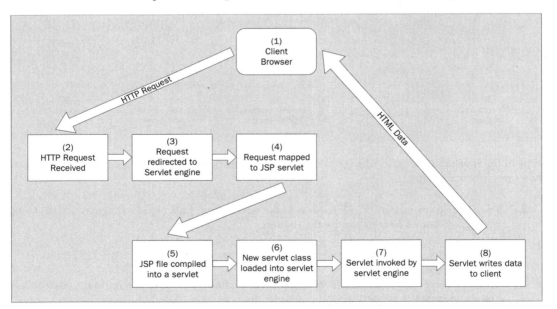

1. The client transmits an HTTP request to the web server. This request includes a URL so the web server knows how to handle the request.

2. The request is received by the web server, which parses the URL from the HTTP request.

3. The web server uses its configuration information and the URL of the request to determine how to process the request. In this example, the request is routed to the servlet container.

4. The servlet container uses its configuration information and the URL of the request to determine which servlet should process the request. In this example, the JSP interpreter is itself a servlet and the servlet container is configured to route requests for JSP pages to it.

5. The JSP servlet compiles the JSP source into a servlet. That is, it generates Java source code for a new servlet based on the JSP text. The new Java servlet is compiled into a class file.

6. The new servlet is loaded into the servlet container the same way a hand-coded servlet would be loaded. Note that if the JSP has been used before and it hasn't been garbage collected, Steps 5 and 6 may not be necessary.

7. The JSP servlet redirects the request to the new servlet. The container has set up the input and output streams to the client for the servlet. Any other relevant state information is also passed to the new servlet.

8. The new servlet generated from the JSP source parses the URL and session information, generates its response and writes the data back to the client.

Because they are so closely related, JSPs and servlets are often used together to build a web application. Java developers can write servlets that use databases or Enterprise JavaBeans to collect and manage the application data and web page designers can use familiar tools like HTML or XML to construct attractive pages. This allows both the page designers and the Java developers to concentrate on what they do best.

Implementing Servlets

All of the classes and interfaces that make up the servlet technology are in the standard extension packages javax.servlet and javax.servlet.http. As mentioned above, developing a servlet requires writing a Java class that implements the javax.servlet.Servlet interface. This interface specifies the few methods that all servlets must implement. In practice, most servlets extend the javax.servlet.http.HttpServlet class, which includes methods for handling HTTP requests. We'll look first at a short example, and then at the javax.servlet.Servlet interface and then at the javax.servlet.http.HttpServlet class.

A Simple HTTP Servlet

First of all, let's look at an example. The code below shows a simple HTTP servlet. When it receives a request, it responds with a list of the HTTP request parameters and their values.

```
//helloservlet.java
import javax.servlet.*;
import javax.servlet.http.*;
import java.io.*;
import java.util.*;

public class HelloServlet extends HttpServlet {

  public void doGet(HttpServletRequest request,
                    HttpServletResponse response) throws ServletException,
                    IOException {
```

```
            response.setContentType("text/html");
            PrintWriter out = response.getWriter();

            // Start the HTML document
            out.println("<html>");

            // Set the title of the document
            out.println("<head><title>HelloServlet</title></head>");

            // Start the document body
            out.println("<body>");
            out
              .println("<p>HelloServlet received a GET request. The parameters
                        follow.</p>");

            Enumeration params = request.getParameterNames();
            while (params.hasMoreElements()) {
              String param = (String) params.nextElement();
              out.println("<p>");
              out.println(param + "=" + request.getParameter(param));
              out.println("</p>");
            }
            out.println("</body></html>");
        }
    }
```

This servlet uses the default implementation of all of the methods in HTTPServlet except for doGet(), which it overrides. The doGet() method is called when the servlet receives an HTTP GET request from a client. So, when the appropriate URL is typed into the browser address window, the browser generated a GET request to the server. The server then called this servlet's doGet() method.

The doGet() method of this servlet does several things. First, these lines set the content-type header to text/html and start the HTML document by writing the opening tags and the title:

```
            response.setContentType("text/html");
            PrintWriter out = response.getWriter();

            // Start the HTML document
            out.println("<html>");

            // Set the title of the document
            out.println("<head><title>HelloServlet</title></head>");

            // Start the document body
            out.println("<body>");
```

The following lines print each of the URL parameters and its value within the body of the document:

```
            Enumeration params = request.getParameterNames();
            while (params.hasMoreElements()) {
              String param = (String) params.nextElement();
              out.println("<p>");
              out.println(param + "=" + request.getParameter(param));
              out.println("</p>");
            }
```

The last line of the doGet() method completes the HTML document by printing the closing tags.

```
out.println("</body></html>");
```

This is what the output of HelloServlet looks like in a browser. The URL query parameters (?param1=value1&param2=value2) are parsed by the servlet and printed to the HTML output stream.

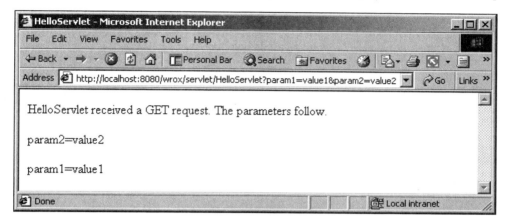

The text has been interpreted by the browser as HTML and rendered as such. We can view the page source to see the raw output of the servlet. Here is the raw text that the HelloServlet generated:

```
<html>
<head><title>HelloServlet</title></head>
<body>
<p>The servlet has received a GET. The parameters follow.</p>
<p>
param2=value2
</p>
<p>
param1=value1
</p>
</body></html>
```

As you can see, all of the strings used in the out.println() calls were transmitted to the client browser. Notice the query string part of the URL in the browser address field. The two query string parameters, param1 and param2, have been collected by the servlet container and stored in the HTTPServletRequest object that is passed to the doGet() method. This servlet can retrieve the parameters and their values – value1 and value2 respectively – so it can include them in the HTML document. The servlet could also use the query string parameters for customizing its behavior.

There are many new methods and classes being used here, and next we shall look at the two most important of them: the Servlet interface and HTTPServlet class. In the example above, most of the methods were the default implementations of HTTPServlet, except for the doGet() method. In the following discussion of these implementations, it is hoped that the reader will begin to see some of the possibilities inherent in the servlet package.

The javax.servlet.Servlet Interface

The `javax.servlet.Servlet` interface defines five methods that all servlets must implement. The `init(ServletConfig)` method is called exactly once – when the servlet is first loaded into the web server. The `init()` method is called before any other method, so it can be used to initialize the servlet to make it ready to receive requests. Note that the developer must store the `ServletConfig` object passed as an argument so it can be returned by the `getServletConfig()` method. We will look at the `ServletConfig` object later in this chapter.

The `destroy()` method is called when the servlet is unloaded from the web server. It is the developer's opportunity to free resources like database connections or files before the servlet goes away.

The `getServletInfo()` method is an opportunity for the servlet to return a descriptive string about itself to the servlet container. This may be anything that is descriptive to the web site developer or maintainer. It is not usually communicated to clients.

The `service()` method is the method that does the work. The servlet container calls it when a request that is mapped to this servlet is received. The servlet container passes `ServletRequest` and `ServletResponse` objects to the `service()` method, which it uses to handle the request. We will look at the `ServletRequest` and `ServletResponse` objects and see examples of their use below.

Most people never need to implement `javax.servlet.Servlet` directly. The `javax.servlet.GenericServlet` class implements `javax.servlet.Servlet` and provides a default implementation for each servlet method except `service()`. Its `init(ServletConfig)` method stores the `ServletConfig` so it can be returned by `getServletConfig()` and then calls an `init()` method that has no parameters. Most of the time, you will not override this method to do servlet initialization, but rather override the no-argument `init()`.

The `destroy()` method of `GenericServlet` does nothing. Override it to release any resources held by the servlet.

`GenericServlet`'s `getServletInfo()` method returns the empty string. Override it to have the servlet return a meaningful value.

The `getServletConfig()` method returns the `ServletConfig` passed into the `init(ServletConfig)` method when the servlet was created. This method is not normally overridden.

The javax.servlet.http.HttpServlet Class

The `javax.servlet.http.HttpServlet` class extends `GenericServlet` to include many convenience functions for handling HTTP requests. Most notably, the `service()` method inspects the request and routes it to a method based on the HTTP request method. Each of these methods receives arguments of type `HttpServletRequest` and `HttpServletResponse`, which implement `ServletRequest` and `ServletResponse` respectively. We can see how these are used below:

❑　 `doGet()` – This method can be overridden to process HTTP GET requests. The default implementation returns an HTTP BAD_REQUEST error to the client.

❑ doPost() – This method can be overridden to process HTTP POST requests. The default implementation returns an HTTP BAD_REQUEST error to the client.

❑ doDelete() – This method can be overridden to process HTTP DELETE requests. Clients use HTTP DELETE requests to request that a resource (a URL) be removed from the server. The default implementation returns an HTTP BAD_REQUEST error to the client.

❑ doPut() – This method can be overridden to process HTTP PUT requests. A client can generate an HTTP PUT request to upload file data to the server. The default implementation returns an HTTP BAD_REQUEST error to the client.

❑ doTrace() – This method can be overridden to process HTTP TRACE requests. The default implementation returns a document containing all of the headers sent in the trace request.

❑ doOptions() – This method can be overridden to process HTTP OPTIONS requests. The default implementation generates the required response automatically so this method does not normally need to be overridden.

❑ The getLastModified() method of the HttpServlet class should return the time that the requested resource was last modified. Browser and proxy caches use this value to determine whether a resource should be re-fetched. The default implementation returns a negative number, which indicates that the modification time is unknown. The value is in the same units as System.currentTimeMillis() – which is the number of milliseconds since January 1, 1970.

The javax.servlet.Servlet interface is not bound to any particular protocol so it is very flexible but it doesn't provide much functionality. Since HTTP is the most widely used protocol for web applications, the javax.servlet.http.HttpServlet class is the one most often extended by servlet developers.

ServletRequest and HttpServletRequest

A ServletRequest object is generated by the servlet container and passed to the servlet's service() method. It encapsulates information about the client's request including any query string or POST parameters and an input stream from which the servlet can read the body of the request.

As you can see in the example above, objects of these types are returned as parameters:

```
public void doGet(HttpServletRequest request,
                  HttpServletResponse response) throws ServletException,
                  IOException {
    response.setContentType("text/html");
```

HttpServletRequest extends ServletRequest with methods that are appropriate for HTTP requests. The ServletRequest and HttpServletRequest methods are described below.

Handling the Input Stream

A servlet often needs to read data from the client before it can do its processing. The ServletRequest object has two methods that can be used to read this data. The getInputStream() method returns an InputStream on which the servlet can read the binary request data. Alternatively, the servlet can use the getReader() method to get a buffered stream from which to read text data. Note that only one of getInputStream() or getReader() can be called on a given ServletRequest or an IllegalStateException will be thrown.

Understanding the Content of the Request

A servlet needs to know what kind of data is in the request. The characteristics of the request are made available to the servlet through these `ServletRequest` methods.

The `getContentLength()` method returns the length, in bytes, of the request data or −1 if the length is not known. The `getContentType()` method returns the MIME content type of the request data or `null` if the type is not known. MIME content types are strings that can be used to interpret the data like `image/gif` or `text/html`.

Occasionally, you may need to know whether the request was made using a secure channel. The `isSecure()` `ServletRequest` method returns `true` if this request was made using a secure protocol; HTTPS, for example. The `getAuthType()` method of `HttpServletRequest` returns the name of the authentication scheme used to protect the servlet – for example, BASIC or SSL. This method returns `null` if no authentication scheme was used.

Information About the Requestor and the Request

Sometimes a servlet needs to know some information about the client making the request. It may need to log access from certain hosts or respond with internationalized content, for example. The several `ServletRequest` methods give the servlet information about the request and the client making the request. If your servlet must generate internationalized content, the `getLocale()` method is useful for determining the `Locale` preferred by the requestor. The `getRemoteHost()` method returns the host name of the requestor – for example, `mail.wrox.com`. If the address cannot be resolved to a name, this method returns the IP address of the requestor.

A servlet can also determine information about the protocol of the request using the `ServletRequest` and `HttpServletRequest` methods. We will see this at work in the examples later.

Information About the Server

If a web application is divided among more than one server, a servlet may need to know some information about the server that received the request. The `getServerName()` and `getServerPort()` methods in `ServletRequest` return the host name and network port respectively of the server that received the request. In practice, this information is rarely useful.

Managing Parameters

Depending on the request method, request parameters can come from the URL query string, the POST parameters, or both. Query strings can be used with GET or POST requests while POST parameters are only available in POST requests.

> **Caution: a servlet that reads from the input stream of a POST request can cause the automatic parameter parsing to fail. If you must read from the input stream of a POST request, parse the parameters manually.**

The `ServletRequest.getParameterNames()` returns an `Enumeration` of `String` objects containing the names of the parameters contained in this request. In the case of an HTTP request, this would include the HTTP GET query parameters or the POST form data parameters. The `getParameter(String)` method returns a string containing the value of the specified parameter or `null` if the parameter has no value. If there can be more than one value for a parameter, you must use the `getParameterValues()` method, which returns an array of strings containing the value(s) of the specified parameter.

HTTP Headers

The `HttpServletRequest` extends `ServletRequest` with methods to read the HTTP headers. HTTP headers are used to describe the content and the client's desired handling of the request. The `HttpServletRequest` methods for accessing HTTP headers are as follows:

❑ The `getHeaderNames()` method returns an `Enumeration` of the header names present in this request.

❑ The `getHeader(String)` method returns the value of the requested header name. If the request does not contain a header with that name, `getHeader()` returns `null`.

`HttpServletRequest` also includes the `getIntHeader()` and `getDateHeader()` convenience methods to convert the header values to integers and dates.

Request Attributes

Servlets and the servlet container can associate name-value pair attributes with requests. If the request is passed between servlets using the `RequestDispatcher` techniques explained below, the attributes set in one servlet will propagate to the subsequent servlets. These attributes might include such things as the public key certificate of the requestor or intermediate results associated with the request. The naming convention for attributes follows the naming convention for Java packages in which the name starts with the Internet domain name of the author, for example, `com.wrox.*`.

We will look more closely at attributes later on in the chapter.

ServletResponse and HttpServletResponse

Like the `ServletRequest`, the `ServletResponse` object is constructed by the servlet container and passed to the servlet's `service()` method. It is used by the servlet to communicate its response to the client's request. `ServletResponse` includes an `OutputStream` on which the servlet can write data to the client as well as methods to set other response characteristics. The `HttpServletResponse` class extends `ServletResponse` with methods to set HTTP headers and cookies. Let's look at the important methods of these classes.

Handling the Output Stream

The `ServletResponse` class has two methods that can be used to retrieve the output stream for writing data to the client – `getOutputStream()` and `getWriter()`. They differ in that `getOutputStream()` returns an unfiltered stream suitable for writing binary data while `getWriter()` returns a `PrintWriter` suitable for text. Note that only one of `getOutputStream()` or `getWriter()` can be called on a given `ServletResponse` or an `IllegalStateException` will be thrown.

Controlling the Information About the Response

Servlets need to communicate to their client information that helps the client interpret the response. This information is expressed in the headers to the HTTP response. The headers are sent when data is written to the output stream, so to work properly these methods must be called before any data is written to the output stream.

The `setContentLength(int)` method is used by the servlet to set the content length header for this response. This value should be the length of the content data, in bytes.

The setContentType(String) method is used by the servlet to set the MIME content type header for this response. This should be text/html for HTML documents. The setLocale(Locale) method is used to set the Locale of the response including headers as appropriate. If the servlet doesn't call this method, the default Locale of the server is used.

A servlet can also set arbitrary headers using the setHeader() method. This HttpServletResponse method adds a new header with the specified name and value to the response. This differs from addHeader() in that if a header already exists with this name, the value is replaced with the new value. addHeader() will add the value to the list of values if the header already exists. HttpServletResponse also includes convenience methods for setting integer and date headers.

Controlling the Output Buffering

The ServletResponse object has methods for manipulating the buffer associated with the output stream. We don't usually need to explicitly control the output buffering for a simple servlet, but sometimes it's more efficient to take direct control of the buffering.

Since the headers are sent at the beginning of the output, a larger buffer allows the servlet to queue more output before the headers must be committed. A response is said to be **committed** once the headers have been sent to the client. A smaller buffer consumes less server memory space and may result in a quicker response to the client. The right size depends on the application's requirements. Servlets can use these methods control output stream buffering.

❑ setBufferSize(int) sets the desired buffer size for the output stream. The actual size may be larger.

❑ getBufferSize() returns the actual output buffer size allocated by the servlet container.

❑ flushBuffer() causes the data in the buffer to be immediately written to the client. If the headers have not already been sent, they are sent.

❑ reset() clears all of the data that has been written to the response including headers. If any data have been committed, this method throws a java.lang.IllegalStateException.

❑ isCommitted() returns a boolean indicating whether any data (including headers) have been written to the client.

Sending Status and Error Information

Servlets must communicate to their clients the status of their requests. This status is communicated through HTTP status codes. Some codes indicate errors while others indicate the successful servicing of the request. The codes are defined as static integers in the HttpServletResponse class.

The setStatus() method is used by a servlet to set the status code when there is no error. If there is an error, use the sendError() method, which sends an error response to the client. Calling this method causes the response to be committed so no further output should be written to it. If the response has already been committed, this method throws a java.lang.IllegalStateException. In addition to the error code, sendError() has an optional second parameter that is a descriptive error message. Later in this chapter we'll see some examples of the use of these methods.

Manipulating URLs

Often the response data generated by a servlet contains URLs referencing other web resources. Sometimes the servlet needs to immediately redirect the requestor to another resource. These HttpServletResponse methods enable servlets to create and manipulate URLs and redirect requests.

The encodeURL(String) method returns the URL argument rewritten, if necessary, to support session tracking. We'll look in more detail at session tracking later in this chapter. Similarly, the encodeRedirectURL(String) method rewrites the argument URL to support session tracking. The rules for encoding URLs used for redirection are different, though, so use this method to create arguments for sendRedirect(). sendRedirect(String) sends a temporary redirect response to the client using the specified URL string. Calling this method causes the response to be committed so no further output should be written to it. If this method is called after output is committed, a java.lang.IllegalStateException is thrown.

The Servlet Life Cycle

Now that we've looked at the basic servlet API and seen a simple example, let's look at how servlets are handled by a servlet container. Servlets go through several states as a servlet container uses them. The servlet container can create, use, and destroy servlets based on its configuration and the requests it receives. This figure shows a servlet's progression through its life cycle.

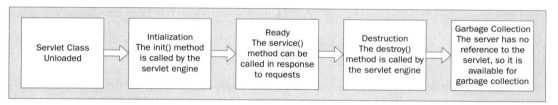

The first action a web server takes is to load the servlet class and call its init() method. As mentioned before, the init() method is called exactly once and is an opportunity for the servlet to initialize expensive resources including things like database connections. Most servlet containers allow the administrator to specify whether a servlet should be initialized when the server starts or only when a request is received. Initializing a servlet when the server starts makes it ready to service requests more quickly because it doesn't need to be loaded when the first request arrives. However, initializing all servlets when the server starts can make it slow to start and use more memory than it would otherwise. As always, the demands of your application determine which is the right strategy.

After the init() method completes, the servlet is in the ready state and is available to service requests using its service() method. When the servlet is to be unloaded from the server, its destroy() method is called. This is the servlet's opportunity to release resources that it acquired during its init() or service() methods. Once the destroy() method completes, there are no remaining references to the servlet so it is available for garbage collection.

The ServletConfig Object

The init() method of a servlet receives a ServletConfig object as its parameter. This object contains information from the servlet container that the servlet can use to configure itself. When a servlet is deployed, it can be configured with deployment parameters called init parameters. These parameters can be used to tell the servlet about the environment in which it will run. init parameters are often used to set JDBC connection strings or other deployment-specific data.

The ServletConfig methods include getInitParameterNames() which returns an enumeration of the names of the servlet init parameters. It returns an empty enumeration if the servlet has no parameters. getInitParameter(String) returns the value for this servlet's specified parameter or null if the parameter has no value. The getServletContext() method returns the ServletContext for this servlet. We will discuss ServletContext in more detail later.

This code will print out the name of the servlet and a list of `init` parameters given to a servlet when it was deployed:

```
private void printConfig(){
  ServletConfig cfg = getServletConfig();
  System.out.println("This servlet's name is "+cfg.getServletName());

  Enumeration enum = cfg.getInitParameterNames();
  while (enum.hasMoreElements()) {
    String name = (String) enum.nextElement();
    String param = cfg.getInitParameter(name);
    System.out.println("Init parameter: "+name+" is set to "+param);
  }
}
```

First, this method fetches the `ServletConfig` for this servlet using the `getServletConfig()` method. Then it prints the name that was given to the servlet by the administrator of the servlet container when this servlet was deployed. Finally, it gets the list of `init` parameters by calling `getInitParameterNames()` and loops through them, calling `getInitParameter()` for each one.

The next example demonstrates some of the functions of the `ServletConfig` and the `ServletContext`. The `ServletConfig` (which we will be discussing in depth later) is passed to the servlet's `init()` method by the servlet container. The `GenericServlet` class implementation of `init()` stores it for us so we don't override it in this example. We will look at the `ServletConfig` and `ServletContext` in the `doGet()` method so we can see the results in a browser.

```
//paramServlet.java
import javax.servlet.*;
import javax.servlet.http.*;
import java.io.*;
import java.util.*;

public class ParamServlet extends HttpServlet {
  public void doGet(HttpServletRequest request,
                    HttpServletResponse response) throws ServletException,
                    IOException {

    // Set the content type header and start the HTML document
    response.setContentType("text/html");
    PrintWriter out = response.getWriter();
    out.println("<html>");
    out.println("<head><title>ParamServlet</title></head>");
    out.println("<body>");

    // fetch the ServletConfig that was stored by init()
    ServletConfig config = getServletConfig();

    out.println("<br>This servlet's name is " + config.getServletName());
    out.println("<br>It's init parameters are :<ul>");
    Enumeration params = config.getInitParameterNames();
    while (params.hasMoreElements()) {
      String name = (String) params.nextElement();
      String value = config.getInitParameter(name);
      out.println("<li>" + name + " = " + value + "</li>");
    }
    out.println("</ul>");

    // Now let's look at the ServletContext
    ServletContext context = config.getServletContext();
```

```
        out.println("<br>The server is " + context.getServerInfo());
        out.println("<br>This server supports servlet version "
                    + context.getMajorVersion() + "."
                    + context.getMinorVersion());

        // Try to read an attribute set in the server (will be null the first time)
        Object obj = context.getAttribute("com.wrox.ParamServletAttribute");
        out.println("<br>The attribute is " + obj);

        // Now set an attribute that can be seen by all servlets in this
        // context (including this one next time)
        context.setAttribute("com.wrox.ParamServletAttribute",
                    "AttributeValue");

        out.println("</body></html>");
    }
}
```

We configured the servlet container to give this servlet these two `init` parameters.

Parameter	Value
Parameter1	Value1
Parameter2	Value2

This is done by editing the `web.xml` file entry for the `ParamServlet`. Since we are running our examples on Tomcat, this file can be found in `C:\jakarta-tomcat-4.0-b7\webapps\wrox\WEB-INF`. The resulting entry looks like this:

```
    <servlet>
        <servlet-name>
            ParamServlet
        </servlet-name>
        <servlet-class>
            ParamServlet
        </servlet-class>
        <init-param>
            <param-name>Parameter1</param-name>
            <param-value>Value1</param-value>
        </init-param>
        <init-param>
            <param-name>Parameter2</param-name>
            <param-value>Value2</param-value>
        </init-param>
    </servlet>
```

The `web.xml` file provided with the examples includes the text above, so you don't need to add it.

Once the servlet container starts up, it can be accessed from a web browser. The response looks like this:

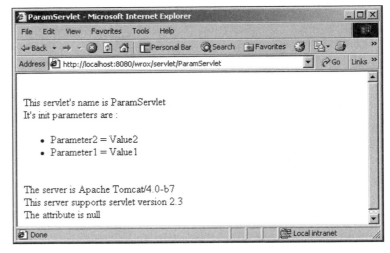

Let's look at what the servlet told us. First, it printed the name of the servlet. Some servlet containers let you give names to servlets. We didn't specify a name when we deployed this servlet, so it defaulted to the class name.

Next the servlet printed its init parameters, which are the same ones we entered in the table above. Then, the servlet printed some information about the servlet container. Normally, you don't care about the servlet container in which your servlet is running, but this one happens to be the Tomcat server, which supports version 2.3 of the servlet API.

The last thing the servlet printed was an attribute that it read from the ServletContext. All servlets in a given web application share the same ServletContext so they can share information by setting attributes in the ServletContext. This servlet first tried to read the attribute. The first time we accessed the servlet, the attribute was null. But, this line of code sets the attribute:

```
context.setAttribute("com.wrox.ParamServletAttribute",
                     "AttributeValue");
```

So the next time we access the servlet, the response looks like this:

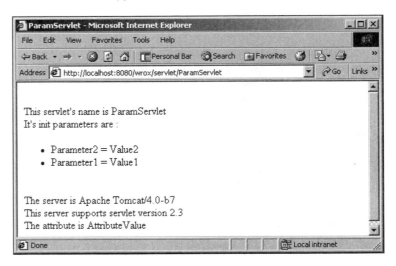

As you can see, the attribute remained set between invocations of the servlet. This example shows a single servlet setting and reading a `ServletContext` attribute, but the `ServletContext` attributes are shared among all of the servlets in a web application.

We will say more on attributes later, but for now it is worth observing that key value pairs can be set through using them.

The ServletContext Object

Web applications are usually built from several components including multiple servlets, JSP pages, and static content (files). The `ServletContext` object is the servlet's view of the entire web application of which it is a part. The `ServletContext` can be accessed from the `ServletConfig` object discussed above using its `getServletContext()` method. The `ServletContext` contains important information about the servlet container and the servlet's environment that the servlet can use to control its processing. `ServletContext` also has attributes that can be set and retrieved by servlets allowing the servlets to communicate with one another. `ServletContext` also has methods that provide version information about the servlet container to the servlet. Let's look at the `ServletContext` methods and see how they are used.

Attributes

The `ServletContext` can hold name-value pairs called attributes that are shared among all of the servlets in a web application. Note that this is different the `ServletRequest` attributes which, as we saw above, are only valid within the scope of a particular request. They are also different to session attributes that we will look at later.

The naming convention for attributes follows the naming convention for Java packages in which the name starts with the Internet domain name of the author, for instance, `com.wrox.*`. The `getAttributeNames()` method returns an `Enumeration` of all of the attribute names available in this `ServletContext`. The `setAttribute(String, Object)` method binds a new name-value attribute pair to this `ServletContext`. If an attribute by that name already exists, it is replaced by this binding. The `getAttribute(String)` method returns the object that the `ServletContext` has associated with the given name and the `removeAttribute(String)` method removes the named attribute.

Servlet Container Version Information

The `ServletContext` object also holds information about the servlet container itself including its name and version as well as the version of the servlet API that it supports. `getMajorVersion()` and `getminorVersion()` return the major and minor version numbers of the servlet API supported by the container. They can be used by the servlet to infer the capabilities of the servlet container. Servlet containers that support the Servlet API 2.3 return 2 from both `getMajorVersion()` and `getMinorVersion()`.

Referencing Other Resources

Servlets usually use other web resources in fulfilling their duties. These resources might be files local to the server, other servlets, or other web resources of unknown type. The `ServletContext` object provides these methods to allow servlets to utilize other resources.

The `getMimeType(String)` method returns the MIME type of the specified file or `null` if the file type is unknown. The MIME types for files are determined by the servlet container and can be configured when the servlet is deployed. Some common MIME types are `text/html`, `text/plain` and `image/jpeg`.

`getRealPath(String)` returns the absolute path for the given URL file path. It returns a string formatted for the host operating system on which the servlet container is running and returns `null` if the URL path cannot be resolved.

The `getResource(String)` method returns a resource URL known to the `ServletContext` at the specified path. This method returns `null` if no resource is known by that name. It is similar to the `getResource()` method in `java.lang.Class`, but allows the servlet container to use methods other than the class loader to locate resources. `getResource()` may be used to locate files such as images that are deployed with the web application. Note that to forward a request or include another web resource in the servlet's response, use `getNamedDispatcher()` described below. `getResourceAsStream(String)` returns an `InputStream` rather than a URL for the requested resource.

Multithreaded Servlets

Some servlet containers will use multiple threads to service requests more efficiently, so it's important that the servlet writer be aware that the servlet might be executing in more than one thread simultaneously. All variables that might be unsafe, if used by more than one thread executing the same servlet, need to be synchronized as explained in Chapter 6, on threads. This means that it will be difficult to hold state data as instance data in the servlet class. We'll see later some other options for holding state data.

Here's an excerpt from a servlet that might have problems in a multithreaded server:

```
public class HelloServlet extends HttpServlet {
    private StringBuffer importantStateData = new StringBuffer("");
    public void doGet(HttpServletRequest request,
                    HttpServletResponse response)
                    throws ServletException, IOException {
    // read and update importantStateData
    ...
```

If the servlet container runs the servlet in multiple threads, `importantStateData` might be used in an inconsistent state.

Sometimes using shared data like this is unavoidable. In these instances, a servlet can implement the `SingleThreadModel` interface to indicate to the servlet container that it's not safe to run this servlet in multiple threads at once. The servlet container will not call the `service()` method of a `SingleThreadModel` servlet until the previous call to `service()` has completed. `SingleThreadModel` is a marker interface. That is, it has no methods, but the servlet container can use the `instanceof` operator to interpret it. This excerpt shows how the servlet could be modified to be safer.

```
public class HelloServlet extends HttpServlet
    implements SingleThreadModel {
    private StringBuffer importantStateData = new StringBuffer("");
    public void doGet(HttpServletRequest request,
                    HttpServletResponse response)
                    throws ServletException, IOException {
        // read and update importantStateData
    ...
```

While this solves the immediate problem, it can make the server much less efficient when heavily loaded. Where possible, it's better to minimize the use of shared variables and use `synchronized` blocks to protect those that remain.

Handling Requests

We've seen a simple example of how a servlet can service a client's request. Now let's look at request handling in more detail.

The two most common requests a servlet will receive are HTTP GET and HTTP POST. In general, a client sends a GET request to retrieve a resource – a read operation. A POST request can be used to update information in the server – a write operation. Most fetches of web pages are GETs and most form submissions are POSTs. The example servlets above responded to GET requests.

The next example shows how to use some of the information available in an HttpServletRequest object. When this servlet receives a GET request, it responds with some information about the request. It prints the protocol being used (HTTP) and the URL that the user referenced to get to the servlet. It also prints the user's IP address and all of the HTTP headers. The headers contain valuable information about the client's capabilities. The last thing on the response page is a small form, which asks for the user's name and favorite color.

```java
//FormServlet.java
import javax.servlet.*;
import javax.servlet.http.*;
import java.io.*;
import java.util.*;

public class FormServlet extends HttpServlet {

  public void doGet(HttpServletRequest request,
                    HttpServletResponse response) throws ServletException,
                    IOException {

    // Identify this response as an HTML document
    response.setContentType("text/html");
    PrintWriter out = response.getWriter();

    // Start the HTML document
    out.println("<html>");

    // Set the title of the document
    out.println("<head><title>FormServlet</title></head>");

    // Start the document body
    out.println("<body>");

    // What protocol are we using?
    out.println("Using protocol: " + request.getProtocol() + "<br>");

    // What URL was requested?
    out.println("The URL you requested is ");
    String my_url =

    // Add the scheme we're using (http)
    request.getScheme() + "://" +

    // Add the hostname and port the server is using
    request.getServerName() + ":" + request.getServerPort() +

    // Add the path to the servlet
    request.getServletPath();
```

```
      out.println(my_url + "<br>");

      // Print the requestor's IP address
      out.println("Your computer is " + request.getRemoteHost() + "<br>");
      out.println("<hr>");

      // Show all the headers
      Enumeration headerNames = request.getHeaderNames();
      while (headerNames.hasMoreElements()) {
        String headerName = (String) headerNames.nextElement();
        String headerValue = request.getHeader(headerName);
        out.println("Header:" + headerName + " = " + headerValue + "<br>");
      }
      out.println("<hr>");

      /* Print a form asking for a name and a favorite color.      */
      /* Note that the ACTION refers the form back to this servlet  */
      /* and the method will be POST rather than GET.               */
      out.println("<FORM METHOD=\"post\" ACTION=\"" + my_url + "\">");
      out.println("<br>");
      out.println("What is your name: <INPUT TYPE=\"text\" NAME=\"name\" >");
      out.println("<br>");
      out.println("What is your favorite color:
            <INPUT TYPE=\"text\" NAME=\"color\" >");
      out.println("<br>");
      out.println("<INPUT TYPE=\"submit\" >");
      out.println("<br>");

      out.println("</FORM>");
      out.println("</body></html>");
  }
}
```

This servlet responds with this page to an Internet Explorer browser. If you have Netscape or some other browser, you can experiment with loading this page. It should return different values for each browser:

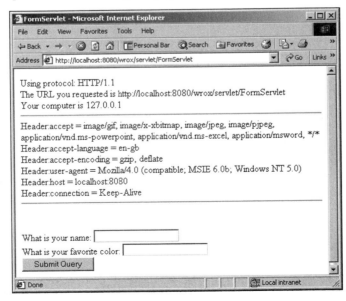

The `user-agent` header tells you what browser version and operating system the client is using. Your servlet might do something different for different versions of browsers.

If we type in a name and favorite color into the form that the servlet generated, however, here's what we see:

The form was submitted by a POST request and we haven't implemented a `doPost()` method yet. Recall that the default implementation of `doPost()` (in `HttpServlet`) responds with an HTTP error `400` (`BAD_REQUEST`). If we want to process the form data, we need to implement `doPost()`. Here's what the `doPost()` method looks like:

```
        out.println("</FORM>");
        out.println("</body></html>");
    }
```

```
    protected void doPost(HttpServletRequest request, HttpServletResponse response)
            throws javax.servlet.ServletException, java.io.IOException {

        // Identify this response as an HTML document
        response.setContentType("text/html");
        PrintWriter out = response.getWriter();

        out.println("<html>");
        out.println("<head><title>FormServlet</title></head>");
        out.println("<body>");

        // Get the values for the "name" and "color" form parameters.
        out.println("Your name is " + request.getParameter("name") + "<br>");
        out.println("Your favorite color is " + request.getParameter("color")
                + "<br>");

        out.println("</body></html>");
    }
}
```

Now when we hit the **Submit Query** button, the servlet reads the name and the favorite color from the form and responds with an appropriate web page:

Generating Responses

We've already seen some examples of how a servlet might generate responses to a client. It can just use the getOutputStream() or getWriter() methods and write data directly to the client.

We also saw how the servlet can set the HTTP headers to tell the client how the data should be interpreted. All of the responses so far have been HTML, so we used the content type "text/html", but a servlet can write any type of data to a client including binary data.

The next servlet reads a GIF image file and sends it to the client as binary data.

```java
//BinaryServlet.java
import javax.servlet.*;
import javax.servlet.http.*;
import java.io.*;
import java.util.*;

public class BinaryServlet extends HttpServlet {
  private static final String filename = "image.gif";
  public void doGet(HttpServletRequest request,
                    HttpServletResponse response) throws ServletException,
                    IOException {

    // Must set the headers before starting the output stream
    response.setContentType("image/gif");
    File f = new File(filename);
    response.setContentLength((int) f.length());

    OutputStream out = response.getOutputStream();

    // read the image data
    FileInputStream fis = new FileInputStream(f);
    byte[] data = new byte[(int) f.length()];
    fis.read(data);

    // write the image data to the client
    out.write(data);

  }
}
```

Notice how the `init()` method uses an `init` parameter to find the image file. This servlet needs some configuration in the `web.xml` file to tell the servlet where to find the `image.gif` file. Open the `web.xml` file in an editor and find the entry for the `BinaryServlet`.

It looks like this:

```
<servlet>
    <servlet-name>
        BinaryServlet
    </servlet-name>
    <servlet-class>
        BinaryServlet
    </servlet-class>
    <init-param>
        <param-name>filename</param-name>
        <param-value>
            C:/jakarta_tomcat_4.0/webapps/wrox/image.gif
        </param-value>
    </init-param>
</servlet>
```

Change the value of the `filename` parameter to the path where you copied the examples to. For instance, here the pathname reflects the path to the image if you have configured Tomcat according to our specifications in Appendix B and downloaded the chapter code as instructed.

Once configured, this is what the servlet looks like in a browser:

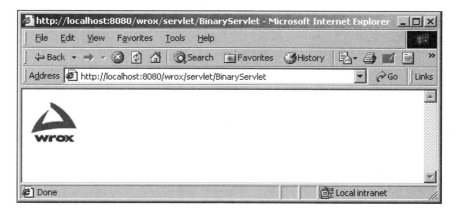

Notice that the servlet sets the content type to `"image/gif"` rather than `"text/html"` as we have seen before. This sets the content-type header to let the browser know that this data is an image in GIF format. It also sets the content length header to the size of the GIF file. It's important, especially for binary data, to set the content length so the client will recognize the end of the response data. As mentioned before, it's also important to remember to set all of the headers that you intend to set before committing any data to the output stream.

Request Forwarding

Sometimes a servlet may need to redirect the request to another servlet or web resource. It's common for a servlet to do some work to collect some data and then redirect the request to another servlet or a JSP for HTML rendering. Here is how a servlet might forward a request to another servlet. It can attach data for the other servlet using the ServletRequest's setAttribute() method.

```
String NEW_LOCATION = "/servlet/NewServlet";
RequestDispatcher dispatcher =
                 getServletContext().getRequestDispatcher(NEW_LOCATION);
request.setAttribute("com.wrox.SomeAttribute", someObject);
dispatcher.forward(request, response);
```

First, this example gets the RequestDispatcher interface for the new location. The servlet container determines the mapping for the new location and returns the appropriate dispatcher.

Next, an attribute called "com.wrox.SomeAttribute" is set in the request. This request will be forwarded to the new location so the attribute will be accessible in the new servlet. The last line causes the request to be sent to the new servlet. If the response had already been committed to the client, forward() will throw a java.lang.IllegalStateException.

When the forwarded request is received by the new servlet, it can access the attribute set in the original servlet like this:

```
Object someObject = request.getAttribute("com.wrox.SomeAttribute");
```

This way, servlets can collaborate on a request with one doing the preliminary processing of a request and storing the results in request attributes. The other servlet reads the attributes and renders the response. This type of forwarding is often used when developing servlets and JSP pages to work together. A servlet will do the data processing to fulfill the request and then forward the data as request attributes to a JSP page for rendering into HTML.

Including Resources

In addition to forwarding the request to another resource, a servlet can also include the output of another resource in its output. The following code shows how the RequestDispatcher can be used to include the output of the new servlet in the output of the current servlet.

```
String NEW_LOCATION = "/servlet/NewServlet";
RequestDispatcher dispatcher =
                 getServletContext().getRequestDispatcher(NEW_LOCATION);
request.setAttribute("com.wrox.SomeAttribute", someObject);
dispatcher.include(request, response);
```

Again, this example first gets the RequestDispatcher object for the new location. Next, an attribute called "com.wrox.SomeAttribute" is set in the request. This request will be sent to the included servlet so the attribute will be accessible in the new servlet. The last line causes the request to be sent to the new servlet and the output of that servlet included in the response. Because the response may already be committed, the included servlet can't set the status code or the headers in the response. Any attempt to set status or headers is ignored.

Managing Sessions

A web application usually needs to keep track of its users. Each page request is received individually but it needs to be associated with other requests so the application can remember the user's past actions and tailor its responses based on them. For example, a shopping application might need to keep track of what items the shopper added to his shopping cart, even though the items might be on different pages. A series of transactions between the server and the client is called a session.

The getSession() method of the HttpServletRequest returns the session associated with the request. When called in its form with no arguments, getSession() creates a new session if no session exists. It has another form, which takes a boolean argument which, if false, will not create a new session and will return null if the session does not yet exist. It is important to call this method before any output response is written or session tracking may not work correctly. The getSession() method returns an HttpSession object, which provides methods for storing attributes and managing the storage of the session data.

Session Attributes

As we saw with the ServletRequest and the ServletContext, the HttpSession object can hold attributes. These attributes are shared among all requests from a particular client, so they might be used to hold information about the user such as the contents of a shopping cart or login information.

These are the HttpSession methods for manipulating session attributes:

❑ getAttributeNames() returns an Enumeration of all of the attribute names that have been set in this session.

❑ setAttribute(String name, Object obj) binds a new name-value attribute pair to this session. If an attribute by that name already exists, it is replaced by this binding.

❑ getAttribute(String name) returns the object that the session has associated with the given name. If there is no attribute for this name, null is returned.

❑ removeAttribute(String name) removes the named attribute from the session. After removeAttribute() is called, any call to getAttribute() with the same name will return null.

Session Management

The HttpSession class has several methods that are useful for monitoring and managing the state of a session. The isNew() method returns true if the client has not yet acknowledged the session by submitting a request with the appropriate session ID. getCreationTime() and getLastAccessedTime() can be used to determine how old the session is and how long it has been idle.

Sessions can be invalidated either by explicit action on the part of a servlet, or based on the expiration of an inactivity timer. A servlet can force the session to be invalidated by calling the HttpSession method invalidate(). If the client does not make a request within the time returned by the getMaxInactiveInterval() method, the session will be invalidated by the servlet container. This is how a server can clean up sessions from idle clients. The maximum inactivity interval for a session can be set by a servlet using the HttpSession setMaxInactiveInterval() and by the deployer in the web.xml file.

The next example illustrates the use of the `HttpSession`. It shows how objects can be bound to the session using `setAttribute()`.

```java
//SessionServlet.java
import javax.servlet.*;
import javax.servlet.http.*;
import java.io.*;
import java.util.*;

public class SessionServlet extends HttpServlet {

  public void doGet(HttpServletRequest request,
                    HttpServletResponse response) throws ServletException,
                    IOException {

    HttpSession session = request.getSession();
    if (session.isNew()) {

      // This is a new session, ask the user for his data
      askForIdentification(request, response);
    } else {

      // This session is not new,
      // respond with the data associated with the session
      clientAlreadyKnown(request, response);
    }
  }

  private void askForIdentification(HttpServletRequest request,
                                    HttpServletResponse response) throws
IOException {
    response.setContentType("text/html");
    PrintWriter out = response.getWriter();
    out.println("<html>");
    out.println("<head><title>SessionServlet</title></head>");
    out.println("<body>");

    // Print a form asking for a name and a favorite color.
    // Notice the use of encodeURL() to make sure the session tracking works
    String my_url = request.getScheme() + "://" + request.getServerName()
                  + ":" + request.getServerPort()
                  + request.getContextPath() + request.getServletPath();
    out.println("<FORM METHOD=\"post\" ACTION=\""
                + response.encodeURL(my_url) + "\">");
    out.println("<br>");
    out.println("What is your name: <INPUT TYPE=\"text\" NAME=\"name\" >");
    out.println("<br>");
    out
      .println("What is your favorite color: <INPUT TYPE=\"text\" NAME=\"color\"
>");
    out.println("<br>");
    out.println("<INPUT TYPE=\"submit\" >");
    out.println("<br>");
    out.println("</FORM>");
    out.println("</body></html>");
  }

  private void clientAlreadyKnown(HttpServletRequest request, HttpServletResponse
response)
          throws javax.servlet.ServletException, java.io.IOException {
```

```
        // inspect the session to get the client's name and favorite color
        HttpSession session = request.getSession();
        String name = (String) session.getAttribute("name");
        String color = (String) session.getAttribute("color");

        response.setContentType("text/html");
        PrintWriter out = response.getWriter();
        out.println("<html>");
        out.println("<head><title>SessionServlet</title></head>");
        out.println("<body>");
        out.println("I know you, " + name + ", your favorite color is "
                + color);
        out.println("</body></html>");
    }

    protected void doPost(HttpServletRequest request, HttpServletResponse response)
            throws javax.servlet.ServletException, java.io.IOException {

        // have to get the session before writing any output
        HttpSession session = request.getSession();

        response.setContentType("text/html");
        PrintWriter out = response.getWriter();

        out.println("<html>");
        out.println("<head><title>SessonServlet</title></head>");
        out.println("<body>");

        // Get the user's name and favorite color from the form
        String name = request.getParameter("name");
        String color = request.getParameter("color");

        // Set two attributes in the session to hold them.
        session.setAttribute("name", name);
        session.setAttribute("color", color);

        out.println("Thanks " + name + ", I like " + color + " too!<br>");
        out.println("</body></html>");
    }
}
```

The servlet above is similar to the `FormServlet` example you saw earlier. It asks the user for their name and favorite color in the `doGet()` method and stores the responses as attributes in the session. Then when this client returns, rather than ask for the information again, it is retrieved from the session. Here's what the form looks like the first time we access the servlet.

The servlet's `doGet()` method is called when the request is received. It checks to see if this session is new, that is, has this client been here before? Since this is my first visit to this site, it calls the private method `askForIdentification()`, further down in the listing, which prints a form for me to fill out. When I submit the form, here is the response:

The form submission was an `HTTP POST`, so the `doPost()` method of the servlet was called. It read the form parameters and stored them in the session using the `setAttribute()` method. The session data will now remain with the session until it is deleted or expires.

If we go and browse some other sites and come back later, the server remembers us and responds with this page:

Just like the first time we visited this site, the `doGet()` method of the servlet was called. This time, however, the session was not new so the private method `clientAlreadyKnown()` was called. It looked up my information in the session object using the `getAttribute()` method and responded with the short page shown above. This example just shows session attributes being preserved between requests to the same servlet, but different servlets can also share session attributes.

Now let's look under the hood and see how servlet containers track sessions. Servlet containers have a few different ways to track sessions so that servlets can associate multiple requests from the same client. In general, a servlet doesn't need to know how the server is tracking the session, but sometimes it's useful to know. The servlet container has three ways it can track sessions: URL rewriting, cookies, and SSL sessions.

URL Rewriting

The servlet container can associate a request with a session by looking for a special URL parameter that it adds to every URL. This URL parameter will be something like **jsessionid=12345678** where the number is a unique arbitrary string. The application servlets don't need to look for this session ID, the servlet container parses it automatically when the request is received and initializes the session. A servlet can find out if the session is being tracked using URL rewriting by using the `isRequestedSessionIdFromURL()` method of the `HttpServletRequest`.

One thing to keep in mind is that if a servlet generates URLs, they need to have the session ID added to them. As mentioned before, the way to do this is to use the encodeURL() method of the HttpServletResponse. It takes a URL string as argument and returns a string with the session ID added if necessary. If the session is being tracked some other way, it will return the argument string unmodified. All URLs emitted from a servlet should be run through the encodeURL() as in the example servlet above.

Cookies

The other common way to track sessions is with cookies. A cookie is a small piece of data that the browser stores on behalf of the server. Once stored, the server can request the cookie from the browser to retrieve the data. This allows the server to store the session ID in the browser and ask for it when needed. Many people have concerns about cookies because they can be used in ways that compromise privacy and security. Because of these concerns, many people disable the cookie feature of their browsers, which forces the server to use another method of session tracking. The servlet container is responsible for handling this situation, so no action is required of the servlet. A servlet can find out if cookies are being used for session tracking with the isRequestedSessionIdFromCookie() method of the HttpServletRequest.

SSL Sessions

The HTTPS protocol is built using Secure Sockets Layer (SSL) encryption technology. Its main purpose is to ensure confidentiality of the data sent between the client and the server, but built into SSL is the capability to associate multiple requests from a client with a single session. Servlet containers can easily use the SSL sessions to define servlet sessions.

What's with All These Attributes?

By now you've noticed that several of the classes involved in writing servlets can hold attributes. The ServletContext, the HttpSession and the ServletRequest each have a setAttribute() method, a getAttribute() method, a getAttributeNames() method, and a removeAttribute() method. Why do we need so many places to store attributes?

Each of these three objects, the ServletContext, the HttpSession and the ServletRequest, has a different **scope**. That is, they each have a different life cycle and are shared differently among servlets and requests. The following table summarizes the scope of the attributes associated with these objects:

	Scope	Description
ServletContext	Application or Global	All servlets within a web application can access these attributes while processing any request for any client. These attributes might include data regarding the configuration of the application as a whole.
HttpSession	Session	These attributes are visible to all servlets within a web application, but are associated with a particular client. These attributes might include information about the user such as access rights or customization parameters.

Table continued on following page

	Scope	Description
`ServletRequest`	Request	These attributes are only maintained while a request is being processed. They can be passed to other servlets if the request is forwarded using the `RequestDispatcher`'s `forward()` or `include()` methods. These attributes might include intermediate data needed to complete the processing of the request.

Exception Handling

Errors and unexpected conditions are inevitable in a web application. Sometimes an error needs to be communicated to the user; maybe he tried to access an invalid or unauthorized page. Sometimes the error is a system error and needs to be reported to the developer or system administrator of the web site. Java servlets have mechanisms for both types of error conditions.

A servlet can communicate errors to the servlet container and web application deployer by throwing an exception during initialization or request processing. It can throw an instance of `javax.servlet.ServletException` to indicate that the servlet should not be placed in active service. A servlet can also throw an instance of `javax.servlet.UnavailableException`. The `UnavailableException` can include a minimum time of unavailability. The servlet container may try to instantiate the servlet again after the minimum time has elapsed.

Errors are communicated to the user through the `HttpServletResponse` object. Sometimes the best response to an error is to send an HTML page describing the error. That way, the user can take corrective action. Other times, you may want to send an HTTP error code that can be interpreted automatically by the browser. As we saw above, the `HttpServletResponse` object has a method called `sendError()` that will send an HTTP error response to the client. It also defines symbolic constants for these codes. HTTP defines several error codes, many of which are familiar to web users. Some of the more common error codes appear in the table below.

Code	Constant in HttpServletResponse	Description
200	SC_OK	No error exists
400	SC_BAD_REQUEST	The request could not be serviced for some reason
403	SC_FORBIDDEN	The client is denied access to the requested service
404	SC_NOT_FOUND	The requested service does not exist
405	SC_METHOD_NOT_ALLOWED	The HTTP request method (GET, POST) is not supported. As we saw in the example above, this is the error code returned by the default implementations of `doGet()` and `doPost()` in `HttpServlet`.

Code	Constant in HttpServletResponse	Description
500	SC_INTERNAL_SERVER_ERROR	Processing the request caused the server to have an unexpected error. This is the error code returned if a servlet class cannot be loaded or if it throws an exception back to the servlet container.

The following code shows how a servlet can return an HTTP error to the client. If the session doesn't contain a bound attribute called "authorized" the servlet returns an error SC_FORBIDDEN (403) to the client.

```
public void doGet(HttpServletRequest request,
                  HttpServletResponse response)
                  throws ServletException, IOException {

  HttpSession session = request.getSession();
  if (session.getAttribute("authorized") == null) {
    response.sendError(HttpServletResponse.SC_FORBIDDEN);
  }
```

If the "authorized" attribute is not set in the session, the user receives a page like this.

The exact contents of the page will vary depending on the particular browser type and version.

The Servlet Log

Error messages that should come to the attention of the developer or web site administrator can be printed to the servlet log. Every servlet container must maintain some mechanism for keeping a log for servlets. It may be as simple as a log file or more elaborate like the UNIX syslog or the Windows Event Log. However it is implemented, the servlet log is a good way for servlets to communicate with the server administrators.

Servlets write to the servlet log through the `ServletContext` object's `log()` method. There are two log methods in the `ServletContext` class. Each takes a string that will be written into the log. One method also takes a `java.lang.Throwable` as a parameter, which is useful if an `Exception` has been thrown. The servlet container will include a stack trace for the `Exception` in the log as well. The following servlet shows how to write to the servlet log:

```
//LogServlet.java
import javax.servlet.*;
import javax.servlet.http.*;
import java.io.*;
import java.util.*;

public class LogServlet extends HttpServlet {

  public void init() throws ServletException {
    getServletContext().log("LogServlet: in the init() method");
  }
  public void doGet(HttpServletRequest request,
                    HttpServletResponse response) throws ServletException,
                    IOException {
    getServletContext().log("LogServlet: in the doGet() method");

    // create an exception and send it to the log
    Throwable throwable = new RuntimeException("An example exception");
    getServletContext().log("Here's what an exception looks like",
                            throwable);
  }
  public void doPost(HttpServletRequest request,
                    HttpServletResponse response) throws ServletException,
                    IOException {
    getServletContext().log("LogServlet: in the doPost() method");
  }
  public void doPut(HttpServletRequest request,
                    HttpServletResponse response) throws ServletException,
                    IOException {
    getServletContext().log("LogServlet: in the doPut() method");
  }
  public void doDelete(HttpServletRequest request,
                       HttpServletResponse response) throws ServletException,
                       IOException {
    getServletContext().log("LogServlet: in the doDelete() method");
  }
  public void destroy() {
    getServletContext().log("LogServlet: in the destroy() method");
  }
}
```

Summary

Servlets are an important part of the Java 2 Platform, Enterprise Edition suite of technologies and provide key features that are important for any complex web application. While they are not the only technology available, they have advantages in terms of speed of execution, portability, and vendor independence that the other technologies can't match.

All servlets implement or extend one of the three important servlet classes: the interface `javax.servlet.Servlet` or one of the abstract classes `javax.servlet.GenericServlet` or `javax.servlet.http.HttpServlet`. The `GenericServlet` class provides a convenient default implementation of most of the `Servlet` interface. The `HttpServlet` class is extended by most servlets because it includes features to support the dominant web protocol: HTTP.

The `ServletRequest` and `ServletResponse` objects are the communication channels between the servlet and the client. Their input and output streams allow the servlet to read and write data directly to the client. The `ServletRequest` can also store attribute data that is passed between servlets as they collaborate to service the request.

The `HttpSession` and the `ServletContext` can also store attribute data. This allows servlets to manage attributes with different scopes enabling data to exist at the request, session, or application visibility.

By using powerful features of Java servlets like session tracking, scoped attributes, and the `ServletContext`, web application developers can create complex applications using the latest in Java technology.

E-mail With JavaMail

E-mail has quickly woven itself into the fabric of our everyday lives. Practically everyone of age in the developed world has access to an e-mail account – this makes it very easy to communicate with co-workers, friends and relatives. In the landscape of application development, there is a recurring requirement to add e-mail functionality to applications. For instance, a web application hosted at an e-commerce site can send an order confirmation to a customer. In a business-to-business scenario, the application can send an e-mail message to a supplier, requesting additional products.

This chapter will cover the use of sockets to send e-mail messages and will examine the JavaMail API, which provides support for sending and receiving e-mail. The API provides a high-level abstraction to the various Internet messaging systems. By using a collection of core classes, a JavaMail application can easily send and receive e-mail messages.

In this chapter, we will

- ❑ Examine e-mail messaging systems
- ❑ Install and configure the JavaMail system
- ❑ Send e-mail using JavaMail (including attachments)
- ❑ Retrieve e-mail from mail servers
- ❑ Develop a web-based mail application

E-Mail Messaging Systems

An e-mail messaging system is composed of mail clients and mail servers. An e-mail client is normally a GUI based application installed on a user's machine – some of the most popular are Netscape Communicator and MS Outlook. There are also a large number of web-based applications that serve as e-mail clients such as Hotmail (http://www.hotmail.com/) and Yahoo! Mail (http://mail.yahoo.com/). An e-mail server is responsible for routing messages to their destination and also storing messages until the user receives them. The diagram below illustrates the process of e-mail transmission:

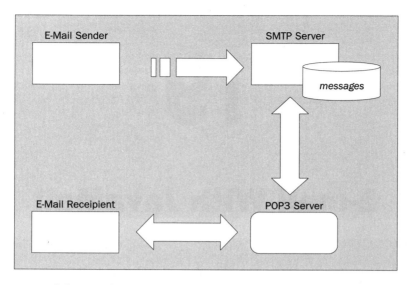

In the diagram, two of the popular Internet protocols are used: Simple Mail Transfer Protocol (SMTP) and Post Office Protocol version 3 (POP3). SMTP defines the process for sending e-mail in a reliable and efficient manner and is defined in RFC 821 (http://www.ietf.org/rfc/rfc821). POP3 defines a mechanism for retrieving messages from a mail server. The POP3 protocol identifies the user and password and retrieves only those messages for the given user. POP3 protocol is defined in RFC 1939 (http://www.ietf.org/rfc/rfc1939).

There also exists another popular mail protocol, Internet Message Access Protocol (IMAP). The IMAP protocol defines a mechanism for accessing and managing messages from more than one computer. With an IMAP e-mail client, you can develop messages online and in a disconnected fashion. Microsoft Exchange Server and Microsoft Outlook are two popular products that support the IMAP protocol. A nice feature of IMAP is the support for concurrent access to shared mailboxes. In contrast, the POP3 protocol only allows single-user access to a mailbox. The IMAP protocol is defined in RFC 2060 (http://www.ietf.org/rfc/rfc2060).

Anatomy of an E-Mail message

An e-mail message is composed of two major sections: headers (containing a set of attributes) and body content – this can be seen in the diagram to the right:

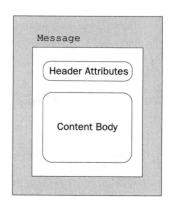

The header contains information about the message, such as the sender, recipient(s), subject and time stamp. The actual text of the message is contained in the body content. Some e-mail messages can also contain multiple sections in the body content to reference attached files. Later in this chapter, we'll cover the techniques for creating multipart messages and attaching files to the e-mail.

Sending E-Mail Manually

Let's say, for example, you do not have access to an e-mail client application. No worries, you can still send e-mail by connecting directly to the SMTP server. As long as you know the commands in the SMTP protocol then you can compose your own e-mail message directly with the SMTP server.

In order to send and receive e-mail messages, you will need network access to an SMTP server and POP3 server. If you are on a corporate network, contact your local network administrators for the names of the SMTP and POP3 servers. If you are using an Internet Service Provider (ISP), then you can contact their technical support desk for these details. It is likely that the names of the SMTP and POP3 server are already configured in your e-mail client.

The SMTP protocol defines a collection of commands, to send your own e-mail message you only need the following commands:

SMTP Command	Description
HELO	Identifies the domain of the sending host such as `j-nine.com`
MAIL	Name of the sender
RCPT	Name of receiver(s)
DATA	Message body of the e-mail

You can use the `telnet` command to communicate with an SMTP server listening on port 25. Below is the conversation between the user and SMTP server. The lines in bold are the ones typed by the user, but you will not see them displayed on screen. You should replace **mymailserver.com** with whichever SMTP server that your e-mail client uses. You must leave a blank line between the subject and the body text otherwise everything will appear in the e-mail header. To send the mail you must place a period "`.`" on a line by itself by typing "*<Enter>*.*<Enter>*" (without the quotes).

```
C:\Beg_Java_Networking\Ch19>telnet smtp.mymailserver.com 25
Connected to smtp.mymailserver.com
Escape character is '^]'
220 smtp.mymailserver.com ESMTP server (Netscape Messaging Server - Version 3.6) ready Tue,
17 July 2001 07:19:14 -0400
HELO j-nine.com
250 smtp.mymailserver.com
MAIL FROM: info@j-nine.com
250 Sender <info@j-nine.com> Ok
RCPT TO: darby@j-nine.com
250 Recipient <darby@j-nine.com> Ok
DATA
354 Ok Send data ending with <CRLF>.<CRLF>
Subject: Direct Connect Test
```

Hi,
How are things going? Hope all is well.
Cheers
.
250 Message received
QUIT
221 smtp.mymailserver.com ESMTP server closing connection
Connection to host lost

Sending E-Mail with Sockets

As you can see, the SMTP server listens on a socket port and accepts text-based commands. Instead of having to manually type in the e-mail message each time, you can develop a Java program to send the e-mail. The Java application will use the `Socket` class defined in the `java.net` package, which we used in earlier chapters. For the SMTP protocol, you simply send the appropriate SMTP commands using sockets as shown in the diagram below.

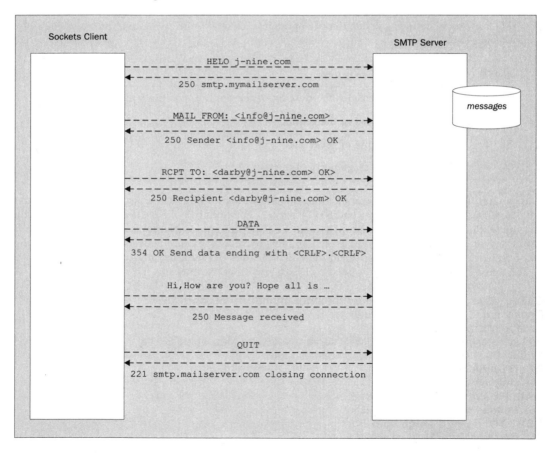

```java
// SocketMail.java

import java.io.BufferedReader;
import java.io.PrintWriter;
import java.io.IOException;
import java.net.Socket;

public class SocketMail {

  public static void send(String smtpHost, String sender,
                          String recipients, String subject, String msg) {

    Socket mailSocket;
    BufferedReader is;
    PrintWriter outToServer;

    try {

      // Step 1:  Connect to SMTP server
      System.out.println("opening connection to server: " + smtpHost);
      mailSocket = new Socket(smtpHost, 25);
      System.out.println("connected");

      // Step 2:  Get an output stream for the socket connection
      outToServer = new PrintWriter(mailSocket.getOutputStream());

      // Step 3:  Compose the message using the SMTP commands
      System.out.println("composing message");
      outToServer.println("MAIL FROM: <" + sender + ">");
      outToServer.println("RCPT TO: <" + recipients + ">");
      outToServer.println("DATA");
      outToServer.println("SUBJECT: " + subject);
      outToServer.println("X-Mailer: SocketMail");
      outToServer.println(msg);
      outToServer.println(".\n");

      outToServer.flush();
      mailSocket.close();
      System.out.println("message sent");
    } catch (IOException exc) {
      System.out.println(exc);
    }
  }

  public static void main(String[] args) {
    if (args.length != 3) {
      System.out.println("Usage:  java SocketMail <smtphost> <from> <to>");
      System.exit(1);
    }

    String smtpHost = args[0];
    String from = args[1];
    String to = args[2];
    String subject = "Test Message";
    StringBuffer theMessage = new StringBuffer();
    theMessage.append("Hello,\n\n");
    theMessage.append("Hope all is well on your end.\n");
    theMessage.append("Cheers!");

    SocketMail.send(smtpHost, from, to, subject, theMessage.toString());
  }
}
```

647

The `SocketMail` program has the following usage syntax:

```
java SocketMail <smtphost> <from> <to>
```

In the command below, provide the name of the SMTP server for your corporate network or Internet Service Provider. Also use your e-mail address for the `from` and `to` arguments.

C:\Beg_Jav_Networking\Ch19>**java SocketMail smtp.mymailserver.com me@mycompany.com me@mycompany.com**

You can test the results of the program by checking your e-mail with an e-mail client.

In the `send()` method, a socket connection is opened to the SMTP server. Recall that the SMTP servers listen on port 25.

```
// Step 1:  Connect to SMTP server
System.out.println("opening connection to server: " + smtpHost);
mailSocket = new Socket(smtpHost, 25);
System.out.println("connected");
```

Once the connection is open, we retrieve the output stream for the socket connection. The output stream is used to send data to the server.

```
// Step 2:  Get an output stream for the socket connection
     outToServer = new PrintWriter(mailSocket.getOutputStream());
```

As you can see in the code snippet below, the program simply sends over the appropriate SMTP commands for the e-mail message.

```
// Step 3:  Compose the message using the SMTP commands
System.out.println("composing message");
outToServer.println("MAIL FROM: <" + sender + ">");
outToServer.println("RCPT TO: <" + recipients + ">");
outToServer.println("DATA");
outToServer.println("SUBJECT: " + subject);
outToServer.println("X-Mailer: SocketMail");
outToServer.println(msg);
outToServer.println(".\n");
```

Finally once everything is complete, the output stream is flushed and the socket connection is closed.

```
     outToServer.flush();
     mailSocket.close();
     System.out.println("message sent");
```

The `SocketMail` class also contains a `main()` method for testing purposes. The actual message attributes and text are defined in the local variables and then transmitted by calling the `send()` method.

```
public static void main(String[] args) {
   if (args.length != 3) {
      System.out.println("Usage:  java SocketMail <smtphost> <from> <to>");
```

```
        System.exit(1);
    }

    String smtpHost = args[0];
    String from = args[1];
    String to = args[2];
    String subject = "Test Message";
    StringBuffer theMessage = new StringBuffer();
    theMessage.append("Hello,\n\n");
    theMessage.append("Hope all is well.\n");
    theMessage.append("Cheers!");

    SocketMail.send(smtpHost, from, to, subject, theMessage.toString());
}
```

That is the basic process for sending text-based e-mail messages to an SMTP server. If you only need to send simple text messages, then you can simple reuse the code from `SocketMail`. However, if you have more sophisticated application requirements such as sending e-mail with attachments, retrieving e-mail from POP3 and others, then you should use the JavaMail API. The JavaMail API was designed to shield the application developer from the low-level e-mail protocols.

Preparing Your System To Use JavaMail

To get started with the JavaMail code examples in this chapter, you will need to follow these steps:

1. Download and install the JavaMail API 1.2 or later from: http://java.sun.com/products/javamail/. Note: all code examples in this chapter are based on JavaMail 1.2.

Once the file is downloaded, extract it to a directory on your file system. For the remainder of this chapter, we'll refer to the JavaMail installation directory as <JAVAMAIL>.

2. Download and install the JavaBeans Activation Framework API: The JavaMail API depends on the JavaBeans Activation Framework (JAF), more details on this later in the chapter. The JavaBeans Activation Framework is available at: http://java.sun.com/products/javabeans/glasgow/jaf.html.

Once the file is downloaded, extract it to a directory on your file system. For the remainder of this chapter, we'll refer to the JAF installation directory as <JAF>.

3. You will also need an application server to run the ezmail application that we will construct in this chapter. Appendix B gives full instructions on how to install Tomcat Version 4.0-b7, which is the version that this code was tested on.

4. Download the sample code for this chapter from the Wrox web site. Visit http://www.wrox.com/ and navigate your way to Beginning Java Networking, download the code file and extract the contents to your hard drive.

The source code for this chapter is organized as shown below:

```
C:\Beg_Java_Networking\Ch19>dir
 Volume in drive C has no label.
 Volume Serial Number is 3803-B844

 Directory of C:\Beg_Java_Networking\Ch19

17/08/2001  13:02    <DIR>          .
17/08/2001  13:02    <DIR>          ..
17/08/2001  11:12    <DIR>          ezmail_webapp
18/07/2001  13:13             1,910 MessageList.java
18/07/2001  07:47             1,462 MessageView.java
17/07/2001  04:05             4,141 my_resume.pdf
17/08/2001  12:55             3,623 QuickMailAttach.java
17/08/2001  12:45             2,608 QuickMailHtml.java
17/08/2001  12:49             2,455 QuickMailText.java
17/08/2001  11:46             1,776 SocketMail.java
17/08/2001  12:43                68 setpaths.bat
```

Sending E-Mail

Sending e-mail with the JavaMail API is fairly straightforward:

Here is the 3-step process for sending e-mail:

1. The first thing you have to do is configure a mail session for the application

2. Once the mail session is configured then you compose the message

3. After the message is composed send it out

Let's walk through each step in detail.

Configure a Mail Session

The JavaMail API defines the `javax.mail.Session` class. The purpose of the `Session` is to hold configuration properties for the mail system and also provide user authentication information. In order to send an e-mail message, you must first get an instance of a `Session` object.

The `Session` class provides a collection of factory methods for getting an instance. Two of the most commonly used methods are described below:

```
public Session getInstance(java.util.Properties)
public Session getDefaultInstance(java.util.Properties)
```

The first method returns a new unshared `Session` object based on the properties and the second returns a shared `Session` object.

The factory methods described above are static methods, which means you can invoke the methods by simply giving the class name and the method. The code snippet below creates a new-shared `Session` object.

```
Properties props = new Properties();
Session mailSession = Session.getDefaultInstance(props);
```

The JavaMail API defines the following properties for a `Session` class:

Property	Description	Default Value
`mail.protocol.host`	The name of the protocol-specific mail server. For example, to connect using the SMTP protocol, this property would be named: `mail.smtp.host`. Overrides the `mail.host` property.	`mail.host`
`mail.protocol.user`	The protocol-specific username. Overrides the `mail.user` property.	`mail.user`
`mail.host`	The name of the default mail server. This value is used for connecting to the mail server if the protocol-specific host property is missing.	`local.machine`
`mail.user`	The username for connecting to the mail server. This value is used if the protocol-specific user property is missing.	`user.name`
`mail.store.protocol`	Specifies the default message access protocol for retrieving messages.	First available protocol in configuration file
`mail.transport.protocol`	Specifies the transport protocol for sending messages.	First available protocol in configuration file
`mail.from`	The return address of the current user.	`username@host machine`
`mail.debug`	Accepts a `Boolean` value (`true`, `false`) for generating debug messages (such as verbose mode).	`false`

When you are sending an e-mail message using the SMTP protocol, you will normally set the `mail.smtp.host` property. The `mail.smtp.host` property will reference the name of the SMTP server on your network. The code snippet below shows how to set the `Properties` object for sending a message using the SMTP protocol. In this example, the SMTP server is named: `smtp.mymailserver.com`.

```
Properties props = new Properties();
props.put("mail.smtp.host", "smtp.mymailserver.com");
Session mailSession = Session.getInstance(props);
```

That's the basic process for getting an instance of a `Session` object. Now let's discuss the use-case for the different factory methods: `getInstance(props)` and `getDefaultInstance(props)`. In general, you should use a shared `Session` object for a single-user desktop application.

Even if the code calls the factory method `Session.getDefaultInstance(props)` multiple times, the JVM returns the reference to the same object.

If you are using JavaMail for a web application using Servlets and JSP, then the `Session.getInstance(props)` method is preferable because it returns a new instance of the `Session` object. This is very important for unique web clients, for example, one of your web clients may access the SMTP server: `smtp.free-mail.com` and another user may access `smtp.mycompany.com`. As you can see, you will need two unique mail sessions to handle the different property values. Also, once you've configured the JavaMail `Session` object, you should store it in the web user's server-side `HttpSession` object.

Compose the Message

All messages in JavaMail inherit from the abstract base class `javax.mail.Message`. The `Message` class itself implements the `javax.mail.Part` interface.

To compose an actual message, you have to create an instance of a `javax.mail.Message` subclass or for Internet mail, use the `javax.mail.internet.MimeMessage` class. The `MimeMessage` class extends the abstract `Message` class and provides support for handling MIME type via the JavaBeans Activation Framework (JAF). The `MimeMessage` is constructed using the `javax.mail.Session` object.

```
Properties props = new Properties();
props.put("mail.smtp.host", "smtp.mymailserver.com");
Session mailSession = Session.getInstance(props);
MimeMessage testMessage = new MimeMessage(mailSession);
```

The table below shows a list of commonly used methods in the `MimeMessage` class.

Method	Description
`void setFrom(Address theSender)`	The sender of the message

`void setRecipient(`
`    Message.RecipientType type,`
`    Address theAddress)`
	Sets recipient of the message. All addresses of the specified type are replaced by the addresses parameter

`void setRecipients(`
`    Message.RecipientType type,`
`    Address[] theAddresses)`
	Sets recipients of the message. All addresses of the specified type are replaced by the addresses parameter

`void addRecipient(`
`    Message.RecipientType type,`
`    Address theAddress)`
	Adds the recipient to the existing recipient list

`void addRecipients(`
`    Message.RecipientType type,`
`    Address[] theAddresses)`
	Adds a collection of the recipients to the existing recipient list

`void setSentDate(java.util.Date theDate)`	The time stamp of the message
`void setSubject(String theSubject)`	The subject of the message
`void setContent(Object theConent,` `                String contentType)`	The content of the message based on a content-type

Addressing the Recipients

The methods `setRecipient()`, `setRecipients()`, `addRecipient()` and `addRecipients()` allow you to specify the type of recipient. The `Message` class defines the following recipient types:

❑   `Message.RecipientType.TO`: Message sent to recipient

❑   `Message.RecipientType.CC`: Recipient is carbon-copied

❑   `Message.RecipientType.BCC`: Recipient is blind carbon-copied (the recipient's name and address cannot be seen by any other recipients)

The methods `addRecipient()` and `addRecipients()` allow you to add recipients to the existing list. The methods `setRecipient()` and `setRecipients()` will replace the recipients on the list. In general, it is a good practice to use the methods `addRecipient()` and `addRecipients()`. By using these methods, you won't accidentally replace/overwrite your recipient list.

Here's a code snippet for addressing an e-mail message. The snippet also sets the date and subject for the message.

```
InternetAddress fromAddress = new InternetAddress("darby@j-nine.com");
InternetAddress toAddress = new InternetAddress("editor@wrox.com");
testMessage.setFrom(fromAddress);
testMessage.addRecipient(javax.mail.Message.RecipientType.TO, toAddress);
testMessage.setSentDate(new java.util.Date());
testMessage.setSubject("Latest and Greatest");
```

Setting the Message Content

The JavaMail API is based on the JavaBeans Activation Framework (JAF). The JAF provides a high-level mechanism for accessing a binary data stream. This is supported by MIME types, data handlers and data sources. In the JavaMail usage scenario, the JAF allows us to construct simple text-based messages and also support e-mail attachments. The attachments are typically a binary file such as an MS Word document or Adobe PDF file. Each binary file has an associated MIME type that can be used by another application.

When you set the content of the message, you also provide the content-type of the message – the method signature:

```
public void setContent(Object theContent, String type)
```

For example, the code snippet below sets the message content to the text string: The eagle has landed.

```
testMessage.setContent("The eagle has landed", "text/plain");
```

When an e-mail client receives this message, it examines the content-type of the message. In this example, the content-type is `text/plain` and the e-mail client renders this message using a textbox.

The JavaMail API also provides a short-cut method for handling text messages. Instead of explicitly stating the content-type, simply call the method:

```
public void setText(String theText)
```

The method `setText()` sets the content of the method and uses `text/plain` as the content-type. In our example, we can set the message content to the string `messageText` using:

```
testMessage.setText(messageText);
```

Later in this chapter, we'll discuss how to attach files to an e-mail message.

Sending a Text Message

The `javax.mail.Transport` class provides functionality for sending the message. The code snippet below shows how to send an e-mail message:

```
Transport.send(testMessage);
```

At this point, the `Transport` object will communicate with the appropriate transport protocol – in this example, we are using the SMTP protocol. Let's create a class called `QuickMailText` that can send e-mail messages:

```java
// QuickMailText.java

import javax.mail.*;
import javax.mail.internet.*;

public class QuickMailText {

  public static void sendMessage(String smtpHost, String from, String to,
                                 String subject,
                                 String messageText) throws MessagingException {

    // Step 1:  Configure the mail session
    System.out.println("Configuring mail session for: " + smtpHost);
    java.util.Properties props = new java.util.Properties();
    props.put("mail.smtp.host", smtpHost);
    Session mailSession = Session.getDefaultInstance(props);

    // Step 2:  Construct the message
    System.out.println("Constructing message -  from=" + from + "  to="
                       + to);
    InternetAddress fromAddress = new InternetAddress(from);
    InternetAddress toAddress = new InternetAddress(to);

    MimeMessage testMessage = new MimeMessage(mailSession);
    testMessage.setFrom(fromAddress);
    testMessage.addRecipient(javax.mail.Message.RecipientType.TO,
                             toAddress);
    testMessage.setSentDate(new java.util.Date());
    testMessage.setSubject(subject);
    testMessage.setText(messageText);
    System.out.println("Message constructed");

    // Step 3:  Now send the message
    Transport.send(testMessage);
    System.out.println("Message sent!");
  }
```

```
      public static void main(String[] args) {
        if (args.length != 3) {
          System.out.println("Usage:  java QuickMailText <smtphost> <from> <to>");
          System.exit(1);
        }

        String smtpHost = args[0];
        String from = args[1];
        String to = args[2];
        String subject = "Test Message - quickmail_text";

        StringBuffer theMessage = new StringBuffer();
        theMessage.append("Hello,\n\n");
        theMessage.append("Hope all is well.\n");
        theMessage.append("Cheers!");

        try {
          QuickMailText.sendMessage(smtpHost, from, to, subject,
                                    theMessage.toString());
        } catch (javax.mail.MessagingException exc) {
          exc.printStackTrace();
        }
      }
    }
```

To run this, and other examples in this chapter you will need to add mail.jar and activation.jar to your classpath. This is accomplished by typing:

C:\Beg_Java_Networking\Ch19>**set classpath=.;<JAVAMAIL>\mail.jar; <JAF>\activation.jar**

The QuickMailText program has the following usage syntax:

```
    java QuickMailText <smtphost> <from> <to>
```

In the command below, provide the name of the SMTP server for your corporate network or Internet Service Provider and use your e-mail address for the from and to arguments.

C:\Beg_Java_Networking\Ch19>**java QuickMailText mymailserver me@mycompany.com me@mycompany.com**

If the program has been compiled and executed correctly you should see a new message in your e-mail client that looks something like this:

Subject: Test Message - quickmail_text

Hello,

Hope all is well.
Cheers!

The class QuickMailText defines the method sendMessage(). The method document and signature is shown below:

```
public static void sendMessage(String smtpHost, String from, String to,
                               String subject,
                               String messageText) throws MessagingException {
```

The body of this method follows the 3-step process for sending e-mail. First, the mail session is configured with a `java.util.Properties` object as shown below:

```
System.out.println("Configuring mail session for: " + smtpHost);
java.util.Properties props = new java.util.Properties();
props.put("mail.smtp.host", smtpHost);
Session mailSession = Session.getDefaultInstance(props);
```

The `java.util.Properties` object contains the name of the SMTP server.

Next, the message is composed using the parameters passed into this method:

```
System.out.println("Constructing message -  from=" + from + "  to="
                   + to);
InternetAddress fromAddress = new InternetAddress(from);
InternetAddress toAddress = new InternetAddress(to);

MimeMessage testMessage = new MimeMessage(mailSession);
testMessage.setFrom(fromAddress);
testMessage.addRecipient(javax.mail.Message.RecipientType.TO, toAddress);
testMessage.setSentDate(new java.util.Date());
testMessage.setSubject(subject);
testMessage.setText(messageText);
System.out.println("Message constructed");
```

Finally, the message is transmitted over the network using the `Transport` class.

```
Transport.send(testMessage);
System.out.println("Message sent!");
```

The `QuickMailText` class also contains a `main()` method for testing. The `main()` method defines local variables for the desired message. It then makes a call to the static method `sendMessage()` as shown below:

```
public static void main(String[] args) {
  if (args.length != 3) {
    System.out.println("Usage:  java QuickMailText <smtphost> <from> <to>");
    System.exit(1);
  }

  String smtpHost = args[0];
  String from = args[1];
  String to = args[2];
  String subject = "Test Message - quickmail_text";

  StringBuffer theMessage = new StringBuffer();
  theMessage.append("Hello,\n\n");
  theMessage.append("Hope all is well.\n");
  theMessage.append("Cheers!");
```

```
    try {
      QuickMailText.sendMessage(smtpHost, from, to, subject,
                                theMessage.toString());
    } catch (javax.mail.MessagingException exc) {
      exc.printStackTrace();
    }
  }

}
```

Notice in the `main()` method that we have to handle the `javax.mail.MessagingException`. A `MessagingException` subclass is thrown if the mail could not be sent.

Sending HTML-Formatted E-Mail

Most e-mail clients support HTML-formatted e-mail. HTML-formatted e-mail allows the sender to construct an e-mail message that contains an embedded HTML page.

Using the JavaMail API it is very easy to send HTML-formatted e-mail. During construction of the actual message text, you can simply build a string that contains the appropriate HTML tags. Also when the content of the message is set, you then specify the content type of `text/html`.

In this example, we'll modify the `QuickMailText` class to support HTML-formatted e-mail. There are only minor modifications that need to be made and these are highlighted below:

```java
// QuickMailHtml.java

import javax.mail.*;
import javax.mail.internet.*;

public class QuickMailHtml {

    public static void sendMessage(String smtpHost, String from, String to,
                                   String subject,
                                   String messageText) throws MessagingException {

        // Step 1:  Configure the mail session
        System.out.println("Configuring mail session for: " + smtpHost);
        java.util.Properties props = new java.util.Properties();
        props.put("mail.smtp.host", smtpHost);
        Session mailSession = Session.getDefaultInstance(props);

        // Step 2:  Construct the message
        System.out.println("Constructing message -  from=" + from + "  to=" + to);
        InternetAddress fromAddress = new InternetAddress(from);
        InternetAddress toAddress = new InternetAddress(to);

        MimeMessage testMessage = new MimeMessage(mailSession);
        testMessage.setFrom(fromAddress);
        testMessage.addRecipient(javax.mail.Message.RecipientType.TO, toAddress);
        testMessage.setSentDate(new java.util.Date());
        testMessage.setSubject(subject);
        testMessage.setContent(messageText, "text/html");
        System.out.println("Message constructed");

        // Step 3:  Now send the message
        Transport.send(testMessage);
```

```
      System.out.println("Message sent!");
    }

    public static void main(String[] args) {
      if (args.length != 3) {
        System.out.println("Usage:  java QuickMailHtml <smtphost> <from> <to>");
        System.exit(1);
      }

      String smtpHost = args[0];
      String from = args[1];
      String to = args[2];
      String subject = "Test Message - quickmail_html";

      StringBuffer theMessage = new StringBuffer();
      theMessage.append("<h2><font color=red>Hello,</font></h2>\n\n");
      theMessage.append("<hr>");
      theMessage.append("<i>Hope all is well.</i>\n");
      theMessage.append("<hr>");
      theMessage.append("<h3><i><font color=blue>Cheers!</font></i></h3>");

      try {
        QuickMailHtml.sendMessage(smtpHost, from, to, subject,
                                  theMessage.toString());
      } catch (javax.mail.MessagingException exc) {
        exc.printStackTrace();
      }
    }
  }
```

As in the previous example you need to provide the name of the SMTP server for your corporate network or Internet Service Provider and use your e-mail address for the `from` and `to` arguments.

C:\Beg_Java_Networking\Ch19>**java QuickMailHtml mymailserver me@mycompany.com me@mycompany.com**

Test the results of the program by checking your e-mail with an e-mail client and you should get something like the screenshot below:

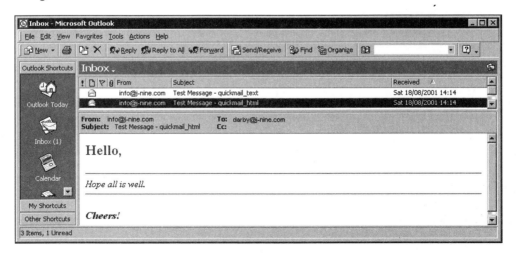

The `sendMessage()` method has the same parameters as before, however, in this version the `messageText` parameter contains the HTML text of the message. The only modification to the `sendMessage()` method is when we actually set the message content. For simple text messages, we called the `setText()` method since it uses the content-type of `text/plain` by default. However, in this example, the message text contains HTML tags so we set the content-type to `text/html`. This is accomplished by calling the `setContent()` method as shown below:

```
testMessage.setContent(messageText, "text/html");
```

As before, the program contains a `main()` method for testing. The only difference is the construction of the message text. A `StringBuffer` object is used instead of a `String` object. In general, if you have a large amount of data to append to a string, then the `StringBuffer` class is more efficient. The code snippet below adds the message text including the HTML tags:

```
StringBuffer theMessage = new StringBuffer();
theMessage.append("<h2><font color=red>Hello,</font></h2>\n\n");
theMessage.append("<hr>");
theMessage.append("<i>Hope all is well.</i>\n");
theMessage.append("<hr>");
theMessage.append("<h3><i><font color=blue>Cheers!</font></i></h3>");
```

When we call the `sendMessage()` method, the `StringBuffer` object is converted to a `String` by calling its `toString()` method:

```
QuickMailHtml.sendMessage(smtpHost, from, to, subject, theMessage.toString());
```

As you can see, there are only a small number of modifications to send HTML-formatted e-mail so you can easily extend this example to use a more complex HTML page.

Sending E-Mail with Attachments

One of the most popular features of e-mail is the ability to attach documents. For example, if you are applying for a new job, there is no need to fax a copy of your resume, simply attach it to the e-mail message. The recipient will then be able to view the document using an appropriate helper application. Friends and relatives also use/exploit e-mail attachments by sending photos of loved ones.

The JavaMail API was designed to support messages that could contain multiple parts. For example, an e-mail message can contain a text part that is normally included in e-mail messages plus parts for the additional files that are attached. The diagram below illustrates the concept of an e-mail message with multiple parts.

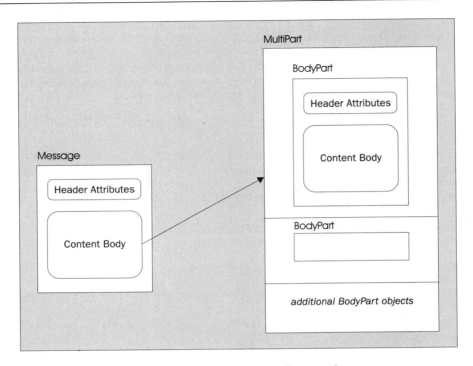

The JavaMail API supports multipart messages with the following classes:

❑ `javax.mail.Multipart`: `Multipart` is an abstract class that defines a container for holding multiple sections of a message. Each section of a `Multipart` message is represented as a `BodyPart`, which is discussed below.

❑ `javax.mail.internet.MimeMultipart`: `MimeMultipart` is a subclass of `Multipart`. It provides MIME-specific support for the headers and attributes.

❑ `javax.mail.BodyPart`: `BodyPart` is an abstract class that implements the `javax.mail.Part` interface. It contains the attributes and content for a message body.

❑ `javax.mail.internet.MimeBodyPart`: `MimeBodyPart` is a subclass of `BodyPart`. It provides the additional support for MIME-specific headers and attributes.

JavaBeans Activation Framework

The JavaMail API utilizes the JavaBeans Activation Framework (JAF) for accessing arbitrary binary content. In particular, the JAF is used during the composition of an e-mail message with various attachments – PDF File, GIF image, MP3 recording.

When attaching a file using the JavaMail API, you will need two classes from the JAF: `DataHandler` and `FileDataSource`. These classes are defined in the package `javax.activation`. The `DataHandler` class provides a high-level mechanism for accessing the content of arbitrary data sources. The `FileDataSource` class is an implementation of the `javax.activation.DataSource` interface, it defines a content type for the data and an access mechanism via input and output streams.

Sending an E-Mail Attachment

Let's modify the `QuickMailText` class so that we can send e-mail attachments.

```java
// QuickMailAttach.java

import javax.mail.*;
import javax.mail.internet.*;

import javax.activation.DataHandler;
import javax.activation.FileDataSource;

public class QuickMailAttach {

  public static void sendMessage(String smtpHost, String from, String to,
                        String subject, String messageText,
                        String fileName) throws MessagingException {

    // Step 1:  Configure the mail session
    System.out.println("Configuring mail session for: " + smtpHost);
    java.util.Properties props = new java.util.Properties();
    props.put("mail.smtp.host", smtpHost);
    Session mailSession = Session.getDefaultInstance(props);

    // Step 2:  Construct the message
    System.out.println("Constructing message -  from=" + from + "  to="
                        + to);
    InternetAddress fromAddress = new InternetAddress(from);
    InternetAddress toAddress = new InternetAddress(to);

    MimeMessage testMessage = new MimeMessage(mailSession);
    testMessage.setFrom(fromAddress);
    testMessage.addRecipient(javax.mail.Message.RecipientType.TO,
                        toAddress);
    testMessage.setSentDate(new java.util.Date());
    testMessage.setSubject(subject);

    // Step 3:  Create a body part to hold the "text" portion of the message
    System.out.println("Constructing 'text' body part");
    MimeBodyPart textBodyPart = new MimeBodyPart();
    textBodyPart.setText(messageText);

    // Step 4:  Create a body part to hold the "file" portion of the message
    System.out.println("Attaching 'file' body part: " + fileName);
    MimeBodyPart fileBodyPart = new MimeBodyPart();
    FileDataSource fds = new FileDataSource(fileName);
    fileBodyPart.setDataHandler(new DataHandler(fds));
    fileBodyPart.setFileName(fds.getName());
    System.out.println("Finished attaching file");

    // Step 5:  Create a Multipart/container and add the parts
    Multipart container = new MimeMultipart();
    container.addBodyPart(textBodyPart);
    container.addBodyPart(fileBodyPart);

    // Step 6:  Add the Multipart to the actual message
    testMessage.setContent(container);
    System.out.println("Message constructed");

    // Step 7:  Now send the message
    Transport.send(testMessage);
```

```
      System.out.println("Message sent!");
   }

   public static void main(String[] args) {
      if (args.length != 4) {
         System.out
            .println("Usage:  java QuickMailAttach <smtphost> <from> <to> <file>");
         System.exit(1);
      }

      String smtpHost = args[0];
      String from = args[1];
      String to = args[2];
      String fileName = args[3];
      String subject = "Test Message - quickmail_attach";

      StringBuffer theMessage = new StringBuffer();
      theMessage.append("Hello,\n\n");
      theMessage.append("Hope all is well.\n");
      theMessage.append("Cheers!");

      try {
         QuickMailAttach.sendMessage(smtpHost, from, to, subject,
                                  theMessage.toString(), fileName);
      } catch (javax.mail.MessagingException exc) {
         exc.printStackTrace();
      }
   }
}
```

The `QuickMailAttach` program has the following usage syntax:

java QuickMailAttach <smtphost> <from> <to> <file>

The code download for this chapter contains a sample PDF file: `my_resume.pdf` for use with this program.

C:\Beg_Java_Networking\Ch19>**java QuickMailAttach mymailserver me@mycompany.com me@mycompany.com my_resume.pdf**

You can test the results of the program by checking your e-mail with an e-mail client and seeing if `my_resume.pdf` has been received.

The `sendMessage()` method contains a new parameter for the name of the file to attach. The attributes of the message (`from`, `to`, `date`) are set in the normal fashion.

The new code appears in step 3. At this point, a body part section is created to hold the actual text of the message.

```
      System.out.println("Constructing 'text' body part");
      MimeBodyPart textBodyPart = new MimeBodyPart();
      textBodyPart.setText(messageText);
```

Next, an additional body part is created to hold a reference to the attached file. This is accomplished using the JAF. The code first creates a `FileDataSource` object based on the file name. The `DataHandler` class serves as an intermediary between the body part object and the data source.

```
System.out.println("Attaching 'file' body part: " + fileName);
MimeBodyPart fileBodyPart = new MimeBodyPart();
FileDataSource fds = new FileDataSource(fileName);
fileBodyPart.setDataHandler(new DataHandler(fds));
fileBodyPart.setFileName(fds.getName());
System.out.println("Finished attaching file");
```

The code block below shows the construction process of a `Multipart` object. Recall that the `Multipart` object is a container for `BodyPart` implementations. In this example, we add the body parts for the text and file. Finally, the `Multipart` object is set as the content for the message.

```
Multipart container = new MimeMultipart();
container.addBodyPart(textBodyPart);
container.addBodyPart(fileBodyPart);

testMessage.setContent(container);
```

As before, the program contains a `main()` method for testing. The only difference is the new local variable is defined as `filename`, which is passed to the `sendMessage()` method.

Storage and Retrieval of Messages

In the previous section, you learned how to send e-mail messages. In this section, you will learn how to retrieve messages using the JavaMail API.

The JavaMail API provides two key classes for retrieving e-mail messages: `Store` and `Folder`.

javax.mail.Store

The `Store` class models a messaging folder system and provides methods for accessing folders for a given mail protocol. The `Store` class is retrieved from the `Session` object. Here is an example of retrieving a `Store` for accessing a POP3 store.

```
Session mailSession = Session.getDefaultInstance(props);
Store msgStore = mailSession.getStore("pop3");
```

The `Store` class can also retrieve messages from an IMAP message store.

Once you have a reference to a `Store`, then you can make a connection as shown in the code snippet below:

```
String host = "mypop3server";
String user = "daz";
String password = "dazzle";
msgStore.connect(host, user, password);
```

javax.mail.Folder

The `Folder` class is a container for messages that can also contain subfolders. A client application communicates with a `Folder` object to retrieve the messages within the folder. Messages stored in the folder are numbered sequentially; it is important to note that the numbering system is one-based. The message numbers are only valid for a given mail session, so if a message within the folder is deleted, then all of the messages are renumbered accordingly.

Folders are retrieved from a `Store` object. The code snippet below shows how to access the root folder of an e-mail system and retrieve the folder named INBOX:

```
Folder inbox = msgStore.getDefaultFolder().getFolder("INBOX");
inbox.open(Folder.READ_ONLY);
```

The `Folder` class defines a rich set of methods; the table below lists some of the most commonly used:

Method	Description
`String getName()`	Returns the name of the folder
`void open(int mode)`	Open the folder using the specified mode: `Folder.READ_ONLY`, `Folder.READ_WRITE`
`int getMessageCount()`	Returns the number of messages in the folder
`Message getMessage(int number)`	Retrieves the designated message (1-based)
`Message[] getMessages()`	Retrieves all of the messages within the folder

Listing Messages

In a typical e-mail program, the application retrieves the e-mail messages and presents the user with a list of the messages. The next program `MessageList.java` demonstrates the techniques to list the messages stored in a folder.

```java
// MessageList.java

import javax.mail.*;

public class MessageList {

  public static void main(String[] args) {
    if (args.length != 3) {
      System.out
        .println("Usage:  java MessageList <pop3host> <user> <password>");
      System.exit(1);
    }

    String host = args[0];
    String user = args[1];
    String password = args[2];

    try {

        // Step 1:  Configure the mail session
        System.out.println("Configuring mail session for: " + host);
        java.util.Properties props = new java.util.Properties();
        props.put("mail.pop3.host", host);
        Session mailSession = Session.getDefaultInstance(props);

        // Step 2:  Retrieve and connect to the Store
        System.out.println("Connecting to message store: " + host);
        Store msgStore = mailSession.getStore("pop3");
        msgStore.connect(host, user, password);
```

```
        System.out.println("Connected!");

        // Step 3:  Retrieve the INBOX  folder
        Folder inbox = msgStore.getDefaultFolder().getFolder("INBOX");
        inbox.open(Folder.READ_ONLY);

        // Step 4:  Retrieve a list of messages
        Message[] msgs = inbox.getMessages();
        FetchProfile profile = new FetchProfile();
        profile.add(FetchProfile.Item.ENVELOPE);
        inbox.fetch(msgs, profile);

        // Step 5:  Display the subject and date for each message
        int count = inbox.getMessageCount();
        for (int i = 0; i < count; i++) {
          System.out.println("Message #" + msgs[i].getMessageNumber());
          System.out.println("Subject: " + msgs[i].getSubject());
          System.out.println("Date: " + msgs[i].getSentDate());
          System.out.println("---------------------------------\n");
        }

        // Step 6:  Close up shop
        inbox.close(false);
        msgStore.close();
      } catch (javax.mail.MessagingException exc) {
        exc.printStackTrace();
      }
    }
  }
```

The `MessageList` program has the following usage syntax:

java MessageList <pop3host> <user> <password>

In the command below, provide the name of the POP3 server for your corporate network or Internet Service Provider and use your username and password. If successful, you should see a list of the contents of your inbox, which will have a similar look to the output shown below:

C:\Beg_Java_Networking\Ch19>**java MessageList mypop3server user password**:
Configuring mail session for: localhost
Connecting to message store: localhost
Connected!
Message #1
Subject: Test Message - quickmail_text
Date: Wed Jul 18 07:08:21 EDT 2001

Message #2
Subject: Test Message - quickmail_html
Date: Wed Jul 18 07:08:39 EDT 2001

Message #3
Subject: Test Message - quickmail_attach
Date: Wed Jul 18 07:08:56 EDT 2001

In the `main()` method, the mail session is configured to use the appropriate mail protocol. Next, the `Store` is retrieved from the session and a connection is made.

```
System.out.println("Connecting to message store: " + host);
Store msgStore = mailSession.getStore("pop3");
msgStore.connect(host, user, password);
```

The `Folder` for `INBOX` is retrieved from the `Store`.

```
Folder inbox = msgStore.getDefaultFolder().getFolder("INBOX");
inbox.open(Folder.READ_ONLY);
```

Now for the fun part, the messages are retrieved from the folder. Instead of retrieving the entire content of each message, we only need the *envelope* information. The *envelope* information contains the headers such as `from`, `to`, `subject`, `date` and other fields. The JavaMail API provides the `FetchProfile` class for configuring the message retrieval.

First, create an empty `FetchProfile` object and then populate it with the appropriate `FetchProfile.Item` fields. The following fields are defined in `FetchProfile.Item`.

FetchProfile.Item	Description
ENVELOPE	The Envelope is a collection of message attributes such as: From, To, Cc, Bcc, ReplyTo, Subject and Date. An implementation may include additional items.
CONTENT_INFO	Information about the message contents: ContentType, ContentDisposition, ContentDescription, LineCount and Size.
FLAGS	A message contains a list of flags. These flags are system-defined and user-defined. An example of a system-defined flag is DELETED, meaning this message is marked for deletion. See javax.mail.Flag for more information.

In this example, we only want to get a list of *envelope* information that contains the headers: `from`, `to`, `subject`, and `date`.

```
Message[] msgs = inbox.getMessages();
FetchProfile profile = new FetchProfile();
profile.add(FetchProfile.Item.ENVELOPE);
inbox.fetch(msgs, profile);
```

Next, the message number, date and subject of each message are displayed in the `for-loop`.

```
int count = inbox.getMessageCount();
for (int i = 0; i < count; i++) {
  System.out.println("Message #" + msgs[i].getMessageNumber());
  System.out.println("Subject: " + msgs[i].getSubject());
  System.out.println("Date: " + msgs[i].getSentDate());
  System.out.println("---------------------------------\n");
}
```

Finally, we close the `Folder` and the `Store` objects.

```
inbox.close(false);
msgStore.close();
```

Viewing Message Contents

Now that you know how to retrieve a list of messages from the server, the next logical step is to view the contents of a given message.

To retrieve a given message from a folder, simply access it using the message number. For example, to retrieve the second message on the mail server, use the code snippet below:

```
int msgNum = 2;
Message theMessage = inbox.getMessage(msgNum);
```

If you simply want to dump the contents of the message to an output stream, then use the `writeTo()` method defined in the `Message` class. Here's an example:

```
theMessage.writeTo(System.out);
```

This method will display the message headers and display the message content. If the content is binary, then it will simply dump the binary content to the output stream.

The `Message` class also provides a number of techniques for accessing the contents of a message. For a simple text message, you can cast the content to `String` and then display it. For example:

```
String text = (String) theMessage.getContent();
```

However, it is good practice to first check the content-type of the message before you retrieve the actual content. Here's an example that verifies that the message has the MIME type `text/*`.

```
if (theMessage.isMimeType("text/*")) {
    String text = (String) theMessage.getContent();
}
```

Recall that you can also receive `Multipart` messages. These are messages that may contain text portions and binary data from attached files. In this case, you cannot simply cast the content to a `String`. The code snippet below checks to see if a message is a `Multipart` message:

```
if (theMessage.isMimeType("multipart/*")) {
    // access each individual body part
}
```

The example below will view the contents of an individual message. The `MessageView.java` program makes use of the `writeTo()` method defined in the `Message` class.

```
// MessageView.java

import javax.mail.*;
```

```
public class MessageView {

   public static void main(String[] args) {
      if (args.length != 4) {
         System.out
            .println("Usage:  java MessageView <pop3host> <user> <password>
<msgnum>");
         System.exit(1);
      }

      String host = args[0];
      String user = args[1];
      String password = args[2];
      int msgNum = Integer.parseInt(args[3]);

      try {

         // Step 1:  Configure the mail session
         System.out.println("Configuring mail session for: " + host);
         java.util.Properties props = new java.util.Properties();
         props.put("mail.pop3.host", host);
         Session mailSession = Session.getDefaultInstance(props);

         // Step 2:  Retrieve and connect to the Store
         System.out.println("Connecting to message store: " + host);
         Store msgStore = mailSession.getStore("pop3");
         msgStore.connect(host, user, password);
         System.out.println("Connected!");

         // Step 3:  Retrieve the INBOX  folder
         Folder inbox = msgStore.getDefaultFolder().getFolder("INBOX");
         inbox.open(Folder.READ_ONLY);

         // Step 4:  Display the subject and date for each message
         if (msgNum <= inbox.getMessageCount()) {
            Message theMessage = inbox.getMessage(msgNum);
            theMessage.writeTo(System.out);
         } else {
            System.out.println("Message number not found");
         }

         // Step 5:  Close up shop
         inbox.close(false);
         msgStore.close();
      } catch (Exception exc) {
         exc.printStackTrace();
      }
   }
}
```

The `MessageView` program has the following usage syntax:

```
java MessageView <pop3host> <user> <password> <msgnum>
```

This program is very similar to the previous `MessageList` program, but with an additional parameter passed into the program for the message number. As well as the arguments you entered in the previous example, this program also needs a message number to be added to the command line.

C:\Beg_Java_Networking\Ch19>**java MessageView mypop3server user password 1**
Configuring mail session for: localhost
Connecting to message store: localhost
Connected!
Message-ID: <5889081.995446898049.JavaMail.Administrator@sterling>
Date: Wed, 18 Jul 2001 05:01:37 -0400 (EDT)
From: tooty@foo.com
To: daz@localhost
Subject: Test Message - quickmail_text
Mime-Version: 1.0
Content-Type: text/plain; charset=us-ascii
Content-Transfer-Encoding: 7bit
Received: from 127.0.0.1 ([127.0.0.1])
      by sterling (JAMES SMTP Server 1.2.1rc2) with SMTP ID 336
      for <daz@localhost>;
      Wed, 18 Jul 2001 05:01:38 -0500

Hello,

Hope all is well.
Cheers!

This code is very similar to MesageList.java, the main difference comes in step 4 where the contents for a given message are displayed. This is accomplished with the code snippet below:

```
if (msgNum <= inbox.getMessageCount()) {
  Message theMessage = inbox.getMessage(msgNum);
  theMessage.writeTo(System.out);
} else {
  System.out.println("Message number not found");
}
```

In this example, the messages remain on the POP3 server. If you would like to remove the messages after you have read them, then you need to mark them for deletion. In order to mark messages for deletion, you will need read/write access on the INBOX.

```
Folder inbox = msgStore.getDefaultFolder().getFolder("INBOX");
inbox.open(Folder.READ_WRITE);
```

Once you have a reference to the INBOX, then retrieve the desired message and mark it for deletion.

```
theMessage = inbox.getMessage(msgNum);
theMessage.setFlag(Flags.Flag.DELETED, true);
```

At this point, the message is only *marked* for deletion; the message still resides on the mail server. To actually delete the message, use the Folder object, inbox and call the close() method with the Boolean parameter set to true.

```
inbox.close(true);
```

As you can see, retrieving messages from a mail server is fairly easy using the JavaMail API. Now that you have the fundamentals covered, we'll develop a web-based e-mail application.

Pulling It All Together: The ezmail Application

Well, you've made it this far! It is safe to assume that you understand the basic techniques to send and receive e-mail. So let's put the JavaMail API to the test and develop a web-based e-mail application similar to Yahoo! Mail and Hotmail. The web application will make use of Java servlets and JavaServer Pages (JSP). See Chapter 18 for a detailed discussion on servlets. We have also briefly mentioned JSPs in Chapter 18, but for more information, we recommend you read *Professional JSP*, published by *Wrox Press*, ISBN: *1861003625*.

The application we are developing is called *ezmail*. A user of the ezmail application can perform the following operations:

❑   View a list of e-mail messages in their inbox

❑   View the text of an e-mail

❑   Compose and send an e-mail

❑   Reply to an e-mail

Below is a screen-shot of a user viewing a list of messages in their inbox:

The ezmail application involves a large number of servlets, JSPs, support classes, and HTML pages. A high-level flowchart for the application is shown opposite. Not all of the components are displayed in this diagram. The detailed components are discussed after the deployment instructions.

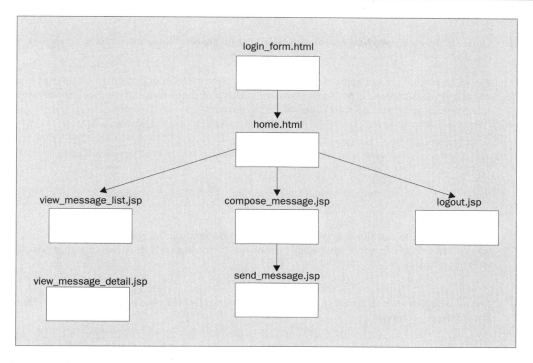

Deploying the Web App – ezmail

You can deploy the ezmail web application on any server that supports Servlets 2.2 and JSP 1.1. Also, the application requires JavaMail 1.2 or higher. You may need to consult the documentation for your application server to verify the JavaMail version. If the application server supports an older version, then simply download the latest version from http://java.sun.com/products/javamail/.

The sample code for the ezmail app is located in the /ezmail_webapp directory of this chapter's code download. This directory has the following structure:

❑   public_html contains all JSP and HTML pages

❑   public_html/WEB-INF contains the application deployment descriptor file: web.xml

❑   public_html/WEB-INF/classes contains compiled code for servlets and supporting classes

❑   public_html/WEB-INF/lib contains Java archive files for the ezmail app

❑   source contains all of the source code for servlets and supporting classes

To deploy the application you will need to follow these steps:

1.   Modify the web.xml file. Move to line 13:

```
<param-value>localhost</param-value>
```

and change the value (localname) to the name of your SMTP server.

2. Define a new web application for your application server. The new application should point to the directory: `/ezmail_webapp/public_html`.

For example, if you are using Tomcat (see Appendix B), then edit the file `<TOMCAT_INSTALL>/conf/server.xml`. Move to the bottom of the file where you see the `<context>` sections and make the following entry:

```
<Context path="/testmail"
            docBase="C:/Beg_Java_Networking/Ch19/ezmail_webapp/public_html"
            crossContext="false"
            debug="0"
            reloadable="true" >
    </Context>
```

You may need to modify the value for `docBase` depending on your installation path. If you're not using Tomcat, then consult your application server's documentation for deploying web applications.

3. Start a web browser and visit the URL http://localhost:<port>/testmail/. You should then see the following screen:

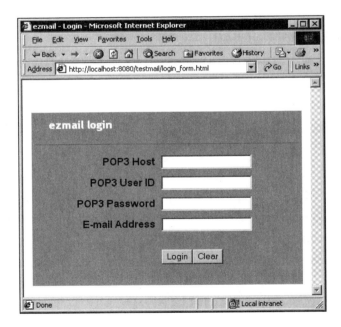

Application Architecture

The ezmail application implements the Model-View-Controller (MVC) design pattern. The MVC pattern strives to decouple application logic from presentation logic. Following this approach, the ezmail application separates application logic from presentation logic using servlets and JSPs. The role of servlets in the MVC pattern is to serve as *controllers* for the application. The servlet controller handles the event processing and performs the appropriate business logic. In a data-driven application, the business logic normally retrieves data from the model. The servlet then forwards the data to a JSP page. The role of JSPs is to provide a view of the data in an HTML page. See the diagram below for their interaction:

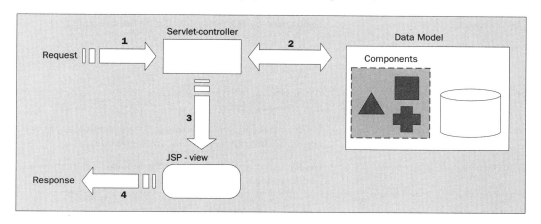

The MVC pattern provides a number of benefits:

❑   Decouples application logic from presentation logic

❑   Minimizes HTML code in the servlet

❑   Minimizes business logic in JSP

❑   Servlets act as a central gateway to the web application

Design patterns are a very popular subject in the developer community. If you would like more details then take a look at *J2EE Patterns Catalog* published at Sun's web site,
http://developer.java.sun.com/developer/technicalArticles/J2EE/patterns/.

Key Players

The ezmail application is composed of a number of key classes, servlets and JSPs. Let's start first with the classes and servlets.

Class / Servlet	Description
MailControllerServlet	The main servlet for the application. Handles the initial web requests and processes the action command. Executes the perform() method on the appropriate Action implementation. Finally, forwards to a destination JSP.

Table continued on following page

Class / Servlet	Description
Action	The standard interface for describing an Action in the ezmail application
LoginAction	Logs the user into the application
ViewMessageListAction	Retrieves a list of messages from the user's inbox
ViewMessageDetailAction	Retrieves the details of a message from the user's inbox
SendMessageAction	Sends an e-mail message to the desired recipient
LogoutAction	Logs the user out of the system
ActionException	Represents an error condition
UserInfo	An entity for the user's pop3host, username, password and e-mail address
MailHelper	Utility class for sending and retrieving e-mail. Code is very similar to previous examples in the chapter.
Constants	Collection of constant strings for actions, destination pages and keys for HttpSession data

The ezmail application also has a number of supporting HTML pages and JSPs. A description of each is given below:

HTML / JSP	Description
login_form.html	Login form for user id, password, and so on
home.html	Contains frames for menu.html and main.html
menu.html	Menu of actions for the user: Inbox, Compose, Logout
main.html	Initial welcome page
compose_message.jsp	Form for composing an e-mail message
send_message.jsp	Confirmation page for a sent message
view_message_list.jsp	Displays a list of messages for a user
view_message_detail.jsp	Displays the details for a given message
detail_nav_links.inc	Navigation links for messages: Reply | Next | Message. This page is included on the view_message_detail.jsp
view_details_error.jsp	Error page for viewing messages
logout.jsp	Logout confirmation page

Defining Actions

In a traditional GUI application, the end-user triggers actions by clicking the mouse on buttons or components on the GUI display. This action/event is passed to a registered event listener/handler. The listener then performs the desired operation. In the ezmail application, the `MailControllerServlet` handles all of the web requests (except in one special case, more on that later). The application architecture defines a standard method for actions/commands. A special parameter named `action` is passed on the URL request to the `MailControllerServlet`. When the servlet retrieves the action parameter it then invokes a registered action listener.

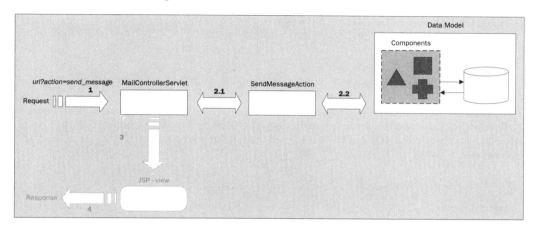

The action listeners are Java classes that implement the `ezmail.Action` interface. The `Action` listeners actually contain the business logic for performing a given operation. The `MailControllerServlet` delegates calls the `Action` listeners. The `Action` listeners invoke methods on utility classes or additional components in the model.

The table below lists the action commands supported by the ezmail application along with their associated `Action` classes and destination pages.

action parameter	Action implementation	Destination Page
login	LoginAction	home.html
view_message_list	ViewMessageListAction	view_message_list.jsp
view_message_detail	ViewMessageDetailAction	view_message_action.jsp
compose	–	compose_message.jsp
send_message	SendMessageAction	send_message.jsp
logout	LogoutAction	logout.jsp

The code for the `Action` interface (`Action.java`) is shown below. This file, and all the Java files required for the ezmail application can be found in the `ezmail_webapp\source` directory of this chapter's code download. The JSP and HTML files can be found in the `ezmail_webapp\public_html` directory.

```
// Action.java

package ezmail;

import javax.servlet.ServletContext;
import javax.servlet.http.HttpServletRequest;
import javax.servlet.http.HttpServletResponse;

public interface Action {

  public void perform(ServletContext servletContext,
                      HttpServletRequest request,
                      HttpServletResponse response) throws ActionException;

}
```

Below is an implementation of the Action interface for sending e-mail. The SendMessageAction class implements the perform() method of the Action interface. Inside of the perform() method the class calls the sendMessage() message of the ezmail.MailHelper class. If the listener needs to share data with a JSP, then the listener has the option of storing the data in the HttpSession object or HttpRequest object. The JSP can easily retrieve the data at a later time from the HttpSession or HttpRequest.

```
// SendMessageAction.java

package ezmail;

import javax.servlet.ServletContext;
import javax.servlet.http.HttpServletRequest;
import javax.servlet.http.HttpServletResponse;
import javax.servlet.http.HttpSession;

import javax.mail.Session;

public class SendMessageAction implements Action {

  public SendMessageAction() {}

  /**
   * Performs the following steps...
   * <ol>
   * <li>....</li>
   * </ol>
   *
   * The data is then placed in the user's session.  The attribute is named
   * <code>Constants.DATA</code>
   */
  public void perform(ServletContext servletContext,
                      HttpServletRequest request,
                      HttpServletResponse response) throws ActionException {

    try {
      HttpSession theHttpSession = request.getSession();

      // retrieve the mail session
      Session mailSession =
        (Session) theHttpSession.getAttribute(Constants.MAIL_SESSION);
      UserInfo theUserInfo =
```

```
                (UserInfo) theHttpSession.getAttribute(Constants.USER_INFO);

            String from = theUserInfo.getE-mailAddress();
            String to = request.getParameter("to");
            String subject = request.getParameter("subject");
            String messageText = request.getParameter("message_text");

            MailHelper.sendMessage(mailSession, from, to, subject, messageText);
        } catch (Exception exc) {
            exc.printStackTrace();
            throw new ActionException(exc.getMessage());
        }
    }

}
```

When the `MailControllerServlet` is initialized, it builds an internal mapping of action commands with their appropriate `Action` implementations. Here's a code snippet from the `MailControllerServlet`'s `init()` method.

```
public class MailControllerServlet extends HttpServlet {
    private HashMap actionTable;
...
    public void init() throws ServletException {
...
        // Create the Action implementations and place in HashMap
        actionTable = new HashMap();
        actionTable.put(Constants.LOGIN_KEY, new LoginAction());
        actionTable.put(Constants.SEND_MESSAGE_KEY, new SendMessageAction());
...
    }
}
```

When the `MailControllerServlet` receives an HTTP request, it looks up the appropriate `Action` implementation from the action mapping table. Once it has a reference to the `Action` implementation, then it invokes the `perform()` method. This is accomplished with the code snippet below:

```
            // retrieve the desired Action implementation
            String actionParam = request.getParameter(Constants.ACTION_PARAM);
            Action tempAction = (Action) actionTable.get(actionParam);

            // now let's perform the action!
            // note:  getServletContext() is inherited from javax.servlet.GenericServlet
            tempAction.perform(getServletContext(), request, response);

            // Dispatch/forward the request to destination page
            String destPage = (String) pageTable.get(actionParam);

            System.out.println("destPage = " + destPage);

            ServletContext context = getServletContext();
            RequestDispatcher dispatcher = context.getRequestDispatcher(destPage);
            dispatcher.forward(request, response);
```

This architecture provides a modular/extensible approach for adding functionality to the web application. To add new functionality to the application, simply implement the `Action` interface and register the new implementation in the `init()` method of the `MailControllerServlet`.

Defining Destination Pages

After the servlet has executed the `perform()` method of the `Action` implementation, it forwards control to the JSP for the rendering of the data. The `MailControllerServlet` determines the destination by looking in the page mapping table. The page mapping table was also initialized in the servlet's `init()` method, similar to the action mapping table. The forwarding process is shown in Step 3 of the diagram below.

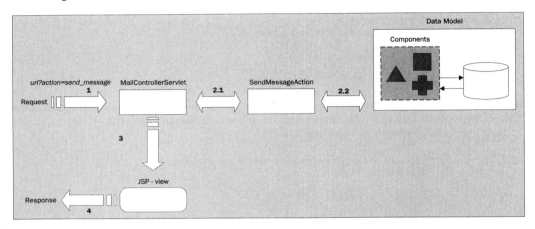

The destination page is typically a JSP file. If the `Action` implementation retrieved data for the JSP, then the JSP can access the data set from the `HttpSession` or `HttpRequest`. The JSP is then responsible for rendering the contents of the data. The process is shown in Step 4 in the diagram above. JSP rendering examples are presented later in this chapter.

Application Interaction

In this section, we'll walk through the actions for **Login**, **View Message List** and **View Message Details**. The remaining actions are very similar in nature. Basically, each action reads URL parameters, executes the `perform()` methods and sends the results to the destination page. The actions are generated from the menu or from internal links in the application. You saw a screenshot containing the menu at the start of this section.

Each link within the application contains a special `action` parameter. This parameter is sent to the `MailControllerServer` for processing. A list of the actions are shown below:

- ❑ `login`
- ❑ `view_message_list`
- ❑ `view_message_detail`
- ❑ `compose`
- ❑ `send_message`
- ❑ `logout`

Logging In

Before the user can send or receive e-mail, they must first login to the application. This allows us to access the correct mailbox based on user id and password. The key players for the `login` action are shown below:

action parameter	Action implementation	Destination Page
login	LoginAction	home.html

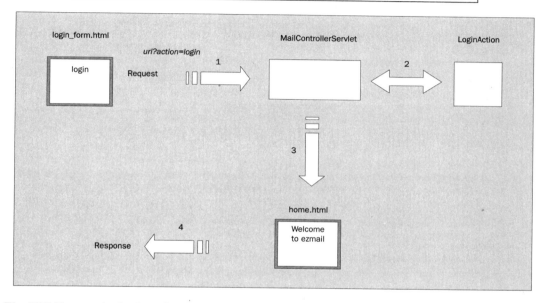

The HTML page, login_form.html prompts the user for the pop3 server name, username, password, and e-mail address. You saw a screenshot of this at the beginning of this section.

When the user selects the Login button, the form data is passed to the `MailControllerServlet`. The form also contains a hidden field for the `action` parameter. The `MailControllerServlet` executes the `perform()` method in the `LoginAction` implementation code.

The `LoginAction` configures a `javax.mail.Session` object based on the parameters login_form.html. The `LoginAction` then constructs a `UserInfo` object to hold the information entered by the user. The `UserInfo` object along with the `javax.mail.Session` object is placed in the `HttpSession` object. The `HttpSession` object is a special server-side object that is unique for a given web user; it is commonly used to track state information for a user. Here's the source code for `LoginAction.java`:

```java
// LoginAction.java

package ezmail;

import javax.servlet.ServletContext;
import javax.servlet.http.HttpServletRequest;
import javax.servlet.http.HttpServletResponse;
```

```
import javax.servlet.http.HttpSession;

import javax.mail.Session;
import javax.mail.Store;
import javax.mail.Folder;

public class LoginAction implements Action {

  public LoginAction() {}

  public void perform(ServletContext servletContext,
                      HttpServletRequest request,
                      HttpServletResponse response) throws ActionException {

    try {
      HttpSession theHttpSession = request.getSession();

      // retrieve data from login form and servlet context
      String pop3host = request.getParameter("pop3host");
      String user = request.getParameter("user");
      String password = request.getParameter("password");
      String e-mailAddress = request.getParameter("e-mail_address");
      String smtphost = servletContext.getInitParameter("smtphost");

      // Configure the mail session
      System.out.println("Configuring mail session");
      java.util.Properties props = new java.util.Properties();
      props.put("mail.smtp.host", smtphost);
      props.put("mail.pop3.host", pop3host);
      Session mailSession = Session.getInstance(props, null);
      System.out.println("Configuring mail session....complete!");

      // create a UserInfo object
      UserInfo info = new UserInfo(pop3host, user, password, e-mailAddress);

      // now let's add user data to the session
      theHttpSession.setAttribute(Constants.MAIL_SESSION, mailSession);
      theHttpSession.setAttribute(Constants.USER_INFO, info);
      theHttpSession.setAttribute(Constants.LOGIN_STATUS,
                                  new Boolean(true));
    } catch (Exception exc) {
      exc.printStackTrace();
      throw new ActionException(exc.getMessage());
    }
  }
}
```

Once the LoginAction has performed its operations, control is passed to the destination page home.html. This HTML page contains two frames. The first frame is menu.html and the second frame is the main.html welcome page.

View Message List

The user can check the contents of their inbox by choosing the Inbox menu option. This will display the header information for each message in a tabular fashion. Each message contains a clickable link for viewing the message body. The key players for the view_message_list action are shown opposite.

action parameter	Action implementation	Destination Page
view_message_list	ViewMessageListAction	view_message_list.jsp

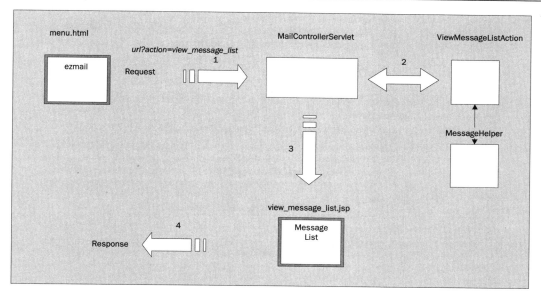

When the user selects the Inbox menu item, a request is passed to the MailControllerServlet. The value of the action parameter is view_message_list and MailControllerServlet executes the perform() method in the ViewMessageListAction implementation code.

The ViewMessageListAction retrieves a list of messages from the user's inbox. The messages are then stored in the user's HttpSession object. This technique allows the JSP page, view_message_list.jsp, to access the messages and list them in an HTML page.

The code for the ViewMessageListAction is shown below. Notice that the MailHelper utility class handles the actual message retrieval. The MailerHelper code is not shown since it is simply a composition of the MessageList and MessageView classes presented earlier in the chapter.

```java
// ViewMessageListAction.java

package ezmail;

import javax.servlet.ServletContext;
import javax.servlet.http.HttpServletRequest;
import javax.servlet.http.HttpServletResponse;
import javax.servlet.http.HttpSession;

import javax.mail.Session;
import javax.mail.Folder;
import javax.mail.Message;

public class ViewMessageListAction implements Action {

  public ViewMessageListAction() {}
```

```
public void perform(ServletContext servletContext,
                    HttpServletRequest request,
                    HttpServletResponse response) throws ActionException {

  try {
    HttpSession theHttpSession = request.getSession();

    // retrieve the mail session
    Session mailSession =
      (Session) theHttpSession.getAttribute(Constants.MAIL_SESSION);
    UserInfo theUserInfo =
      (UserInfo) theHttpSession.getAttribute(Constants.USER_INFO);

    // retrieve the messages from the user's inbox
    Message[] msgs = MailHelper.getMessages(mailSession, theUserInfo);

    // place the messages in the http session
    theHttpSession.setAttribute(Constants.MESSAGE_LIST, msgs);
  } catch (Exception exc) {
    exc.printStackTrace();
    throw new ActionException(exc.getMessage());
  }
}
}
```

The JSP page, `view_message_list.jsp`, displays the messages in an HTML table. Each message has a link for viewing the message details. The link has the `action` command `vie w_message_detail` and also appends the message number. Let's take a look at the JSP code fragment for accessing the list.

```
<!-- view_message_list.jsp (fragment) -->

<%
Message[] theMessages = (Message[]) session.getAttribute(Constants.MESSAGE_LIST);

  if (theMessages.length == 0) {
    out.print("<b>No messages on server.</b>");
    return;
  }
%>
```

As you can see above, the JSP retrieves the list of messages from the `HttpSession`. The messages were stored there by the `ViewMessageListAction` class.

Next, the `view_message_list.jsp` builds an HTML table for the messages. A screenshot of the table output is shown opposite followed by the source code.

#	Sender	Subject	Date
<u>1</u>	info@j-nine.com	<u>Test Message - quickmail text</u>	<u>18. Aug. 2001</u> <u>02:18:18 PM</u>
<u>2</u>	info@j-nine.com	<u>Test Message - quickmail html</u>	<u>18. Aug. 2001</u> <u>02:18:30 PM</u>
<u>3</u>	info@j-nine.com	<u>Test Message - quickmail attach</u>	<u>18. Aug. 2001</u> <u>02:19:20 PM</u>

```
<!-- view_message_list.jsp (fragment) -->

<table border="1" cellspacing="1" cellpadding="5" width="75%">
     <tr>
            <th># </th>
            <th>Sender</th>
            <th>Subject</th>
            <th>Date</th>
     </tr>

<%
     Message currentMessage;
     int messageNum;
     String sender;
     Address[] addressList;
     String date;
     int count = theMessages.length;

     String startLink;
     String endLink;
     for (int i=0; i < count; i++) {
            currentMessage = theMessages[i];
            addressList = currentMessage.getFrom();
            sender = addressList[0].toString();
            date = MailHelper.formatDate(currentMessage.getSentDate());
            messageNum = currentMessage.getMessageNumber();

            startLink = "<a
href='controller?action=view_message_detail&message_num=" + messageNum + "&max=" +
count + "'>";
            endLink = "</a>";
%>
     <tr>
            <td>
                   <%= startLink %><%= messageNum %> <%= endLink %>
            </td>
            <td>
                   <%= startLink %><%= sender %><%= endLink %>
            </td>
            <td>
```

```
                <%= startLink %><%= currentMessage.getSubject() %><%= endLink %>
        </td>
        <td>
                <%= startLink %><%= date %><%= endLink %>
        </td>
    </tr>
<%
    }
%>

    </table>
```

View Message Detail

The user displays the details for a message by selecting the message from the list. The key players for the `view_message_detail` action are shown below.

action parameter	Action implementation	Destination Page
view_message_detail	ViewMessageDetailAction	view_message_detail.jsp

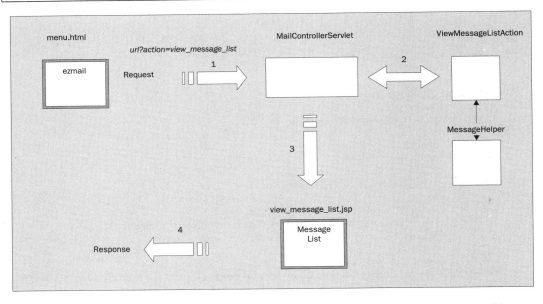

As usual, all of the web requests are routed through the `MailControllerServlet`. The `ViewMessageDetailAction` retrieves the message number from the web request. Recall that the `view_message_list.jsp` file created links for each message. The links included the actual message number.

The code for `ViewMessageDetailAction.java` is shown opposite. Again, the `MailHelper` class handles the actual retrieval of a given message.

```
// ViewMessageDetailAction.java

package ezmail;

import javax.servlet.ServletContext;
import javax.servlet.http.HttpServletRequest;
import javax.servlet.http.HttpServletResponse;
import javax.servlet.http.HttpSession;

import javax.mail.Session;
import javax.mail.Folder;
import javax.mail.Message;

public class ViewMessageDetailAction implements Action {

  public ViewMessageDetailAction() {}

  public void perform(ServletContext servletContext,
                      HttpServletRequest request,
                      HttpServletResponse response) throws ActionException {

    try {
      HttpSession theHttpSession = request.getSession();

      // retrieve the mail session
      Session mailSession =
        (Session) theHttpSession.getAttribute(Constants.MAIL_SESSION);
      UserInfo theUserInfo =
        (UserInfo) theHttpSession.getAttribute(Constants.USER_INFO);

      // retrieve the messages from the user's inbox
      int messageNum =
        Integer.parseInt(request.getParameter("message_num"));
      Message theMsg = MailHelper.getMessage(mailSession, theUserInfo,
                                             messageNum);

      // place the messages in the http session
      theHttpSession.setAttribute(Constants.CURRENT_MESSAGE, theMsg);
    } catch (Exception exc) {
      exc.printStackTrace();
      throw new ActionException(exc.getMessage());
    }
  }

}
```

Once the ViewMessageDetailAction retrieves the message, control is passed to the view_message_detail.jsp for display. The JSP retrieves the message from the HttpSession using the following code fragment:

```
<!-- view_message_detail.jsp (fragment) -->
<%
    Message theMessage = (Message)
                    session.getAttribute(Constants.CURRENT_MESSAGE);
    ...
%>
```

The JSP then displays the message sender, subject, date and subject. Navigation links are included at the top and bottom of the text message. This allows the user to reply to the current message, move to the previous or next message. An output of the `view_message_detail.jsp` is shown below:

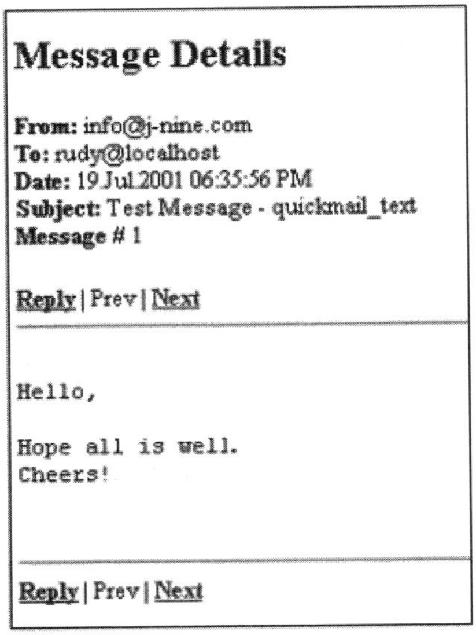

Summary

In this chapter, you learned how to send e-mail messages using the JavaMail API. This consisted of configuring a mail session, populating the values of a `Message` object and then sending it using the `Transport` object. You also learned how easy it was to send HTML-formatted e-mail and attachments.

The chapter also covered techniques for retrieving messages from a mail server. You created special `FetchProfiles` to retrieve the header information for displaying a top-level list. Then, you learned how to retrieve individual messages and access their content.

The chapter integrated the technologies presented by developing a web-based e-mail application. Servlets and JSPs were used to send and retrieve messages. During the construction of the application, you learned about application design patterns and architecture.

Armed with this information on the JavaMail API, you are now ready to add e-mail functionality to your applications.

Messaging with JMS

In any enterprise, many applications are used to support the business processes. Just as departments of enterprises need to communicate with each other to get their work done, different applications will need to communicate with each other to achieve the same. The communication between applications within one enterprise is sometimes called **enterprise messaging**. Other forms of communication between applications also exist, examples of these forms are:

❑   Business to business: Here applications belonging to different enterprises interact

❑   Inter-application: Here an application is a distributed solution with components (perhaps viewed as an application) on several different pieces of hardware

Enterprise messaging applications exchange information using the concept of message passing. This means an application will inform another application it wants something done by sending a message to it. For example, a sales department would send a copy of an order to the finance department for it to send out a bill.

This chapter explains the basics of using enterprise messaging with Java applications. It will cover the different techniques for enterprise messaging and make clear what the respective advantages and drawbacks are. At the end of the chapter, you will be able to implement enterprise messaging in your own applications.

In particular, this chapter will cover:

❑   Message oriented middleware

❑   Hub and spoke architecture

❑   Java Messaging Service (JMS)

Enterprise Messaging

Before getting started on programming enterprise messaging applications, we must examine the basic models on which our applications will be built. The explanations will often refer to the scenario of the interaction between a sales application and a finance application. For instance, the sales application might send details of an order to a finance application so the customer can be billed. This finance application could then send a payment history back.

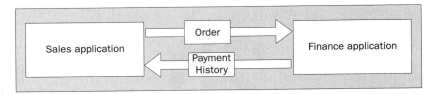

Enterprise messaging is the communication between different applications within the same company and there are many ways to achieve this communication.

To get a more complete picture of the various methods we'll look at some of the common ones:

- ❑ Raw network
- ❑ Remote procedure calls (RPC)
- ❑ Electronic Mail
- ❑ Message Oriented Middleware (MOM)

Raw Network Communication

The use of raw network communication techniques, such as named pipes or TCP/IP sockets, form the basis for all the other techniques. Achieving communications between applications using this low-level technique is the most time-consuming for a programmer to accomplish. As a programmer you spend a lot of time dealing with adverse network conditions and how best to cope with such situations on top of processing the messages. Some examples of the problems you have to solve include the temporary loss of a connection, requiring you to reconnect and the encoding of your information into a byte format that is understood at the destination. The received information also needs to be transformed from an array of bytes to a convenient programming object like a string or integer. The main advantage of using raw network communication techniques is the potential of high data throughput. An example of this is a live streaming application that needs continuous video feeds.

Remote Procedure Calls

To make it easier for programmers to invoke methods in other applications, remote procedures calls were devised (see Chapter 16 for more details on doing RPC calls with Java by using Remote Method Invocation, RMI). This communication technique deals with the data encoding issues and most network communication aspects, like opening a TCP/IP port. Remote procedure calls (RPC) make it easy to invoke a specific piece of logic within another application. The logic in the remote application must be exposed as a method suitable for invocation through RPC.

Although RPC is a powerful method for network programming, it does have some important disadvantages. Applications communicating with one another using RPC need to be running at the same time. Upgrades and configuration changes that require an application to be temporarily offline may result in errors in the other application. Maintenance should thus be planned at the same time or the logic that uses RPC will have to be intelligent enough to retry the invocation later.

Applications that use RPC must run at a similar speed if overall performance is to be guaranteed, as each component should be able to handle requests at a comparable rate. Going back to our example, you will see that the finance application should be able to process orders just as fast as the sales application, otherwise the sales application is slowed down in its order intake.

Electronic Mail

To allow applications to run at a different speed one could make use of mail. Mail is an asynchronous way of exchanging messages – if the sales application mailed the order to the finance application then it can continue processing new orders, while the finance application can take its time processing the order, so you will not be billed so fast.

Mail abstracts raw network aspects from the programmer and it has several ways to encode information with the use of MIME or XML messages, however it has a big disadvantage in that it is not *reliable*. The chance of a mail message being lost, certainly within the same enterprise, can be very small but it is a possibility. If the sales department processes an order and the items are shipped, you will want the absolute guarantee that the finance department will bill that customer.

Also, keep in mind that electronic mail (e-mail) is a method of communication between people, or between software applications and people. However, it is not ideally suited for communication between software applications or software components. Although programs shuffle the data from place to place, the actual writing of the message and more importantly the interpretation of a received message is done by a human. E-mail has no means for helping applications interpret the received message or invoke a new action within that application.

Message Oriented Middleware

The communication techniques provided by **message oriented middleware** (MOM) deal with all the issues described earlier. MOM allows for reliable message exchange between applications. It also abstracts all network problems from the application programmer. Message-exchange can be achieved asynchronously and synchronously. In most cases, MOM implementations support multiple message formats and provide tools to encode and decode information within a message.

All this additional functionality can affect performance and this form of intracompany communication is not always the best solution. If an application needs to stream data continuously to another application, the use of raw network communication techniques will be a wiser choice.

Message oriented middleware is software that connects otherwise separate applications through the passing of messages. The software creates an infrastructure that insulates the application developer from the details of the various operating systems and network interfaces.

Message oriented middleware has several key concepts:

- ❑ Clients
- ❑ Message agents
- ❑ Destinations
- ❑ Messages

The messaging system is often a peer-to-peer facility. This means that a **messaging client** can send messages to, and receive messages from, any other messaging client. There is no central server that distributes the messages, as with e-mail.

A **messaging agent** provides facilities for creating, sending, and receiving messages. Each client connects to its own messaging agent to make use of these facilities. The messaging agent will see to it that a message is delivered to the requested **destination** or other client.

Messages are not sent to applications or message agents directly, but to an abstract location called a **destination**, this is a unique address within the message oriented middleware software. A messaging agent is needed to send messages to, or read messages delivered to a specific destination. A destination can point to a location on the same machine or anywhere on the network.

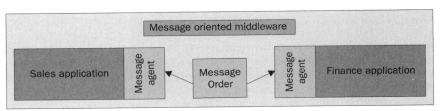

Illustrated in the diagram above is the structure of the sales/finance application we discussed in the last section if it was implemented using message oriented middleware.

A message can be separated into roughly two parts. One part, referred to as the **message header**, contains information intended only for the message agent. The other part, referred to as the **message body** or **payload**, holds information intended for the target-application or message receiving application.

The message header instructs the messaging agent on where to deliver the message and how it should be transported. The header also contains other instructions, like indications about the desired assurances or the number of times a delivery was attempted. Other information describes the return address (also a destination) to which the target-application should send its response (if any).

The message body is mostly left untouched by the MOM software. However, transformations are made on the information intended for the target application if the platform on which the application runs, requires such transformations. The transformation should only involve changes in byte ordering when crossing big endian and little endian boundaries or when the character encoding differs (like ASCII or Unicode).

> **Transformation of a message body does not occur when using the Java API.**
> **Regardless of operating system or hardware platform, Java always uses the same byte ordering (big endian) and character encoding (Unicode).**

Hub and Spoke Architecture

Creating applications that use enterprise messaging requires a design that spans across the several applications communicating with each other. This overall design is often referred to as **system architecture**.

As you let more and more applications communicate with enterprise messaging, your architecture can slowly grow to be a mesh of one-to-one connections between applications. The figure below shows such a mesh between applications. Each arrow indicates a set of destinations known to each application.

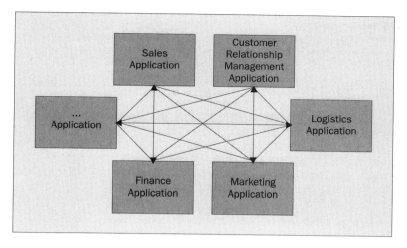

Each enterprise messaging application may need to create a connection for each application within your company. When a new application is created, every existing application that requires interaction with this new application, needs to be modified. Several solution strategies for dealing with this mesh of connections may immediately pop into your mind. You might think of creating additional end-points to prepare your application for possible future expansion. However, this leads to unnecessary message sending when no expansion is created. The strategy is also useless after all the end-points have been used up.

One of the solutions to this problem is the **hub and spoke architecture**. This architecture defines a central application, called a **message broker** *or* **message server**, to be the destination of all applications. It is the responsibility of the message broker to route messages to the correct target application based on information within the message. The message broker is not part of the message oriented middleware software, but a separate application, so the argument mentioned earlier stating that message oriented middleware does not have a central server still holds, however the use of the hub and spoke architecture does introduce such an application.

Message brokers differ in level of complexity. Simple ones are only capable of forwarding messages, more advanced ones have the additional capability of transforming the message content from one format to another format by rearranging them or adding information. The most complex message brokers offer administrative capabilities, like logging, and they can perform alternative transformations or forwarding if error conditions occur. Some can even be configured to expect a level of service from an application, meaning that if an application doesn't respond to a send message within a certain timeframe or with a specific message (format), the message broker can take alternative actions. These could include resending the message or contacting an administrator. Any new application added to the enterprise messaging system will only require changes in the message broker.

When you look at the architecture you can make an analogy with a hub (message broker) and spokes (applications) of a wheel. The next figure illustrates this architecture. As you can see this is a simpler architecture. For instance, adding a new module doesn't require changes to the other modules. Nor do the individual modules now have to know where the others are or how to communicate with them.

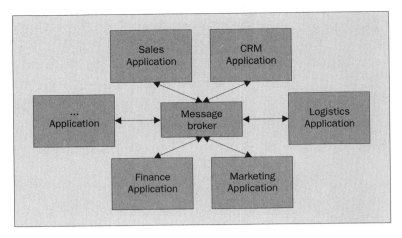

There is an easy way to use the hub and spoke architecture without having to buy or create a message broker application. You can use the publish and subscribe domain of Java Messaging Service (JMS). Note that Java Messaging Service (JMS) implementations are not free. The one provided with Java 2 Platform, Enterprise Edition (J2EE) reference implementation is not suitable for production use. If you do have another J2EE implementation, which is supplied with most application servers, you can use the publish and subscribe domain. Also, note that most message broker applications cost several times the cost of an application server.

The Java Message Service (JMS)

The first part of this chapter gave you the run-down on what enterprise messaging is, what technologies you can use and some of the architectures that are possible. The remaining sections will guide you through programming enterprise messaging applications with the use of the **Java Messaging Service (JMS)**. Two examples will be used to demonstrate program applications or software components that can communicate with each other via messages. But before we get to that we must examine the JMS in detail.

The Java Message Service is a Java API that allows applications to create, send, receive, and read messages. The API defines a common set of interfaces and associated semantics that allow programs written in the Java programming language to communicate with message oriented middleware.

Java Messaging Service (JMS) applications are capable of communicating with heterogeneous applications that are written in other programming languages, run on other operating systems or machine architectures. This is because messages, created with the JMS API, can match most formats used by existing, non-JMS applications. The non-Java and non-JMS application will need to access their messages through means provided by the Java Messaging Service (JMS) vendor-implementations. Examples of these are proprietary APIs or other standards like the CORBA Messaging Service from the Object Management Group (OMG).

The use of the JMS API in your programs will give them the flexibility to switch between messaging implementations. This is similar to the way the use of the JDBC API makes your programs flexible in switching between database management systems. This portability is only valid if your applications use only JMS and not the vendor-specific API for communications with MOM.

The advent of Java Messaging Service also brought about a consensus on what components are used in messaging. One messaging system would require the use of a separate configuration-component, while another incorporated the configuration options within methods of the message client directly. Previously, conceptually similar components would also be called something different across messaging systems. With the creation of the unified API for various messaging strategies, JMS minimized the set of components that a Java language programmer must learn to create enterprise messaging products.

The behavior of messaging systems is different. Some systems provide only facilities for delivering messages to a client as they arrive (push model), while others only support means for clients to actively request messages (pull model). The semantic specifications within JMS remove these differences, by describing completely how and when messages arrive at clients. Semantics are also defined at a low level with various rules, for instance on how and when the properties of a message header are (can be) set. At the high level the specifications divide the behavior of key components within the two *messaging domains*.

Messaging Domains in JMS

Java Messaging Service (JMS) describes the many difference in messaging systems with just two **messaging domains**.

- ❑ Point-to-Point
- ❑ Publish and Subscribe

The **point-to-point** domain has a lot of similarity to the postal service; addresses are predefined and messages sent to a specific address are mostly intended for one person. This domain uses **message queues** instead of postal addresses as destinations. Each message is addressed to a specific queue; clients extract messages from the queue(s) established to hold their messages. Similar to postal addresses, you will find that queues are generally predefined, so they are known at design time. Just as with a queue at the checkout in the supermarket, the first to arrive will be helped (delivered) first.

The **publish and subscribe** (or *Pub/Sub)* domain is built around the idea of a content hierarchy. It lets clients, called **publishers**, send messages to a node located somewhere within a content hierarchy. **Subscribers** are clients that subscribe to a node in the content hierarchy in order to receive messages, published to this particular node. The system takes care of distributing messages arriving from a node's multiple publishers to its multiple subscribers. Publishers and subscribers are generally anonymous and may dynamically publish or subscribe to a content hierarchy. Messages intended for several clients or messages intended for unknown clients are best sent using the publish and subscribe domain of Java Messaging Service (JMS).

The JMS Specification defines rules for compliance for each domain. A standalone JMS provider may implement one or both domains. A Java 2 Platform, Enterprise Edition (J2EE) provider must implement both domains. Most current implementations of the JMS API provide support for both the point-to-point and publish/subscribe domains. JMS clients are allowed to combine the use of both domains in a single application.

Application Architecture

Previous we defined the key components of a MOM-based messaging service: clients, message agents, destinations, and messages. Java Messaging Service (JMS) refines these key components and adds a few more.

JMS calls a messaging system that implements the interfaces and provides administration and control features, a JMS **Provider**. Message clients are separated into the JMS clients and non-JMS clients categories. JMS clients are programs or components written in the Java programming language and that send and receive messages by using the JMS API. All other programs, regardless of their programming language, are considered non-JMS clients. Communication between clients of both categories is possible; the JMS Provider is tasked to solve this problem. JMS introduces another key component, called **administered objects**; these are preconfigured JMS objects such as destinations or **connection factories**. They are created and configured by an administrator for use by client applications. Later on, the benefits and such of administered objects will be explained further.

Java Messaging Service calls clients that send messages **message producers** and clients that receive messages **message consumers**. Depending on the message domain used within your program the JMS API refers to message producers, message consumers and destinations differently. The table below supplies an overview of the way JMS refers to key components of MOM within a particular messaging domain.

JMS	Point to point domain	Pub/Sub domain
Destination	Queue	Topic
Message producer	QueueSender	TopicPublisher
Message consumer	QueueReceiver	TopicSubscriber

What's Not in JMS

At this point, the Java Messaging Service (JMS) might seem the ideal solution for all your enterprise application needs; however, JMS does not completely cover every aspect of large distributed intracompany communications software.

The specification does not address the following functionality:

❑ Wire protocol: Vendors are allowed to implement JMS with no restrictions made on the wire protocol (network communication protocol) used. A message sent from one vendor does not need to be interpretable by another vendor simply by reading the network message. The exchange between different implementations is only required at the API level, using code.

❑ Administration: **Administered objects** are a core piece of Java Messaging Service (JMS). The storage and removal of these objects are done through the Java Naming and Directory Interface (JNDI). Apart from storage of Java objects, administration also involves other activities like the configuration of wire protocol resources (IP numbers, sockets etc.).

❑ Security: JMS is part of the Java 2 Platform, Enterprise Edition (J2EE) so most security aspects (such as login) are delegated to other parts of the platform. Controlling privacy and integrity of messages or the way digital signatures or keys should be used or distributed among clients are not specified within JMS. JMS considers security to be a JMS provider-specific feature that is configured by an administrator. Clients should not control security aspects through the JMS API.

❑ Resilience: Enterprise messaging applications usually need a high level of service. This means high availability and reliability, preferably achieved by using load balancing and fault tolerance capabilities of the messaging product. A popular way to support these capabilities in a messaging product involves combining multiple, cooperating clients into one critical service. How such clients work together to be a single, unified service is not defined in the JMS specification – this is left to providers to realize.

Choosing a resilience level can be achieved in a variety of ways, more hardware (RAM or processors), making use of OS features (duplicate processes), or software capabilities, such as clustering. When solving a resilience 'problem', any of these solutions might be the right one, taking into account budget, current environment, company standards, business ambitions, available time, experience etc. Considering all these options means that choosing a JMS provider is not an easy task.

❑   Error/Advisory Notification: Clients receive messages asynchronously from most MOM products informing them of problems or system events. A standard for system messages or notifications does not exist in the JMS specification. Conformance to the guidelines defined by JMS will prevent clients from using these messages. Good JMS clients are not allowed to depend on any system messages. Any portability problems introduced by the use of or the dependency on error/ advisory notifications through messages is thus prevented by conformance to the Java Messaging Service (JMS) specification.

❑   Triggering: The arrival of a message or the signaling of a problem (like no more room for messages) will likely need a particular client to be running, and there's no guarantee that it will be. Some JMS providers support such triggering mechanism through their own administrative facilities; JMS however does not provide a mechanism for triggering the execution of a client.

❑   Persistent message storage: Messages sent through an enterprise messaging system will conform to a certain type definition. The type definition describes for instance the fields present in a message and in what sequence they can be found. These type definitions may be stored within a repository by messaging products. There are no means to define type definitions or store them in repositories using the JMS API.

The list of functionalities that are not a part of the Java Messaging Service (JMS) specification may seem a long one. Not having these functionalities however does not mean that the specification of JMS is incomplete. In fact, JMS describes only those things that directly relate to messaging. Because the focus lies on just the kind of producers, consumers, message formats, associated behavior and so on, implementing and using JMS only requires knowledge of messaging. This results in a low learning curve for using Java Messaging Service (JMS).

Also, bear in mind that JMS is part of the Java 2 Platform, Enterprise Edition (J2EE). The other functionalities mentioned above, are most likely a required part of an enterprise messaging application. The J2EE contains the necessary standards for most of these functionalities. Mentioning them in the Java Messaging Service (JMS) specification would mean that this specification would redefine standards that are already implemented elsewhere.

Anatomy of JMS Messages

Before delving into the depths of the Java Messaging Service (JMS) API, this section focuses on the fundamental part of any messaging service: the *messages*. You have read about enterprise messaging, message oriented middleware and had an introduction to the Java Messaging Service (JMS). This section discusses mainly the anatomy of messages within the context of the JMS specification.

When discussing message exchange between applications, the JMS specification defines its own terms – consume and produce.

❑ The term **consume** is defined as the receipt of a message by a JMS client. This in turn means that a JMS provider has received a message through the MOM and has given the message to the client. The specification makes no difference in the term consume, even though it does distinguish between asynchronous and synchronous receipt of messages.

❑ The term **produce** means the sending of a message in the most general sense, without regard to the way the message is distributed among destinations by the messaging system. In conclusion, produce stands for the giving of a message to a JMS provider with the intent that the provider should deliver it to one or more destinations that then consume this message.

Properties

In a previously, messages were described as consisting of a **header** and a **body**: the header contains instructions intended for MOM; the body contains the information intended for the target application(s). The JMS specification adds another part to a message called **properties**. The properties section defines addition of optional fields that can be added to the message header. The order in which property values are stored, is not defined.

The value of a property can be any primitive Java language type (boolean, byte, short, int, long, float, double) or of type java.lang.String. The JMS specification supports automatic transformations between property values. The transformations occur when using the typed property retrieval methods, which follow the pattern get<Type>Property(). If a conversion cannot be performed, a MessageFormatException will be thrown. In cases of String to numeric conversion problems a NumberFormatException will be thrown.

Properties are divided into three categories:

❑ **Standard**: These properties are non-mandatory attributes of any JMS message, but have a standardized name and meaning

❑ **Provider specific**: These properties are mainly intended for providers to send additional information with messages, helping them process the messages correctly to non-JMS clients

❑ **Application specific**: These are used by the sending and receiving applications to help with their message processing

Java Messaging Service (JMS) specifies several standard properties that are not mandatory. The optional header fields have property names that are prefixed by the text 'JMSX'.

The following table shows most of the standard properties in a JMS message, who sets their value and what they are used for.

Name	Set by	Use
JMSXUserID	Provider just before a message is produced	Identifies the user of the sending application
JMSXAppID	Provider just before a message is produced	Identifies the sending application

Name	Set by	Use
JMSXDeliveryCount	Provider just before a message is consumed	The number of attempts made to deliver the message (starts with 1)
JMSXRcvTimestamp	Provider just before a message is consumed	The time the message is delivered to the consumer
JMSXGroupID	Client	The identity of message group
JMSXGroupSeq	Client	Indicates the sequence number of the message in a message group (starts with 1)

The value for JMSXRcvTimestamp is set by the provider just before consumption of the message by the consumer. The provider is part of the JMS implementation and should not be confused with the producer or sending application of the message.

The names of provider-specific properties are prefixed with the text "JMS_<vendor_name>", the values and the types stored under these names are determined by the vendors of messaging software. Provider-specific properties can be used to store information needed to support JMS with provider-native clients. They are not intended to help coordinate JMS-to-JMS messaging.

The last categories of JMS message properties are the application-specific ones – these are any name-value pairs stored where the name is not prefixed with "JMS_<vendor_name>" or "JMSX". The main use of application-specific properties is to help the message consuming application to distinguish the type of message received without having to process the (larger) message body.

Body

Many different types of message bodies are currently in use with message oriented middleware. The Java Messaging Service (JMS) specification defines a JMS message for the most common ones.

A JMS provider is required to transform messages received by non-JMS clients into the "best" message type. This means for instance that if possible a character message should result in an object of the type TextMessage. If no transformation is achievable then the provider should convert the message into a ByteMessage. A provider is required to accept, from a client, messages whose implementation differs from the provider's implementation. The JMS provider must handle these "foreign" message implementations but you must expect that handling these "foreign" messages may not be as efficient as for its own messages.

The complete list of message types and their body contents is:

- ❑ ByteMessage: If the body contains a stream of uninterpreted bytes.

- ❑ StreamMessage: If the body contains a stream of Java primitives.

- ❑ MapMessage: For an unordered list of name-value pairs.

- ❑ TextMessage: If the body contains a java.lang.String object.

- ❑ ObjectMessage: If the body contains a serializable Java object.

The body of a consumed (received) message is always read-only. The body of a produced (sent) message can be changed without fear of changing the just transmitted message. This feature is useful if multiple messages need to be sent to the same destination. For instance, a book transmitted chapter by chapter can be send to the same location by using the same message object.

Header

All messages have a set of required header fields. Their values have meaning to both client and provider. Header fields can be used to route or identify messages. The Java Messaging Service (JMS) specification only defines those header fields that are transmitted to JMS clients.

Name	Purpose
JMSDestination	This holds the destination to which the message is being sent.
JMSDeliveryMode	Used to specify the delivery mode when the message was sent.
JMSMessageID	This field uniquely identifies each message sent by a particular provider.
JMSTimestamp	This holds the time a message was given to a JMS Provider to be sent. The field does not hold the time the message was actually transmitted. The actual send may occur later due to transactions or other client-side queuing of messages.
JMSCorrelationID	This contains a value used to link or correlate one message with another. This is mostly used as a means to link a response message with its request message.
JMSReplyTo	This holds a destination supplied by a client when the message was sent. Any reply should be sent to this destination.
JMSRedelivered	The JMSRedelivered header field indicates if a message was delivered to the client earlier, but the client did not acknowledge its receipt.
JMSType	Holds a message type identifier supplied by a client when a message is sent. The values are not standardized by JMS and contain anything from text, typecode:1345, my birthday. The value has only meaning to the sending and receiving applications.
JMSExpiration	Holds the sum of the time-to-live value specified on the send method and the current GMT. When a message is received, its JMSExpiration header field contains this same value.

The JMS API

The following class diagram summarizes the responsibilities of the different interfaces in the Java Messaging Service (JMS) API:

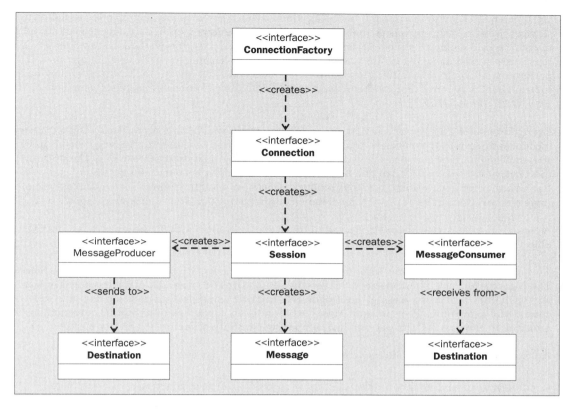

If you read the class diagram from top to bottom you will see the setup-procedure typically followed by a JMS client:

❑   Use the `ConnectionFactory` to create a `Connection`

❑   Use the `Connection` to create a `Session`

❑   Use the `Session` to create a `MessageProducer` or `MessageConsumer`

❑   Use the `Session` to create a `Message`

❑   Use the `MessageProducer` to send the message to a destination

❑   Use the `MessageConsumer` to receive a message from a destination

A `ConnectionFactory` or `destination` is stored in the Java Naming and Directory Interface (JNDI) as **administered objects**. Therefore, JMS applications usually use JNDI to obtain the `ConnectionFactory` and the `Destination`. This practice allows for highly portable applications as any vendor-specific code is removed from the application. Although this practice is advisable, it is by no means mandatory. Other techniques, like property files in combination with dynamic class loading, also create highly portable applications. These techniques could be used when no JNDI service is available. The use of JNDI does give some added benefits since it can be configured to restrict the access of its resources.

JNDI is an API used to provide the Java programmer with a single interface to naming and directory services. Most relevant here is the naming service part as it allows a unified naming scheme for all sorts of data. In JMS connection factories and destinations are stored by the JNDI interface under a previously agreed name. At runtime, applications can retrieve connections or destinations from JNDI by performing a lookup. The application can find the objects registered with JNDI wherever they happen to be, even if they move. For more information on JNDI you can consult *Professional Java Data by Wrox Press, ISBN 1861004109.*

Even after creating a `Connection`, message delivery is not yet possible. In order to send a message (produce) to, or retrieve messages (consume) from a `Destination`, the `Connection` needs to be started. The interface contains a `start()` method for a programmer to achieve this. The `Connection` can be used to create more than one `Session` this allows multiple concurrent access to `Destinations` from within your applications by means of multithreading. The concurrent use of the same resource (`Destination`) will have to be coordinated within your application.

A `Session` creates a `MessageProducer` or `MessageConsumer` with the help of a `Destination` object. A `MessageProducer` or `MessageConsumer` cannot be used on more than one `Destination`.

To specify which message you wish to receive from a `Destination`, you can use a **Message Selector**. The Message Selector filters message delivery to a `MessageConsumer` by matching message header and properties values of a message arriving at a `Destination` following rules defined in a SQL 92 conditional expression. The syntax of Message Selector can contain familiar SQL92 constructions like grouping of expressions with parenthesis, comparisons with the value `null` and more.

An example of SQL 92 conditional expression for a Message Selector is:

```
JMSType = 'order' AND (customer IN ('gold', 'platinum') OR amount >= 220371)
```

Point-to-Point Messaging Example

With our first example we'll explore the point-to-point messaging domain. Based on the same enterprise messaging scenario discussed earlier (a finance and sales application), the section will show how to send and receive messages with JMS. After we have looked at the code, instructions on setting up the environment and running the code are given. The Java 2 Platform, Enterprise Edition (J2EE version 1.3 Beta) reference implementation on Microsoft Windows 2000 Professional was used as the JMS implementation for these examples, but it should work equally well on other platforms, once your environment is set-up correctly.

Creating the Application

The Sales application sends an order to the finance application with the help of a `BasicMessageSender` object. This utility class can be used to send a text message (a `String`) to a supplied queue destination. The `BasicMessageSender` class hides away all the Java Messaging Service (JMS) steps needed before a message can be sent. The use of this utility class (which is a part of the API so is portable across JMS providers) makes the code in `SalesApplication.java`, which is used to send a message, look fairly simple.

```
// SalesApplication.java

package com.wrox.p2p;
```

```
import javax.naming.*;
import javax.jms.*;

public class SalesApplication {
  public SalesApplication() {}
  public static void main(String[] args) {
    try {
      BasicMessageSender sender = new BasicMessageSender("SalesQFactory",
            "FinanceInQ");
      sender.sendMessage("The order XML document");
      sender.cleanup();
    } catch (NamingException namingEx) {
      namingEx.printStackTrace();
    } catch (JMSException jmsEx) {
      jmsEx.printStackTrace();
    }
  }
}
```

When the sales application constructs a `BasicMessageSender` object, it specifies two parameters. The first parameter is the name queried for in the JNDI directory to get the `QueueConnectionFactory` administered object. The second parameter specifies the name of the `Queue` (a `Destination`) administrated object. The sales application then uses the `sendMessage()` method of the `BasicMessageSender` object to send one or more text messages to the queue.

The `BasicMessageSender` uses several JMS resources; the sales application can clear these resource by calling the `cleanup()` method. After this method is called, the `BasicMessageSender` object should no longer be used. Inadvertent use of the `BasicMessageSender` object will lead to a `java.lang.NullPointerException`. Naturally, there are much better mechanisms to indicate an invalid use of the object, but this simple way will at least inhibit incorrect use of the `BasicMessageSender` class in your own applications. If the sales application did not call the `cleanup()` method, the utility class would call it when it is garbage collected.

Finally some exceptions are caught and any problems with producing the message are simply reported to the console.

Now le'ts look at the code for the `BasicMessageSender` class, which contains most of the functionality for actually sending the messages:

```
// BasicMessageSender.java

package com.wrox.p2p;

import javax.naming.*;
import javax.jms.*;

public class BasicMessageSender {

  protected QueueConnection _connection;
  protected QueueSession _session;
  protected QueueSender _sender;
  protected String _jndiQueueName;
```

```
    protected String _jndiQueueFactoryName;

    public BasicMessageSender(String jndiQueueFactoryName,
                              String jndiQueueName)
            throws NamingException, JMSException {
      _jndiQueueName = jndiQueueName;
      _jndiQueueFactoryName = jndiQueueFactoryName;
      initialize();
    }

    protected void initialize() throws NamingException, JMSException {
      Context ctx = new InitialContext();
      QueueConnectionFactory queueConnectionFactory =
        (QueueConnectionFactory) ctx.lookup(_jndiQueueFactoryName);
      Queue outQueue = (Queue) ctx.lookup(_jndiQueueName);
      _connection = queueConnectionFactory.createQueueConnection();
      _session = _connection.createQueueSession(false,
                                        Session.AUTO_ACKNOWLEDGE);
      _sender = _session.createSender(outQueue);
    }
```

The `initialize()` method retrieves the administered objects from the JNDI directory and creates a `QueueConnection` object, a `QueueSession` object and a `QueueSender` object. The `QueueSession` object is constructed with two parameters. The first indicates if transaction control is necessary, the second parameter indicates who will acknowledge any messages it receives (the consumer or the client). The `BasicMessageSender` uses the basic parameter values, which result in a non-transactional `QueueSession`, which automatically sends acknowledgements when required. Any problems (such as exceptions) that arise are left to the user of a `BasicMessageSender` object to deal with.

```
    public void sendMessage(String theMessageBody) throws JMSException {
      if (_sender != null) {
        _connection.start();
        TextMessage message = _session.createTextMessage();
        message.setText(theMessageBody);
        _sender.send(message);
      }
    }
```

The second method that needs some explaining, deals with the sending of messages and is appropriately named `sendMessage()`. First the method checks that the sender is not `null` then it starts the connection. Messages can only be exchanged when the connection is started.

The Java Messaging Service (JMS) specification states that multiple requests to start a connection that has already been started, may not result in any problems so our code should work fine. However, you might feel more comfortable with having an initialization construction like the one given below:

```
if (!_alreadyStarted)
{
  _connection.start();
  _alreadyStarted = true;
}
```

It is very likely that the JMS provider has thus already implemented a similar construction. A cautious programmer may add the above code, just to be safe though.

Next, the method creates a new `TextMessage` object. The message body is filled using the `setText()` method. The method concludes with the sending of the message using the `send()` method.

```java
public void finalize() {
  try {
    cleanup();
  } catch (JMSException jmsEx) {

    // ignore this error
  }
}
public void cleanup() throws JMSException {
  if (_connection != null) {
    _connection.close();
  }
}
}
```

Again any problems are left to the user of the `BasicMessageSender` object to deal with. The user will need to catch the `JMSException` to deal with the problems, and devise its own problem solving strategy. The simplest might be trying again and if still unsuccessful, let a human deal with it, not your code. Finally there is a `cleanup()` method, which as before deals with releasing system resources.

Messages are usually sent with the intention of them eventually being received. The receiver of the order messages sent by the sales application is the finance application. This application receives the order messages placed on the queue `FinanceInQ`. Once again a utility class, this time `BasicMessageReceiver`, is used. The `BasicMessageReceiver` class helps the Finance application by abstracting all the Java Messaging Service (JMS) steps that need to take place for receiving a text message. The message code needed within the `FinanceApplication.java` is thus elegantly simple.

```java
// FinanceApplication.java

package com.wrox.p2p;

import javax.jms.*;
import javax.naming.*;

public class FinanceApplication {
  public FinanceApplication() {}
  public static void main(String args[]) {
    try {
      BasicMessageReceiver receiver =
        new BasicMessageReceiver("FinanceQFactory", "FinanceInQ");
      String message = receiver.receiveMessage(1);
      System.out.println("The message is: \"" + message + "\"");
      receiver.cleanup();
    } catch (NamingException namingEx) {
      namingEx.printStackTrace();
    } catch (JMSException jmsEx) {
      jmsEx.printStackTrace();
    }
  }
}
```

The use of the `BasicMessageReceiver` class is similar to the use of the `BasicMessageSender` class. The finance application first needs to create a `BasicMessageReceiver` object supplying the names of the administered objects `QueueConnectionFactory` and `Queue` within the JNDI directory. Next the `BasicMessageReceiver` is asked to retrieve the first message available on the queue `FinanceInQ`. The parameter of the `receiveMessage()` method indicates the number of milliseconds one is prepared to wait before the method should return. A value lower than zero indicates a willingness to wait indefinitely for a message. This parameter value should be used with some caution. If no message is available and the required amount of time has passed, the method returns with a `null` value.

> **The Java Messaging Service (JMS) specification defines a method `receiveNoWait()` if a polling mechanism is needed. This method will return immediately returning the value `null` if no message was available.**

The object releases any resources it has claimed and performs any additional cleanup operations with the `cleanup()` method; then the exceptions are caught. The `BasicMessageReceiver` object should not be used after calling this method. Similar to the `BasicMessageSender` class any inadvertent use will lead to a `java.lang.NullPointerException`.

Next you will find the code for the `BasicMessageReceiver` class:

```java
// BasicMessageReceiver.java

package com.wrox.p2p;

import javax.naming.*;
import javax.jms.*;

public class BasicMessageReceiver {

  protected QueueConnection _connection;
  protected QueueSession _session;
  protected QueueReceiver _receiver;
  protected String _jndiQueueName;
  protected String _jndiQueueFactoryName;

  public BasicMessageReceiver(String jndiQueueFactoryName, String jndiQueueName)
        throws NamingException, JMSException {
    _jndiQueueName = jndiQueueName;
    _jndiQueueFactoryName = jndiQueueFactoryName;
    initialize();
  }

  protected void initialize() throws NamingException, JMSException {
    Context ctx = new InitialContext();
    QueueConnectionFactory queueConnectionFactory =
      (QueueConnectionFactory) ctx.lookup(_jndiQueueFactoryName);
    Queue outQueue = (Queue) ctx.lookup(_jndiQueueName);
    _connection = queueConnectionFactory.createQueueConnection();
    _session = _connection.createQueueSession(false,
                                        Session.AUTO_ACKNOWLEDGE);
    _receiver = _session.createReceiver(outQueue);
  }
```

The first interesting part is the `initialize()` method. This method retrieves the administered objects from the JNDI directory and creates a `QueueConnection` and `QueueSession` object just as the `initialize()` method does in the `BasicMessageSender` class. The difference between the Message Receiver and the `BasicMessageSender` class in this method is found in the last line of code. This line creates the `QueueReceiver` object and stores the reference in a member field.

```
    public String receiveMessage(long millisecondTimeout)
            throws JMSException {
      String result = null;
      if (_receiver != null) {
        _connection.start();
        if (millisecondTimeout < 0) {
          millisecondTimeout = 0;
        }
        Message message = (Message) _receiver.receive(millisecondTimeout);
        if (message != null && message instanceof TextMessage) {
          result = ((TextMessage) message).getText();
        }
      }
      return result;
    }
```

The `receiveMessage()` method checks if there is a `QueueReceiver` object and starts the connection. Next, it checks the requested timeout and sets it to a minimum value if needed. The method continues by waiting for a message for the requested amount of time. The resulting message, if any, is checked for its type and the text in the message body is extracted and returned.

```
    public void finalize() {
      try {
        cleanup();
      } catch (JMSException jmsEx) {

        // ignore this error
      }

    }

    public void cleanup() throws JMSException {
      if (_connection != null) {
        _connection.close();
        _connection = null;
      }
    }
  }
```

The way the `BasicMessageReceiver` class is constructed has the advantage that it can be used to illustrate the minimal steps needed to receive a text message. Using this class in your programs will mean you can receive text messages from other applications with very little effort.

The supplied utility classes intentionally focus on sending and receiving messages with text in the message body. The exchange of text messages will become the most important form of enterprise messaging, with the increasing popularity of XML. The utility classes in this example (`BasicMessageSender` and `BasicMessageReceiver`) could be used within a total XML enterprise messaging environment. The applications can freely create their own XML documents for transmission or process an incoming XML document in a way that is appropriate.

Setting Up the Environment

To run the code in this example we must set up the environment variables and start the J2EE server that will pass the messages between the applications. If you do not have Java 2 Platform, Enterprise Edition visit: http://java.sun.com/j2ee/ where you will be able to download the latest release.

To set up the environment execute the following commands in sequence:

1. Open a command line window and set up the environment variables with the commands:

C:\Beg_Java_Networking\Ch20>**SET J2EE_HOME=C:\j2sdkee1.3**

Replace `C:\j2sdkee1.3` *with the location where J2EE is installed.*

C:\Beg_Java_Networking\Ch20>**SET PATH=%J2EE_HOME%\bin;%PATH%**

2. Start the J2EE server by giving the command:

C:\Beg_Java_Networking\Ch20>**j2ee**

If the startup is successful you should see something similar to the following output, in the command window:

J2EE server listen port: 1050
Redirecting the output and error streams to the following files:
C:\j2sdkee1.3\logs\benhi1\j2ee\j2ee\system.out
C:\j2sdkee1.3\logs\benhi1\j2ee\j2ee\system.err
J2EE server startup complete.

3. Open a new command line window and again set up the environment with the following commands:

 C:\Beg_Java_Networking\Ch20>**SET J2EE_HOME=C:\j2sdkee1.3**

Replace C:\j2sdkee1.3 with the location where J2EE is installed.

C:\Beg_Java_Networking\Ch20>**SET PATH=%J2EE_HOME%\bin;%PATH%**

4. Add an administered object, QueueConnectionFactory, for the SalesApplication, giving it the name SalesQFactory, with the command:

C:\Beg_Java_Networking\Ch20>**j2eeadmin -addJmsFactory SalesQFactory queue**

5. Add an administered object, QueueConnectionFactory, for the FinanceApplication, called FinanceQFactory, with the command:

C:\Beg_Java_Networking\Ch20>**j2eeadmin -addJmsFactory FinanceQFactory queue**

6. Add an administered object, a Queue, to communicate with the FinanceApplication object:

C:\Beg_Java_Networking\Ch20>**j2eeadmin -addJmsDestination FinanceInQ queue**

7. Add an administered object, a `Queue`, to communicate with the `SalesApplication` object:

C:\Beg_Java_Networking\Ch20>**j2eeadmin -addJmsDestination SalesInQ queue**

8. You can verify the correct execution of the setup commands by following the following steps (check if the bolded lines appear in your list):

C:\Beg_Java_Networking\Ch20>**j2eeadmin -listJmsDestination**

This should produce something like the following output – the important lines have been bolded:

```
JmsDestination
--------------
< JMS Destination : jms/Topic , javax.jms.Topic >
< JMS Destination : FinanceInQ , javax.jms.Queue >
< JMS Destination : SalesInQ , javax.jms.Queue >
< JMS Destination : jms/Queue , javax.jms.Queue >
```

C:\Beg_Java_Networking\Ch20>**j2eeadmin -listJmsFactory**

This should produce the following output – again the important lines have been bolded:

```
JmsFactory
----------
< JMS Cnx Factory : FinanceQFactory , Queue , No properties >
< JMS Cnx Factory : SalesQFactory , Queue , No properties >
< JMS Cnx Factory : jms/QueueConnectionFactory , Queue , No properties >
< JMS Cnx Factory : QueueConnectionFactory , Queue , No properties >
< JMS Cnx Factory : TopicConnectionFactory , Topic , No properties >
< JMS Cnx Factory : jms/TopicConnectionFactory , Topic , No properties >
```

Now that we have established a common environment, we can run our point-to-point messaging domain example.

Running the Application

❑ Make sure all the files listed below are stored in the C:\Beg_Java_Networking\com\wrox\p2p directory:

```
BasicMessageSender.java
BasicMessageReceiver.java
FinanceApplication.java
SalesApplication.java
```

❑ In the same command window used to test the j2ee server (or another one with the same environment variables setup) enter the following commands to compile the code:

C:\Beg_Java_Networking\Ch20>**SET CLASSPATH=.;%JAVA_HOME%\jre\lib\rt.jar;%J2EE_HOME%\lib\j2ee.jar;%J2EE_HOME%\lib\locale**

C:\Beg_Java_Networking\Ch20>**javac com\wrox\p2p*.java**

❑ First, we send a message using the sales application:

C:\Beg_Java_Networking\Ch20>**java -Djms.properties=%J2EE_HOME%\config\jms_client.properties com.wrox.p2p.SalesApplication**

If this is successful the following message will be displayed:

Java(TM) Message Service 1.0.2 Reference Implementation (build b13)

❑ Next, we run the finance application which will extract the message from the message queue:

C:\Beg_Java_Networking\Ch20>**java -Djms.properties=%J2EE_HOME%\config\jms_client.properties com.wrox.p2p.FinanceApplication**

The following output should be displayed if the message has been received:

Java(TM) Message Service 1.0.2 Reference Implementation (build b13)
The message is: "The order XML document"

From this output we can see that the finance application has received the message from the sales application via the message queue.

How Could This Example Be Extended?

Now we have looked at the code and run the example, let's take some time to consider what else could be done to extend this application. The intention of the previous example was to demonstrate sending messages in the simplest possible way. However, in a real world implementation some other issues might need to be considered.

The thing to remember when using the BasicMessageReceiver class is the way it receives messages. As mentioned before the utility class can be used to receive text messages. Messages sent in one of the other available formats (like MapMessage or StreamMessage) will also be removed from the queue by the receiveMessage() method of the BasicMessageReceiver object (referenced by the member field _receiver). These messages don't pass the type check within the receiveMessage() method and will subsequently be lost with the method returning a null value. To deal with this problem one could remove the type check and deal directly with a java.lang.ClassCastException. This exception, when caught, will still not allow you to undo the message removal though.

Creating a message selector that uses the message property JMSType is not an option either as the property needs to be set explicitly by the sending party. The value of the message property JMSType is not automatically set by the messaging software. The Java Messaging Service (JMS) specification does not define a set of standard values for this property either. Applications can use this standard property to transmit an indication of the type of message body used. Possible values for this property can be text, stream, order, payment history, type=13452, some XML document. Messaging applications will use this field to help identify the type of message received.

A way to resolve the message-loss problem is by changing the initialize() method. If you create the QueueSession to be transactional, you can prevent the removal of the message from the Queue when the message is not of the correct type.

The modifications that would be needed in the source code are highlighted in the shortened listing given next:

```
public class BasicMessageReceiver
{
    ...
  protected void initialize() throws NamingException, JMSException {
    Context ctx = new InitialContext();
    QueueConnectionFactory queueConnectionFactory =
      (QueueConnectionFactory) ctx.lookup(_jndiQueueFactoryName);
    Queue outQueue = (Queue) ctx.lookup(_jndiQueueName);
    _connection = queueConnectionFactory.createQueueConnection();
    _session = _connection.createQueueSession(true,
                                      Session.AUTO_ACKNOWLEDGE);
    _receiver = _session.createReceiver(outQueue);
  }

  public String receiveMessage(long millisecondTimeout)
        throws JMSException {      {
    ...
    Message message = (Message) _receiver.receive(millisecondTimeout);
    if (message != null && message instanceof TextMessage) {
      result = ((TextMessage) message).getText();
      _session.commit();
    } else {
      _session.rollback();
    }
  }
  return result;
  }
    ...
}
```

So essentially, what we are doing here is removing queued messages within a transaction, the transaction commits (thus removing the message) if the message is of the correct type, otherwise the transaction rolls back and the message stays on the queue.

When sending a message to an application, the sending application might want to receive a message indicating the result of message processing by the receiving application. This return (or "reply") message needs to be correlated to a specific message transmission within the sending application. For example, the sales application would like to receive a message informing it if the customer pays his bills on time. A customer with a good payment record could then be marked for discount or better yet late payers could be marked for additional charges.

The supplied utility classes, presented in this paragraph, are only convenient for sending and receiving text messages that have little or no correlation with each other. There is no way to specify that an application will want to receive a specific reply message with the help of a BasicMessageReceiver. The Java Messaging Service (JMS) API contains its own utility class (QueueRequestor) to achieve this. The QueueRequestor class has a method request(), which takes as its only parameter a Message object. The return value is the reply message. The JMS utility class uses temporary queues as reply destinations. The class only expects one reply message to be sent.

There are several types of queues within the JMS specification. The queues used in the example are permanent queues. Permanent queues exist beyond the lifetime of a JMS client. In the example, the queues were created with the help of the `j2eeadmin` tool that stored the queues within the JNDI directory. JMS clients can use these queues for as long as they reside within the JNDI directory. The JMS specification prefers that queues are obtained from a JNDI directory and that they are created by administrators. The specification does allow the direct creation of queues by JMS clients. Creating permanent queues with the `QueueSession.createQueue()` method is provided for situations where clients need to dynamically create permanent queues. The parameter passed, however, is not standardized, so it is clearly provider-specific. JMS software that relies on the use of this method is not portable between providers.

The JMS API also allows the creation of temporary queues – these exist only for as long as the `QueueConnection` object is open. They are mainly used in synchronous point-to-point message exchanges. Clients that use temporary queues are still portable.

Publish and Subscribe Messaging Example

You have learned about the point-to-point messaging domain, the publish/subscribe domain is next. We will have to create a set of utility classes to help with messaging within this domain. The sales application uses a `BasicTopicPublisher` class to publish a message to a certain topic. The creation of a `BasicTopicPublisher` object can only be done if one supplies the JNDI names for the `TopicConnectionFactory` and the `Topic` administered objects. A call to the method `publishMessage()` will result in the publication of the text message to the topic.

```java
// SalesApplication.java

package com.wrox.pubsub;

import javax.naming.*;
import javax.jms.*;

public class SalesApplication {
  public SalesApplication() {}
  public static void main(String[] args) {
    try {
      BasicTopicPublisher publisher =
        new BasicTopicPublisher("SalesTFactory", "OrderT");
      publisher.publishMessage("The order XML document");
      publisher.cleanup();
```

The first thing you might notice is the absence of a second topic. This value `OrderT` is used to retrieve the topic from the JNDI directory. In the point-to-point messaging domain there was a need to create two JMS destinations, in the form of queue objects. Each of the applications used one of the queues. Point-to-point messaging is best characterized as address-focused messaging. Messaging within the publish/subscribe messaging domain is best characterized as content-focused messaging. The subject of a message is viewed as more important compared to the addressee. Java Messaging Service allows multiple subscribers to receive the same message published to a topic. Multiple publishers are allowed to send (publish) their messages to the same topic. The method `cleanup()` is used to clean up any resources used by the utility class.

```java
    } catch (NamingException namingEx) {
      namingEx.printStackTrace();
    } catch (JMSException jmsEx) {
```

```
            jmsEx.printStackTrace();
        }
    }
}
```

Finally any exceptions are caught and simply printed out to the command line.

Now let's examine the code of the utility class `BasicTopicPublisher`. This class performs the actual functionality of publishing the message.

```java
// BasicTopicPublisher.java

package com.wrox.pubsub;

import javax.naming.*;
import javax.jms.*;

public class BasicTopicPublisher {
    protected TopicConnection _connection = null;
    protected TopicSession _session = null;
    protected TopicPublisher _publisher = null;
    protected String _jndiTopicName = null;
    protected String _jndiTopicFactoryName = null;
    public BasicTopicPublisher(String jndiTopicFactoryName,
                               String jndiTopicName) throws NamingException,
                               JMSException {
        super();
        _jndiTopicName = jndiTopicName;
        _jndiTopicFactoryName = jndiTopicFactoryName;
        initialize();
    }
    protected void initialize() throws NamingException, JMSException {
        Context ctx = new InitialContext();
        TopicConnectionFactory topicConnectionFactory =
            (TopicConnectionFactory) ctx.lookup(_jndiTopicFactoryName);
        Topic topic = (Topic) ctx.lookup(_jndiTopicName);
        _connection = topicConnectionFactory.createTopicConnection();
        _session = _connection.createTopicSession(false,
                                            Session.AUTO_ACKNOWLEDGE);
        _publisher = _session.createPublisher(topic);
    }
```

In a similar way to previous utility classes presented in this chapter, all initialization work is done in the appropriately named `initialize()` method. The initialisation of a `MessagePublisher` resembles a `BasicMessageSender`. First the `InitialContext` is obtained so the JNDI directory can be accessed. Next the value stored under the name `_jndiTopicFactoryName` is retrieved from the directory; the resulting value is interpreted as a `TopicConnectionFactory`. After obtaining the `TopicConnectionFactory`, the JMS destination or the topic is retrieved from the directory by querying it with the value `_jndiTopicName`. Following these steps is the first Java Messaging Service (JMS) API call, which creates the `TopicConnection`. The next API call (`createTopicSession()`) opens a non-transactional session, that will automatically do any acknowledgements required. The final line of code in the method `initialize()` creates the `TopicPublisher`.

```
    public void publishMessage(String theMessageBody) throws JMSException {
      if (_publisher != null) {
        _connection.start();
        Message message = _session.createTextMessage(theMessageBody);
        _publisher.publish(message);
      }
    }
```

The `BasicMessageSender` class has a `sendMessage()` method to transmit messages. The equivalent of this method in the `BasicTopicPublisher` class is named `publishMessage()`. This method has the same parameter, which serves as the body of the text message published to the topic. The method starts with a check if a publisher is available. Next it starts the connection and creates a `TextMessage` object by calling the `createTextMessage()` method of the `TopicSession` member field (`_session`). The method concludes by publishing the message to the topic.

```
    public void finalize() {
      try {
        cleanup();
      } catch (JMSException jmsEx) {
        // ignore this error
      }

    }
    public void cleanup() throws JMSException {
      if (_connection != null) {
        _connection.close();
      }
    }
  }
```

A `finalize()` method is implemented to ensure that when garbage is collected a cleanup is tried again. A call to the `cleanup()` method results in the release of any Java Messaging Service (JMS) resources, by closing the `TopicConnection` stored in the member field `_connection`.

Receiving messages in the publish and subscribe messaging domain is more difficult than in the point-to-point messaging domain. The main difficulty lies in the event-driven nature of publish and subscribe model. When an application wants to receive messages published to a topic, it creates a `TopicSubscriber` object. With this object it needs to register a `MessageListener`. This `MessageListener` has a method called `onMessage()`. This method is called by the JMS provider when a message is published to the topic. An application is not able to actively wait for a message to be delivered as with the `receive()` method of a `BasicMessageReceiver`.

Here we use a very simple `MessageListener` implementation called `BasicTextMessageListener`. This class implements the single method in the `javax.jms.MessageListener` interface (`onMessage()`). The implementation first checks the type of message passed, then it simply extracts the message body and prints this to the console.

```
// BasicTextMessageListener.java

package com.wrox.pubsub;

import javax.jms.*;
```

```java
public class BasicTextMessageListener implements MessageListener {

  public BasicTextMessageListener() {}

  public void onMessage(Message message) {
    if (message != null && message instanceof TextMessage) {
      try {
        System.out.println(((TextMessage) message).getText());
      } catch (JMSException jmsEx) {
        jmsEx.printStackTrace();
      }
    }
  }
}
```

> In the section on point-to-point messaging we highlighted the possibility of messages being lost, when the application retrieves a message from the queue that was not in its desired format. To solve this problem the **BasicMessageReceiver** class was expanded with some transaction logic. Using the publish and subscribe messaging domain will never result in message loss. There is no need to add special transaction logic to keep messages from being lost when they are of the wrong type. A message published to a topic results in delivery of this message to each of the **TopicSubscribers.**

The code dealing with setting up a TopicSubscriber is compacted in another utility class called BasicTopicSubscriber:

```java
// BasicTopicSubscriber.java

package com.wrox.pubsub;

import javax.naming.*;
import javax.jms.*;

public class BasicTopicSubscriber {
  protected TopicConnection _connection = null;
  protected TopicSession _session = null;
  protected TopicSubscriber _subscriber = null;
  protected String _jndiTopicName = null;
  protected String _jndiTopicFactoryName = null;
  public BasicTopicSubscriber(String jndiTopicFactoryName,
                              String jndiTopicName) throws NamingException,
                              JMSException {
    super();
    _jndiTopicName = jndiTopicName;
    _jndiTopicFactoryName = jndiTopicFactoryName;
    initialize();
  }
  protected void initialize() throws NamingException, JMSException {
    Context ctx = new InitialContext();
    TopicConnectionFactory topicConnectionFactory =
      (TopicConnectionFactory) ctx.lookup(_jndiTopicFactoryName);
    Topic topic = (Topic) ctx.lookup(_jndiTopicName);
```

```
    _connection = topicConnectionFactory.createTopicConnection();
    _session = _connection.createTopicSession(false,
                                      Session.AUTO_ACKNOWLEDGE);
    _subscriber = _session.createSubscriber(topic);
}
```

The `initialize()` method of the `BasicTopicSubscriber` class obtains the required
`TopicConnectionFactory` and `Topic` administered objects from the JNDI directory. Next it creates
the `TopicConnection`, `TopicSession` and `TopicSubscriber` objects.

```
public void subscribe(MessageListener messageListener)
        throws JMSException {
    _connection.stop();
    _subscriber.setMessageListener(messageListener);
    _connection.start();
}
```

A user of the `BasicTopicSubscriber` class will need to invoke the `subscribe()` method to
register a `MessageListener`. The class first stops the `TopicConnection` referenced by
`_connection`. Next it registers the `MessageListener` implementation passed as a parameter. The
`subscribe()` method concludes by starting the `TopicConnection` again.

The starting and stopping of the connection is necessary because of the event-driven nature of the
publish and subscribe messaging domain. No messages will be delivered to any
`MessageListener` registered with help of this connection, when the connection is stopped.
Dealing with changes to the `MessageListener` on a running connection is undefined by the Java
Messaging Service (JMS) specification.

```
public void finalize() {
    try {
        cleanup();
    } catch (JMSException jmsEx) {
        // ignore this error
    }
}
public void cleanup() throws JMSException {
    if (_connection != null) {
        _connection.close();
    }
}
}
```

We now come to the final component of the publish/subscribe messaging domain example – the finance
application. A few things to take note of when looking at the code is the need to create a
`BasicTextMessageListener` object and this is subscribed to the topic with an object of type
`BasicTopicSubscriber`.

```
// FinanceApplication.java

package com.wrox.pubsub;

import javax.naming.*;
import javax.jms.*;
```

```
import java.io.*;

public class FinanceApplication {

  public FinanceApplication() {}
  public static void main(String[] args) {

    try {
      BasicTextMessageListener messageListener =
        new BasicTextMessageListener();

      BasicTopicSubscriber subscriber =
        new BasicTopicSubscriber("FinanceTFactory", "OrderT");

      subscriber.subscribe(messageListener);

      while (true) {
        char s = (char) System.in.read();
        if (s == 'q') {
          subscriber.cleanup();
          System.exit(0);
        }
      }
    } catch (NamingException namingEx) {
      namingEx.printStackTrace();
    } catch (JMSException jmsEx) {
      jmsEx.printStackTrace();
    } catch (IOException ioEx) {
      ioEx.printStackTrace();
    }
  }
}
```

The main() method of the finance application is somewhat different than the previous main() methods shown. The finance application needs to listen to message events sent by the JMS provider. To prevent the finance application from stopping prematurely a small loop is built into the main method. The loop continuously reads characters from the console and exits the application when a 'q' character is typed. The loop ensures the small finance application will only stop after the user indicates it can. In an enterprise messaging application such a loop will no doubt not be needed. The loop is added to the finance application to allow the testing of code.

Setting Up the Environment

If it is not already running, start the J2EE server in the same way described for the last example. Open up a new command line window and set up the environment variables as before; then:

❑ Add an administered object, TopicConnectionFactory, for the sales application with the command:

C:\Beg_Java_Networking\Ch20>**j2eeadmin -addJmsFactory SalesTFactory topic**

❑ Add an administered object, TopicConnectionFactory, for the finance application with the command:

717

```
C:\Beg_Java_Networking\Ch20>j2eeadmin -addJmsFactory FinanceTFactory topic
```

❑ Add an administered object, a `Topic`, so applications that have interesting messages about the topic can publish them. Applications interested in messages related to the topic can subscribe to it to be kept informed.

```
C:\Beg_Java_Networking\Ch20>j2eeadmin -addJmsDestination OrderT topic
```

Before moving on to examine the Java code, you can verify the correct execution of the setup commands by following the following steps (check if the bolded lines appear in your list):

❑ After the setup instructions run this command:

```
C:\Beg_Java_Networking\Ch20>j2eeadmin -listJmsDestination
```

This should yield something similar to the output below; the important line have been bolded:

```
JmsDestination
--------------
< JMS Destination : jms/Topic , javax.jms.Topic >
< JMS Destination : OrderT , javax.jms.Topic >
< JMS Destination : jms/Queue , javax.jms.Queue >
```

❑ After the setup instructions run this command:

```
C:\Beg_Java_Networking\Ch20>j2eeadmin -listJmsFactory
```

This should yield something similar the output below, the important line have been bolded:

```
JmsFactory
----------
< JMS Cnx Factory : FinanceTFactory , Topic , No properties >
< JMS Cnx Factory : SalesTFactory , Topic , No properties >
< JMS Cnx Factory : jms/QueueConnectionFactory , Queue , No properties >
< JMS Cnx Factory : QueueConnectionFactory , Queue , No properties >
< JMS Cnx Factory : TopicConnectionFactory , Topic , No properties >
< JMS Cnx Factory : jms/TopicConnectionFactory , Topic , No properties >
```

Now that we have established a common environment, lets run the code.

Running the Application

❑ Make sure all the files listed below are stored in the
`C:\Beg_Java_Networking\Ch20\com\wrox\pubsub` directory:

```
BasicTextMessageListener.java
BasicTopicPublisher.java
BasicTopicSubscriber.java
FinanceApplication.java
SalesApplication.java
```

❑ In the same window used to set up the environment enter the following commands to compile the classes:

C:\Beg_Java_Networking\Ch20>**SET CLASSPATH=%J2EE_HOME%\lib\j2ee.jar;%J2EE_HOME%\lib\locale;.**

C:\Beg_Java_Networking\Ch20>**javac com\wrox\pubsub*.java**

❑ First we subscribe to the message service with the finance application:

C:\Beg_Java_Networking\Ch20>**java -Djms.properties=%J2EE_HOME%\config\jms_client.properties com.wrox.pubsub.FinanceApplication**

If this is successful the following message will be displayed:

Java(TM) Message Service 1.0.2 Reference Implementation (build b13)

❑ Next we publish a message with the sales application, this must run in a new command line window. Don't forget to set up the environment variables:

C:\Beg_Java_Networking\Ch20>**java -Djms.properties=%J2EE_HOME%\config\jms_client.properties com.wrox.pubsub.SalesApplication**

❑ Now the sales application has published a message, we check the window to the subscribing application (the finance application) to see if has been received. If everything has gone to plan, we should see the following message:

The order XML document

From this output we can see that the finance application received the message.

❑ To quit the finance application type the character 'q' and press return.

Summary

This chapter covered working with message queues and many aspects surrounding enterprise messaging. The chapter started with a look at alternatives to enterprise messaging, detailing their strengths and weaknesses. Message oriented middleware was presented as the ideal solution for enterprise messaging and the strengths and weaknesses of this solution were given.

Next came a high-level introduction to message oriented middleware. The introduction covered the key components found in message oriented middleware:

❑ Clients

❑ Message agents

❑ Destinations

❑ Messages

Some high-level application architecture variants were then discussed. The discussion presented an architectural solution that resembles the hub and spoke structure of a wheel.

The rest of the chapter focused on the Java Messaging Service (JMS) covering the different ways to accomplish enterprise messaging with JMS. Each method is called a messaging domain. The messaging domains in Java Messaging Service (JMS) are **"point to point"** and **"publish and subscribe"**.

The chapter described the anatomy of JMS messages, before exposing you to some useful, practical examples. The chapter gave examples for both messaging domains of JMS. The examples made use of the utility classes `BasicMessageSender`, `BasicMessageReceiver`, `BasicTopicPublisher`, `BasicTopicSubscriber`, and `BasicTextMessageListener` for sending and receiving messages. These utility classes are constructed in such a way that reuse in other (your) applications would require few changes.

Networking in JDK 1.4

Java is still a growing language, adapting to the needs of an expanding programming horizon. With this in mind, we shall examine Sun's release of JDK 1.4 and its implications for networking performance and other related issues. Though still in Beta at the time of writing (with the anticipated official release scheduled for late 2001), the J2SE 1.4 API includes many new features that enhance and extend the Java networking model.

In this chapter we will:

- ❑ Introduce the new buffer and channel classes
- ❑ Explore selectable channels, selectors and selection keys
- ❑ Build a scalable server application using the new non-blocking I/O facilities
- ❑ Examine some of the expanded features in the java.net package
- ❑ Finish with an overview of various minor and underlying enhancements

New I/O API

Designed to co-exist with the already familiar Java I/O packages discussed in Chapter 5, Sun has introduced a completely new I/O API (cleverly referred to as **NIO**) with the release of Java 1.4. Considering that Java had originally been intended for use in embedded systems, I/O was not a major focus in its design. This, along with the added layer of abstraction introduced by the use of a virtual machine, had made I/O one of Java's weaker facets. The NIO packages have been designed to address these issues by providing developers with fast, scalable I/O operations on streams and binary data.

As detailed in the public review draft JSR 51 (http://www.jcp.org/jsr/detail/51.jsp), the NIO API will enable the creation of "production quality web and application servers". To achieve this level of functionality and performance, the NIO classes rely heavily on the underlying operating system and hardware to optimize data handling. Additionally, unlike the old java.io implementations, many of the new class methods are not synchronized (leaving this to the developer to implement as needed) in order to maximize efficiency.

The NIO packages include buffer classes, channels, and selectors as well as character encoding/decoding functionality. Though located in the `java.util` package, new support for regular expressions adds powerful character sequence pattern matching that works hand in hand with the NIO capabilities.

Enhancements have also been made to the existing I/O classes in order to take advantage of the new packages. Here is a summary of what the new packages offer:

❑   `java.nio`: Defines a variety of buffer classes that provide the underlying data handling for the NIO packages

❑   `java.nio.channels`: Includes channels for I/O connectivity and selectors for implementing multiplexing

❑   `java.nio.channels.spi`: Support classes for the `channels` package

❑   `java.nio.charset`: Classes for encoding and decoding character sequences

❑   `java.nio.charset.spi`: Support classes for the `charset` package

❑   `java.util.regex`: Pattern matching for character sequences

❑   `java.lang.CharSequence`: By implementing this interface, `Strings`, `StringBuffers` and `CharBuffers` can be used for pattern matching

Though Sun states that they do not intend to deprecate the original Java I/O package (at least not in the near future), they do hope that developers will adopt and eventually migrate to the new packages. To fully understand the implications of the NIO packages, we'll look at some of its core functionality before delving into the relayed networking issues.

New Foundation Classes: Buffer and Channels

Within the NIO packages, two core classes – `Buffer` and `Channels` – form the foundations. The `Buffer` class provides a completely new underlying mechanism for handling large data sets, and the `Channels` class represents a new abstraction for I/O connectivity. In the next few sections we'll look at the fundamentals of buffers and channels. Once we have an understanding of these classes, we'll explore some of their extended capabilities.

Buffers

One of the central building blocks of the NIO packages is the **Buffer** (`java.nio.Buffer`). The abstract `Buffer` class provides the basic underlying support for all other types of buffer classes.

In its most basic form, a buffer is simply a container for raw byte data. The basic difference between a buffer and more familiar data storage classes such as arrays or lists, is that a buffer can be used to represent data that resides elsewhere. As we shall see later on, a buffer can be used to *map* a file's data into memory or to contain application data so that it can be manipulated as if it were a file. Structurally, a buffer is a (seemingly) continuous allotment of memory, which can be accessed sequentially using a number of properties.

The byte data within a buffer can be manipulated 'as is' or be represented as a primitive data type (such as int, `float`, and so on). Because a number of primitive types can be represented in the data, we say that a buffer contains elements since primitive types can be of differing byte lengths. In this way, when iterating through a buffer and accessing its elements, the properties will be adjusted by the appropriate number of bytes and we needn't be concerned about the data's type and length.

Finally, a key point to keep in mind (as it will highlight the significance of the buffer classes later on) is that a buffer's data is stored in memory and, though it can be used to represent file data, is not stored on disk. To put it another way, a buffer is a virtual representation of file data (or application data that you wish to manipulate as if it were a file) and it is this feature that provides the basis for improving Java's I/O performance.

The Byte Buffer

The **byte buffer** (`java.nio.ByteBuffer`) is a concrete implementation of the core abstract `Buffer` class and serves as the launching point for almost all operations that use buffers. For this reason, we'll take some time to get familiar with a byte buffer's basic functionality. Note that, because the `ByteBuffer` subclasses `Buffer`, its properties and navigation methods are all situated within the parent `Buffer` class (as described above). For this reason, we'll introduce the specifics of navigating and manipulating a buffer as we explore the practical uses of the `ByteBuffer`.

Though we might be tempted to think of a byte buffer as just another storage medium, along the same lines as an array or a set, it should really be viewed as a more primitive storage space. The reason for this will become clear as we begin to examine the byte buffer, which as it turns out, is quite straightforward.

The `ByteBuffer` class allows you to:

❑ Create new buffers

❑ Add data to a buffer

❑ Retrieve data from a buffer

❑ Navigate the data within a buffer

So what's all the fuss about? Well, the great thing about `ByteBuffer` is not what it can do, but rather what you can do with it.

> **The essence of a byte buffer is that it can be used as a target or source of I/O operations. Since a buffer can be used to virtually represent the contents of a file, an application can have I/O type functionality without the overhead of actual disk access.**

This is achieved by **mapping** a byte buffer to data in a resource (a file) such that you can manipulate data contained within the resource without the overhead of repeated I/O accesses to the resource directly. However, this behavior goes hand in hand with the channel classes so we'll continue this discussion in the sections on channels, later on. For now, let's look at instantiating and navigating a byte buffer.

Creating a Byte Buffer

There are several ways to create a new byte buffer. The most common is to use the static `allocate()` method as in the following example.

```
ByteBuffer buffer = ByteBuffer.allocate(1024);
```

This creates a new byte buffer instance that can store up to 1024 bytes of information. The buffer returned by the `allocate()` method is **non-direct**, which is to say that it does not employ any of the underlying optimizations of a **direct** buffer. With a direct buffer, the JVM will attempt to use native I/O operations, the result of which is a reduction of intermediary copying, resulting in a dramatic increase in efficiency. To create a more highly optimized direct buffer we would use the static `allocateDirect()` method as shown below:

```
ByteBuffer directBuffer = ByteBuffer.allocateDirect(1024);
```

There is a greater overhead when creating direct buffers, however, and so their use should be limited to situations where the buffer will remain in use for an extended period.

Finally, a byte buffer can be created by 'wrapping' an array of bytes. In this instance, the byte buffer and the byte array remain coupled so that modifications to one will be reflected in the other. Here's a look at the static `wrap()` method.

```
byte[] bytes = new byte[1024];
ByteBuffer buffer = ByteBuffer.wrap(bytes);
```

Once we have created a byte buffer there are a variety of `put()` and `get()` methods for adding and accessing single elements, as well as bulk `put()` and `get()` methods for inserting larger chunks of data. We will take a closer look at these methods in the next section, since they rely on an understanding of navigating through the data within the buffer.

There is also a `slice()` method that can be used to create a new byte buffer. The new byte buffer will represent a subsequence (beginning at the current position) of the 'sliced' buffer. As with the `wrap()` method, the sliced buffer's content is coupled to the original section of data from which it was created.

Navigating Buffers

There are several properties used to navigate and manipulate a buffer. Specifically, a buffer has a capacity, limit, position and mark. The diagram below shows a buffer and an example of its properties in action, so refer to it as we examine each property in detail.

The **capacity** is generally unchanging, and is defined when the buffer is created. It simply refers to the number of bytes allotted to the buffer when it was instantiated. For example, the following byte buffer will have a capacity of 1024 bytes:

```
ByteBuffer buffer = ByteBuffer.allocate(1024);
```

The **limit** is a variable parameter that indicates the point separating data that is to be read/written and data that should not be read/written. By default, the limit is equal to the capacity, however, it can be convenient to set this so that the limit equals the index of the last byte of data added to a buffer. In this way, any future reads will not venture into unused areas of the buffer.

The **position** represents the point at which the next read/write will commence and can be set anywhere from 0 to the limit of a buffer. This is the parameter that is usually of the most interest when manipulating buffers. A common mistake is to forget to ensure that the position is set before reading data, particularly in a case where you fill a buffer up with data from one source and then immediately read it out to another source.

Finally, you can set a **mark** to indicate a point to which the position is to return to, upon calling a buffer's reset() method (note that a mark cannot be set higher than the current position, therefore, reset() can only move the position back). For instance, a mark can be handy for iterating over a portion of a buffer.

These four properties of a buffer can be thought of as a hierarchy, as shown below:

0 <= mark <= position <= limit <= capacity

The following few lines of code create and manipulate a byte buffer. The buffer's properties after this code is executed, are reflected in the diagram below.

```
ByteBuffer buffer = ByteBuffer.allocate(8);
buffer.put((byte) 145);
buffer.put((byte) 146);
buffer.mark();
buffer.put((byte) 147);
buffer.put((byte) 148);
// Four bytes have been written to position = 4
buffer.limit(6);
```

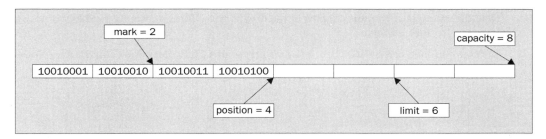

Before delving into more extensive examples using buffers, it would be well worth the time to examine the Java NIO API to get a sense of how various method calls modify the values of properties. The table below is a quick reference of how each property is affected after several common actions. For instance, calling clear() on a buffer resets its position to zero, its limit to the capacity and any mark is removed. As well, when adding data to a buffer, the position moves with each byte written and before the data can be read out of the buffer, the position must be moved backwards (by using the rewind() method, for example).

Buffer Action	Mark	Position	Limit	Capacity
Create using allocate(n)	None	Position = 0	Limit = n	Capacity = n
Create using wrap(byte[n])	None	Position = n	Limit = n	Capacity = n
reset()	No change	Position = mark	No change	No change
clear()	Removed	Position = 0	Limit = capacity	No change

Table continued on following page

Buffer Action	Mark	Position	Limit	Capacity
flip()	Removed	Position = 0 (after limit is set)	Limit = current position	Capacity = current position
rewind()	Removed	Position = 0	No change	No change

Setting Up and Running the Examples

Though you have been compiling and running examples throughout the preceding chapters, this chapter relies on the new classes in the J2SE 1.4 release. Therefore, running and compiling these examples will require that you download and install the 1.4 SDK located at Sun's web site (http://java.sun.com/j2se/1.4).

Here are the settings that we will assume when demonstrating the examples in this chapter.

❑ **Install** the J2SE 1.4 in the directory C:\jdk1.4>. This is the default installation, so if you are running the j2sdk-1_4_0-beta-win.exe download program this is where JDK will be installed automatically.

❑ Save the examples from this chapter in the directory C:\Beg_Java_Networking\Ch21 as you start to work on them

❑ Run the supplied batch file jdk1_4.bat to set your classpath, path and Java_Home without permanently changing your system settings:

```
rem jdk1_4.bat
set JAVA_HOME=C:\jdk1.4
set CLASSPATH=.;C:\jdk1.4\lib
set PATH=C:\jdk1.4\bin;
```

Working with Buffers

In this example, we're simply going to create a byte buffer and then put it through its paces. There's nothing too exciting about this program, but we will monitor the various parameters of this program (capacity, limit, and so on) to get a feel for how various actions affect them.

```java
// BufferTest.java

import java.nio.*;

public class BufferTest
{
    public static void showParameters(ByteBuffer buffer, String message){

        System.out.println();
        System.out.println("" + message);
        System.out.println("Capacity: " + buffer.capacity ());
        System.out.println("Limit: " + buffer.limit());
        System.out.println("Position: " + buffer.position());
        System.out.println("Remaining: " + buffer.remaining());
    }

    public static void main(String[] args)
```

```
        {
            ByteBuffer buffer = ByteBuffer.allocate(512);
            showParameters(buffer, "Buffer Allocated:");

            buffer.putFloat(1.1f);
            buffer.putFloat(2.2f);
            buffer.mark();
            buffer.putFloat(3.3f);
            showParameters(buffer, "Added three floats and " +
                                  "placed a mark at the 8th byte:");

            buffer.reset();
            showParameters(buffer, "Reset the buffer:");

            buffer.getFloat();
            showParameters(buffer, "Get a float (moving the " +
                                  "position ahead):");
            buffer.rewind();
            showParameters(buffer, "Rewind the buffer:");

            buffer.flip();
            showParameters(buffer, "Flip the buffer:");

            buffer.limit(8);
            showParameters(buffer, "Set the limit to 8 bytes and " +
                                  "try to add 9 bytes:");
            try
            {
                byte[] bytes = new byte[9];
                buffer.put(bytes);
            }
            catch(BufferOverflowException boe)
            {
                System.out.println("Buffer Overflow: " + boe);
            }
        }
    }
}
```

Running the program from the command prompt should produce the following output:

C:\Beg_Java_Networking\Ch21>**java BufferTest**

Buffer Allocated:
Capacity: 512
Limit: 512
Position: 0
Remaining: 512

Added three floats and placed a mark at the 8th byte:
Capacity: 512
Limit: 512
Position: 12
Remaining: 500

Reset the buffer:
Capacity: 512
Limit: 512
Position: 8

Remaining: 504

Get a float (moving the position ahead):
Capacity: 512
Limit: 512
Position: 12
Remaining: 500

Rewind the buffer:
Capacity: 512
Limit: 512
Position: 0
Remaining: 512

Flip the buffer:
Capacity: 0
Limit: 0
Position: 0
Remaining: 0

Set the limit to 8 bytes and try to add 9 bytes:
Capacity: 8
Limit: 8
Position: 0
Remaining: 8
Buffer Overflow: java.nio.BufferOverflowException

The first thing our program does is to create a new byte buffer using the `allocate()` method (if you recall, this means that our byte buffer is going to be a non-direct buffer).

```
// create buffer with capacity of 512 bytes
ByteBuffer buffer = ByteBuffer.allocate(512);
```

The output reveals its initial state immediately after instantiation. As expected, the capacity is equal to 512, the limit equals the capacity and the position is 0. The next action that the application takes is to add three `float` values (4 bytes each in length) to the buffer. So that we can reference it later, we also set a mark after adding the second float.

```
//add three 4 byte floats, put a mark after the second float.
buffer.putFloat(1.1f);
buffer.putFloat(2.2f);
buffer.mark();
buffer.putFloat(3.3f);
```

Notice how the position has changed to reflect the fact that we've just added 12 bytes of information. As well, the remaining number of bytes has been reduced accordingly. The next action calls the buffer's `reset()` method:

```
buffer.reset();
```

The `reset()` method simply sets the position equal to the mark that we set earlier (at the 8th byte). Now we call the buffer's `getFloat()` method. This method returns a float value (which we ignore) and moves the position forward by four bytes.

After calling the `rewind()` method in the next step, the position has been returned to zero and the mark we set earlier has been discarded (though we can't really see this from the output).

The `flip()` method, however, changes all the parameters. It basically 'crops' the buffer based on the buffer's position when the method was called and then sets the position to zero. The interesting (though rather impractical) thing about our example is that the buffer's position was at zero when we 'flipped' it. Therefore, until we set the limit to a positive integer, our buffer is useless! That's what our last step does.

Finally, to end with a bang, we purposely cause the buffer to throw a `BufferOverflowException` by setting the limit to 8 bytes and then trying to add 9 bytes of data using the `put()` method.

```
buffer.limit(8);
showParameters(buffer, "Set the limit to 8 bytes and " +
                       "try to add 9 bytes:");
try
{
    byte[] bytes = new byte[9];
    buffer.put(bytes);
}
catch(BufferOverflowException boe)
{
    System.out.println("Buffer Overflow: " + boe);
}
```

Though this example is rather straightforward, it's well worth trying it out to get a feel for how each of the method calls affects each property. As you begin to use buffers in more advanced ways, understanding how to navigate a buffer will help to avoid any number of irritating bugs.

Beyond the Byte Buffer

The buffer class itself is an abstract class from which the byte buffer and an assortment of primitive "wrapper" buffers are derived. These "wrapper" buffers are used to represent a **view** of the raw byte data that a byte buffer contains.

For instance, imagine you've read in a file containing thousands of floating point numbers and its data is now contained within a byte buffer (as raw byte data – we haven't parsed them to floats). At some point, you might want to have this data in its floating-point format in order to carry out some calculations. To facilitate this, you can simply ask the byte buffer to return a view of itself as a **float buffer** (`java.nio.FloatBuffer`).

As with the `slice()` and `wrap()` methods, a view is intrinsically tied to the original byte buffer, so that any changes to one will be reflected in the other. Each of the Java primitive types (such as `char`, `int`, `double`, and so on) can be represented as a view of a buffer.

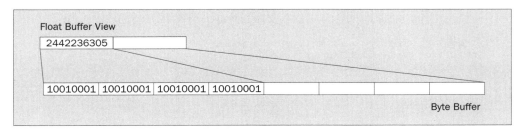

The buffer feature we are discussing begins to reveal the connection between the buffer classes and the channel classes we are about to look at. The byte buffer subclass, namely a **mapped byte buffer** (java.io.MappedByteBuffer) has the added benefit (as the name would imply) in that it can be *mapped* to a region of a file. This provides the functionality of disk-based I/O operations but with the efficiency that comes from performing these operations on data held in memory. The benefit of this approach is that you can have the simplicity of working with the file directly using gets and puts, and so on, but are saved the hassle and overhead of reading in the entire file and then saving it again. In short, you get the efficiency of manipulating the data in memory but the convenience of handling the data at its source. For instance, at any point you can call a mapped byte buffer's force() method to write any changes to the buffer's content back to the file that it is mapped to.

A View and Mapped Byte Buffer Example

In the following example, we will demonstrate the use of a mapped byte buffer, as well as the use of a buffer view, to manipulate the data. One thing to note is that though we have yet to explore the channel classes, our example requires that we get a sneak preview of a file channel. In this example we'll focus on the use of buffers – we'll look at the channel classes in the next section.

```java
// FloatSum.java

import java.io.*;
import java.nio.*;
import java.nio.channels.*;

public class FloatSum {
  private static void createFile(File file) throws IOException {

    // Get the channel from the input stream to the file.
    FileOutputStream fos = new FileOutputStream(file, false);
    FileChannel fileChannel = fos.getChannel();

    ByteBuffer buffer = ByteBuffer.allocate(512);
    buffer.putFloat(1.1f);
    buffer.putFloat(2.2f);
    buffer.putFloat(3.3f);

    /* Flip the buffer so that we only write the 12 bytes of
       data that we just added instead of 512. */
    buffer.flip();

    fileChannel.write(buffer);
    fileChannel.close();
  }

  private static void sum(File file) throws IOException {

    // Get the channel from the input stream to the file.
    FileInputStream fis = new FileInputStream(file);
    FileChannel fileChannel = fis.getChannel();

    // Map the contents of the file into memory.
    int size = (int) fileChannel.size();
    MappedByteBuffer mappedBuffer = fileChannel.map(FileChannel.MAP_RO, 0,
            size);

    // Get a view of the data as FloatBuffer
    FloatBuffer floatBuffer = mappedBuffer.asFloatBuffer();
    floatBuffer.rewind();
```

```
      // Perform the search
      float total = 0.0f;
      while (floatBuffer.hasRemaining()) {
        float next = floatBuffer.get();
        System.out.println("" + next);
        total += next;
      }

      // Close the channel and print the results.
      fileChannel.close();
      System.out.println("Total: " + total);
    }

  public static void main(String[] args) {
    if (args.length < 1) {
      System.err.println("Usage: text file of floats...");
      return;
    }

    File file = new File(args[0]);
    try {
      createFile(file);
      sum(file);
    } catch (IOException ioe) {
      System.err.println("Error: " + ioe);
    }
  }
}
```

Running the above code from the command prompt will produce this output:

C:\Beg_Java_Networking\Ch21>**java FloatSum floats.dat**
1.1
2.2
3.3
Total: 6.6000004

For convenience, the first thing that the program does is to call its createFile() method to create a file containing properly formatted float data. The application will need this later on (you saw how we also called it as a parameter on the command line). This method takes a file (named floats.dat in this instance) as its parameter and will use this file to store several floats.

After getting a reference to the file using a fileChannel() (we will go into more detail on this in the next section), the application creates a byte buffer with a capacity of 512 bytes. Then, three float variables are added to the buffer using the put() method.

```
    // Create a byte buffer and put three floats in it.
    ByteBuffer buffer = ByteBuffer.allocate(512);
    buffer.putFloat(1.1f);
    buffer.putFloat(2.2f);
    buffer.putFloat(3.3f);

    /* Flip the buffer so that we only write the 12 bytes of
       data that we've just added (instead of 512 bytes). */
    buffer.flip();
```

Before we write the buffer out to the file, notice that we call the buffer's flip() method. This avoids one of those 'gotchas' that can turn up later as an irritating bug in an application. Recall (from our preceding discussion on buffer navigation) that after putting data into a buffer, the position moves ahead with each call to put(). Now, if we do not return the buffer to the zero position before we write the buffer to the file, the write will commence from the current position (which, unless we call rewind() or similar, will be *ahead* of the data). Therefore, nothing will get written to the file. Here's an example:

1. The position equals 3 after three calls to put()

2. A call to write() will commence from the current position, therefore, only data after element 3 up to the buffer's limit will be written

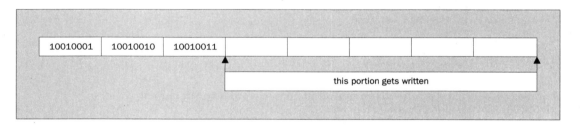

3. By calling the flip() method immediately after the calls to put(), the position gets set to 0 and the limit gets set to the previous position (which was 3). Now, a call to write() will write out the appropriate data.

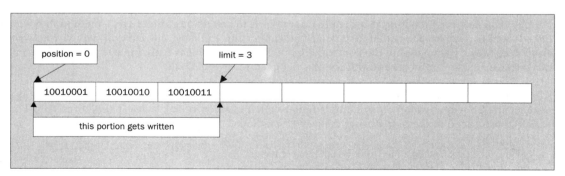

Another benefit of using flip() (as opposed to calling the buffer's rewind() method) is that we avoid writing the unused portion of the buffer to the file. This could have been achieved by manipulating a *view* of the byte buffer, as well. In this instance, we would have created an array of floats and then added these to a float buffer view using the put() method. Notice that we first create a new byte buffer with a capacity of 12 (or three floats * four bytes) and then get a view of this buffer as a float buffer. This technique is outlined opposite and can be used in place of the above code.

```
float[] floats = { 1.1f, 2.2f, 3.3f };
ByteBuffer buffer = ByteBuffer.allocate(floats.length * 4);
FloatBuffer floatBuffer = buffer.asFloatBuffer();
floatBuffer.put(floats);
```

Recalling the fact that a view and its originating byte buffer are coupled, the values put into the float buffer view are also reflected in the byte buffer.

The last step in creating the float.dat file is to call the file channel's write() method, and then close the channel.

The next function that the application carries out is to sum the floats within the floats.dat file by calling the sum() method. The sum() method takes the same floats.dat file as its parameter and gets a handle to it using a file channel just as the createFile() method did. Once the application has a file channel representing the floats.dat file, it creates a mapped byte buffer, which will contain the data from that file as raw bytes.

```
// Map the contents of the file into memory
int size = (int) fileChannel.size();
MappedByteBuffer mappedBuffer = fileChannel.map(FileChannel.MAP_RO, 0,
        size);
```

A mapped byte buffer cannot be instantiated directly, since it is directly associated with a file. Therefore, creating a mapped byte buffer is achieved by calling a channel's map() method.

The three parameters passed to the map() method in our example indicate that the mapping will be read-only (FileChannel.MAP_RO), start from the beginning of the file (0) and end at the end of the file (size). In other words, we're mapping the entire file instead of a sub section, so that we can read all of the data.

Now that we have the data mapped into our buffer, we can create a float view of the data so that we can manipulate the data as float primitives.

```
// Get a view of the data as FloatBuffer
FloatBuffer floatBuffer = mappedBuffer.asFloatBuffer();
floatBuffer.rewind();

// Perform the search
float total = 0.0f;
while(floatBuffer.hasRemaining())
{
    float next = floatBuffer.get();
    System.out.println("" + next);
    total += next;
}
```

This allows the application to simply iterate through the float buffer and add up the data values without the need to parse or cast the data as it is retrieved from the buffer. Notice that, by using a float buffer, we can simply call the get() method without concerning ourselves with the fact that a float is 4 bytes in length – all of the buffer's properties will adjust themselves appropriately. This is another benefit to using a view to process raw byte data as a primitive type.

As it has been hinted at in the preceding example, NIO buffers do, in fact, have a direct connection to the upcoming channel classes. Though buffers can be instantiated in isolation, one of the major benefits of using a buffer is to map it to file – this is the starting point for the following discussion on channels.

Channels

According to Sun, the `Channel` interface is the "nexus for I/O operations", and represents an open connection to another entity. Less formally, you can think of a channel as the Swiss army knife of connectivity, capable of communicating with hardware devices, files, sockets or simply another program module.

There are several concrete classes using this concept available, namely:

- ❑ `FileChannel`
- ❑ `SelectableChannel`
- ❑ `SocketChannel`
- ❑ `ServerSocketChannel`
- ❑ `DatagramChannel`

Before we explore the details of these classes, we should address the issue of how the NIO channels interact with the `java.io` classes that we are more used to dealing with.

In order to bring the two APIs together, the `java.io.FileInputSteam`, `FileOutputStream` and `RandomAccessFile` classes have a new method, called `getChannel()`. The `getChannel()` method returns a `FileChannel` instance associated with the already existing stream and is in an *open* state until it is explicitly closed.

Therefore, to start making use of the NIO packages, a common starting point would be to create a new stream in the usual fashion and then create a channel from the stream. The following example shows a straightforward data transfer from one file to another using channels. Note that this could have been done by transferring one byte at a time in a loop, however, the `transferTo()` and `transferFrom()` methods can be optimized by the underlying OS to take advantage of any cached file data. This results in some very speedy data transfers.

```java
// Transfer.java

import java.io.*;
import java.nio.channels.*;

public class TransferTest {
  private static void transfer(File from, File to) throws IOException {

    FileInputStream fis = new FileInputStream(from);
    FileChannel inChannel = fis.getChannel();

    FileOutputStream fos = new FileOutputStream(to, false);
    FileChannel outChannel = fos.getChannel();

    inChannel.transferTo(0, (int) inChannel.size(), outChannel);

    outChannel.close();
    fos.close();
    inChannel.close();
    fis.close();
  }
```

```
    public static void main(String[] args) {
      try {
        transfer(new File("from.txt"), new File("to.txt"));
      } catch (IOException ioe) {
        System.err.println("Error: " + ioe);
      }
    }
  }
}
```

Before running this code you will need to create a file called from.txt containing a few lines of plain text and save it in the C:\Beg_Java_Networking\Ch21 directory. When you run the program from the command prompt a file called to.txt will be created.

C:\Beg_Java_Networking\Ch21>**java Transfer**

The application commences by creating two File instances (as handles to the to.txt and from.txt files) and passes them to the transferTo() method. This method creates a file input stream using the from.txt file and a file output stream using the to.txt file. From these streams, two corresponding channels are created.

```
FileInputStream fis = new FileInputStream(from);
FileChannel inChannel = fis.getChannel();

FileOutputStream fos = new FileOutputStream(to, false);
FileChannel outChannel = fos.getChannel();
```

Note that because the inChannel was created using an input stream, it is read-only. Similarly, the outChannel is only available for writing. Using either channel inappropriately will cause a NonReadableChannelException or NonWritableChannelException to be thrown.

To transfer the data, the application uses the inChannel's transferTo() method. The parameters passed to the transferTo() method indicate that the bytes, from the zero position of the channel up to the channel's size, should be transferred to the outChannel. In other words, that it should transfer all of the data of the file associated with the inChannel to the file associated with the outChannel.

```
inChannel.transferTo(0, (int)inChannel.size(), outChannel);
```

After the data is transferred, both channels are closed. One thing to note is that during the read or write from a channel, any other thread that attempts a read or write on the channel will block. Other I/O operations on the channel will be handled according to the channel's type.

Pattern Matching and Character Sets

Though regular expression style pattern matching is at a bit of a tangent to networking issues, most experienced network programmers will attest to its usefulness when dealing with large amounts of character data.

In light of this and since this functionality has (finally!) been added in the J2SE 1.4 release, we'll work through an example using the new Pattern (java.util.regex.Pattern) and Matcher (java.util.regex.Matcher) classes in conjunction with the file I/O using file channels. This example will introduce the use of the java.nio.charset package in conjunction with **character buffers** (java.nio.CharBuffer).

The next example involves working with regular expressions and character buffers. Before running the program you will need to create another text file containing several lines of text and saved as `lines.txt` in the `C:\Beg_Java_Networking\Ch21` directory.

```java
// LineCounter.java

import java.util.regex.*;
import java.io.*;

import java.nio.*;
import java.nio.charset.*;
import java.nio.channels.*;
import java.nio.channels.spi.*;

public class LineCounter {
  public static void count(String file) throws IOException {

    /*
     * Open the file using FileInputStream and get a channel
     * from the input stream.
     */
    FileInputStream fis = new FileInputStream(file);
    FileChannel fileChannel = fis.getChannel();

    // Map the file in memory for speedy access.
    int size = (int) fileChannel.size();
    MappedByteBuffer buffer = null;
    try {
      buffer = fileChannel.map(FileChannel.MAP_RO, 0, size);
    } catch (IOException e) {
      System.out.println("Please, make sure the file is valid.");
      System.exit(1);
    }
    finally {
      fileChannel.close();
    }

    Charset charset = Charset.forName("ISO-8859-1");
    CharsetDecoder decoder = charset.newDecoder();
    CharBuffer lines = decoder.decode(buffer);

    // Pattern used to parse the lines.txt file into lines.
    Pattern linePattern = Pattern.compile(".*\r?\n");

    // Determine the number of lines.
    Matcher matcher = linePattern.matcher(lines);
    int numberOfLines = 0;
    for (; matcher.find(); numberOfLines++) {

      // empty loop since we are just counting lines.
    }
    fileChannel.close();

    System.out.println("Number of lines: " + numberOfLines);
  }

  public static void main(String[] args) {

    if (args.length == 0) {
      System.err.println("Syntax: java LineCounter " + "[file to count]");
```

```
            System.exit(1);
        }
        try {
            LineCounter.count(args[0]);
        } catch (IOException ioe) {
            System.err.println("Error: " + ioe);
            System.exit(1);
        }
    }
}
```

Running the program will produce an output stating the number of lines of text in your `lines.txt` file. For example, if `lines.txt` contained 2 lines of text then the following output should appear:

C:\Beg_Java_Networking\Ch21>**java LineCounter lines.txt**
Number of lines: 2

The `LineCounter` example begins by passing the file name from the command line to the application's `count()` method. This method creates a file channel and then maps the entire contents of the file using a mapped byte buffer, just as we did in previous examples. Since we are going to be counting the number of lines in the file, we will have to search the data for new line characters. To do this we have to view the data as character data instead of raw bytes. This is achieved by specifying a **character set** (`java.nio.charset.CharSet`) and using a character set decoder (`java.nio.charset.CharsetDecoder`) to obtain a view of the data as a character buffer.

```
Charset charset = Charset.forName("ISO-8859-1");
CharsetDecoder decoder = charset.newDecoder();
CharBuffer lines = decoder.decode(buffer);
```

Now that the data is represented as character data, the application can define a regular expression using a pattern and use this, along with a matching object to find pattern matches in the file. The regular expression here says to match any number of characters (that's the `.*` bit), followed by an optional `\r` (that's the `\r?` bit) and a `\n`.

```
// Pattern used to parse the lines.txt file into lines.
Pattern linePattern = Pattern.compile(".*\r?\n");

// Determine the number of lines.
Matcher matcher = linePattern.matcher(lines);
int numberOfLines = 0;
for(; matcher.find(); numberOfLines++)
{
    // empty loop since we are just counting lines.
}
```

The matcher's `find()` method will continue to return the next match found until it reaches the end of the file, therefore we can use it as the test parameter in the `for` loop and simply count the number of iterations to get a line count for the file. The key features in this example are the use of the decoder object to create a character view of the file's data, the creation of a pattern to look for in the data, and using a `Matcher` object to return the matches found.

Note, if you do not have a new line character at the end of your last line of text then the program will report one less line of text than you would expect.

Building a Non-Blocking I/O API

The introduction of a non-blocking I/O facility to Java is one of the primary motivations for the creation of the NIO packages. By using a "select and poll" approach, the new `java.nio.channels.SelectableChannel`, `java.nio.channels.Selector` and `java.nio.channels.SelectionKey` classes facilitate multiplexed, non-blocking I/O. With the next few sections, we'll explore each of these classes and learn how to use them to create a non-blocking server application.

Selector Overview

As with any discussion that starts to involve parallel processing or multithreading, selectors can be troublesome. However, with an understanding of the motivation behind using selectors, we are well on the way to creating non-blocking servers that will make you the life of the party – well, something like that.

One of the drawbacks of the current Java I/O capability is that generally all I/O operations will block (be put on hold, basically) until the requested operation can be carried out. This isn't really a concern in a simply linear system, but if an application has to handle multiple I/O requests, performance can diminish significantly.

Until now, the most effective solution (short of defining our own I/O classes) was to spawn a separate thread for each request, thereby freeing up the main application thread to handle the next I/O request. But even with this scenario, there is a processing overhead in creating each new thread (though it's still far more efficient than creating a completely new process), especially since each request may need some preprocessing as well. With Java 1.4 we can use selectors to avoid this problem.

Let's consider some different situations in which the selector model can be applied.

A Real World Selector Analogy

For our purposes, the following analogy will be that of a grocery store. Customers will be our I/O requests, the thread(s) handling these requests are the cashiers and collecting the items on shopping lists will represent processing for each request.

Now let's look at the various (efficient or otherwise) ways that we can buy groceries. Analogous to the simple linear system mentioned above, imagine a store where a customer takes a number upon entering the store. The only cashier on duty calls out the number of the next customer to be served and then rings that customer through. If the customer is still shopping, the cashier waits until they can be rung through. As you can see, this isn't very efficient (even if the cashier gives up after a while – or times out – a lot of time is lost).

Mimicking the process of spawning multiple threads, the store could choose to add a new cashier for every customer. This is quite efficient (though expensive), since customers must wait only as long as it takes the cashier to set up at their station (count the cash, log in, and so on). However, an even more effective system (and thankfully the one most shoppers encounter) is one in which customers line up at the cashier's till only when they are ready to be rung through (and the cashier asks "Who's next?"). This forms the basis of how selectors work.

Selectors As Multiplexors

The selector class acts as a multiplexor for selectable channel objects and can be used to create the efficient "who's next" scenario described above. A selectable channel (the customer) registers itself with a selector (the cashier), which gets represented as a selection key (like taking a number in our grocery store example, except that these keys are simply for identification and not for prioritizing requests). All of the channels that are registered with a particular selector are maintained in the selector's key set and can be retrieved as a Set via the selector's keys() method. Similarly, the process of determining "who's next" is done through the selector's select() method (all selected keys are maintained in a selected keys Set as well and is returned by calling a selector's selectedKeys() method).

There is one other point to note about this implementation – there is also a canceled key Set (though it is not publicly available) that maintains a set of channels that have been processed in some way and are simply waiting to be de-registered. This is necessary since the act of de-registering a channel may cause the operation to block and the use of an intermediate canceled key set allows channels to maintain the requirement of being asynchronously closable. We'll see selectors in action when we look at socket channels and server socket channels.

Selectable Channels

The selectable channel poses more of a challenge than the file channel that we have been using – but this is a good thing. The added complexity stems from its use of the selectors and selection keys we just looked at. They allow a selectable channel to be multiplexed (that is, create the illusion of parallel processing within a single thread of control) and, in this manner, SelectableChannel classes represent the basis for non-blocking I/O implementations.

From the first incarnations of the Java language, the lack of support for non-blocking I/O has been an Achilles' heel when it came to creating scalable servers. Previously, the only solution was to spawn separate threads that could wait for the socket connection to complete its request. Now, using a "select and poll" scheme, it is possible to create true non-blocking, scalable servers using a limited number of threads. Functionality is available through the java.nio.channels.DatagramChannel class, java.nio.channels.SocketChannel class and java.nio.channels.ServerSocketChannel, which have their basis in the SelectableChannel.

As with the Java I/O stream-based classes (such as java.io.FileInputStream), the datagram socket, socket and server socket channels can be created by calling the getChannel() method of the corresponding socket class.

The distinguishing feature of a selectable channel (as opposed to a file channel, for instance) is that it can be placed in a **non blocking** mode. When configured in this manner and registered with selector, a selectable channel will not block, and any attempt to cause the channel to block will make it throw an IllegalBlockingModeException. Though this may seem confusing at the moment, the next few sections will show how these classes are utilized in an application.

Building a Non-Blocking, Scalable Server

The basic structure of our server will be not unlike those we've already seen in Chapter 9. The main difference is the addition of the "select and poll" mechanism prior to the accept() method in order to prevent incoming requests from causing the main thread to block. As discussed earlier, this can be implemented using the non-blocking mode of a selectable channel in conjunction with a selector and selection keys. This will also overcome the need to spawn a new thread for each request, which (though a very clean design) is not truly scalable.

Our server example is going to provide one of the Internet's core services – to serve up a "Quote of the Day" to anyone who asks. For clarity, our first client is going to make requests from the command line, but it would prove to be a simple exercise to create a small applet interface that anyone could include in a web page. You would have to make sure that the applet code resided on the same server as our quote server. This is a simple matter of having users include a specific applet tag referencing a central applet as opposed to porting the applet source to their own server and referencing that.

To create a quote server you must begin by creating a file called `quotes.txt` containing several quotes using the following format. Save this in the `C:\Beg_Java_Networking\Ch21` directory.

> Text of the quote all on one line (no breaks)
> - author of the quote all on one line
> Text of the quote all on one line
> - author of the quote all on one line
> and so on...

```java
// QuoteServer.java

package com.wrox.quote;

import java.net.*;
import java.util.*;
import java.util.regex.*;
import java.io.*;

import java.nio.*;
import java.nio.charset.*;
import java.nio.channels.*;
import java.nio.channels.spi.*;

public class QuoteServer {

  // Define a default port
  private static final int DEFAULT_PORT = 7236;

  // Pattern used to parse the quotes.txt file into lines.
  private static Pattern linePattern = Pattern.compile(".*\r?\n");

  /*This must be a member variable so that we can close it
    in the classes finalizer method. */
    private FileChannel fileChannel;

  /*
   * The buffer that will be associated with the fileChannel
   * to hold the quote.txt data.
   */
  private CharBuffer quotes;

  /* The number of lines / 2 since a quote consists of
      a line for the quote and a line for the author. */
  private int numberOfQuotes;

  public QuoteServer() throws IOException {
    init();
  }
```

Map the quote file into a `charBuffer`. For a large-scale implementation you'll want to use a more scalable solution such as a relational database.

```java
private void init() throws IOException {

    /* Open the file using FileInputStream and get a channel
       from the input stream. */
    FileInputStream fis = new FileInputStream("quotes.txt");
    fileChannel = fis.getChannel();

    // Map the file in memory for speedy access.
    int size = (int) fileChannel.size();
    MappedByteBuffer buffer = fileChannel.map(FileChannel.MAP_RO, 0, size);

    /* Decode the byte buffer into a character buffer. We'll
       use the HTML standard Latin 1 character set. */
    Charset charset = Charset.forName("ISO-8859-1");
    CharsetDecoder decoder = charset.newDecoder();
    quotes = decoder.decode(buffer);

    // Determine the number of quotes in the file for future reference.
    Matcher matcher = linePattern.matcher(quotes);
    for (numberOfQuotes = 0; matcher.find(); numberOfQuotes++) {

      // empty loop since we are just counting lines.
    }

    /* Because each quote has an associated author on the next line,
       divide this number by 2 */
    numberOfQuotes /= 2;
}

/* This method is the actual server that listens, accepts
   and responds to client requests. */
public void listen(int port) throws Exception {

    System.out.println("Quote Server listening on port " + port + ".");

    // Create a non-blocking server socket
    ServerSocketChannel serverChannel = ServerSocketChannel.open();
    serverChannel.configureBlocking(false);

    // Use the host and port to bind the server socket
    InetAddress inetAddress = InetAddress.getLocalHost();
    InetSocketAddress socketAddress = new InetSocketAddress(inetAddress,
            port);
    serverChannel.socket().bind(socketAddress);

    // The Selector for incoming requests
    Selector requestSelector = SelectorProvider.provider().openSelector();

    /* Put the server socket on the selectors 'ready list'.
       No need to retain the SelectionKey returned. */
    serverChannel.register(requestSelector, SelectionKey.OP_ACCEPT);
```

In the `while` loop, any registered operation will be returned by the `select()` method. The `select()` method itself will block until a channel is ready.

```
      while (requestSelector.select() > 0) {
        System.out.println("Connection Accepted...");

        // A request has been made and is ready for I/O.
        Set requestKeys = requestSelector.selectedKeys();

        Iterator iterator = requestKeys.iterator();
        while (iterator.hasNext()) {
          SelectionKey requestKey = (SelectionKey) iterator.next();

          // Get the socket that's ready for I/O
          ServerSocketChannel requestChannel =
            (ServerSocketChannel) requestKey.channel();

          // This shouldn't block
          Socket requestSocket = requestChannel.accept();

          // Send a quote to the client
          PrintWriter out = new PrintWriter(requestSocket.getOutputStream(),
                                            true);
          out.println(getNextQuote());
          out.close();

          iterator.remove();
        }
      }
    }
```

Here is where we will show off a bit of the NIO classes and get a random quote:

```
    private String getNextQuote() {

      // Select a number from 0 to the max number of quotes.
      int quoteIndex = (((int) (Math.random() * numberOfQuotes)) * 2);
      ;

      // Iterate through the quotes up until quoteIndex;
      Matcher matcher = linePattern.matcher(quotes);
      for (int i = 0; matcher.find() && i < quoteIndex; i++) {

        // empty loop since we are just counting lines.
      }

// The next two matched (lines) are the quote that we want.
      String quote = matcher.group().trim();
      matcher.find();
      quote += "\n" + matcher.group().trim();

      return quote;
    }

    // Make sure that we close our FileChannel.
    protected void finalize() throws Throwable {
      try {
        fileChannel.close();
      }
      finally {
        super.finalize();
      }
```

```
      }

      public static void main(String[] args) {
        int port = DEFAULT_PORT;

        if (args.length > 0) {
          try {
            port = Integer.parseInt(args[0]);
          } catch (NumberFormatException nfe) {
            System.err.println("Syntax: java QuoteServer [port "
                              + "number to accept connections on.]");
            System.exit(1);
          }
        }

        try {
          new QuoteServer().listen(port);
        } catch (Exception e) {
          System.err.println("Error: " + e);
        }
      }
    }
```

Compile and run the program from the command prompt using the following commands:

C:\Beg_Java_Networking\Ch21>**javac com\wrox\quote\QuoteServer.java**

C:\Beg_Java_Networking\Ch21>**java com.wrox.quote.QuoteServer**
Quote Server listening on port 7236.

Other than the above listening message, nothing much will be returned for now. In the following sections we will create a client to access the server.

There are only four logical programming blocks within the quote server:

❑   Get any parameters from the command line

❑   Map the quotes.txt file into memory (as in the previous example)

❑   Start listening for and process requests

❑   Return a randomly selected quote to the client

Gathering the parameters from the command line is fairly obvious, though it is always nice to try and handle this as gracefully as possible.

Mapping the quotes.txt file into memory uses the same logic (and practically the same code) as in the previous LineCounter example. There are a couple of things to note in this implementation, however. First, this operation is done in the init() method (which is called from the constructor). This way, the mapping is only done once – when the class is initialized. This could be done in a static initializer, but, since you generally only have one instance of a server running, this would be an unnecessary step.

Next, the file channel is declared so that it has class scope. This is done out of necessity since the file channel must remain open while that class utilizes the character buffer that is mapped to it. Therefore, in order to properly close this resource, the file channel must be accessible from the finalize() method.

745

A final detail is the initial loop used to count the number of quotes in the file. This provides an upper limit when we randomly select what quote we will send to the client.

The getNextQuote() method is a simple modification of the LineCounter example. It uses a random number and the number of quotes calculator in the init() method to iterate through the quote file and return a random selection.

The heart of the QuoteServer application is its listen() method. These are the basic steps involved:

1. Create a ServerSocketChannel and set it to non-blocking mode

2. Bind the server channel to the local host and specified port

3. Get a selector and register the server channel with it

4. Wait for the selector to select something

5. Accept the connection and create a socket

6. Respond to the request with a random quote

The only steps that are unique to the new API are Steps 1, 3, and 4; the other steps are fairly standard when creating a simple server. Let's look at the listen() method in more detail.

The server socket channel can be instantiated by simply calling its static open() method. Once we have an instance of the channel we can set it to non-blocking mode. Remember, this is one of the key functions that allow us to create a multiplexed server.

```
ServerSocketChannel serverChannel = ServerSocketChannel.open();
serverChannel.configureBlocking(false);
```

After the server channel is bound to a host and port in the usual fashion, we request a selector from the default selector provider and open it. Conveniently we can do all of this with just one assignment.

```
Selector requestSelector = SelectorProvider.provider().openSelector();
```

We've now registered the selector with the ServerSocketChannel. Notice that we also include an OP_ACCEPT parameter. This defines the operation that our ServerSocketChannel is interested in. We can now test for selections before calling the ServerChannel's accept() method (which would immediately block until a connection is requested from a client). Now, the application simply polls the selector's select() method to see if any operations have been added to its selectedKeys set (in our case, when a client makes a request on the ServerSocketChannel that we registered).

```
serverChannel.register(requestSelector, SelectionKey.OP_ACCEPT);
while (requestSelector.select()> 0)
{
    // Only get here if one or more requests are made and they are ready for
    // I/O.
}
```

Once a selection has been added (multiplexing), then we can assume that any registered objects in the selector's `selectedKeys` set are ready to perform I/O and will probably not block when `accept()` is invoked. Unfortunately, accessing our `ServerSocketChannel` is a bit messy and requires iterating through the selected keys (there should only be one `ServerSocketChannel` that we registered earlier), casting out our channel and calling its `accept()` method to handle the request.

One last thing we have to do is to remove the channel from the selected keys, to ensure that it won't be processed again.

```
Set requestKeys = requestSelector.selectedKeys();

Iterator iterator = requestKeys.iterator();
while(iterator.hasNext())
{
    SelectionKey requestKey = (SelectionKey) iterator.next();

    // Get the socket that's ready for I/O
    ServerSocketChannel requestChannel = (ServerSocketChannel)
                                    requestKey.channel();
    // This shouldn't block
    Socket requestSocket = requestChannel.accept();

    // Send a quote to the client

    iterator.remove();
}
```

Finally, the application retrieves the next quote and sends it to the client.

The Quote Client

To retrieve our inspiring quotes, we need to create a client that can make a connection to our quote server, request a quote, and then translate the incoming data into something useful. To handle this task, we'll create an application client that runs on the command line. To do this you will have to start up an additional command prompt window to the one the quote server is running in and run the `jdk1_4.bat` file.

```
// QuoteClient.java

package com.wrox.quote;

import java.io.*;
import java.net.*;
import java.nio.*;
import java.nio.channels.*;
import java.nio.charset.*;

public class QuoteClient
{
    private static final int DEFAULT_PORT = 7236;

    // The buffer to hold the incoming data
    private static ByteBuffer buffer = ByteBuffer.allocateDirect(1024);

    //Asks for a quote
    private static void requestQuote(String host,
```

```
                                    int port) throws IOException
    {

        InetSocketAddress socketAddress = new InetSocketAddress(
                                            InetAddress.getByName(host),
                                            port);
        SocketChannel socketChannel = null;

        try
        {
            // Connect to the Quote Server
            socketChannel = SocketChannel.open();
            socketChannel.connect(socketAddress);

            buffer.clear();
            socketChannel.read(buffer);

            buffer.flip();
            Charset charset = Charset.forName(" ISO-8859-1");
            CharsetDecoder decoder = charset.newDecoder();
            CharBuffer charBuffer = decoder.decode(buffer);
            System.out.print(charBuffer);
        }
        finally
        {
            if(socketChannel != null)
            {
                socketChannel.close();
            }
        }
    }

    public static void main(String[] args)
    {

        if(args.length == 0)
        {
            System.err.println("Syntax: java QuoteClient " +
                               "[QuoteServer host] [port number " +
                               "to request a connection on.]");
            System.exit(1);
        }

        // Get the host from the command line.
        String host = args[0];
        int port = DEFAULT_PORT;

        // Check to see if a port number was supplied.
        if(args.length == 2)
        {
            try
            {
                port = Integer.parseInt(args[1]);
            }
            catch(NumberFormatException nfe)
            {
                System.err.println("Syntax: java QuoteClient " +
                                   "[QuoteServer host] [port number " +
                                   "to request a connection on.]");
                System.exit(1);
```

```
            }
        }

        // Make a request.
        try
        {
            QuoteClient.requestQuote(host, port);
        }
        catch(Exception e)
        {
            System.err.println("Error: " + e);
        }
    }
}
```

To see a random quote you must compile the code and run the program from the command prompt as follows:

C:\Beg_Java_Networking\Ch21>**javac com\wrox\quote\QuoteClient.java**

C:\Beg_Java_Networking\Ch21>**java com.wrox.quote.QuoteClient localhost (*or IP address*)**

> **Depending on your machine's configuration you may want to specify its actual IP address in order to locate your server running at the same address. To get this information on an NT machine, for instance, you can type the command `ipconfig` at a command prompt.**

The QuoteClient's core functionality is in the requestQuote() method. The code is rather straightforward in this instance; however, since we are using the new socket channel class and buffers, we should touch on a couple of points – specifically the buffer's clear() and flip() methods. The data received from the QuoteServer is in a raw byte form. Therefore, we must read it into a byte buffer. Before this is done, however, we call the buffer's clear() method to make sure that any limits, positions and markers are all reset. This ensures that we are writing to the buffer from the beginning.

After the buffer has been populated with data, the buffer.flip() call conveniently puts the limit to the end of the current data (sets it to the current position) and then sets the position to zero. This way, when we read the data from the buffer, we will be starting from the beginning and we will only read the data contained (as opposed to reading all 1024 bytes allocated when the buffer was created). To output the quote in a legible fashion we use an instance of CharSetDecoder to decode the byte data into a character buffer and then output this to the command line.

Datagram Channels

As with socket and server socket channels, the addition of the DatagramChannel class (java.nio.channels.DatagramChannel), offers new functionality for datagram connectivity. Though we have explored datagrams in Chapter 9, we'll revisit them here in the context of the NIO packages.

In the following example, we use the datagram channel to send a number of datagrams to a waiting receiver. This is quite different from the normal technique of using a `DatagramPacket` object (`java.net.DatagramPacket`) in which the data and receiver are specified when that packet is created. The main difference is that once the datagram packet is created, it is sent to the receiver specified in the constructor. With the datagram channel, the packets are not sent until the channel's `send()` method is called.

```java
// DatagramReceiver.java

package com.wrox.datagram;

import java.net.*;
import java.util.*;
import java.io.*;

import java.nio.*;
import java.nio.charset.*;
import java.nio.channels.*;
import java.nio.channels.spi.*;

public class DatagramReceiver
{

    private static final int DEFAULT_PORT = 7236;

    public static void main(String[] args)
    {
        int port = DEFAULT_PORT;

        if(args.length > 0)
        {
            try
            {
                port = Integer.parseInt(args[0]);
            }
            catch(NumberFormatException nfe)
            {
                System.err.println("Syntax: java DatagramServer [port " +
                                    " number to accept connections on.]");
                System.exit(1);
            }
        }

        try
        {
        DatagramChannel channel = DatagramChannel.open(port);
        System.out.println("Listening for datagrams...");
        while(true)
        {
            ByteBuffer buffer = ByteBuffer.allocate(512);
            SocketAddress sender = channel.receive(buffer);

            if(sender != null)
            {
                buffer.flip();
                System.out.println("Message from: " + sender);

                // decode a message
                Charset charset = Charset.forName("ISO-8859-1");
                CharsetDecoder decoder = charset.newDecoder();
```

```
                    CharBuffer message = decoder.decode(buffer);

                    System.out.println("received: " + message);
                }
            }
        }
        catch(IOException ioe)
        {
            System.err.println("Error: " + ioe);
        }
    }
}
```

To compile and run the `DatagramReceiver` program from the command prompt type:

C:\Beg_Java_Networking\Ch21>**javac com\wrox\datagram\DatagramReceiver.java**

C:\Beg_Java_Networking\Ch21>**java com.wrox.datagram.DatagramReceiver**

The following code is for `com\wrox\datagram\DatagramSender.java`.

```
// DatagramSender.java

package com.wrox.datagram;

import java.io.*;
import java.net.*;
import java.nio.*;
import java.nio.channels.*;
import java.nio.charset.*;

public class DatagramSender
{
    private static final int DEFAULT_PORT = 7236;

    // Send a datagram
    private static void sendDatagram(String host,
                                     int port) throws IOException
    {

        InetSocketAddress socketAddress = new InetSocketAddress(
                                          InetAddress.getByName(host),
                                          port);
        DatagramChannel channel = null;
        Charset charset = Charset.forName("ISO-8859-1");
        String[] messages = { "One", "Two", "Three", "Four", "Five" };

        try
        {
            channel = DatagramChannel.open();
            channel.connect(socketAddress);

            for(int i=0; i<messages.length; i++)
            {
                // create a message
                CharBuffer buffer = CharBuffer.allocate(512);
                CharsetEncoder encoder = charset.newEncoder();
                buffer.put(messages[i]);
```

```
                    buffer.flip();
                    ByteBuffer message = encoder.encode(buffer);
                    channel.send(message, null);
                }
            }
            finally
            {
                if(channel != null)
                {
                    channel.close();
                }
            }
        }

        public static void main(String[] args)
        {
            if(args.length == 0)
            {
                System.err.println("Syntax: java DatagramClient " +
                                    "[DatagramServer host] [port number to " +
                                    "request a connection on.]");
                System.exit(1);
            }

            // Get the host from the command line.
            String host = args[0];
            int port = DEFAULT_PORT;

            // Check to see if a port number was supplied.
            if(args.length == 2)
            {
                try
                {
                    port = Integer.parseInt(args[1]);
                }
                catch(NumberFormatException nfe)
                {
                    System.err.println("Syntax: java DatagramClient " +
                                        "[Server host] [port number to " +
                                        "request a connection on.]");
                    System.exit(1);
                }
            }

            try
            {
                DatagramSender.sendDatagram(host, port);
            }
            catch(Exception e)
            {
                System.err.println("Error: " + e);
            }
        }
    }
```

With `DatagramReceiver` running in one command prompt window you need to run
`DatagramSender` in a different window using these commands:

C:\Beg_Java_Networking\Ch21>**javac com\wrox\datagram\DatagramSender.java**

C:\Beg_Java_Networking\Ch21>**java com.wrox.datagram.DatagramSender localhost (*or IP address)***

You should then see output similar to that shown below, in the DatagramReceiver window.

Listening for datagrams...
Message from: /192.168.10.134 : 2459
received: One
Message from: /192.168.10.134 : 2459
received: Two
Message from: /192.168.10.134 : 2459
received: Three
Message from: /192.168.10.134 : 2459
received: Four
Message from: /192.168.10.134 : 2459
received: Five

The Datagram Receiver application is rather basic – all of its functionality is contained within the main() method. A DatagramChannel is instantiated by calling the static open() method and passing it the port on which the receiver is to listen.

The application then enters a loop, creates a byte buffer to hold the incoming data, and calls the datagram's receive() method. This method will block until a datagram is received on the port specified when the DatagramChannel was instantiated. When a datagram arrives, the receive() method returns the sender's address and populates the byte buffer with the datagram's contents.

To finish processing, the receiver application does a quick check to make sure the sender's InetAddress is not null and then decodes the byte buffer data just as we have seen in previous examples.

The datagram sender application begins by examining the arguments passed in on the command line to retrieve the port and host for the receiver application, and then calls the sendDatagram() method. The sendDatagram() method uses its port and host arguments to instantiate an InetAddress object specifying the location of the datagram receiver.

To create and send our datagram, a DatagramChannel is used. We instantiate a new channel by calling the datagram's static open() method. Then we reverse the decoding process we've seen in previous examples and *encode* the string data using a **charset encoder** (java.nio.charset.Encoder). The result of this operation is a byte buffer representing the string data as raw bytes, which can be passed to the datagram channel's send() method. Notice that we pass a null value instead of a valid InetAddress to the send() method. This is perfectly fine since we have already supplied the channel with the receiver InetAddress when we call the channel's connect() method.

java.net Enhancements

J2SE 1.4 also includes enhancements within the java.net packages, which, in some cases, fill some gaps and, in others, aid in helping the language conform more closely to several RFC specifications. Among the many changes, the addition of support for Internet Protocol version 6 (IPv6) addressing and the new URI class are particularly notable.

Internet Protocol Version 6

With the exponential growth of the Internet, what seemed like an endless supply of IP addresses turned out to be rather limited indeed. Having been referred to as the "new y2k problem", the rapidly depleting address space of the original 32-bit Internet address has led to the creation of a new address standard as specified in RFC 2373 (http://www.ietf.org/rfc/rfc2373.txt).

Though it has been a topic of much debate, the new, larger address space, namely **Internet Protocol version 6** (IPv6), will eventually become the *de facto* Internet addressing protocol. We should also note that the newer protocol also addresses many other weaknesses of the IPv4 design, such as providing facilities for authentication and encryption.

Though a thorough dissection of the IPv6 protocol is beyond the scope of this book, the reader may wish to explore the RFC 2373 specifications to get a better sense of all the details. For now, we'll simply concern ourselves with the new J2SE 1.4 support for IPv6 addresses and how they co-exist with the IPv4 addressing (`java.net.InetAddress`) we learned about in Chapter 8.

In the following sections we will revisit some of the concepts introduced in the previous chapters but this time explore some of the topics in more detail, in order to get a better understanding of the motivations for and implementations of IPv6.

The IPv6 Address Structure

First, let's have a look at the actual construction of an IPv6 address. We've already seen this in Chapter 8, but for completeness we'll mention it again here. While the IPv4 address consists of 32 bits of data, to ensure plenty of addresses to go around in the foreseeable future, an IPv6 address contains 128 bits of data. To account for the large number of integer digits required to make up a 128-bit address, the IPv6 address is typically represented using groups of four hexadecimal numbers separated by colons. For instance, a typical address may look like this:

```
EEA3:DE40:0000:0000:0000:0034:0000:FE2D
```

Of course, even this is a lot to remember so there are abbreviations. We won't enumerate the rules here (they are discussed in RFC 2373), but you should keep this in mind if you see something like the above written like so.

```
EEA3:DE40::0034:0:15.14.2.13
```

One thing that should be pointed out is that the last 32 bits of the address are often represented in traditional IPv4 notation using decimals and periods. This is a small nod towards the fact that both types of address must co-exist for the time being, as we will see in the next section.

Handling Two Protocols

Obviously, the Internet community cannot simply declare some future date as "International Change Your Internet Protocol Day". Though I'm sure this would be quite festive, much of the hardware and software that makes up the Internet is still IPv4-centric and will be for some years to come. Having foreseen this problem, the IPv6 specification contributors created a scheme so that IPv4 nodes can extract the portion of the IPv6 address that is useful to them. This is achieved by way of embedding an IPv4 address within the 128-bit IPv6 address (recall the decimal notation permitted in the previous address example?). These embedded addresses have two forms, namely, the **IPv4-compatible IPv6 address** and the **IPv4-mapped IPv6 address**.

The IPv4-compatible address is used for **tunneling** IPv6 addresses over routers, and has the form

```
80 bits                                16 bits   32 bits
| 0000.....              ...0000 |        0000 | 12.34.12.34 |
```

and the IPv4-mapped address uses the form

```
80 bits                                16 bits   32 bits
| 0000.....              ...0000 |        FFFF | 12.34.12.34 |
```

for representing an IPv4 address within a valid IPv6 address. This means that an IPv4-only router, for example, can still understand the address.

However, this is not the end of the story. As the need for a transition to the newer address space increases, more and more schemes are being introduced to ensure that all goes smoothly. For example, nodes (routers and so on) may employ a **dual–protocol stack** that will allow them to handle either addressing scheme independently. Now that we have an overview (albeit cursory) of the implications for, and motivations behind, IP addressing, let's have a look at its impact on the Java language.

Programming Implications

The complexity of almost all the issues raised in the preceding discussion are handled 'behind the scenes' within the J2SE 1.4 API. Understanding these issues will make the usefulness of many of the new classes and methods more obvious when you encounter them for the first time.

To facilitate the two addressing protocols, `java.net.Inet4Address` and `java.net.Inet6Address` have been added to the `java.net` package as subclasses of `InetAddress`. Through polymorphism, applications need not worry about what type of address they are dealing with until a protocol-specific behavior is required. For the most part, applications will still use the `InetAddress` for most basic functions (notice in the Quote examples, that the `InetAddress` references are all pretty standard).

There are, of course, some caveats that come with this. Specifically, it is recommended that `InetAddress` be instantiated using a *host name* or *IPv6 literal address* (by "literal" we simply mean in its numeric form as given in the examples above). In short, avoid using IPv4 literal addresses since they will eventually be an invalid address format.

Address Resolving

Unfortunately, there are not a lot of example applications that we can write to demonstrate IPv6 addressing. Though Java has added the necessary functionality, most systems have yet to implement IPv6. But to get a feel for what we've been talking about, the following example will allow you to input an address and then it will output the type of address that it resolves to (either IPv4 or IPv6).

```java
// AddressTester.java

import java.net.*;

public class AddressTester {

    public static void main(String[] args) {
```

```
        if(args.length == 0) {
            System.err.println("Syntax: java AddressTester " +
                               "[node address]");
            System.exit(1);
        }

        try {
            InetAddress inetAddress = InetAddress.getByName(args[0]);

            if(inetAddress instanceof Inet4Address) {
                System.out.println("IPv4 Address: " + inetAddress);
            }
            else if(inetAddress instanceof Inet6Address) {
                System.out.println("IPv6 Address: " + inetAddress);
            }
            else {
                System.out.println("Unknown Address type.");
            }
        }
        catch(Exception e) {
            System.err.println("Error: " + e);
        }
    }
}
```

Run the program from the command prompt using the command below. Try a couple of different addresses to see the differing results:

C:\Beg_Java_Networking\Ch21>**java AddressTester 12.12.12.12**
IPv4 Address: /12.12.12.12

C:\Beg_Java_Networking\Ch21>**java AddressTester EEA3:DE40::0034:0:15.14.2.13**
IPv6 Address: /[eea3:de40::34:0:f0e:20d]

This example is pretty basic. The address is retrieved from the command line and then it is used to instantiate a new InetAddress. Then the application attempts to cast this address to an Inet4Address and an Inet6Address. The instanceof operator determines the type of address that was passed to the application and the appropriate print statement is output.

Uniform Resource Identifier

JDK 1.4 introduces a new class called java.net.URI – this class can be used to represent any URI that is compliant with RFC 2396 (http://www.ietf.org/rfc/rfc2396.txt). The only connection between the URI and the URL classes (covered in Chapters 4 and 12) is the URI method toURL(), which returns a URL instance based on the URI. Otherwise, these two classes operate completely independently. Sun's motivation behind the URI class is that it should act strictly as an identifier. This is in contrast to the URL class, which has capabilities not only for identifying a resource, but also for looking up the host and opening a connection to the resource specified by the URL.

Many of the methods of the URI class are simply accessor methods for retrieving the various parts of the URI instance. However, there are three methods (normalize(), resolve() and relativize()) available for **normalization**, **resolution** and **relativization** of a URI instance. Basically, the normalize() method is used to strip a hierarchical URI instance of any extraneous "." and ".." characters from the path, as shown below:

```
URI uri = new URI("./docs/./index");
URI normalizedURI = uri.normalize();
```

This results in the `normalizedURI` being `"docs/index"`.

Both the `resolve()` and `relativize()` methods take a second URI as a parameter and use it to construct a new URI. Resolution combines a relative URI with a base URI to create an absolute URI. As an example of where this method might be useful, consider an application that needs to be portable across several domains. The application could define a domain-specific base URI and make all others relative to this base URI.

The `resolve()` method can then be used to construct absolute URIs using the base and relative URIs as shown below:

```
URI baseURI = new URI("http://joe@somewhere.com:80/docs/");
URI relativeURI = new URI("public/home");
URI absoluteURI = baseURI.resolve(relativeURI);
```

This results in the `absoluteURI` being:

```
http://joe@somewhere.com:80/docs/public/home
```

Relativization is basically the reverse of resolution. This method takes an absolute URI and attempts to create a relative URI using a base URI of some sort:

```
URI baseURI = new URI("http://joe@somewhere.com:80/docs/");
URI absoluteURI = new URI("http://joe@somewhere.com:80/docs/public/home");
URI relativeURI = baseURI.relativize(absoluteURI);
```

This results in the `relativeURI` having the value `public/home`.

Many of the methods for the URI class are centered on parsing the various syntactic pieces of the URI. The rules by which a string is parsed into a URI generally conform to the RFC 2396 and, as a result, can be rather complex. In light of this, we have not tried to define every nuance of the parsing rules as such, but rather we've considered URI construction and methods related to various syntaxes.

Creating and Manipulating URIs

This example demonstrates the various parts of a URI that we have just looked at. Notice the nomenclature for each URI part and how it corresponds to a particular method call. Also, the example defines several URIs and manipulates them using the `normalize()`, `resolve()`, and `relativize()` methods.

```
// URITest.java

import java.net.*;

public class URITest {
  public static void main(String[] args) {
    try {
      URI sampleURI = new URI("http://joe@somewhere.com:80/docs"
                            + "/public/home/index.html?id=1#ref");
```

```
            System.out.println("\nDefine and examine sampleURI:\n  " + sampleURI);

            System.out.println("  Scheme: " + sampleURI.getScheme());
            System.out.println("  Scheme-specific-part: "
                              + sampleURI.getSchemeSpecificPart());
            System.out.println("  Fragment: " + sampleURI.getFragment());
            System.out.println("  Authority: " + sampleURI.getAuthority());
            System.out.println("  User Info: " + sampleURI.getUserInfo());
            System.out.println("  Port: " + sampleURI.getPort());
            System.out.println("  Path: " + sampleURI.getPath());
            System.out.println("  Query: " + sampleURI.getQuery() + "\n");

            URI baseURI = new URI("http://joe@somewhere.com:80/docs/");
            System.out.println("Define baseURI:\n  " + baseURI + "\n");

            URI publicURI = new URI("docs/../public/home");
            System.out.println("Define publicURI:\n  " + publicURI + "\n");
            System.out.println("Normalize publicURI:\n  " + publicURI.normalize()
                              + "\n");
            URI absoluteURI = baseURI.resolve(publicURI);
            System.out.println("Resolve publicURI against baseURI:\n  "
                              + absoluteURI + "\n");

            URI adminURI = new URI("http://joe@somewhere.com:80"
                                 + "/docs/admin/home");
            System.out.println("Define adminURI:\n  " + adminURI + "\n");
            URI relativeURI = baseURI.relativize(adminURI);
            System.out.println("Relativize adminURI against baseURI:\n  "
                              + relativeURI);
        } catch (URISyntaxException use) {
            System.out.println("Error: " + use);
        }
    }
}
```

Run the program from the command prompt like this:

C:\Beg_Java_Networking\Ch21>**java URITest**

Define and examine sampleURI:
 http://joe@somewhere.com:80/docs/public/home/index.html?id=1#ref
 Scheme: http
 Scheme-specific-part: //joe@somewhere.com:80/docs/public/home/index.html?id=1
 Fragment: ref
 Authority: joe@somewhere.com:80
 User Info: joe
 Port: 80
 Path: /docs/public/home/index.html
 Query: id=1

Define baseURI:
 http://joe@somewhere.com:80/docs/

Define publicURI:
 docs/../public/home

Normalize publicURI:
public/home

Resolve publicURI against baseURI:
http://joe@somewhere.com:80/docs/public/home

Define adminURI:
http://joe@somewhere.com:80/docs/admin/home

Relativize adminURI against baseURI:
admin/home

Within the `main()` method, the application defines a lengthy `sampleURI` and then examines how the URI has been parsed by calling several methods to examine each of its various parts. After running the example as is, try changing the `sampleURI` by altering the scheme or user information, and see what happens.

In the second half of the application, we implement normalization, resolution and relativization. Be sure to consider this functionality closely, as determining what to resolve (or relativize) against what, can be potentially confusing.

Other New Features

Though we have gone into extensive details on several new features of the J2SE 1.4 release, there are innumerable minor changes as well some rather significant "under the hood" enhancements. The following section introduces a few of these enhancements. Some of the security enhancements are dealt with in much more detail in Chapter 14.

Unconnected/Unbound Socket Support

In previous JDK releases, the instantiation of a socket or server socket required that it be bound immediately through the constructor of a class. With J2SE 1.4, sockets and server sockets can be created, manipulated, and then bound using an `InetAddress`, allowing you to configure options before making a connection and, perhaps more significantly, to work better with the new channel classes. In our `QuoteServer` example, for instance, we implicitly created a new server socket, configured the blocking and then used `bind()` on the socket.

```
// Create a non-blocking server socket
ServerSocketChannel serverChannel = ServerSocketChannel.open();
serverChannel.configureBlocking(false);

// Use the host and port to bind the server socket
InetAddress inetAddress = InetAddress.getLocalHost();
InetSocketAddress socketAddress = new InetSocketAddress(inetAddress,
        port);
serverChannel.socket().bind(socketAddress);
```

Similarly, in the previous `DatagramSender` example, notice that we specified an address for the intended receiver when we called the channel's `connect()` method. This makes each call to `send()` (or `receive()`) more efficient, because any security checks have already been handled by the `connect()` method.

```
channel = DatagramChannel.open();
channel.connect(socketAddress);

for(int i=0; i<messages.length; i++)
{
    // create a message to send
...
    channel.send(message, null);
}
```

Socket Out Of Band Data Support

When sending data using a socket, situations may arise where the application may want to interrupt the current I/O operation and send an urgent message. This is commonly referred to as **out of band (OOB)** data. The socket class has been modified to provide *limited* support for this type of service with the addition of two methods – sendUrgentData() and setOOBInline().

Though the sendUrgentData() method takes a single integer as a parameter, it actually only sends a single byte of information (the lower eight bits of the integer). According to the API, the OOB data is sent after any preceding writes to the socket's output stream and before any other writes occur. On the receiving end, the socket must be enabled to accept the OOB data using the setOOBInline() method. However, doing so only instructs the socket to not dispose of this data. It does not provide any special handling of the OOB data; therefore, this would have to be handled using a custom protocol, for example.

SOCKS Protocol Version 5

As mentioned in Chapters 7, firewalls are an essential networking security component. In order to communicate between the exterior and interior of a firewall, a proxy server and a protocol of some sort must be used. The most common protocol in use today is the **SOCKS protocol**. Implementing the use of this protocol within a Java application is not so much a matter of programming, as it is of setting properties:

```
Properties properties = System.getProperties();
properties.put("yourSocksProxyPort","1080");
properties.put("yourSocksProxyHost","socks.yourdomain.com");
System.setProperties(properties);
```

You can achieve the same results using command line arguments when starting your application:

```
java -DyourSocksProxyPort=1080 -DyourSocksProxyHost=yourSocksdomain.com
```

Once these properties are set, all socket communication will automatically use the specified SOCKS proxy server. The feature that is unique to J2SE 1.4 is that applications can use either SOCKS version 4 (with IPv4 addressing) or SOCKS version 5 (IPv6 addressing) and will **auto-negotiate** the appropriate version.

URLConnection

Along with **improved http streaming performance**, the abstract java.net.URLConnection class has had several methods added which are, therefore, available to the java.net.HttpURLConnection and java.net.JarURLConnection subclasses.

Three new methods have been added:

```
addRequestProperty()
getRequestProperties()
getHeaderFields()
```

The latter two methods simply return immutable map objects containing the request or header names as the map keys and their associated values. The `addRequestProperty()` method provides a facility to add new name/value pairs to the URL connection. This is convenient for adding new request properties, but the method will not overwrite values of existing keys.

Additionally, the `getErrorStream()` method of the `HttpURLConnection` class has been enhanced for improved handling of server errors returned in the event of connection failure. For instance, if an HTTP connection fails, but the server has sent a default help page or contact page (in place of a bleak 'file not found' message), it can be retrieved using this stream.

Summary

Though we have covered many of the new features in the J2SE 1.4 release, the material was selectively chosen to provide a foundation for network-specific issues. The reader is encouraged to explore the rest of the new packages and classes added in this Java release as well as to explore the classes and packages introduced here.

The topics covered in this chapter included:

- ❑ Creating, manipulating and navigating buffers

- ❑ Viewing byte buffers as primitive data types

- ❑ Use of channels to extend the functionality of I/O streams

- ❑ File channels and mapped byte buffers

- ❑ Using selectable channels (socket and server socket channels) in server applications

- ❑ Datagram connectivity using channels

- ❑ New support for IPv6

- ❑ URIs and the URI class

Some of the key issues to keep in mind are the new I/O abstractions provided by the channel classes, and the use of buffers to enhance data handling. The use of selectors and selection keys in creating multiplexed, scalable servers also formed a significant portion of the material covered. The reader is invited to experiment with the new features included in the JDK 1.4 release, which is currently in Beta.

Java Network Connectivity Exceptions

Exceptions are a basic consideration when designing and writing Java programs as they are used to signal serious problems upon execution. This is particularly important when developing network programs since so many components are involved when a program makes a connection to another program across a network or even on the same machine.

Without exceptions it can be difficult to locate network problems or provide adequate handling of exceptional situations in your program. Java has developed ways of addressing these problems. Java 1.0 threw a `SocketException` whenever a socket-related error occurred, JDK 1.1 added three new subclasses of `SocketException` that provide more information about the cause of the problem: `BindException`, `ConnectException` and `NoRouteToHostException` (no new subclasses have been added to `SocketException` up to and including JDK 1.4). In addition, the `java.net` package contains a number of exceptions that provide detailed information about what went wrong with URLs or the use of a specific protocol such as HTTP, to make it easier to find problems in your source code or to react appropriately to erroneous input.

In this appendix, we will focus on exceptions thrown in the `java.net` package and the tools you can use to analyze them. Covering every exception related to RMI, JMS, Servlets, and CORBA and how to debug them, taking into consideration the many existing application servers and Integrated Development Environment (IDE) debuggers, would provide enough material to fill an entire book of its own. A good place to investigate a specific Java networking-related problem you have (after consulting this appendix) is to search the forums in the Java Developer Connection at http://developer.java.sun.com/developer/ or to search the Usenet archives at http://groups.google.com/.

In this appendix you will learn how to:

❑   Work with Java exceptions in your program

❑   Place debug code into your program

❑   Detect network connectivity problems that lead to an error that is indicated by an exception from the `java.net` package being thrown

All of this will give you an insight into debugging and analyzing networking problems using exceptions, and how you can avoid mistakes commonly made in network programs.

Handling Exceptions in Java

Exceptions in Java are thrown when an error is detected. Exceptions have the following advantages:

- ❑ Exceptions are superior to return codes when local and encapsulated handling of the error is not guaranteed

- ❑ Exception handling separates the detection mechanism from the handling policy to make source code more readable and better structured

- ❑ Exceptions cannot be ignored by a programmer – a try/catch block has to be provided

- ❑ Exceptions can easily pass large amounts of information to the handler point (there is no limitation to a single return code)

When To Use Exceptions

Exceptions incur processing overhead when they are thrown, so they should only be used in error situations that are truly exceptional. For example, you have a class which encapsulates a telephone directory and you provide a method called searchEntry() to look for an entry based on the last name (which is passed as a parameter). You should not throw an exception in searchEntry() to indicate that the entry cannot be found, in this case it is preferable to return null to indicate that the entry cannot be found as this is not an unexpected error.

Java Exception Syntax

When an error is detected, the detecting method creates an exception and throws it using the throw keyword. Another method that detects an exception is a try block, which can either:

- ❑ Handle the exception in a catch block that follows the try block

    or

- ❑ Pass it on to the calling method by declaring that the method in which the exception may occur is capable of throwing that particular exception

In general, it is better to catch an exception as early as possible, which makes it easier to handle – you do not have to provide exception handling code along the entire call hierarchy, and you can usually react in a more meaningful way.

When you catch an exception, you can try to recover from it and continue processing, or you can report the problem. The following lines are taken from HTTPRequest.java, which was used in the SimpleHTTPServer example that was featured in Chapter 13, however exception handling has been improved:

```
try
{
    PrintStream os = PrintStream(clientconnection.getOutputStream());
    BufferedReader br = new BufferedReader(new
      InputStreamReader(clientconnection.getInputStream()));
    ...
    StringTokenizer st = new StringTokenizer(request);
    String header_method = st.nextToken();
    ...
}
catch (IOException ioe)
{
    System.err.println(e.getMessage());
    e.printStackTrace(System.err);
}
catch (NoSuchElementException nse)
{
    ...
}
catch (Exception e)
{
    ...
}
finally
{
    try
    {
        clientconnection.close();
    }
    catch (IOException e)
    {
        // Handle or ignore this exception
    }
}
```

The statements in the `try` block can throw many different exceptions. The Java exception syntax allows you to design and implement error-handling code that is as detailed or as general as required. In the above example we are interested in reporting a `NoSuchElementException` that may be thrown by the `st.nextToken()` statement, because it indicates that an HTTP client provides a request string that does not comply with the HTTP protocol. It is important to report or log this.

When To Use a finally Block

The `finally` block is also used correctly here. A `finally` block should be used when resource clean-up needs to be done. The statements in a `finally` block are always executed, irrespective of exceptions that may occur. Consider how the following example makes us save many lines of code by using a `finally` block:

At first, it might look just fine to include the `clientconnection.close()` into the `try` block like this:

```
try
{
    PrintStream os = new PrintStream(clientconnection.getOutputStream());
    BufferedReader br = new BufferedReader(new
      InputStreamReader(clientconnection.getInputStream()));
    .
```

```
        .
        .
        .
    StringTokenizer st = new StringTokenizer(request);
    String header_method = st.nextToken();
    clientconnection.close();
}
```

On second thought, it means that we have to repeat the statement `clientconnection.close()` in all our `catch` blocks as well, to properly release the resources associated with the socket. The better approach is to provide a `finally` block like this:

```
finally
{
    if (clientconnection != null)
        clientconnection.close();
}
```

Exception Class Hierarchy

All exceptions in Java are descendants of the `Throwable` class. The following diagram shows the class hierarchy of Java exceptions:

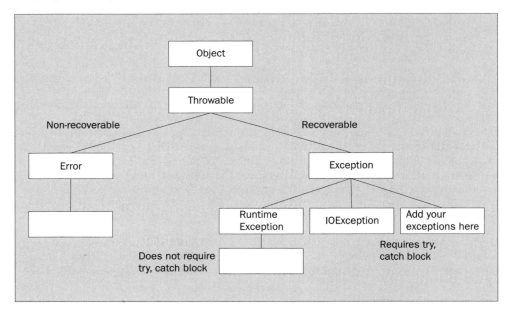

Exceptions that you define in your program typically extend `Exception` so that they require a `try/catch` block.

The following source code shows how you can extend the `Exception` class in your program to force the user of your exception to provide a meaningful error message, by not overriding the no-arguments constructor.

```
class MyNetworkException extends Exception {

    public MyNetworkException(String msg)
    {
        // Calls the superclass constructor to construct an Exception
        // with the specified detail message
        super(msg);
    }
}
```

Java defines a number of `RuntimeException` subclasses, which do not have to be used with a `try/catch` block. These `RuntimeException` subclasses include `IllegalArgumentException`, `NullPointerException`, `IndexOutOfBoundsException` or `SecurityException`. The reason these exceptions do not require `try/catch` blocks is that these exceptions are typically the result of coding errors, which have hopefully been eliminated by the time you deploy an application. Wrapping every method that accesses an array into a `try/catch` block to catch an `IndexOutOfBoundsException` would render the source code unreadable.

java.net Exceptions

All `java.net` exceptions are subclasses of `IOException`.

BindException

A `BindException` is thrown if you try to construct a `Socket`, `ServerSocket` or `DatagramSocket` on a local port and address that is already in use by another program. For instance, if you already have an HTTP server running on port 80 of your system, and you try to start `SimpleHTTPServer` (see Chapter 13) on port 80, then a `BindException` will be thrown when `SimpleHTTPServer` tries to construct the `ServerSocket`.

You can use the utility `netstat` to find out which TCP and UDP ports and addresses are currently in use on a system. `netstat` is available on Linux, UNIX and Microsoft Windows platforms. If the parameters `an` are used then all connections are displayed and IP addresses are displayed numerically:

C:\Beg_Java_Networking>**netstat -an**

Active Connections

Proto	Local Address	Foreign Address	State
TCP	0.0.0.0:21	0.0.0.0:0	LISTENING
TCP	0.0.0.0:23	0.0.0.0:0	LISTENING
TCP	192.168.1.1:80	0.0.0.0:0	LISTENING
TCP	0.0.0.0:135	0.0.0.0:0	LISTENING
TCP	0.0.0.0:445	0.0.0.0:0	LISTENING
TCP	0.0.0.0:777	0.0.0.0:0	LISTENING
TCP	0.0.0.0:1047	0.0.0.0:0	LISTENING
TCP	0.0.0.0:1052	0.0.0.0:0	LISTENING
TCP	0.0.0.0:4585	0.0.0.0:0	LISTENING
TCP	0.0.0.0:8008	0.0.0.0:0	LISTENING
TCP	0.0.0.0:9494	0.0.0.0:0	LISTENING

```
TCP   9.21.31.252:23      9.26.138.190:1643   ESTABLISHED
TCP   9.21.31.252:139     0.0.0.0:0           LISTENING
TCP   9.21.31.252:4582    9.21.28.151:445     TIME_WAIT
TCP   9.21.31.252:4585    9.26.4.21:445       ESTABLISHED
UDP   0.0.0.0:135         *:*
UDP   0.0.0.0:445         *:*
UDP   0.0.0.0:1027        *:*
UDP   0.0.0.0:1038        *:*
UDP   0.0.0.0:1044        *:*
```

The output suggests that there is an FTP server running on port 21, a Telnet server on port 23 and an HTTP server on port 80, however we cannot be sure. `netstat` only tells us that there is a server running and listening on these ports. An educated guess was made, since we know that these ports are used by default for the above-mentioned well-known services. All UDP sockets have `*:*` in the `Foreign Address` column and nothing in the `State` column because UDP is a connectionless protocol (see Chapter 10).

Most servers listen for incoming requests on all IP addresses (which is indicated by 0.0.0.0 in the above list) while other servers may choose to listen just on one address, such as the server on port 80 which is bound to the local IP address 192.168.1.1. You can find out how many IP addresses your system has by using the utility `ipconfig` under Microsoft Windows or `ifconfig` under Linux and UNIX.

Using `ipconfig` on a networked Windows 2000 Professional system gave the following output:

C:\Beg_Java_Networking>**ipconfig /all**

Windows 2000 IP Configuration

```
        Host Name . . . . . . . . . . . . . . . . : pwwin2k
        Primary DNS Suffix  . . . . . . . . . . . :
        Node Type . . . . . . . . . . . . . . . . : Hybrid
        IP Routing Enabled. . . . . . . . . . . . : Yes
        WINS Proxy Enabled. . . . . . . . . . . . : No
        DNS Suffix Search List. . . . . . . . . . : ibm.com
```

Ethernet adapter Local Area Connection:

```
        Connection-specific DNS Suffix  . . :
        Description . . . . . . . . . . . . . . . . : IBM 10/100-EtherJet-PCI-Adapter
        Physical Address. . . . . . . . . . . . . : 00-60-94-25-3C-1F
        DHCP Enabled. . . . . . . . . . . . . . . : No
        IP Address. . . . . . . . . . . . . . . . . : 192.168.1.1
        Subnet Mask . . . . . . . . . . . . . . . . : 255.255.255.0
        Default Gateway . . . . . . . . . . . . . :
        DNS Servers . . . . . . . . . . . . . . . . : 205.207.148.33
                                                      205.207.148.13
```

Ethernet adapter Internet Connection":

```
        Connection-specific DNS Suffix  . . : aci.on.ca
        Description . . . . . . . . . . . . . . . . : Realtek RTL8139(A) PCI-Adapter
```

```
Physical Address . . . . . . . . . . . . : 00-00-CB-59-47-BD
DHCP Enabled . . . . . . . . . . . . . . : Yes
Autoconfiguration Enabled . . . . . . : Yes
IP Address . . . . . . . . . . . . . . . . : 66.38.169.66
Subnet Mask . . . . . . . . . . . . . . : 255.255.255.0
Default Gateway . . . . . . . . . . . . : 66.38.169.1
DHCP Server . . . . . . . . . . . . . . : 205.207.148.250
DNS Servers . . . . . . . . . . . . . . : 205.207.148.33
                                          205.207.148.13
Lease Obtained . . . . . . . . . . . . : Saturday, 30. June 2001 14:58:00
Lease Expires . . . . . . . . . . . . . : Saturday, 30. June 2001 18:58:00
```

The output indicates that there are two Ethernet adapters on this system. One is connected to an internal LAN and the other is connected to a cable modem. The system is set up as a router, which means IP data packages will be forwarded from one IP address to the other (this computer shares its Internet connection with the other computers connected to the internal LAN). If you have more than one computer at home, you will likely want to have a similar setup which enables you to test your network programs under many different aspects (from behind a firewall, using private IP addresses, and so on).

ConnectException

A `ConnectException` is thrown if the remote host refuses a connection, usually because the host is busy or no process is listening on the remote port. For instance, this exception will be thrown when you attempt a connection to a server socket, which has already reached its connection backlog (the default backlog value for the `ServerSocket` constructor is 50).

After you have made sure, using `netstat`, that the server is listening on the port you are trying to connect to, restart the server to verify if you can reproduce the problem when you are the first client to establish a connection. This way you can rule out a problem that is related to the backlog limit being reached.

If you still receive a `ConnectException`, then you need to verify your server setup to make sure that all your server-side security settings (such as the ones specified in your policy files) are correct and effective.

MalformedURLException

A `MalformedURLException` is thrown if the parsing of a URL revealed a problem. It does not indicate an actual network connectivity problem.

Common mistakes resulting in a `MalformedURLException` include:

❑   Leaving out the protocol ("`www.wrox.com/`" instead of "`http://www.wrox.com/`")

❑   Specifying an invalid protocol ("`www://wrox.com`")

❑   Leaving out the colon ':' (`http//www.wrox.com/`)

Most web browsers allow you to enter a server's IP address, rather than a URL; however, when the browser then actually requests the page, it will prefix the most likely protocol based on the address – if the server name starts with "`ftp`", it will add "`ftp://`" otherwise it will add "`http://`".

A `MalformedURLException` will not be thrown if:

❑ The host name is invalid ("www.java-rules.com"). An `UnknownHostException` will be thrown instead.

❑ The path is invalid ("http://www.fbi.gov/x-files"). If you had requested a document through an `HttpURLConnection`, a `FileNotFoundException` would be thrown instead.

NoRouteToHostException

A `NoRouteToHostException` is thrown if an error occurred while attempting to connect a socket to a remote server, and the remote host cannot be reached because of the following reasons:

❑ An intervening firewall prevents a direct connection

❑ An intermediate router is down

❑ The host does not exist or is not connected

❑ The connection has timed out because of a slow or congested network, or too many routers along the route

The first check you would want to make is to use `telnet` to see if the server exists and responds to an incoming connection. `ping` and `traceroute` (or `tracert` on Microsoft Windows) can help you to examine the details of a network connection to a remote host, with respect to its actual response time and route. When trying to `ping` a South African host (http://www.paradisefound.co.za/) from North America, you will get a similar output to this:

C:\Beg_Java_Networking>**ping www.paradisefound.co.za**

Pinging www.paradisefound.co.za [196.2.153.70] with 32 bytes of data:

Request timed out.
Request timed out.
Reply from 196.2.153.70: bytes=32 time=1392ms TTL=233
Request timed out.

Ping statistics for 196.2.153.70:
    Packets: Sent = 4, Received = 1, Lost = 3 (75% loss),
Approximate round trip times in milli-seconds:
    Minimum = 1392ms, Maximum = 1392ms, Average = 1392ms

This does not necessarily mean that the connection is so unreliable that 75% of the packets actually get lost. It could also imply that the timeout should be increased for the time to wait for each reply – this is achieved using the parameter -w:

C:\Beg_Java_Networking>**ping www.paradisefound.co.za -w 2000**

With the timeout increased, all packets were received with a maximum round trip time of almost 2 seconds (this sample was been taken at a time when Internet traffic was at its worst, which was on a weekday during a time where in both time zones the business day had not ended).

The `tracert` utility can be used to follow the actual route to a remote host. It will help you to analyze which part of the route caused the problem.

C:\Beg_Java_Networking>**tracert www.paradisefound.co.za**

Tracing route to www.paradisefound.co.za [196.2.153.70]
over a maximum of 30 hops:

```
 1   <10 ms    20 ms    10 ms  gw-xtreme19.aci.on.ca [66.38.169.1]
 2    10 ms    10 ms    10 ms  ssr8-1-gw.aci.on.ca [205.207.148.46]
 3    10 ms    10 ms    20 ms  mt-ahe-12-e1-0.mt.sfl.net [206.221.252.81]
 4    10 ms    10 ms    10 ms  mtdist3-v587.mt.sfl.net [209.135.97.189]
 5    10 ms   <10 ms    10 ms  216.18.63.141
 6    10 ms    10 ms    20 ms  216.18.63.70
 7    10 ms    10 ms    20 ms  216.18.63.13
 8    10 ms    10 ms    10 ms  h66-59-191-14.gtconnect.net [66.59.191.14]
 9    20 ms    10 ms    10 ms  VLN.Serialx-x-x.GWx.POPx.ALTER.NET [157.130.159.253]
10    20 ms    20 ms    20 ms  POS4-1.XR2.TOR2.ALTER.NET [152.63.131.150]
11    20 ms    10 ms    10 ms  294.ATM2-0.TR2.TOR2.ALTER.NET [152.63.128.58]
12    30 ms    30 ms    20 ms  137.at-5-1-0.TR2.NYC8.ALTER.NET [152.63.7.121]
13    30 ms    30 ms    40 ms  284.ATM7-0.XR2.BOS1.ALTER.NET [152.63.20.181]
14    31 ms    40 ms    30 ms  190.ATM7-0.GW3.BOS1.ALTER.NET [146.188.177.221]
15    30 ms    30 ms    30 ms  uunet-co-za-whitinsville-gw.alter.net [157.130.221.86]
16    50 ms    40 ms    50 ms  s1-1-1.cr1.nyc1.us.uu.net [196.30.229.10]
17    40 ms    50 ms    40 ms  fe4-0-0.ir1.nyc1.us.uu.net [196.30.121.243]
18  1181 ms  1182 ms  1182 ms  tun0.ir1.cpt1.za.uu.net [196.30.121.214]
19  1242 ms  1262 ms  1352 ms  srp1-0-0.cr1.cpt1.za.uu.net [196.30.200.194]
20  1192 ms  1201 ms  1182 ms  atm6-0sub560.cr1.plz1.za.uu.net [196.30.229.94]
21  1182 ms  1191 ms  1202 ms  mweb-pe.cust-gw.iafrica.net [196.7.186.6]
22  1192 ms  1201 ms  1192 ms  pel-36-2.mweb.co.za [196.2.153.5]
23  1242 ms     *      1292 ms  net-52-006.mweb.co.za [196.2.52.6]
24  1251 ms  1272 ms  1332 ms  net-153-070.mweb.co.za [196.2.153.70]
Trace complete.
```

What is of interest is the dramatic change between router number 17 and 18. By looking at the host names of the routers, we can guess that this connection will use a direct long distance connection between the United States and South Africa, which is the bottleneck. However, this is no more than an educated guess. IP does not provide information on how to find out the actual physical location of a server (because it is hardly ever relevant). Try to run `tracert` to a server that you expect to be physically close to your location. You might be surprised about the number of hops over routers it takes to get there, you may even find that some web sites are physically located in a different country to where you thought they would be.

An extension called DNS LOC attempts to add location information as an optional feature to DNS described in RFC 1876. (see http://www.ietf.org/rfc/rfc1876.txt for details), but it is not widely used.

Time-To-Live (TTL) is a counter that is stored in the control information of each IP packet and specifies the maximum number of routers the packet is allowed to pass before it is discarded – every router that passes an IP packet from one subnet to another decrements this counter. This feature makes sure that no IP packet can travel an IP network forever. When you see (ttl=number!) next to the times (not in this example), it indicates an asymmetric path, which means the TTL of the packets `tracert` gets back does not match what it sent, which means that a packet takes one route going in one direction and a different route coming back.

It is important to understand the impact of the Internet on your networking programs. Unlike an office workgroup or a telephone connection (which do not use dynamic routing), the Internet cannot guarantee bandwidth and response time, thus you may experience drastic performance changes even throughout the lifetime of a connection. Hence, it is important to choose appropriate timeouts for socket communication using the `setSoTimeout()` method for a `Socket`, `ServerSocket` or `DatagramSocket` object. It is in general a good idea to test your program under a worst-case network scenario (a physically distant peer, client or server at a high-traffic time) to make sure timeouts are handled appropriately.

ProtocolException

A `ProtocolException` is thrown to indicate an error in the underlying protocol such as HTTP when you choose an incorrect HTTP request method or when the behavior of a client is not as expected by the protocol. For example, this error occurs when you try to post data to an HTTP server and you get redirected. Follow these steps to handle redirection in your program:

1. Disable redirection before creating a `URLConnection` using the `HttpURLConnection.setFollowRedirects(false)` static method

2. Create a new `HttpURLConnection` to the redirected location:

```
int i = conn.getResponseCode();
if (i >= 300 && i <= 399)
  conn = new URL(conn.getHeaderField("Location")).openConnection();
```

SocketException

A `SocketException` is thrown to indicate an error in an underlying protocol such as TCP or UDP. This exception can be thrown for many different reasons, which can also be platform dependent. This means it may be a problem on one platform such as Microsoft Windows NT, but it may not be a problem on Linux or vice versa.

A common error is when a single socket is used from concurrently executing threads. Even if you make sure by means of synchronization that two threads do not use a socket connection at the same time, this may still cause an exception, because the underlying TCP/IP implementation may not support this. You should avoid this in your design.

For instance, the following example reads from an `HttpURLConnection` in two threads. While it is obviously not a good idea in this case, because the sequence of the reads is non-deterministic, it is less obvious that this may lead to unexpected exceptions being thrown when reading from or writing to a socket (such as an `IOException` telling you that the connected stream is closed, when in fact you have not explicitly closed it). However, this example may still run okay on your system.

```
import java.net.*;
import java.io.*;

public class ReadURL implements Runnable
{
    private static ReadURL application;
    private BufferedReader rd;
```

```java
public static void main(String[] args)
{
    try
    {
        application = new ReadURL();
        Thread thread = new Thread(application);
        thread.start();
        application.printLine();

    } catch (IOException e) {
        System.out.println(e);
    }
}

public ReadURL() throws IOException
{
    URL requestURL = new URL("http", "www.ibm.com", "/index.html");
    HttpURLConnection conn = (HttpURLConnection)
        requestURL.openConnection();
    rd = new BufferedReader(new InputStreamReader(conn.getInputStream()));
}

private void printLine() throws IOException
{
    String HTTPResponse = rd.readLine();
    System.out.println("Main Thread:" + HTTPResponse);
}

public void run()
{
    try
    {
        String HTTPResponse = rd.readLine();
        System.out.println("2nd Thread:" + HTTPResponse);
    } catch (IOException e) {
        System.out.println(e);
    }
}
}
```

In peer applications where your program is both a server and a client, it is a good idea to create a socket pair (one to be the communication endpoint where your program acts as the client, and one to be the communication endpoint where your program acts as the server).

A good debugging approach to understand a SocketException is to build a simple prototype that models your application, for example, a server and a client that just make a connection or (if possible) to attempt a connection to a known and working product such as an HTTP server. This lets you focus on resolving connection problems in your program first and you can rule out a malfunctioning server. You can also provide debug code in your application that shows the control flow and the value of variables (up until the point the SocketException is thrown).

UnknownHostException

An `UnknownHostException` is thrown to indicate that the numeric IP address of a host could not be determined by its name. This indicates an address resolution problem. Check your `hosts` file to make sure it contains all entries that are not resolved by a DNS server (such as entries that identify hosts in your private network which uses private IP addresses). A `hosts` file is a simple text file, which for instance is located on a Windows 2000 system in the `C:\WINNT\system32\drivers\etc` directory. It contains numeric IP addresses and their corresponding host names. Whenever a host name is resolved, this is the first place TCP/IP searches to resolve a name. Use `nslookup` to determine if a host-name gets resolved as expected (`nslookup` is not available on some Windows platforms).

To make sure that TCP/IP is correctly installed and working on your machine, use the following call:

```
System.out.println(java.net.InetAddress.getLocalHost());
```

This should print the host-name and IP address of your local system.

UnknownServiceException

An `UnknownServiceException` is thrown to indicate that either the MIME type returned by a `URLConnection` does not make sense or the application is attempting to write to a read-only `URLConnection`.

For instance, when you run the following lines of code and attempt the `conn.getOutputStream()` call:

```
URL requestURL = new URL("http", "www.ibm.com", "/index.html");
HttpURLConnection conn = (HttpURLConnection)
    requestURL.openConnection();

// Read in response line
BufferedReader rd = new BufferedReader(new
    InputStreamReader(conn.getInputStream()));
BufferedWriter wr = new BufferedWriter(new
    OutputStreamWriter(conn.getOutputStream()));
```

Output is generally disabled for a `URLConnection`, unless you enable it using `setDoOutput(true)`.

Summary

This appendix has provided you with a selection of common networking problems. It is very likely that you will encounter one or more of the problems or exceptions discussed in this appendix, when writing networking programs. The techniques how to analyze these problems and how to manage debug information in your source code to debug them, will enable you to easily solve these problems and also to tackle problems specific to other Java networking areas such as RMI, JMS, Servlets, and CORBA.

Installing and Configuring Tomcat 4.0

In this appendix we'll discuss the basics of how to install and configure Tomcat 4.0, the latest version of the open-source JSP and Servlet Reference Implementation. Tomcat 4.0 is the main web container that is used in this book.

Installing Tomcat 4.0

While there are many Servlet and JSP engines available (as of this writing, Sun's "Industry Momentum" page at http://java.sun.com/products/jsp/industry.html lists nearly 40), we have chosen to focus our attention on Tomcat 4.0. Tomcat is produced by the Apache Software Foundation's Jakarta project, and is freely available at http://jakarta.apache.org/tomcat/.

Since Tomcat is primarily used by programmers, its open-source development model is of particular benefit as it brings the developers and users close together. If you find a bug, you can fix it and submit a patch; if you need a new feature, you can write it yourself, or suggest it to the development team. Tomcat is also the reference implementation of the JSP and Servlet specifications, version 4.0 supporting the latest Servlet 2.3 and JSP 1.2 versions. (Version 3.2.1 is the current version of the Servlet 2.2/JSP 1.1 reference implementation.) Many of the principal developers are employed by Sun Microsystems, who are investing considerable manpower into ensuring that Tomcat 4.0 provides a high-quality, robust web container with excellent performance.

A Word On Naming

The naming of Tomcat 4.0 components can be a little confusing, with the names **Tomcat**, **Catalina**, and **Jasper** all flying around. So, to avoid any problems with terminology:

❑ **Catalina** is a Servlet container – that is, an environment within which Java Servlets can be hosted

❑ **Jasper** is the JSP component of Tomcat – in fact, it's just a Servlet that understands how to process requests for JSP pages

❑ **Tomcat** comprises Catalina, plus Jasper, plus various extra bits and pieces including batch files for starting and stopping the server, some example web applications, and mod_webapp

❑ **mod_webapp** is the component that will allows you to connect Tomcat to the Apache web server. Catalina includes a web server of its own, but you may also wish to connect it to an external web server to take advantage of Apache's extra speed when serving static content, or to allow you to run JSP or Servlet-based applications alongside applications using other server-side technologies such as PHP. As of this writing mod_webapp is in alpha-testing, but expect it to become stable soon. In time, connectors for other major web servers should also appear.

Basic Tomcat Installation

These steps describe installing Tomcat 4.0 on a Windows 2000 system, but the steps are pretty generic; the main differences between platforms will be the way in which environment variables are set.

As this book goes to press, the latest 'milestone' version of Tomcat 4 is the Beta 7 release.

❑ You will need to install the Java 2 Standard Edition software development kit, if you have not already done so; JDK 1.3 can be downloaded from http://java.sun.com/j2se/1.3/. Tomcat 4.0 Beta 7 is also compatible with JDK 1.4 – in fact, it assumes that this is the default JDK. It will run successfully on lower versions, however.

❑ Download a suitable Tomcat 4.0 binary release from http://jakarta.apache.org/tomcat/ – the file will be called something like jakarta-tomcat-4.0-xx.zip. (Other archive formats are available which may be more suitable if you are on a UNIX-type platform.)

❑ Unzip the file you downloaded into a suitable directory. On a Windows machine, unzipping into C:\ will create a directory named C:\jakarta-tomcat-4.0-xx containing the Tomcat 4.0 files.

❑ Create CATALINA_HOME and JAVA_HOME environment variables pointing to the directories where you installed the Tomcat and Java 2 SDK files – typical values are C:\jakarta-tomcat-4.0-xx for CATALINA_HOME and C:\jdk1.3 for JAVA_HOME.

Under Windows 2000, environment variables are set using the System control panel. On the Advanced tab, click on the Environment Variables... button. In the resulting dialog box, add CATALINA_HOME and JAVA_HOME as system variables:

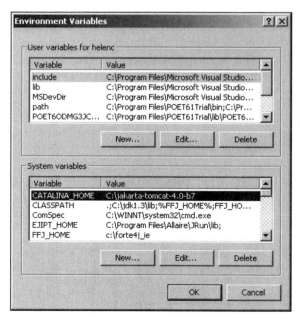

These environment variables allow Tomcat to locate both its own files (using CATALINA_HOME), and the Java 2 SDK components it needs, notably the Java compiler, (using JAVA_HOME).

If you are using Windows 98, environment variables are set by editing the C:\autoexec.bat file. Add the following lines:

```
set CATALINA_HOME=C:\jakarta-tomcat-4.0-xx
set JAVA_HOME=C:\jdk1.3
```

Under Windows 98 you will also need to increase the environment space available, by right-clicking on your DOS prompt window, selecting **Properties**, going to the **Memory** tab, and setting the initial environment to 4096 bytes.

❑   Start Tomcat by running the startup.bat batch file (startup.sh on Unix-type systems), which can be found in the %CATALINA_HOME%\bin directory (in other words, the bin directory inside the directory where Tomcat is installed).

Tomcat will start up and print some status messages:

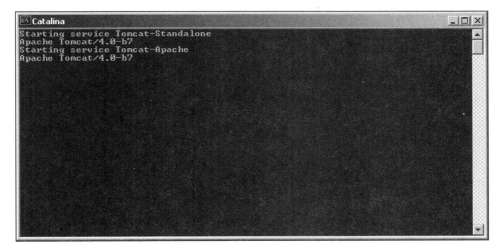

❑   We now have Tomcat 4.0 up and running, using its internal web server (on port 8080). Point your web browser at http://localhost:8080/; you should see the default Tomcat home page:

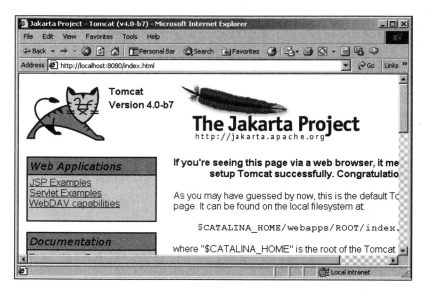

Spend some time exploring the examples and documentation provided with Tomcat.

❑ To shut down Tomcat, run the shutdown.bat batch file (shutdown.sh on Unix-type systems), again from the %CATALINA_HOME%\bin directory

The Tomcat 4.0 Directory Structure

Looking inside our Tomcat installation directory we find a few text files, and various directories:

❑ bin contains Windows batch files and Unix shell scripts for starting and stopping Tomcat, and for other purposes, together with the bootstrap.jar JAR file needed for the first stage of starting Tomcat

❑ classes is not created by default, but if it exists any .class files it contains will be visible to all web applications

❑ common contains Java code needed by all parts of Tomcat: .jar files (Java library files) in the common\lib directory, and .class files in common\classes. Notable among the .jar files is servlet.jar, which contains the classes defined by the Servlet 2.3 and JSP 1.2 specifications. You will need to have servlet.jar listed in your CLASSPATH environment variable when compiling classes (for example, Servlets) that use these APIs

❑ conf contains Tomcat's configuration files, notably server.xml (used to configure the server – which host-name and port number to use, which web applications to deploy, etc.) and the server-wide web.xml

> **Note that settings in the server-wide web.xml file (located in %CATALINA_HOME%\conf) apply to the whole server, but that this behavior is not mandated by the Servlet specification. Applications making use of it will not be portable to other servlet containers.**

❏ jasper contains .jar files containing parts of the JSP engine.

❏ lib is populated with various .jar files (library files) required by web applications, including parts of the JSP engine. You can add your own .jar files here and they will be visible to all web applications

❏ logs is where Tomcat places its log files. Logging is configured in server.xml

❏ server contains the files comprising Catalina, and other required libraries: .jar files in server\lib, and .class files in server\classes

❏ webapps is the location where Tomcat looks for web applications to deploy. Any .war file placed here, or any expanded web application directory structure stored within the directory, will automatically be deployed when Tomcat starts up

The URL path under which the application is deployed will correspond to the name of the .war file or directory; for example, if you place a myapplication.war file or a myapplication directory within webapps, Tomcat will automatically deploy it as http://localhost:8080/myapplication/

The automatic deployment settings may not suit your application, in which case you may prefer to store the application outside the webapps directory and configure it as desired using server.xml

❏ work is used by Tomcat to store temporary files, notably the .java source files and compiled .class files created when processing JSPs

The illustration to the right demonstrates the relationship these folders have with one another. Note that the Servlet example web application (wrox) from Chapter 18 has been placed in the webapps folder:

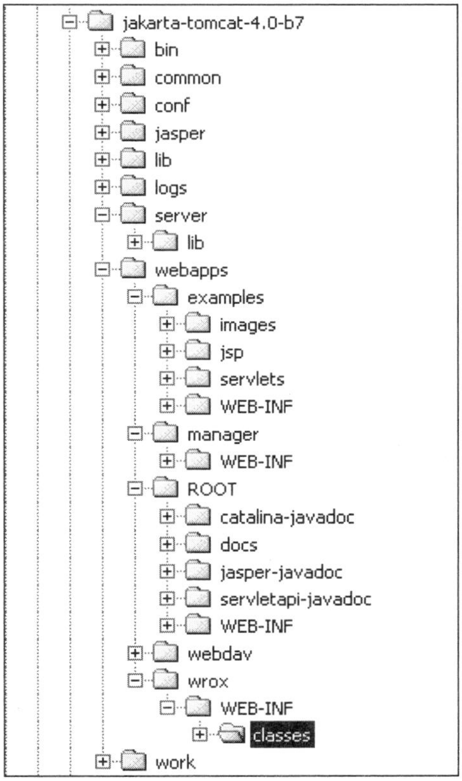

Tomcat 4.0 Configuration

The Tomcat documentation has improved considerably compared to early versions and should be your first stop if you need to configure Tomcat in any way. However, there are a few steps that are sufficiently common that we cover them here.

Deploying a Web Application

There are two ways to tell Tomcat to deploy a web application:

❑ As mentioned above, you can deploy an application simply by placing a `.war` file or an expanded web application directory structure in the `%CATALINA_HOME%\webapps` directory.

❑ However, the default settings may not be suitable for your application, in which case it will be necessary to edit `%CATALINA_HOME%\conf\server.xml` and add a `<Context>` element for your application.

The default `server.xml` file is well commented, and you should read these to familiarize yourself with the contents of this file. Various additional elements, not shown or described here but included in the default `server.xml`, provide for logging and other similar functionality, and define authentication realms. The default `server.xml` also includes commented-out sections illustrating how to set up a secure (HTTPS) connector, and to set up database-driven authentication realms. It also includes elements that work together with the `mod_webapp` Apache module.

The outline structure of `server.xml` is as follows:

```
<Server>
  <Service>
    <Connector/>
    <Engine>
      <Host>
        <Context/>
      </Host>
    </Engine>
  </Service>
</Server>
```

At the top level is a `<Server>` element, representing the entire Java Virtual Machine. It may contain one or more `<Service>` elements:

```
<Server port="8005" shutdown="SHUTDOWN" debug="0">
```

A `<Service>` element represents a collection of one or more `<Connector>` elements that share a single 'container' (and therefore the web applications visible within that container). Normally, that container is an `<Engine>` element:

```
<Service name="Tomcat-Standalone">
```

A `<Connector>` represents an endpoint by which requests are received and responses are returned, passing them on to the associated `<Container>` (normally an `<Engine>`) for processing. This `<Connector>` element creates a non-secure HTTP/1.1 connector, listening on port `8080`:

```
<Connector className="org.apache.catalina.connector.http.HttpConnector"
           port="8080" minProcessors="5" maxProcessors="75"
           acceptCount="10" debug="0"/>
```

An `<Engine>` element represents the Catalina object that processes every request, passing them on to the appropriate `<Host>`:

```
<Engine name="Standalone" defaultHost="localhost" debug="0">
```

The `<Host>` element is used to define the default virtual host:

```
<Host name="localhost" debug="0" appBase="webapps">
```

A `<Context>` element is used to define an individual web application:

```
<Context path="/examples" docBase="examples" debug="0"
         reloadable="true">
</Context>
```

The attributes of the `<Context>` element are:

- ❑ `path` determines the URL prefix where the application will be deployed. In the example above, the application will be found at `http://localhost:8080/examples/`.

- ❑ `docBase` specifies the whereabouts of the `.war` file or expanded web application directory structure for the application. Since a relative file path is specified here, Tomcat will look in its `webapps` directory (this was configured in the `<Host>` element, above) but an absolute file path can also be used.

- ❑ `debug` specifies the level of debugging information that will be produced for this application

- ❑ `reloadable` intimates whether the container should check for changes to files that would require it to reload the application. When deploying your application in a production environment, setting its value to `"false"` will improve performance, as Tomcat will not have to perform these checks.

```
    </Host>

  </Engine>

 </Service>

 <!-- Snip details of service for the mod_webapp connector -->

</Server>
```

Getting Help

If you need help with Tomcat 4.0, and this appendix and the documentation just haven't helped, your first port of call should be the Tomcat web site, http://jakarta.apache.org/tomcat/. There are two mailing lists dedicated to Tomcat issues:

- ❑ tomcat-user, for Tomcat's users – this is where you can ask questions on configuring and using Tomcat. The Tomcat developers should be on hand to help out as necessary.

- ❑ tomcat-dev, which is where the developers themselves lurk. If you decide to get stuck in with contributing to improving Tomcat itself, this is where the action is.

Index

A Guide to the Index

The index is arranged hierarchically, in alphabetical order, with symbols preceding the letter A. Most second-level entries and many third-level entries also occur as first-level entries. This is to ensure that users will find the information they require however they choose to search for it.

U

p2p.wrox.com
The programmer's resource centre

A unique free service from Wrox Press
with the aim of helping programmers to help each other

Wrox Press aims to provide timely and practical information to today's programmer. P2P is a list server offering a host of targeted mailing lists where you can share knowledge with your fellow programmers and find solutions to your problems. Whatever the level of your programming knowledge, and whatever technology you use, P2P can provide you with the information you need.

ASP Support for beginners and professionals, including a resource page with hundreds of links, and a popular ASP+ mailing list.

DATABASES For database programmers, offering support on SQL Server, mySQL, and Oracle.

MOBILE Software development for the mobile market is growing rapidly. We provide lists for the several current standards, including WAP, WindowsCE, and Symbian.

JAVA A complete set of Java lists, covering beginners, professionals, and server-side programmers (including JSP, servlets and EJBs)

.NET Microsoft's new OS platform, covering topics such as ASP+, C#, and general .Net discussion.

VISUAL BASIC Covers all aspects of VB programming, from programming Office macros to creating components for the .Net platform.

WEB DESIGN As web page requirements become more complex, programmer sare taking a more important role in creating web sites. For these programmers, we offer lists covering technologies such as Flash, Coldfusion, and JavaScript.

XML Covering all aspects of XML, including XSLT and schemas.

OPEN SOURCE Many Open Source topics covered including PHP, Apache, Perl, Linux, Python and more.

FOREIGN LANGUAGE Several lists dedicated to Spanish and German speaking programmers, categories include .Net, Java, XML, PHP and XML.

How To Subscribe

Simply visit the P2P site, at **http://p2p.wrox.com/**

Select the 'FAQ' option on the side menu bar for more information about the subscription process and our service.